CLOUD COMPUTING

CLOUD COMPUTING

BUSINESS TRENDS AND TECHNOLOGIES

Igor Faynberg
Hui-Lan Lu
Dor Skuler

This edition first published 2016

Registered office
John Wiley & Sons Ltd, The Atrium, Southern Gate, Chichester, West Sussex, PO19 8SQ, United Kingdom

For details of our global editorial offices, for customer services and for information about how to apply for permission to reuse the copyright material in this book please see our website at www.wiley.com.

Library of Congress Cataloging-in-Publication Data

Faynberg, Igor.
Cloud computing : business trends and technologies / Igor Faynberg, Hui-Lan Lu, Dor Skuler, Alacatel-Lucent.
pages cm
Includes bibliographical references and index.
ISBN 978-1-118-50121-4 (cloth)
1. Cloud computing. I. Lu, Hui-Lan. II. Skuler, Dor. III. Title.
QA76.585.F38 2016
004.67′82–dc23

2015022953

A catalogue record for this book is available from the British Library.

ISBN: 9781118501214

Set in 10/12pt Times by Aptara Inc., New Delhi, India

1 2016

Contents

About the Authors

This book was written while the authors worked in the *CloudBand* Business Unit at Alcatel-Lucent. *CloudBand,* founded by Dor Skuler, is a market-leading platform for Network Functions Virtualization (NFV).

Igor Faynberg, Adjunct Professor in the Computer Science Department of Stevens Institute of Technology, is a Bell Labs Fellow. At the time of writing this book, he was a senior architect in charge of NFV security, reporting to the Chief Technology Officer of *CloudBand.*

Previous to that he had held various staff and managerial positions in Bell Labs and Alcatel-Lucent business units. In his Bell Labs career, he has influenced the development of several software technologies—from mathematical programming to Intelligent Network and Internet/PSTN convergence to virtualization. He has contributed to and held various leadership positions in the Internet Engineering Task Force (IETF), International Telecommunication Union (ITU), and European Telecommunication Standardization Institute (ETSI), where he presently serves as Chairman of the ETSI NFV Security working group. He has served on technical committees of several IEEE conferences, and he holds numerous patents for the inventions related to technologies that he had developed.

Igor has also co-authored two books and numerous refereed papers. He holds a Mathematics Diploma from Kharkov University, Ukraine, and MS and PhD degrees in Computer and Information Science from the University of Pennsylvania.

Hui-Lan Lu is a Bell Labs Fellow at Alcatel-Lucent, where she has conducted research and development in various areas, including mathematical programming, service creation, IP multimedia communication, quality of service in converged networks, and security.

She has been also involved in strategic standards efforts in the IETF, ITU, and ETSI. More recently, she has served as Rapporteur for the ETSI NFV case study of *OpenStack* security and Vice Chairman of ITU-T SG 13 (the lead study group on Cloud Computing and future networks).

Hui-Lan has co-authored a book on converged networks and services, and numerous refereed papers. She holds a PhD degree in physics from Yale University in New Haven and has over 40 patents.

Dor Skuler formerly served as Senior Vice President and General Manager of the *CloudBand* Business Unit at Alcatel-Lucent, which he founded. Prior to this role, Dor served as Vice President of Strategy and Head of Corporate Development for Alcatel-Lucent in its corporate headquarters in Paris. Previously Dor had held entrepreneurial roles such as General Manager of Mobile Security, a new venture in Alcatel-Lucent's Bell Labs and Enterprise Business Divisions.

Before joining Alcatel-Lucent, Dor served as Vice-President of Business Development and Marketing at *Safend*, an endpoint security company. Dor also founded and served as President of *Zing Interactive Media*, a venture-backed startup company in the field of mobile interactive media.

Dor holds a Master's of Science in Marketing and an MBA in International Business. Dor was selected in Global Telecom Business' "40 under 40" list in 2009, 2011 and 2013 and is often invited to speak in industry events and is interviewed by the global press.

Acknowledgments

A book of this scope and size could not have been written without help from many people. We acknowledge much stimulation that came from early discussions with Markus Hofmann who headed the Bell Labs research effort in the Cloud. We have had incisive discussions on various topics of networking with Mark Clougherty, Vijay Gurbani, and Dimitri Stiliadis.

We have been much influenced and supported by David Amzallag (then CTO of *CloudBand*), particularly on the topic of operations and management.

Our first steps in addressing Cloud security were made together with Doug Varney, Jack Kozik, and Herbert Ristock (now with *Genesys*). We owe much of our understanding of the subject to our *CloudBand* colleagues—Ranny Haibi, Chris Deloddere, Mark Hooper, and Avi Vachnis. Sivan Barzilay has reviewed Chapter 7, to which she has contributed a figure; we also owe to her our understanding of TOSCA.

Peter Busschbach has reviewed Chapter 3 and provided insightful comments.

A significant impetus for this book came from teaching, and the book is intended to be an assigned text in a graduate course on Cloud Computing. Such a course, taught in the Stevens Institute of Technology, has been developed with much encouragement and help from Professor Daniel Duchamp (Director of Department of Computer Science), and many useful suggestions from Professor Dominic Duggan. Important insight, reflected in the course and in the book, came from graduate students who had served over the years as teaching assistants: Bo Ye (2012); Wa Gao (2013); Xiaofang Yu (2014); and Saurabh Bagde and Harshil Bhatt (2015).

It is owing to meeting (and subsequent discussions with) Professor Ruby Lee of Princeton University that we have learned of her research on *NoHype*—an alternative to traditional virtualization that addresses some essential security problems.

The past two years of working in the European Telecommunications Standardization Institute (ETSI) Network Function Virtualization (NFV) Industry Specification Group have contributed significantly to our understanding of the demands of the telecommunications industry. In particular, deep discussions of the direction of NFV with Don Clarke (Cable Labs), Diego Garcia Lopez (Telefonica), Uwe Michel (Deutsche Telekom) and Prodip Sen (formerly of Verizon and then HP) were invaluable in forming our perspective. Specifically on the subject of NFV security we owe much to all participants in the NFV Security group and particularly to Bob Briscoe (BT) and Bob Moskowitz (Verizon).

We got much insight into the US standards development on this topic in our conversation with George W. Arnold, then Director of Standards in National Institute of Standards and Technology (NIST).

It has been a great delight to work under the cheerful guidance of Ms Liz Wingett, our Project Editor at John Wiley & Sons. Her vigilant attention to every detail kept us on our feet, but the manuscript improved with every suggestion she made. As the manuscript was being prepared for production, Ms Audrey Koh, Production Editor at John Wiley & Sons, has achieved a feat truly worthy of the Fifth Labor of Hercules, going through the proofs and cleaning up the Augean Stables of stylistic (and, at times, even factual) inconsistencies.

To all these individuals we express our deepest gratitude.

1

Introduction

> If the seventeenth and early eighteenth centuries are the age of clocks, and the later eighteenth and the nineteenth centuries constitute the age of steam engines, the present time is the age of communication and control.
>
> **Norbert Wiener** (from the 1948 edition of *Cybernetics: or Control and Communication in the Animal and the Machine*).

It is unfortunate that we don't remember the exact date of the extraordinary event that we are about to describe, except that it took place sometime in the Fall of 1994. Then Professor Noah Prywes of the University of Pennsylvania gave a memorable invited talk at Bell Labs, at which two authors[1] of this book were present. The main point of the talk was a proposal that AT&T (of which Bell Labs was a part at the time) should go into the business of providing computing services—in addition to telecommunications services—to other companies by actually running these companies' data centers. "All they need is just to plug in their terminals so that they receive IT services as a utility. They would pay anything to get rid of the headaches and costs of operating their own machines, upgrading software, and what not."

Professor Prywes, whom we will meet more than once in this book, well known in Bell Labs as a software visionary and more than that—the founder and CEO of a successful software company, *Computer Command and Control*—was suggesting something that appeared too extravagant even to the researchers. The core business of AT&T at that time was telecommunications services. The major enterprise customers of AT&T were buying the *customer premises equipment* (such as private branch exchange switches and machines that ran software in support of call centers). In other words, the enterprise was buying things to run on premises rather than outsourcing things to the network provider!

Most attendees saw the merit of the idea, but could not immediately relate it to their day-to-day work, or—more importantly—to the company's stated business plan. Furthermore, at that very moment the Bell Labs computing environment was migrating from the Unix

[1] Igor Faynberg and Hui-Lan Lu, then members of the technical staff at Bell Labs Area 41 (Architecture Area).

Cloud Computing: Business Trends and Technologies, First Edition. Igor Faynberg, Hui-Lan Lu and Dor Skuler.

programming environment hosted on mainframes and Sun workstations to Microsoft Office-powered personal computers. It is not that we, who "grew up" with the Unix operating system, liked the change, but we were told that this was the way the industry was going (and it was!) as far as office information technology was concerned. But if so, then the enterprise would be going in exactly the *opposite* way—by placing computing in the hands of each employee. Professor Prywes did not deny the pace of acceptance of personal computing; his argument was that there was much more to enterprises than what was occurring inside their individual workstations—payroll databases, for example.

There was a lively discussion, which quickly turned to the detail. Professor Prywes cited the achievements in virtualization and massive parallel-processing technologies, which were sufficient to enable his vision. These arguments were compelling, but ultimately the core business of AT&T was networking, and networking was centered on telecommunications services.

Still, telecommunications services were provided by software, and even the telephone switches were but peripheral devices controlled by computers. It was in the 1990s that virtual telecommunications networking services such as *Software Defined Networks*—not to be confused with the namesake development in data networking, which we will cover in Chapter 4—were emerging on the purely software and data communications platform called *Intelligent Network*. It is on the basis of the latter that Professor Prywes thought the computing services could be offered. In summary, the idea was to combine data communications with centralized powerful computing centers, all under the central command and control of a major telecommunications company. All of us in the audience were intrigued.

The idea of computing as a public utility was not new. It had been outlined by Douglas F. Parkhill in his 1966 book [1].

In the end, however, none of us could sell the idea to senior management. The times the telecommunications industry was going through in 1994 could best be characterized as "interesting," and AT&T did not fare particularly well for a number of reasons.[2] Even though Bell Labs was at the forefront of the development of all relevant technologies, recommending those to businesses was a different matter—especially where a proposal for a radical change of business model was made, and especially in turbulent times.

In about a year, AT&T announced its trivestiture. The two authors had moved, along with a large part of Bell Labs, into the equipment manufacturing company which became Lucent Technologies and, 10 years later, merged with Alcatel to form Alcatel-Lucent.

At about the same time, Amazon launched a service called *Elastic Compute Cloud* (*EC2*), which delivered pretty much what Professor Prywes had described to us. Here an enterprise user—located anywhere in the world—could create, for a charge, *virtual* machines in the "Cloud" (or, to be more precise, in one of the Amazon data centers) and deploy any software on these machines. But not only that, the machines were *elastic*: as the user's demand for computing power grew, so did the machine power—magically increasing to meet the demand—along with the appropriate cost; when the demand dropped so did the computing power delivered, and also the cost. Hence, the enterprise did not need to invest in purchasing and maintaining computers, it paid only for the computing power it received and could get as much of it as necessary!

As a philosophical aside: one way to look at the computing development is through the prism of dialectics. As depicted in Figure 1.1(a), with mainframe-based computing as the

[2] For one thing, the regional Bell operating companies and other local exchange carriers started to compete with AT&T Communications in the services market, and so they loathed buying equipment from AT&T Network Systems—a manufacturing arm of AT&T.

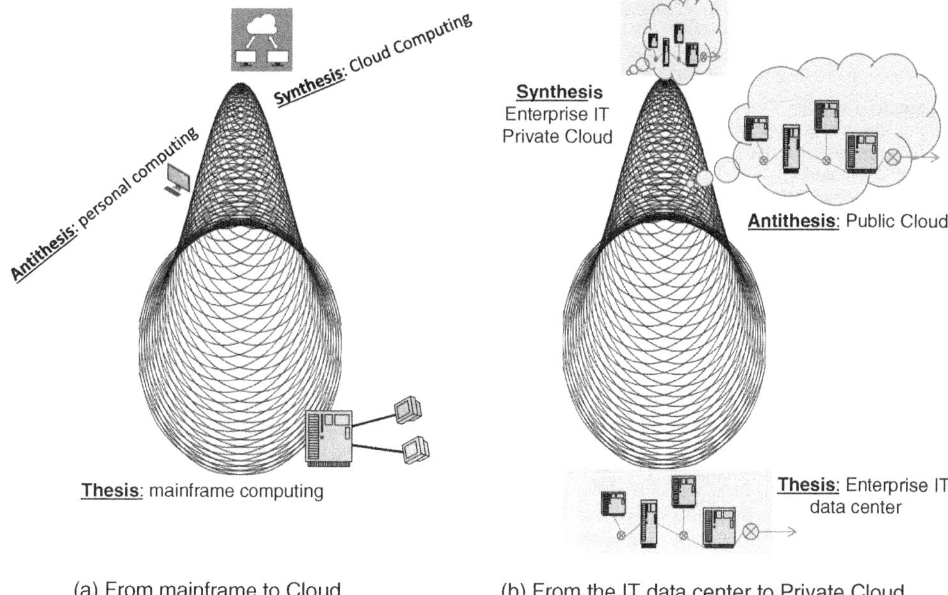

Figure 1.1 Dialectics in the development of Cloud Computing: (a) from mainframe to Cloud; (b) from IT data center to Private Cloud.

thesis, the industry had moved to personal-workstation-based computing—the *antithesis*. But the spiral development—fostered by advances in data networking, distributed processing, and software automation—brought forth the Cloud as the *synthesis*, where the convenience of seemingly central on-demand computing is combined with the autonomy of a user's computing environment. Another spiral (described in detail in Chapter 2) is depicted in Figure 1.1(b), which demonstrates how the *Public Cloud* has become the *antithesis* to the *thesis* of traditional IT data centers, inviting the outsourcing of the development (via "*Shadow IT*" and *Virtual Private Cloud*). The synthesis is *Private Cloud*, in which the Cloud has moved computing back to the enterprise but in a very novel form.

At this point we are ready to introduce formal definitions, which have been agreed on universally and thus form a standard in themselves. The definitions have been developed at the National Institute of Standards and Technology (NIST) and published in [2]. To begin with, Cloud Computing is defined as a model "for enabling ubiquitous, convenient, on-demand network access to a shared pool of configurable computing resources (e.g., networks, servers, storage, applications, and services) that can be rapidly provisioned and released with minimal management effort or service provider interaction." This Cloud model is composed of five essential characteristics, three service models, and four deployment models.

The five essential characteristics are presented in Figure 1.2.

The three service models, now well known, are Software-as-a-Service (SaaS), Platform-as-a-Service (PaaS), and Infrastructure-as-a-Service (IaaS). NIST defines them thus:

1. *Software-as-a-Service* (*SaaS*). The capability provided to the consumer is to use the provider's applications running on a Cloud infrastructure. The applications are accessible from various client devices through either a thin client interface, such as a web browser

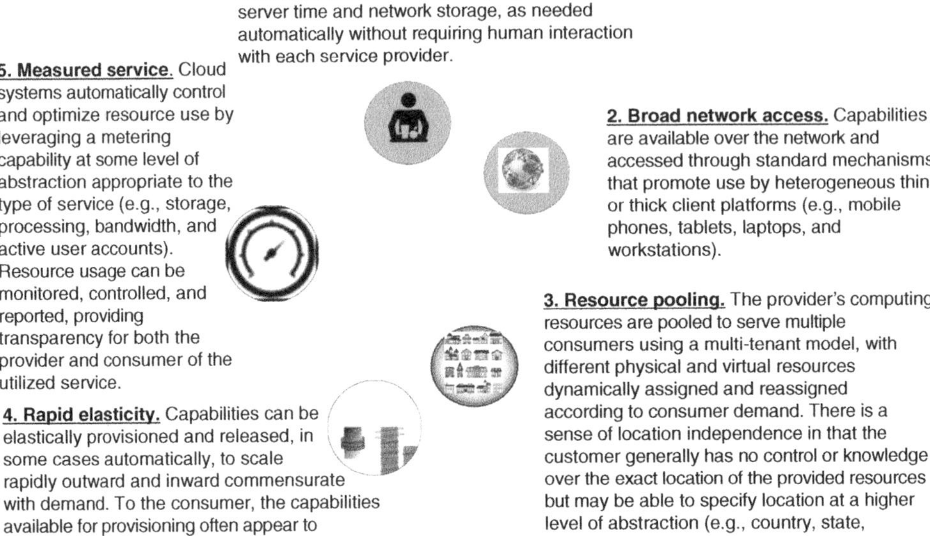

1. On-demand self-service. A consumer can unilaterally provision computing capabilities, such as server time and network storage, as needed automatically without requiring human interaction with each service provider.
2. Broad network access. Capabilities are available over the network and accessed through standard mechanisms that promote use by heterogeneous thin or thick client platforms (e.g., mobile phones, tablets, laptops, and workstations).
3. Resource pooling. The provider's computing resources are pooled to serve multiple consumers using a multi-tenant model, with different physical and virtual resources dynamically assigned and reassigned according to consumer demand. There is a sense of location independence in that the customer generally has no control or knowledge over the exact location of the provided resources but may be able to specify location at a higher level of abstraction (e.g., country, state, or data center).
4. Rapid elasticity. Capabilities can be elastically provisioned and released, in some cases automatically, to scale rapidly outward and inward commensurate with demand. To the consumer, the capabilities available for provisioning often appear to be unlimited and can be appropriated in any quantity at any time.
5. Measured service. Cloud systems automatically control and optimize resource use by leveraging a metering capability at some level of abstraction appropriate to the type of service (e.g., storage, processing, bandwidth, and active user accounts). Resource usage can be monitored, controlled, and reported, providing transparency for both the provider and consumer of the utilized service.

Figure 1.2 Essential characteristics of Cloud Computing. *Source:* NIST SP 800-145, p. 2.

(e.g., web-based e-mail), or a program interface. The consumer does not manage or control the underlying Cloud infrastructure including network, servers, operating systems, storage, or even individual application capabilities, with the possible exception of limited user-specific application configuration settings.

2. *Platform-as-a-Service* (*PaaS*). The capability provided to the consumer is to deploy onto the Cloud infrastructure consumer-created or acquired applications created using programming languages, libraries, services, and tools supported by the provider. The consumer does not manage or control the underlying Cloud infrastructure including network, servers, operating systems, or storage, but has control over the deployed applications and possibly configuration settings for the application-hosting environment.
3. *Infrastructure-as-a-Service* (*IaaS*). The capability provided to the consumer is to provision processing, storage, networks, and other fundamental computing resources where the consumer is able to deploy and run arbitrary software, which can include operating systems and applications. The consumer does not manage or control the underlying Cloud infrastructure but has control over operating systems, storage, and deployed applications; and possibly limited control of select networking components (e.g., host firewalls).

Over time, other service models have appeared—more often than not in the marketing literature—but the authors of the well-known "Berkeley view of Cloud Computing" [3] chose to "eschew terminology such as 'X as a service (XaaS),'" citing the difficulty of agreeing "even among ourselves what the precise differences among them might be," that is, among the services for some values of X...

Finally, the four Cloud deployment models are defined by NIST as follows:

1. *Private Cloud.* The Cloud infrastructure is provisioned for exclusive use by a single organization comprising multiple consumers (e.g., business units). It may be owned, managed, and operated by the organization, a third party, or some combination of them, and it may exist on or off premises.
2. *Community Cloud.* The Cloud infrastructure is provisioned for exclusive use by a specific community of consumers from organizations that have shared concerns (e.g., mission, security requirements, policy, and compliance considerations). It may be owned, managed, and operated by one or more of the organizations in the community, a third party, or some combination of them, and it may exist on or off premises.
3. *Public Cloud.* The Cloud infrastructure is provisioned for open use by the general public. It may be owned, managed, and operated by a business, academic, or government organization, or some combination of them. It exists on the premises of the Cloud provider.
4. *Hybrid Cloud.* The Cloud infrastructure is a composition of two or more distinct Cloud infrastructures (private, community, or public) that remain unique entities, but are bound together by standardized or proprietary technology that enables data and application portability (e.g., Cloud bursting for load balancing between Clouds).

Cloud Computing is not a single technology. It is better described as a business development, whose realization has been enabled by several disciplines: computer architecture, operating systems, data communications, and network and operations management. As we will see, the latter discipline has been around for as long as networking, but the introduction of Cloud Computing has naturally fueled its growth in a new direction, once again validating the quote from Norbert Wiener's book that we chose as the epigraph to this book.

As Chapter 2 demonstrates, Cloud Computing has had a revolutionary effect on the information technology industry, reverberating through the telecommunications industry, which followed suit. Telecommunications providers demanded that vendors provide software only, rather than "the boxes." There have been several relevant standardization efforts in the industry, and—perhaps more important—there have been open-source software packages for building Cloud environments.

Naturally, standardization was preceded by a significant effort in research and development. In 2011, an author[3] of this book established the *CloudBand* product unit within Alcatel-Lucent, where, with the help of Bell Labs research, the telecommunications Cloud platform has been developed. It was in the context of *CloudBand* that we three authors met and the idea of this book was born.

We planned the book first of all as a textbook on Cloud Computing. Our experience in developing and teaching a graduate course on the subject at the Stevens Institute of Technology taught us that even the brightest and best-prepared students were missing sufficient knowledge in Central Processing Unit (CPU) virtualization (a subject that is rarely taught in the context of computer architecture or operating systems), as well as a number of specific points in data communications. Network and operations management has rarely been part of the modern computer science curriculum.

[3] Dor Skuler, at the time Alcatel-Lucent Vice President and General Manager of the *CloudBand* product unit.

In fact, the same knowledge gap seems to be ubiquitous in the industry, where engineers are forced to specialize, and we hope that this book will help fill the gap by providing an overarching multi-disciplinary foundation.

The rest of the book is structured as follows:

- Chapter 2 is mainly about "what" rather than "how." It provides definitions, describes business considerations—with a special case study of *Network Function Virtualization*—and otherwise provides a bird's eye view of Cloud Computing. The "how" is the subject of the chapters that follow.
- Chapter 3 explains the tenets of CPU virtualization.
- Chapter 4 is dedicated to networking—the nervous system of the Cloud.
- Chapter 5 describes network appliances, the building blocks of Cloud data centers as well as private networks.
- Chapter 6 describes the overall structure of the modern data center, along with its components.
- Chapter 7 reviews operations and management in the Cloud and elucidates the concepts of orchestration and identity and access management, with the case study of *OpenStack*—a popular open-source Cloud project.
- The Appendix delves into the detail of selected topics discussed earlier.

The references (which also form a bibliography on the respective subjects) are placed separately in individual chapters.

Having presented an outline of the book, we should note that there are three essential subjects that do not have a dedicated chapter. Instead, they are addressed in each chapter inasmuch as they concern that chapter's subject matter.

One such subject is security. Needless to say, this is the single most important matter that could make or break Cloud Computing. There are many aspects to security, and so we felt that we should address the aspects relevant to each chapter within the chapter itself.

Another subject that has no "central" coverage is standardization. Again, we introduce the relevant standards and open-source projects while discussing specific technical subjects. The third subject is history. It is well known in engineering that many existing technical solutions are not around because they are optimal, but because of their historical development. In teaching a discipline it is important to point these out, and we have tried our best to do so, again in the context of each technology that we address.

References

[1] Parkhill, D.F. (1966) *Challenge of the Computer Utility*. Addison-Wesley, Reading, MA.

[2] Mell, P. and Grance, T. (2011). Special Publication 800-145: The NIST Definition of Cloud Computing. Recommendations of the National Institute of Standards and Technology. US Department of Commerce, Gaithersburg, MD, September, 2011.

[3] Armbrust, M., Fox, A., Griffith, R., *et al.* (2009) Above the Clouds: A Berkeley view of Cloud Computing. Electrical Engineering and Computer Sciences Technical Report No. UCB/EECS-2009-2A, University of California at Berkeley, Berkeley, CA, February, 2009.

2

The Business of Cloud Computing

In this chapter, we evaluate the business impact of Cloud Computing.

We start by outlining the IT industry's transformation process, which historically took smaller steps—first, virtualization and second, moving to Cloud. As we will see, this process has taken place in a dialectic spiral, influenced by conflicting developments. The centrifugal forces were moving computing out of enterprise—"*Shadow IT*" and *Virtual Private Cloud.* Ultimately, the development has synthesized into bringing computing back into the transformed enterprise IT, by means of *Private Cloud.*

Next, we move beyond enterprise and consider the telecommunications business, which has been undergoing a similar process—known as *Network Functions Virtualization (NFV),* which is now developing its own *Private Cloud* (a process in which all the authors have been squarely involved).

The Cloud transformation, of course, affects other business sectors, but the purpose of this book—and the ever-growing size of the manuscript—suggests that we draw the line at this point. It is true though that just as mathematical equations applicable to one physical field (e.g., mechanics) can equally well be applied in other fields (e.g., electromagnetic fields), so do universal business formulae apply to various businesses. The impact of Cloud will be seen and felt in many other industries!

2.1 IT Industry Transformation through Virtualization and Cloud

In the last decade the IT industry has gone through a massive transformation, which has had a huge effect on both the operational and business side of the introduction of new applications and services. To appreciate what has happened, let us start by looking at the old way of doing things.

Traditionally, in the pre-Cloud era, creating software-based products and services involved high upfront investment, high risk of losing this investment, slow time-to-market, and much ongoing operational cost incurred from operating and maintaining the infrastructure. Developers were usually responsible for the design and implementation of the whole system: from the selection of the physical infrastructure (e.g., servers, switching, storage, etc.) to the software-reliability infrastructure (e.g., clustering, high-availability, and monitoring mechanisms) and

---

Cloud Computing: Business Trends and Technologies, First Edition. Igor Faynberg, Hui-Lan Lu and Dor Skuler.

communication links—all the way up to translating the business logic into the application. Applications for a given service were deployed on a *dedicated* infrastructure, and capacity planning was performed separately for each service.

Here is a live example. In 2000, one of the authors[1] created a company called *Zing Interactive Media*,[2] which had the mission to allow radio listeners to interact with content they hear on the radio via simple voice commands. Think of hearing a great song on the radio, or an advertisement that's interesting to you, and imagine how—with simple voice commands—you could order the song or interact with the advertiser. In today's world this can be achieved as a classic Cloud-based SaaS solution.

But in 2000 the author's company had to do quite a few things in order to create this service. First, of course, was to build the actual product to deliver the service. But on top of that there were major investments that were invisible to the end user:[3]

(A) Rent space on a hosting site (in this case we rented a secure space (a "*cage*") on an AT&T hosting facility).
(B) Anticipate the peak use amount and develop a redundancy schema for the service.
(C) Specify the technical requirements for the servers needed to meet this capacity plan. (That involves a great deal of shopping around.)
(D) Negotiate vendor and support contracts and purchase and install enough servers to meet the capacity plan (some will inevitably be idle).
(E) Lease dedicated *T1*[4] lines for connectivity to the "cage" and pay for their full capacity regardless of actual use.
(F) Purchase the networking gear (switches, cables, etc.) and install it in the "cage."
(G) Purchase and install software (operating systems, databases, etc.) on the servers.
(H) Purchase and install load balancers, firewalls, and other *networking appliances*.[5]
(I) Hire an IT team of networking experts, systems administrator, database administrator, and so on to maintain this setup.
(J) (Finally!) Deploy and maintain the unique software that actually delivered Zing Interactive Media's service.

Note that this investment had a huge upfront cost. This was incurred prior to the launching of the service and provided no differentiation whatsoever to the product. Out of necessity, the investment was made with the peak use pattern in mind—not even the median use pattern. And even with all these precautions, the investment was based on an educated guess. In addition, as the service succeeded, scaling it up required planning and long lead times: servers take time to arrive, access to the hosting site requires planning and approvals, and it takes weeks for the network provider to activate newly ordered communication links.

We will return to this example later, to describe how our service could be deployed today using the Cloud.

---

[1] Dor Skuler.
[2] For example, see www.bloomberg.com/research/stocks/private/snapshot.asp?privcapId=82286A.
[3] These actions are typical for all other products that later turned into SaaS.
[4] *T1* is a high-data-rate (1.544 Mbps) transmission service in the USA that can be leased from a telecom operator. It is based on the *T-carrier* system originally developed at Bell Labs and deployed in North America and Japan. The European follow-up on this is the *E-carrier* system, and the *E1* service offered in Europe has a rate of 2.048 Mbps.
[5] We discuss networking appliances in Chapter 5.

The example is quite representative of what enterprise IT organizations have to deal with when deploying services (such as e-mail, virtual private networking, or enterprise resource planning systems). In fact, the same problems are faced by software development organizations in large companies.

When starting a new project, the manager of such a development follows these steps:

(A) Make an overall cost estimate (in the presence of many uncertainties).
(B) Get approvals for both budget and space to host the servers and other equipment.
(C) Enter a purchase request for new hardware.
(D) Go through a procurement organization to buy a server (which may take three months or so).
(E) Open a ticket to the support team and wait until the servers are installed and set up, the security policies are deployed, and, finally, the connectivity is enabled.
(F) Install the operating system and other software.
(G) Start developing the *actual* value-added software.
(H) Go back to step A whenever additional equipment or outside software is needed.

When testing is needed, this process grows exponentially to the number of per-tester dedicated systems. A typical example of (necessary) waste is this: when a software product needs to be stress tested for scale, the entire infrastructure must be in place and waiting for the test, which may run for only a few hours in a week or even a month.

Again, we will soon review how the same problems can be solved in the Cloud with the Private Cloud setup and the so-called "*Shadow IT*."

Let us start by noting that today the above process has been streamlined to keep both developers and service providers focused only on the added value they have to create. This has been achieved owing to *IT transformation* into a new way of doing things. Two major enablers came in succession: first, virtualization, and, second, the Cloud itself.

Virtualization (described in detail in the next chapter) has actually been around for many years, but it was recently "rediscovered" by IT managers who looked to reduce costs. Simply put, virtualization is about consolidation of computing through the reuse of hardware. For example, if a company had 10 hardware servers, each running its own operating system and an application with fairly low CPU utilization, the virtualization technology would enable these 10 servers to be replaced (without any change in software or incurring a high-performance penalty) with one or two powerful servers. As we will see in the next chapter, the key piece of virtualization is a *hypervisor*, which emulates the hardware environment so that each operating system and application running over it "thinks" that it is running on its own server.

Thus, applications running on under-utilized dedicated physical servers[6] were gradually moved to a virtualized environment enabling, first and foremost, server consolidation. With that, fewer servers needed to be purchased and maintained, which respectively translated into savings in *Capital Expenditure (CapEx)* and Operational Expenditure (OpEx). This is a significant achievement, taking into account that two-thirds of a typical IT budget is devoted

[6] A server was considered under-utilized if the application that ran on it incurred on average 5–10% utilization on a typical x86 processor.

to maintenance. Other benefits include improvements in availability, disaster recovery, and flexibility (as it is much faster to deploy virtual servers than physical ones).

With all these gains for the providers of services, the consumers of IT services were left largely with the same experience as before—inasmuch as the virtualization setups just described were static. Fewer servers were running, with higher utilization. An important step for sure, but it did not change the fundamental complexity of consuming computing resources.

The Cloud was a major step forward. What the Cloud provided to the IT industry was the ability to move to a service-centric, "pay-as-you-go" business model with minimal upfront investment and risk. Individuals and businesses developing new applications could benefit from low-cost infrastructure and practically infinite scale, allowing users to pay only for what they actually used. In addition, with Cloud, the infrastructure is "abstracted," allowing users to spend 100% of their effort on building their applications rather than setting up and maintaining generic infrastructures. Companies like Amazon and Google have built massive-scale, highly efficient Cloud services.

As we saw in the previous chapter, from an infrastructure perspective, Cloud has introduced a platform that is multi-tenant (supporting many users on the same physical infrastructure), elastic, equipped with a programmable interface (via API), fully automated, self-maintained, and—on top of all that—has a very low total cost of ownership. At first, Cloud platforms provided basic infrastructure services such as computing and storage. In recent years, Cloud services have ascended into software product implementations to offer more and more generic services—such as load-balancing-as-a-service or database-as-a-service, which allow users to focus even more on the core features of their applications.

Let us illustrate this with an example. Initially, a Cloud user could only create a virtual machine. If this user needed a database, that would have to be purchased, installed, and maintained. One subtle problem here is licensing—typically, software licenses bound the purchase to a limited number of physical machines. Hence, when the virtual machine moves to another physical host, the software might not even run. Yet, with the *database-as-a-service* offered, the user merely needs to select the database of choice and start using it. The tasks of acquiring the database software along with appropriate licenses, and installing and maintaining the software, now rest with the Cloud provider. Similarly, to effect load balancing (before the introduction of *load-balancer-as-a-service*), a user needed to create and maintain virtual machines for the servers to be balanced and for the load balancer itself. As we will see in Chapter 7 and the Appendix, the current technology and Cloud service offers require that a user merely specifies the server, which would be replicated by the Cloud provider when needed, with the load balancers introduced to balance the replicas.

The latest evolution of Cloud moves the support for application life cycle management, offering generic services that replace what had to be part of an application itself. Examples of such services are *auto-deployment*, *auto-scaling*, *application monitoring*, and *auto-healing*.

For instance, in the past an application developer had to create monitoring tools as part of the application and then also create an algorithm to decide when more capacity should be added. If so, the tools would need to setup, configure and bring on-line the new virtual machines and possibly a load balancer. Similarly, the tools would need to decide whether an application is healthy, and, if not, start auto-healing by, for example, creating a new server, loading it with the saved state, and shutting down the failed server.

Using the new life-cycle services, all the application developers need to do now is merely declare the rules for making such decisions and have the Cloud provider's software perform

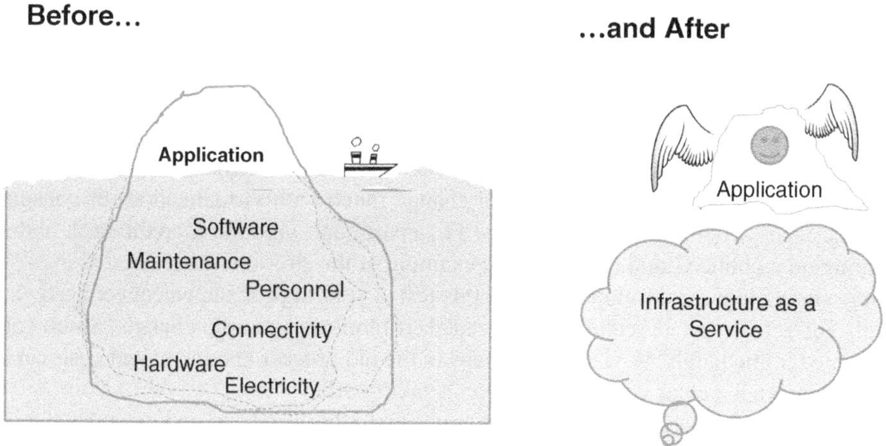

Figure 2.1 Investment in an application deployment—before and after.

the necessary actions. Again, the developer's energy can be focused solely on the features of the application itself.

The technology behind this is that the Cloud provider essentially creates generic services, with the appropriate *Application Programmer's Interface* (*API*) for each service. What has actually happened is that the common-denominator features present in all applications have been "abstracted"—that is, made available as building blocks. This type of modularization has been the principle of software development, but what could previously be achieved only through rigidly specified procedure calls to a local library is now done in a highly distributed manner, with the building blocks residing on machines other than the application that assembles them.

Figure 2.1 illustrates this with a metaphor that is well known in the industry. Before the Cloud, the actual value-adding application was merely the tip of an iceberg as seen by the end user, while a huge investment still had to be made in the larger, invisible part that was not seen by the user.

An incisive example reflecting the change in this industry is *Instagram*. Facebook bought Instagram for one billion dollars. At the time of the purchase, Instagram had 11 employees managing 30 million customers. Instagram had no physical infrastructure, and only three individuals were employed to manage the infrastructure within the Amazon Cloud. There was no capital expense required, no physical servers needed to be procured and maintained, no technicians paid to administer them, and so on. This enabled the company to generate one billion dollars in value in two years, with little or no upfront investment in people or infrastructure. Most company expenses went toward customer acquisition and retention. The Cloud allowed Instagram to scale automatically as more users came on board, without the service crashing with growth.

Back to our early example of Zing Interactive Media—if it were launched today it would definitely follow the Instagram example. There would be no need to lease a "cage," buy a server, rent T1 lines, or go through the other hoops described above. Instead, we would be able to focus only on the interactive radio application. Furthermore, we would not need to hire database administrators since our application could consume a database-as-a-service function.

And finally, we would hire fewer developers as building a robust scalable application would be as simple as defining the life cycle management rules in the relevant service of the Cloud provider.

In the case of software development in a corporation, we are seeing two trends: Shadow IT and Private Cloud.

With the Shadow IT trend, in-house developers—facing the alternative of either following the process described above (which did not change much with virtualization) or consuming a Cloud service—often opted to bypass the IT department, take out a credit card, and start developing on a public Cloud. Consider the example of the stress test discussed above—with relatively simple logic, a developer can run this test at very high scale, whenever needed, and pay only for actual use. If scaling up is needed, it requires a simple change, which can be implemented immediately. Revisiting the steps in the old process and its related costs (in both time and capital), it's clear why this approach is taking off.

Many a Chief Information Officer (CIO) has observed this trend and understood that it is not enough just to implement virtualization in their data centers (often called Private Cloud, but really they were not that). The risks of Shadow IT are many, among them the loss of control over personnel. There are also significant security risks, since critical company data are now replicated in the Cloud. The matter of access to critical data (which we will address in detail in the Appendix) is particularly important, as it often concerns *privacy* and is subject to regulatory and legal constraints. For instance, the US Health Insurance Portability and Accountability Act (HIPAA) [7] has strict privacy rules with which companies must comply. Another important example of the rules guarding data access is the US law known as the *Sarbanes–Oxley Act (SOX)*,[8] which sets standards for all US public companies' boards and accounting firms.

These considerations, under the threat of Shadow IT, lead CIOs to take new approaches. One is called *Virtual Private Cloud*, which is effected by obtaining from a Cloud provider a secure area (a dedicated set of resources). This approach allows a company to enjoy all the benefits of the Cloud, but in a controlled manner, with the company's IT being in full control of the security as well as costs. The service-level agreements and potential liabilities are clearly defined here.

The second approach is to build true private Clouds in the company's own data centers. The technology enabling this approach has evolved sufficiently, and so the vendors have started offering the full capabilities of a Cloud in software products. One example, which we will address in much detail in Chapter 7 and the Appendix, is the open-source project developing Cloud-enabling software, *OpenStack*. With products like that the enterprise IT departments can advance their own data center implementation, from just supporting virtualization to building a true Cloud, with services similar to those offered by a Cloud provider. These private Clouds provide internal services internally, with most of the benefits of the public Cloud (obviously with limited scale), but under full control and ultimately lower costs, as the margin of the Cloud provider is eliminated.

The trend for technology companies is to start in a public Cloud and then, after reaching the scale-up plateau, move to a true private Cloud to save costs. Most famous for this is *Zynga*—the gaming company that produced *Farmville*, among other games. Zynga started out with Amazon, offering its web services. When a game started to take off and its use patterns

---

[7] www.hhs.gov/ocr/privacy/

[8] www.gpo.gov/fdsys/pkg/PLAW-107publ204/html/PLAW-107publ204.htm

became predictable, Zynga moved it to the in-house Cloud, called *zCloud*, and optimized for gaming needs. Similarly, eBay has deployed the OpenStack software on 7000 servers that today power 95% of its marketplace.[9]

It should now be clear that the benefits of the Cloud are quite significant. But the Cloud has a downside, too.

We have already discussed some of the security challenges above (and, again, we will be addressing security throughout the book). It is easy to fall in love with the simplicity that the Cloud offers, but the security challenges are very real, and, in our opinion, are still under-appreciated.

Another problem is control over hardware choices to meet reliability and performance requirements. Psychologically, it is not easy for developers to relinquish control over the exact specification of the servers they need and choices over which CPU, memory, form factor, and network interface cards are to be used. In fact, it is not only psychological. Whereas before a developer could be assured of meeting specifications, now one should merely trust the Cloud infrastructure to respond properly to an API call to increase computing power. In this situation, it is particularly important to develop and evaluate overarching software models in support of highly reliable and high-performance services.

As we will see later in this book, Cloud providers respond to this by adding capabilities to reserve-specific (yet hardware-generic) configuration parameters—such as number of CPU cores, memory size, storage capacity, and networking "pipes."

Intel, among other CPU vendors, is contributing to solving these problems. Take, for example, an application that needs a predictable amount of CPU power. Until recently, in the Cloud it could not be assured with fine granularity what an application would receive, which could be a major problem for real-time applications. Intel is providing API that allows the host to guarantee a certain percentage of the CPU to a given virtual machine. This capability, effected by assigning a virtual machine to a given processor or a range of processes—so-called *CPU pinning*—is exposed via the hypervisor and the Cloud provider's systems, and it can be consumed by the application.

As one uses higher abstraction layers, one gains simplicity, but as one consumes generic services, one's ability to do unique things is very limited. Or otherwise put, if a capability is not exposed through an API, it cannot be used. For example, if one would like to use a specific advanced function of a load balancer of a specific vendor, one is in trouble in a generic Cloud. One can only use the load balancing functions exposed by the Cloud provider's API, and in most cases one would not even know which vendor is powering this service.

The work-around here is to descend the abstraction ladder. With the example of the last paragraph, one can purchase a virtual version of the vendor's load balancer, bring it up as a virtual machine as part of your project, and then use it. In other words, higher abstraction layers might not help to satisfy unique requirements.

2.2 The Business Model Around Cloud

Cloud service providers, such as Google or Amazon, are running huge infrastructures. It is estimated that Google has more than one million physical servers and that Amazon Cloud is providing infrastructure to 1.5–2 million virtual machines. These huge data centers are

[9] See www.computerweekly.com/news/2240222899/Case-study-How-eBay-uses-its-own-OpenStack-private-Cloud

built using highly commoditized hardware, with very small operational teams (only tens of people in a shift manage all Google's servers) leveraging automation in order to provide new levels of operational efficiencies. Although the infrastructure components themselves are not highly reliable (Amazon is only providing 99.95% SLA), the infrastructure automation and the way applications are written to leverage this infrastructure enable a rather reliable service (e.g., *Google search engine* or *Facebook Wall*) for a fraction of the cost that other industries bill for similar services.

Cloud provides a new level of infrastructure efficiencies and business agility, and it achieves that with a new operational model (e.g., automation, self-service, standardized commodity elements) rather than through performance optimization of infrastructure elements. The CapEx investment in hardware is less than 20% of the total cost of ownership of such infrastructures. The rest is mainly operational and licensing cost. The Cloud operational model and software choices (e.g., use of open-source software) enable a dramatic reduction in total cost—not just in the hardware, as is the case with virtualization alone.

Let us take a quick look at the business models offered by Cloud providers and software and service vendors, presented respectively in the subsections that follow.

2.2.1 Cloud Providers

Cloud offers a utility model for its services: computing, storage, application, and operations. This comes with an array of pricing models, which balance an end user's flexibility and price. Higher pricing is offered for the most flexible arrangement—everything on demand with no commitment. Better pricing is offered for reserved capacity—or a guarantee of a certain amount of use in a given time—which allows Cloud providers to plan their capacity better. For example, at the time of writing this chapter, using the Amazon pricing tool on its website we have obtained a quote from AWS for a mid-sized machine at $0.07 per hour for on-demand use. Reserved capacity for the same machine is quoted at $0.026—a 63% discount. This pricing does not include networking, data transfers, or other costs.[10]

Higher prices are charged for special services, such as the Virtual Private Cloud mentioned earlier. Finally, the best pricing is *spot pricing*, in which it is the Cloud provider who defines when the sought services are to be offered (that is, at the time when the provider's capacity is expected to be under-utilized). This is an excellent option for off-line computational tasks. For the Cloud providers, it ensures higher utilization.

One interesting trend, led by Amazon AWS, is the constant stream of price reductions. As Amazon adds scale and as storage and other costs go down, Amazon is taking the approach of reducing the pricing continuously—thereby increasing its competitive advantage and making the case, for potential customers, for moving to the Cloud even more attractive. In addition, Amazon continuously adds innovative services, such as the higher application abstraction mentioned above, which, of course, come with new charges. Additional charges are also made for networking, configuration changes, special machine types, and so forth.

For those who are interested in the business aspects of the Cloud, we highly recommend Joe Weinman's book [1], which also comes with a useful and incisive website[11] offering,

[10] The cited prices were obtained on January 20, 2015. For current prices, see http://aws.amazon.com/ec2/pricing/.
[11] www.Cloudonomics.com/

among many other things, a set of simulation tools to deal with structure, dynamics, and financial analysis of utility and Cloud Computing. We also recommend another treatise on Cloud business by Dr. Timothy Chou [2], which focuses on software business models.

2.2.2 *Software and Service Vendors*

To build a Private Cloud, a CIO organization needs to create a data center with physical servers, storage, and so on.[12] Then, in order to turn that into a Cloud, it has the choice of either purchasing the infrastructure software from a proprietary vendor (such as *VMware*) or using open-source software. OpenStack, addressed further in Chapter 7, is an open-source project that allows its users to build a Cloud service that offers services similar to Amazon AWS.

Even though the software from open-source projects is free for the taking, in practice—when it comes to large open-source projects—it is hard to avoid costs associated with the maintenance. Thus, most companies prefer not to take software directly from open-source repositories, instead purchasing it from a vendor who offers support and maintenance (upgrades, bug fixes, etc.). Companies like *Red Hat* and *Canonical* lead this segment. Pricing for these systems is usually based on the number of CPU sockets used in the Cloud cluster. Typically, the fee is annual and does not depend on the actual use metrics.

In addition, most companies use a professional services firm to help them set up (and often also manage) their Cloud environments. This is usually priced on a per-project time and material basis.

2.3 Taking Cloud to the Network Operators

At the cutting edge of the evolution to Cloud is the transformation of the telecommunications infrastructure. As we mentioned earlier, the telecommunications providers—who are also typically regulated in their respective countries—offer by far the most reliable and secure real-time services. Over more than 100 years, telecommunications equipment has evolved from electro-mechanical cross-connect telephone switches to highly specialized digital switches, to data switches—that make the present telecommunications networks. Further, these "boxes" have been interconnected with specialized networking appliances[13] and general-purpose high-performance computers that run operations and management software.

The *Network Functions Virtualization (NFV)* movement is about radically transforming the "hardware-box-based" telecom world along Cloud principles.[14]

First, let us address the problem that the network operators wanted to solve. While most of what we know as "network function" today is provided by software, this software runs on dedicated "telecom-grade" hardware. "Telecom grade" means that the hardware is (1) specifically engineered for running in telecommunications networks, (2) designed to live in the network for over 15 years, and (3) functional 99.999% (the "five nines") of the time (i.e., with about 5 minutes of downtime per year). This comes with a high cost of installation and maintenance

[12] The structure of data centers is discussed in Chapter 6.

[13] Described in Chapter 5.

[14] In the interests of full disclosure, as may be inferred from their short biographies, the authors are among the first movers in this space, and therefore their view is naturally very optimistic.

of customized equipment. Especially when taking into account Moore's "law," according to which the computing power doubles every 18 months, one can easily imagine the problems that accompany a 15-year-long commitment to dedicated hardware equipment.

With increased competition, network providers have been trying to find a solution to reducing margins and growing competition. And that competition now comes not only from within the telecom industry, but also from web-based service providers, known as *Over-The-Top (OTT)*.

Solving this problem requires a new operational model that reduces costs and speeds up the introduction of new services for revenue growth.

To tackle this, seven of the world's leading telecom network operators joined together to create a set of standards that were to become the framework for the advancement of virtualizing network services. On October 12, 2012, the representatives of 13 network operators[15] worldwide published a White Paper[16] outlining the benefits and challenges of doing so and issuing a call for action.

Soon after that, 52 other network operators—along with telecom equipment, IT vendors, and technology consultants—formed the *ETSI NFV Industry Specifications Group (ISG)*.[17]

The areas where action was needed can be summarized as follows. First, *operational improvements*. Running a network comprising the equipment from multiple vendors is far too complex and requires too much overhead (compared with a Cloud operator, a telecom network operator has to deal with the number of spare parts—which is an order of magnitude higher).

Second, *cost reductions*. Managing and maintaining the infrastructure using automation would require a tenth of the people presently involved in "manual" operations. With that, the number of "hardware boxes" in a telecom network is about 10,000(!) larger than that in the Cloud operator.

Third, *streamlining high-touch processes*. Provisioning and scaling services presently require manual intervention, and it takes 9 to 18 months to scale an existing service, whereas Cloud promises instant scaling.

Fourth, *reduction of development time*. Introducing new services takes 16 to 25 months. Compare this to several weeks in the IT industry and to immediate service instantiation in the Cloud.

Fifth, *reduction of replacement costs*. The respective lifespans of services keep shortening, and so does the need to replace the software along with the hardware, which is where the sixth—and last—area comes in.

Sixth, *reduction of equipment costs*. (The hint lies in comparing the price of the proprietary vendor-specific hardware with that of the commodity off-the-shelf x86-based servers.

To deal with the above problem areas, tried-and-true virtualization and Cloud principles have been called for. To this end, the NFV is about integrating into the telecom space many of the same Cloud principles discussed earlier. It is about first virtualizing the network functions pertinent to routing, voice communications, content distribution, and so on and then running them on a high-scale, highly efficient Cloud platform.

The NFV space can be divided into two parts: the *NFV platform* and the *network functions* running on top of it. The idea is that the network functions run on a common shared platform (the NFV platform), which is embedded in the network. Naturally, the network is what makes

---

[15] AT&T, BT, CenturyLink, China Mobile, Colt, Deutsche Telekom, KDDI, NTT, Telecom Italia, Telefonica,Telstra, and Verizon.

[16] https://portal.etsi.org/NFV/NFV_White_Paper.pdf

[17] www.etsi.org/technologies-clusters/technologies/nfv

a major difference between a generic Cloud and the NFV, as the *raison d'être* of the latter is delivering network-based services.

The NFV is about replacing physical deployment with virtual, the network functions deployed *dynamically, on demand* across the network on *Common Off-The-Shelf (COTS)* hardware. The NFV platform automates the installation and operation of Cloud nodes, orchestrates mass scale-distributed data centers, manages and automates application life cycles, and leverages the network. Needless to say, the platform is open to all vendors.

To appreciate the dynamic aspect of the NFV, consider the *Content Delivery Networking (CDN)* services (all aspects of which are thoroughly discussed in the dedicated monograph [3], which we highly recommend). In a nutshell, when a content provider (say a movie-streaming site) needs to deliver a real-time service over the Internet, the bandwidth costs (and congestion) are an obstacle. A working solution is to replicate the content on a number of servers that are placed, for a fee, around various geographic locations in an operator's network to meet the demand of local users. At the moment, this means deploying and administering physical servers, which comes with the problems discussed earlier. One problem is that the demand is often based on the time of day. As the time for viewing movies on the east coast of the United States is different from that in Japan, the respective servers would be alternately under-utilized for large periods of time. The ability to deploy a CDN server dynamically to data centers near the users that demand the service is an obvious boon, which not only saves costs, but also offers unprecedented flexibility to both the content provider and the operator.

Similar, although more specialized, examples of telecommunications applications that immediately benefit from NFV are the *IP Multimedia Subsystem (IMS)* for the *Third Generation (3G)* [4] and the *Evolved Packet Core (EPC)* for the *Fourth Generation (4G)* broadband wireless services [5]. (As a simple example: consider the flexibility of deploying—among the involved network providers—those network functions[18] that support roaming).

Network providers consider the NFV both disruptive and challenging. The same goes for many of the network vendors in this space.

The founding principles for developing the NFV solution are as follows:

- The NFV Cloud is distributed across the operator's network, and it can be constructed from elements that are designed for zero-touch, automated, large-scale deployment in central offices[19] and data centers.
- The NFV Cloud leverages and integrates with the networking services in order to deliver a full end-to-end guarantee for the service.
- The NFV Cloud is open in that it must be able to facilitate different applications coming from different vendors and using varying technologies.
- The NFV Cloud enables a new operational model by automating and unifying the many services that service providers might have, such as the distributed Cloud location and the application life cycle (further described in Chapter 7). The NFV Cloud must provide a high degree of security. (On this subject, please see the White Paper published by TMCnet, which outlines the authors' vision on this subject.[20])

---

[18] Such as the proxy Call Session control function (P-CSCF) in IMS.

[19] A central office is a building that hosts the telecommunication equipment for one or more switching exchanges.

[20] www.tmcnet.com/tmc/whitepapers/documents/whitepapers/2014/10172-providing-security-nfv.pdf

No doubt, this latest frontier shows us that the Cloud is now mature enough to change even more traditional industries—such as the energy sector. In coming years, we will see the fundamental effect of the Cloud on these industries' financial results and competitiveness.

References

[1] Weinman, J. (2012) *The Business Value of Cloud Computing*. John Wiley & Sons, Inc, New York.

[2] Chou, T. (2010) *Cloud: Seven Clear Business Models*, 2nd edn. Active Book Press, Madison, WI.

[3] Hofmann, M. and Beaumont, L.R. (2005) *Content Networking: Architecture, Protocols, and Practice* (part of the Morgan Kaufmann Series in Networking). Morgan Kaufmann/Elsevier, Amsterdam.

[4] Camarillo, G. and García-Martín, M.-A. (2008) *The 3G IP Multimedia Subsystem (IMS): Merging the Internet and the Cellular Worlds*, 3rd edn. John Wiley & Sons, Inc, New York.

[5] Olsson, M., Sultana, S., Rommer, S., *et al.* (2012) *EPC and 4G Packet Networks: Driving the Mobile Broadband Revolution*, 2nd edn. Academic Press/Elsevier, Amsterdam.

3

CPU Virtualization

This chapter explains the concept of a virtual machine as well as the technology that embodies it. The technology is rather complex, inasmuch as it encompasses the developments in computer architecture, operating systems, and even data communications. The issues at stake here are most critical to Cloud Computing, and so we will take our time.

To this end, the name of the chapter is something of a misnomer: it is not *only* the CPU that is being virtualized, but the whole of the computer, including its memory and devices. In view of that it might have been more accurate to omit the word "CPU" altogether, had it not been for the fact that in the very concept of virtualization the part that deals with the CPU is the most significant and most complex.

We start with the original motivation and a bit of history—dating back to the early 1970s—and proceed with the basics of the computer architecture, understanding what exactly *program control* means and how it is achieved. We spend a significant amount of time on this topic also because it is at the heart of security: it is through manipulation of program control that major security attacks are effected.

After addressing the architecture and program control, we will selectively summarize the most relevant concepts and developments in operating systems. Fortunately, excellent textbooks exist on the subject, and we delve into it mainly to highlight the key issues and problems in virtualization. (The very entity that enables virtualization, a *hypervisor*, is effectively an operating system that "runs" conventional operating systems.) We will explain the critical concept of a process and list the operating system services. We also address the concept of *virtual memory* and show how it is implemented—a development which is interesting on its own, while setting the stage for the introduction of broader virtualization tasks.

Once the stage is set, this chapter will culminate with an elucidation of the concept of the virtual machine. We will concentrate on hypervisors, their services, their inner workings, and their security, all illustrated by live examples.

Cloud Computing: Business Trends and Technologies, First Edition. Igor Faynberg, Hui-Lan Lu and Dor Skuler.

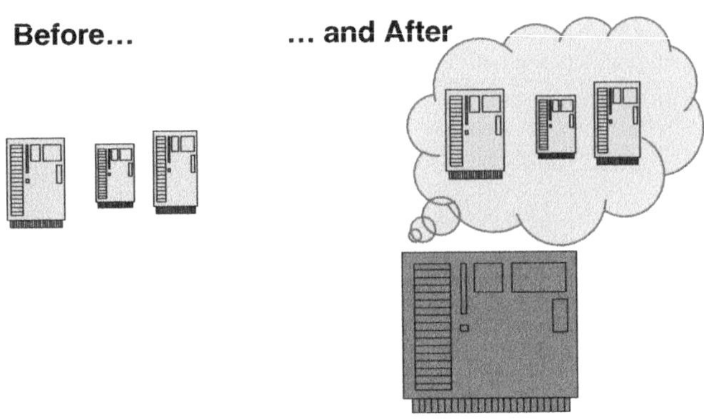

Figure 3.1 A computing environment before and after virtualization.

3.1 Motivation and History

Back in the 1960s, as computers were evolving to become ever faster and larger, the institutions and businesses that used them weighed up the pros and cons when deciding whether to replace older systems. The major problem was the same as it is now: the cost of software changes, especially because back then these costs were much higher and less predictable than they are now. If a business already had three or four computers say, with all the programs installed on each of them and the maintenance procedures set in place, migrating software to a new computer—even though a faster one than all the legacy machines combined—was a non-trivial economic problem. This is illustrated in Figure 3.1.

But the businesses were growing, and so were their computing needs. The industry was working to address this problem, with the research led by IBM and MIT. To begin with, *time sharing* (i.e., running multiple application processes in parallel) and *virtual memory* (i.e., providing each process with an independent full-address-range contiguous memory array) had already been implemented in the IBM System 360 Model 67 in the 1960s, but these were insufficient for porting multiple "whole machines" into one machine. In other words, a solution in which an operating system of a stand-alone machine could be run as a separate user process now executing on a new machine was not straightforward. The reasons are examined in detail later in this chapter; in a nutshell, the major obstacle was (and still is) that the code of an operating system uses a privileged subset of instructions that are unavailable to user programs.

The only way to overcome this obstacle was to develop what was in essence a *hyper* operating system that *supervised* other operating systems. Thus, the term *hypervisor* was coined. The joint IBM and MIT research at the Cambridge Scientific Center culminated in the *Control Program/Cambridge Monitor System* (*CP/CMS*). The system, which has gone through four major releases, became the foundation of the IBM VM/370 operating system, which implemented a hypervisor. Another seminal legacy of CP/CMS was the creation of a user community that pre-dated the open-source movement of today. CP/CMS code was available at no cost to IBM users.

IBM VM/370 was announced in 1972. Its description and history are well presented in Robert Creasy's famous paper [1]. CMS, later renamed the *Conversational Monitor System*, was part of it. This was a huge success, not only because it met the original objective of porting multiple systems into one machine, but also because it effectively started the virtualization industry—a decisive enabler of Cloud Computing.

Since then, all hardware that has been developed for minicomputers and later for microcomputers has addressed virtualization needs in part or in full. Similarly, the development of the software has addressed the same needs—hand in hand with hardware development.

In what follows, we will examine the technical aspects of virtualization; meanwhile, we can summarize its major achievements:

- Saving the costs (in terms of space, personnel, and energy—note the green aspect!) of running several physical machines in place of one;
- Putting to use (otherwise wasted) computing power;
- Cloning servers (for instance, for debugging purposes) almost instantly;
- Isolating a software package for a specific purpose (typically, for security reasons)—without buying new hardware; and
- Migrating a machine (for instance, when the load increases) at low cost and in no time—over a network or even on a memory stick.

The latter capability—to move a virtual machine from one physical machine to another—is called *live migration*. In a way, its purpose is diametrically opposite to the one that brought virtualization to life—that is, consolidating multiple machines on one physical host. Live migration is needed to support elasticity, as moving a machine to a new host—with more memory and reduced load—can increase its performance characteristics.

3.2 A Computer Architecture Primer

This section is present only to make the book self-contained. It provides the facts that we find essential to understanding the foremost virtualization issues, especially as far as security is concerned. It can easily be skipped by a reader familiar with computer architecture and—more importantly—its support of major programming control constructs (procedure calls, interrupt and exception handling). To a reader who wishes to learn more, we recommend the textbook [2]—a workhorse of Computer Science education.

3.2.1 CPU, Memory, and I/O

Figure 3.2 depicts pretty much all that is necessary to understand the blocks that computers are built of. We will develop more nuanced understanding incrementally.

The three major parts of a computer are:

1. The *Central Processing Unit* (*CPU*), which actually executes the programs;
2. The computer *memory* (technically called *Random Access Memory* (*RAM*)), where both programs and data reside; and
3. *Input/Output* (*I/O*) devices, such as the monitor, keyboard, network card, or disk.

All three are interconnected by a fast network, called a *bus*, which also makes a computer expandable to include more devices.

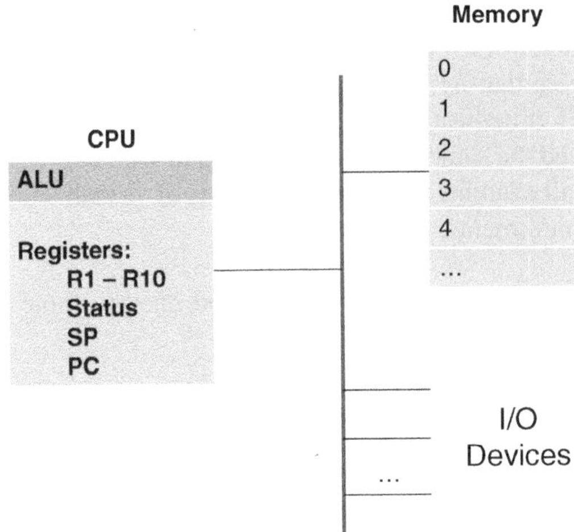

Figure 3.2 Simplified computer architecture.

The word *random* in RAM (as opposed to *sequential*) means that the memory is accessed as an array—through an index to a memory location. This index is called a *memory address*.

Note that the disk is, in fact, also a type of *memory*, just a much slower one than RAM. On the other hand, unlike RAM, the memory on the disk and other permanent storage devices is persistent: the stored data are there even after the power is turned off.

At the other end of the memory spectrum, there is much faster (than RAM) memory inside the CPU. All pieces of this memory are distinct, and they are called *registers*. Only the registers can perform operations (such as addition or multiplication—*arithmetic* operations, or a range of bitwise *logic* operations). This is achieved through a circuitry connecting the registers with the *Arithmetic and Logic Unit* (*ALU*). A typical mode of operation, say in order to perform an arithmetic operation on two numbers stored in memory, is to first transfer the numbers to registers, and then to perform the operation inside the CPU.

Some registers (we denote them R1, R2, etc.) are general purpose; others serve very specific needs. For the purposes of this discussion, we identify three registers of the latter type, which are present in any CPU:

1. The *Program Counter* (*PC*) register always points to the location memory where the next program instruction is stored.
2. The *Stack Pointer* (*SP*) register always points to the location of the stack of a *process*—we will address this concept in a moment.
3. The *STATUS register* keeps the execution control state. It stores, among many other things, the information about the result of a previous operation. (For instance, a flag called the *zero bit* of the STATUS register is set when an arithmetical operation has produced zero as a result. Similarly, there are positive-bit and negative-bit flags. All these are used for branching instructions: JZ—jump if zero; JP—jump if positive; JN—jump if negative. In turn, these instructions are used in high-level languages to implement conditional *if* statements.) Another—quite essential to virtualization—use of the STATUS register, which

we will discuss later, is to indicate to the CPU that it must work in *trace* mode, that is execute instructions one at a time. We will introduce new flags as we need them.

Overall, the set of all register values (sometimes called the *context*) constitutes the state of a program being executed as far as the CPU is concerned. A program in execution is called a *process*.[1] It is a very vague definition indeed, and here a metaphor is useful in clarifying it. A program can be seen as a cookbook, a CPU as a cook—using kitchen utensils, and then a process can be defined as the act of cooking a specific dish described in the cookbook.

A cook can work on several dishes concurrently, as long as the state of a dish (i.e., a specific step within the cookbook) is remembered when the cook switches to preparing another dish. For instance, a cook can put a roast into the oven, set a timer alarm, and then start working on a dessert. When the alarm rings, the cook will temporarily abandon the dessert and attend to the roast.

With that, the cook must know whether to baste the roast or take it out of the oven altogether. Once the roast has been attended to, the cook can resume working on the dessert. But then the cook needs to remember where the dessert was left off!

The practice of multi-programming—as maintained by modern operating systems—is to store the state of the CPU on the process stack, and this brings us to the subject of CPU inner workings.

We will delve into this subject in time, but to complete this section (and augment a rather simplistic view of Figure 3.2) we make a fundamental observation that modern CPUs may have more than one set of identical registers. As a minimum, one register set is reserved for the *user* mode—in which application programs execute– and the other for the *system* (or *supervisory*, or *kernel*) mode, in which only the operating system software executes. The reason for this will become clear later.

3.2.2 How the CPU Works

All things considered, the CPU is fairly simple in its concept. The most important point to stress here is that the CPU itself has no "understanding" of any program. It can deal only with *single* instructions written in its own, CPU-specific, *machine code*. With that, it keeps the processing state pretty much for this instruction alone. Once the instruction has been executed, the CPU "forgets" everything it had done and starts a new life executing the next instruction.

While it is not at all necessary to know all the machine code instructions of any given CPU in order to understand how it works, it is essential to grasp the basic concept.

As Donald Knuth opined in his seminal work [3], "A person who is more than casually interested in computers should be well schooled in machine language, since it is a fundamental part of a computer." This is all the more true right now—without understanding the machine language constructs one cannot even approach the subject of virtualization.

Fortunately, the issues involved are surprisingly straightforward, and these can be explained using only a few instructions. To make things simple, at this point we will avoid referring to

---

[1] In some operating systems, the term *thread* is what actually denotes the program execution, with the word *process* reserved for a set of threads that share the same memory space, but we intentionally do not distinguish between processes and threads here.

the instructions of any existing CPU. We will make up our own instructions as we go along. Finally, even though the CPU "sees" instructions as bit strings, which ultimately constitute the machine-level code, there is no need for us even to think at this level. We will look at the text that encodes the instructions—the assembly language.

Every instruction consists of its operation code *opcode*, which specifies (no surprise here!) an operation to be performed, followed by the list of operands. To begin with, to perform any operation on a variable stored in memory, a CPU must first load this variable into a register.

As a simple example: to add two numbers stored at addresses 10002 and 10010, respectively, a program must first transfer these into two CPU registers—say *R1* and *R2*. This is achieved with a *LOAD* instruction, which does just that: loads something into a register. The resulting program looks like this:

```
LOAD R1 @10002
LOAD R2 @10010
ADD R1, R2
```

(The character "@" here, in line with assembly-language conventions, signals *indirect* addressing. In other words, the numeric string that follows "@" indicates an address from which to load the value of a variable rather than the value itself. When we want to signal that the addressing is *immediate*—that is, the actual value of a numeric string is to be loaded—we precede it with the character "#," as in *LOAD R1, #3.*)

The last instruction in the above little program, *ADD*, results in adding the values of both registers and storing them—as defined by our machine language—in the second operand register, R2.

In most cases, a program needs to store the result somewhere. A *STORE* instruction—which is, in effect, the inverse of *LOAD*—does just that. Assuming that variables x, y, and z are located at addresses 10002, 10010, and 10020, respectively, we can augment our program with the instruction *STORE R2, @10020* to execute a C-language assignment statement: $z = x + y$.

Similarly, arithmetic instructions other than ADD can be introduced, but they hardly need any additional explanation. It is worth briefly mentioning the *logical instructions*: *AND* and *OR*, which perform the respective operations bitwise. Thus, the instruction *OR R1, X* sets those bits of R1 that are set in X; and the instruction *AND R1, X* resets those bits of R1 that are reset in X. A combination of logical instructions, along with the *SHIFT* instruction (which shifts the register bits a specified number of bits to the right or to the left, depending on the parameter value, while resetting the bits that were shifted), can achieve any manipulation of bit patterns.

We will introduce other instructions as we progress. Now we are ready to look at the first—and also very much simplified—description of a CPU working mechanism, as illustrated in Figure 3.3. We will keep introducing nuances and important detail to this description.

The CPU works like a clock—which is, incidentally, a very deep analogy with the mechanical world. All the operations of a computer are carried out at the frequency of the impulses emitted by a device called a *computer clock*, just as the parts of a mechanical clock move in accordance with the swinging of a pendulum. To this end, the speed of a CPU is measured by the clock frequency it can support.

All a CPU does is execute a tight infinite loop, in which an instruction is fetched from the memory and executed. Once this is done, everything is repeated. The CPU carries no memory of the previous instruction, except what is remaining in its registers.

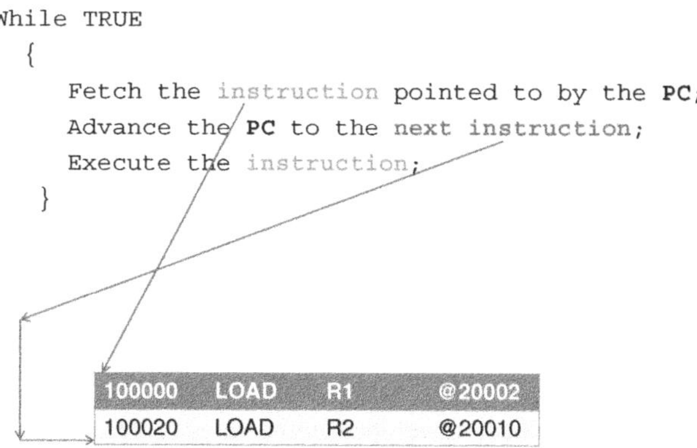
While TRUE
{
Fetch the instruction pointed to by the PC;
Advance the PC to the next instruction;
Execute the instruction;
}
100000 LOAD R1 @20002
100020 LOAD R2 @20010

Figure 3.3 A simplified CPU loop (first approximation).

If we place our little program into memory location 200000,[2] then we must load the PC register with this value so that the CPU starts to execute the first instruction of the program. The CPU then advances the PC to the next instruction, which happens to be at the address 200020. It is easy to see how the rest of our program gets executed.

Here, however, for each instruction of our program, the *next* instruction turns out to be just the next instruction in the memory. This is definitely not the case for general programming, which requires more complex control-transfer capabilities, which we are ready to discuss now.

3.2.3 In-program Control Transfer: Jumps and Procedure Calls

At a minimum, in order to execute the "if–then–else" logic, we need an instruction that forces the CPU to "jump" to an instruction stored at a memory address different from that of the next instruction in contiguous memory. One such instruction is the *JUMP* instruction. Its only operand is a memory address, which becomes the value of the PC register as a result of its execution.

Another instruction in this family, *JNZ* (*Jump if Non-Zero*) effects conditional transfer to an address provided in the instruction's only operand. *Non-zero* here refers to the value of a *zero* bit of the STATUS register. It is set every time the result of an arithmetic or logical operation is zero—a bit of housekeeping done by the CPU with the help of the ALU circuitry. When executing this instruction, a CPU does nothing but change the value of the PC to that of the operand. The STATUS register typically holds other conditional bits to indicate whether the numeric result is positive or negative. To make the programmer's job easier (and its results faster), many CPUs provide additional variants of conditional transfer instructions.

More interesting—and fundamental to all modern CPUs—is an instruction that transfers control to a procedure. Let us call this instruction *JPR* (*Jump to a Procedure*). Here, the CPU helps the programmer in a major way by automatically storing the present value of the PC (which, according to Figure 3.3, initially points to the next instruction in memory) on the

[2] At this point we intentionally omit defining the memory unit (i.e., *byte* or *word*) in which the addresses are expressed.

stack[3]—pointed to by the SP. With that, the value of the SP is changed appropriately. This allows the CPU to return control to exactly the place in the program where the procedure was called. To achieve that, there is an operand-less instruction, *RTP* (*Return from a Procedure*). This results in popping the stack and restoring the value of the PC. This must be the last instruction in the body of every procedure.

There are several important points to consider here.

First, we observe that a somewhat similar result could be achieved just with the JUMP instruction alone; after all, a programmer (or a compiler) could add a couple of instructions to store the PC on the stack. A JUMP—to the popped PC value—at the end of the procedure would complete the task. To this end, everything would have worked even if the CPU had had no notion of the stack at all—it could have been a user-defined structure. The two major reasons that modern CPUs have been developed in the way we describe here are (1) to make procedure calls execute faster (by avoiding the fetching of additional instructions) and (2) to enforce good coding practices and otherwise make adaptability of the ALGOL language and its derivatives straightforward (a language-directed design). As we have noted already, the recursion is built in with this technique.

Second, the notion of a process as the execution of a program should become clearer now. Indeed, the stack traces the control transfer outside the present main line of code. We will see more of this soon. It is interesting that in the 1980s, the programmers in Borroughs Corporation, whose highly innovative—at that time—CPU architecture was ALGOL-directed, used the words *process* and *stack* interchangeably! This is a very good way to think of a process—as something effectively represented by its stack, which always traces a single thread of execution.

Third, this structure starts to unveil the mechanism for supporting multi-processing. Assuming that the CPU can store all its states on a process stack and later restore them—the capability we address in the next section—we can imagine that a CPU can execute different processes concurrently by switching among respective stacks.

Fourth—and this is a major security concern—the fact that, when returning from a procedure, the CPU pops the stack and treats as the PC value whatever has been stored there means that if one manages to replace the original stored value of the PC with another memory address, the CPU will *automatically* start executing the code at that memory address. This fact has been exploited in distributing computer *worms*. A typical technique that allows overwriting the PC is when a buffer is a parameter to a procedure (and thus ends up on the stack). For example, if the buffer is to be filled by reading a user-supplied string, and the procedure's code does not check the limits of the buffer, this string can be carefully constructed to pass both (1) the worm code and (2) the pointer to that code so that the pointer overwrites the stored value of the PC. This technique has been successfully tried with the original *Morris's worm of 1988* (see [4] for a thorough technical explanation in the context of the worm's history unfolding).[4] We will address security in the last section of this chapter.

For what follows, it is important to elaborate more on how the stack is used in implementing procedure calls.

---

[3] The stack is typically set in higher addresses of the memory, so that it "grows" down: Putting an item of n memory units on the stack results in *decreasing* the value of SP by n.

[4] At that time, it exploited the vulnerability of a Unix finger utility. It is surprising that the same vulnerability still remains pertinent!

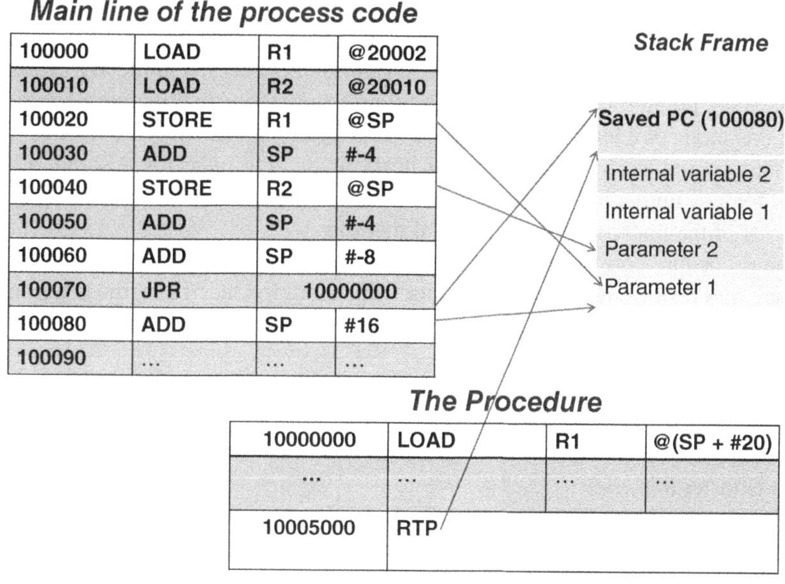

Main line of the process code
100000 LOAD R1 @20002
100010 LOAD R2 @20010
100020 STORE R1 @SP
100030 ADD SP #-4
100040 STORE R2 @SP
100050 ADD SP #-4
100060 ADD SP #-8
100070 JPR 10000000
100080 ADD SP #16
100090 ... ...
Stack Frame
Saved PC (100080)
Internal variable 2
Internal variable 1
Parameter 2
Parameter 1
The Procedure
10000000 LOAD R1 @(SP + #20)
... ...
10005000 RTP

Figure 3.4 The process stack and the procedure call.

With a little help from the CPU, it is now a programmer's job (if the programmer writes in an assembly language) or a compiler's job (if the programmer writes in a high-level language) to handle the parameters for a procedure. The long-standing practice has been to put them on the stack *before* calling the procedure.

Another essential matter that a programmer (or a compiler writer) must address in connection with a procedure call is the management of the variables that are local to the procedure. Again, a long-standing practice here is to allocate all the local memory on the stack. One great advantage of doing so is to enable recursion: each time a procedure is invoked, its parameters and local memory are separate from those of the previous invocation.

Figure 3.4 illustrates this by following the execution of an example program,[5] along with the state of the process stack at each instruction. Here, a procedure stored at location 1000000 is called from the main program. The procedure has two parameters stored at locations 20002 and 20010, respectively.

The first six instructions implement the act of pushing the procedure parameters on the stack. (Note that we consider each parameter to be four units long, hence *ADD SP #-4*; of course, as the stack—by convention—diminishes, the value of the stack pointer is decreased.)

The seventh instruction (located at the address 100060), prepares the internal memory of the procedure on the stack, which happens in this particular case to need eight units of memory for the two, four-unit-long variables.

In the eighth instruction, the procedure code is finally invoked. This time the CPU itself pushes the value of the PC (also four bytes long) on the stack; then, the CPU loads the PC with the address of the procedure. At this point, the procedure's *stack frame* has been established.

[5] This example program is intentionally left unoptimized.

Execution of the first instruction of the procedure results in retrieving the value of the first parameter, which, as we know, is located on the stack, exactly 20 units above the stack pointer. Similarly, another parameter and the internal variables are accessed indirectly, relative to the value of the stack pointer. (We intentionally did not show the actual memory location of the stack: with this mode of addressing, that location is irrelevant as long as the stack is initialized properly! This is a powerful feature in that it eliminates the need for absolute addressing. Again, this feature immediately supports recursion, as the same code will happily execute with a new set of parameters and new internal memory.)

When the procedure completes, the RTP instruction is executed, which causes the CPU to pop the stack and restore the program counter to its stored value. Thus, the program control returns to the main program. The last instruction in the example restores the stack to its original state.

A minor point to note here is that a procedure may be a *function*—that is, it may return a value. How can this value be passed to the caller? Storing it on the stack is one way of achieving that; the convention of the *C*-language compilers though has been to pass it in a register—it is faster this way.

This concludes the discussion of a procedure call. We are ready to move on to the next level of detail of CPU mechanics, motivated by the new forms of control transfer.

3.2.4 Interrupts and Exceptions—the CPU Loop Refined

So far, the simple CPU we have designed can only deal with one process. (We will continue with this limitation in the present section.) The behavior of the process is determined by the set of instructions in its main line code—and the procedures, to which control is transferred—but still in an absolutely predictable (sometimes called "deterministic" or "synchronous") manner. This type of CPU existed in the first several decades of computing, and it does more or less what is needed to perform in-memory processing. It has been particularly suitable for performing complex mathematical algorithms, so long as not much access to I/O devices is needed.

But what happens when an I/O request needs to be processed? With the present design, the only solution is to have a subroutine that knows how to access a given I/O device—say a disk or a printer. We can assume that such a device is *memory-mapped*: there is a location in main memory to write the command (read or write), pass a pointer to a data buffer where the data reside (or are to be read into), and also a location where the status of the operation can be checked. After initiating the command, the process code can do nothing else except execute a tight loop checking for the status.

Historically, it turned out that for CPU-intensive numeric computation such an arrangement was more or less satisfactory, because processing I/O was an infrequent action—compared with computation. For business computing, however—where heavy use of disks, multiple tapes, and printers was required most of the time—CPU cycles wasted on polling are a major performance bottleneck. As the devices grew more complex, this problem was further aggravated by the need to maintain interactive device-specific protocols, which required even more frequent polling and waiting. (Consider the case when each byte to a printer needs to be written separately, followed by a specific action based on how the printer responds to processing the previous byte.) For this reason, the function of polling was transferred into the CPU loop at the expense of a change—and a dramatic change at that!—of the computational model.

The gist of the change is that whereas before a subroutine was called from a particular place in a program determined by the programmer (whether from the main line or another subroutine), now the CPU gets to call certain routines *by itself*, acting on a communication from a device. With that, the CPU effectively *interrupts* the chain of instructions in the program, which means that the CPU needs to return to this chain exactly at the same place where it was interrupted. More terminology here: the signal from a device, which arrives asynchronously with respect to the execution of a program, is appropriately called an *interrupt*; everything that happens from that moment on, up to the point when the execution of the original thread of instruction resumes, is called *interrupt processing*.

Of course, the actual code for processing the input from a device—the *interrupt handling routine*—still has to be written by a programmer. But since this routine is never explicitly called *from* a program, it has to be placed in a specified memory location where the CPU can find it. This location is called an *interrupt vector*. Typically, each device has its own vector—or even a set of vectors for different events associated with the device. (In reality this may be more complex, but such a level of detail is unnecessary here.) At initialization time, a program must place the address of the appropriate interrupt routine in the slot assigned to the interrupt vector. The CPU jumps to the routine when it detects a signal from the device. When the interrupt is *serviced*, the control is returned to the point where the execution was interrupted—the execution of the original program is resumed.

This mechanism provides the means to deal with the external events that are asynchronous with the execution of a program. For reasons that will become clear later, the same mechanism is also used for handling certain events that are actually *synchronous* with program execution. They are synchronous in that they are caused by the very instruction to be executed (which, as a result, may end up being *not* executed). Important examples of such events are:

- A computational exception (an attempt to divide by zero).
- A memory-referencing exception (such as an attempt to read or write to a non-existent location in memory).
- An attempt to execute a non-existing instruction (or an instruction that is illegal in the current context).
- (A seemingly odd one!) An explicit in-line request (called a *trap*) for processing an exception. In our CPU this is caused by an instruction (of the form *TRAP <trap number>*) which allows a parameter—the trap number—to associate a specific interrupt vector with the trap, so that different trap numbers may be processed differently.

The fundamental need for the trap instruction will be explained later, but one useful application is in setting breakpoints for debugging. When a developer wants a program to stop at a particular place so that the memory can be examined, the resulting instruction is replaced with the trap instruction, as Figure 3.5 illustrates. The same technique is used by hypervisors to deal with non-virtualizable instructions, and we will elaborate on this later too.

Figure 3.6 illustrates the following discussion.

We are ready to modify the simplistic CPU loop of Figure 3.3. The new loop has a check for an interrupt or exception signal. Note that, as far as the CPU is concerned, the processing is quite deterministic: the checking occurred exactly at the end of the execution of the present instruction, no matter when the signal arrived. The CPU's internal circuitry allows it to determine the type of interrupt or exception, which is reflected in the interrupt number x. This

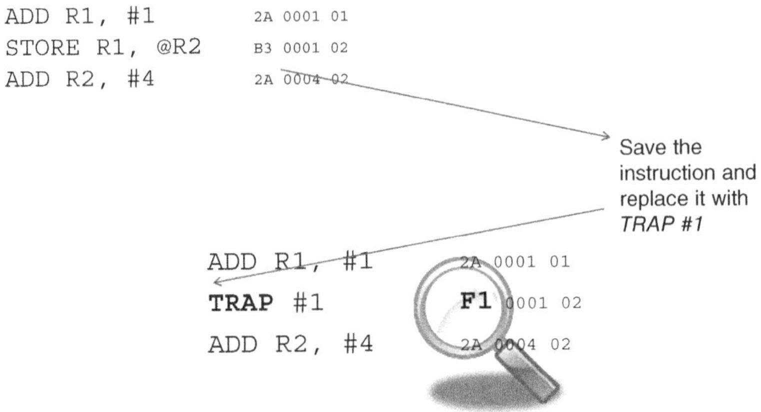

Figure 3.5 Setting a breakpoint.

number serves as the index to the interrupt vector table.[6] There is an important difference between processing interrupts and processing exceptions: an instruction that has caused an exception has *not* been executed; therefore, the value of the PC to be stored must remain the same. Other than that, there is no difference in processing between interrupts and exceptions, and to avoid pedantic repetition, the rest of this section uses the word "interrupt" to mean "an interrupt or an exception."

The table on the left in Figure 3.6 indicates that the interrupt service routine for processing interrupt x starts at location 30000000. The CPU deals with this code similarly to that of a procedure; however, this extraordinary situation requires an extraordinary set of actions! Different CPUs do different things here; our CPU does more or less what all modern CPUs do.

To this end, our CPU starts by saving the present value of the STATUS register on the process stack. The reason is that whatever conditions have been reflected in the STATUS register flags as a result of the previous instruction will disappear when the new instruction is executed. For example, if the program needs to branch when a certain number is greater than another, this may result in the four instructions as follows:

- Two instructions to load the respective values into R0 and R1.
- One instruction to subtract R1 from R0.
- One last instruction to branch, depending on whether the result of the subtraction is positive.

The execution of the last instruction depends on the flag set as a result of the execution of the third instruction, and so if the process is interrupted after that instruction, it will be necessary for it to have the flags preserved when it continues.

---

[6] In early CPUs the interrupt vector table typically lay in low memory, often starting with address 0. Modern CPUs have a special register pointing to this table, which can be put anywhere in the memory. It may be useful to observe at this point, even though we are still only dealing with a one-user/one-process execution, that in a multi-user environment a crucial task of operating systems and hypervisors is to protect access to certain parts of memory. We will start addressing this point with the next CPU loop modification.

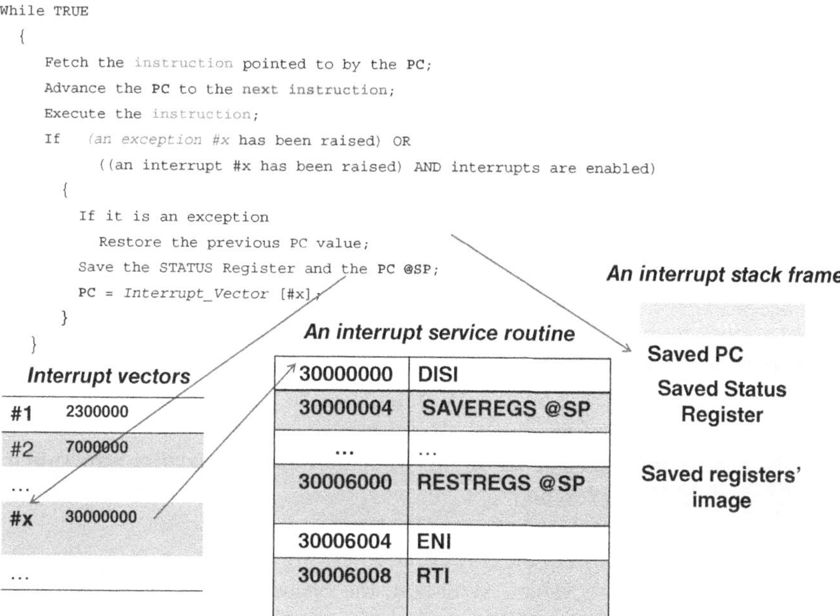
While TRUE
{
Fetch the instruction pointed to by the PC;
Advance the PC to the next instruction;
Execute the instruction;
If (an exception #x has been raised) OR
((an interrupt #x has been raised) AND interrupts are enabled)
{
If it is an exception
Restore the previous PC value;
Save the STATUS Register and the PC @SP;
PC = Interrupt_Vector [#x];
}
}
Interrupt vectors
#1 2300000
#2 7000000
...
#x 30000000
...
An interrupt service routine
30000000 DISI
30000004 SAVEREGS @SP
... ...
30006000 RESTREGS @SP
30006004 ENI
30006008 RTI
An interrupt stack frame
Saved PC
Saved Status Register
Saved registers' image

Figure 3.6 The second approximation of the CPU loop.

After saving the STATUS register, the CPU saves the value of the PC, just as it did with the procedure call stack frame. Then it starts executing the interrupt service routine.

The first instruction of the latter must be the *DISI* (*Disable Interrupts*) instruction. Indeed, from the moment the CPU discovers that an interrupt is pending—and up to this instruction—everything has been done by the CPU itself, and it would not interrupt itself! But the next interrupt from the same device may have arrived already. If the CPU were to process it, this very interrupt routine would be interrupted. A faulty device (or a malicious manipulation) would then result in a set of recursive calls, causing the stack to grow until it overflows, which will eventually bring the whole system down. Hence, it is necessary to disable interrupts, at least for a very short time—literally for the time it takes to execute a few critical instructions.

Next, our sample interrupt service routine saves the rest of the registers (those excluding the PC and the STATUS register) on the stack using the *SAVEREGS* instruction.[7] With that, in effect, the whole state of the process is saved. Even though all the execution of the interrupt service routine uses the process stack, it occurs independently of—or concurrently with—the execution of the process itself, which is blissfully unaware of what has happened.

The rest of the interrupt service routine code deals with whatever else needs to be done, and when it is finished, it will restore the process's registers (via the *RESTREGS* instruction) and *enable interrupts* (via the penultimate instruction, *ENI*). The last instruction, *RTI*, tells the CPU to restore the values of the PC and the STATUS register. The next instruction the CPU will execute is exactly the instruction at which the process was interrupted.

[7] Again, different CPUs handle this in different ways. Some automatically save all the registers on the stack; some expect the interrupt routine to save only what is needed.

(Typically, and also in the case of our CPU, there is a designated STATUS register flag (bit) that indicates whether the interrupts are disabled. DISI merely sets this flag, and ENI resets it.)

An illustrative example is a debugging tool, as mentioned earlier: a tool that allows us to set breakpoints so as to analyze the state of the computation when a breakpoint is reached.[8] The objective is to enable the user to set—interactively, by typing a command—a breakpoint at a specific instruction of the code, so that the program execution is stopped when it reaches this instruction. At that point the debugger displays the registers and waits for the next command from the user.

Our debugging tool, as implemented by the *command_line( )* subroutine, which is called by the TRAP #1 service routine, accepts the following six commands:

1. *Set <location>*, which sets the breakpoint in the code to be debugged. Because this may need to be reset, the effect of the command is that
   (a) both the instruction (stored at <location>) and the value of <location> are stored in the respective global variables, and
   (b) the instruction is replaced with that of TRAP #1.

   Figure 3.5 depicts the effect of the command; following convention, we use hexadecimal notation to display memory values. With that, the opcode for the TRAP #1 instruction happens to be *F1*.
2. *Reset*, which returns the original instruction, replaced by the trap, to its place.
3. *Register <name>, <value>*, which sets a named register with its value. The images of all CPU registers (except the PC and the STATUS register, which require separate handling) are kept in a global structure *registers_struct* so when, for instance, a user enters a command: *Register R1, 20*, an assignment "*registers_struct.R1 = 20;*" will be executed.
4. *Go*, to start executing the code–based on the respective values of the registers stored in *registers_struct*.
5. *Show <memory_location>, <number_of_units>*, which simply provides a core dump of the piece of memory specified by the parameters.
6. *Change <memory_location>, <value>*, which allows us to change the value of a memory unit.

Both the *Go( )* procedure and the interrupt vector routine *TRAP_1_Service_Routine( )* are presented in Figure 3.7. We will walk through them in a moment, but first let us start with the initialization. In the beginning, we:

1. Store the address of the pointer to the *TRAP_1_Service_Routine( )* at the interrupt vector for the *TRAP #1* instruction. (This location, which depends on a particular CPU, is supplied by the CPU manual.)
2. Execute the *TRAP #1* instruction, which will result in the execution of the *TRAP_1_Service_Routine( )*. The latter calls the *command_line( )* procedure, which prompts the user for a command and then interprets it.

[8] Later in this chapter we will define the term *introspection*. The mechanism we are about to describe is a simple example of introspection.

The *Go()* code

```
Go()
 {
    #DISI; /* disable interrupts */
    registers_struct.SP =
       registers_struct.SP +4;

   #RESTREGS @registers_struct;
   #STORE PC  @SP+8;
   #STORE STATUS @SP+4
     /* place the PC and Status in
        their proper place within
        the stack frame */

   #ENI; /* enable interrupts */
   #RTI;
 }
```

The service routine for *TRAP #1*

The TRAP #1 vector stores the address of the TRAP_1_Service Routine:

```
#DISI; /*disable interrupts*/
#SAVEREGS @registers_struct;
#ENI;  /*enable interrupts */
display(registers_struct, PC,
 STATUS);
command_line();
```

Figure 3.7 Go( ) and the interrupt service routines.

Now we can start debugging. Say we want a program, whose first instruction is located at memory address 300000, to stop when it reaches the instruction located at address 350000.

We type the following three commands:

```
>Register PC, 300000
>Set 350000
>Go
```

When the interpreter invokes Go( ), it first pops the stack to make up for the debugger's command-line procedure frame (With our design, we will never return from this call by executing RTP.). Then it transfers the register values stored in *registers_struct* to the CPU. The same task is repeated separately for the PC and the STATUS registers, whose values must be modified on the stack to build the proper stack frame. Finally, the RTI instruction is executed.

This will get the program moving. When it reaches the trapped instruction, our TRAP handler will be invoked. As a result, we will see the values of the registers and a prompt again. We can examine the memory, possibly change one thing or another, replace the trapped instruction, and maybe set another trap.

Note that the Go( ) procedure has, in effect, completed interrupt handling: the RTI instruction has not been part of the trap service routine. We can have more than one program in memory, and by modifying the registers appropriately, we may cause another program to run by "returning" to it.

This is a dramatic point: we have all we need to run several processes concurrently!

To do so, we allocate each process appropriate portions of memory for the stack and for the rest of the process's memory, called a *heap*, where its run-time data reside. We also establish

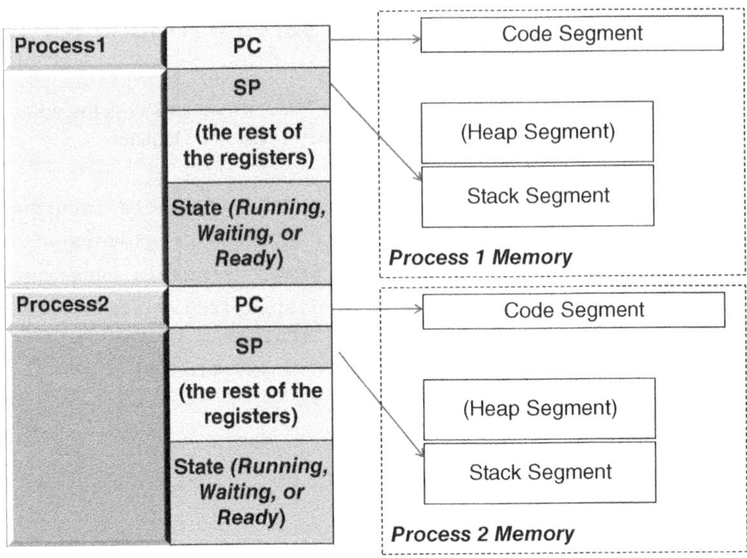

Figure 3.8 The process table.

the proper stack frame. In the latter, the value of the PC must point to the beginning of the process's code, and the value of the SP must point to the process's stack. (The rest of the registers do not matter at this point.) We only need to execute the last three instructions of Figure 3.5; the magic will happen when the RTI instruction is executed![9]

And thus, with the CPU described so far—however simple it may be—it is possible to make the first step toward virtualization, that is multi-processing. With this step, multiple processes (possibly belonging to different users) can share a CPU. This is the view of multi-processing "from outside." The "inner" view—a process's view—is that the process is given its own CPU as a result.

The perception of owning the CPU is the first step toward virtualization. But the ideal of "being virtual" cannot quite be achieved without virtualizing memory, that is making a process "think" that it has its own full memory space starting from address 0.

These two aspects—the CPU and memory virtualization—are addressed in the next two sections. It turns out that adding new capabilities requires changes to the architecture. As the needs of multi-processing become clear, our CPU will further evolve to support them.

3.2.5 Multi-processing and its Requirements—The Need for an Operating System

Let us consider the case of only two processes. To keep track of their progress, we create and populate a data structure—an array, depicted in Figure 3.8—each entry of which contains:

[9] The effect of the RTI instruction here is similar to that of the charlatan's flute in Igor Stravinsky's *Petrushka* [5]: when finally touched by the flute, after magic preparations, the inert puppets become alive and start to dance.

- The complete set of values of a process's registers (with the PC initially pointing to the respective program's code segment, and the SP pointing to the stack).
- The state of the process, which tells us whether the process is (a) *waiting* for some event (such as completion of I/O), (b) *ready* to run, or (c) in fact, *running*. Of course, only one of the two processes can be in the latter state. (For this matter, with one CPU, only one process can be running, no matter how many other processes there are.)
- The segment and page table pointers (see Section 3.2.6), which indirectly specify the address and size of the process *heap* memory (that is, the memory allocated for its global variables).

It is easy to imagine other entries needed for housekeeping, but just with that simple structure—called the *process table*—we can maintain the processes, starting them in the manner described at the end of the previous section and intervening in their lives during interrupts.

It is also easy to see that *two*, for the number of processes, is by no means a magic number. The table can have as many entries as memory and design allow.

The program that we need to manage the processes is called an *operating system*, and its objectives set a perfect example for general management: the operating system has to accomplish much but whatever it does must be done very fast, without noticeably interfering with the lives of the processes it manages.

The major events in those lives occur during interrupts. To this end, the operating system at this point is but a library—a set of procedures called from either the main line of code or the interrupt service routines. Incidentally, the system could even allocate CPU fairly equally among the processes by processing clock interrupts and checking whether a CPU-bound process has exceeded its share of time—the time it is allowed to own the CPU. (This share is called *quantum*. Its value, assigned at the configuration time, allows us to support the CPU virtualization claim: that a CPU with a speed of θ Hz,[10] when shared among N processes, will result in each process being given a virtual CPU of θ/N Hz.)

Overall, the operating system is responsible for the creation and scheduling of the processes and for allocating resources to them. In a nutshell, this is achieved by carefully maintaining a set of queues. In its life, a process keeps changing its state. Unless the process is executing, it is waiting for one thing or another (such as a file record to be read, a message from another process, or a CPU—when it is ready to execute). The operating system ensures that each process is in its proper queue at all times. We will keep returning to the subject of operating systems, but this subject requires an independent study. Fortunately, there are excellent and comprehensive textbooks available [6, 7], which we highly recommend.

Getting back to the architecture at our disposal, we note three fundamental problems.

The first problem is that a user program must somehow be aware of specific addresses in memory where its code and data reside, but these addresses are never known until run time. We defer the resolution of this problem until the next section.

The second problem is that, at the moment, we have no way to prevent a process from accessing another process's memory (whether for malicious reasons or simply because of

[10] The speed of the CPU is measured in terms of the clock frequency it can support. In this respect it is very much like a musician playing to a specific metronome setting. The music (instruction execution) is the same, but it can be played faster or slower, depending both on the requirements of the musical piece and the abilities of the player.

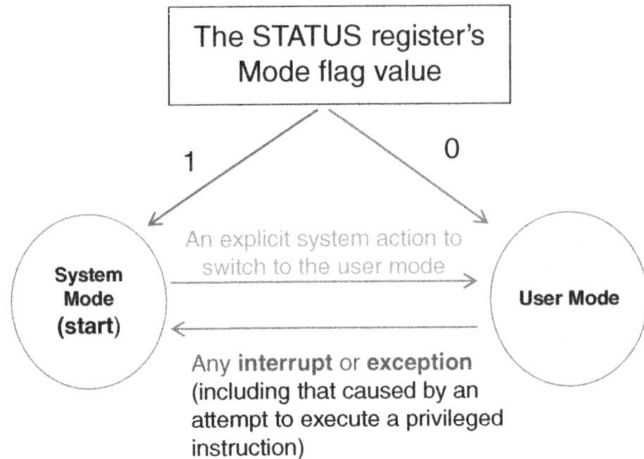

Figure 3.9 The CPU mode state machine.

a programmer's error). Even worse, each process can access the operating system data too, because at this point it is in no way different from the user data.

The third problem is that we cannot prevent processes from executing certain instructions (such as disabling interrupts). If a user can disable interrupts in its program, the computer may become deaf and mute. Incidentally, this is a fine—and extremely important—point that needs some elaboration. Since the system code we discuss is only a library of system routines, it is being executed by one or another process. Indeed, either the process's program calls the respective library procedure directly or it is called during the interrupt—which is processed on the interrupted process's stack. Yet, it is intuitively obvious that *only* the system code, not the user program code, should be allowed to disable the interrupts. Hence the problem here, again, is that the user code so far has been indistinguishable from the system code.

The last problem has been addressed by recognizing that the CPU must have (at least) two *modes* of execution: the *user mode* and the *system mode*. The former is reserved for user programs and some non-critical system code. The latter is reserved for the critical operating system code (or *kernel*). With that, certain instructions must be executed only in the system mode. Correspondingly, both CPUs and modern operating systems have evolved to support this principle.

How can we implement it? We observe that the system code has been invoked when either:

1. It is called explicitly from a user's program, or
2. An interrupt (or an exception) has occurred.

To ensure that system processing is entered only through a designated *gate*, we postulate that all system calls be made via an exception—by executing the TRAP instruction. (Now we have fulfilled the promise made earlier to explain the further use of this instruction!) Every procedure that needs access to system resources or external devices must do so. This reduces the first case above to the second: Now the system code can be invoked only via an interrupt or exception.

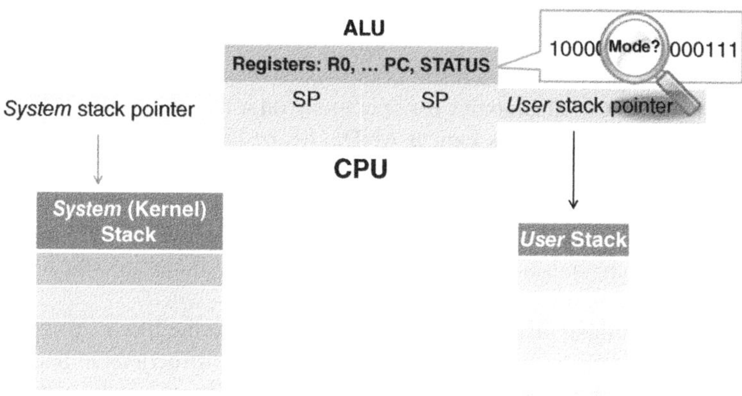

Figure 3.10 The modified CPU and the two process stacks.

We further postulate that the CPU is (1) to start in the system mode and (2) automatically enter the system mode whenever an interrupt or exception is processed. With that, the CPU may switch from system into user mode only when explicitly instructed (by the kernel) to do so.

In what follows, the main idea is to ensure that what a process can do in the user mode is limited only by what can affect this very process—and no other process or the operating system. To achieve that, we first need to make the CPU aware of what code it is running—the user code or the operating system code. Second, we need to restrict the actions that can be performed in the user mode. Again, the guiding principle is that the CPU starts in the system mode and switches to the user mode only when explicitly instructed to do so. While it is in the user mode, the CPU's actions must be restricted.

We make the CPU aware of the operating mode by introducing a new *mode* flag in the STATUS register, which is a bit indicating the system mode (when set) or the user mode (when reset). Figure 3.9 depicts the state machine that governs the transitions between the system and user states.

We further modify our CPU by adding a new stack pointer register, so we have two now—one (called the *system SP*) for the system mode and the other (called the *user SP*) for the user mode. Figure 3.10 illustrates this modification. The register name (or rather encoding) in instructions intentionally remains invariant over the choice of register, but the CPU knows which register to use because of the *mode* flag in the STATUS register.

With that change, an operating system can now maintain **two** stacks—one for executing the system code and one for executing the user code. The notion of maintaining two stacks may appear stunningly complex at first, yet it actually simplifies the operating system design. It has been implemented with great success in the Unix operating system, with the design explained in Bach's prominent monograph [8]. (The attentive reader may ask right away which stack is used to save the CPU state at interrupt. The answer is: the system stack. The first thing that happens at interrupt or exception is that the CPU switches to the system mode, which automatically activates the system stack pointer.)

Next, we introduce *privileged* instructions: those instructions that can be executed successfully only when the CPU is in the system mode. RTI, DISI, and ENI are the first three instructions in this set. The reason for RTI being privileged is that it causes restoration of the STATUS register, and hence may cause a transition to the user mode. As we postulated earlier, this transition may happen *only* as a result of the system code execution.

Now, DISI and ENI are mnemonics for operations on a flag in the STATUS register. With our CPU, any instruction (such as logical AND, OR, or LOAD) that alters the value of the STATUS register is declared privileged. Similarly, any instruction that changes the value of the system stack pointer is privileged by design, since the user code has no way even to refer to the system SP.

The context in which an instruction is used is an important factor in determining whether it needs to be privileged or not.

To this end, we postulate that all instructions that deal with the I/O access (present in some CPUs) are privileged. We will discuss handling privileged instructions in Section 1.2.7; first we need to understand the issues in virtual memory management, which necessitates a whole new class of privileged instructions.

3.2.6 Virtual Memory—Segmentation and Paging

The modern notion of memory being *virtual* has two aspects. First, with virtual memory a process must be unaware of the *actual* (physical memory) addresses it has been allocated. (Instead, a process should "think" that it and its data occupy the same addresses in memory every time it runs.) Second, the process must "think" that it can actually access *all addressable* memory, the amount of which typically far exceeds that of the available physical memory. (It is still uncommon, to say the least, to expect a computer with 64-bit addressing to have two exabytes—2×10^{18} bytes—of actual memory!)

Except for the need for some advanced hardware address-translation mechanism, common to enabling both aspects, there are significant differences in their respective requirements.

We start with the first aspect. Even in the case of a two-process system, as Figure 3.8 demonstrates, it is clear that the segments allocated to them will have different addresses. Yet, with our CPU, each instruction has its pre-defined address in memory, and the memory allows absolute addressing too. And so, if the code of Process 2 has an instruction LOAD R1, 30000 but the data segment for this process starts at location 5000, the instruction must somehow be changed. One potential approach here is to effectively rewrite the program at load time, but this is impracticable. A far better approach is to employ a tried-and-true electrical engineering *midbox* trick, depicted in Figure 3.11. This figure modifies Figure 3.2 with a translation device, called a *Memory Management Unit* (*MMU*), inserted between the CPU and the bus. This device has a table that translates a logical (i.e., virtual) address into an actual physical address. (In modern CPUs, this device has actually been integrated into the CPU box.)

Suppose a process has been programmed (or compiled) with the following assumptions:

- its code starts at location x;
- the user stack starts at location y;
- the system stack starts at location z; and
- the heap starts at location t.

Each of these is a contiguous piece of memory—a segment. In fact, even smaller segments can be thought of and used in practice. For instance, it is very convenient to put all initialization

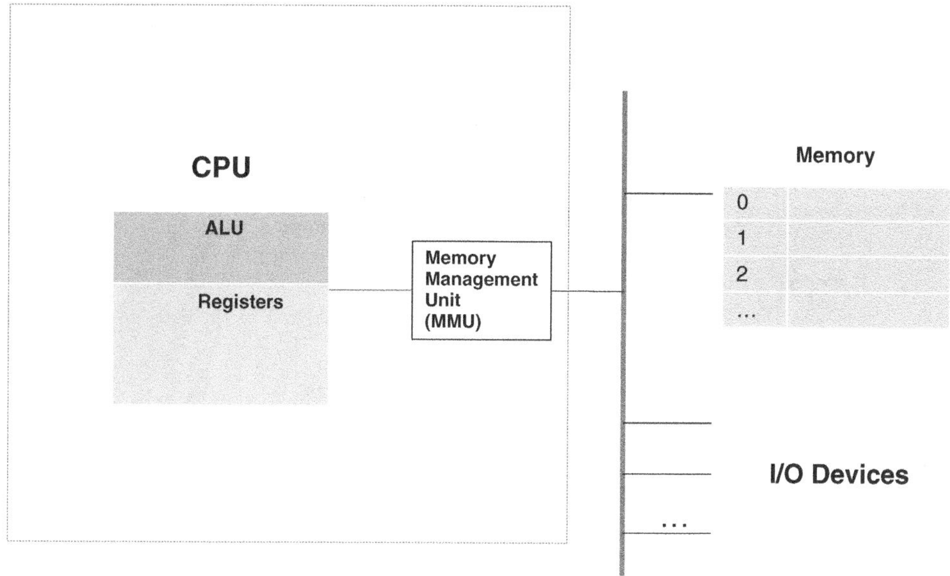

Figure 3.11 Introducing the MMU.

code in one place in memory (which can later be reused after initialisation is completed). Segments are enumerated and referred to by their numbers.

At the time of loading the process, the operating system brings its code into location x', while allocating both stack segments and the heap memory segment starting at addresses y', z', and t', respectively. A segment number is an index into the MMU table. One entry in this table is the *segment base register* (e.g., x' or y'), which the operating system fills out. The MMU has the circuitry to translate a logical address into a physical address. Thus, the logical address a in the code segment gets translated into $a - x + x'$, which is the sum of the segment base register, x', and the offset within the code segment, $(a - x)$. This translation can be performed very fast by hardware, so its effect on timing is negligible.

The MMU also helps to ensure that no process can read or write beyond the segment allocated to it. For that there is another entry in the MMU table: the size of the segment memory which the operating system has allocated. Continuing with the example of the above paragraph, if X is the size of the code segment, then the inequality $a - x < X$ must hold for each address a. If this does not happen, an exception is generated. Again, the comparison with a constant is performed so fast by the MMU circuitry that its effect is negligible.

Figure 3.12 summarizes the MMU address translation process. We should add that an MMU can do (and typically does) much more in terms of protection. For example, in the segment table it may also contain the flags that indicate whether a segment is executable (thus preventing accidental "walking over" the data, as well as preventing attacks where malicious code is placed into a data segment so as to be executed later). Additional flags can indicate whether it is read only, can be shared, and so on. This allows much versatility. For example, an operating system library may be placed into a read-only code segment available to all processes.

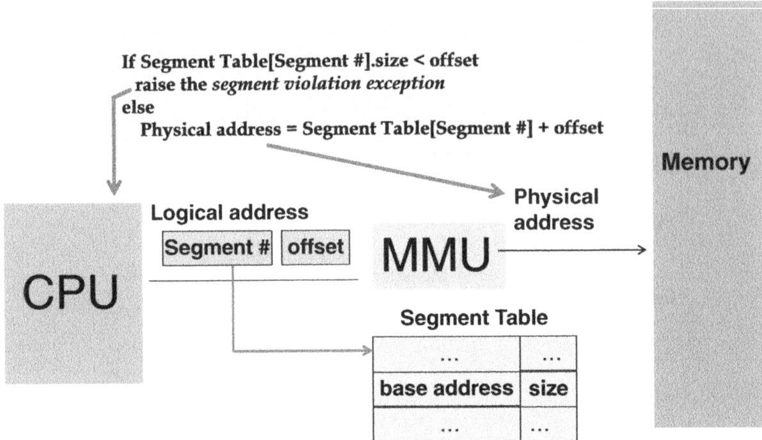

Figure 3.12 Segmentation: The MMU translation processing.

The MMU is typically accessed through its *registers*. It hardly needs an explanation why only privileged instructions may access the MMU entries!

The second aspect of memory virtualization—that is, creating the perception of "infinite" memory—is much more complex, and we will describe it only schematically here. Either of the operating system books [7, 8] does an excellent job of explaining the details.

To begin with, the technology employed here also solves another problem—memory fragmentation. With several processes running, it may be impossible for the operating system to find a *contiguous* memory segment to allocate to yet another process; however, cumulatively there may be enough "holes" (i.e., relatively small pieces of unused memory) to provide enough contiguous memory, should these "holes" be merged into a contiguous space.

To achieve that, another type of MMU is used. It works as follows. The logical memory is treated as an array of blocks called *pages*. All pages have the same size (which is always chosen to be an exponent of 2, so that with the maximum addressable memory n and page size f there are exactly n/f logical pages). Similarly, the actual physical memory is treated as an array of physical *frames*, all of the same size, which is the same as the page size. Each process has a page table, which—for the moment—maps each logical page into a corresponding frame in physical memory. The MMU uses this table to perform the translation.

Figure 3.13 demonstrates a case where, with the help of the MMU, scattered pieces of memory make up what appears to a process to be a contiguous segment. (The page size is actually a *fragmentation unit*. In other words, no memory fragment larger than or equal to the page size is left unused.)

Suppose that a process needs to access what it thinks is address $5 \times page\_size + 123$. As the figure shows, this address is interpreted as belonging to page number 6, with offset 123. The MMU table maps page 6 into the physical frame 21. Ultimately, the address is translated to $20 \times page\_size + 123$, which is the actual physical location.

Providing contiguous memory is a fairly simple feature. The most ingenious feature of paging though is that it supports the case when the number of frames in the memory is fewer than the total number of pages used by all active processes. Then, even the logical address

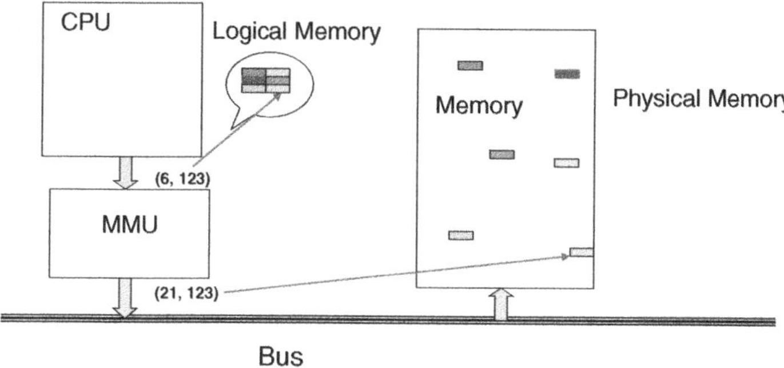

Figure 3.13 Paging—establishing contiguous memory.

space of a single process may be larger than the whole physical memory! To achieve that, the operating system maps the process memory to a storage device (typically, a disk). As Figure 3.14 shows, some pages (called *resident* pages) are kept in the physical memory, while other pages are stored on the disk. When a logical address that corresponds to a non-resident page is referenced by a process, it must be brought into physical memory.

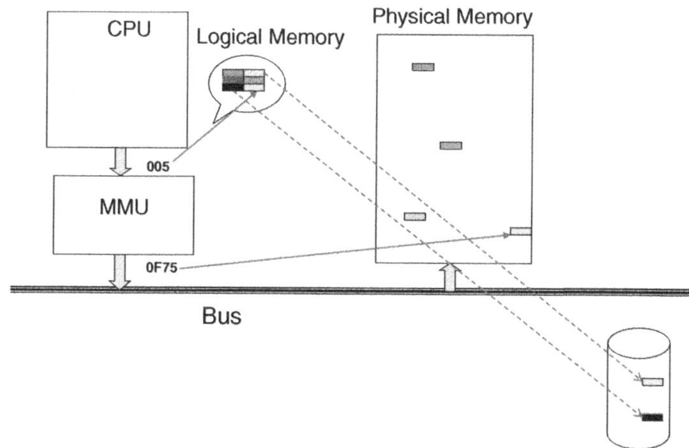

Figure 3.14 Storing pages on the disk to achieve the "infinite" memory illusion.

Of course, when all the frames in memory are occupied, it is a zero-sum game: if a page is to be brought into memory, some other page must be evicted first. The choice of the page to be evicted is made by a page-replacement algorithm employed by the operating system. This choice is crucial to performance, and hence substantial research into the problem has been carried out over a period of decades. Its results, now classic, can be found in any operating systems text.

Incidentally, the actual memory/storage picture is not just black-and-white—that is, fast but relatively small and volatile RAM and relatively slow but voluminous and long-lasting

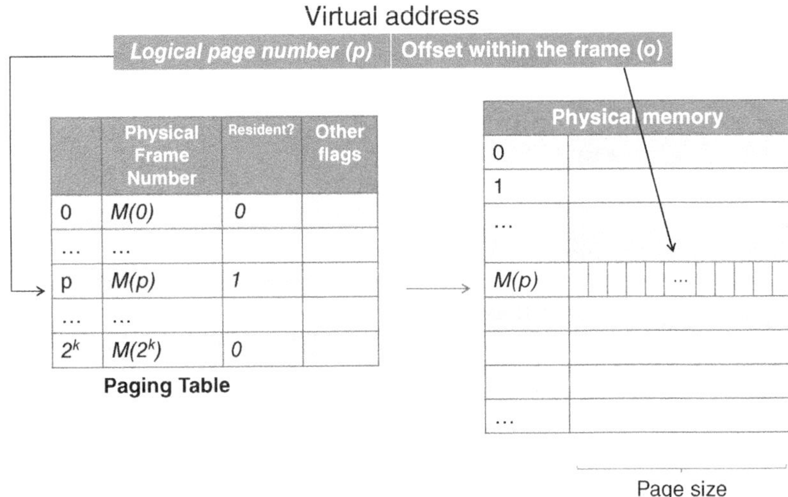

Figure 3.15 Page table and virtual address in-memory translation.

disk storage. In Chapter 6 we introduce and discuss different types of storage solution, which together fill in the spectrum between the two extremes and establish the hierarchy of memory.

The page table depicted in Figure 3.15 provides a few hints as to the translation implementation. The left-most bits of a virtual address provide the logical page number; the rest is the offset, which remains invariant. If a page is resident, as indicated by the respective flag in the table, the translation is straightforward (and rather fast). If it is non-resident, the MMU generates an exception—the *page fault*.

To process a page fault, the operating system needs to find a page to evict. (The page-replacement algorithms use other flags stored at the page table.) Then, the page to be evicted may be written to the disk and, finally, the page that is waiting to be referenced will be read from its place on the disk into the memory frame. If this looks like a lot of work, it is! But with what has been learned about paging, it is made rather efficient. While virtual memory is slower than real memory, complex heuristics-based algorithms make it *not that much* slower. It is also worthy of note that process page tables can grow large—much larger than the extent an MMU may fit in, which brings into place additional machinery employed in this type of translation.

Again, just as segment tables do, page tables also employ memory protection—a page may be executable only, read only, writable, or any combination of these. And, as in the case of segment tables, all instructions that are involved in changing page tables are privileged.

A final note to relate different pieces of this section: segmentation can be combined with paging. For instance, each segment can have its own page table.

3.2.7 Options in Handling Privileged Instructions and the Final Approximation of the CPU Loop

An important question to ask at this point is what the CPU does when it encounters a privileged instruction while in the user mode. (How could a privileged instruction end up in a user's

```
While TRUE
  {
     Fetch an instruction pointed to by the PC;

     If the instruction is valid AND
        the instruction is appropriate for the present mode AND
        the parameters are valid for the operation
          {
             Advance the PC to the next instruction;
             Execute the instruction;
          }
      else
         raise an appropriate exception;
     If (an exception #x has been raised) OR
        (an interrupt #x has been raised) AND interrupts are enabled
       {
         Save the STATUS register and PC on the system stack (@SP);
         Switch to the system mode;
         PC = Interrupt_Vector[x];
       }
  }
```

Figure 3.16 CPU loop—the final version.

program? Of course no legitimate compiler will produce it, but it may end up there because of an assembly programmer's mistake or because of malicious intent. And it *will* end up there because of full virtualization—the subject we explore in Section 3.3.)

All existing CPUs deal with this situation in one of two ways. When a CPU encounters a privileged instruction while in the user mode, it either (1) causes an exception or (2) ignores the instruction altogether (i.e., skips it without performing any operation—just wasting a cycle).

Either way, it is ensured that a user program will be incapable of causing any damage by executing a privileged instruction; however, case 2 causes problems with virtualization. We will dwell on this problem later, when studying hypervisors.

By design, our little CPU,[11] which we have been developing for quite a while now, *does* cause an exception when it encounters a privileged instruction while in the user mode. In this way, the CPU provides a clear mechanism to indicate that something went wrong. It also helps improve security. As far as security considerations are concerned, detecting an attempt at gaining control of the system may be essential for preventing other, perhaps more sophisticated, attempts from the same source. Ignoring a "strange" instruction does not help; taking the control away from the program that contains it does.

With that, we arrive at the third—and final—approximation of the CPU loop, shown in Figure 3.16. The first major change, compared with earlier versions, is that each instruction is examined at the outset. If it cannot be recognized, or has wrong parameters, or if it is

[11] Such a design decision was made when developing the M68000 processor family [9]. In fact, our example CPU reflects several features of that remarkable machine.

inappropriate for the present mode (i.e., if it is a privileged instruction and the CPU is running in the user mode), an exception is raised. Another change is that when the CPU starts processing an interrupt or an exception, it changes to the system mode, and also switches to the system stack. (As far as timing is concerned, the STATUS register is saved before the CPU mode is switched, of course. So the CPU could return to the mode in which it was interrupted.) Again, the registers are saved at the system stack—not the user stack—which is yet another security measure. With good design, the user code can neither touch nor even see the system data structures.

3.2.8 More on Operating Systems

The CPU that we have constructed so far supports virtualization inasmuch as each process can "think" of owning the whole CPU (even though a slower one), all I/O devices, and infinite, uniformly addressed memory. The physical machine is governed by the operating system software, which creates and maintains user processes. An operating system is characterized by the services that it provides.

We have addressed such services as CPU access and memory management. The latter extends to long-term memory—the establishment and maintenance of a file system on a disk. A disk is just one of the I/O devices managed by an operating system. A monitor, keyboard, and printer are examples of other devices. Yet another example is a network drive. A process gets access to a device only through the operating system.

While a process has seeming ownership of the CPU, memory, and devices, it needs to be aware of other processes. To this end, all modern operating systems have mechanisms for *interprocess communication*, which allows processes to exchange messages. Combined with data communications, this capability enables communications among processes that are run on different machines, thus creating the foundation for *distributed computing*.

The services are built in layers, each layer serving the layer immediately above it. If the file system service is implemented on top of the data networking service, then it is possible to map a process's file system across disks attached to different computers, with the process never being aware of the actual location of the device and consequently the location of a specific file record.

A process requests an operating system service via a *system call*. This call—to a programmer—is just a procedure call. Invariably, the corresponding procedure contains a *trap* instruction, which causes a break in process execution. Figure 3.17(a) contains pseudo-code for an example *Service_A* routine. All it does is push the *Service_A* mnemonics on the user stack and pass control to the system via *TRAP 1*.

The process will resume when the *TRAP 1* exception is processed, as depicted in Figure 3.17(b). The handler reads the top of the process's stack to determine that service A is requested and then calls the *Service_A_System* routine. As shown in Figure 3.17(c), the latter proceeds in the system mode, likely calling other system procedures. When finished, it returns to the exception handler of Figure 3.17(b), which at the end passes control back to the user program code via the RTI instruction. (You may remember that the value of the STATUS register, with the mode flag indicating the user mode, was saved at the time of the interrupt. The switch to the user mode is effected merely by restoring that value.)

It is important to understand that a user process goes through a sequence of instructions that alternate between the user program code and the system code; however, the user program

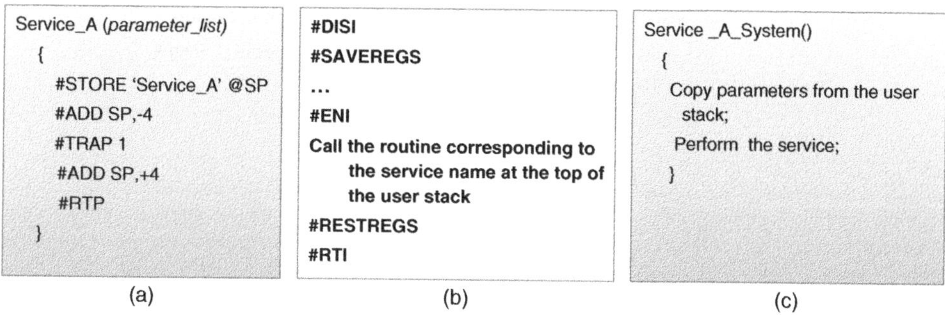

Figure 3.17 System call processing: (a) the *Service_A* routine—user part; (b) the *TRAP 1* service routine; (c) the *Service_A* routine—system part.

has no knowledge or control of the system data structures or other processes' data (unless, of course, other processes intentionally share such data).

We briefly note that when a service routine starts an I/O operation, it typically does not wait until the operation completes. Instead, it parks the process in a queue for a specific event from this device and passes control to a *scheduler* so that another process can run. To this end, a *time-slice* interrupt may result in exactly the same treatment of the interrupted process, if the operating system determines that the process's quantum has been reached. In this way, the operating system can ensure that the CPU has been allocated fairly to all processes.

At this point it is appropriate to explain the difference between the terms *process* and *thread.* A process is assigned resources: its memory space, devices, and so on. Initially, these resources were associated with a *single thread of control.* Later, the term *process* became associated only with the address space and resources—not the thread of execution. With that, multiple tasks (threads) can execute *within* a process, all sharing the same resources. Sometimes, threads are also called light-weight processes, because context switching of threads is a much less involved procedure (no need to reload page tables, etc.) than that of processes. Unfortunately, this terminology is not used consistently.

The evolution of the operating systems has been influenced by two factors: application needs and hardware capabilities (and, consequently, hardware price). When considering the implementation specifics, there is still a gray area within which it is impossible to postulate whether a given function is performed in hardware or in the operating systems.

Advances in data networking have resulted in distributing the operating system functions among different nodes in the network. This has actually been a trend in the 1990s and 2000s, until Cloud Computing took over. With that, the trend seems to be reversed (with effort concentrating on one—virtual—machine), while advancing in spirit (the virtual machine can easily migrate across the network from one machine to another).

Throughout the history of operating systems the general problem of security (as well as the narrower problem of privacy) has been addressed constantly. Interestingly enough, it was addressed even when it was a non-issue—that is, in the absence of networking and at a time when very few people even had access to computers. The history of operating systems has demonstrated though what the overall history of mankind has also demonstrated: the best idea and the best design do not necessarily win. To this end, MIT's *Multiplexed Information*

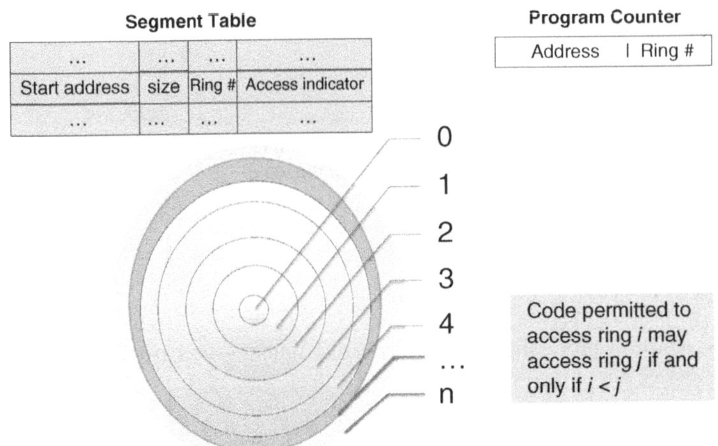

Figure 3.18 Graham's security rings (hardware support).

and Computing Service (*Multics*) [10] operating system's feature set has never ended up fully in a ubiquitous commercial product, although Multics has influenced the design of several operating systems—most notably the Unix operating system.

Multics took security seriously. Robert Graham, a Multics contributor and a visionary, wrote in his seminal 1968 paper [11] (which very much predicted the way things turned out to be almost half a century later): "The community of users will certainly have diverse interests; in fact, it will probably include users who are competitive commercially. The system will be used for many applications where sensitive data, such as company payroll records, will need to be stored in the system. On the other hand, there will be users in the community who wish to share with each other data and procedures. There will even be groups of users working cooperatively on the same project. ... Finally, there will be public libraries of procedures supplied by the information processing utility management. Indeed, a primary goal of such a system is to provide a number of different users with flexible, but controlled, access to shared data and procedures."

Graham's design, which has been implemented in Multics, specified protection rings. We start with a simplified scheme, as depicted in Figure 3.18. Revisiting the segment table discussion of Section 3.2.6, we can further refine the permission to access a segment.

The decision to focus on a per-segment rather than a per-page protection scheme was deliberate. In Graham's lucid prose: "a segment is a logical unit of information of which a user is cognizant," while "a page is a unit of information which is useful to the system for storage management and is thus invisible to the user." The idea of the protection scheme is based on the military principle of *need to know*, defined by the respective clearance level. At a given clearance level, those who have it may access the information at any lower clearance level but not the other way round; hence the representation of the privilege levels as a set of concentric rings. The smallest ring (ring 0) has the highest privilege level. (The graphical significance of this is that the higher the privilege level the smaller the set of those who are granted access at this level, so smaller circles delineate rings with higher privilege levels.)

Graham presents two models in [11]. The first is simple and straightforward; the second is more complex as it provides an optimization.

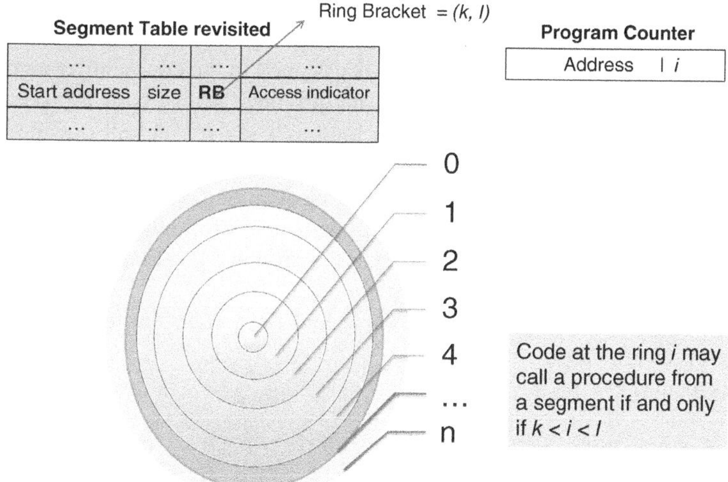

Figure 3.19 Optimization with non-disjoint security rings.

Both models require a change to the segment table. The access indicator field for both models contains four independent flags:

- *User/System* flag—indicates whether the segment can be accessed in the user mode.
- *Read/Write* flag—indicates whether the segment can be written to.
- *Execute* flag—indicates whether the segment can be executed.[12]
- *Fault/No fault* flag—indicates whether accessing the segment results in an exception no matter what (an extra level of protection, which overwrites all other flags).

The PC register is augmented with the ring number indicating the privilege level of the code. In addition, each segment table entry is augmented by a reference to the ring structure, but here the models differ.

In the first model, each segment is now assigned its ring number to indicate its privilege, as shown in the segment table entry. Note that this scheme results in different privileges assigned to *disjoint* sets of segments.

Let us consider a code segment. If the segment's access ring value is i, the code in the segment may access only a segment whose access ring value is $j > i$. (Of course, this is only the first line of defense. Access is further restricted by the values of the access indicator flags.) Jumps out of a segment require special intervention of the system, so all of them cause an exception.

While this model works, Grahams shows that it can be made more efficient if the requirement that the rings be disjoint is relaxed to allow execution of shared routines at the privilege level of the caller—but not higher. This observation results in the second model, depicted in Figure 3.19.

[12] There are fine points in [11] that reflect on the meaning of particular combinations of flag values. For instance, the respective flag values of *read* and *execute* denote code that cannot self-modify.

Here, the ring number in a segment table entry is replaced with two numbers, which respectively indicate the lower and upper bound of the segment's *ring bracket.* All code in a segment—intended to be a procedure library—is assigned to the consecutive segments in the bracket. Thus, when a procedure executing at the privilege level i calls a procedure whose access bracket is $[k, l]$ no exception occurs as long as $k < i < l$. A call outside the bracket limits results in an exception.

So far we have considered only the transfer of control among code segments, but the use of ring brackets can be extended further to the data segments as follows. If a data segment has a ring bracket $[k, l]$ then an instruction executing at the privilege level i may

- write to this segment as long as it is writable and $i \leq k$ (i.e., the instruction has higher privilege level than the segment) or
- read this segment if $k < i \leq l$.

The instruction may not access the segment at all if $i > l$.

Multics specifies eight protection rings. The number of rings is restricted by hardware. Back in the 1980s, the Data General Eclipse MV/8000 CPU had a three-bit ring indicator in the PC. (See [12] for a well-written story about this.)

All that development was foreseeing the future—which is happening right now. The renewed interest in protection, in view of virtualization, has made many computer scientists nostalgic for the 1970s and 1980s.

On this note, we conclude our primer. To summarize:

- A process as a unit has its own virtual world of resources: a CPU, an "infinite" memory, and all I/O devices.
- A process relies on an operating system—the government of a physical machine, which ensures that all processes are treated fairly.
- The operating system kernel is the only entity that can execute privileged instructions. The kernel is entered as a result of processing an interrupt or an exception (including a trap).
- A physical machine may execute more than one process.
- A process may be aware of other processes, and it may communicate with them.

The next section explains how this can be taken to the next level of abstraction so as to develop a virtual machine of the type shown in Figure 3.1.

3.3 Virtualization and Hypervisors

Let us revisit our objectives.

By introducing virtualization we want, first of all, to save the cost—in terms of space, energy, and personnel—of running several machines in place of one. An increasingly important aspect here is the *green* issue: as a rule, one machine uses less energy than several machines.

Yet another objective of virtualization is to increase CPU utilization. Even with multiprocessing, a CPU is almost never fully utilized. Long before the term "Cloud Computing" was coined, it was observed that the machines that ran web servers had low CPU utilization. Running several servers on their respective virtual machines, now grouped on one physical machine that used to run a single server, allowed them to get good use of this single machine while saving money on energy and hardware.

Other objectives include cloning the computing environment (such as a server) for debugging, at low cost; migrating a machine—for instance, in response to increasing load; and isolating an appliance (again a server is a good example) for a specific purpose without investing in new hardware.

As far as security is concerned, isolation is a boon for analyzing an unknown application. A program can be tested in a virtual machine, and consequently any security risk it poses will be isolated to this virtual machine. Granted, this wonderful feature depends on the security of the hypervisor itself, which we address in the last section of this chapter.

In our opinion, the very emergence of Cloud Computing as the business of providing computing services as a utility has also been an outcome (rather than an objective) of virtualization. Of course, it was not virtualization alone but rather a combination of virtualization and availability of fast networks, but we feel that virtualization technology has played a major role here.

We start with a general assumption—based on the traditional CPU architectures—that an operating system kernel by itself cannot create an isolated virtual machine. With the fairly recent CPU virtualization extensions, however, this assumption no longer holds, and later we will review a special case of the *Kernel-based Virtual Machine* (*KVM*) hypervisor, which—as its name suggests—is indeed kernel based.

From the onset of virtualization, the software charged with creating and maintaining virtual machines has been called the *Virtual Machine Monitor* (*VMM*) or *hypervisor*. Both terms are used interchangeably in the literature; in the rest of this book, we will use only the latter term. The *virtual machine* environment is created by a *hypervisor*.

3.3.1 Model, Requirements, and Issues

The classical abstract model for addressing the resources needed by processes executing on virtual machines, as presented in [13], has been known for over 40 years. In this model, two functions are employed—one visible to the operating system and the other visible only to a hypervisor. The former function maps process IDs into (virtual) resource names; the latter one maps virtual resource names into physical resource names. Such mapping is recursive, allowing several virtual machine layers on top of physical hardware. Whenever a fault (i.e., a reference to an unmapped resource) occurs, an exception results in passing control to the next-layer hypervisor. This model has provided a foundation for the systematic study and implementation of virtualization.

A major follow-up was the work [14], which has become a classic and made the names of its authors—Dr. Gerald Popek and Dr. Robert Goldberg—forever associated with virtualization, as in "Popek and Goldberg virtualization requirements." It is worth examining this remarkable paper in some detail.

To begin with, the major task of the paper was to state and demonstrate "sufficient conditions that a computer must fulfill in order to host" a hypervisor. To this end, the authors have developed a formal model of a machine and proved their conclusions mathematically. The model is an abstraction of the third-generation CPU architecture; IBM 360, Honeywell 6000, and DEC PDP-10 are specific examples, as is the CPU we have developed earlier in this chapter. The model does not take interrupts into account, as these are non-essential to the subject, but traps are modeled thoroughly.

The paper outlines the three essential characteristics of a hypervisor (the authors used the term *VMM*): "First, the VMM provides an environment for programs which is essentially identical with the original machine; second, programs run in this environment show at worst only minor decreases in speed; and last, the VMM is in complete control of system resources."

The first characteristic, often referred to as the *fidelity requirement*, states that a program run on a virtual machine must produce the same result as it would produce running on a real machine.

The second characteristic results in the *efficiency requirement*: software emulation of CPU instructions is ruled out in favor of their direct execution by the "hard" CPU. The authors voice this requirement by stating that a "statistically-dominant" subset of instructions must be executed directly by a real processor.

The third characteristic is translated into the following *resource control requirements*:

1. No program running on a virtual machine may access resources that were not explicitly allocated to it by a hypervisor.
2. A hypervisor may take away from a virtual machine any resource previously allocated to it.

Now we can introduce the formal model of [14]. (This part can be skipped without jeopardizing the understanding of either the principles or the results of the work.) The model is based on the definition of the state of the machine $S = \langle E, M, P, R \rangle$ as a quadruple, where E is the state of memory, M is the CPU mode (i.e., user or system mode), P is the value of the PC, and R is the "relocation-bound register." (In the case of our CPU, this is actually the whole MMU, but early third-generation CPUs had effectively only one segment and consequently only one relocation register.) The model makes the memory locations $E[0]$ and $E[1]$ the effective stack for saving the $\langle M, P, R \rangle$ triplet. The instruction i can be viewed as a mapping of the state space into itself, so we can write

$$i(E_1, M_1, P_1, R_1) = (E_2, M_2, P_2, R_2).$$

The instruction is said to *trap* if the storage is left unchanged, except for the top of the stack:

$$E_2[0] = (E_1, P_1, R_1); \text{(saved status)}$$
$$(M_2, P_2, R_2) = E_2[1].$$

An instruction is said to *memory-trap* if it traps when accessing out-of-bound memory.

With that, the instructions are classified as follows:

1. An instruction is called *privileged* if it does not memory-trap, but traps only when executed in user mode.
2. An instruction is called *control-sensitive* if it attempts to change the amount of memory available or affects the CPU mode.
3. An instruction is called *behavior-sensitive* if its execution depends on the value of controls set by a control-sensitive instruction. The examples provided by the authors are (1) the IBM 360 *Load Real Address* (*LRA*) instruction, which is location-sensitive and (2) the PDP-11/45 *Move From Previous Instruction Space* (*MFPI*) instruction, which is mode-sensitive. (The latter instruction is one of that machine's four instructions copying on the current stack the data from the operand address in the previous address space as indicated by the CPU mode. The CPU we have defined does not have such a capability.)

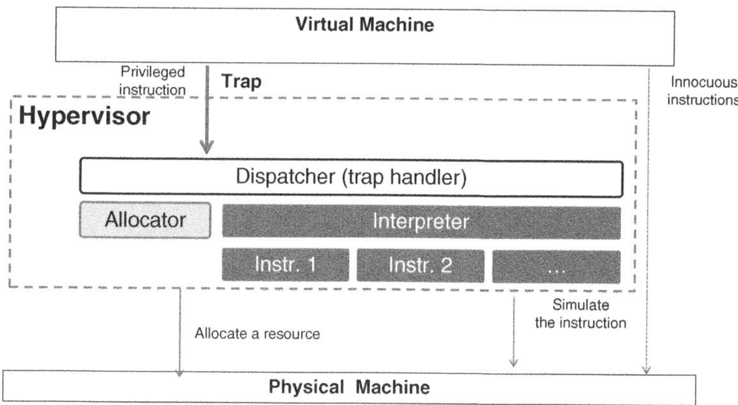

Figure 3.20 Hypervisor structure—after Popek and Goldberg. Data from [14].

4. An instruction is called *sensitive* if it is either behavior-sensitive or control-sensitive. Otherwise, it is called *innocuous*.

Sure enough, formalizing the definition of the sensitive instructions involves a considerable amount of notational complexity, which the authors call an "unfortunately notation-laden tangent." The theory developed based on this notation allows us to prove formally that a hypervisor can be constructed if all sensitive instructions are privileged, which is the main result of the paper.

With that, the hypervisor is constructed as depicted in Figure 3.20.

All innocuous instructions in the code executed by the virtual machine are executed immediately by the CPU of the physical machine. An attempt to execute a privileged instruction results (by definition) in a trap, for which the *Dispatcher* is the service routine. If an instruction requires resource allocation, the dispatcher calls the *Allocator*. Ultimately, a trapped instruction is emulated by the *Interpreter*, which is but a library of emulation routines, one for each instruction.

The model of [14] was not specifically concerned with time sharing, although the authors point out that the CPU itself is a resource that the Allocator can take care of.

Indeed, today hypervisors act in a time-shared environment, as depicted in Figure 3.21.

In this architecture, a hypervisor is responsible for maintaining the virtual machines and allocating resources to each such machine, in accordance with the three virtualization requirements.

Each virtual machine runs its own operating system (called a *guest operating* system), which in turn handles the user processes. A hypervisor gets all the interrupts and exceptions. Among the latter there are traps that correspond to system calls.

Some interrupts (such as alarm interrupts that deal with time sharing among multiple machines) are handled by the hypervisor itself, with the result that a virtual machine that has exceeded its time quantum is stopped, and the CPU is given to another virtual machine.

All the interrupts and exceptions that are specific to a virtual machine, including the system calls that emanated from this machine's user processes, are passed to the guest operating system.

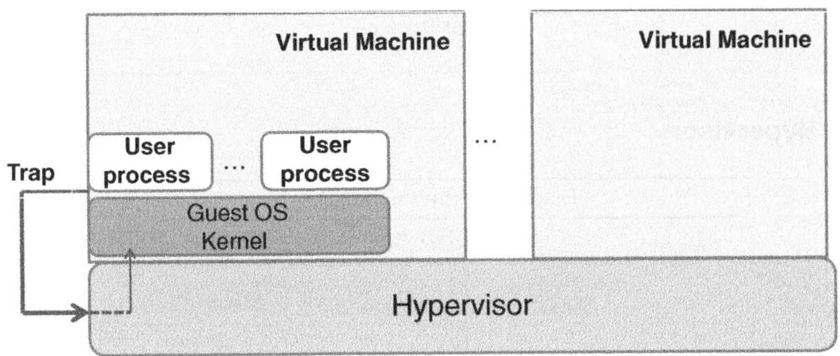

Figure 3.21 General virtualization architecture.

But where does the hypervisor run? So far, we have assumed that it runs directly on the physical machine. Such hypervisors are called *Type-1* (or, sometimes, *bare-metal*) hypervisors. In contrast, a hypervisor that is running on top of an operating system is called a *Type-2* hypervisor. This classification is depicted in Figure 3.22.

We will return to this taxonomy when considering specific case studies later in this chapter.

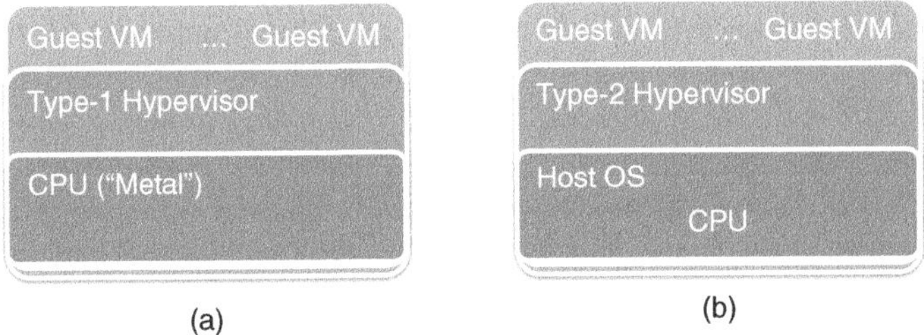

Figure 3.22 Type-1 and Type-2 hypervisors.

So far, we have been concentrating only on CPU virtualization issues. Needless to say, other virtualization elements—such as the virtualization of I/O device access—are by no means trivial, especially when real-time operation is concerned. As far as memory virtualization is concerned, even though it has been solved by operating systems at the process level, this turns out to be another non-trivial issue because of the necessity for a hypervisor to maintain its own "shadow" copies of page tables.

Still, the hardest problem is presented by those CPUs that are non-virtualizable in Popek and Goldberg's terms. Of these, the one most widely used is the x86 processor.

3.3.2 The x86 Processor and Virtualization

This workhorse of servers and personal computers alike has descended from the original Intel 8086 CPU, whose 1979 model (8088) powered the first IBM PC. At that time, the 8088's sharply-focused deployment strategy—personal computing—could not be concerned with virtualization. (What is there to virtualize on a machine designed for a single user?)

In contrast, the Motorola M68000 processor—a rival of the 8088, and the CPU of Apple Macintosh, Atari, and Amiga computers as well as the AT&T Unix PC workstation—had its architecture geared for virtualization from scratch. To this end, the M68000 processor had only one instruction that was non-virtualizable.

This instruction allowed it, while being executed in the user mode, to transfer the value of the STATUS register to a general register. In the CPU we developed earlier in this chapter, its equivalent is *LOAD R1, STATUS*. This instruction is behavior-sensitive in the Popek and Goldberg taxonomy because it allows a user program to discover which mode it is running in. The danger here is as follows: suppose a VM is running an operating system that is carefully designed with security in mind. One feature of this operating system is to halt its execution once it finds out that its kernel code runs in the user mode. Since the STATUS register has the mode flag, any operating system that implements this feature will halt.

With the goal for M68000 to equip micro- and even minicomputers that could run multiple operating systems, Motorola quickly remedied this problem. The M68010 processor, released in 1982, made this instruction trap when executing in the user mode, just as all other instructions did.[13]

As it happened, it was the x86 CPU—not the M68010—that took over the computing space, even though its instruction set, carefully developed with backward compatibility in mind, contained non-virtualizable instructions. For instance, the 32-bit processor instruction set of the Intel Pentium CPU has 17 instructions[14] identified in [15] as non-virtualizable. These instructions fall into three classes. (Ultimately, it is the classes themselves that are important to understand in order to appreciate the problem because, while instructions vary among the processors, the classes are more or less invariant.) Let us look at the classes in the Intel Pentium example.

The first class contains instructions that read and write the values of the global and local segment table registers as well as the interrupt table register, all three of which point to their respective tables. A major problem is that the processor has only one register for each of these, which means that they need to be replicated for each virtual machine; mapping and special translation mechanisms are needed to support that. The respective effect on performance is obvious given that these mechanisms must be brought to motion on each read and write access.

The second class consists of instructions that copy parts of the STATUS register into either general registers or memory (including the stack). The problem here is exactly the same as in the case of the M68000 described above: The virtual machine can find out what mode it is running in.

The third class contains instructions that depend on the memory protection and address relocation mechanisms. To describe this class, it is necessary to introduce the *code privilege*

[13] The 68010 had several other properties that aided virtualization, among them the ability to configure the location of the interrupt vectors (previously always kept in low memory) and handling the "bus-error" exception—on which the implementation of virtual memory depends—in such a way that the instruction that caused it could continue (rather than restart from the beginning) after the memory was "repaired."

[14] More often than not, the reference is to the number of such instructions being 17, but there are arguments against this specific number depending on what is counted—based on side-effects. It is more effective to look at the classes of affected instructions.

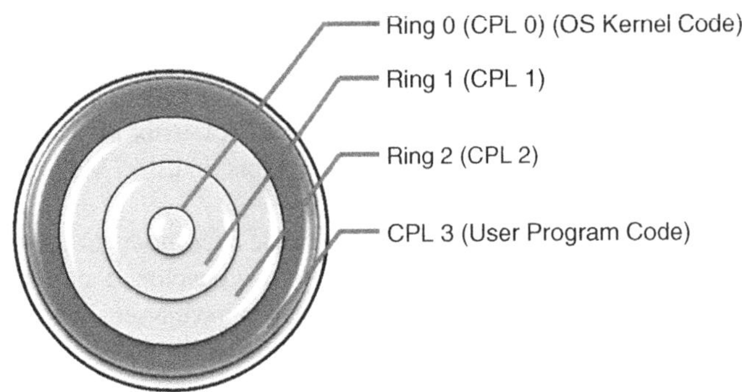

Figure 3.23 Intel privilege level rings.

level (*CPL*) in the x86 instruction set. There are four privilege levels, from 0 to 3, in descending privilege order, as shown in Figure 3.23. Therefore, code running at a higher privilege level has access to the resources available to code running at lower privilege levels; thus running at CPL 0 allows access to all the resources at CPL 1, CPL 2, and CPL 3. (In retrospect, in order to reflect the definition of higher privilege, it would have been more accurate to depict CPL 0 in the outer ring, CPL 1 in the next ring, and so on, but the long-standing practice is to assign the rings as depicted.) The practice of two-level operating systems has been to execute the system code at CPL 0 and the user code at CPL 3.

Returning to the discussion of the third class of non-virtualizable instructions, it consists of instructions that reference the storage protection system, memory, or address relocation systems. Naturally, this class is rather large because even basic instructions (similar to our LOAD instruction) have variants in which segment registers are accessed.

But the instructions that check access rights or segment size from a segment table need to ensure that the current privilege level and the requested privilege level are both greater than the privilege level of a segment. That poses an execution problem, because a virtual machine does not execute at CPL 0.

Jumps, including procedure calls, pose further problems, in part because they are much more sophisticated than the JUMP and JPR instructions defined for our simplistic CPU earlier in this chapter. In the x86 architecture, there are two types of jump: *near jumps* and *far jumps*. Each of these two types is further subdivided into two classes: jumps to the same privilege level and jumps to a different privilege level. Ditto for procedure calls, and there are also *task switches*. As [15] explains, the problem with calls to different privilege levels and task switches is caused by comparing privilege levels of operations that do not work correctly at user level.

There is yet another class of non-virtualizable instructions—those that are supposed to be executed only in the system mode, which they do, but neither execute nor trap when an attempt is made to execute them in the user mode. These instructions are sometimes also called *non-performing*. The problem with these is too obvious to discuss it here.

We define *full virtualization* as a computation environment that is indistinguishable from that provided by a standalone physical CPU. One important characteristic of full virtualization is that it requires no modification to an operating system to be run by the virtual machine created in the environment. It is clear that full virtualization cannot be achieved on the unmodified x86 CPU.

Aside from emulating the CPU in software at every single instruction, which is impracticable, there are two major ways of dealing with non-virtualizable instructions, which we will discuss in the next section. Ultimately, this is all that can be done as far as software is concerned.

Yet, with the changes to x86 that have extended its virtualization capabilities, it has become possible to move on to the pure hardware-assisted virtualization approach. The only problem here is that the x86 processor has been manufactured by several companies—Intel, Cyrix, Advanced Micro Devices, and VIA Technologies among them—and while the behavior of the basic instruction set is standardized among the manufacturers, the virtualization mechanisms are not. Early approaches to virtualization extensions by Intel (VT-x) [16] and AMD (Pacifica and later AMD-V) [17] have been well described and compared in [18].

Although the extensions differ among manufacturers, their common capability is the provision of the new *guest operating mode*, in which software can request that certain instructions (as well as access to certain registers) be trapped. This is accompanied by the following two features (as summarized in [19]), which enable virtualization:

- *Hardware state switch*, triggered on a transition into and out of the guest operating mode, which changes the control registers that affect processor operation modes and the memory management registers.
- *Exit reason* reporting on a transition from the guest operating mode.

These features enable full virtualization. Before we return to this, let us address some generic approaches to non-virtualizable CPUs.

3.3.3 Dealing with a Non-virtualizable CPU

The common denominator of all solutions here is modification of the original binary code. The differences are in the timing of modifications to the code: whether these modifications take place at run time or before run time, via global pre-processing.

With *binary rewriting*, the virtualization environment software inspects, in near-real time, a set of instructions likely to be executed soon. Then it replaces the original instructions with traps, passing control to the hypervisor, which calls—and executes in the privileged mode—a routine that emulates the problematic instruction. This mechanism works exactly as the debugging tool that we described earlier in Section 3.2.4 (which was the reason for describing the tool in the first place), and, predictably, it may interfere with other debugging tools. As [20] points out, this potential interference necessitates storing the original code in place. This technique avoids pre-processing of the operating system binary code.

With *paravirtualization*, pre-processing is necessary. Pre-processing replaces all privileged instructions with so-called *hypercalls*, which are system calls that trap directly into the hypervisor. In effect, paravirtualization involves binary rewriting too, just that it performed prior to execution (rather than in real time) and on the whole of the operating system's binary code (rather than on a select subset of the instruction stream).

This provides a software interface to a virtual machine that differs from the interface to the actual hardware CPU interface. The modified guest operating system always runs in ring 1 now. Note that the application code remains unchanged as a result. Another advantageous feature of the paravirtualization technique is that it works (although slower than needed) even with full, hardware-assisted virtualization, so the virtual machine can easily migrate from a CPU that does not support full virtualization to one that does without any change. (There is a speed penalty though: in a paravirtualized system the system calls, destined for the OS kernel, first end up in a hypervisor, which then needs to interact back-and-forth with the kernel.)

There are other interesting advantages to paravirtualization. A notable one is handling of timers. All modern operating systems rely on clock interrupts to maintain their internal timers, a feature that is particularly essential for real-time media processing. For this, even an idle virtual machine needs to process the clock interrupts. With paravirtualization, the virtual machine code is changed to request a notification at the specified time; without it, the hypervisor would need to schedule timer interrupts for idle machines, which, according to the authors of [19], is not scalable.

Another advantage is in working with multi-processor architectures. Until now we have assumed there to be only one CPU in our simplified computer architecture, but this is not necessarily the case with modern machines. Conceptually, an operating system deals with multiple CPUs in the same way it deals with one; with modular design, it is just the scheduler and the interrupt handlers that need to be fully aware of the differences. Without delving into the depths here, we note that x86-based multi-processor architectures use the *Advanced Programmable Interrupt Controller* (*APIC*) for interrupt redirection in support of *Symmetric Multi-Processing* (*SMP*). Accessing APIC in virtual mode is expensive because of the transitions into and out of the hypervisor (see [19] for a code example). With paravirtualization, which has the full view of the code, the multiple APIC access requests can be replaced with a single hypercall.

A similar effect can be achieved when handling I/O devices. Overall, as the reader has probably noticed, paravirtualization is, in effect, a type of compilation, and as such it has all the code optimization advantages that compilers have enjoyed.

Unfortunately, there are certain disadvantages to paravirtualization too. The authors of [19] note that they "experienced significant complexity of software-only paravirtualization" when porting the x86-64 Linux to Xen, and think that the root cause of this complexity is in forcing "kernel developers to handle virtual CPU that has significant limitations and different behaviors from the native CPU." Such "behaviors" require, among other things, new interrupt and exception mechanisms,[15] as well as new protection mechanisms.

Interestingly enough, in some cases—where applications are I/O-intensive or need large amounts of virtual memory—paravirtualization results in a faster execution than full virtualization would have done. This observation resulted in the development of *hybrid virtualization*. The idea is to add new features not by modifying the paravirtualization interface but by introducing "pseudo-hardware," that is a kernel interface to what appears (to the kernel) to be a hardware module. Thus, the paravirtualization interface per se is kept to the minimum. New

[15] The protection mechanism problems arise when a kernel address space needs to be shared. The ring-level protection cannot be employed as the kernel no longer runs in ring 0, hence the need for the "overhead of stitching address space between any transition between the application and the kernel" [21].

"pseudo-hardware" interfaces are created for memory management (in particular, the MMU) and all I/O devices.

Now we are ready to discuss I/O virtualization in more detail.

3.3.4 I/O Virtualization

Not unlike dogs, I/O devices have evolved to recognize one owner—a *single* operating system on the physical machine. Making them respond to multiple owners has proved to be non-trivial. As [22] puts it, "most hardware doesn't natively support being accessed by multiple operating systems (yet)."

While much attention has been given to CPU virtualization per se, handling of I/O in the virtual environment has not been much of a concern. The assumption was that the hypervisor itself should be able to take care of performing actual I/O, while making virtual machines "believe" that they own the devices.

Granted, in a way, I/O virtualization has been around for a long time, ever since operating systems introduced the practice of *spooling*, which interfaces to slow devices (such as a printer, a plotter, or the now extinct punch card machine). (Originally, the noun *SPOOL* was an acronym for *Simultaneous Peripheral Operations On-Line*, but by the late 1970s it had already become a verb.) To implement spooling, an operating system provides a process with what looks like a fast interface to a device, while in reality the original request is properly formatted and stored on the disk along with all other queued requests, which the system processes asynchronously. In addition, the operating system provides a process with a uniform device interface for each device type (disk, tape, terminal, etc.); the operations specific to each device are "hidden" in the drivers. Such a development supported decoupling between logical and physical devices, ensuring portability. (See [23] for more details.)

Another aspect of I/O virtualization emerged with the growth of fast local area networks. With the networking approach, devices can be shared among the machines on a network. For instance, it is enough for only one machine on a network to have printers (or sometimes even a disk). That machine would receive the I/O requests over the network and execute them on behalf of the senders, sending back the result when needed. This is carried out using Internet transport layer protocols—the *Transmission Control Protocol* (*TCP*) or the *User Datagram Protocol* (*UDP*)—both described in Chapter 4. Foreseeing disk-less Cloud devices, memory paging was performed over the network where only one machine had a real disk. The industry has developed a standard (IETF RFC 3720) for transmitting the *Small Computer Systems Interface* (*SCSI*) message exchanges over the TCP protocol. (SCSI was designed for access to peripheral devices. This development is covered in detail in Chapter 6 as part of the discussion of storage.)

It is interesting to observe the duality in the I/O virtualization development. Since several virtual machines reside on a single physical machine, on the one hand there is a need to share a single I/O device among all these virtual machines; on the other hand, there is a need to emulate the presence of a computer network on this physical machine. We will address the last point in much detail later; for now we observe that as a minimum it is necessary to maintain the network drivers on every virtual machine.

Short of allowing a virtual machine direct access to a device, a hypervisor can support I/O either by (1) directly emulating devices or (2) using paravirtualized drivers (effectively

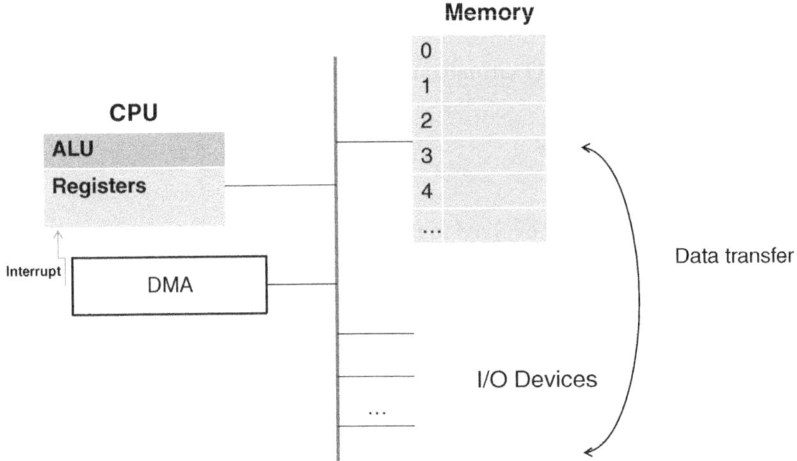

Figure 3.24 Direct Memory Access (DMA).

splitting the device driver into two parts: the VM front-end part and the hypervisor back-end part), as discussed in the previous section.

In fact, some level of emulation is always needed—and is always present in hypervisors—the emulation of the low-level firmware[16] components, such as graphic and network adapters or *Basic Input/Output System* (*BIOS*) adapters.

BIOS is a good example of where the complexities start. It is typically implemented on a hardware chip, and it provides access to the (physical) machine hardware configuration. Under normal circumstances, BIOS is responsible, among other things, for selecting the booting device and booting the system. There is only one BIOS on a physical machine, and so its function must be replicated by a hypervisor for each virtual machine. It is hard to underestimate the potential security problems with giving full access to hardware to all virtual machines, which makes its emulation in a hypervisor a non-trivial task!

Of all the above options, the one that employs direct access to I/O devices—and is therefore called *directed I/O*—is the fastest. To understand the challenges in its implementation, we first need to augment the computer architecture of Figure 3.2. Figure 3.24 expands the architecture by introducing the *Direct Memory Access* (*DMA*) device now present in every CPU.

This is what DMA is needed for: a device (or, to be precise, a part of the device called a *device controller*) often needs to transfer a large stream of bytes to or from main memory. A disk and a network driver are good examples of devices with such needs. Had the CPU itself been involved in the task of dealing with these I/O streams, it would not have had sufficient time to do its main job—executing instructions. DMA is there to take on this task, and it works as follows. DMA has access to both the devices and the memory bus. As the computer clock ticks to drive the cycles in the machine operation, the DMA may "steal" some cycles periodically to perform the memory transfer on behalf of the CPU or, alternatively—especially in the case of

[16] Firmware is a microprogram driving a hardware chip; sometimes it is hard-coded (non-erasable), in other cases it can be modified by the user.

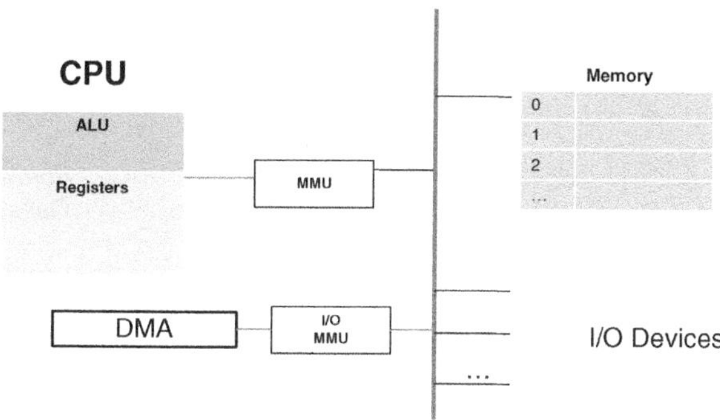

Figure 3.25 I/O MMU.

a large transfer—the DMA may take the memory bus away from the CPU for the duration of the transfer. (In the latter case, the CPU would work with its own fast memory cache instead of the main memory, which gets updated later.) In a nutshell, the DMA is delegated the task of data transfer between the memory and the CPU, and in some architectures it is even used for intra-memory data transfer. When DMA is finished, it interrupts the CPU.

The DMA problem with I/O virtualization is that in the traditional architecture DMA writes to the "real" (i.e., not virtual) memory. If this approach were followed slavishly, directed I/O would give a virtual machine unprotected access to the physical memory, which is shared among several virtual machines. This would be a flagrant security violation. In fact, this would also violate the isolation principle, since software in one virtual machine could hurt all other virtual machines.

To deal with this problem, a type of MMU (appropriately called the *I/O MMU*—sometimes also spelled *IOMMU*) is employed, as depicted in Figure 3.25. Similarly to the MMU of Figure 3.11, where the MMU performs virtual-to-real memory translation for the CPU, the I/O MMU performs this function for DMA. With that, the memory space is partitioned among the devices, and the translation and partitioning caches are typically included with hardware, which often provides memory protection. (For an example, see [21] for a description of the Intel VT-D approach.)

This approach supports virtual machine isolation and provides a degree of security. Yet, as [021] points out, the challenge here is posed by dynamic translation mappings. The issues are similar to general paging, and the overarching problem is the performance penalty resulting from the extra work that the hypervisor needs to perform. In fact, this work needs to be performed before DMA has finished a memory transfer, which brings yet another problem of the tolerable delay in DMA operations. The performance problems associated with employing I/O MMU have been analyzed in an earlier paper [24].

Directed I/O still remains an active research problem, as does the overall I/O virtualization subject. The well-known "Berkeley View of Cloud Computing" [25]—in its catalog of obstacles to Cloud deployment—lists[17] "performance unpredictability." The I/O virtualization hinges on sharing I/O devices, and it is the dependency that stubbornly remains problematic.

[17] As the obstacle number 5.

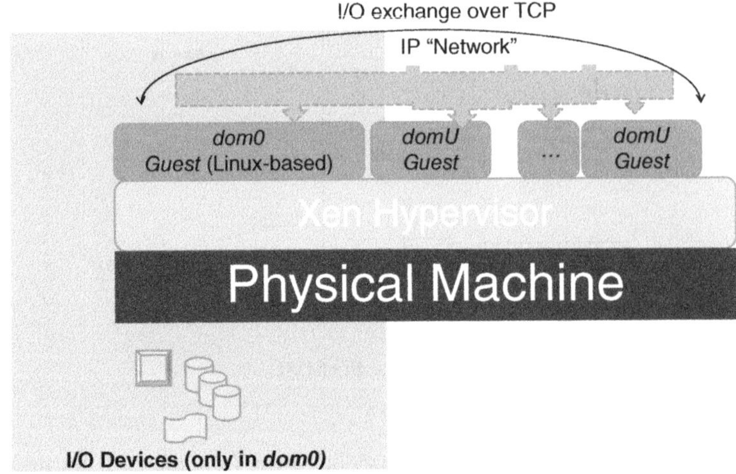

Figure 3.26 Virtual machine I/O support in Xen.

(On the contrary, sharing main memory and CPU has proven to work well.) Fortunately, there are ideas for overcoming this problem, and the earlier success of IBM mainframes keeps one hopeful.

On this optimistic note, we finish our review of virtualization concepts and technologies. Now we can illustrate the implementation of these concepts and technologies with specific examples of popular hypervisors.

3.3.5 Hypervisor Examples

In this section we illustrate the concepts discussed so far using several examples of widely used hypervisors: Xen hypervisor, KVM hypervisor, as well as hypervisors developed by VMware and Oracle. We conclude the section with a description of the *NOVA microhypervisor*, which will provide a natural segue to the section on hypervisor security that follows.

We start with the *Xen hypervisor*, comprehensively described in [22]. (The open-source code for Xen is hosted at www.xen.org.) Xen is a Type-1 ("bare-metal") hypervisor. It is operating-system agnostic, and it can, in fact, run concurrently guest VMs that use different operating systems.

As far as the virtualization taxonomy is concerned, Xen supports both paravirtualized and fully virtualized guests, respectively called PV and HVM. (The latter acronym stands for "Hardware-assisted Virtualization Mode." Of course, HVM can be used only on processors that support full virtualization extensions—both Intel and AMD processor extensions are supported.)

For guests running in HVM, Xen emulates low-level hardware and firmware components—such as graphic, network, and BIOS adapters, using techniques described in the previous section. Predictably, emulation often results in degraded performance. Xen deals with this by creating yet another mode, called PV-on-HVM (or PVHVM), in which an HVM guest is paravirtualized only partly.

Xen's approach to handling physical I/O devices is straightforward and elegant. To explain it, we need to introduce, with the help of Figure 3.26, the Xen *domain* concept.

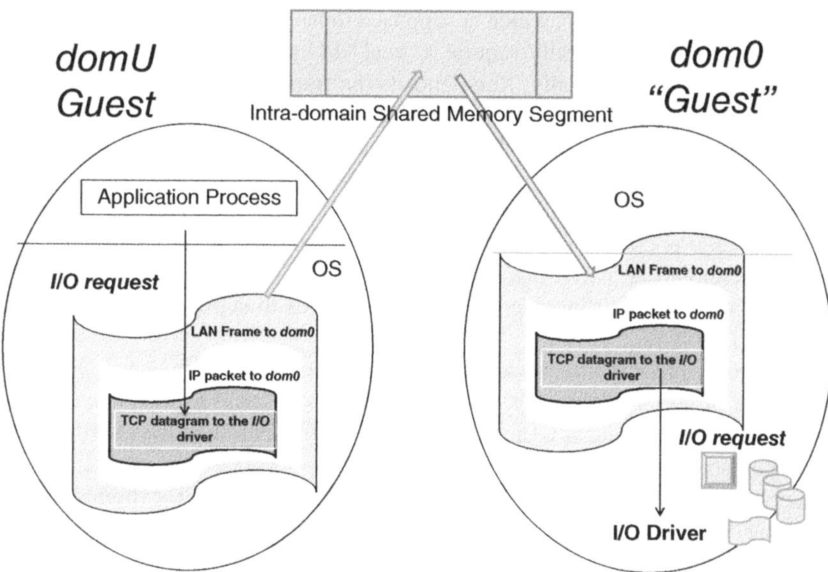

Figure 3.27 Xen network I/O optimization using shared memory.

Xen creates a special environment—called a *domain*—for each guest. "Normal" guests (which amount to all but one specialized guest) each run in their own unauthorized domain, *domU*. One specialized domain, *Domain 0* (or *dom0*), is reserved for a privileged guest—which probably should have been called a "virtualized host" because it is part of the control system that hosts all other virtual machines. To this end, Domain 0 is created at Xen boot time, and it is restricted to running specific operating systems (typically Linux, but other systems are also supported—with new ones added from time to time). Domain 0 is also the place where policies are specified. Separation of mechanisms and policies that control the use of the mechanisms is a Xen design principle. A Xen hypervisor executes the mechanisms according to the policy configured in *dom0*.

As far as the I/O is concerned, the trick is that all physical devices are attached only to the *dom0* guest which handles them—with the unique privileges it has been assigned. That solves the problem of the I/O devices recognizing only one owner. All other guests understand that their machines have no I/O devices attached but that all such devices are on the machine where the *dom0* guest resides. This is not a problem, because all the virtual machines are network-addressable and hence network I/O can be used.

Figure 3.27 illustrates the operation of I/O in Xen. When a guest in *domU* needs to communicate with a device, it uses the upper half of the split I/O driver.[18]

The I/O request is sent via TCP to *dom0* using the network module. In the process, a TCP datagram is constructed, which is enveloped into an IP packet. The IP packet is then

[18] A *split driver* is a common term for all mechanisms implementing asynchronous I/O processing. In the network I/O case, the *upper half* of the driver is responsible for hiding the location of a device (as well as the fact that a device is not present on the given machine) from the process that needs to perform I/O processing. The upper half is responsible for sending I/O requests to the machine where the devices are located—as well, of course, as for receiving the results. The *lower half* of the driver takes care of the actual devices.

encapsulated in a link-layer *frame*, which is supposed to be sent over the Local Area Network (LAN)—an act that would normally require a "real" I/O performed by the network driver. Instead of emulating a LAN literally, Xen deposits the frame into a common (to both *domU* and *dom0*) memory segment on the physical machine. (This is an act of optimization, which does introduce a security risk and therefore requires a careful protection scheme.)

Dom0 receives the frame on the "LAN," peels off the link-, network-, and transport-layer packaging, and handles the I/O request to the actual I/O driver which handles the respective device. When the I/O is complete, *dom0* sends it back through the network by reversing the above process. It should be noted that the actual operation is more complex than its rather simplistic rendition here, as it involves multiple exchanges in support of a TCP session, as specified by the TCP.

KVM (the acronym is sometimes spelled in small letters) exploits the new guest operating mode, mentioned earlier in this chapter. Like Xen, KVM is a Type-1 hypervisor;[19] unlike Xen, KVM creates a virtual machine as a Linux process—running over the Linux kernel. Like Xen, KVM is an open-source project.[20]

KVM supports full native virtualization on the extended x86 CPUs (both Intel VT and AMD-V), as well as on other processors, the list of which continues to grow.[21] In addition to the full native virtualization, KVM also supports paravirtualization for the Linux and Microsoft Windows operating system-based guests in the form of a paravirtualized network driver. With the help of the *Quick EMUlator* (*QEMU*),[22] a patched version of KVM works with Mac OS X.

Again, with the KVM architecture [19], a virtual machine is created through the same interface as a regular Linux process. In fact, each virtual CPU *appears* to the administrator as a regular Linux process. This is largely a matter of the user interface though.

KVM provides device emulation using a modified version of QEMU, which emulates BIOS as well as extended bus extensions, disk controllers (including those of SCSI), network cards, and other hardware and firmware components.

Specifically, a virtual machine is created by opening a Linux device node (*/dev/kvm*). As a new process, the machine has its own memory, separate from that of the process that created it. In addition to creating a new virtual machine, /dev/kvm provides the controls for allocating memory to it, accessing the machine's CPU registers, and interrupting the CPU.

Using Linux's memory management capabilities, the kernel configures the guest address space from non-contiguous pages (as illustrated schematically in Figure 3.13). The user space can also be mapped into physical memory, which helps in emulating DMA.

KVM modifies Linux by introducing a new execution mode, *guest mode*, with the transition diagram depicted in Figure 3.28. (The two other modes supported by Linux, similar to the Unix operating system, are the *kernel* and *user* modes.)

This works as follows. The user-level code issues a system call via the Linux *ioctl*( ) function, with the request to execute the guest code. In response, the kernel causes the execution of the guest code in the guest mode. This continues until an exit event (such as a request for an I/O instruction, or an interrupt, or a time-out) occurs. When the CPU exits guest mode, it returns to

---

[19] We will return to this statement later, as in this case the difference between a Type-1 and a Type-2 hypervisor blurs.

[20] www.linux-kvm.org/page/Main_Page

[21] Please see www.linux-kvm.org/page/Processor_support

[22] QEMU is a free-source CPU emulator available at qemu.org (see http://wiki.qemu.org/Main_Page).

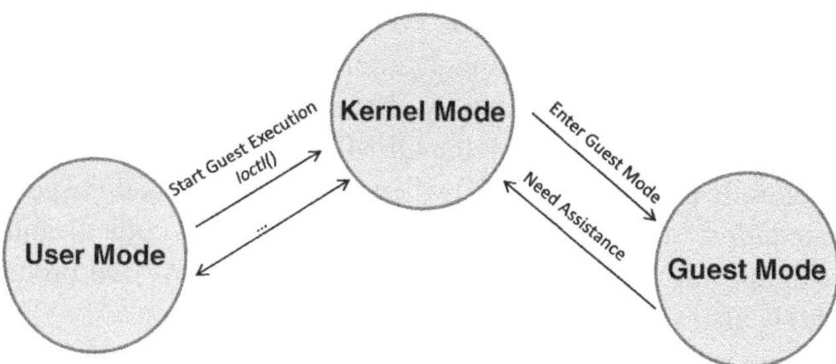

Figure 3.28 The state transition diagram for the KVM modes.

the kernel mode. The kernel processes the event, and depending on the result, either resumes the guest execution or returns to the user.

As [19] observes, tight integration into Linux helps both developers and end users of KVM to reclaim Linux's many capabilities (such as scheduling, process management, and assignment of virtual machines to specific CPUs).

We stated earlier that KVM is a Type-1 hypervisor, but there is a difference in opinion in the developers' community on that. Some people argue that since KVM is administered via a Linux interface, and, in fact, a virtual machine appears as a Linux process, it is a Type-2 hypervisor. Here the fine line is demarcated by the privilege ring in which the hypervisor runs, and it so happens that the Linux subsystem embodied by KVM has the highest privilege. (Needless to say it runs on bare metal, but so does any code—unless it is interpreted by software. The defining difference, in our opinion, is the privilege granted to the hypervisor code.)

But whereas the issue of KVM being a Type-1 hypervisor is questioned, there are pure Type-2 hypervisors: the VMware® *Workstation* and the Oracle *VM VirtualBox*®.[23] (In contrast, the VMware ESX and ESXi hypervisors are Type 1.)

The paper [18] that we cited in the review of the x86 virtualization also provides a comprehensive description of the VMware Workstation hypervisor (the authors of [18] prefer to use the term VMM). Unlike Xen, the VMware Workstation handles the problem of non-trapping privileged instructions in near real time by scanning the binary image and replacing problematic instructions either with traps or with direct procedure calls to a library. (Remember that the difference here is that Xen, which employs paravirtualization, achieves a similar result by pre-processing the operating system code; VMware requires no such pre-processing—the code is changed on the fly after the image has been loaded.)

Another Type-2 hypervisor, Oracle VM VirtualBox (comprehensively described in its User Manual [26]) employs a combination of techniques that are different from both paravirtualization and full software emulation (although it uses the latter in special circumstances).

The VirtualBox software, through its ring-0 kernel driver, sets up the host system so that the guest code runs natively, with VirtualBox lurking "underneath" ready to assume control whenever needed. The user (ring-3) code is left unmodified, but VirtualBox reconfigures the guest so that its system (ring-0) code runs in ring 1. The authors of [26] call this "a dirty

[23] The VirtualBox software was initially developed by Innotek GmbH, a company that was acquired later by Sun Microsystems, which in turn was acquired by Oracle Corporations.

trick," but there is nothing dirty about it since ring 1 on x86 has typically been left unused. When the system code (now running in ring 1) attempts to execute a privileged instruction, the VirtualBox hypervisor intercepts control. At that point, the instruction can be given to the host OS to execute or it can be run through the QEMU recompiler.

One interesting example mentioned in [26] when recompilation is invoked by VirtualBox—using its own *disassembler*[24] to analyze the code—is "when guest code disables interrupts and VirtualBox cannot figure out when they will be switched back on." All protected-mode code (such as BIOS code) is also recompiled.

It is important to note that all hypervisors mentioned so far support live migration. The problem here is non-trivial, as live migration involves copying the virtual machine memory while this memory can still be modified (the machine naturally needs to continue running on the old host until all the memory is copied), so it is a multi-pass process, in which careful synchronization between the old and new hosts is needed. Besides memory transfer, there are other aspects to live migration, to which we will return later in this book.

Meanwhile, new hypervisors such as *NOVA* [27] are being developed as a result of the research effort to address OS security by making the OS kernel as small and simple as possible. (Just to quantify this, the Xen hypervisor has about 150,000 lines of code,[25] while the NOVA hypervisor has only 9000.[26]) (There is a table in [27], in which the code sizes of most hypervisors mentioned in this section are compared.)

Although NOVA does not prevent paravirtualization, the authors of [28] state: "We do not use paravirtualization in our system, because we neither want to depend on the availability of source code for the guest operating systems nor make the extra effort of porting operating systems to a paravirtualization interface." Nor does NOVA use binary translation; it relies solely on hardware support for full virtualization.

NOVA represents the third generation of *microkernel* (or *μ-kernel*) systems—the operating systems that provide only the most basic capabilities to an application: memory and process management as well as interprocess communications. The idea behind this approach is that the rest of the operating system capabilities, including file system management, can be performed by an application itself trapping to the kernel when a sensitive action needs to be performed. Microkernels were initially developed in connection with LANs, but later security—which requires simplicity in software—has become the major driver.

The NOVA microhypervisor is to a hypervisor what a microkernel is to a kernel. It provides only basic mechanisms for virtualization, virtual machine separation, scheduling, communication, and management of platform resources. The rest is moved up. To this end, each virtual machine has its own associated virtual-machine monitor, which runs as an unprivileged user application on top of the microhypervisor. This architecture is depicted in Figure 3.29.

Note that this architecture is drastically different from all others that we have reviewed so far in that the hypervisor is split into a monolithic microkernel part and the user part replicated for each virtual machine. What is essential here is that the microkernel is specifically designed with security in mind: the decomposition of the hypervisor minimizes the amount of privileged code.

[24] A disassembler is a program that converts binary code to assembly-level code. In this case, it is used to analyze a program.

[25] http://wiki.xen.org/wiki/Xen_Overview

[26] http://os.inf.tu-dresden.de/~us15/nova/

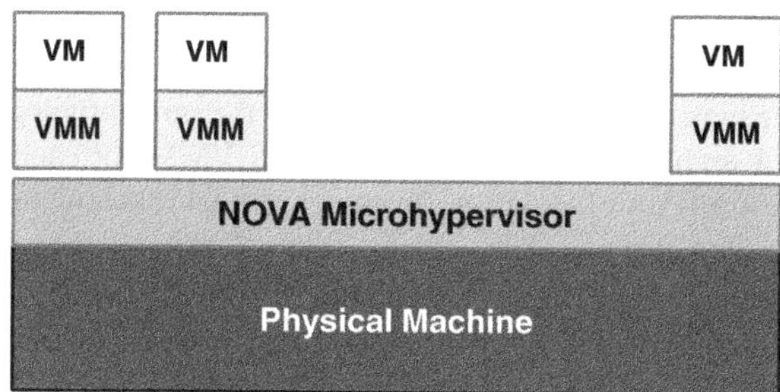

Figure 3.29 NOVA architecture (simplified).

This does not come without a cost, however, as the authors of [28] note: "By implementing virtualization at user level, we trade improved security … for a slight decrease in performance."

This discussion leads us to the subject of the next (and last) section in this chapter.

3.3.6 Security

Security is by far the most complex matter in Cloud Computing. Cloud Computing combines multiple technologies, and so all the threats endemic to each of these technologies are combined, too. The matter is further complicated by the different security demands of different service and deployment models. This necessitates a three-pronged approach to security in Cloud Computing: (a) understanding the security threats and evaluating the risks—along with their respective mitigation mechanisms—brought in by each of the technologies involved (operating systems, virtualization, data networking at the routing and switching layers, web applications, to name just the major ones); (b) analyzing the risks and mechanisms in light of a specific service model and specific deployment model; and (c) developing the holistic security picture. We will address generic security mechanisms systematically in a separate chapter, while the technology-specific pieces belong in the chapters where the respective technologies are described. Thus, the present chapter deals only with virtualization security, which ultimately boils down to hypervisor security.

The motivation for paying attention to hypervisor security should be obvious now. A hypervisor is a single point of security failure; if it is compromised, so are all the virtual machines under its control. How can it get compromised? For example, just as a carefully constructed *worm* (discussed in Section 3.2.3) "escapes" a user process's code and takes over the computer resources that only an operating system may control, so can a malicious guest code in an attack that, in fact, is called an *escape* [27] break out of a virtual machine to take control of the hypervisor and, consequently, all other virtual machines on the same physical host.

Assuming for the moment that the host hardware has been fully protected against tampering and that the booting process is safe, the attacks can come in the form of maliciously modified operating system and device drivers that schedule DMA to write—in the absence of I/O MMU—into the "wrong" memory. The devil here is in the rather complex detail of the interface between a virtual machine and the host, which provides, in the words of [27], "the attack surface that can be leveraged by a malicious guest operating system to attack the virtualization layer." If there is a vulnerability in the interface (and, as is well known, no complex software specification exists without having one), it can be exploited so that a virtual machine takes over the hypervisor—or rather executes at the same privilege level. (This is the reason why the NOVA architecture provides a dedicated VMM for each virtual machine, a feature that adds an extra layer of isolation. Even if a virtual machine takes over its VMM, which runs as an unprivileged application, there is still no damage to the top-level hypervisor.)

When the booting process is compromised (typically through manipulation of unprotected firmware), it is possible to install malicious programs that run with the highest privilege—"at the root" in Unix parlance, whence comes a common name for this type of program—a *rootkit*. The worst part of it is that typically, rootkits cannot even be detected.

A synopsis of the rootkit history is presented in [29]. Rootkits started as "Trojan horses"[27] that ran at the user level without doing much more harm than just hiding themselves, but, with the appearance of administrative tools that had the ability to detect them, morphed into kernel-level malicious programs. Just when the intrusion-detecting tools followed them there, so new ways had to be found to avoid detection.

Rootkits—or rather non-malicious programs exhibiting rootkit-like stealth—have been used for seemingly legitimate purposes (enforcement of copyright protection being a notorious example), but this appears to be a gray area as far as laws are concerned. There is substantial academic research into rootkits, which aims at discovering the vulnerabilities the rootkits may exploit. The *SubVirt* project, described in [29], has been developed jointly by Microsoft and the University of Michigan. The *Virtual Machine-Based Rootkit* (*VMBR*) is one outcome of the project. VMBR inserts itself between the hypervisor and the target operating system by manipulating the system boot sequence. This can be achieved either through "a remote vulnerability" (unspecified in the paper) or social engineering (fooling the user, bribing the vendor, or corrupting "a bootable CD-ROM or DVD image present on a peer-to-peer network"). Once the root privileges are gained, VMBR is installed on the disk (which requires some massaging of the disk blocks and the data they already contain). At that point, the boot records are also cleverly modified—in a way that avoids actual detection of the modification. To achieve this, the boot blocks are manipulated "during the final stages of shutdown, after most processes and kernel subsystems have exited." Both Microsoft Windows XP and Linux operating systems have been reported to be invaded in this way, with gory technical detail presented in [29]. As far as the hypervisors go, the proof-of-concept VMBR is reported to be implemented on Linux/VMware and Microsoft Windows/VirtualPC platforms.

Perhaps VMBR would have remained an obscure academic exercise, had it not been for a clear case of practicality which the researches made by also implementing a nice array of services (such as "a keystroke *sniffer*, a *phishing* web server, a tool that searches a user's file system for sensitive data, and a detection countermeasure which defeats a common VMM detection technique"). The researchers also demonstrated that their VMBR was effective in modifying an observable state of the system, which made it very hard to detect—so hard that "one of the authors accidentally used a machine which had been infected by our proof-of-concept VMBR without realizing that he was using a compromised system!"

A key point of the resulting defense strategy to detect these types of rootkit is to run detection software at a layer below VMBR so that it can "read physical memory or disk and

[27] A Trojan horse is a program that purports to be another—typically well-known—program.

look for signatures or anomalies that indicate the presence of a VMBR, such as a modified boot sequence." Protection at this level can also be implemented in firmware. Prevention, using secure boot techniques, is also recommended and, in our opinion, it is the best course of action; however, if a safe boot medium (i.e., a shrink-wrapped CD-ROM) has already been poisoned through a social engineering scheme, that won't help.

While the SubVirt VMBR was implemented for the standard (non-virtualizable x86 CPU), another research project produced the *Blue Pill* VMBR, designed for the fully virtualizable AMD chip. (For detail and references, see Joanna Rutkowska's blog.[28]) The Blue Pill code has been freely distributed, but there has been significant controversy around the project, motivating many a company to block access to these pages on its corporate network.

So far, we have reviewed cases where malicious software either "took over" the hypervisor or otherwise was executed at the hypervisor level. It turns out that even taking control of a hypervisor per se may be unnecessary for inflicting damage; it may be sufficient instead to exploit vulnerabilities in virtual machine isolation.

An unobtrusive (passive) attack, in which an adversary learns what is supposed to be secret information, may inflict serious damage. To this end, it is important to learn and remember how much the information about the inner workings of a physical computer—even what looks like innocuous information—may reveal. There is a whole series of *side-channel attacks* in which hardware (e.g., CPU, memory, or devices) usage patterns can be used to reveal—with differing degrees of difficulty–various secrets, including cryptographic keys.

The very information on the specific physical host residence of a virtual machine must be kept secret. (As we learn later in the book, this is very similar to the long-standing practice by network and service providers of keeping the network infrastructure secret.) This explains why the authors of [30][29] caused a significant stir in the industry by reporting their experiments using a well-known service of a major Cloud provider, specific to the Xen hypervisor (and based on comparisons of *dom0* IP addresses).

The researchers had demonstrated that it was "possible to map the internal Cloud infrastructure, identify where a particular target VM is likely to reside, and then instantiate new VMs until one is placed co-resident with the target." Once instantiated, the machines mounted cross-VM side-channel attacks to learn (through CPU data caches) the CPU utilization measurements. Various attacks that can be mounted based on these data—including *keystroke timing* (in which the times between two successive keystrokes allow you to guess a typed password)—are also described in [30].

Among the recommended approaches to mitigating risk, the authors of [30] mention obfuscation of both the internal structure of Cloud providers' services and the placement policy. For example, providers might inhibit network-based co-residence checks. Another, somewhat vague, recommendation is to "employ blinding techniques to minimize the information that can be leaked." The problem with that is that it is next to impossible to predict what type of information can be used as a side-channel. The best solution, in authors' opinion, is "simply to expose the risk and placement decisions directly to users." With that, a user may require a dedicated physical machine and bear the costs. Unfortunately, this defies the principles of

[28] http://theinvisiblethings.blogspot.com/2006/06/introducing-blue-pill.html

[29] We highly recommend reading this fascinating paper in full, while suggesting that a reader unfamiliar with IP networking defer that until studying Chapter 4, which provides the necessary networking background.

Cloud Computing. Side-channel attacks are considered somewhat far-fetched at the moment; however, the argument for the protection of the *information* on a Cloud provider's infrastructure is important, sound, and timely. Later in the book, we will address mechanisms for achieving that.

To conclude this chapter, we cite the NIST recommendations [27] pertinent to hypervisors:

- Install all updates to the hypervisor as they are released by the vendor. Most hypervisors have features that will check for updates automatically and install the updates when found. Centralized patch management solutions can also be used to administer updates.
- Restrict administrative access to the management interfaces of the hypervisor. Protect all management communication channels using a dedicated management network, or authenticate and encrypt the management network communications using FIPS 140-2 validated cryptographic modules.[30]
- Synchronize the virtualized infrastructure to a trusted authoritative time server.
- Disconnect unused physical hardware from the host system. For example, a removable disk drive might occasionally be used for backups or restores but it should be disconnected when not actively being used. Disconnect unused NICs[31] from any network.
- Disable all hypervisor services such as clipboard or file sharing between the guest OS and the host OS unless they are needed. Each of these services can provide a possible attack vector. File sharing can also be an attack vector on systems where more than one guest OS share the same folder with the host OS.
- Consider using introspection capabilities[32] to monitor the security of each guest OS. If a guest OS is compromised, its security controls may be disabled or reconfigured so as to suppress any signs of compromise. Having security services in the hypervisor permits security monitoring even when the guest OS is compromised.
- Consider using introspection capabilities to monitor the security of activities occurring among guest OSs. This is particularly important for communications which in a non-virtualized environment were carried over networks and monitored by network security controls (such as network firewalls, security appliances, and network Intrusion Detection and Prevention Solution (IDPS) sensors).
- Carefully monitor the hypervisor itself for signs of compromise. This includes using self-integrity monitoring capabilities that hypervisors may provide, as well as monitoring and analyzing hypervisor logs on an ongoing basis.

Incidentally, there is an argument in the industry that augmenting hypervisor with introspection services may provide additional attack vectors if only because of the increased size of code. Performance is often cited as a problem too.

An alternative is to develop a privileged appliance—a VM that provides introspection services through a hypervisor-exposed API. This takes care of the performance concerns

[30] We will discuss this in detail later in the book.

[31] NIC stands for *Network Interface Controller*, a device that connects a computer to a LAN (at a physical layer).

[32] The term *introspection capabilities* refers to the capabilities of a hypervisor that are above and beyond its normal function of administering VMs. These capabilities include monitoring the traffic among the VMs, access to file systems, memory, program execution, and all other activities that can help detect intrusion.

(since the services are performed at the appliance's expense) as well as the hypervisor-code-creep concern. But exposing introspection API may be dangerous in its own way if the access to this API is not controlled to limit it only to the appliance.

Yet another approach to introspection, which works in a controlled environment (such as Private Cloud), is to avoid hypervisor altogether and instead install root-kit-like agents in each virtual machine. These agents monitor the VM behavior and log it.

The research on virtualization security is ongoing. A novel and promising approach, called *NoHype*, is being investigated at Princeton University [31, 32]. Here a hypervisor merely prepares the environment for a virtual machine to run and then assigns it to a specific CPU core, which would be "owned" by this machine. This approach can accommodate particularly sensitive situations where the highest level of VM isolation (short of using a standalone computer) is needed.

References

[1] Creasy, R.J. (1981) The origin of the VM/370 time-sharing system. *IBM Journal of Research and Development*, **25**(5), 483–490.

[2] Tanenbaum, A.S. (2006) *Structured Computer Organization*, 5th edn. Pearson Prentice Hall, Upper Saddle River, NJ.

[3] Knuth, D. (1997) *Art of Computer Programming, Volume 1: Fundamental Algorithms*, 3rd edn. Addison-Wesley Professional, New York.

[4] Eichin, M.W. and Bochlis, J.A. (1989) With microscope and tweezers: An analysis of the Internet virus of November 1988. Proceedings of the 1989 IEEE Symposium on Security and Privacy, May 1–3, Cambridge, MA, pp. 326–343.

[5] Stravinsky, I. (1988) *Petrushka*, First Tableau (full score). Dover Publications, Mineola, NY, p. 43.

[6] Tanenbaum, A.S. (2007) *Modern Operating Systems*, 3rd edn. Prentice Hall, Englewood Cliffs, NJ.

[7] Silberschatz, A., Galvin, P.B., and Gagne, G. (2009) *Operating System Concepts*, 8th edn. John Wiley & Sons, New York.

[8] Bach, M.J. (1986) *The Design of the Unix Operating System*. Prentice Hall, Englewood Cliffs, NJ.

[9] Motorola (1992) *Motorola M68000 Family Programmer's Reference Manual*. Motorola, Schaumburg, IL.

[10] Organick, E.I. (1972) *The Multics System: An Examination of Its Structure*. MIT Press, Boston, MA.

[11] Graham, R.M. (1968) Protection in an information processing utility. *Communications of the ACM*, **11**(5), 365–369.

[12] Kidder, T. (1981) *The Soul of a New Machine*. Atlantic, Little, Brown, Boston, MA.

[13] Goldberg, R.P. (1973) Architecture of Virtual Machines, 2nd edn. Proceedings of the AFIPS National Computer Conference, June 4–8, Montvale, NJ, pp. 74–112. http://flint.cs.yale.edu/cs428/doc/goldberg.pdf.

[14] Popek, G.J. and Goldberg, R.P. (1974) Formal requirements for virtualizable third generation architectures. *Communications of the ACM*, **17**(7), 412–421.

[15] Robin, J.S. and Irvine, C.E. (2000) Analysis of the Intel Pentium's ability to support a secure Virtual Machine Monitor. Proceedings of the 9th USENIX Security Symposium, August 14–17, Denver, CO, pp. 129–144.

[16] Intel Corporation (2010) Intel® 64 and IA-32 Architectures, Software Developer's Manual, Volume 3A: System Programming Guide, Part 1. Order Number: 253668-034US, March.

[17] Advanced Micro-Devices (2012) AMD64 Technology. AMD64 Architecture Programmer's Manual, Volume 3: General-Purpose and System Instructions. Publication No. 24594 3.19. Release 3.19, September.

[18] Adams, K. and Agesen, O. (2006) A comparison of software and hardware techniques for x86 virtualization. ASPLOS-XII Proceedings of 12th International Conference on Architectural Support for Programming Languages and Operating Systems, New York, pp. 412–421.

[19] Kivity, A., Kamay, Y., Laor, D., *et al.* (2007) kvm: The Linux Virtual Machine Monitor. Proceedings of the Linux Symposium, June 27–30, Ottawa, Ont., pp. 225–230.

[20] Nakajima, J. and Mallick, A.K. (2007) Hybrid-virtualization—enhanced virtualization for Linux. Proceedings of the Linux Symposium, June 27–30, Ottawa, Ont., pp. 86–97.

[21] Intel (2006) Intel® virtualization technology for directed I/O. Intel® Technology Journal, 10(03). ISSN 1535-864x, August 10, 2006, Section 7.
[22] Chisnall, D. (2007) *The Definitive Guide to the Xen Xypervisor*. Prentice Hall Open Source Development Series, Pearson Education, Boston, MA.
[23] Waldspurger, C. and Rosenblum, M. (2012) I/O virtualization. *Communications of the ACM*, **55**(1), 66–72.
[24] Ben-Yehuda, M., Xenidis, J., Ostrowski, M., *et al.* (2007) The price of safety: Evaluating IOMMU performance. Proceedings of the Linux Symposium, June 27–30, 2007, Ottawa, Ont., pp. 225–230.
[25] Armbrust, M., Fox, A., Griffith, R., *et al.* (2009) Above the Clouds: A Berkeley view of Cloud computing. Electrical Engineering and Computer Sciences Technical Report No. UCB/EECS-2009-2A, University of California at Berkeley, Berkeley, CA, February 10.
[26] Oracle Corporation (n.d.) Oracle VM VirtualBox® User Manual. www.virtualbox.org/manual/.
[27] Scarfone, K., Souppaya, M., and Hoffman, P. (2011) Guide to Security for Full Virtualization Technologies. Special Publication 800-125, National Institute of Standards and Technology, US Department of Commerce, January.
[28] Steinberg, U. and Kauer, B. (2010) NOVA: A microhypervisor-based secure virtualization architecture. Proceedings of the 5th European Conference on Computer Systems (EuroSys'10), Paris, pp. 209–222.
[29] King, S.T.; Chen, P.M., Wang, Y., *et al.* (2006). SubVirt: Implementing malware with virtual machines. Proceedings of the 2006 IEEE Symposium on Security and Privacy (S&P'06), Oakland, CA, pp. 327–341.
[30] Ristenpart, T., Tromer, E., Shacham, H., and Savage, S. (2009) Hey, you, get off of my Cloud: Exploring information leakage in third-party compute Clouds. Proceedings of CCS'09, November 9–13, 2009, Chicago, IL.
[31] Keller, E., Szefer, J., Rexford, J., and Lee, R.B. (2010) NoHype: Virtualized Cloud infrastructure without the virtualization. *ACM SIGARCH Computer Architecture News*, **38**(3), 350–361.
[32] Szefer, J., Keller, E., Lee, R.B., and Rexford, J. (2011) Eliminating the hypervisor attack surface for a more secure Cloud. Proceedings of the 18th ACM Conference on Computer and Communications Security, ACM, pp. 401–412.

4

Data Networks—The Nervous System of the Cloud

This chapter picks up just at the point where Chapter 3 left off. There we had already mentioned data networking more than once, always with a forward reference. No postponement anymore!

Data networking refers to a set of technologies that enable computer-to-computer communications. The ultimate result is that two processes located on different computers can talk to one another. This, in turn, supports *distributed processing*. As you may remember, this is an operating system task to enable interprocess communications on the same machine. Transferring this capability across machines—over a network—naturally involves operating systems, too.

In fact, the disciplines of data communications and operating systems have been evolving side by side since the 1960s. In earlier systems, the data communication capabilities were added by means of both (a) new device drivers for physical network access and (b) specialized libraries for interprocess communications across the network (which differed from those provided by the kernel for interprocess communications within the machine). It is interesting that, in these early days, achieving over-the-network interprocess communications was not an end in itself[1] but rather the means of accessing remote resources—typically, files. *File transfer* was a major data networking application. Another one was *transaction systems* (such as those employed in banking or airline reservations), in which a user would type a command that caused an action in a database located on a remote machine and then get a response from this machine.

Toward the end of the 1980s, the operating systems evolution proceeded along two branches: (1) *network operating systems*, which provide an environment in which users can access remote resources while being aware of their being remote; and (2) *distributed operating systems*, which provide an environment in which users access remote resources in exactly the same way they access local resources. This development—which is very interesting in itself—and its results are well described in [1]. In addition, we recommend [2] as an encyclopedic reference to

[1] As it would have been for voice or text communications, had those been considered back then.

Cloud Computing: Business Trends and Technologies, First Edition. Igor Faynberg, Hui-Lan Lu and Dor Skuler.

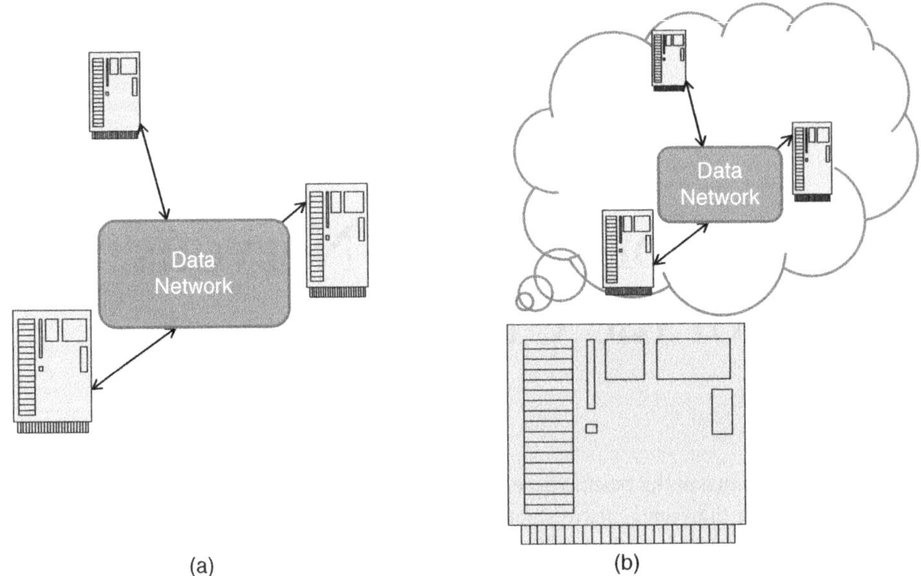

Figure 4.1 Dual aspects of networking in Cloud Computing.

distributed computing. In more than one way, the objectives of these developments were very similar to those of Cloud Computing inasmuch as these objectives included support of *migration*, which is three-pronged: *data migration* involves moving a file or its portion to the accessing machine; *computation migration* involves invoking a computation on a remote machine—where the required data reside—with the result returned to the accessing machine; *process migration* involves the execution of a program on a remote machine (e.g., for the purposes of load balancing). Cloud Computing, of course, augments the latter capability with full virtual machine (rather than process) migration. Yet, there is an emerging trend in which new applications are run on dedicated inexpensive microprocessors; here, the CPU virtualization component becomes much less relevant in achieving elasticity, while the data networking component remains prominent.

The ever-growing size of the manuscript does not allow us to concentrate on distributed processing in any detail. Fortunately, there are well-known monographs (including the references that we just mentioned) on the subject. In the rest of this chapter, we will deal with distributed computing primarily in the context of the World-Wide Web.

Going back to data networking, it requires, at a minimum, physical interconnection of computers, as depicted in Figure 4.1(a). Naturally, interconnection in this form is an essential aspect of Cloud Computing, as it effects the data exchange (1) within a Cloud; (2) between any two federating Clouds; and (3) between any computer that needs to access the Cloud and the Cloud.

It is interesting to observe a duality present in Figure 4.1(b). (We have actually referred to it more than once in the previous chapter.) Here, as the physical machines "turn" into virtual machines, consolidated on a single physical machine, all the networking software must remain unchanged, and so the "physical network," now located within the same physical machine, is effectively simulated by the hypervisor.

As far as the introduction to data networking is concerned, we have tried to make this book as self-contained as possible.

We start with an overview of data networking, using the classical *Open Systems Interconnection* (*OSI*) model developed by the International Organization for Standardization (ISO). The OSI reference model is the best universal tool for explaining both the principles of data communication and its major issues. All data communication protocols fit (more or less) within this model, and often the very question of where a particular protocol fits leads to a deeper understanding of the issues involved.

Following the discussion of the model, we introduce the *Internet Protocol* (*IP*) and review the Internet protocol suite. In the course of this review, it should become apparent that even though the Internet was designed around specific paradigms and with only a few applications in view, it was made fairly extensible. We demonstrate this extensibility with examples—which we will need later—of the standardized means to achieve *Quality of Service* (*QoS*), a capability to support "data pipes" of specific capacity.

An important issue—deserving a separate section (although a separate book could easily be dedicated to it) is that of addressing and routing in IP-based networks. Following that we have a section on *Multi-Protocol Label Switching* (*MPLS*), which almost leaps out of the IP context, by effectively introducing a technology that synthesizes circuit switching with packet switching.

The next step, building on the previously discussed capabilities, introduces a new dimension to virtualization. This dimension deals with network virtualization rather than computer virtualization. Instead of building a separate private network, an enterprise can use a set of mechanisms for carving out from a provider's network—or the Internet—what looks and feels like a dedicated private network, that is a *Virtual Private Network* (*VPN*). This capability has been carried over from public telephone networks (see [3] for the detail and history), which provided an enterprise with a unique numbering plan so that telephone calls were made in the same manner whether the two callers were in adjacent offices or in different countries.

In the case of data networks—and at this point it is accurate to say that telephony has become just another application of data networking, so we are approaching a situation in which there are really no other networks except data networks—the VPN variants are depicted in Figure 4.2. A private network, which is completely owned by an enterprise, is shown in Figure 4.2(a). Typically, such a network spans a single enterprise campus. If an enterprise has two campuses, the two networks can be interconnected through a "pipe," as shown in Figure 4.2(b). (Incidentally, this is one of the means of interconnection provided by the Cloud carrier actor described in the NIST reference architecture discussed earlier.) Figure 4.2(c) depicts a scenario in which different islands of an enterprise (campus networks or even individual users) access a carrier's public network or the Internet to form a VPN.

Further development of this topic, undertaken in a separate section, introduces the subject of a *Software-Defined Network* (*SDN*), which gives greater control to network providers for centralized decision making about routing and forwarding of data packets.

As is the case with the previous chapter, we conclude the present one with an overview of network security, although this time it is limited in scope to only network layer security.

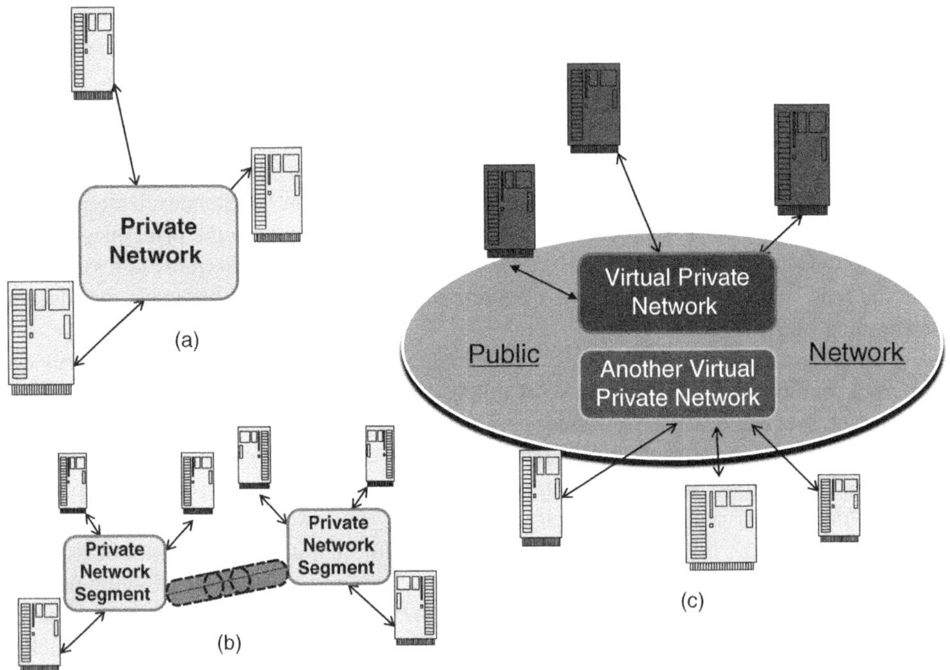

Figure 4.2 Private and virtual private networks.

4.1 The OSI Reference Model

This model (first published in 1984 and subsequently revised 10 years later [4]) has successfully applied a divide-and-conquer approach to the complex problem of making two different processes, executing at different hosts, communicate with each other. Even though many of the actual OSI standards ended up abandoned in favor of the Internet standards (see [5], which explains very well the reasons as well as the history of the effort), the model lives on.[2]

Figure 4.3 highlights the key aspects of the model. To begin with, the endpoints are structured as seven-layer entities, each layer being an independent module, responsible for a particular communication function.

There are two aspects to the model: the first aspect relates to intermachine communications; the second to processing within a single machine. In the remainder of this section we will discuss these aspects, followed by a functional description of each layer.

4.1.1 Host-to-Host Communications

As a separate module, each layer is designed to "talk" directly to its counterpart (the point that the dotted lines in Figure 4.1 illustrate). A set of messages pertinent to a particular layer, combined with the rules defining the order of the messages is called a *protocol*. For

[2] To this end, many OSI concepts and even protocols have ended up synthesized in the Internet protocol suite.

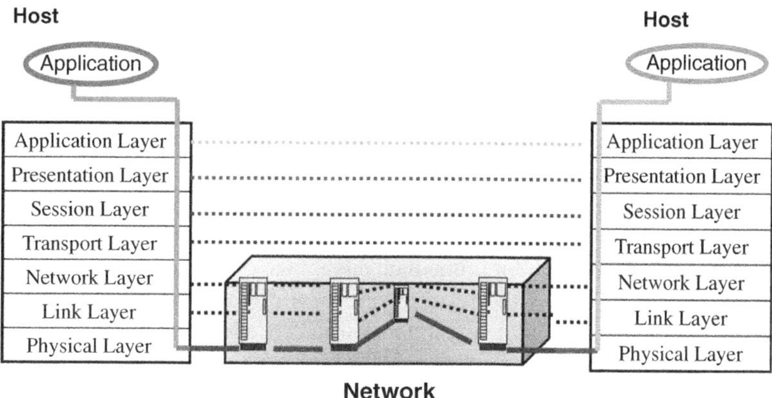

Figure 4.3 The OSI reference model.

example, a file transfer (perhaps the earliest data communication application) may require a protocol that contains a message for copying a given file as well as a set of operation status messages—including error messages.

While the actual transfer of a message is relegated to the layer immediately below, terminating with a physical layer which relies on the physical medium for data transfer, the "direct" intra-layer message (called the *protocol data unit*) is presented to the receiving module at the endpoint intact.

The endpoint entities are identified by the layer's addressing scheme. Thus, an application layer's endpoints are identified by the application-defined addressing scheme, the session layer's endpoints by the session-layer addressing scheme, and so on. The chief rule for maintaining modularity is that a given layer is *not* supposed to have any knowledge of what happens below it—beyond what is specified in the interlayer interface. (As often happens with rules, this particular one has been broken, as we will see very soon, when discussing Internet protocols.)

The meaning of endpoints differs among different layers. For the layers from application down to session layer, the interlocutors are application processes, represented in the model through *application entities*. For the transport layer, the endpoints are the machines themselves. But the network layer is altogether different—as Figure 4.1 demonstrates—in that it relays each protocol data unit through multiple machines until that unit reaches the intended recipient host.

The delivery model deserves special attention, as there are two competing modes for it. In one mode—called *connectionless*—the network works like a postal system. Once an envelope with the address of the recipient is deposited into the system, it may pass multiple relay stations, until it ends up in the post office that serves the recipient. It used to be (and maybe still is?) that people carried on chess games by correspondence. With each turn in the game, the correspondent who made a move would write down that move in a letter, send it to his or her counterpart, and wait for the latter's move. Note that the route the envelopes travel may differ from one envelope to another, subject to mail pick-up regulations and transport availability. Playing chess by correspondence was a slow thing.

The other mode—called *connection-oriented*—took after telephony. A typical application sample here is a telephone conversation. In the classic *Public Switched Telecommunications Network* (*PSTN*) of the previous century, the telephone switches established an end-to-end route (called a *circuit*) among themselves, connecting the two telephones. Once established, the circuit would last for as long as the conversation continued. In addition, the PSTN could establish, on a customer's request, a semi-permanent circuit, connecting various pieces of the customer's enterprise, thus establishing a type of VPN. This model is natural for physical "on-the-wire" connections, but it has been applied to data communications where *virtual circuits* are defined in the network layer.[3] An immediate advantage of the connection-oriented mode, compared with connectionless, is the relative ease of traffic engineering (i.e., guaranteeing the upper bounds of the end-to-end delay and its variance, called *jitter*). An immediate disadvantage is the potential waste of resources required to maintain a circuit. Going back to the chess game example, the game would definitely have moved faster if the players had used the telephone instead of mail, but it would have been much more expensive while also tying up telephone lines that would be idle while the players thought about their next moves.

We will return to this topic repeatedly. As we will see, both models are still alive and well, having evolved in synthesis. The evolution of these models in telephone networks and the Internet has been described in [3]. We note finally that the highest layer at which the machines comprising the so-far-observed network operate, for the purposes of the OSI model, is the network layer. We will call these machines *network elements*. Often, network elements are also called *switches* or *routers*—the distinction comes historically from the respective model: connection-oriented or connectionless.

Finally, the link layer and the physical layer both deal with a single physical link and thus connect either (1) the two network elements or (2) a network element and the endpoint host.

4.1.2 Interlayer Communications

Our experience in teaching data communications and operating systems has proven that the understanding of the computation model (i.e., what is being called within the context of an application process and under what circumstances) is central both to the overall understanding of data communications and to the understanding of each protocol involved.

We should note right away that a given model does not imply an implementation, although any implementation is based on one or another model. Ultimately, thinking about a specific implementation of any abstract idea is a good step toward understanding this idea. We will make one step from what the standard specifies toward developing an actual implementation.

According to the OSI model, each layer provides a well-defined *service* to the layer above. The service is a set of capabilities, and the capabilities are implemented by passing the information between the layers.

The key questions here are how a communicating process interacts with the layers of Figure 4.3, and how these layers interact with one another on a single machine (host).

The OSI specification states that in order to transmit its protocol data unit to its peer, a layer sends a *request* to the underlying layer. The layers interact strictly according to the layering structure, without bypassing the ranks. The incoming protocol data (from the peer layer) is

[3] Again, we refer the reader to the excellent textbook [5] for a detailed explanation of the technologies and protocols.

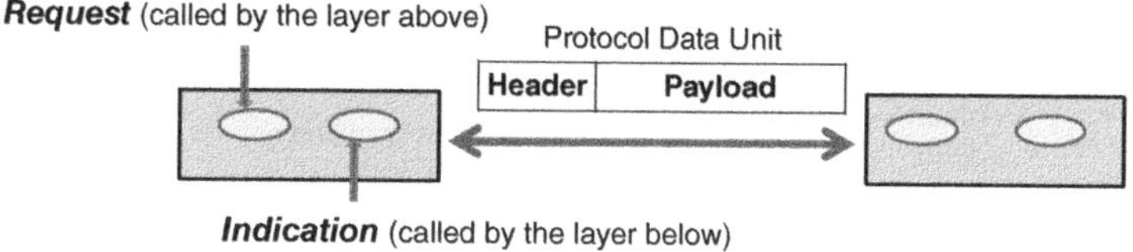

Figure 4.4 *Requests* and *indications* as methods of the layer class.

carried in an *indication* from the underlying layer. Consequently, each layer receives a *request* from the layer above and sends its own request to the layer below; similarly, each layer receives an indication from the layer below and sends its own indication to the layer above. This model is concise, but it is abstract enough to allow drastically different implementations.

Let us start with a straightforward but rather inefficient implementation, in which each layer is implemented as a separate process[4] and the messages are passed using interprocess communications. This results in rather slow operation, and there is an inherent difficulty. Since indications and requests are asynchronous,[5] a simplistic implementation—possibly dictated by the message-passing capabilities of a given operating system—may end up with at least two processes (or two threads within a single process) for each layer. One process (or thread) would execute a tight loop waiting for the indications and propagating them up, and the other waiting for the requests and propagating them down. A slightly better approach is to wait for *any* message (either from the layer above or the layer below) and then process it accordingly.

One way to describe an efficient computational model, with the help of Figure 4.4, is to define a layer as a *class* with two methods: *request* and *indication*, along with the appropriate data structures and constants dictated by the layer's functional requirements. The *request* method is to be invoked only by the layer above; the *indication* method is to be invoked only by the layer below.

According to the OSI model, for each layer, two objects of the respective class are to be instantiated at the hosts and network elements. The objects exchange *protocol data units*, as defined in the protocol specification of the layer.

When a layer sends a protocol data unit, it attaches to it a *header* that further describes the payload that follows. Then it invokes the *request* method of the layer below, passing the protocol data unit to it. In our computation model, the request action starts with the application process itself, and so all the subsequent calls are performed in the context of this process (the application entity).

An invocation of a layer's request method from the layer above will, at a certain point, result in this layer's invocation of the request method of the layer below. It does not, however, *necessarily* result in that action—for instance, the layer's required behavior may be such that it needs to accumulate data to a certain point, before invoking the request method of the layer below. Conversely, when the request method is invoked, it can result in several request

---

[4] We have observed an attempt at such implementation; the resulting performance was so disastrous that the project ended up being scrapped.

[5] A request from an application process to the application layer is generated when this process needs to send data, and it is fairly easy to see how the rest of the requests are chained to the original request. The *indications*, however, are generally caused by messages received from the network.

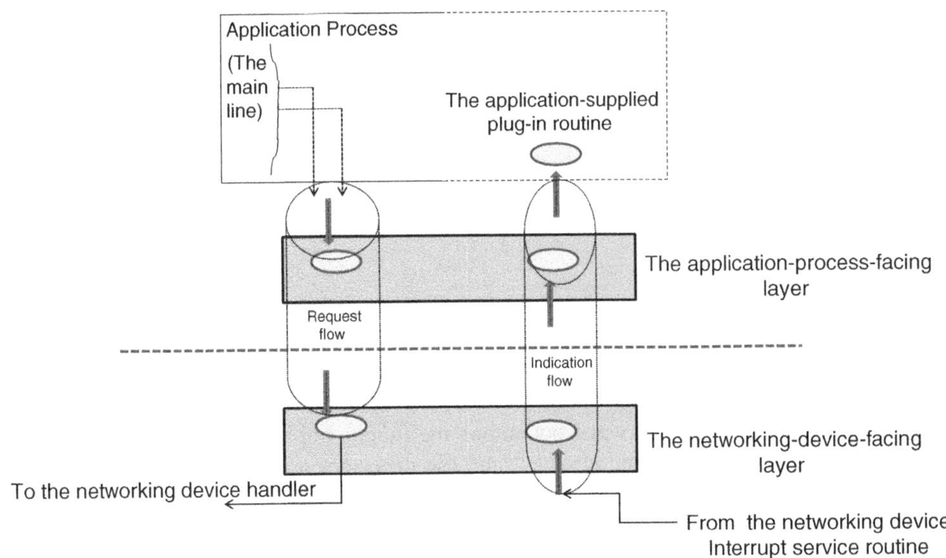

Figure 4.5 Summary of the overall computational model.

invocations at the layer below—as may be required by the necessity to break a large protocol data unit into smaller ones carried in the layer below. (For example, a huge file may not be sent in a single protocol data unit, and so a request to copy a file from one machine to another would typically result in several data units sent. We will see more examples later.)

The same consideration applies to invoking the *indication* method. Just as the messages to be sent out at a higher level may need to be broken into smaller units for processing at the layer below, so the received messages may need to be assembled before they are passed to the layer above.

We know that the first request in the chain is invoked by the application process. But who invokes the first indication? Naturally, the one whose job it is to watch the device that receives data from the network! As we know, the CPU already watches for the device signals, which suggests that the first indication method should be invoked by the relevant interrupt service routine, with the rest of the invocations propagating from there.

Now that we get into the subject of devices, it is appropriate to note that the link and physical layers have typically been implemented in hardware, as are parts of the network layer in network elements. Therefore, the actual device-facing interface may need to be maintained in the upper layers. And, as we will see from the Internet discussion, some applications skip a few top layers altogether, so the application process may face a layer that is lower than the application layer. This is reflected in the overall model depicted in Figure 4.5.

Note that this model has a clear place for the indication as a method provided by the application. (We have omitted the word "process," because the process is defined by the main line of code of the application program.) The indication method is exported by the application program as a plug-in routine, and so it ends up being invoked not by the application process, but by the operating system as part of the interrupt processing.

In conclusion, we repeat that what we have described is just a model rather than a prescription for an implementation. The purpose of any model is to elucidate all aspects of a conception; in the case of OSI interlayer exchanges, the major issue is the asynchronous nature of the indications. As a matter of fact, quite a few years ago, one of the authors was part of a team at Sperry Univac which implemented the OSI protocol suite variant on a Varian Data Machines minicomputer in exactly the way described above. To be precise, the link and physical layers were implemented on hardware (a separate board); the rest were object libraries.[6] This implementation, however, was dictated by the absence of an interprocess communications mechanism in the operating system.

4.1.3 Functional Description of Layers

We will follow the model top down, starting with the application layer. Not surprisingly, there is not much in the standard description of the latter; however, its major functions—in addition to the data transfer—include identification of the interlocutors via an appropriate addressing scheme, authentication, authorization to enter the communications, and negotiation of the quality-of-service parameters. (We will discuss the last point in detail in the context of IP networks.)

Another important function is the establishment of the *abstract syntax* context, which refers to a translation of data structures (originally defined in a high-level language) to bit strings. The necessity for this came from the earliest days of data communications, starting with character encodings. The IBM terminals used the *Extended Binary Coded Decimal Interchange Code (EBCDIC)*, which was the *lingua franca* of IBM operating systems, while the Bell System teletypes used the *American Standard Code for Information Interchange* (*ASCII*) whose genes came from telegraphy. Minicomputer operating systems adapted ASCII, which was also the standard for a virtual teletype terminal.

Character representation remains an important issue, and it resulted in new standards related to *internationalization* of the Internet, but this issue is only the tip of the iceberg when it comes to representation of data structures. For one thing, the machines' architectures differed in how the bits were read within an octet (a byte), with both options—left to right and right to left—prevalent. Furthermore, the order of bytes within a computer word (whether 16 or 32 bit) differs among the architectures, too, as does the representation of signed integers and floating-point numbers. Hence the necessity for a mechanism to construct (by the sender) and interpret (by the receiver) the on-the-wire bit string, which is what the abstract syntax context is for.

Finally, the OSI standard distinguishes at the application layer between connectionless and connection-oriented modes of operation. The security functions (oddly)—along with functions for establishing the responsibility for error recovery and synchronization—are assigned to the connection-oriented mode only.

Starting with the presentation layer, all layers provide specific services to the layer directly above. The presentation layer's services are the identification of all available *transfer syntaxes*

[6] To be precise, there were no object-oriented languages in use at the time, so strictly speaking what was implemented was a library of subroutine calls, which were compiled in separate modules—one module per layer. Each module corresponded to a program, which had its own data structures along the procedure libraries. The data was visible only to the procedures within the module.

(i.e., the layouts of the on-the-wire bit strings) and selection of the transfer syntax to use. Beyond that, the presentation layer provides the pass to the session layer, effectively translating the session payload by mapping the transfer syntax into the abstract syntax. Negotiation of the transfer syntax is a function of the presentation layer. It is useful to look at the computation aspect here: each payload-carrying request to the presentation layer results in the invocation of a request to the session layer and, conversely, each payload-carrying indication to the session layer results in the invocation of a request to the presentation layer. Both are processed synchronously, with the presentation layer translating the payload.[7]

The session layer provides a duplex connection between two processes (via their respective *presentation entities*), identified by session addresses. The session-layer services include the establishment and release of the connection and data transfer, as well as the connection resynchronization, management, and relevant exception reporting. In addition, there is a *token management* service, which allows the communicating processes to take turns in performing control functions. The session layer permits a special, *expedited* service for shorter session protocol data units, in support of quality-of-service requirements.[8]

The above services only relate to the connection-oriented mode. In the connectionless mode, the session-layer services reduce merely to a pass-through to the transport layer.

The transport layer actually implements the capabilities in support of the services defined for the layers above. The stated objective of the OSI design was to optimize "the use of the available network-service to provide the performance required by each session-entity at minimum cost."

The services that the transport layer provides to the session layer actually do not differ in their description from those defined for the session layer, but the transport layer is the one that is doing the job. One interesting feature is session multiplexing, as demonstrated in Figure 4.6.

Here the three sessions—AC, BD, and EF—are multiplexed into the transport-layer connection between the hosts X and Y. (Unfortunately, from the very onset of the OSI standardization the model has not been implemented consistently, standing in the way of interoperability. As we will see, the Internet model dispensed with the distinction between the session and transport layers altogether.) In turn, the transport layer can multiplex transport connections to network-layer connections. The latter can also be split when necessary.

Additional unique functions of the transport layer include the transport protocol data unit sequence control, segmenting and concatenation of the transport control data units, flow control, and error detection and recovery, all of these augmented by expedited data transfer and quality-of-service monitoring. This set of functions guarantees, in connection-oriented mode, a controllable, end-to-end error-free pipe.[9]

---

[7] Such "thinness" of the presentation layer resulted, as we will see, in it being abandoned by the designers of the US Department of Defense Advanced Research Projects Agency Network (ARPANET) protocols, which later made the Internet protocol suite. Yet, the function was introduced into the Internet applications-layer protocols later—when the growing set of applications required it—with varying options for the abstract transfer syntax.

[8] Initially, the Internet had rejected the concept of quality-of-service provision, but, as we will see shortly, it eventually accepted it, and even used the OSI terminology. The Internet, however, has specified quality-of-service support in the transport and network layers.

[9] In the connection-oriented mode, of the above functions, only end-to-end error detection and monitoring of the quality of service are present.

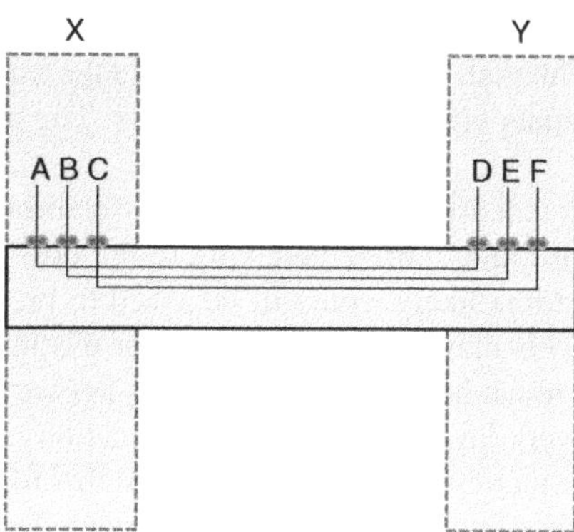

Figure 4.6 Session multiplexing in the OSI transport layer.

To achieve this is a major feat, as the connectionless network may deliver the data units out of order or lose some of them altogether. The establishment and tearing down of the transport-layer connection is a non-trivial problem in itself (as can be learned from Chapter 6 of [5]).

Once the connection is established, the transport layer must enumerate all the data units it sends[10] and then keep track of the acknowledgments from the peer site that contain the sequence numbers of the received data units. All unacknowledged protocol data units need to be retransmitted. On the receiving side, for every two protocol data units with non-consecutive sequence numbers, the transport layer must wait to collect all the units that fill that gap before passing the data to the session layer. There are complex heuristics involved in tuning multiple parameters, particularly the timer values, and the overall scheme is further complicated by the need for recovery procedures for the cases where one or both of the hosts crash during data transfer.

Error detection and correction involves computing a standard hash function (such as a checksum) for the transport protocol data unit. The sender sends the computed quantity (typically as part of a header) and the receiver computes the function over the received message and compares the result with the quantity computed by the sender. In the simplest case, where no error correction is involved, if the comparison fails, the received message is discarded and no acknowledgment is sent back. The absence of an acknowledgment eventually causes the sender to retransmit the message.

Error correction employs special hash functions whose results carry "redundant" bits so that it is possible to reconstruct corrupted bits in the payload. *Cyclical redundancy check* (*CRC*) is a typical class of hash functions used for error proto-correction, but CRC performs best when computed in hardware. Jumping ahead again, we note that in the Internet, *Transmission Control Protocol* (*TCP*)—a simple type of checksum—is used for this purpose, and so error correction is achieved through retransmission.

[10] Naturally, the sequence numbers have a defined size, and so their arithmetic must be carried out modulo some number M, which brings yet another design problem: to ensure that no messages with the same sequence number are outstanding at any time.

The basic service that the network layer provides to the transport layer is transfer of data between transport entities. With that, the purpose is to shield the transport layer from the detail of relaying its protocol data units via the network elements. The network layer protocol data units are called *packets.*

In the network, the packets that arrive from the host may be broken into smaller pieces and sent on their way on different routes. (Imagine taking to the post office a parcel that weighs a ton to be mailed overseas. Most likely, you will be asked to break it into separate, smaller parcels. After that, some parcels may end up going to their destination by boat, while others will be flown.) This is pretty much how the connectionless network layer mode works.

In the OSI model, the network layer supports both connection-oriented and connectionless modes of operation, but these modes are very different, and this makes the OSI network layer rather complex. (In the Internet model, the connection-oriented mode was initially rejected altogether, but once it was introduced, the network layer became complex, too.)

In the connection-oriented mode, the network connection establishment phase results in the end-to-end *virtual circuit* traversing the network. In other words, a route from one host in the network is set up once for the duration of the connection, so all packets on the given virtual circuit traverse the same network elements. This helps in engineering the network and guaranteeing—for each connection—its specific quality-of-service parameters, such as throughput and end-to-end transit delay (and its variation). Furthermore, the connection-oriented mode allows the transport layer to outsource the lion's share of its function to the network layer. The main disadvantage of this mode is the expense involved in tying up the resources in the network elements for the duration of the connection. If the endpoints need to exchange a short message only once in a blue moon, there is no need to establish and maintain a connection which would remain idle most of the time. However, if short connections need to be set up often then the connection setup time becomes a factor to consider. Another disadvantage is a single point of failure: if a network element crashes, all virtual circuits that pass through it are broken, and all respective sessions are terminated. These disadvantages were not detrimental to the telecommunications business, as shown by the Public Service Data Networks (PSDN), based on a set of ITU-T X-series recommendations (most notably X.25 [6], which specifies the network layer).

A little historical detour is worthwhile here. The study of connection-oriented services was neither an academic nor a standardization exercise. By the end of the 1960s, there was an urgent need to connect computers in geographically separate parts of an enterprise. At the time, the telecommunications companies that already had vast networks, to which the enterprises were physically connected, were in a unique position to satisfy this business need.

In the 1970s, following the analogy with the Public Switched Telephone Networks (PSTN) service, the *Public Data Network* (*PDN*) services were developed. The *Datran Data Dial* service, which became operational in the USA in 1974 and later was provided by the Southern Pacific Communications Company,[11] had a virtual circuit with error rate no worse than one bit in 10^7 bits transmitted [7]. After that, PDN services continued to grow. In the 1980s, telephone

[11] A predecessor of Sprint Nextel Corporation, Southern Pacific Communications Company was a unit of the Southern Pacific Railroad, which owned a substantial right of way. There is an adage that the transportation and telecommunications industries always compete, but in the case of SPC both industries were one.

companies started to develop the *Integrated Services Digital Network* (*ISDN*), which provides pipes combining circuit-switched voice with X.25-based packet-switched data, the latter to be delivered over the PDN virtual circuits. In the 1990s, ISDN was deployed in several countries in Europe and in Japan, and standardization proceeded to prepare the world for broadband ISDN, in which the network layer employs X.25-like frame relay and *Asynchronous Transfer Mode* (*ATM*) protocols, both providing virtual circuits although based on different technologies. These developments culminated in the mid-1990s, but in the late 1990s it was clear that the World Wide Web, and with it the Internet, had won. The network layer in the Internet standards at that time had no place for the ISO-like connection-oriented model, although, as we will see later, it started to develop something similar.

In the *connectionless* mode, the network layer, in general, is not responsible for the data that are handed to it beyond the best effort to deliver it to its destination. Once a *packet* is received by a network element, it merely passes it down to its neighbor. The decision to select this neighbor is dictated by the packet's destination address and the network layer's *routing table*, which can be provisioned or built dynamically using one or another *routing algorithm*. A routing algorithm computes the *shortest path* to the destination. "Short" here refers not to the geographic distance, but to that defined by the weight assigned to each link. (The metrics here range from a link's capacity to its current load.) Routing demands truly distributed computation: all routers participate in this computation by advertising their presence and propagating the information about their links. (Once again we refer the reader to [5] for comprehensive coverage of the subject, including a bibliography.) In the simplest case, a technique, initially considered in ARPANET and called *flooding*, was used. With that technique, there are no routing tables. A network element simply resends the packet it received to each of its neighbors—except, of course, the neighbor that was the source of the packet.)

Whether connectionless or connection oriented, the network layer is the first, among those considered so far, whose operation is based on *relaying* rather than point-to-point communications. In fact, in the early networks (and in an early version of the OSI model), the network layer was the only one that was explicitly based on relaying. With that the OSI explicitly forbids relaying in the layers below the application layer and above the network layer.

Now that we are ready to discuss the lower layers of the OSI reference model, we will have to go back and forth between the link layer and the physical layer. Here is why. The later version of the OSI reference model standard diplomatically states: "The services of the Physical Layer are determined by the characteristics of the underlying medium … ," but the link layer remains a catch-all for these services. There is nothing wrong with that *per se*, as the link layer has a clear and unique function, but for pedagogical reasons it is much better to elucidate the aspects of this function in view of the very characteristic of the underlying medium.

Going back to the early days of data networking, the physical connections (such as a twisted pair, or a circuit leased from a telephone company, or focused microwave links, or a satellite link) were all point to point. With that, data transfer along lines could have a significant error rate, especially when long-distance analog lines were involved. Analog transmission required modems at the endpoints, and it had an error rate two orders of magnitude higher than that of digital transmission.

Again, some historical review is in order. As late as the 1980s and early 1990s, only an analog service was available to individual telephone company subscribers at home; however, digital

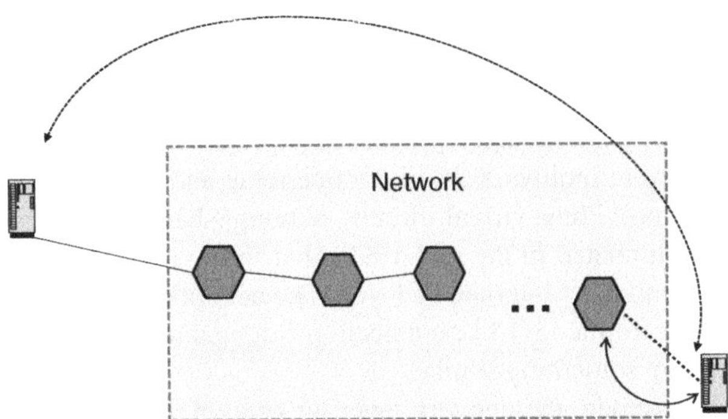

Figure 4.7 The case for error correction at the link layer.

services were available to corporate subscribers.[12] The Western Union *Broadband Exchange Service* was successfully launched in Texas in 1964. According to [7], at the beginning of the 1970s Multicom and Caducée followed with similar services in Canada and France, respectively, providing "full-duplex, point-to-point switched service at speeds up to 4800 bits per second, while providing low bit error rates which had previously only been generally available on private lines." These services, in fact, were the beginning of the PDN service—at the physical layer.

The physical-layer service is essentially a raw bit stream. Let us consider first point-to-point connection. In this case, the function of the link layer is almost identical to that of the transport layer: a connection between two endpoints needs to be established, and then the protocol data units are exchanged between the stations. On the sending side, the link layer encapsulates the network payload into *frames*, which are fed bit by bit to the physical layer. The payload in the frames is accompanied by error-correcting codes. As we observed, a connection can be faulty, especially on a long-distance analog dial-up line, employing modems at both ends. Error correction was thus an essential service provided by the link layer for this type of medium.

Error correction at the link layer was criticized by people who believed that the job done at the transport layer was sufficient; Figure 4.7 illustrates the counter-argument. Here, what can be fixed by local retransmission on a faulty link when error correction is employed has to be made up by retransmission across the network when it is not. The situation gets even worse when there are several faulty links in the path of a message.

Meanwhile, toward the mid-1970s the physical media changed in a major way.

Starting with the invention of the LAN [8], broadcast media proliferated. Figure 4.8 depicts four types: the *bus*, *star*, and *wireless* LANs actually share a single medium; the *ring* LAN combines a series of bit repeaters.

This development changed the requirements for the link layer in more than one way. First, broadcast demands unique link-layer identities, which must be explicitly carried in every frame. Second, LANs operate at much higher bit rates, enabling voice and video traffic, and hence it made sense to develop quality-of-service parameters to allocate bandwidth according to

[12] This was, in fact, one serious impediment to the deployment of ISDN in the United States. ISDN required a digital subscriber line.

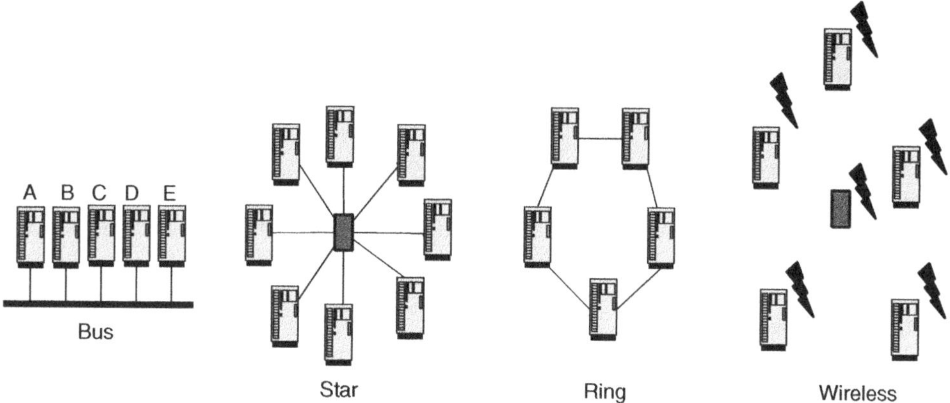

Figure 4.8 Broadcast media configurations.

specific traffic priorities. Third, the very nature of the broadcast results in pushing an essential network layer function—locating the receiver of a message (within the LAN perimeter, of course)—down to the link and physical layers. Fourth, while accepting some network-layer function, the link layer could easily delegate the function of maintaining a connection to the transport layer. To this end, the word "link" in the link layer almost became a misnomer. Fifth, the shared media required a special set of functions for access control, which made a distinct *sublayer* of the link layer. Sixth, broadcast media—as opposed to point-to-point links—demanded the implementation of security mechanisms to protect data.

We will return to LAN in Chapter 6, when discussing storage.

4.2 The Internet Protocol Suite

A 1974 paper [9] by Vint Cerf and Bob Kahn laid the ground for what became the Internet protocol suite.[13] The paper itself, which pre-dates the creation of the ISO OSI standards project by three years, is a model of crystal-clear and concise technical approach. It enumerates all aspects of the networking problems present at the moment, deduces the requirements for an overarching solution, and produces a solution by systematically applying the minimalistic approach.

It is worth following the original motivation and the resulting requirements as presented in [9]. The paper observes that the data communications protocols that operate within a *single* packet-switched network already exist, and then enumerates and examines the five internetworking operation issues.

The first issue is addressing. Recognizing that multiple networks with "distinct ways of addressing the receiver" exist, the paper stresses the need for a "uniform addressing scheme ... which can be understood by each individual network."

[13] As its name implies, the paper describes a solution to *internetworking* of all packet-switched networks—both existing and future ones.

The second issue is the maximum packet size. Because the maximum size of a single data unit that a given network can accept differs among networks, and the smallest such maximum size "may be impractically small" to agree on as a standard, it offers the alternative of "requiring procedures which allow data crossing a network boundary to be reformatted into smaller pieces."

The third issue is the maximum acceptable end-to-end delay for an acknowledgment on whose expiration the packet can be considered lost. Such delay values vary among the networks; hence the need for "careful development of internetwork timing procedures to insure that data can be successfully delivered through the various networks."

The fourth issue is mutation and loss of data, which necessitates "end-to-end restoration procedures" for the recovery.

Finally, the fifth issue is the variation among the networks in their "status information, routing, fault detection, and isolation." To deal with this, "various kinds of coordination must be invoked between the communicating networks."

To deal with the first issue, a uniform internetwork address is proposed, in which a "TCP address"[14] contains the network identifier and the TCP identifier, which in turn specify the host within that network, and the *port*—which is a direct pipe to a communicating process.

To deal with the second issue, the concept of a *gateway* connecting two networks is proposed. Being aware of each of the two networks it connects, the gateway mediates between them by, for example, fragmenting and reassembling the packets when necessary. The rest of the issues are dealt with entirely end to end. The paper specifies in much detail the procedures for retransmission and duplicate detection—based on the sliding windows mechanism already used by the French Cyclade system.

In the conclusion, the paper calls for the production of a detailed protocol specification so that experiments can be performed in order to determine operational parameters (e.g., retransmission timeouts).

In the next six years, quite a few detailed protocol specifications that followed the proposal were developed for the ARPANET. In the process, the protocol was broken into two independent pieces: the Internetworking Protocol (IP) dealt with the packet structure and the procedures at the network layer; the Transmission Control Protocol (TCP) dealt with the end-to-end transport layer issues. Even though other transport protocols were accepted for the Internet, the term TCP/IP has become the norm when referring to the overall Internet protocol suit.

In 1981, the stable standard IP (IP version 4 or IPv4) was published in [10] as the US Department of Defense Internet Protocol.[15] This protocol is widely used today, although a newer standard—IPv6—is being deployed, and the IETF has even been working on developing versions past that.

[14] The acronym in the paper refers to the "Transmission Control Program"—the protocol combining what we call the TCP and IP today.

[15] Later, after the Internet Engineering Task Force (IETF) was formed in 1986, this document was published as Request for Comments (RFC) 791. All IETF RFCs are available free of charge at www.ietf.org. In the rest of this book, we refer to the IETF RFCs strictly by number since it is straightforward to locate them: an RFC referred to by number *N* is located at http://tools.ietf.org/html/rfc*N*. Thus, RFC 791, for example, is at http://tools.ietf.org/html/rfc791.

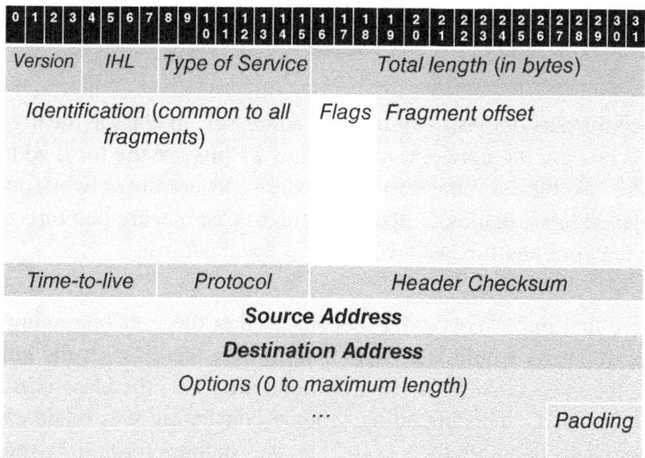

Figure 4.9 The IPv4 packet header.

4.2.1 *IP—The Glue of the Internet*

Figure 4.9 displays the structure of the IPv4 packet, which—quite amazingly—has remained unchanged even though some fields have been reinterpreted, as we will see soon.

It is essential to understand the fields, since IPv4 is still the major version of the protocol deployed in the Internet (and consequently used in the Cloud).

We start with the IPv4 solution to the Internet addressing problem, as that problem was listed first in Cerf and Kahn's original vision that we discussed earlier. Each IP packet has a source and a destination address, which are of the same type—a 32-bit string representing a pair:

$$< Networkaddress, Hostaddress >.$$

It is important to emphasize that by its very definition, an IP address is *not* an address of a host in that it is not unique to a host. A host may be *multi-homed*, that is reside on more than one network; in this case, it will have as many IP addresses as there are networks it belongs to.[16] Similarly, a router, whose role is to connect networks, has as many distinct IP addresses as there are networks it interconnects.

In fact, RFC 791 even allows a host attached to only one network to have several IP addresses: "a single physical host must be able to act as if it were several distinct hosts to the extent of using several distinct internet addresses." Conversely, with *anycast* addressing (which was not even envisioned at the time of RFC 791, but which we will encounter later), a common IP address is assigned to multiple hosts delivering the same service—for the purpose of load balancing.

[16] The network—these days, it is almost invariably a LAN—does provide a unique Layer 2 address to the host, which is hard-coded in the NIC hardware. Chapter 3 introduced this acronym in connection with the NIST security requirements, but it used the concept even earlier—when describing device emulation. To this end, NICs are emulated in XEN because all VM device traffic is "routed" to Domain 0 over IP.

Back to the IP address logical structure. With the initial design, the network address *Class* tag had three values: A, B, and C. To this end, RFC 791 states:

> "There are three formats or classes of internet addresses: in class a, the high order bit is zero, the next 7 bits are the network, and the last 24 bits are the local address; in class b, the high order two bits are one-zero, the next 14 bits are the network and the last 16 bits are the local address; in class c, the high order three bits are one-one-zero, the next 21 bits are the network and the last 8 bits are the local address."

First, we observe that the *Class* tag has been placed at the very beginning of the address. The parsing of the IP string would start with determining the class. If the leftmost bit of the IP address is "0," the class is A; if the first two bits are "10", the class is B; and if the first three bits are "110," it is C. This encoding scheme convention was made easily extensible. (For example, later Class D—with the "1110" tag, was defined for *multicast* addresses.[17])

Second, the idea of the class-based scheme was to have many small (Class C) networks, fewer Class B networks—which have more hosts, and only 128 huge Class A networks. This idea was very reasonable at the time. Figure 4.10 depicts the map of the Internet ca. 1982, as created by the late Jon Postel.[18]

About 10 years later, however, the IETF identified three major problems, both unanticipated and unprecedented, which occurred with the growth of the Internet. First, the address space of mid-sized Class B networks was becoming exhausted. Second, the routing tables had grown much, too large for routers to maintain them, and—worse—they kept growing. Third, the overall IP address space was on its way to being exhausted.

The last problem, by its very nature, could not be dealt with in the context of the IPv4 design, but the first two problems could be fixed by doing away with the concept of a class. Thus, the *Classless Inter-Domain Routing* (*CIDR*) scheme emerged, first as an interim solution (until IPv6 took over) and then (since IPv6 has not taken over) as a more or less permanent solution. After the publication of three successive RFCs, it was published in 2006 as IETF Best Current Practice, in RFC 4632.[19]

CIDR gets rid of the class tag, replacing it with a specific "network mask" that delineates the prefix—the exact number of bits in the network part of the address. With that, the assignment of prefixes was "intended to follow the underlying Internet topology so that aggregation can be used to facilitate scaling of the global routing system." The concept of CIDR aggregation is illustrated in Figure 4.11.

Network A, identified by its prefix *x*, aggregates the address space of its *subnets*—networks B and C, whose prefixes are, respectively, *x0* and *x1*. Thus, to reach a host in any subnet, the routers on the way only need to find the longest matching prefix.

By 2006, the Internet provider business was sufficiently consolidated, and so it made sense to assign prefixes. Consequently, the "prefix assignment and aggregation is generally done according to provider-subscriber relationships, since that is how the Internet topology

---

[17] See RFC 5771 (http://tools.ietf.org/html/rfc5771).

[18] Jon Postel, in addition to his many services to Internet development, administered the Internet Assigned Numbers Authority (IANA) until his untimely death in 1998.

[19] http://tools.ietf.org/html/rfc4632

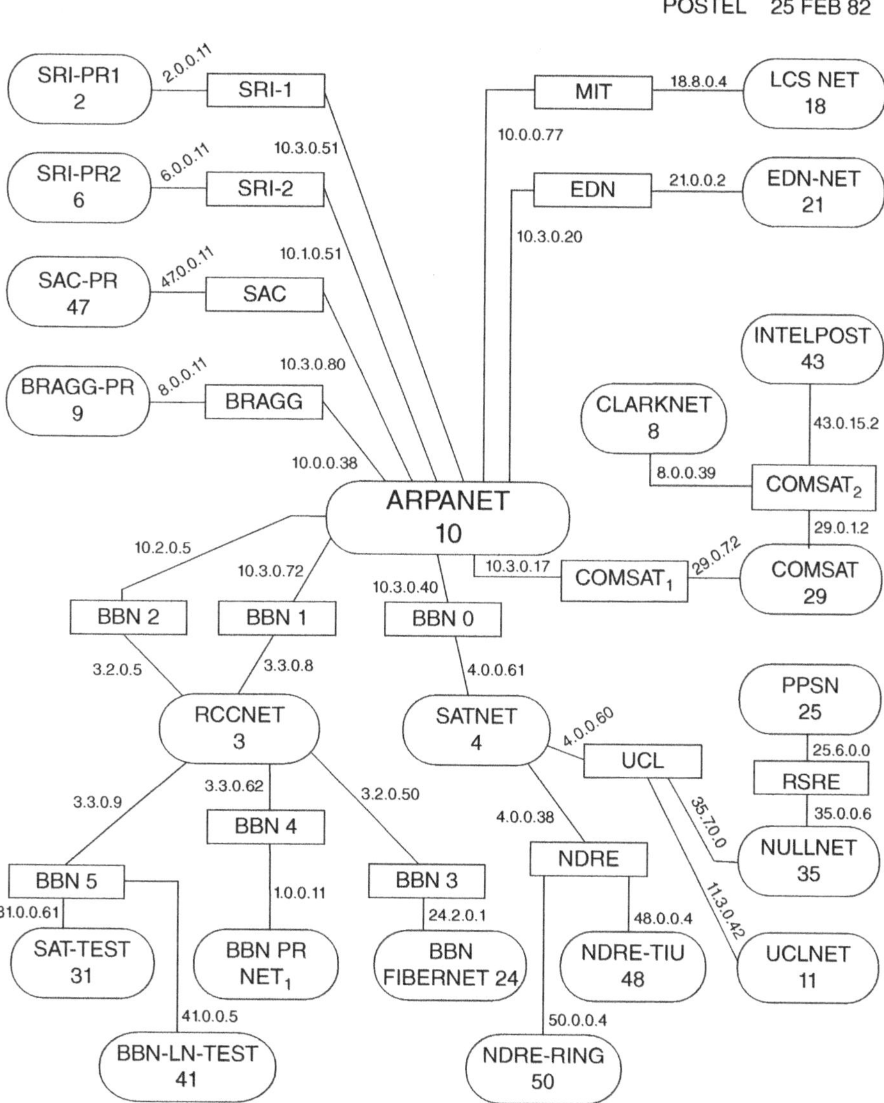

Figure 4.10 Jon Postel's map of the Internet in 1982. *Source:* http://commons.wikimedia.org/wiki/File%3AInternet_map_in_February_82.png. By Jon Postel [Public domain], via Wikimedia Commons.

is determined." Of course, the strategy was to be backward-compatible with the class-based system, and, as we will see shortly, this is exactly how the addressing works.

The prefixes are specified by the number of bits in the network portion of an IP address. The mask is appended to an IP address along with the "/" character. At this point, it is necessary to reflect on the IP address specification. Even though the semantics of an IP address is a pair of integer numbers, the IP addresses have traditionally been spelled out in decimal notation, byte

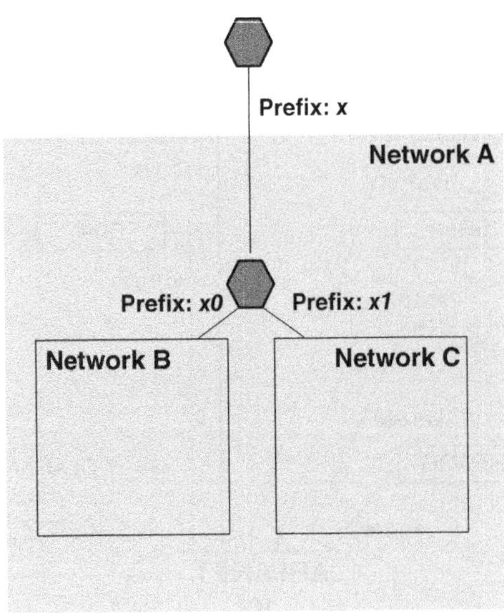

Figure 4.11 CIDR aggregation.

by byte, separated by dots as in 171.16.23.42. The mask is spelled out the same. Considering the above address (which belongs to Class B), its network mask is 255.255.0.0, and so the full address in the prefix notation is 171.16.23.42/16. Similarly, a Class C address 192.16A99.17 has a mask of 255.255.255.0 and is specified as 192.16A99.17/A.

Figure 4.12 demonstrates how an existing Class B network can be broken into four subnets internally.

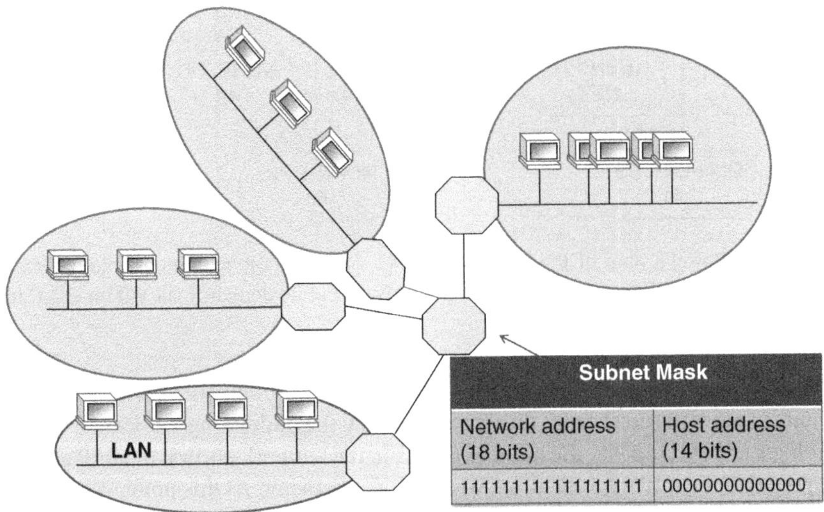

Figure 4.12 "Subnetting" a Class B network.

At this point, we must recognize that we have veered off the RFC 791 by fast-forwarding 20 years ahead. Now we get back to the discussion of the rest of the IP header fields of Figure 4.9.

The first field is *version*, and it defines the structure of the rest of the header. It appears to be the most wasteful field in terms of the IP header real estate. The four bits were assigned to indicate the protocol version; as helpful as they were in experimentation, only two versions—IPv4 and IPv6—have been used in all these years. Yet the IP was designed to live forever, and it makes sense to anticipate a couple of new versions becoming widely used every 30 years or so.

The *Internet Header Length* (*IHL*) is just what it says it is: the length of the Internet header in 32-bit words. This is, in effect, a pointer to the beginning of the IP payload.

The *type-of-service* field has been designed to specify the quality of service parameters. It is interesting that even though the only applications explicitly listed in this (1981!) specification are telnet and FTP, the packet precedence had already been thought through and, as the document reports, implemented in some networks. The major choice, at the time, was a three-way tradeoff between low delay, high reliability, and high throughput. These bits, however, have been reinterpreted later as differentiated services; we will discuss the new interpretation in the next section.

Total length specifies the length of the packet, measured in bytes. (The length of the header is also counted.) Even though the field is 16 bits long, it is recommended that the hosts send packets longer than 576 bytes only if they are assured that the destination host is prepared to accept them. At the time of this writing the maximum packet size of 65,535 is already considered limiting, but in 1981 long packets were expected to be fragmented. To this end, the next three fields deal with fragmentation matters.

The *identification* field provides the value intended to "aid in assembling the fragments of a datagram." (There were attempts to redefine it.) The *flags* field (the first bit still left unused) contains the DF and MF 1-bit fields, which stand respectively for Don't Fragment and More Fragments. The former flag instructs the router to drop the packet (and report an error) rather than fragment it; the latter flag indicates that more fragments are to follow. The fragment offset is the pointer to the place of the present fragment in the original payload. (Thus the first fragment has the offset value of 0.) It is important to note that IPv6 has dispensed with fragmentation altogether. Instead, it requires that the packet be sent over a path that accepts it.

The *Time-To-Live* (*TTL*) field is there to prevent infinite looping of a packet. Since the original Internet envisioned no circuits, the Internet routers applied the "best-effort" practice when forwarding a packet toward its destination. *Routing protocols* make routers react to changes in the network and change the routing tables, but propagation of such changes can be slow. As a result, packets may end up in loops. The value of TTL is used to determine whether a packet is vagrant. This field is "mutable" in that it is updated by each router. Originally, it was set to the upper bound of the time it might take the packet to traverse the network, and each router was supposed to modify it by subtracting the time it took to process the packet. Once the value reached zero, the packet was supposed to be discarded. The semantics of the field has changed slightly: instead of being measured in fractions of a second (which is somewhat awkward to deal with), it is measured in number of hops.

The *protocol* field specifies the transport-layer protocol employed. Going back to the computational model we discussed at the beginning of this chapter, it is necessary to determine which procedure to call (or which process to send it to) on reception of the packet by the host.

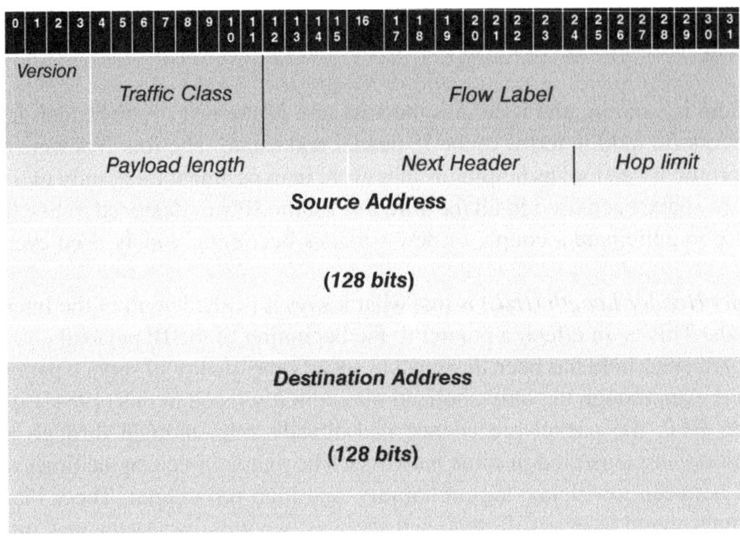

Figure 4.13 The IPv6 basic packet header (after RFC 2460).

The *header checksum* is computed at each router by adding all the 16-bit words of the header (presumably while they are arriving), using 1's complement addition, and taking the 1's complement of the sum. When the packet arrives, the checksum computed over the whole header must be equal to zero, if there were no errors—because the header already includes the previously computed checksum. If the resulting value is non-zero, then the packet is discarded. (Note that only the header is checked at the network layer; verification of the payload is the job of upper layers.) If the router needs to forward the packet it recomputes the checksum, after the TTL value is changed.

Only at this point do the source and destination addresses appear in the header, followed by the *options* field. The latter field is optional; it has not been used much recently. (In the past, one typical use was to spell out explicit routes.) Finally, the packet is padded with a sufficient number of bits to stay on the 32-bit boundary (in case the options don't end with a full 32-bit word).

This completes our overview of the IPv4 header. It should be clear now how IPv4 solves the original problem of network interconnection. In the process, we have also mentioned several new problems, among them IP address space exhaustion. We have not discussed security, which is an elephant in the room and in need of a separate chapter (to fill in all the prerequisites). Another big problem is the absence of clear support for what is called "quality of service." We will deal with this problem at length in Section 4.3; however, we mention it now because IPv6, which we are going to address next, has provided an improvement over IPv4.

The (*basic*) IPv6 header is depicted in Figure 4.13.

What is perhaps most noticeable from the first, cursory glance at the IPv6 header is that it appears to be simpler than that of IPv4. Indeed, it is! Some fields have been dropped or made optional, which makes it not only easier to comprehend, but also faster to execute. The header is extensible in that new headers (which can be defined separately, thus improving modularity) are linked together in an IP packet by means of the *next header* field. Hence the word "basic" in the definition of the header.

The major change, of course, is brought about by quadrupling the IP address size—from 32 to 128 bits. Besides the obvious benefit of a much greater number of addressable notes, this also supports addressing hierarchy. IPv6 improves the scalability of multicast routing by supporting the definition of the scope of a multicast address. IPv6 also formally defines the *anycast* address.

The IPv4 *time-to-live* field is now appropriately renamed the *hop limit*; the *type-of-service* field is renamed *traffic class*. The latter field supports quality of service, as does the new field called *flow label*. Again, we will return to this subject and cover it in detail, but it is worth mentioning right now that this field supports a capability that in effect is equivalent to that of providing a virtual circuit.

RFC 2460,[20] which defines the basic IPv6 header, describes this flow labeling capability as follows: "A new capability is added to enable the labeling of packets belonging to particular traffic "flows" for which the sender requests special handling, such as non-default quality of service or 'real-time' service." The main reason for adding this capability was to correct a layering violation committed in an IPv4-based solution, which we will review later.

The rest of the IPv6 header's specifications (beyond the basic header) are referenced in RFC 2460.[21] As a final note, even though IPv6 is not fully deployed, there are IPv6 networks as well as IPv6-capable devices. The IPv6 networks can be interconnected through IPv4, by means of tunneling. After all, IP has been developed with the primary goal of interconnecting networks!

So far, we have only briefly mentioned the routing protocols, whose job is to compute routing maps. Let us take a look at Figure 4.14. To begin with, no routing is needed in LANs, even though each host uses IP. (LANs can be interconnected further by Layer-1 and Layer-2 switches, to build even larger LANs called *metropolitan-area networks*. They can further be organized into *wide-area networks* using circuit-switched technology (such as a leased telephone line) or virtual-circuit-switched technology (such as frame relay or *Asynchronous Transfer Mode* (*ATM*) technologies, or *Multi-Protocol Label Switching (MPLS)*, which we will discuss later.) The moment routers are involved, however, they need to learn about other routers in the network.

The question is: "Which network?" For sure, no router can hold the routing map of the whole Internet. Small networks that employ only a few routers can provision in them static routing maps. Routers within a larger network need to implement one or another *interior routing gateway protocol*. The constrained space of this book does not allow any further discussion of these.[22] The case of *exterior routing* among *Autonomous Systems* (*ASs*), however, is particularly important to Cloud Computing, because it is involved in offering "data pipe" services. The idea here is similar to the development of geographic maps: a country map to show the highways interconnecting cities (exterior routing) and another type of map to show the streets in a city (interior routing).

---

[20] www.ietf.org/rfc/rfc2460.txt

[21] The full implementation of IPv6 must include/support the following headers: Hop-by-Hop Options, Routing (Type 0), Fragment, Destination Options, Authentication, and Encapsulating Security Payload.

[22] Once again, we refer the reader to [1].

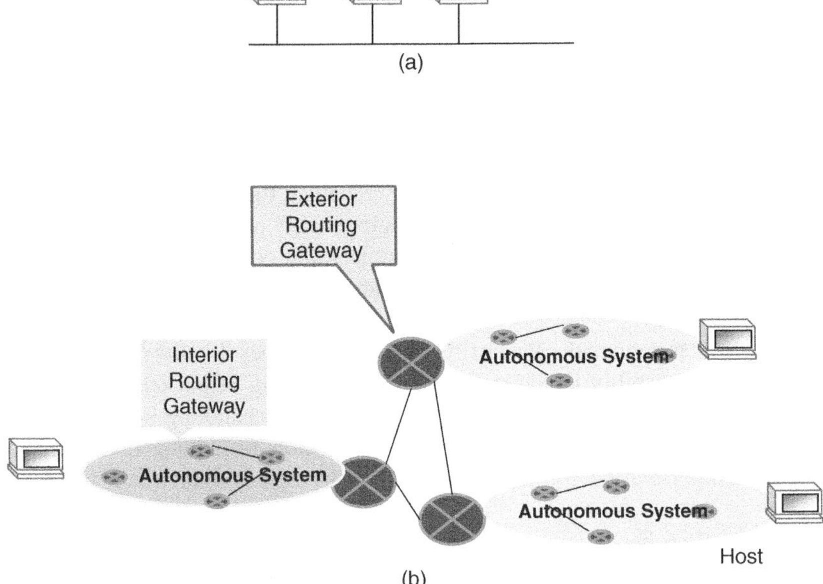

Figure 4.14 Routing protocol classification: (a) LAN, no routing needed; (b) routing within and among autonomous systems.

As Figure 4.15 shows, each AS is assigned—by its respective Regional Internet Authority (RIR)[23]—a number called the Autonomous System Number (ASN). To the rest of the world, an AS is represented by routers called border gateways, which exchange information as defined by the Border Gateway Protocol (BGP). The BGP (whose current version is 4) is specified in the RFC 1771.[24]

In the past, an "autonomous system" meant an Internet Service Provider (ISP), but this has changed with time. Now an ISP may have several separate ASs within it. According to RFC 1930,[25] "The classic definition of an Autonomous System is a set of routers under a single technical administration, using an interior gateway protocol and common metrics to route packets within the AS, and using an exterior gateway protocol to route packets to other ASs."

The networks under a single technical administration have grown and otherwise evolved into using multiple interior gateway protocols and multiple metrics. The quality of *sameness*

[23] RIRs distribute geographically the blocks issued by IANA. RIRs, in alphabetical order along with their jurisdictions, are as follows: *African Network Information Centre* (*AfriNIC*) (Africa); *American Registry for Internet Numbers* (*ARIN*) (the United States, Canada, parts of the Caribbean region—not including those covered by LACNIC below, and Antarctica); *Asia-Pacific Network Information Centre* (*APNIC*) (Pacific Asia, Australia, New Zealand, and islands in the region); *Latin America and Caribbean Network Information Centre* (*LACNIC*) (Latin America and parts of the Caribbean region); and *Réseaux IP Européens Network Coordination Centre* (*RIPE NCC*) (Europe—except for the European part of Russia, Central Asia, the Middle East, and Russia).

[24] www.ietf.org/rfc/rfc1771.txt

[25] www.ietf.org/rfc/rfc1930.txt

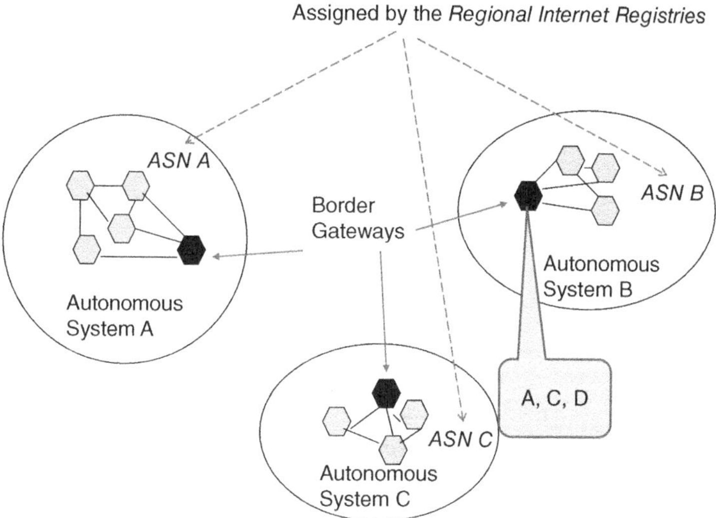

Figure 4.15 Autonomous systems and border gateways.

though has remained as long as two conditions are met: (1) the network *appears* to other networks to have a coherent interior routing plan (i.e., it can deliver a packet to the destination IP address belonging to it) and (2) it can tell which networks are reachable *through* it. The latter factor is non-trivial as not every network may allow the traffic from all other networks to flow through it, and, conversely, a given network may not want its traffic to pass through certain networks. We will return to this later.

Taking these changes into account, RFC 1930 redefines an AS as "a connected group of one or more IP prefixes run by one or more network operators." With that, this group must have "a *single* and *clearly defined* routing policy." The word *policy* is key here, reflecting a major difference between the interior and exterior routing objectives. In interior routing, the objective is to compute a complete map of the network and—at the same time—to determine the most efficient route to every network element.

Hence, when two *interior* routers get connected, they exchange information about all reachable nodes they know about (and then, based on this information, each router recomputes its own network map); conversely, when a router loses a connection, it recomputes its map and advertises the change to its remaining neighbors. In both cases, the routers that receive the news compute their respective maps and propagate the news to their remaining neighbors, and so forth.

This is not the case with exterior routing, where decisions on what information to propagate are made based on policies and agreements. Let us return to Figure 4.15. Here, an autonomous system B knows how to reach autonomous systems A, C, D, and E. It is neither necessary nor expected that B advertise to C automatically all the networks it knows. For example, in order for B to advertise E to C:

1. The policy of E must *not* exclude C from its transit destinations.
2. B must agree to route traffic from E to C.

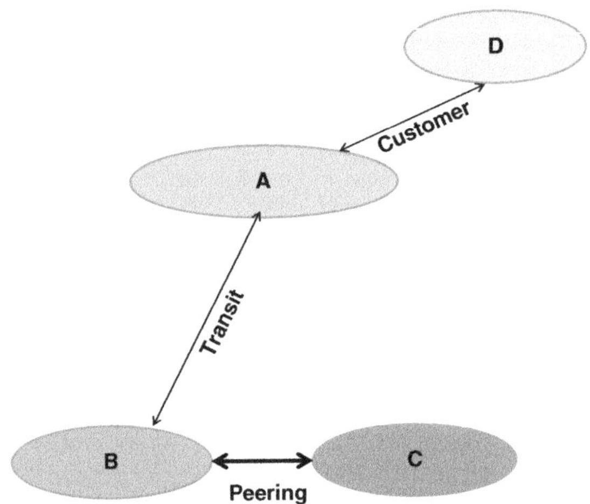

Figure 4.16 Transit and (settlement-free) peering relationships.

3. C must agree to accept traffic from E.
4. E must agree to accept traffic from C (there is symmetry).

There is, in fact, a taxonomy of relationships between ASs, as depicted in Figure 4.16.

Here we enter the business territory. We should note right away that the Internet is unregulated, and—to a great extent—self-organized. It has been and is being shaped by business. Contrary to popular belief, the Internet has never been and is not free. In its earlier days it was paid for largely by the US government, which explains the flat structure of Figure 4.10. Much has changed since then!

At the bottom of the food chain, the ISP customers pay their respective ISPs for connection to the Internet.

Smaller ISPs achieve interconnection by paying for a *transit* relationship, which combines two services: (a) advertising the routes to others (which has the effect of soliciting traffic toward the ISP's customers) and (b) learning other ISPs' routes so as to direct to those the traffic from the ISP's customers. The traffic is billed upstream—that is, a transit network bills for the traffic it receives and pays for the traffic that leaves it.

In *peering*, only the traffic between the networks and their downstream customers is exchanged and neither network can see upstream routes over the peering connection. Some networks are transit free and rely only on peering.

Initially, the word "peering" meant that the two parties involved did not exchange any money—one major difference from the transit relationship. Later the terminology was compromised, and the notion of a *settlement* in a peering connection appeared. There is a comprehensive article by Geoff Huston (then of Telstra) [11], which describes the business nuances of the matter.[26]

[26] A year after this article was published, in June 2000, the authors attended Geoff's talk at the Internet Society conference, where he reviewed the financial structure of the ISP business, and concluded that it was a commodity business approaching a crisis. The crisis was later known as the "dot-com bust."

Ultimately, the initial concept of peering has been reinstalled with the modifier "settlement free." The (very large) service providers that have full access to the Internet through settlement-free peering comprise the *Tier-1 network*.

Two networks can be interconnected through private switches, but when there are more than two service providers in a region, it is more efficient to interconnect the peering networks over the *Internet Exchange Points (IXPs)*—which are typically operated independently. At the moment of this writing there are over 300 IXPs.

It is rather instructive to take a look at a specific policy of a Tier-1 network provider.

AT&T has published the respective document, called "AT&T Global IP Network Settlement-Free Peering Policy."[27] This document (we are looking at the October 2012 official version) first lists the company's objective "to interconnect its IP network with other Internet backbone providers on a settlement-free basis when such interconnection provides tangible benefits to AT&T and its customers." Then it provides the relevant ASNs: AS7018, for private peering in the USA; AS2685, in Canada; and AS2686, in Latin America. The requests for peering by an ISP must be submitted in writing with information on which countries the ISP serves, in which IXPs it has a presence, the set of ASNs and prefixes served, and the description of the traffic.

Specific requirements are spelled out for peering (in the USA), with AS7018. To begin with, the peer operator must have "a US-wide IP backbone whose links are primarily OC192 (10 Gbps) or greater," and interconnect with AT&T in at least three points in the USA—one on the East Coast, one in the Central region, and one on the West Coast. In addition, the candidate peer must interconnect with AT&T in two "non-US peering locations on distinct continents where peer has a non-trivial backbone network." A customer of AS7018 may not be a settlement-free peer.

The bandwidth and traffic requirements are spelled out: "Peer's traffic to/from AS7018 must be on-net only and must amount to an average of at least 7 Gbps in the dominant direction to/from AT&T in the US during the busiest hour of the month." With that, "the interconnection bandwidth must be at least 10 Gbps at each US interconnection point." The in-AT&T/out-AT&T traffic ratio is limited to no more than 2:1.

One benefit of peering is cooperation in resolving security incidents and other operational problems. To this end, the candidate peer is expected to cooperate in this and back up its ability to do so by having "a professionally managed 24×7 [Network Operations Center] NOC."

Finally, we must consider the routing policy requirements—which are of special interest to us inasmuch as they illustrate the constraints of exterior routing:

1. The peer must announce a consistent set of routes at each point of interconnection.
2. The peer may not announce transit or third-party routes—only its own routes and the routes of its customers. With that, the peer customer's routes must be filtered by prefix.
3. The forbidden activities include "pointing a default route … or otherwise forwarding traffic for destinations not explicitly advertised, resetting next-hop, selling or giving next-hop to others."

[27] www.corp.att.com/peering/

Taking business concerns and resulting policies into account, BGP is the protocol for exchanging the AS reachability information. Executing BFP results in constructing a directed acyclic (i.e., loop-free) graph of AS connectivity, which represents the combined policies of all ASs involved. To ensure this, RFC 1771 requires that a "BGP speaker advertise to its peers ... in neighboring ASs only those routes that it itself uses." This inevitably leads to the "hop-by-hop" routing, which has limitations as far as policies are concerned. One such limitation is the inability to enforce *source routing* (i.e., spelling out a part or all of the routing path). Yet, BGP does support all policies consistent with the "hop-by-hop" paradigm.

Unlike any other routing protocol, BGP needs reliable transport. It may look strange at first glance that a routing protocol is actually an application-layer protocol, but it is! Routing is an application that serves the network layer. (Similarly, network management applications serve the network layer—as they do all other layers as well.) Border gateways do not necessarily need to be interconnected at the link layer, and hence fragmentation, retransmission, acknowledgment, and sequencing—all functions of the reliable transport layer—need to be implemented. Another requirement is that the transport protocol supports a *graceful close*, ensuring that all outstanding data be delivered before the connection is closed. Perhaps not surprisingly, these requirements have been met by the TCP[28] introduced earlier in this chapter, and so BGP is using TCP for transport. To this end, the TCP port 179 is reserved for BGP connections.

And now that we have started to talk about transport protocols, it is high time we move on to discussing the rest of the protocols in the IP suite.

4.2.2 The Internet Hourglass

The metaphor of Figure 4.17 belongs to Steve Deering, then a member of the Internet Architecture Board, who developed it further in his presentation[29] on the state of the Internet protocol at the Plenary Session of the 51st IETF meeting in London, on August 8, 2001.

Noting that the Internet had reached middle age just as he himself had, Dr. Deering suggested that at such an age it is appropriate to watch one's waist.

The waist of the Internet is the IP. There are quite a few link-layer protocols—each corresponding to the respective physical medium—that run below the IP, and there are even more protocols that run above, at the transport layer and, especially, the application layers. The IP, however, used to be one protocol, and a very straightforward protocol at that. The Internet works as long as two maxims belonging to Vint Cerf hold: *IP on Everything* and *Everything on IP*.[30]

In the rest of this section, we will take a very brief—and woefully incomplete—tour of the Internet protocol suite, simply to develop the perspective. We will revisit some of these protocols and discuss them in more detail later in the book.

---

[28] Note here the difference between the TCP and the initial *Transmission Control Program* vision, where the present IP and TCP were combined.

[29] www.ietf.org/proceedings/51/slides/plenary-1/

[30] At a 1992 meeting, Vint Cerf, who makes a point of always dressing in a three-piece suit, stripped off his jacket, vest, tie, and (white) shirt. Underneath, he was wearing a T-shirt with the Gothic print: "IP on Everything." Five years later, at a meeting with Lucent Technologies researchers at MCI Worldcom headquarters, Vint Cerf presented Bob Martin, then Lucent CTO, with a T-shirt of the same vintage. Dr. Martin asked if wearing this T-shirt would help him get a taxi, to which Dr. Cerf wryly replied: "Not if the driver cares about his rugs."

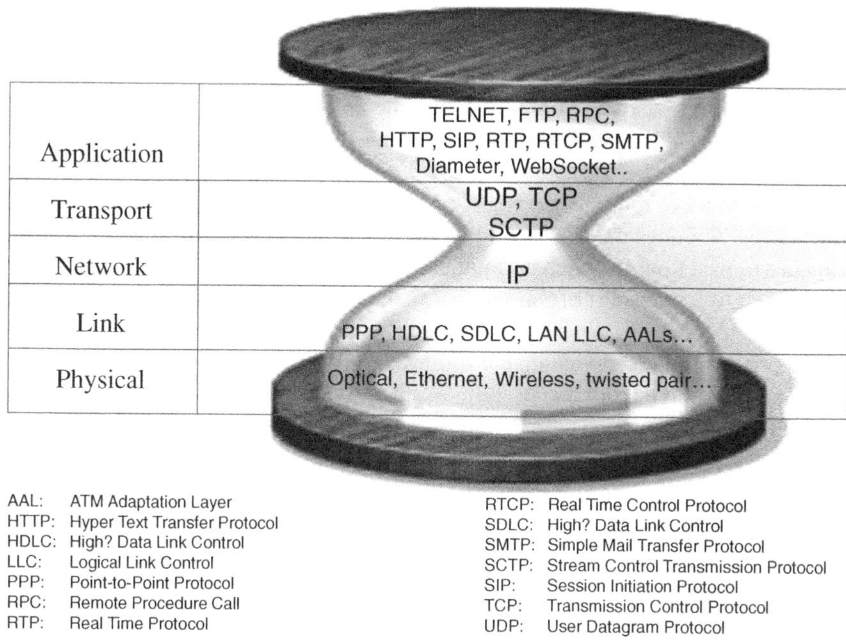

AAL: ATM Adaptation Layer
HTTP: Hyper Text Transfer Protocol
HDLC: High? Data Link Control
LLC: Logical Link Control
PPP: Point-to-Point Protocol
RPC: Remote Procedure Call
RTP: Real Time Protocol
RTCP: Real Time Control Protocol
SDLC: High? Data Link Control
SMTP: Simple Mail Transfer Protocol
SCTP: Stream Control Transmission Protocol
SIP: Session Initiation Protocol
TCP: Transmission Control Protocol
UDP: User Datagram Protocol

Figure 4.17 The Internet hourglass.

Physical media span both wireline and wireless LANs, copper and optical fiber links, as well as longer-haul wireless broadcast to communicate with satellites. On point-to-point lines, such as twisted pair, we have the IETF Point-to-Point (PPP) protocol, as well as the ISO High-Level Data Link Control (HDLC) protocol. In the deployment of the IBM Systems Network Architecture (SNA), another supported Layer-2 protocol is Synchronous Data Link Control (SDLC)—a progenitor of HDLC and pretty much all other data link control protocols. LANs invariably employ the IEEE standard Logical Link Control (LLC) protocol family, which also carries SDLS genes.

ATM networks are a special matter. As we mentioned earlier in this chapter, ATM networks were positioned to be *the* Layer-3 networks. In 2001, even though IP had pretty much won the battle, the notion that an ATM switch was a peer of an IP router was still shared by part of the industry. Hence the complaint of Dr. Deering about the growing waist of the network layer. In a dramatic development, the ATM was finally relegated to the link layer as far as the IP is concerned: ATM Adaptation Layer (AAL) protocols were treated as Layer-2 protocols in the hour-glass model. IP on everything!

To this end, the IP can run on top of the IP, too. The technique of *encapsulating* an IP packet within another IP packet (in other words, making an IP packet a payload of another IP packet by attaching a new IP header) is perfectly legal, and has been used effectively in creating a kind of virtual private network. Dr. Deering lovingly referred to this property of the IP as its waist being "supple," and reflected this in one of his slides by depicting the waist of the hourglass twisted into a spiral.

At the transport layer there are three protocols, all developed by the IETF. In addition to TCP, which effectively combines the session- and transport-layer services, guaranteeing end-to-end in-sequence, error-free byte-stream delivery, and also special mechanisms to detect network congestion (and adjust to it by exponentially reducing the amount of data sent), there are two other protocols: the *User Datagram Protocol* (*UDP*) and the *Stream Control Transmission Protocol* (*SCTP*).

The UDP, specified in RFC 768,[31] is a connectionless protocol, which provides no delivery guarantees whatsoever. Nor does the UDP require any connection setup. UDP is indispensable in implementing fast transactions in which the application layer performs error control. Another core function of the UDP is transport of "streaming media" (i.e., voice or video packets). The UDP is much better at this because losing an occasional video frame has a much less adverse effect on the perception of video service than a frame "saved" by retransmission (which then causes significant variation in the delay).

The SCTP deserves a more detailed description here, because we will need to refer to it later. It is also important to elucidate why the Internet ended up with two different reliable transport-layer protocols. To begin with, the SCTP was developed as part of the IETF Internet/PSTN interworking movement described in [3]. The initial objective of the SCTP was to transport *Signaling System No. 7* messages over the Internet, and so the work took place in the IETF SIGTRAN working group. Later, some application protocols—not related to telephony—specified the SCTP as the transport mechanism of choice, primarily because of its built-in reliability. The protocol is defined in RFC 4960,[32] and as is often the case, there are other related RFCs.

Just as TCP does, SCTP provides error-free, non-duplicated transfer of payload, employing data fragmentation and network congestion avoidance. The SCTP has also addressed the following TCP limitations:

- TCP combines reliable transfer with in-sequence delivery, but the need to separate these two features was clear at the end of the last century. SCTP allows an application to choose either of these features or both.
- TCP treats the payload as a byte stream. This forces an application to use the push facility to force message transfer at the end of the application-defined record. In contrast, SCTP deals with "data chunks" which are transmitted at once. (SCTP does provide an option to bundle chunks.)
- TCP is not effective with *multi-homing* (i.e., a host's attachment to more than one network) while SCTP explicitly supports it, as we will demonstrate shortly.
- TCP has been vulnerable to synchronization denial-of-service attacks. SCTP has addressed this by maintaining the state of initialization in a special data structure (a *cookie*).

Multi-homing is illustrated by the example of Figure 4.18. Here, process X has an SCTP session with process Y. Just as in the case of TCP, SCTP provides a single port for each process (p_X for process X and p_Y for process Y) as the interface to transport-layer services.

What makes the example of Figure 4.18 very different from earlier scenarios is that the respective hosts on which the processes run are multi-homed. The host where the process X

[31] http://tools.ietf.org/html/rfc768

[32] http://tools.ietf.org/html/rfc4960.txt

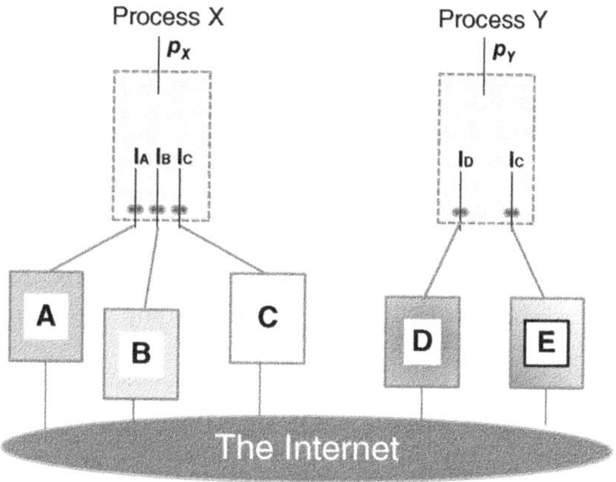

Figure 4.18 Multi-homing with SCTP.

runs is attached to three networks, A, B, and C; the host where the process Y runs is attached to two networks, D and E. Consequently, the former host has three IP addresses (I_A, I_B, and I_C); the latter host has two IP addresses (I_D and I_E). The unique and new capability that SCTP adds is *demultiplexing*—over all involved networks—of the stream of packets received from a process combined with multiplexing of the packets received from these networks on their way to the process. This feature improves reliability as well as performance. The effect on improving the performance is clear when considering what happens when one of the available networks is congested.

The SCTP has slightly—but notably—redefined the semantics of a session, which it calls an *association*. Whereas a TCP session is a quadruple (I_S, P_S, I_D, P_D) defined by the source IP address, source port number, destination IP address, and destination port number, in the SCTP association $(<I_S>, P_S, <I_D>, P_D)$, the quantities $<I_S>$ and $<I_D>$ are respectively the *lists* of source and destination addresses.

To conclude, we note that SCTP has been implemented in major operating systems, and it has been prescribed by 3GPP as the transport-layer protocol of choice for a variety of application protocols that require high reliability. (One example is *Diameter*—a protocol for authentication, authorization, and accounting.)

A small representative subset of the application-layer protocols is listed in Figure 4.17. These protocols have been developed in response to specific needs: *Simple Mail Transfer Protocol* (*SMTP*) for e-mail; telnet for remote connections to mainframe accounts through a virtual terminal; *File Transfer Protocol* (*FTP*) for file transfer; *Simple Network Management Protocol* (SNMP) for remote management of network elements and devices, and so forth.

The *Hyper-Text Transfer Protocol* (HTTP) not only defined and enabled the World-Wide Web, but, as we will see later, it has also influenced the creation of a new universal style of accessing resources and invoking remote operations on them. This style has become central for accessing Cloud Computing applications. A limitation of HTTP is that only an HTTP client can start a conversation with a server; the latter may only respond to the client. For full-duplex client-to-server channels, the *WebSocket* protocol and API have been developed and standardized by the IETF and W3C, respectively.

A decade earlier, a similar capability—receipt of server notifications—was built into the IETF *Session Initiation Protocol* (*SIP*), which was developed for the creation and management of multimedia sessions. The 3GPP *IP Multimedia Subsystem* (*IMS*), which signals the foundation of third- and fourth-generation wireless networks (and also landline next-generation networks) has been based on SIP.

The actual real-time media transfer is performed by the IETF *Real Time Protocol* (*RTP*). To this end, the (initially unforeseen) need to support real-time communications has resulted in the QoS development, described in the next section. In his talk, Steve Deering referred to this development as "putting on weight," and the accompanying slide depicted a much wider-waisted hourglass!

4.3 Quality of Service in IP Networks

The somewhat enigmatic term *Quality of Service* (*QoS*) actually refers to something rather specific and measurable. For our purpose, this "something" boils down to a few parameters, such as bandwidth, delay, and delay variation (also called *jitter*). Adherence to certain values of these parameters makes or breaks any service that deals with audio or video.

In the early days of data communications, there was virtually no real-time application in sight that was, too sensitive to delay or delay variation. Telephony (even though digitized) was in the hands of telephone companies only, and it relied on connection-oriented transport, which provided constant bit-rate transfer. The 1980s vision of telephone companies for the *Integrated Services Digital Network* (*ISDN*) (see [3] for history and references) left the voice traffic to traditional switching, while the data traffic was to be offloaded to a packet network. With the bandwidth promise growing, the *Broadband ISDN* plan envisioned the use of the ATM connection-oriented switches. To this end, a detailed study and standardization of QoS provisioning and guarantees was first performed in the context of ATM, as described in [5].

Standardization of the QoS support for the IP networks, undertaken in the 1990s, was in a way reactive to the ISDN, but it was revolutionary. The very term *Integrated Services Packet Network* was coined by Jonathan Turner, who wrote in his truly visionary work [12]: "In this paper, I argue that the evolutionary approach inherent in current ISDN proposals is unlikely to provide an effective long-term solution and I advocate a more revolutionary approach, based on the use of advanced packet-switching technology. The bulk of this paper is devoted to a detailed description of an Integrated Services Packet Network (ISPN), which I offer as an alternative to current ISDN proposals." Further theoretical support for this vision has been laid out in [13]. Ultimately, the standards for the integrated services model—in particular the *Resource ReSerVation Setup Protocol* (*RSVP*)—were developed by the IETF in the late 1990s. The integrated services model effectively establishes—although only temporarily—a virtual circuit, with the routers maintaining the state for it.

Sure enough, the ISDN did not end up as "an effective long-term solution," but the ISPN revolution ran into difficulties—which we will explain later when discussing the technology—just at a time when the standard was being developed. The antithesis was the *differentiated services* movement (the name itself being a pun on "integrated services"), which took over the IETF in March 1998. The differentiated services model implied no virtual circuit. Routers keep no state, but they treat the arriving packets according to their respective classes, as encoded in IP packets themselves.

Ultimately, the integrated services model was found unscalable, and it was not deployed as such. The differentiated services model won; however, this happened because an altogether new virtual-circuit-based network element technology, *Multi-Protocol Label Switching* (*MPLS*) won, in itself synthesizing the Internet and ATM approaches. It is with MPLS that the integrated services and differentiated services models found their synthesis: A variant of the RSVP is used to establish the circuit; and differentiated services are used to maintain guaranteed QoS on the circuit.

The rest of this section first describes the traffic model and the QoS parameters, and then explains the integrated and differentiated services models and protocols. The section culminates—and ends—with the description of MPLS.

4.3.1 Packet Scheduling Disciplines and Traffic Specification Models

Just as the cars traveling on a highway maintain constant speed, so do the bits traveling over a wire. Variation in traffic speed takes place when the cars have to slow down or stop—where the roads merge or intersect; similarly, network traffic speed variation takes place at its "intersections"—in the routers.

A router needs to examine an arriving packet to determine the interface at which it needs to be forwarded toward its destination—that adds to the delay already caused by the I/O processing within the router. Given that packets arrive simultaneously on several interfaces, it is easy to see how a router can become a bottleneck. The packets end up in one or another queue, waiting to be forwarded. As long as the lengths of the queued packets add up to the assigned router memory limit, the packets inside the router are only delayed, but when this limit is reached, the router needs to *drop* them.

A router can shape the traffic it receives by treating packets differently according to their respective types—employing *packet scheduling disciplines*, which select the order of packet transmission. (At the moment, we have intentionally used the abstract term *type* without specifying how the type is determined. We will discuss a packet classification for each special case introduced in subsequent sections.)

Figure 4.19 illustrates the three major packet scheduling disciplines:

- With *best effort*, the packets are sent on a first-come, first-served basis; they are dropped when queues become, too large;
- With *fair queuing*, the packets are queued separately for each packet type and transmitted round-robin to guarantee each type an equal share of bandwidth. Here, the traffic type with statistically larger packets will end up letting lighter-type traffic go first; and
- With *weighted fair queuing*, round-robin scheduling is also employed, but the bandwidth is allocated according to each type's priority. The difference with fair queuing is that instead of transmitting an equal number n of bytes from each queue, nw_t bytes are transmitted from the queue associated with type t. A larger weight w_t is assigned to a higher priority queue.

It turns out (as is proven in [14]) that it is possible to guarantee upper bounds on the end-to-end delay and buffer size for each type.

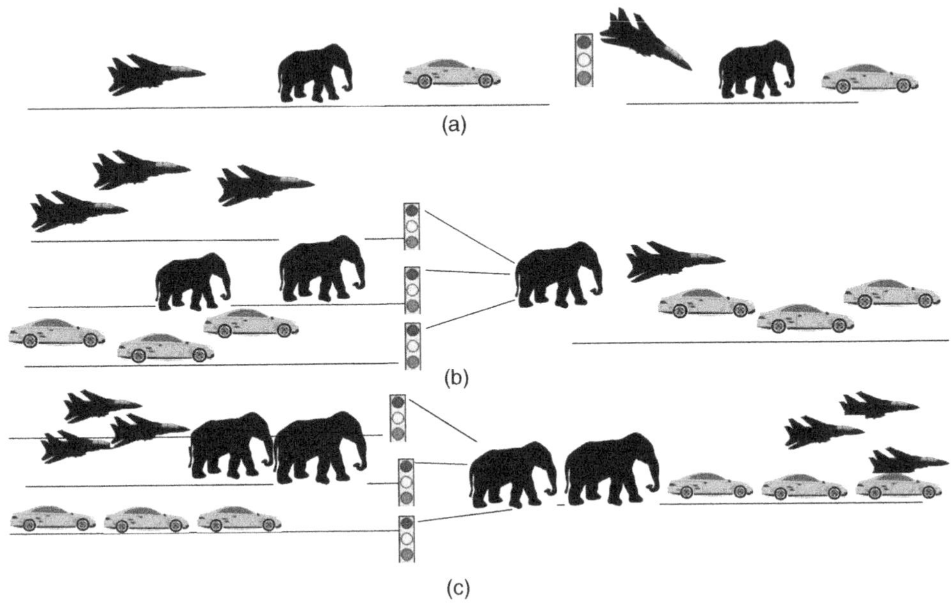

Figure 4.19 Packet scheduling disciplines: (a) best effort; (b) fair queuing; (c) weighted fair queuing.

When enough routers are stressed to their limit, the whole network gets congested. This situation is well known in transportation and crowd control; in both cases *admission control* is employed at entrances to congested cities or crowded places.

The two traffic specification models used in network admission are based on an even simpler analogy (depicted in Figure 4.20)—a bucket with a small hole in the bottom. The hole symbolizes the entrance to the network. When the bucket is full, the water starts overflowing, never reaching the "network."

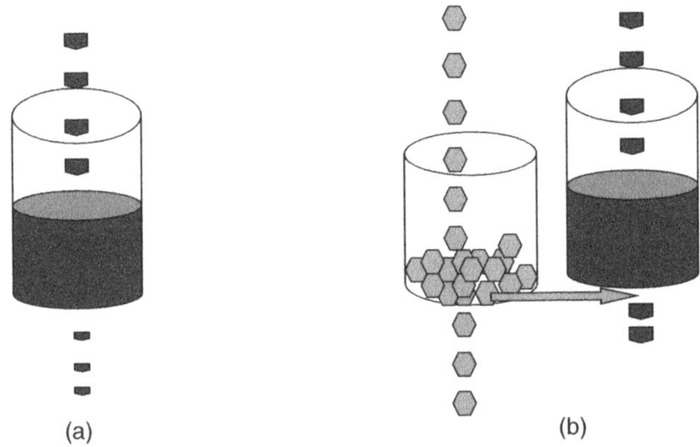

Figure 4.20 Traffic specification models: (a) leaky bucket; (b) token bucket.

Now envision a host playing the role of the spigot, inserting packets into the access control "bucket," which is a network-controlled queue of size β bytes (the bucket depth). The queue is processed at a rate ρ bytes/sec.

With the *leaky bucket model*, once the bucket is full, the packets that arrive at a higher rate than ρ and cause overflow end up being dropped. This model eliminates traffic *bursts*—the traffic can enter the network no faster than at a constant rate.

The *token bucket model* is designed to allow bursts. Here the flow out of the bucket is controlled by a valve. The state of the valve is determined by the condition of the token bucket. The latter receives quantities called tokens at a rate of r tokens/sec, and it can hold b tokens. (The tokens stop arriving when the bucket is full.) Now, when exiting the token bucket, a token opens the output valve of the main bucket (Figure 4.20(b)), to allow the output of one byte, at which point the valve is closed. Consequently, no traffic is admitted when the token bucket is empty. Yet, if there is no traffic to output, the bottom hole of the token bucket is closed, and so the tokens are saved in the bucket until they start to overflow. The difference from the leaky bucket model is that now bursts—up to the token bucket size—are allowed.

The volume $V(t)$ of the admitted traffic over time t is bounded thus:

$$V(t) \leq rt + b.$$

Hence, the maximum burst M can last for $(M - b)/r$ seconds.

By placing a token bucket after a leaky bucket that enforces rate R, one can shape the traffic never to exceed that rate while allowing controlled bursts.

4.3.2 Integrated Services

The type by which packets are distinguished in the integrated services model is defined by *flows*. A flow is a quintuple: (*Source IP address*, *Source Port*, *Protocol*, *Destination Port*, *Destination IP address*). Protocol designates the transport protocol. At the time the model was defined there were only two such protocols: TCP and UDP. (SCTP was defined later, and—because of its multiplexing feature—it does not fit exactly, unless the definition of a flow is extended to allow the source and destination of IP addresses to be sets of IP addresses.) Note that the layering principle gets violated right here and now, since the router has to inspect the IP payload.

In the simplest case, a flow is a simplex (i.e., one-way) end-to-end virtual circuit provided by the network layer to the transport layer; however, the integrated services envisioned multicast, so in the general case the virtual circuit here is a tree, originating at a point whence the packets are to be sent.

The integrated services framework was carefully built to supplement IP, but to support it, the IP routers had to be changed in a major way. The change included the necessity of making reservations—to establish the circuits and then to maintain these circuits for as long as they are needed.

The IETF 1994 integrated services framework, laid out in RFC 1633,[33] defined a new router function, called *traffic control*, which has been implemented with three components: *admission*

[33] www.ietf.org/rfc/rfc1633.txt

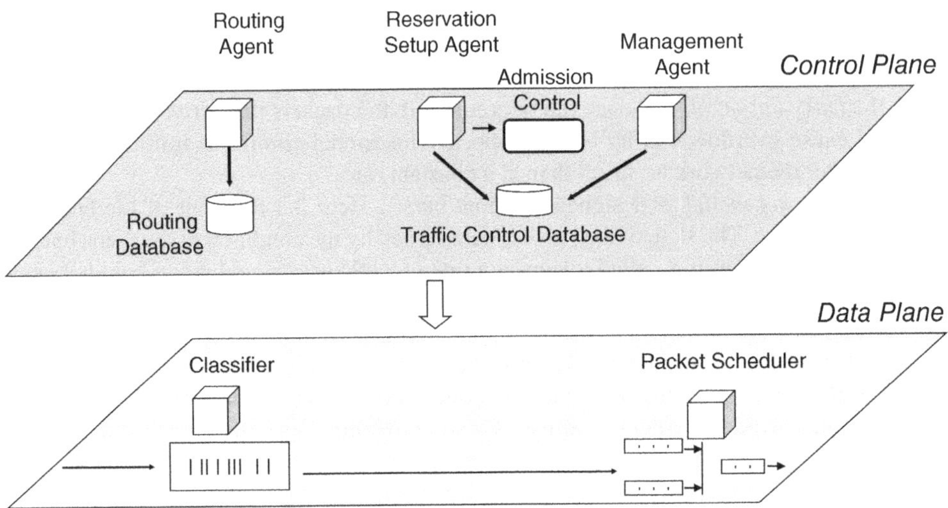

Figure 4.21 The integrated services model (after RFC 1631).

control, *classifier*, and *packet scheduler*. (Incidentally, the same terminology has largely been reused by the differentiated services framework.)

The role of admission control is to decide whether a new flow can get the requested QoS support. It is possible that several flows belong to the same type and receive the same QoS treatment. The classifier then maps incoming packets to their respective types—also called *classes of service*. Finally, the packet scheduler manages the class-arranged packet queues on each forwarding interface and serializes the packet stream on the forwarding interfaces.

The above entities are set up in the router and also at the endpoint hosts. The integrated services are brought into motion by the RSVP, which creates and maintains, for each flow, a flow-specific state in the endpoint hosts and routers in between. We will discuss RSVP in more detail shortly, but the general idea is that the receiving application endpoint specifies the QoS parameters in terms of a flow specification or *flowspec*, which then travels through the network toward the source host.[34] While traveling through the routers, the flowspec needs to pass the admission control test in each router; if it does, the reservation is accepted and so the *reservation setup agent* updates the state of the router's traffic control database.

Figure 4.21, which presents a slight modification of the architectural view of RFC 1631, explains the interworking of the elements above. There is a clear distinction between the *control plane*, where signaling takes place asynchronously with actual data transfer and the *data plane*, where the packets are moving in real time. It is interesting that the authors of RFC 1631 envisioned the reservations to be done by network management, that is without employing a router-to-router protocol. The routing function of the routers is unrelated to forwarding.

[34] If this arrangement looks strange, consider a streaming video application as it was envisioned in the 1990s. Presumably the receiving endpoint should subscribe to the service (and maybe even pay the network for the QoS it requires), and so it is only reasonable for it to start the reservation.

$$D = \begin{cases} \dfrac{(b-M)(p-R)}{R(p-r)} + \dfrac{M + \sum_{i \in Path} C_i}{R} + \sum_{i \in Path} D_i & (p > R \geq r), \\[2ex] \dfrac{M + \sum_{i \in Path} C_i}{R} + \sum_{i \in Path} D_i & (R \geq p \geq r). \end{cases}$$

from TSpec:

r: token rate
p: peak rate
b: token bucket depth

M: maximum packet size

from Rspec:

R: service rate

Figure 4.22 The end-to-end worst-case delay D (after RFC 2212).

The *Integrated Services* model deals with two end-to-end services: *guaranteed service* and *controlled-load service* on a per-flow basis.

The guaranteed service provides guaranteed bandwidth and bounds on the end-to-end queuing delay for *conforming* flows. The conformance is defined by the *traffic descriptor* (*TSpec*), which is the obligation of the service to the network. The obligation of the network to the application is defined in the *service specification* (*RSpec*).

TSpec is based on the token bucket model, and contains five parameters:

- *token rate r* (bytes/sec);
- *peak rate p* (bytes/sec);
- *token bucket depth b* (bytes);
- *minimum policed unit m* (bytes) (if a packet is smaller, it will still count as *m* bytes); and
- *maximum packet size M*.

RSpec contains two parameters: *service rate R* (bytes/sec) and—to introduce some flexibility in the scheduling—the *slack term S* (μsec), which is the delay a node can add while still meeting the end-to-end delay bounds.

Figure 4.22 provides the formula for the worst-case delay for the guaranteed service in terms of the TSpec and RSpec parameters. Two additional router-dependent variables here are

C_i: the overhead a packet experiences in a router i due to the packet length and transmission rate; and

D_i: a rate-independent delay a packet experiences in a router i due to flow identification, pipelining, etc.

Unlike the guaranteed service, the controlled-load service is best described in terms of what it does *not* allow to happen, which is visible queuing delay or visible congestion loss. The definition is left quite ambiguous—no quantitative guarantees—because admission control is

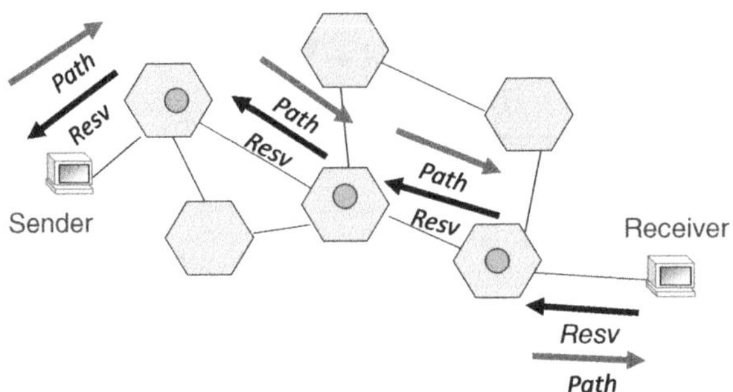

Figure 4.23 An example of the RSVP exchange.

left to implementation. (Sometimes, this service is called a *better-than-the-best-effort* service.) With this service, costly reservations are avoided, and routers rely on statistical mechanisms. Consequently, only TSpec (which limits the traffic that an application can insert into the network) but not RSpec (which spells out the network obligation) is required for the controlled-load service.

In 1997, the IETF completed the standards for integrated services and specified the RSVP for that purpose[35] in a series of RFCs from RFC 2205 through RFC 2216.

Figure 4.23 provides a simple example of the use of the RSVP. The host on the receiving side of the integrated services starts reservations with the *RESV message*. This message carries the flow descriptor, time value (needed for refreshing, as we will explain in a moment), the destination IP and port addresses, protocol number, and other parameters. The requests are propagated *upstream* through the routers until they reach the host that is to provide the service.

The latter host responds with the *PATH* message, which is propagated downstream and installs the state in the router. This message contains the flow identification, the sender TSpec, the time value, and other parameters. (Incidentally, for the purposes of security, both the RESV and PATH messages contain cryptographic proof of their integrity—that is, proof that they have not been tampered with.) As a result of PATH propagation, all routers install the state of the reservation (indicated by a small circle in Figure 4.23). The fact that keeping the state in the network has been accepted signifies a considerable compromise of the early Internet principles; however, the state has been declared *soft*. It is kept for as long as the RESV and PATH messages keep arriving within a specified time period—and indeed the procedure is to keep issuing those for the duration of a session. This should explain the need for the time value in both messages. If the exchange stops, the state is destroyed.

The session can also be torn down with a *PATHtear* message. The full set of RSVP messages is contained in the table of Figure 4.24.

As we will see shortly, RSVP got another life beyond integrated services.

[35] As we mentioned earlier, RSVP extensions have been used for different control-plane purposes, which go far beyond those of integrated services.

MESSAGE	Direction
PATH	downstream (sender to receiver)
RESV	upstream (receiver to sender)
PATHerr	upstream (in response to *PATH*)
RESVErr	downstream (in response to *RESV*)
PATHTear	downstream
RESVTear	upstream
RESVConf	downstream (in response to a specific request within *RESV)*

Figure 4.24 Summary of the RSVP messages.

4.3.3 Differentiated Services

Differentiated services were called that to emphasize the difference from the integrated services which, as we have mentioned, had in turn been named after the ISDN. (Hence the etymology here still points to telephone networks.) Nevertheless, the services as such are pretty much the same in both models, just that the means of enabling them differ. The major reason for developing a new model was the concern that the integrated services model—with its reservation and state mechanisms—would not scale in large-core networks.

Just as in the integrated services model, the service (as far as QoS is concerned) is characterized by its end-to-end behavior. But no services are defined here. Instead, the model supports a pre-defined set of service-independent building blocks. Similarly, the forwarding treatment is characterized by the behavior (packet scheduling) at each router, and the model defines forwarding behaviors (rather than end-to-end behaviors).

Another drastic difference is the absence of any signaling protocol to reserve QoS. Consequently, no state is to be kept in the routers. Furthermore, there is no flow-awareness or any other virtual-circuit construct in this model. The type of traffic to which a packet belongs (and according to which it is treated) is encoded in the packet's IP header field (*Type of Service*, in IPv4; *Class of Service*, in IPv6). These types are called *classes*, and the routing resources are allocated to each class.

Instead of signaling, network provisioning is used to supply the necessary parameters to routers. Well-defined forwarding treatments can be combined to deliver new services.

Class treatment is based on service-level agreements between customers and service providers. Traffic is policed at the edge of the network; after that, class-based forwarding is employed in the network itself.

Let us look at some detail. Each *Per-Hop-Behavior* (*PHB*) is assigned a 6-bit *Differentiated Services Codepoint* (*DSCP*). PHBs *are* the building blocks: all packets with the same codepoint make a *behavior aggregate*, and receive the same forwarding treatment. PHBs may be further combined into *PHB groups*.

The treatment of PHBs is identical in all routers within a *Differentiated Service* (*DS*) domain. Again, for the purposes of QoS provision, the origination and destination addresses, protocol IDs, and ports are irrelevant—only the DSCPs matter.

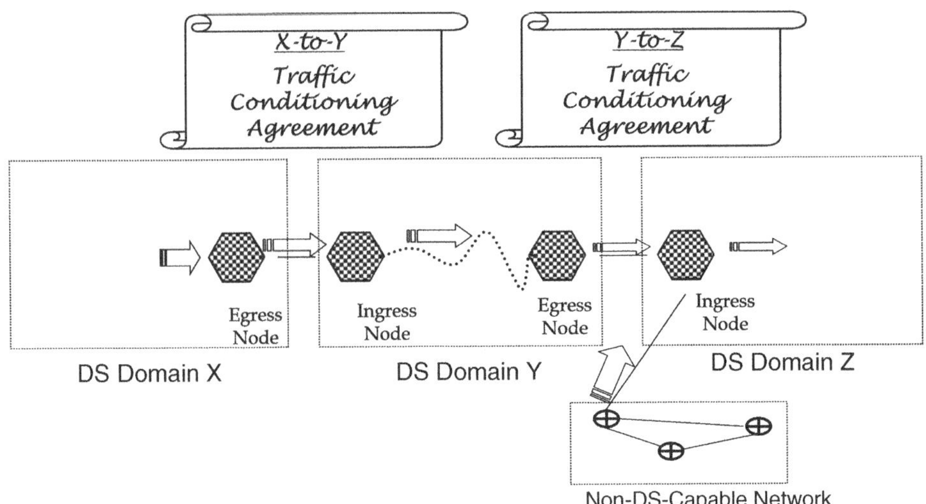

Figure 4.25 Traffic conditioning at the edges of DS domains. *Source:* Reprinted from [3] with permission of Alcatel-Lucent, USA, Inc.

Services are specified in a *Service-Level Agreement* (*SLA*) between a customer and a service provider as well as between two adjacent domains. An SLA specifies the traffic as well as security, accounting, billing, and other service parameters. A central part of an SLA is a *Traffic Conditioning Agreement* (*TCA*), which defines traffic profiles and the respective policing actions. Examples of these are token bucket parameters for each class; throughput, delay, and drop priorities; and actions for non-conformant packets.

Figure 4.25 illustrates the concepts. SLAs can be static (i.e., provisioned once) or dynamic (i.e., changed via real-time network management actions).

As far as the PHB classification is concerned, the default PHB group corresponds to the good old best-effort treatment. The real thing starts with the *Class Selector* (*CS*) PHB group (enumerated CS-1 through CS-8, in order of ascending priority).

The next group is the *Expedited Forwarding* (*EF*) PHB group, belonging to which guarantees the departure rate of the aggregate's packet to be no less than the arrival rate. It is assumed that the EF traffic may pre-empt any other traffic.

The *Assured Forwarding* (*AF*) PHB group allocates (in ascending order) priorities to four classes of service, and also defines three dropping priorities for each class of service (as the treatment for out-of-profile packets).

Figure 4.26 provides a self-explanatory illustration of the semantics of assured forwarding: for each transportation class, its priority as well as the dropping priority for its elements is spelled out.

The operations of the model inside a router are explained in Figure 4.27.

The major elements of the architecture are: Classifier, Meter, Marker, Dropper, and Shaper.

The Classifier functions are different at the edge of the network and in its interior nodes. In the boundary nodes located at the edge of the network, the Classifier determines the aggregate to which the packet belongs and the respective SLA; everywhere else in the network, the Classifier only examines the DSCP values.

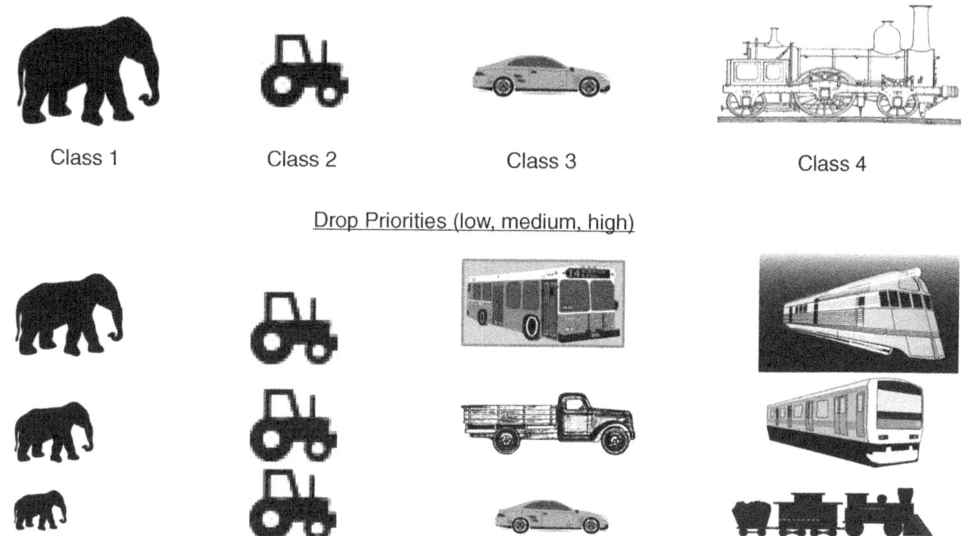

Figure 4.26 An example of an AF specification.

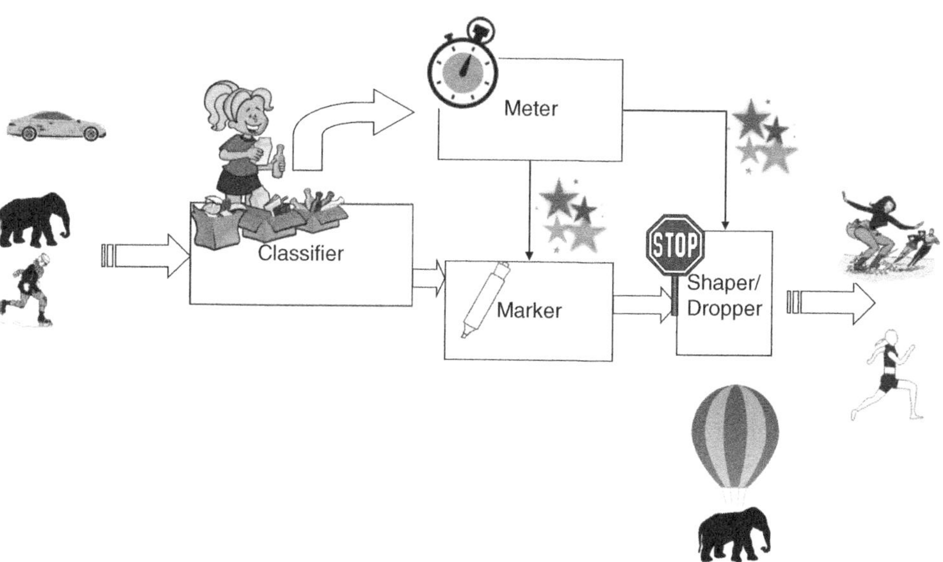

Figure 4.27 The inside view of DS. *Source:* RFC 2475.

The Meter checks the aggregate (to which the incoming packet belongs) against the Traffic Agreement Specification and determines whether it is in or out of the class profile. Depending on particular circumstances, the packet is either marked or just dropped.

The Marker writes the respective DSCP in the DS field. Marking may be done by the host, but it is checked (and is likely to be changed when necessary) by the boundary nodes. In some cases, special DSCPs may be used to mark non-conformant packets. These doomed packets may be dropped later if there is congestion. Depending on the traffic adherence to the SLA profile, the packets may also be promoted or demoted.

The Shaper delays non-conformant packets until it brings the respective aggregate in compliance with the traffic profile. To this end, shaping often needs to be performed between the egress and ingress nodes.

To conclude, we provide a long-overdue note on the respective standards. Altogether there are more than a dozen differentiated services RFCs published by the IETF at different times. RFC 2474[36] maps PHBs into DS codepoints of the IP packets. The idea of combining integrated services, in edge networks and differentiated services, in core networks has been exploited in RFC 2998.[37] With the particular importance of network management here, we highly recommend reading RFC 3279[38] and RFC 3280[39], which respectively define the management information base (i.e., the set of all parameters) in the routers and explain the network management operation.

4.3.4 *Multiprotocol Label Switching (MPLS)*

In his IP hourglass presentation, Dr. Deering referred to MPLS—along with several technologies it enabled—as "below-the-waist-bulge," lamenting that it is "mostly reinventing, badly, what IP already does (or could do, or should do)." Maybe so, but IP did not provide a straightforward virtual-circuit switching solution. This is not surprising, given that such a solution would have contradicted the fundamental principles of the Internet.

Given that in the mid-1990s, ATM switches as well as frame relay switches were around something had to be done to synthesize the connection-oriented and connectionless technologies. The synthesis, then called "tag switching," was described in [15], which stated in no uncertain terms an objective to simplify "the integration of routers and asynchronous transfer mode switches by employing common addressing, routing, and management procedures."

The IETF MPLS Working Group has been active since 1997, and it has been among the busiest IETF working groups, having published over 70 RFCs.[40]

We will start our overview of MPLS by identifying, with the help of Figure 4.28, the difference between routing and switching.

Imagine walking in a strange city, map in hand, toward a landmark at a given address. To get to the landmark one needs to determine where exactly one is at the moment, find this place as well as the landmark on the map, find a combination of streets that looks like the shortest

---

[36] www.ietf.org/rfc/rfc2474.txt
[37] www.ietf.org/rfc/rfc299A.txt
[38] www.ietf.org/rfc/rfc3279.txt
[39] www.ietf.org/rfc/rfc3280.txt
[40] The full list of past and present MPLS work items can be found at http://tools.ietf.org/wg/mpls/.

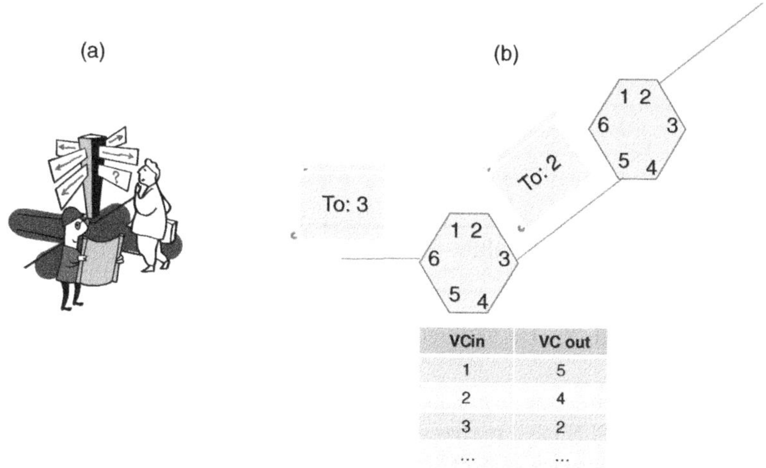

VCin	VC out
1	5
2	4
3	2
...	...

Figure 4.28 Routing and switching.

way to get to the landmark, and start walking, checking street names at corners, as depicted in Figure 4.28(a), and making decisions where to turn. This takes time, and an outdated map may further complicate the affair. This is pretty much what the routing problem is. And if walking is problematic, everyone who has driven under these circumstances knows how ineffective this may be (with other drivers blowing their horns all around!).

However, when all one has to do is follow the signs toward the landmark—whether on foot or driving—finding the destination is straightforward. This is the case with switching over a pre-determined circuit. The circuit does not have to be permanent (consider the case of real-estate signs marking the direction toward an open house or detour signs placed only for the duration of a road repair). Another metaphor is the route designation for US highways. To travel from Miami to Boston, one only needs to follow the Interstate Route 95, which actually extends over several different highways—even named differently. The interchanges are well marked though, and with a car's driver following the signs (rather than looking at the map), the car switches from one highway to another while always staying on the route.

Similarly, with datagram switching, a network node never has to determine the destination of a datagram in order to forward it to the next node. Instead, the datagram presents a (locally significant) interface number—a virtual circuit ID, so that the datagram is forwarded exactly on the interface it names. For example, the node on the left of Figure 4.28(b) has received a datagram to be forwarded on interface 3. The node's switching map indicates that the next node's interface to forward the datagram on is 2, and so the virtual circuit ID 3 is replaced by that of 2 on the next hop. With that, the datagrams follows a pre-determined "circuit."

This is exactly how MPLS works. First, a *Label-Switched Path* (*LSP*)—a virtual end-to-end circuit—is established; then the switches (also called MPLS-capable routers) and then *switching* (rather than routing) IP packets, without ever looking at the packet itself. Furthermore, an LSP can be established along any path (not necessarily the shortest one), a feature that helps traffic engineering.

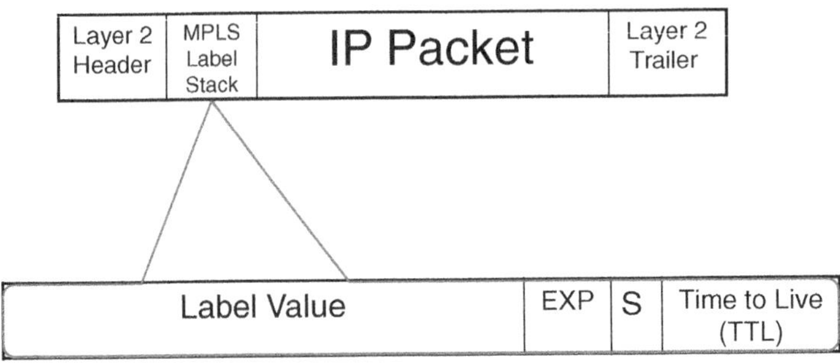

Figure 4.29 The location and structure of the MPLS label.

The locally significant circuit is designated by a *label*. (Hence the "L" in MPLS.) As Figure 4.29 demonstrates, the MPLS label prefixes the IP packet within the link-layer frame, sitting just where one would otherwise expect to see the link-layer header. In terms of the ISO reference mode, that fact alone would have put MPLS squarely in Layer 2 had it not been for the actual, "real" link layer running over the physical circuit. For this reason, MPLS is sometimes referred to as "Layer-2.5 technology." The situation is further complicated because the labels can be stacked, for the purposes of building virtual private networks. (As is typical with virtual things, recursion comes in.) For the purposes of this section though, we always assume that the stack contains one and only one label.

The structure of the MPLS label is defined in RFC 3032.[41] The label contains four fields:

- *Label Value* (20 bits), which is the actual virtual circuit ID;
- *Traffic Class* (*TC*) (3 bits),[42] which is used for interworking with *diffserv* and for explicit congestion marking;
- *S* (1 bit) is a Boolean value indicating whether the present label is the last on the label stack; and
- *Time-to-Live* (*TTL*) (8 bits), which has the same purpose and the same semantics as its namesake field in IPv4. (The IP packet is not examined in MPLS.)

The way the label is used is rather straightforward. The label value serves as an index into the internal table (called the *Incoming Label Map* (*ILM*)) of the MPLS switch, which, among other things, contains the outgoing label value, the next hop (i.e., the index to the forwarding interface), and the state information associated with the path. Then the new link-layer frame is formed, with the new outgoing label inserted before the IP packet.

One interesting question here: Where in this framework is it essential that the payload be an IP packet? The answer is that it is not essential at all. For the moment—as we are addressing

[41] www.ietf.org/rfc/rfc3032.txt

[42] This field was initially called *EXP* (for "experimental"), even though the original plan was to experiment with encoding QoS classes. Since there was no agreement on what those were, a political compromise to use the catch-all "experimental" designation was reached. Such indecision proved to be dangerous though, as other standards organizations interpreted the name of the field as an invitation to "experiment" with the field by themselves. Prompted by the impending loss of control over the standard, the IETF moved to rename the field, which was accomplished by the publication of RFC 5462 (www.ietf.org/rfc/rfc5462.txt).

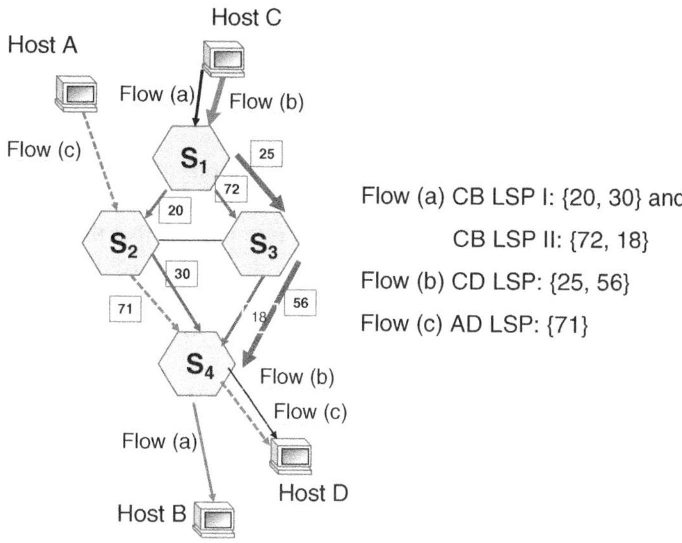

Figure 4.30 An example of label assignment to flows and LSPs.

the use of MPLS within IP networks—we naturally look at everything from the IP point of view, but we will shortly use the fact that any payload—including an ATM cell and the Ethernet frame—can be transferred with MPLS. This, finally, explains the "multi-protocol" part in the name "MPLS." Yet MPLS was invented with IP networks in mind, and its prevalent use is in IP networks. To emphasize that, the MPLS standards call an MPLS switch a *Label-Switched Router* (LSR).

While the process of switching is fairly simple, the overall problem of engineering, establishing, and tearing down end-to-end circuits is exceedingly complex. It took the industry (and the IETF in particular) many years to resolve this, and work on many other aspects of it—especially where it concerns optical networking—is continuing.[43]

Figure 4.30 illustrates the mapping of labels to LSPs along with some of their important properties. To begin with, all LSPs (just like the integrated services flows) are simplex. Our example actually deals only with flows, and we have three to look at:

- *Flow (a)* originates in host C and terminates in host B. For the purposes of *load balancing* (an important network function to which we will return more than once in this book) there are two LSPs. LSP I traverses three LSRs—S_1, S_2, and S_4—the last two assigning the flow labels 20 and 30, respectively. Similarly, LSP II, which traverses S_1, S_3, and S_4, has labels 72 and 18 assigned to the same flow.

[43] In addition to the IETF, work on MPLS has progressed in several industrial fora (such as the ATM Forum and Frame Relay Forum) concerned with other protocols of the "multi" part. These fora have now merged into the *BroadBand Forum* (*BBF*) (www.broadband-forum.org/technical/ipmplstechspec.php). In addition, some MPLS standardization has been worked in ITU-T. See [16] for an overview of QoS in packet-switching networks as related to early ITU-T work on the subject.

- *Flow (b)* originates in host C and terminates in host D, also traversing LSRs S_1, S_3, and S_4, and it assigns labels 25 and 56 to the flow.
- *Flow (c)* originates in host A and terminates in host D, traversing LSRs S_2 and S_4, the latter switch assigning the flow label 71.

Each label in the *Label-Switched Path* (*LSP*) has a one-to-one association with a *Forwarding Equivalence Class* (*FEC*), which is in turn associated with the treatment the packets receive. An FEC is defined by a set of rules. For instance, a rule may be that the packets in the FEC match a particular IP destination address, or that they are destined for the same egress router, or that they belong to a specific flow (just as in the example of Figure 4.30). Naturally, different FECs have different levels of scalability. The classification of FEC packets is performed by the ingress routers.

At this point, we are ready to address—very briefly—the issue of forming LSPs. One simple rule here, which follows from the fact that only a specific LSR knows how to index its own incoming label map, is that the labels are assigned *upstream*—that is, from the sink to the source, similarly to the way reservations are made with RSVP.

In fact, RSVP in its new incarnation with extension for traffic engineering—called RSVP-TE—has become a standard protocol for label distribution. Because RSVP was originally designed to support multicast, the development of RSVP-TE reignited interest in broadband multicast.

Before RSVP-TE though, another protocol, appropriately called the *Label Distribution Protocol* (*LDP*), was designed for label distribution. Later, the designers of LDP had to take traffic engineering into account, too, and the resulting LDP extension was called *Constraint-based Routing LDP* (*CR-LDP*). It hardly makes things simpler, but BGP has introduced its own extension for managing LSPs.

Figure 4.31 gives an example of a simple explicit route setup with CR-LDP and RSVP-TE, concentrating on their similarities rather than their differences. The requests (emphasized in bold) flow upstream, while the assignment of labels proceeds downstream. In addition to setting up the LSPs, both protocols support the LSP tunnel rerouting, applying the "make-before-break" principle, and provide pre-emption options.

Except for support for multicast, which, again, was the original feature of RSVP-TE, the differences between CR-LDP and RSVP-TE are fairly insignificant. In short, these are manifest in the underlying protocols (CR-LDP needs TCP or UDP, while RSVP-TE runs directly over IP); the state installed in an LSR (CR-LDP installs hard state, while RSVP-TE—true to its original design—installs soft state); LSP refresh (performed only by RSVP-TE); and security options (RSVP-TE has its own authentication mechanism).

To conclude, in less than 20 years since its inception, MPLS has gone a long way. First, it enabled peer-to-peer communication with ATM and frame relay switches. It also introduced a means of supporting Internet traffic engineering (e.g., offload, rerouting, and load balancing), accelerated packet forwarding, and—as we will see in the next section—provided a consistent tunneling discipline for the establishment of virtual private networks.

The MPLS technology, by means of its extension called *Generalized MPLS* (*GMPLS*) has also evolved to support other switching technologies (e.g., those that involve time-division multiplexing and wavelength switching). There is an authoritative book [17] on this subject. As we move to WAN virtualization technologies—the subject of the next section—it is appropriate to note that MPLS has proven to be the technology of choice in this area.

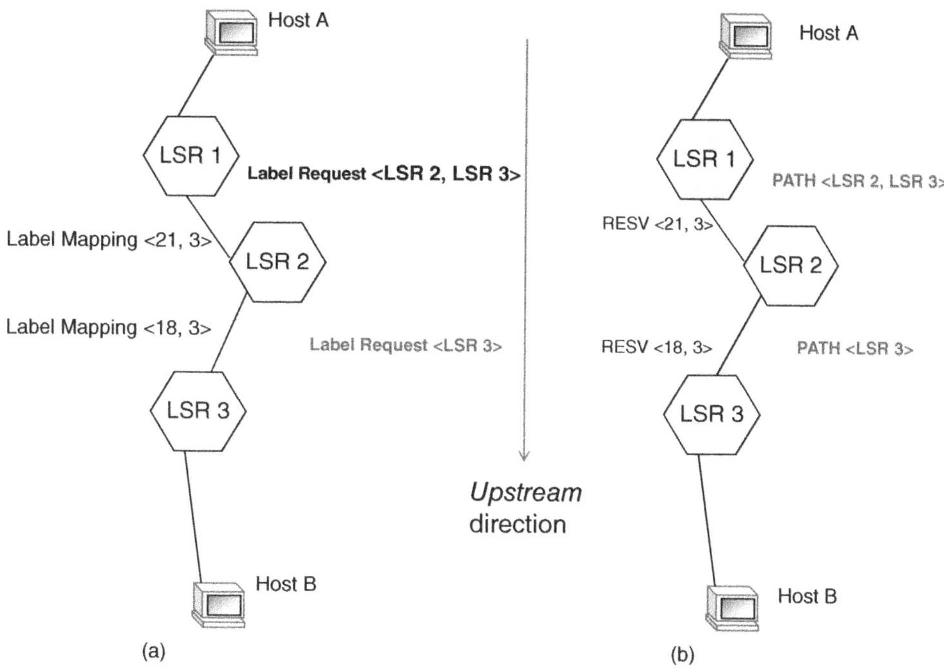

Figure 4.31 Examples of the explicit route setup with (a) CR-LDP and (b) RSVP-TE.

4.4 WAN Virtualization Technologies

As we mentioned in the Introduction, the need for virtual data networking pre-dated PDN times; PDN was, in fact, created to address the need for companies to have what *appears* to be their own separate private networks.

To this end, all that the term *virtualization* means, when applied to data networks, is just an environment where something is put on top of the existing network—as an *overlay*—to carve out of it non-intersecting, homogeneous pieces that, for all practical purposes, are private networks. In other words, each of these pieces has an addressing scheme defined by the private network it corresponds to, and it operates according to the network policies.

The association of endpoints forming a VPN can be achieved at different OSI layers. We consider Layer-1, Layer-2, and Layer-3 VPNs.

The *Layer-1 VPN* (*L1VPN*) framework, depicted in Figure 4.32, and standards have been developed by the IETF and ITU-T. The framework is described in RFC 4847,[44] which also lists related documents. L1VPN is defined as a "service offered by a core Layer 1 network to provide Layer 1 connectivity between two or more customer sites, and where the customer has some control over the establishment and type of the connectivity." The model is based on GMPLS-controlled traffic engineering links. With that, the data plane (but not the control plane) is circuit switched.

[44] www.ietf.org/rfc/rfc4847.txt

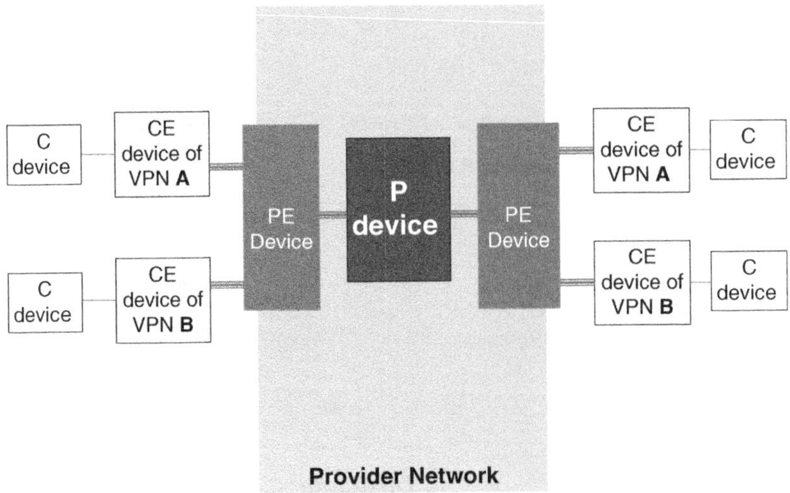

Figure 4.32 Layer-1 VPN framework (after RFC 4847).

The customer devices, *C devices*, are aggregated at a *Customer Edge* (*CE*) device, which is a VPN endpoint. (There are two VPNs, named A and B in the figure.) A CE device can be a *Time Division Multiplexing* (*TDM*) switch, but it can also be a Layer-2 switch or even a router. The defining feature of a CE device is that it be "capable of receiving a Layer-1 signal and either switching it or terminating it with adaptation."

In turn, a CE device is attached to a *Provider Edge* (*PE*) device, which is the point of interconnection to the provider network through which the L1VPN service is dispensed. A PE device can be a TDM switch, an optical cross-connect switch, a photonic cross-connect switch, or an Ethernet private line device (which transports Ethernet frames over TDM). PE devices are themselves interconnected by switches, called *Provider* (*P*) devices.

The VPN membership information is defined by the set of CE-to-PE GMPLS links. Even though the CE devices belong to a customer, their management can be outsourced to a third party, which is one of the benefits of Layer-1 VPN. Another benefit is "small-scale" use of transmission networks: several customers share the physical layer infrastructure without investing in building it.

Layer-2 VPNs have two species. One species is a simple "pseudo-wire," which provides a point-to-point link-layer service. Another species is LAN-like in that it provides a point-to-multipoint service, interconnecting several LANs into a WAN. Both species use the same protocols to achieve their goals, so we will discuss the use of these protocols only for the second species—virtual LAN (VLAN).

To begin with, there are two aspects to virtual LANs. The first aspect deals with carving a "real" (not-emulated) LAN into seemingly independent, separate VLANs. The second aspect deals with gluing instead of carving, and it deals with connecting LANs at the link layer.

Figure 4.33 illustrates the VLAN concept. The hosts that perform distinct functions—drawn in Figure 4.33(a) with different shapes—share the same physical switched LAN. The objective is to achieve—by software means—the logical grouping of Figure 4.33(b), in which each function has its own dedicated LAN. To this end, the logical LANs may even have

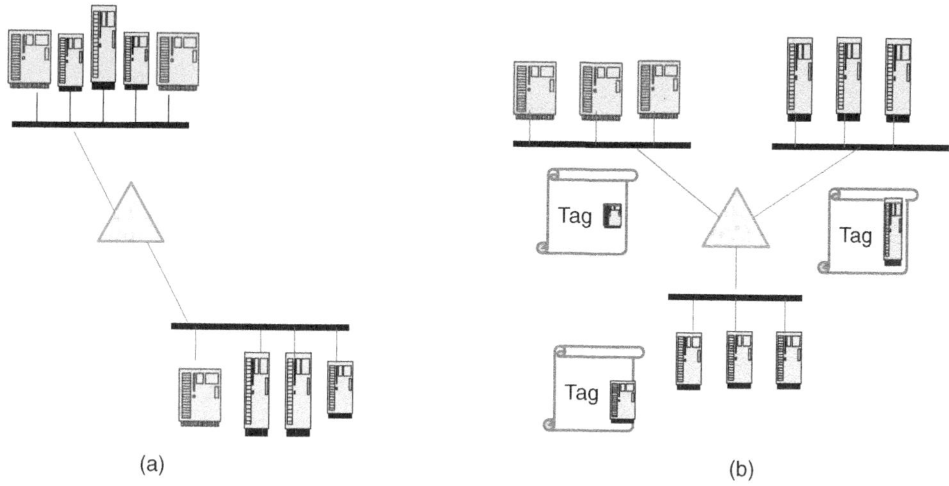

Figure 4.33 The VLAN concept: (a) physical configuration; (b) logical configuration.

different physical characteristics so that, for example, multimedia terminals get a higher share of bandwidth.

This is achieved by means of VLAN-aware switches that meet the IEEE 802.1Q[45] standard. The switches recognize the *tags* that characterize the class (i.e., VLAN) to which the frame belongs and deliver the frame accordingly.

VLANs can be extended into WAN Layer-2 VPNs by means of *pseudo-wire* (as defined in RFC 3985[46]), where a bit stream—in the case of LANs, a frame—is transmitted over a packet-switched network.

Figure 4.34, which reuses the terminology of Figure 4.32, demonstrates the framework. The difference here is that the Layer-2 frames are tunneled through the PSN over an emulated (rather than a real) circuit.

A pseudo-wire can naturally be established over an MPLS circuit, but the presence of an MPLS is not a requirement. There is an older—and in a way competing—technology for carrying link-layer packets over an IP network in the form of the *Layer Two Tunneling Protocol (L2TP)*. Originally, as described in [3], L2TP was developed among the first mechanisms in support of PSTN/Internet integration, enabling a connection between a host and the Internet router over a telephone line. It aims to carry PPP frames with a single point-to-point connection. Now in its third version, the L2TPv3 as specified in RFC 3931[47] still retains the call setup terminology, but the scope of its application has been extended to support Ethernet-based VLAN.

Finally, Layer-3 VPNs are not much different conceptually—they also involve tunneling, but at Layer 3. The PEs in this case don't have to deal with the LAN-specific problems, but there is another set of problems that deal with duplicate addresses. Each Layer-2 network address card has a unique Layer-2 address; however, this is not the case with IP addresses. The reasons for that will become clear later, when we introduce *Network Address Translation*

[45] http://standards.ieee.org/getieee802/download/802.1Q-2005.pdf
[46] www.ietf.org/rfc/rfc3985.txt
[47] http://tools.ietf.org/html/rfc3931

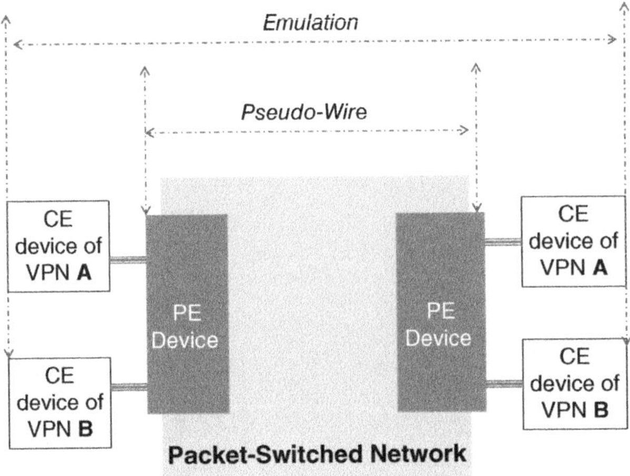

Figure 4.34 Pseudo-wire emulation edge-to-edge network reference model (after Figure 2 of RFC 3985).

(*NAT*) appliances, but the fact is that it is possible for two private networks to have overlapping sets of IP addresses, and hence the provider must be able to disambiguate them.

RFC 2547[48] describes a set of techniques in which MPLS is used for tunneling through the provider's network and extended BGP advertises routes using *route distinguisher* strings, which allow disambiguation of duplicate addresses in the same PE.

Another approach is the *virtual router* architecture introduced in RFC 2917.[49] Here, MPLS is also used for tunneling, but no specialized route-advertising mechanism is needed. Disambiguation is achieved by using different labels in distinct routing domains.

By now, the role and benefits of MPLS in constructing VPNs, especially in view of its traffic engineering capabilities in support of QoS, should be evident. We can now explain the need for stacking MPLS labels, a need that arose precisely because of VPN requirements.

Figure 4.35(a) depicts two distinct LANs interconnected by an MPLS LSP in a private network. Consider now interworking this arrangement with a VPN, as shown in Figure 4.35(b). As the LSP enters the ingress PE, the latter can *push* its own label (preserving the original label, which has no significance in the provider network and thus tunneled through it along with the payload). That label is *popped* at the egress PE, and so the packet returns to the private network with the original label that now has a meaning for the rest of the LSP.

We will return to VPN when discussing modern Cloud data centers.

4.5 Software-Defined Network

The very idea of SDN—a centrally managed network—has been around from the beginning of networking. (One could argue that it has been around from the beginning of mankind,

[48] www.ietf.org/rfc/rfc2547.txt

[49] https://tools.ietf.org/html/rfc2917

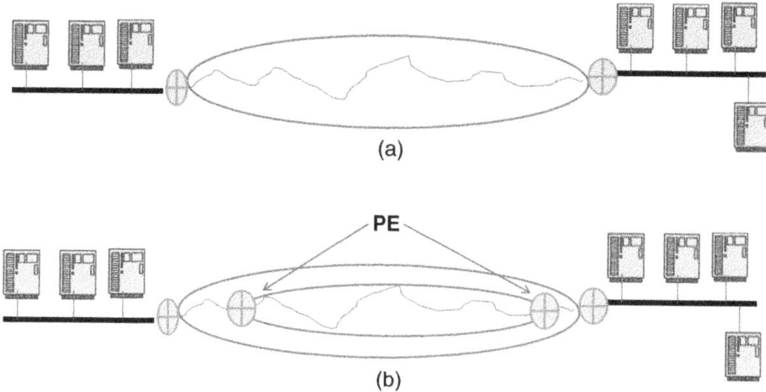

Figure 4.35 Label stacking in provider-supported VPN: (a) LSP in a single network; (b) LSP traversing a provider network.

as it involves the benefits of central planning and management versus those of agility and robustness of independent local governments.) It should be clear though that the point of the argument revolving around the idea of SDN is not central management in general, but the real-time central management of routing.

To this end, the initial SDN development is very similar to that of the PSTN *Intelligent Network (IN)* [18]. Telephone networks were always centrally managed, but the telephone switches established calls through co-operation among themselves. In the 1970s, they evolved so that the call establishment was performed *out-of-band* of the voice circuitry—via a separate packet network. Toward the 1990s, call control was increasingly separated from all-software service control. The latter started with a simple address translation (not unlike that performed by the Internet domain name servers, which we will address in detail later in this book), but evolved toward executing complex service logic programs.

The trajectory of that evolution was leading toward switches becoming mere "switching fabric," with all other functions moving into the general computers that would exercise complete control over call and service logic, combining IN and network management. The *Telecommunications Information Networking Consortium (TINA-C)*[50] had worked for seven years (from 1993 to 2000) on this vision, providing the architecture, specifications, and even software. Although the direction was right, the vision never materialized simply because the "switching fabric" dissolved in the Internet—its functions taken on by the LAN switches[51] and IP routers. That was the beginning of the end for telephone switches as such.

In the late 1990s, the progress of work (described in detail in [3]) in several IETF working groups resulted in clear standards for telephone switches to be effectively decomposed into pieces that spoke to both PSTN and IP. The "switching" though was a function of an IP

[50] www.tinac.com/index.htm

[51] In fact, it was known from Bell Labs experiments in the 1980s that telephony can be deployed over the Ethernet LAN with no other "switching fabric" than generic LAN. In 1994, Alon Cohen and Lior Haramaty of Vocaltec filed a patent application for a specialized voice-over-IP transceiver. The patent was granted in 1998.

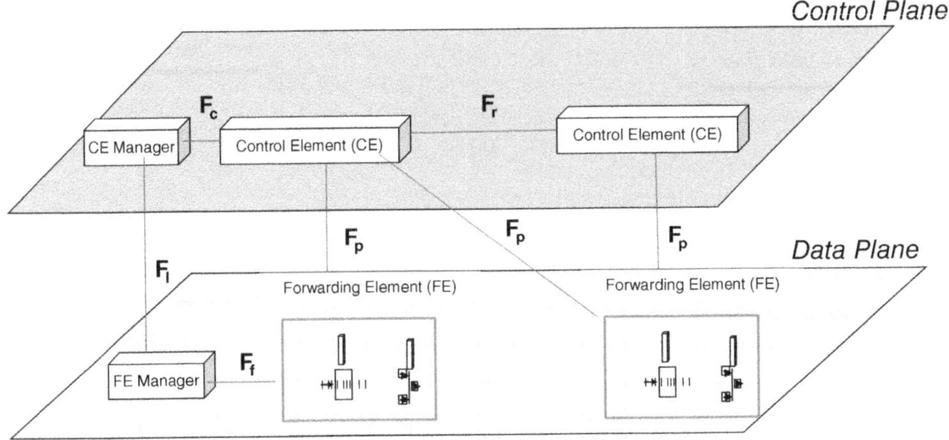

Figure 4.36 The ForCES architecture (after RFC 3746).

router. Thus, a *SoftSwitch* concept was born,[52] whose very name reflected the idea of its programmability, which came naturally as only general-service computers were needed to control it. The *Session Initiation Protocol/Intelligent Network* (*SIN*) design team led by Dr. Hui-Lan Lu in the IETF transport area has demonstrated how all PSTN-based services can be both reused and enhanced with the soft switch. The result of this work—at the time largely unnoticed, since 3GPP was completing a related but much more powerful effort standardizing the *IP Multimedia Subsystem* (*IMS*) for mobile networks—was RFC 3976.[53] In contributing to the RFC, its leading author, Dr. Vijay Gurbani, supplied the research that was part of his PhD thesis. As the IMS became a success, the name SoftSwitch disappeared, as did the industry's efforts to enhance or even maintain PSTN switches.

With the telephone switches gone, the attention of researchers turned toward IP routers. The latter started as general-purpose computers (Digital Equipment Corporation PDP-10 minicomputers, for example, which BBN had deployed in 1977 in ARPANET), but, by 2000, they had become complex, specialized hardware devices[54] controlled by proprietary operating systems. Then the push came to separate the forwarding part of the router (the "switching fabric" that requires specialized hardware) from the part that performs signaling and builds routing tables.

The IETF started the discussion on the *Forwarding and Control Element Separation* (*ForCES*) working group charter in 2000, with the ForCES framework published as RFC 3746[55] in 2004. Figure 4.36 reproduces the ForCES architecture.

[52] At the time, also the project of the International SoftSwitch Consortium.

[53] www.ietf.org/rfc/rfc3976.txt

[54] The complexity has been driven by the ever-growing real-time performance requirements. Particularly, the forwarding part (i.e., data plane) had to be so fast, that even the fastest bus architectures could not keep up with demand. Hence many a fast router ended up using good old crossbar switches ... just as the telephone switches did. *Le roi est mort; vive le roi!*

[55] https://tools.ietf.org/html/rfc3746

RFC 5810[56] defines the protocol (or rather protocols) for the interfaces—called, in the ITU-T tradition, *reference points* between the pairs of elements. The transaction-oriented protocol messages are defined for the *Protocol Layer* (*PL*), while the *Protocol Transport Mapping Layer* (ForCES TML) "uses the capabilities of existing transport protocols to specifically address protocol message transportation issues." Specific TMLs are defined in separate RFCs.

By 2010 there were several implementations of the ForCES protocol, three of which are reported on and compared with one another in RFC 6053.[57] The ForCES development was taken to new heights with the *SoftRouter* project at Bell Labs. In the SoftRouter architecture, described in [19], the control plane functions are separated completely from the packet forwarding functions. There is no static association; the FEs and CEs find one another dynamically. When an FE boots, it discovers a set of CEs that may control it, and dynamically binds itself to the "best" CE. A seeming allusion to SoftSwitch is actually a direct reference. As the authors of [19] state: "The proposed network evolution has similarities to the SoftSwitch based transformation of the voice network architecture that is currently taking place. The SoftSwitch architecture ... was introduced to separate the voice transport path from the call control software. The SoftRouter architecture is aimed at providing an analogous migration in routed packet networks by separating the forwarding elements from the control elements. Similar to the SoftSwitch, the SoftRouter architecture reduces the complexity of adding new functionality into the network."

The next significant step came as an action reflecting the common academic sentiments: the Internet architecture was "ossified," and it was impossible to change it; it was, in fact, hard to teach students practical aspects of networking when there was no access to real networks to experiment at scale. The *Global Environment for Network Innovations* (*GENI*) project[58] has addressed this by establishing a wide project for programmable networks, which use virtualization—including network overlays—so as to allow "network slicing" in order to give individual researchers what appears to be a WAN to experiment with.

Somewhat downscaling the concept to a campus network, eight researchers issued, in 2008, what they called a "white paper" [20].[59] The proposal of the paper was called *OpenFlow*.

Having observed that the flow tables in the present Ethernet switches and routers have common information, the authors of [20] proposed exploiting this so as to allow flow tables to be programmed directly. Systems administrators could then *slice* the campus network by partitioning the traffic and allocating the entries in the flow table to different users. In this way, researchers "can control their own flows by choosing the routes their packets follow and the processing they receive. In this way, researchers can try new routing protocols, security models, addressing schemes, and even alternatives to IP."

According to [20], the ideal OpenFlow environment looks as depicted in Figure 4.37, which we intentionally drew in the context of the previous figure to demonstrate the progress of the development. Here the controller process, which is implemented on a general computer, maintains a secure transport-layer channel with its counterpart process in the switch. The latter

[56] www.rfc-editor.org/rfc5810.txt
[57] www.rfc-editor.org/rfc/rfc6053.txt
[58] www.geni.net/?page_id=2
[59] The paper was an editorial note submitted to the *ACM Computer Communications Review*, and was not peer reviewed.

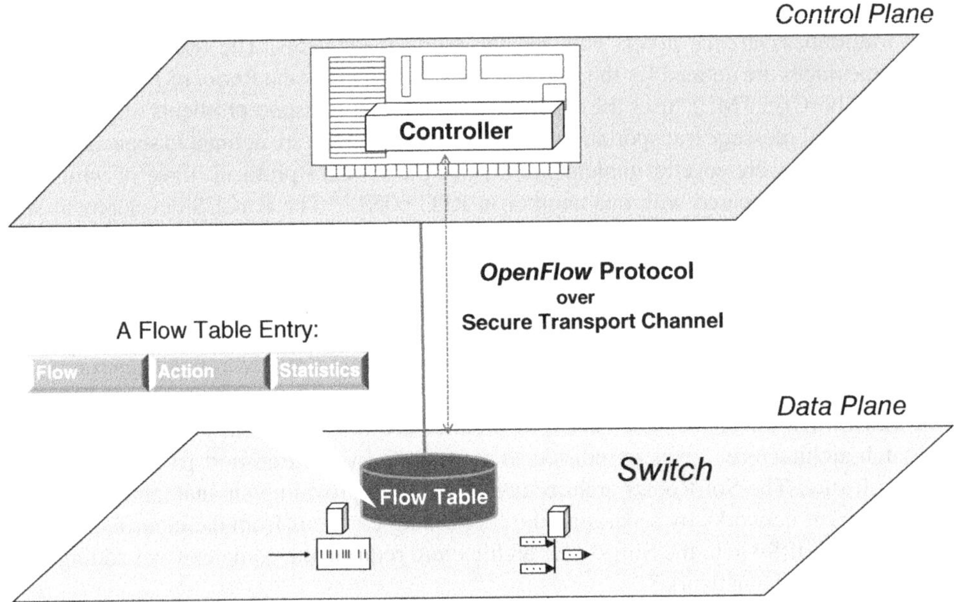

Figure 4.37 The OpenFlow switch.

process is responsible for the maintenance of the flow table. The OpenFlow protocol, through which the flow table is maintained, is exchanged between these two processes.

A *flow* has a broad definition: it can be a stream of packets that share the same quintuple (as defined in the integrated services) or VLAN tag, or MPLS label; or it can be a stream of packets emanating from a given Layer-2 address or IP address.

In addition to the header that defines the flow, a flow table entry defines the *action* to be performed on a packet and the *statistics* associated with each flow (number of packets, number of bytes, and the *time* since the last packet of the defined flow arrived). The action can be either sending a packet on a specific interface, or dropping it, or—and here is where things become new and interesting—sending it to the controller(!) for further inspection. It is obvious how this feature can benefit researchers, and its benefit for law enforcement is equally obvious.

Thus, the industry moved even further toward transforming the data-networking architecture into a fully programmable entity—coming, within the space of 20 years, to the realization of IN and TINA-C plans. In 2008, the OpenFlow Consortium was formed to develop the OpenFlow switch specifications. The membership of the consortium, as [20] reports, was "open and free for anyone at a school, college, university, or government agency worldwide." Yet the Consortium restricted, in an effort to eliminate vendor influence, its welcome to those individual members who were "not employed by companies that manufacture or sell Ethernet switches, routers or wireless access points." The situation changed in 2011, when the work of the Consortium was taken over by the *Open Networking Foundation* (*ONF*),[60] which has

[60] https://www.opennetworking.org/

a large and varied enterprise membership including both network operators and vendors. A special program supports research associates whose membership is free of charge.

4.6 Security of IP

There are many aspects to network security, and we will keep returning to this subject throughout the book to introduce new aspects. Just to mention a couple of things that are the subject of later chapters, there are *firewalls* (which are but police checkpoints for the IP traffic) and there are *Network Address Translation* (*NAT*) devices (whose purpose is to hide the internal structure of the network, and which are often combined with firewalls). Then there are mechanisms for access management, and different cryptographic mechanisms for different OSI layers. We highly recommend [21] as a comprehensive—and beautifully written—monograph on network security. For the purposes of this chapter, which is mainly concerned with the network layer, we will deal with one and only one aspect: IP security.

Security was not a requirement when IP was first designed, and so IP packets crisscrossed the Internet from sources to destinations in the clear. As long as the Internet was the network for and by researchers, the situation was (or at least was thought to be) fine.

The fact is though that anyone on a broadcast network (or with access to a switch) can peek inside a packet (if only to learn someone else's password); people with more advanced means can also alter or replay the packets. Furthermore, it is easy for anyone to inject into the network arbitrary packets with counterfeit source IP addresses.

The suite of protocols known as IP security (IPsec) was developed to provide security services at the network layer. An important reason for developing security at the network layer is that existing applications can stay unchanged, while new applications can still be developed by people blissfully unaware of the associated complexity. Addressing security at the layers below provides only a hop-by-hop solution—because of the routers in the end-to-end path. (Addressing it at the transport layers initially appeared redundant, and would have remained redundant, had the network not been "broken"—as will become evident later.

IPsec is specified in a suite of IETF RFCs whose relationship is depicted in Figure 4.38. Understanding the relationship is important to the practical use of IPsec as it provides several services (authentication, confidentiality protection, integrity protection, and anti-replay) which can be mixed and matched to fit specific needs.

Cryptography (see [22] for not only an explanation of the algorithm but also the code) provides the foundation for these services. To this end, IPsec supports a range of cryptographic algorithms to maximize the chances of two involved endpoints having a common supported algorithm.[61] It also allows new algorithms to be added as they emerge and supplant those that are found to be defective. For example, the latest IPsec requirements for cryptographic algorithms, as specified in RFC 7321,[62] mandate support for the *Advanced Encryption Standard* (*AES*) in light of the weakness of the *Data Encryption Standard* (*DES*), and support

[61] A *NULL* encryption algorithm—which does for encryption as much as its name suggests—is included for developers' convenience. It even has its own RFC 2410 (www.rfc-editor.org/rfc/rfc2410.txt), which is very entertaining to read. (A citation: "Despite rumors that the National Security Agency suppressed publication of this algorithm, there is no evidence of such action on their part. Rather, recent archaeological evidence suggests that the *NULL* algorithm was developed in Roman times, as an exportable alternative to Caesar ciphers.")

[62] www.rfc-editor.org/rfc/rfc7321.txt

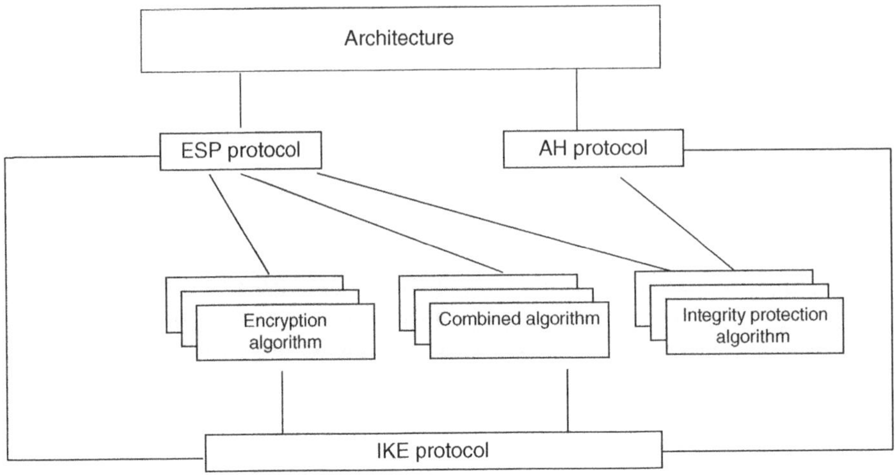

Figure 4.38 Relationship among the IPSec specifications (after RFC 6071).

for *Keyed-Hashing for Message Authentication* (*HMAC*) based on *Secure Hash Algorithm-1* (*SHA-1*), because of the weakness of *Message Digest 5* (*MD5*). Such open, full embrace of state-of-the-art cryptography seems natural today, but it actually took many years to achieve because of governmental restrictions that varied across different countries; cryptography has invariably been considered part of munitions, and its export has been regulated. Commercial and civilian users, if not banned from using cryptographic technology all together, were restricted to using weak and inadequate algorithms. Some governments had even mandated *key escrow* (i.e., disclosing keys to authorities). Given the global nature of the Internet, this situation did not help Internet security, and it prompted the IETF to publish an informational RFC to voice its concerns. This RFC[63] was assigned number 1984[64] intentionally.

Central to IPsec is the notion of *security association*. A security association is but a simplex end-to-end session that is cryptographically protected. Hence, a bidirectional session will need two security associations at least. To establish a security association involves the generation of cryptographic keys, choosing algorithms, and selecting quite a few parameters. In unicast, a security association is identifiable by a parameter known as the *Security Parameters Index* (*SPI*).

IPsec consists of two parts: *security association management* and *packet transformation*. The security association management part deals with authenticating IPsec endpoints and then setting up and maintaining security associations. An essential procedure here is negotiation of security services and agreement on the related security parameters. The whole procedure

[63] www.rfc-editor.org/rfc/rfc1984.txt

[64] As an echo of RFC 1984, the IETF later published RFC 2804 (www.rfc-editor.org/rfc/rfc2804.txt), declaring its stance on wiretapping standards.

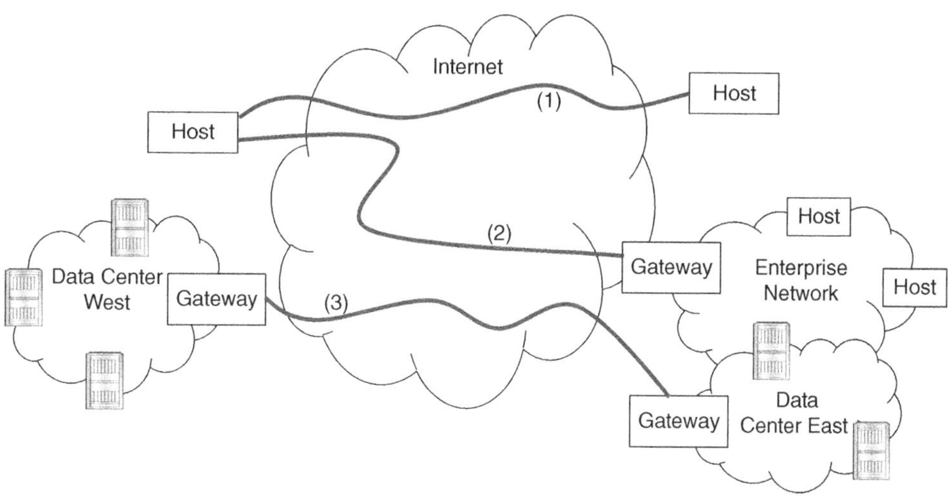

Figure 4.39 IPSec scenarios.

is performed at the beginning of an IPsec session and then, once in a while, afterward for a liveliness check. The corresponding protocol is complex, and its definition has gone through several iterations. Its present version, the *Internet Key Exchange Protocol version 2* (*IKEv2*), is specified in RFC 7296.[65] For a vivid explanation of how IKE works (and how it should have worked), [21] is again the best if not the only source.

The packet transformation part deals with the actual application of previously agreed on cryptographic algorithms to each packet. There are two distinct protocols for that task (which unfortunately reflects more on the standard's politics than necessity). One protocol, called *Authentication Header* (*AH*), is defined in RFC 4302.[66] AH provides connectionless integrity protection, data origin authentication, and an anti-replay service. But true to its name, it does not provide confidentiality protection.

In contrast, the second protocol, *Encapsulating Security Payload* (*ESP*), defined in RFC 4303,[67] does provide confidentiality protection as well as all other security services. As a result, ESP is far more widely used than AH. ESP is computationally intensive though, because of all this cryptographic work that it performs. There is hardware to speed this up, and since operating systems know best how to deal with this hardware, ESP has been implemented as part of the kernel in major operating systems.

Through ESP, secure communication becomes possible for three scenarios, explained below with the help of Figure 4.39.

The first scenario is *host-to-host.* Two mutually-authenticated hosts set up a session with each other using their pubic IP addresses over the Internet. Outsiders cannot eavesdrop or alter the traffic between them—as though there is a private communication line in use.

The second scenario is *host-to-gateway.* A remote host connects to a security gateway of an enterprise network over the Internet. The gateway has access to all other machines in

[65] www.rfc-editor.org/rfc/rfc7296.txt
[66] www.rfc-editor.org/rfc/rfc4302.txt
[67] www.rfc-editor.org/rfc/rfc4303.txt

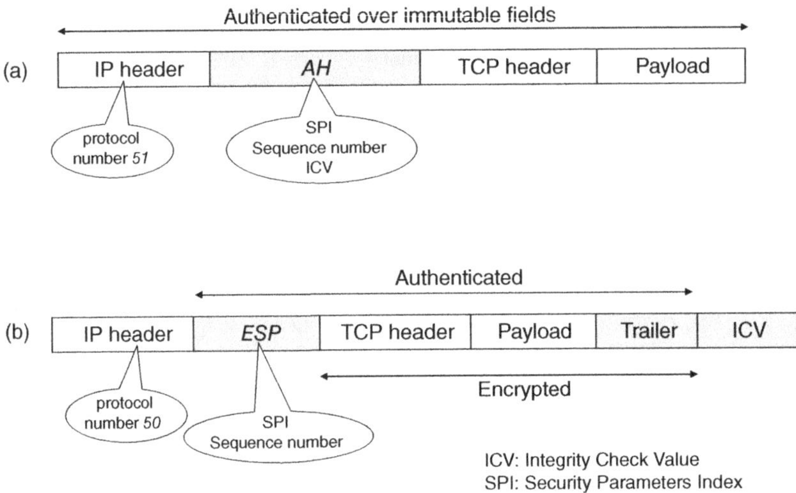

Figure 4.40 IPsec in transport mode in IPv4.

the network, and so once a tunnel is established, the host can communicate with them, too. This scenario is typical for the enterprise VPN access. (Returning to VPNs for a moment, it is precisely the mechanism of this scenario that enables secure IP-over-IP VPN. A private telephone circuit is replaced here by an IPsec tunnel.) As in the first scenario, the traffic is protected, but, unlike in the first scenario, the host may have a second IP address, which is significant only within the enterprise. In this case, the gateway also has two IP addresses—one for the hosts on the rest of the Internet, and one for the enterprise. The significance of this will become clear after we discuss NATs in the next chapter.

The third and last scenario is *gateway-to-gateway*. Two remote enterprise campuses are stitched over the Internet through their respective security gateways into an integral whole. This scenario is particularly relevant to Cloud Computing, since two data centers can be interconnected in exactly the same way. In essence, this scenario is similar to the second one, the only difference being that the tunnel carries aggregate rather than host-specific traffic.

IPsec supports two operational modes: transport and tunnel. In transport mode, each packet has only one IP header, and the IPsec header (either AH or ESP) is inserted right after it. To indicate the presence of the IPsec header, the protocol field in the IP header takes on the protocol number of AH or ESP. Figure 4.40 depicts the packet structure of IPsec in transport mode for IPv4. For an AH packet, the integrity check covers the immutable fields of the IP header, such as version, protocol, and source address.[68] The integrity check value is part of the authentication header, which also carries an SPI and a sequence number. The SPI serves as an index to a security association database entry that contains the parameters (e.g., the message authentication algorithm and key) for validating the AH packet. The purpose of the sequence number, which is unique for each packet, is replay protection. Note that the IPsec header does

[68] There is a serious complication here, which is caused by NATs, and therefore can be addressed only later when we discuss these.

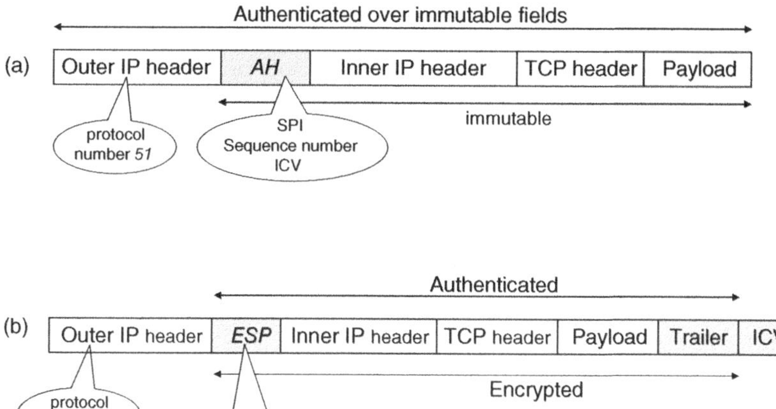

Figure 4.41 IPsec in tunnel mode in IPv4.

not contain information about what mode is in use. The information is stored in the security association database.

For an ESP packet, the integrity check covers everything beyond the IP header. Furthermore, the integrity check value is not part of the ESP header. It is supplied in a separate field.

In tunnel mode, there are two IP headers: an "inner" IP header carrying the ultimate IP source and destination addresses, and an "outer" IP header carrying the addresses of the IPsec endpoints. Figure 4.41 depicts the respective packet structures. (Figure 4.41 (a) is illustrative but not precisely correct. In addition to the immutable fields shown there, there are other immutable fields–such as Source IP address.)

One may wonder about the usefulness of AH given that ESP can do everything that AH can but not the other way around. One argument is that AH offers slightly more protection by protecting the IP header itself. Another argument is that AH works better with firewalls (which, again, we will discuss later). There are other arguments, too, but what matters in the end is that the main reason for using IPsec is confidentiality protection, and this is not a service that AH can provide. As far as the IPsec scenarios are concerned, the transport mode applies to scenario 1, while the tunnel mode applies to the rest.

So far, we have addressed the operation of IPsec only with IPv4. We can only say that the operation of IPsec with IPv6 is not really very different, except, of course, for the headers. In the space of this book we cannot delve into the intricacies of IPv6. Again, [21] has done an excellent job on that, elucidating the aspects caused by the IETF politics.

References

[1] Tanenbaum, A.S. and Van Steen, M. (2006) *Distributed Systems: Principles and Paradigms*, 2nd edn. Prentice Hall, Englewood Cliffs, NJ.

[2] Birman, K.P. (2012) *Guide to Reliable Distributed Systems: Building High-Assurance Applications and Cloud-Hosted Services*. Springer-Verlag, London.

[3] Faynberg, I., Lu, H.-L., and Gabuzda, L. (2000) *Converged Networks and Services: Internetworking IP and the PSTN*. John Wiley & Sons, New York.
[4] International Organization for Standardization (1994) International Standard ISO/IEC 7498-1: Information Technology—Open Systems Interconnection—Basic Reference Model: The Basic Model. International Organization for Standardization/International Electrotechnical Commission (ISO/IEC), Geneva. (Also published by the International Telecommunication Union—Telecommunication Standardization Sector (ITU-T) as ITU-T Recommendation X.200 (1994 E).
[5] Tanenbaum, A.S. and Wetherall, D.J. (2011) *Computer Networks*, 5th edn. Prentice Hall, Boston, MA.
[6] ITU-T (1996) ITU-T Recommendation X.25 (formerly CCITT), Interface between Data Terminal Equipment (DTE) and Data Circuit-terminating Equipment (DCE) for terminals operating in the packet mode and connected to public data networks by dedicated circuit. International Telecommunication Union, Geneva.
[7] Halsey, J.R., Hardy, L.E., and Powning, L.F. (1979) Public data networks: Their evolution, interfaces, and status. *IBM Systems Journal*, **18**(2), 223–243.
[8] Metcalfe, R.M. and Boggs, D. (1976) Ethernet: Distributed packet switching for local computer networks. *Communications of the ACM*, **19**(7), 395–405.
[9] Cerf, V. and Kahn, R. (1974) A protocol for packet network intercommunication. *IEEE Transactions on Communications*, **4**(5), 637–648.
[10] Information Sciences Institute, University of South California (1981) DoD Standard Internet Protocol. (Published by the IETF as RFC 791), Marina Dely Rey.
[11] Huston, G. (1999) Interconnection, peering and settlements—Part II. *The Internet Protocol Technical Journal*, **2**(2), 2–23.
[12] Turner, J.S. (1986) Design of an integrated services *packet* network. *IEEE Journal on Selected Areas in Communications*, **SAC-4**(A), 1373–1380.
[13] Clark, D.D., Shenker, S.S., and Zhang, L. (1992) Supporting real-time applications in an integrated services packet network: Architecture and mechanism. SIGCOMM '92 Conference Proceedings on Communications Architectures & Protocols, pp. 14–26.
[14] Stiliadis, D. and Varma, A. (1998) Latency-rate servers: A general model for analysis of traffic scheduling algorithms. *IEEE/ACM Transactions on Networking (TON)*, **6**(5), 611–662.
[15] Rekhter, Y., Davie, B., Rosen, E., *et al.* (1997) Tag switching architecture overview. *Proceedings of the IEEE*, **85**(12), 1973–1983.
[16] Lu, H.-L. and Faynberg, I. (2003) An architectural framework for support of quality of service in packet networks. *Communications Magazine, IEEE*, **41**(6), 98–105.
[17] Farrel, A. and Bryskin, I. (2006) *GMPLS: Architecture and Applications*. The Morgan Kaufmann Series in Networking. Elsevier, San Francisco, CA.
[18] Faynberg, I., Gabuzda, L.R., Kaplan, M.P., and Shah, N. (1996) *The Intelligent Network Standards: Their Applications to Services*. McGraw-Hill, New York.
[19] Lakshman, T., Nandagopal, T., Sabnani, K., and Woo, T. (2004) The SoftRouter Architecture. ACM SIGCOM HotNets, San Diego, CA. http://conferences.sigcomm.org/hotnets/2004/HotNets-III%20Proceedings/lakshman.pdf.
[20] McKeown, N., Anderson, T., Balakrishnan, H., *et al.* (2008) OpenFlow: Enabling innovation in campus networks. *ACM SIGCOMM Computer Communication Review*, **38**(2), 69–74.
[21] Kaufman, C., Perlman, R., and Speciner, M. (2002) *Network Security: Private Communications in a Public World*. Prentice Hall PTR, Upper Saddle River, NJ.
[22] Schneier, B. (1995) *Applied Cryptography: Protocols, Algorithms, and Source Code in C*. John & Wiley Sons, New York.

5

Networking Appliances

All the appliances described here are the building blocks of modern data centers. They enable both the establishment of network boundaries and the deployment of applications. In both physical and virtual form, they also enable Cloud Computing inasmuch as networking is its essential component.

The first critical network appliance, described in Section 5.1, is the *Domain Name System* (*DNS*) server. To access any resource on the Internet (a web page, a mailbox, a telephone to receive a call), one ultimately needs to specify an IP address of the resource. An application, however, is not supposed to know it (and rarely does). Instead, it uses a *resource locator*—a character string specified according to the application-layer naming scheme. The locator is then translated by the DNS into an associated IP address in real time. A few benefits of such an arrangement, beyond supporting names that are easy for humans to remember, is that it supports resource mobility and can also be utilized, in support of elasticity, for *load balancing*—that is, the distribution of effort among several servers that perform identical operations. But, the translation service is not the only benefit of DNS—it is also used for *service discovery*, which makes the DNS infrastructure particularly critical for networking and Cloud Computing.

The second appliance described in this chapter is called a *firewall*. Firewalls are major implements of security—particularly when it comes to network isolation and protection.

Third comes the discussion of the *Network Address Translation* (*NAT*) appliance—one that is as controversial as it is necessary, what with the fast-depleting IPv4 address space. Although NATs are almost exclusively implemented in firewalls, they are different in their function.

We conclude the chapter with a brief review of the *load balancer* appliance, which in large part enables elasticity of the Cloud. Inasmuch as the space of this manuscript allows, we review different flavors of load balancing, finishing with the load balancing performed solely by DNS servers.

5.1 Domain Name System

The major motivation for developing DNS came from e-mail, or rather its particular implementation. Even though e-mail has existed as a service in one from or another since the

---

Cloud Computing: Business Trends and Technologies, First Edition. Igor Faynberg, Hui-Lan Lu and Dor Skuler.

mid-1960s it was Ray Tomlinson[1] who, while developing the e-mail package for the TENEX operating system, defined a *resource locator* of the form <*user*>@<*host*>, in which the "@" character separates the ASCII-encoded user name and host name. This form of addressing became standard in the ARPANET in 1972, when e-mail support was incorporated into the *File Transfer Protocol* (*FTP*), as codified in RFC 385.[2]

Of course, for e-mail to function, it was essential that the host name be translated into a proper IP address. Each host kept a copy of the translation file, which apparently was not much of a problem at the time: in 1971, there were only 23 hosts on the ARPANET. But two years later, in 1973, Peter Deutsch wrote in RFC 606:[3] "Now that we finally have an official list of host names, it seems about time to put an end to the absurd situation where each site on the network must maintain a different, generally out-of-date, host list for the use of its own operating system or user programs."

Indeed, that "absurd situation" came to an end. After several RFCs written in response to RFC 606,[4] a one-pager RFC 625,[5] published on March 7, 1974, confirmed that the Stanford Research Institute (now SRI Corporation[6]) will keep the master copy of the host translation file, called *HOST.txt*, which will be made available to other hosts. RFC 625 insisted that (1) the file be maintained in the ASCII text form and (2) the FTP protocol be used to access the file.

Seven years later, that solution started to look absurd, too, but for a very different reason. The culprit was the e-mail addressing system, now standardized, in which the sender had to spell out the whole relaying path to the receiver.[7] Not only was this process cumbersome, but it was technically impossible for any human to find the right path when a given path failed.

DNS history was made on January 11, 1982, when 22 Internet engineers participated in a meeting called by Jon Postel[8] "to discuss a few specific issues in text mail systems for the ARPA Internet." RFC 805,[9] from which the above quotation is taken, is a remarkable record of the discussion and decisions. The first specific issue mentioned was relaying of e-mail, and the RFC listed several proposals, noting that "One of the interesting ideas that emerged from this discussion was that the '*user@host*' model of a mailbox identifier should, in principle, be replaced by a '*unique-id@location-id*' model, where the unique-id would be a globally unique id for this mailbox (independent of location) and the location-id would be advice about where to find the mailbox." This idea was not pursued because "... it was recognized that the

[1] http://openmap.bbn.com/~tomlinso/ray/firstemailframe.html

[2] www.rfc-editor.org/rfc/rfc385.txt

[3] www.rfc-editor.org/rfc/rfc606.txt

[4] In those days, the RFC series seemed not only to inform or postulate but also to serve the development community as a discussion medium.

[5] www.rfc-editor.org/rfc/rfc625.txt

[6] www.sri.com/

[7] In 1981, Jon Postel published the first version of the *Simple Mail Transfer Protocol* (*SMTP*) in RFC 788 (www.rfc-editor.org/rfc/rfc78Atxt). The relaying of e-mail was accomplished by specifying the relaying path explicitly. (The RFC gives an example of the "*TO:*" field as *TO: <@A, @B, C@D.*)

[8] Dr Postel and Dr Mockapetris are the two men who led the DNS development. With that, the general idea and concept apparently belonged to Dr Postel, and the design and subsequent program management to Dr Mockapetris.

[9] www.rfc-editor.org/rfc/rfc805.txt

'user@host' model was well established and … so many different elaborations of the 'user' field were already in use."[10]

There was agreement, however, "that the current '*user@host*' mailbox identifier should be extended to user@host.domain, where '*domain*' could be a hierarchy of domains. In particular, the 'host' field would become a 'location' field and the structure would read (left to right) from the most specific to the most general." It was the job of specialized databases—*name servers*—to store the information related to domains and provide it when queried. The most remarkable part of this vision was (and, in our opinion, still is) the concept of separation of a service from the host that provides that service. Ultimately, this enabled the implementation of the World-Wide Web 25 years later, followed by that of IP telephony, IPTV, and, ultimately, the Cloud. With only e-mail as a solid reference point, envisioning a system that would support a multitude of abstract services is an act that fits the definition of a genius in the narrative of Vladimir Nabokov's novel, *Gift* [1]: "Genius is an African who dreams up snow." RFC 882 says: "We should be able to use names to retrieve host addresses, mailbox data, and other as yet undetermined information."

With respect to the envisioned queries, three separate services were identified, but the agreement was that only one of these services—the one that translated the hostname location-id into the respective IP address—was essential at the moment. It was also recognized that the name servers could return other information (such as that for mail procedures employed at the host), although this information could be obtained in other ways, too.

A critical architecture decision was made on the issue of *central* vs. *distributed* implementation of the name query: "It is recognized that having separate servers for each domain has administrative and maintenance advantages, but that a central server may be a useful first step. It is also recognized that each distinct database should be replicated a few times and be available from distinct servers for robust and reliable service." It was in this document that the name *recursive server* first appeared, in the context of the following example:

> "Suppose that the new mailbox specification is of the form USER@HOST.ORG.DOMAIN. e.g., Postel@F.ISI.IN. A source host sending mail to this address first queries a name server for the domain IN (giving the whole location 'F.ISI.IN'). The result of the query is either (1) the final address of the destination host (F.ISI), or (2) the address of a name server for ISI, or (3) the address of a forwarder for ISI. In cases 1 and 3, the source host sends the mail to the address returned. In case 2, the source host queries the ISI name server and … (recursive call to this paragraph)."

With a few major requirements for the system coming out of that meeting, its design principles and implementation considerations were respectively laid out in RFC 882[11] and RFC 883,[12] both authored by Paul Mockapetris, who took on the task of designing DNS. Both documents[13]

---

[10] In effect, the idea was to make the address a combination of two identifiers: the *uniform resource name* (*URN*)—the unique e-mail identity of a mailbox—together with the *uniform resource locator*. As we will soon see, these identifiers were later developed independently.

[11] www.rfc-editor.org/rfc/rfc882.txt

[12] www.rfc-editor.org/rfc/rfc881.txt

[13] These RFCs were superseded by RFC 1034 (www.rfc-editor.org/rfc/rfc1034.txt) and RFC 1035 (www.rfc-editor.org/rfc/rfc1035.txt).

were published in November 1983, and at the same time Jon Postel published the project management document, RFC 881,[14] with the plan to both complete the rollout of DNS in ARPANET and discontinue the maintenance of the HOST.TXT file a year after—in December 1984.

The first issue of DNS software, *Berkeley Internet Domain Name* (*BIND*), was released by the University of California at Berkeley. Later versions of BIND were written at Digital Equipment Corporation, and, finally, the development of BIND moved into the *Internet Systems Consortium*.[15] It is now an open-source project.

In the years that followed, the standards have evolved along with their implementations, but the changes were incremental, except for one major change concerned with security. Indeed, security was neither a requirement nor a concern initially—scalability was. Hence, security was an add-on, unfortunately, and it was specified as a reaction after a serious vulnerability was exploited. A security solution, called *DNSSEC* (which we will discuss in more detail later), had been published by the IETF in 2005, although there were serious problems in the way of its deployment. DNSSEC is also only a partial solution. As we will see, a number of threats can be mitigated with firewalls, but much still depends—and will depend—on consistent implementations of security practices by both network providers and their customers. To this end, Cloud can help implement and enforce security policies consistently.

The rest of this section explains the DNS architecture and operation, and then—as an important aside—also introduces the top-level domain classification and the issue of internationalization of domain names. The discussion of security issues and DNSSEC is in the last section.

5.1.1 Architecture and Protocol

The components of the DNS architecture are depicted in Figure 5.1. The component that is closest to the end user is the *resolver*, which the application process queries. The resolver is expected to be (and typically is) part of an operating system, and therefore no protocol between the application process and the resolver is defined for the interface between the two. It is rather a matter of an application program interface.

A resolver, in turn, gets the information the process needs by querying one or more *name servers*. The responses are stored in the local cache, as it is natural to expect that there be more than one reference to resources in a particular domain. The cache keeps the information for a time not to exceed the value of the *Time-To-Live* (*TTL*) parameter of the record it stores. When the query arrives at the resolver, it first checks if it has the record in the cache. If not, it starts querying the name servers using the DNS protocol (which, by the way, operates over UDP, using standard port 50[16]).

The name servers implement the *domain name space* and they contain the *resource records* associated with the names. The DNS has been designed for the exponential growth of the name space in time; consequently, the domain name space is implemented as a tree structure. As RFC 1034 puts it, "Conceptually, each node and leaf of the domain name space tree names

[14] www.rfc-editor.org/rfc/rfc881.txt

[15] www.isc.org/

[16] For long queries, TCP is used, but this is an exception.

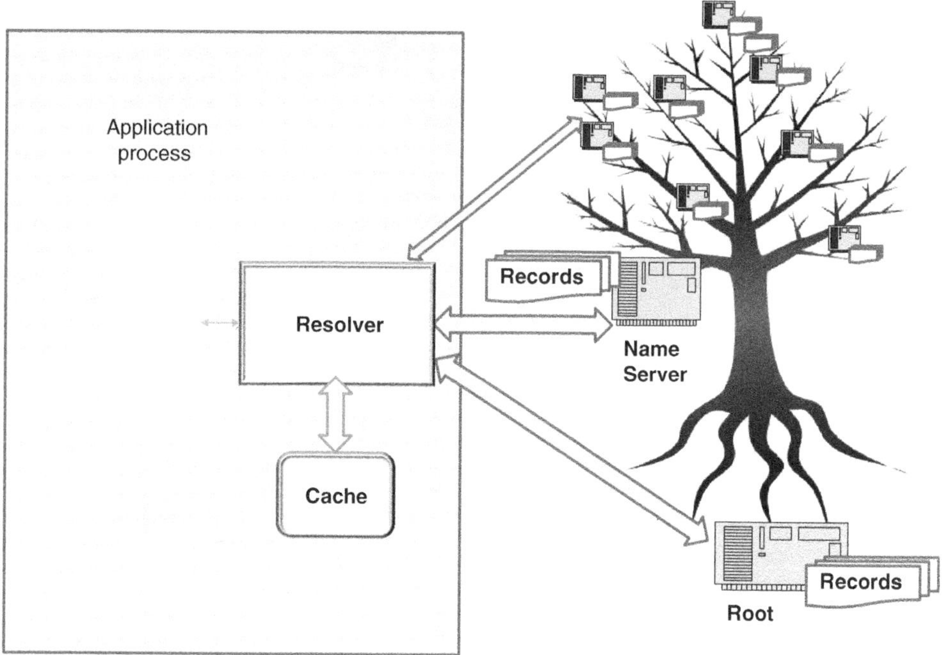

Figure 5.1 DNS components.

a set of information, and query operations are attempts to extract specific types of information from a particular set."

Figure 5.2 elucidates this model further. A name server is responsible for a subset of the domain space, called a *zone*, and this name server is called an *authority* (or an *authoritative name server*) for that zone. In addition to providing zone-related information, a name server provides addresses to other name servers—outside its zone.

A zone administrator can create other zones, thus establishing another branch in the tree. According to RFC 1034, "the database is partitioned at points where a particular organization wants to take over control of a sub-tree. Once an organization controls its own zone it can unilaterally change the data in the zone, grow new tree sections connected to the zone, delete existing nodes, or delegate new subzones under its zone."

To ensure reliability, redundancy is introduced by keeping several identical *slave* name servers in the zone, which are automatically updated by the *master* server.

The syntax of the *domain name*, which is an alphanumeric string, corresponds strictly to the domain name space tree in that a locator of every resource spells out the full path from the root of the tree. Each node of the tree has a *label* (up to 63 bytes in length). Note that the root label is of length *zero*—it is an empty string. The domain name is a sequence of labels spelled—by a long-established convention stemming from early e-mail addressing—from right to the left. Hence the rightmost label always corresponds to the top-level domain.

Let us look at an example, www.stevens.edu, and ask what exactly the label of the top-level domain is here. (No, it is *not* "edu"!) Actually, it is an empty string—as it is supposed to be,

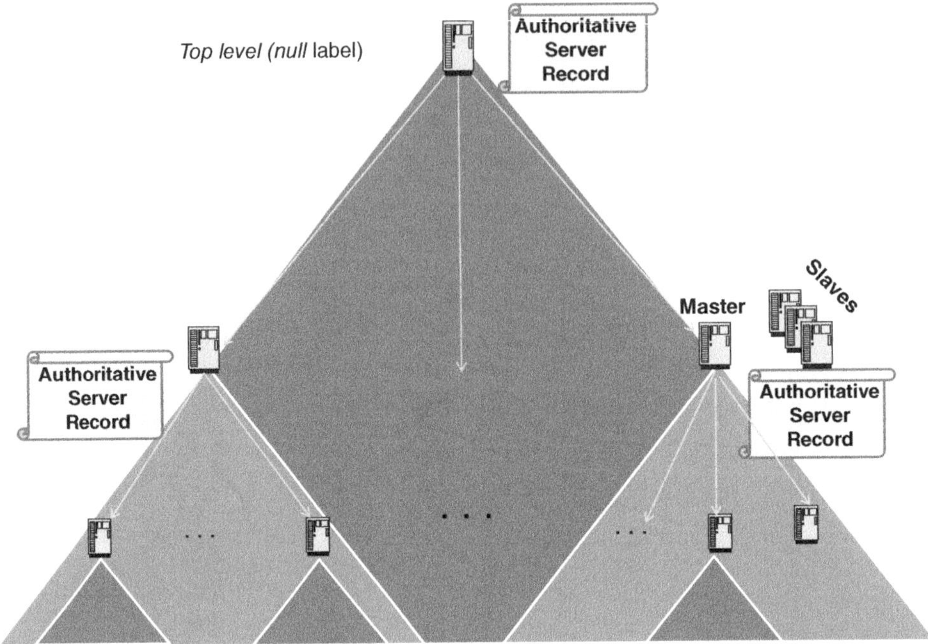

Figure 5.2 The domain name space tree.

by definition, but the above address is technically misspelled, even though existing browsers would make up for that. In other words, the correct (or *fully qualified*) name would have the dot (.) on the right—as in 'www.stevens.edu.' The dot is almost invariably omitted now (it looks a bit redundant, and it is), but in the early days this omission was of concern for a potential security problem raised by RFC 1535.[17]

Labels are case-insensitive.[18] Thus, www.StEVenS.eDU is resolved the same way as www.stevens.edu. By definition, a *hostname* is a domain name that has at least one IP address associated with it. Not every domain name is a hostname (e.g., neither *.com* nor *.edu* is). With the domain name internationalization, the way in which domain names are expressed has grown to adapt to multiple languages and their respective alphabets.

We have mentioned the client side of DNS so far only in the context of the resolver, which keeps querying the servers[19] until it finds the address. But the need to smooth the network traffic—especially in the presence of short, simple queries—demanded the introduction of a

[17] www.ietf.org/rfc/rfc1535.txt. Back then, BIND resolvers, upon encountering a name that was not fully specified, attempted to resolve it by searching a list of fully formed domains until a match was found. That made it possible to end up in an unexpected place. Thus, the location of "host.edu.com" could be returned when resolving "host.edu." An attacker could register the "host.edu" name under the .com domain and impersonate the intended domain. This specific problem has been solved; nonetheless the example is very illustrative of the vulnerabilities in DNS.

[18] Please see clarification related to escape sequences and other delicacies in RFC 4343 (www.tools.ietf.org/rfc/rfc4343.txt).

[19] As we saw earlier, this—essentially iterative—process was called *recursive* early in the definition of DNS, and the name has stuck.

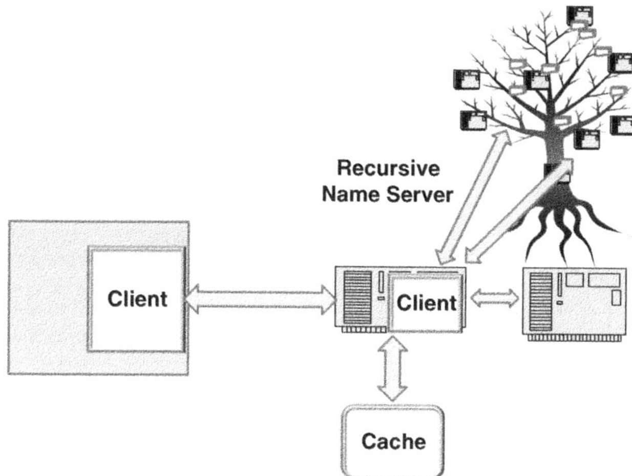

Figure 5.3 A recursive name server.

name server that can operate in the "recursive mode" (that is, itself act as a client, querying multiple servers before returning an answer). A recursive name server (depicted in Figure 5.3) also caches answers. Unfortunately, both cache-keeping and open recursive service provision have become enablers of security attacks, which we will review later in this chapter.

The default (and mandatory-to-implement) mode for a name server is non-recursive. In this mode, it answers queries using only local information. It responds by providing either (a) an answer, (b) an error, or (c) a referral to another server. To use the recursive mode, both clients and the server must agree to it.

To demystify the DNS operation, we will introduce the basics of the DNS protocol.

Figure 5.4 presents the common format of both DNS queries and DNS responses. Aligned on the 16-bit boundary are the main sections of the protocol data unit.

The most involved section is the *Header*, which contains the:

- identification (*ID*) of the unit, so as to correlate replies with outstanding queries;
- tag bit (*QR*), which indicates whether the unit is a query or a response;
- *OPCODE*, which specifies the query;[20]
- flag (*AA*), which is meaningful only in responses that indicate whether the response is authoritative;
- *truncation* flag (set if the message has been truncated because it was longer than permitted by the domain);
- two flags—*Recursion Desired* (*RD*) and *Recursion Available* (*RA*), of which the former is used only in a query directing the name server to pursue the query recursively, and the latter comes in responses indicating whether the server actually supports recursive queries—the Z-bit is reserved for future use and expected to be zero;
- *RCODE*, which specifies the response code; and

[20] DNS, for example, was initially designed to support inverse queries, but this feature has been deprecated.

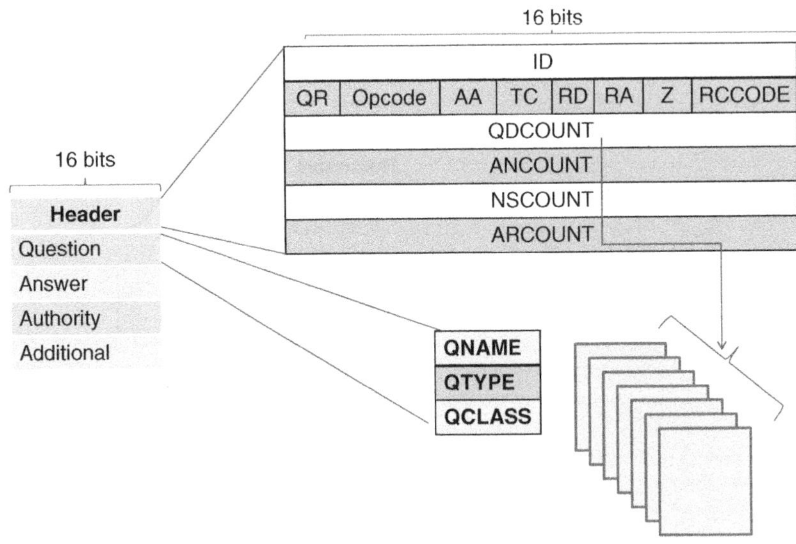

Figure 5.4 The DNS query/response format. Source: RFC 1035.

- *QDCOUNT*, *ANCOUNT*, *NSCOUNT*, and *ARCOUNT*, integers respectively specifying the number of entries in the subsequent sections (*Question*, *Answer*, *Authority*, and *Additional*).

The *Question* section is an array (of size *QDCOUNT*) of records that contain *QNAME* (a domain name), *QTYPE* (more on this when we discuss the resource records), and *QCLASS*, which for all practical purposes always has a value of *IN* (for Internet).[21]

The *Answer*, *Authority*, and *Additional* sections are identical in that each contains a set of *Resource Records* (*RRs*).

The RR structure is demonstrated in Figure 5.5, which is for the most part self-explanatory. The record TYPE is one field, which has been gaining new values. One example is *A*—for IPv4 addresses, later supplemented by *AAAA*—for IPv6 addresses. Other examples are *Start of Authority* (*SOA*), *CERT* (for cryptographic certificates), and *SERV* (for services). The latter, specified by RFC 2782,[22] allows us to specify the location of servers performing specified services. This feature can be very helpful both with e-mail and IP telephony, where a resource locator (explained later in this section) can be used to discover a specific domain-offering service.

Playing with the strings may become complex (as all compiler writers know). One problem, depicted in Figure 5.6, is *circular dependencies*, which arise when a name server returns a name reference that points back to the original domain to be resolved. For this, RFC 1035 postulates that in such cases *glue* (i.e., actual addresses) be specified in the referral.

---

[21] The IETF has discouraged the use of alternative root name servers in RFC 2826 (www.ietf.org/rfc/rfc2826.txt), and highly controversial *AlterNIC* and *eDNS* root servers have been closed. Attempts to build alternative root servers still exist; one of them being for "bit" *bitcoin* operations (http://dot-bit.org/Main_Page).

[22] www.ietf.org/rfc/rfc2782.txt

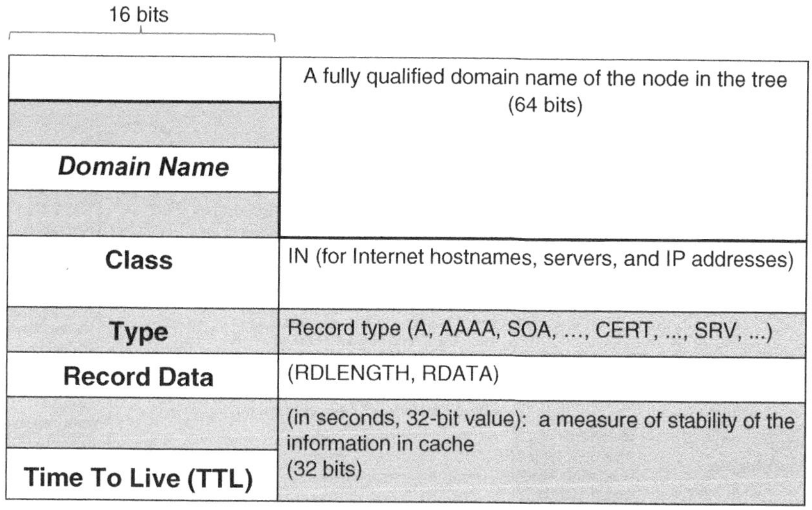

16 bits

Field	Description
Domain Name	A fully qualified domain name of the node in the tree (64 bits)
Class	IN (for Internet hostnames, servers, and IP addresses)
Type	Record type (A, AAAA, SOA, ..., CERT, ..., SRV, ...)
Record Data	(RDLENGTH, RDATA)
Time To Live (TTL)	(in seconds, 32-bit value): a measure of stability of the information in cache (32 bits)

Figure 5.5 The RR structure. Source: RFC 1035.

The *Time-to-Live* (*TTL*) parameter is one interesting example where an early (1983) specification had to be changed. It was found that a 16-bit integer was, too small to specify the appropriate time value in seconds, and so the field grew to 32 bits.

Figure 5.7 provides an example of resolving a query to a recursive name server to find an IP address of the domain www.cs.stevens.edu.

The process starts from the root, **h.root-servers.net** [12A63.2.53]. (The significance of the letter "h" in front of the name is explained in the next section.) The response contains a set of referrals to the servers supporting the ".edu" domain. One such referral record is "edu. 172800 IN NS d.edu-servers.net." (Note the high value of TTL—the higher the level, the more stable the records are.)

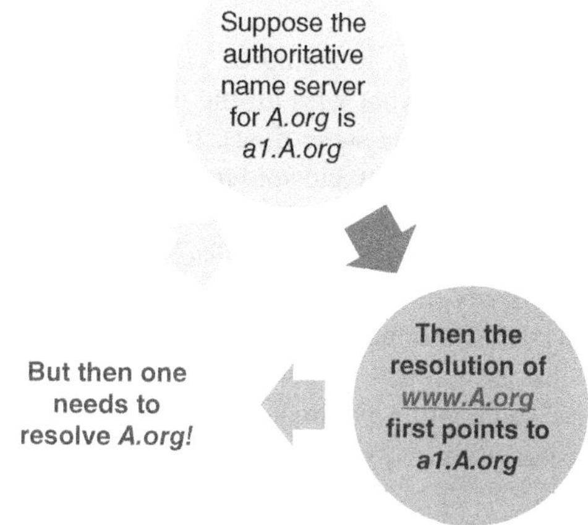

Figure 5.6 Circular dependencies.

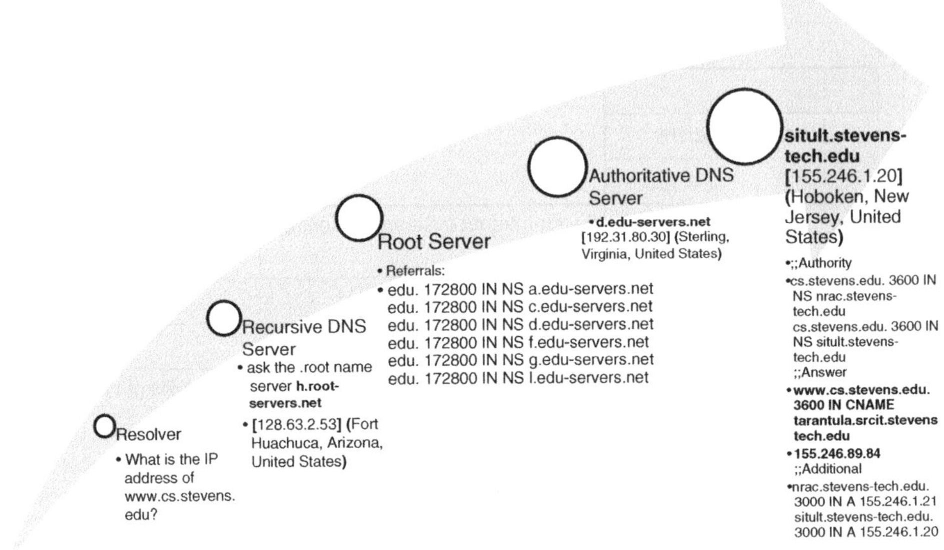

Figure 5.7 A sample name resolution.

The query to the referred server resolves to the authoritative name servers (later supplemented by their IP addresses as *glue*) and then the canonical (i.e., primary) domain name record: *www.cs.stevens.edu. 3600 IN CNAME tarantula.srcit.stevens-tech.edu*, which we encounter for the first time now. This feature is needed to support alias names, as a given domain can provide different services under different names. CNAME merely points to the canonical domain name (in our example, *tarantula.srcit.stevens-tech.edu*). The next query must have that name. Finally, we get the IP address in the A record (*155.246.89.8*).

5.1.2 DNS Operation

Based on what we have reviewed so far, it should be clear that running a top-level domain server is a formidable technical task (what with all the databases that need to be replicated across the borders and kept secure at the same time). But technical complexities aside, the mere fact that domain names can be bought and sold has naturally complicated things.

Once DNS was adopted, Jon Postel founded the *Internet Assigned Numbers Authority* (*IANA*),[23] which has, among its many tasks, administered the root zone. In 1998, IANA became a department of the newly created *Internet Corporation for Assigned Names and Numbers* (*ICANN*),[24] which performs, among other services under a US government contract: "(1) the coordination of the assignment of technical protocol parameters including the management of the address and routing parameter area (ARPA) top-level domain; (2) the administration of certain responsibilities associated with Internet DNS root zone management

[23] www.iana.org/about

[24] www.icann.org/en/about/welcome

System Name	IP Addresses	Manager
a.root-servers.net	198.41.0.4, 2001:503:ba3e::2:30	VeriSign, Inc.
b.root-servers.net	192.228.79.201	University of Southern California (ISI)
c.root-servers.net	192.33.4.12	Cogent Communications
d.root-servers.net	199.7.91.13, 2001:500:2d::d	University of Maryland
e.root-servers.net	192.203.230.10	NASA (Ames Research Center)
f.root-servers.net	192.5.5.241, 2001:500:2f::f	Internet Systems Consortium, Inc.
g.root-servers.net	192.112.36.4	US Department of Defence (NIC)
h.root-servers.net	128.63.2.53, 2001:500:1::803f:235	US Army (Research Lab)
i.root-servers.net	192.36.148.17, 2001:7fe::53	Netnod
j.root-servers.net	192.58.128.30, 2001:503:c27::2:30	VeriSign, Inc.
k.root-servers.net	193.0.14.129, 2001:7fd::1	RIPE NCC
l.root-servers.net	199.7.83.42, 2001:500:3::42	ICANN
m.root-servers.net	202.12.27.33, 2001:dc3::35	WIDE Project

Figure 5.8 Root name systems. Source: Internet Assigned Number Authority, www.iana.org

such as generic (gTLD) and country code (ccTLD) Top-Level Domains; [and] (3) the allocation of Internet numbering resources ..."

The *Top-Level Domain* (*TLD*) names correspond to the DNS root zone. The information about all top TLDs is replicated on 13 root servers (or rather *root systems*, as we will explain shortly) named by the respective letters of the alphabet—"A" through "M." Each of these servers has a name, starting from this letter, to which the suffix "*.root-servers.net*" is appended. To initialize the cache of a resolver (or a recursive DNS server), one can obtain a *hint* file with the appropriate IP addresses from www.internic.net/zones/named.root. The systems, along with their respective operators, and the contact IPv4 and IPv6 addresses, are listed in Figure 5.8.

It is a common mistake to think that the servers are single hosts (although this was the case long ago). With one exception,[25] they are replicated among different servers around the world, with the total number presently approaching 400. For this reason, the word "server" is a misnomer, and it is much better to refer to a *system* instead. (The L-system alone has 146 servers covering all continents!) In fact, most root systems operate as networks—they have AS numbers and enter peering agreements. Often, anycast IP addressing is used to find the machine that is the closest to the issuer of the query. There is a fascinating site, www.root-servers.org/, which provides detailed information on the location and operation of the root domain.

[25] *B.root-servers.net* has a single location.

There is no *master* system or master server at the top domain.[26] All root systems (or rather, actual hosts within each of them) have the same knowledge about the address records of the name servers authoritative for all existing TLDs. All the hosts are updated from the same set of files maintained by the administering organization, VeriSign Inc. (as a contractor). The DNS root operates under the authority of the *National Telecommunications and Information Administration* (*NTIA*), an agency of the US Department of Commerce.

5.1.3 Top-Level Domain Labels

Edu is an example of a TLD, whose use is reserved for accredited colleges and universities. *Mil* and *gov* are other examples of top-level domains with strictly controlled registries; these are respectively reserved for the US military and US government agencies. Some domains, such as *com* or *biz* (for business), were initially reserved for one purpose (in our example, commercial companies), but ended up being open to all. Ditto for *net*, which was initially created to designate networks but ended up being used for all kinds of purposes.

The history of the control over top-level domain names became rather tumultuous around 1998—with e-commerce developing and different groups (including a group of IETF engineers and Internet enthusiasts, who thought that the Internet belonged to *them*) asserting themselves. We have neither the space nor the time to address this history here, suffice it to note that ICANN was created for, among other things, managing TLDs. (The excerpt from the ICANN mission statement cited earlier should become clear now.)

ICANN distinguishes several groups of TLDs. The *generic* ones (gTLD) include the labels we use most, such as *com*, *net*, *edu*, and so on. The *country code TLDs* (*ccTLDs*) are based on the two-character ISO country codes. The *infrastructure TLDs* (under the name *arpa*, which the reader may remember from the ICANN mission statement) are used mostly for the reverse look-up of IP addresses. CcTLDs also exist in their respective internationalized versions (which we will discuss shortly), as does a special *test* domain created for testing internationalization. Finally, RFC 2606[27] defines domains created for nothing else but testing, self-reference, and reference as examples:[28] "... four domain names are reserved as listed and described below ...

- '.test' is recommended for use in testing of current or new DNS related code;
- '.example' is recommended for use in documentation or as examples;
- '.invalid' is intended for use in online construction of domain names that are sure to be invalid and which [sic] it is obvious at a glance are invalid;
- '.localhost' has traditionally been statically defined in host DNS implementations as having an A record pointing to the loop-back IP address and is reserved for such use."

As we noted before, some gTLDs (such as *.com* or *.net*) ended up registering anyone and anything, and so judging by the label alone it is impossible to infer much about the entity

---

[26] In the early days of DNS, the A server (which was then just a server) was the master.

[27] www.ietf.org/rfc/rfc2606.txt

[28] This has been done to avoid copyright and trademark violation and to prevent other potential legal problems when one uses "real" domain names in examples.

registered under the domain. Such gTLDs are called *unsponsored*, as opposed to *sponsored* gTLDs (such as *.edu*, *.mil*, or *.int*—the latter reserved for international organizations created by treaties), which have specific communities or interest groups associated with such domains. It is a community for a sponsored gTLD that defines the policies determining eligibility for registration and enforces such policies.

And even then there are problems. An interesting and often-cited example is a gTLD named *.xxx*, dedicated to pornography and sponsored by the *International Foundation for Online Responsibility* (*IFFOR*). The domain was finally approved by ICANN in 2011 after a long controversy (just six years before then, the ICANN Board voted against the approval). The argument for its creation was that if a site is explicitly dedicated to pornography, it is easy to block it when needed (e.g., by parents or a company's IT organization). The counter-argument was that nothing prevented the same material from being redistributed in a non-sponsored site (such as *.com*). The most interesting fact about this site is that there are at least two examples of registrants whose content has nothing to do with pornography. One is www.kite.xxx, which focuses "100% on kite sports with an eye for product design." There is a speculation that the site was created tongue-in-cheek merely to point out that there is no restriction on the domain; another speculation is that being present in *that* gTLD is a good attention-getter. Go figure ...

But even stranger things happen on that domain! According to the March 19, 2012 article in *The Register*®[29], the domain registered as *PopeBenedict.xxx* was to promote ... Islam. Apparently, this was a clear case of cyber-squatting as "A Turkish cyber-squatter has registered at least a dozen variants of Pope Benedict's name as .xxx internet domains ..." All domains were offered for sale. The registrar then reserved the names that might deal with religion (such as *anglican.xxx*, *vatican.xxx*, or *jewish.xxx*) so as to prevent their registration.

Things are not quite simple to understand with the ccTLD either. What does it take to register under a particular country name? It turns out that there is no simple answer. Some countries require proof of citizenship for registration (e.g., Albania for TLD *.al*). Others (e.g., Estonia for *.ee* or Germany for *.de*) require only the physical presence in the country of a local administrative contact. Still there are countries, such as Eritrea, that offer no registry services at all. To make things more confusing, countries can sell their TLDs. A well-known example is Tokelau's sale of its domain, *.tk*, to a Dutch company DOT.TK, which was reported to host spammers by Darren Pauli in his online article.[30]

An important development in the history of domain names is their *internationalization*, or the ability of users to employ the scripts of their respective languages. There are two aspects to this: (1) the encoding of a native script so that it can be displayed on a monitor by a browser (as in .中国); (2) the interworking of the script with the actual DNS use.

Support for internationalized scripts on terminals and keyboards has been around since the 1970s. There were various proprietary implementations around—for computer terminals built by various manufacturers—but a standard encoding scheme called *Unicode* has been developed for that purpose by the Unicode Consortium.[31] As for interworking with DNS, apparently the first proposal was published as an IETF Internet Draft in 1996 by M. Dürst[32].

---

[29] www.theregister.co.uk/2012/03/19/pope_benedict_cybersquatter

[30] http://m.zdnet.com.au/pacific-atoll-a-phishing-haven-339313909.htm

[31] www.unicode.org

[32] Available at http://tools.ietf.org/id/draft-duerst-dns-i18n-00.txt.

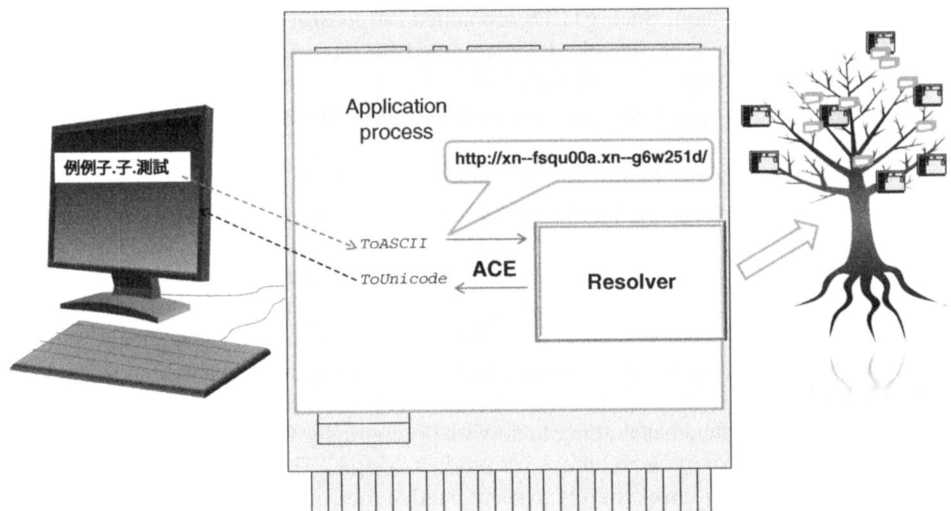

Figure 5.9 Domain name internationalization components. Source: RFC 3490.

Much has been achieved since then, with the major standard for *Internationalizing Domain Names in Applications* (*IDNA*) published as RFC 3490.[33] The overarching idea is the addition of new features without any modification of the existing infrastructure. In other words, only application programs change—not the DNS system. To this end, the latter uses *only* ASCII-encoded (not Unicode-encoded) labels.

Figure 5.9 demonstrates the components and illustrates the operation of IDNA.

When the user types in the domain name in whatever language or script he or she chooses, it is the job of the application (typically, the browser) to convert the Unicode labels into *ASCII-Compatible-Encoding* (*ACE*) strings, and vice versa. The mapping is specified by *Punicode*, defined in RFC 3492[34] in 2003 and later updated. The *ToASCII* algorithm converts the Unicode-encoded string into a unique ASCII-encoded string, and appends the result to the four-character prefix ("*xn–*"), so all IDNA labels start with these four characters. Conversely, the *ToUnicode* algorithm strips off the ACE prefix and converts the rest into a Unicode-encoded string.

It is the browser's job to perform conversions so that the whole DNS system—starting from the resolver—remains unaffected.[35] *ToASCII* is executed on a string received from the user; *ToUnicode* is executed on a string received from the resolver.

A major problem with internationalization (as is typical for all major computing problems) is security, and the specific problem here is spoofing. Even with plain ASCII, some characters (e.g., "l" and "1") look alike in certain fonts. This could be exploited: one might create a

[33] www.ietf.org/rfc/rfc3490.txt

[34] www.ietf.org/rfc/rfc3492.txt

[35] Actually, Punicode was designed to be applied not only to the domain labels but also to other strings used by various applications so as to provide support for internationalized URIs, which will be discussed later in the book.

www.paypa1.com site that looks exactly like the *www.paypal.com* site and lure (for instance, through e-mail) unsuspecting people to it, who will thus divulge their passwords.[36]

With internationalization, things get more serious. Can the reader see the difference between *www.paypal.com* and *www.paypal.com*? The authors certainly can't. Both strings look exactly the same on paper and on the computer screen, which is exactly the problem—the second domain name actually contains a Cyrillic character "*a*" in place of the same-looking Latin alphabet character. (The character was entered into this manuscript in Unicode). If we compare the bit strings that correspond to these domain names, we find that they are different. Words that are spelled the same but have different meanings are called *homographs*. This definition has been broadened in computing to indicate strings that look the same. An ACM Communications article [2] reported on an existing *homographic* attack and warned of their possibilities in the internationalized domain name system.

Perhaps attacks could be prevented if all browsers forbade the use of combinations of Unicode characters that belong to different alphabets in the same label, but this would be hard to enforce. The solution is for the domain name registrars to forbid the practice of mixing characters from different alphabets by refusing to register domain names that contain such mixes. This suggests that a hierarchy of internationalized domain names be created and placed under the respective authorities.

A separate top-level domain of the NDS was created for internationalization. It is called *Internationalized country code Top-Level Domain (IDN ccTLD)*.

The ICANN Board approved the establishment of an internationalized top-level domain name working group in December 2006. A bit less than three years after that, they started accepting applications for top-level internationalized domain names from representatives of countries and territories. Figure 5.10 provides a few examples of the internationalized country code domain names.

Going back to our example, the (bad) *paypal* label should be disallowed for registration in all countries that employ the Cyrillic alphabet. (Just a few examples of such countries are Belarus, Bulgaria, Kazakhstan, Mongolia, Russia, Serbia, and Ukraine. Fortunately, everything seems to work, for the corresponding domain www.xn–pypl-53dc.com still does not exist!)

5.1.4 DNS Security

As is the case with the early Internet development, things were built to be used ... by those who had built them. The fact that everything worked was both amazing and sufficient. No one suspected that the system would be abused (and, sure enough, in the early days there was no clear financial gain in abusing it either). As a consequence, DNS—on which all applications depended—was designed in particular with no protection against potential attackers in mind. The idea, perhaps utopian, was that the Internet community would always be benevolent. Jon Postel put forward his famous robustness principle in RFC 760 (published back in 1980): "In general, an implementation should be conservative in its sending behavior, and liberal in its receiving behavior." The last clause means that if a PDU received is badly formed but could be interpreted, it should be accepted rather than rejected. Unfortunately, this magnanimous attitude has been exploited.

[36] To prevent this, eBay Inc. had actually reserved the *Paypa1* domain name, and so DNS resolves it into www.paypal.com.

Domain	Sponsoring organization
.تونس	Agence Tunisienne d'Internet
.中国	China Internet Network Information Center
.中國	China Internet Network Information Center
рф	Coordination Center for TLD RU (Russia)
.భారత్	National Internet Exchange of India
.ভারত	National Internet Exchange of India
.срб	Serbian National Register of Internet Domain Names (RNIDS)
.சிங்கப்பூர்	Singapore Network Information Centre (SGNIC) Pte Ltd

Figure 5.10 Examples of internationalized country code top domain names. Source: Internet Assigned Number Authority, www.iana.org

The motivation for exploiting DNS vulnerabilities is simple and similar to the motivation for robbing banks: one does it because this is where the money is. If an attacker can somehow fool the recursive name server (or a resolver) into accepting a bad record pointing to the attacker's site (instead of the bank's site), one can learn a good deal about the bank's customer (including his or her password) who visited the attacker's site. Repeating the same trick (which is exactly what software is good at) on many customers and then using the obtained passwords to withdraw money ends up effectively equivalent to robbing the bank.

The major problem with the original DNS design was (and still is) that the records obtained by resolvers or recursive name servers are not authenticated.[37] Ultimately, a response is considered to be valid as long as it matches the QueryID, the requestor's port number, and the original query. If a process (called the *man-in-the-middle*) can intercept a DNS request, it can respond with whatever records it makes up. The originator of the request cannot observe any difference. Creating a *man-in-the-middle* is not always possible, so attacks went to the next level of sophistication.

With a *cache poisoning* attack (thoroughly reviewed in [3]), the attacker guesses the QueryID and the port number (we will explain how in a moment) and then returns the "responses" to the popular queries (which need to be guessed, too). As a result, the resolver's cache is "poisoned"—for a long TTL-specified time—with the attacker's IP address. Now, guessing the QueryID is fairly easy as long as these are changed incrementally. (An attacker can keep issuing its own queries to determine it.) The port number can be easy to guess, too, as long as it is not changing. Hence the countermeasure has been to randomize the QueryID (using a pseudo-random number generator) as well as the port numbers, although randomizing the port numbers is not that easy as we will see later in this chapter when discussing NAT boxes.

[37] Incidentally, most records are *still* not authenticated.

Still, nothing prevents attackers from sending many "responses" with random QueryIDs, and such attacks have been reported to be effective.

Furthermore, as late as 2008—long after the IETF published its DNS security extension standard—a new vulnerability was discovered, where the whole zone could be spoofed. Specifically, the attacker can configure a name server claiming that it is authoritative for a given zone. (There is nothing wrong or dangerous with the ability to do so per se, because the name servers higher in the hierarchy won't point to it.) Then the attacker sends "responses" with authority records, which delegate to the authoritative server for the zone to be spoofed. The name of the authoritative server will actually be correct, but the *glue* will provide the attacker's IP address instead.

There are remedies against this particular attack, too (and so name servers constantly get patched as a reaction to any given attack), but there are surprisingly straightforward solutions to a broad class of DNS security problems. RFC 3833[38] provides a comprehensive catalogue of the attacks.

Perhaps the simplest solution is to use an authenticated channel between the client and the name server, so that the origin of each record is clear. To this end, an IPsec channel would do the job.

The other, more generic solution is to authenticate each DNS record so that the client can check its origin. In 1997, the IETF developed a solution and published the first standard (RFC 2065, now obsolete) specifying the *DNS Security extension* (*DNSSEC*). The work on the standard continued, with the present set of specifications (*DNSSEC-bis*) contained in RFCs 4033–4035.

The scheme is to use public-key cryptography and verify the chain of trust top down, starting with the authoritative name server for the root. DNSSEC actually provides not only a record's origin authentication but also its *integrity assurance* (against any modification en route to the client). To enable this, DNSSEC adds new resource record types:

1. *Resource Record Signature* (*RRSIG*);
2. *DNS Public Key* (*DNSKEY*);
3. *Delegation Signer* (*DS*); and
4. *Next Secure* (*NSEC*).

DNSSEC also modifies the message header by adding new flags. Overall, these modifications end up in much larger DNS response messages, a result that can unfortunately be exploited in the denial-of-service attacks discussed later in this chapter.

The purpose of the new resource record types is described in what follows.

The RRSIG record stores the digital signature for the respective DNS RRset. The situation is somewhat complicated by allowing more than one private key to sign a zone's data (as may be required by different algorithms). It is the job of a *security-aware resolver* to learn a zone's public keys. This can be achieved by configuring a *trust anchor* (a public key or its hash that serves as a starting point for building the authentication chain to the DNS response). The security-aware resolver can learn the anchor either from its configuration or in the process of normal DNS resolution. It is for the latter purpose that the *DNSKEY RR* is introduced. With

[38] www.ietf.org/rfc/rfc3833.txt

that, a security-aware resolver authenticates zone information by forming an authentication chain from a new *DNSKEY* to an already known *DNSKEY*. For this process to work, the resolver must, of course, be configured with at least one trust anchor.

The *DS RR* is used for signing delegations across zone boundaries; it contains the public keys of the delegated child zone. Not that complexity always helps security, but RFC 4033 notes that "DNSSEC permits more complex authentication chains, such as additional layers of DNSKEY RRs signing other DNS RRs within a zone."

In the default mode of operation, the authentication chain is constructed down from the root to the leaf zones, but DNSSEC allows local policies to override the default mode.

So far, we have described how DNSSEC deals with positive responses. In contrast, *NSEC RR* is used for signing negative responses. RFC 4033 explains: "The NSEC record allows a security-aware resolver to authenticate a negative reply for either name or type non-existence with the same mechanisms used to authenticate other DNS replies ... Chains of NSEC records explicitly describe the gaps, or 'empty space', between domain names in a zone and list the types of RRsets present at existing names."

As is true for every chain, a trust chain is as strong as its weakest link, and if this link happens to be at the root, then *every* chain would be weak. For this reason, the security of the top domain name servers is a major concern. ICANN has resolved this by scripting a ceremony[39] for signing the root, where multiple personas with interesting sounding names (such as Ceremony Administrator, Crypto-Officer, Safe Security Controller, Internal Witness, and so on) are choreographed into performing the required steps. These steps include ensuring that the safe for key storage is initially empty,[40] bringing the key-generation equipment into the room, generating and signing the key—producing the certificates, backing up the keys on a smart card, and storing the recovery key material (in tamper-proof hardware security modules), which are then placed in various safe-deposit boxes. All of this is done in front of the auditors, and each step is carefully documented in one or another log. Of course, all participants are themselves authenticated through their respective government-issued IDs. Different rooms have different entry permits—not everyone may enter the safe room, for example. Conversely, until the end of the ceremony or a pre-defined break, no one may leave the ceremony room. There are also procedures for annual inventories of the recovery material.

Unfortunately, the DNS system itself can be used in a denial-of-service attack (without breaking its own security), which we will discuss in the next section as part of a family of such attacks.

The importance of DNS to the Internet is hard to overestimate. The notion of "Internet governance" pretty much means the management of the DNS root and the top domain name space. As it happens, some DNS pioneers had a very different idea of Internet governance in the 1990s. The dramatic events that took place then are described in a well-researched monograph [4], whose authors—Professors of Law at Harvard University and Columbia University, respectively—also provide their opinions on the subject of Internet governance.

There has been much controversy surrounding ICANN, but we believe it is important to point out how much ICANN *has* achieved. To cite [4]: "... [ICANN] has decentralized the sale and distribution of domain names, resulting in a dramatic drop in the price of registration. It has established an effective mechanism for resolving trademark dispute that has diminished

[39] http://data.iana.org/ksk-ceremony/1/ceremony1-script-annotated.pdf

[40] For this task a flash light is prescribed, which is part of the equipment.

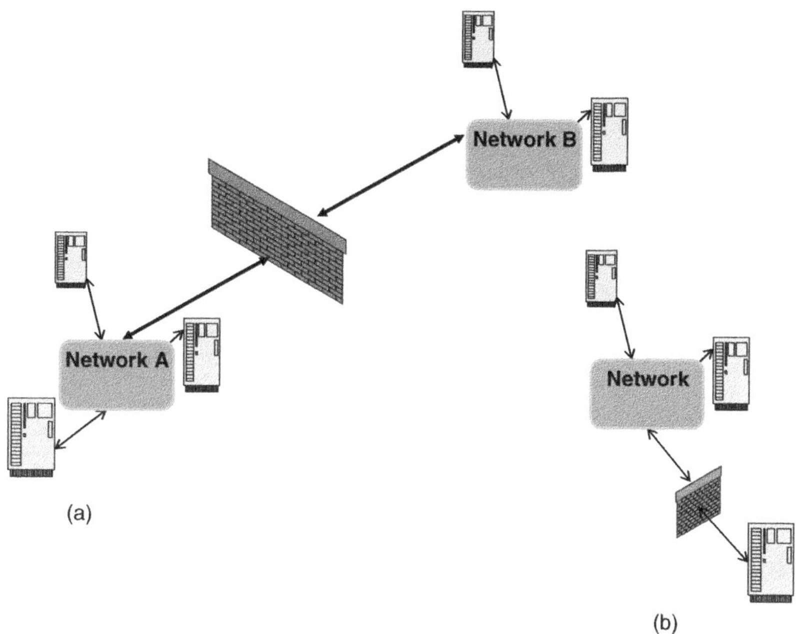

Figure 5.11 Firewalls: (a) a firewall between two networks; (b) a firewall protecting a single host.

the problem of 'cybersquatting' … And it has maintained enough stability in the naming and numbering system that people rarely worry about the Internet collapsing." Who could ask for anything more?

5.2 Firewalls

NIST publication [5] defines a firewall as a program device that controls "… the flow of network traffic between networks or hosts that employ differing security postures."

There are three aspects to this definition. First, a firewall does not *need* to be a "box"—a concept that we will elaborate on further when discussing network function virtualization. Second, as Figure 5.11 demonstrates, a firewall may stand between two networks as well as between a single host and a network. (To this end, a firewall may be supplied by an operating system, or—as we will see later—by a hypervisor, in a purely "soft" form.) Third, a firewall may not necessarily stand only between two different networks; different sections (or *zones*) of a single network—the sections that respectively employ different security policies—must be guarded separately.

The last point, illustrated in Figure 5.12, is essential. It is commonplace that "a firewall is the first line of defense," but an important question to ask is: who is the attacker? For instance, an attack[41] can come from inside an organization, and the first line of

[41] An "attack" here does not necessarily involve a violent act whose objective is to destroy the infrastructure; it could merely be an attempt to get information that must be kept secret. We will look at some common threats and the attacks through which they are realized shortly.

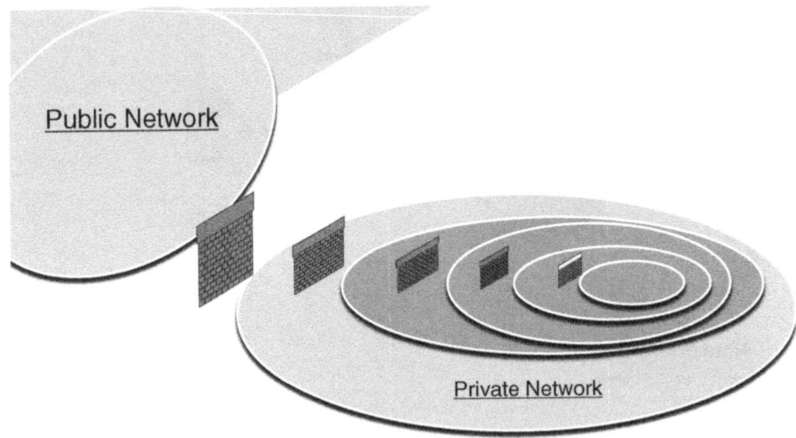

Figure 5.12 Interconnecting networks with different security postures.

defense here is to guard each part of the organization's network according to its respective policies.

Firewalls are not there only to keep the "bad traffic" out. As we will see, their other purpose is to prevent inappropriate traffic from leaving the network. The notion of propriety is defined by security policies, and it changes with time and legal requirements. Interestingly, limiting the traffic that leaves a network is not necessarily a matter of secrecy; just as parents are responsible for the bad behavior of their children, so may the organizations be responsible in which malevolent traffic originates.

The early history of firewalls is described in [6]. The firewall technology appeared much later than the data communications technologies reviewed in the earlier chapters of this book—as is the case with most security developments, the improvements in firewalls were reactive. The first firewalls merely separated LANs (and were intentionally built into the routers rather than into the Layer-2 switches so as to terminate traffic broadcast altogether). As [6] observes, these early firewalls were not deployed with security concerns in mind. True to the original meaning of a firewall (the means to prevent the spread of a fire from one room or building to another), the idea was merely to prevent the spread of local network problems, most of which at that time were caused by misconfiguration.

Firewalls as network security engines came to life in the early 1990s. Initially these were routers augmented with the capability to execute *filtering rules* that restricted certain destination and origin addresses. Meanwhile, research was conducted at Digital Equipment Corporation and AT&T Bell Laboratories on combining packet filtering with *application gateways* (Figure 5.13). The first commercial firewall is reported to have been sold in 1991.

An application gateway does more than its name (a euphemism by all measures!) implies—it examines the network traffic at the application layer while remaining a part of what is effectively a network-layer device and continuing to examine the network and transport-layer datagrams. Of course, the idea is not only to examine traffic, but also to follow up on the examination by restricting it (i.e., dropping suspicious packets). One other—essential—task that started to be performed by firewalls at that time was *logging*. Information on potential attacks was and remains invaluable.

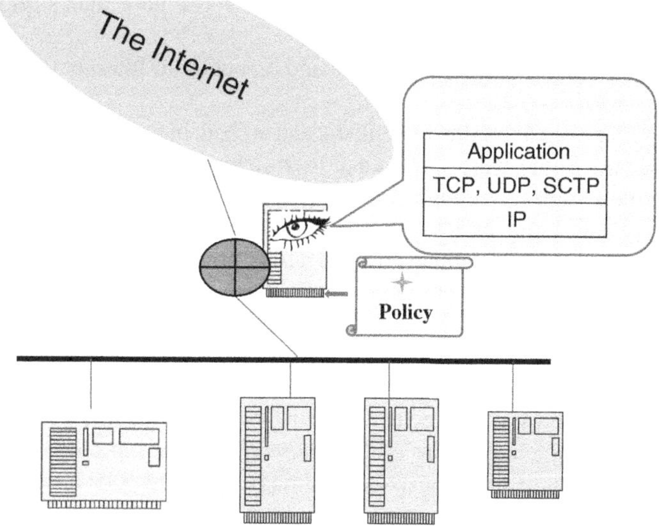

Figure 5.13 An application gateway.

As far as Internet architecture purists are concerned, the firewalls are an abomination. First of all, the application gateway development was a flagrant violation of the layering principle. Second, it resulted in breaking communications without informing the endpoints, which could not possibly deduce why the traffic between them was lost and therefore would be likely to assume network congestion and act accordingly.[42]

Yet, the introduction of application-layer firewalls (or application gateways) was widely embraced not only by the network administrators but also by the researchers and architects of the Internet. The authors of [7], one of whom[43] was an avid Internet enthusiast—later elected to the Internet Architecture Board and heading the IETF Security Area—wrote in its first (1994) edition: "... We feel that firewalls are an important tool that can minimize the danger, while providing most—but not necessarily all—of the benefits of a network connection."

Note that the above statement pre-dates the World-Wide Web, e-commerce, the Internet bubble, and the wholesale movement to IP-based networking by telecommunications providers, banks, newspapers, advertisers, and criminals. To understand the threats addressed then, we need to look at Internet applications ca. the late 1980s. These included

1. file transfer;
2. e-mail (which, incidentally, transferred pretty much text only—attachments, still encoded in ASCII, became fashionable later);
3. remote teletype (pure ASCII text) terminal services (via the *telnet* protocol);
4. remote login package (including remote shell execution);

[42] This particular effect was later mitigated by employing an even worse "abomination" called a *reverse proxy*, which we will discuss later.

[43] Dr Steve Bellovin, back then a Bell Labs colleague and now Professor of Computer Science at Columbia University and CTO of the US Federal Trade Commission.

5. name service (via *finger* protocol)—what would pass as a poor man's *presence* package; and
6. *Usenet*—a bulletin-board discussion service and precursor to Internet fora.

Even with these services, incredibly simplistic and archaic in today's view, there were plenty of security problems. Some were fairly easy to anticipate (unauthorized access to remote computers via remote login), although still considerably hard both to prevent and prosecute. Abuse by hackers was more or less limited to stealing software and occasional e-mails, although the latter did not have as much effect as it does now because at the time intercompany communications were still carried out mostly in the form of printed memoranda, face-to-face meetings, and telephone calls (which were pretty secure when made with plain old telephony).

These seemingly meager (but actually yet unexploited) means of abuse had tremendous effect with the 1988 Internet Worm attack, in which a Cornell University graduate student, who claimed that he had only attempted to determine the size of the Internet, cleverly exploited bugs in the respective implementations of the *sendmail* and *finger* protocols in the ubiquitous Berkeley Unix version, as well as the vulnerabilities caused by poor host administration, to infect a huge number of hosts with a program that kept replicating itself. The process running the program was designed to be—and would have been—unnoticed had it not been for the fact that because of a miscalculation the program replicated itself, too many times, starting new processes and eventually choking a huge number of hosts. The attack is described in great detail in [8]. It caused enough of a sensation to warrant US Congress's request to the Government Accountability Agency to investigate the matter. The resulting report [9] makes very interesting reading. It also demystifies the origin of the damage estimates[44] floating on the Web. The specific recommendations presented in the report are marked as "not implemented"; however, reaction to the incident has been far-reaching.

One major outcome of the incident was that the Defense Advanced Research Projects Agency charged the Software Engineering Institute (SEI), a federally funded research center at Carnegie Mellon University, with creating the CERT® program[45] "to quickly and effectively coordinate communication among experts during security emergencies in order to prevent future incidents and to build awareness of security issues across the internet community." This program is still very effective in detecting security problems and analyzing product vulnerabilities.

The Internet Worm incident also helped the cause of firewall advocates in vendor companies by hinting that there was going to be a market in security products. This market has surely grown with the advance of the World-Wide Web, as have the attacks on the Internet. Accordingly, different types of firewalls and their respective hybrids have been built to protect new applications and to respond to new threats.

---

[44] The report says: "No official estimates have been made of how many computers the virus infected, in part because no one organization is responsible for obtaining such information. According to press accounts, about 6,000 computers were infected. This estimate was reportedly based on an MIT estimate that 10 percent of its machines had been infected, a figure then extrapolated to estimate the total number of infected machines. But, not all sites had the same proportion of vulnerable machines as MIT did. A Harvard University researcher who queried users over the Internet contends that a more accurate estimate would be between 1,000 and 3,000 computers infected. Similar problems exist in trying to estimate virus-related dollar loss. The total number of infected machines is unknown, and the amount of staff time expended on virus-related problems probably differed at each site. The Harvard University researcher mentioned earlier estimated dollar losses to be between $100,000 and $10 million."

[45] www.cert.org/faq/

In what follows, we review the motivation (which, in many cases, was to respond to an attack) for introducing a specific firewall technology as well as its brief description. To this end, we discuss

1. the basics of network perimeter control (including VPNs);
2. stateless firewalls;
3. atateful transport-layer firewalls; and
4. application-layer firewalls.

5.2.1 Network Perimeter Control

It is a well-known practice that each organization that owns a network must have a security policy dictated by the business needs of the organization. The formal expression of such policy and its translation into something on which computers, in general, and firewalls, in particular, can act is the subject of ongoing research and development. For the purposes of this chapter, we merely list the issues that can be translated into the rules to be applied by firewalls.

The first issue is specification of the entities outside the network that can access the resources (for example, web servers, or telephony gateway servers) in the network. For each resource, the sets of respective network entities, users, or user groups for that resource.

The second issue is the specification of the time limit for accessing any given resource. A simple example is the specification of a contiguous time period or a set of contiguous time periods. When the access to resources is charged for, the problem is much more complex.

The third issue is the specification of the *operations* that are allowed to be performed on resources[46] (for instance, where a certain parameter is read-only, or its value can also be changed). As these may depend on specific users (for instance, a network manager employed by the network owner should be allowed to do much more than a customer), they are also specified as part of the access rule.

The fourth issue is the specification of the type of authentication that is required for a particular user. (We believe that this is by far the most complex subject around which the discipline and the industry of identity management—reviewed further in this book—has been built.)

The fifth issue is the specification of what types of exceptional (or even routine) data need to be logged and what acts should be cause for an immediate alarm.

The above five issues become ten when replicated to specify access from inside the network to the resources outside. We mentioned in the introduction to this section, and it is important to keep in mind, that the term "protection" when applied to a firewall has a dual meaning. Keeping bad packets out of the network is only one part of the problem; an equally important problem is restricting emigration: preventing certain packets from leaving the network. (The latter concept may appear peculiar[47] at first sight, but consider the implications of confidential data leaking out of a company or of its employees visiting dangerous sites. Another important example: network providers are expected to prevent IP address spoofing by blocking IP traffic with source addresses not used within their respective networks.)

[46] It does sound abstract, but in time we will look at very specific examples of such operations in the context of RESTful API.

[47] Although not to a person who has ever traveled out of the former Soviet Union or its satellite countries! The scrutiny to which luggage, as well as its owners, was subject on *leaving* the country often far exceeded that applied when entering it. An outbound customs inspection could last for hours, and it was not unheard of for people to miss their flights or trains altogether.

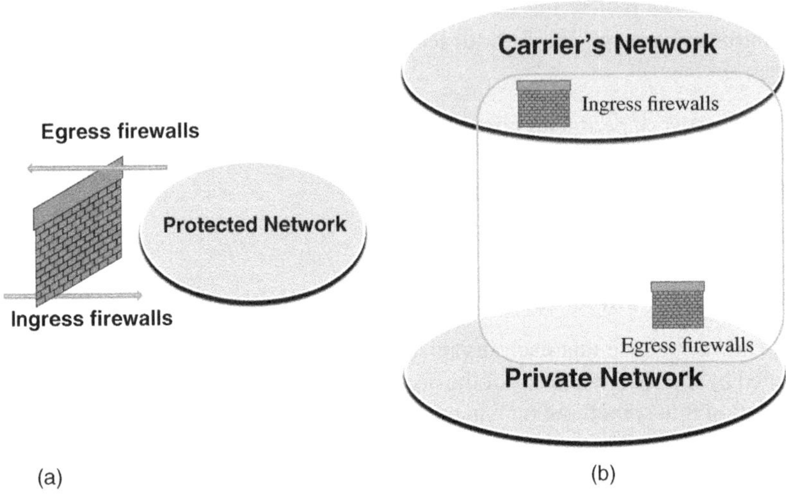

Figure 5.14 Ingress and egress filtering: (a) interfaces; (b) split CPE.

Policy specifications are then translated into rules. The firewalls must interpret the rules, which is a non-trivial problem studied in the discipline of *logic programming*. A well-known problem here is *feature interaction* (a rule addressing one feature may contradict a rule supporting another feature, leading to unanticipated consequences in real-time operation). It is expected that the policy description language will help specify the rules unambiguously and ensure that they can be applied in a non-order-dependent manner.

Again, two sets of policies—and consequently two sets of rules—apply: the policy that controls the admission of inbound traffic specifies *ingress filtering*; the "emigration" policy that specifies which packets may not leave the network protected by the firewall specifies *egress filtering*. This distinction is illustrated in Figure 5.14(a).

In effect then, there are two different firewalls that deal with the inbound and outbound traffic, respectively. When a carrier provides the firewall service in the *Customer Premises Equipment* (*CPE*), it makes sense to split it, as Figure 5.14(b) demonstrates, so that the ingress firewall is physically located within the carrier's network. Not only is bandwidth in the access saved that way, but security is enhanced, too, since the carrier is much better equipped to mitigate certain denial-of-service attacks against the enterprise. Both points apply to home networking, which we will discuss later in this book in the context of network function virtualization.

Finally, when speaking of the "network perimeter," we should return to the VPN discussion of Chapter 4 and recall that a network may actually be an archipelago (cf. Figure 4.2). There are two aspects to that:

1. The islands of the archipelago must be kept indistinguishable from one another (and from the "mainland") as far as the security policy is concerned.
2. Given that each island is surrounded by potentially hostile waters, there is no such thing as one firewall separating "us and them."

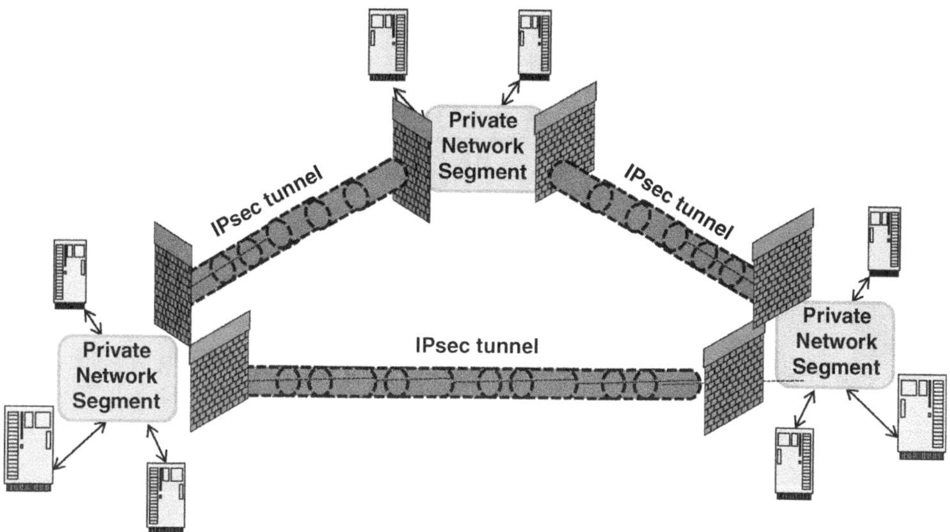

Figure 5.15 Layer-3 VPN with firewalls.

The first aspect is addressed by the fact that each island is indeed protected by one or more firewalls—one for each outside connection, which, of course, must implement the same policy as far as ingress and egress access is concerned. The second aspect is dealt with by employing IPsec to connect the firewalls, so that each tunnel is secure (independent of the underlying network implementation). See Figure 5.15.

Now we are ready to review the services that the firewalls deliver. The simplest and oldest of all such services—a stateless firewall service—only filters IP packets based on the source and destination IP addresses, and, sometimes, on the protocol type.

5.2.2 *Stateless Firewalls*

To give a good example why it is important to restrict traffic based on the protocol number (and not only on the IP address), we need to introduce, briefly, another protocol—the *Internet Control Message Protocol* (*ICMP*), defined in RFC 792[48] and updated in several other RFCs, notably for IPv6. ICMP has its own protocol number (which is, in fact, 1); it is not, however, a transport protocol for it does not carry arbitrary end-to-end payload. Its job is mainly to signal reachability problems among routers, although it was cleverly put to good use in applications such as *ping* (which allows us to determine if a host is present) and *traceroute* (which finds all the routers on a path to a host). Unfortunately, ICMP was also used in a series of DoS attacks[49], starting with the 1997 *smurf* attack (allegedly perpetrated by a high-school student).

The attack, illustrated in Figure 5.16, is directed against a given server, whose IP address is known. The attacker spoofs this address in an ICMP *echo* request sent to a block of broadcast addresses. The routers obligingly propagate the request and, when terminating at

[48] www.ietf.org/rfc/rfc0792.txt

[49] http://hackepedia.org/?title=Tfreak

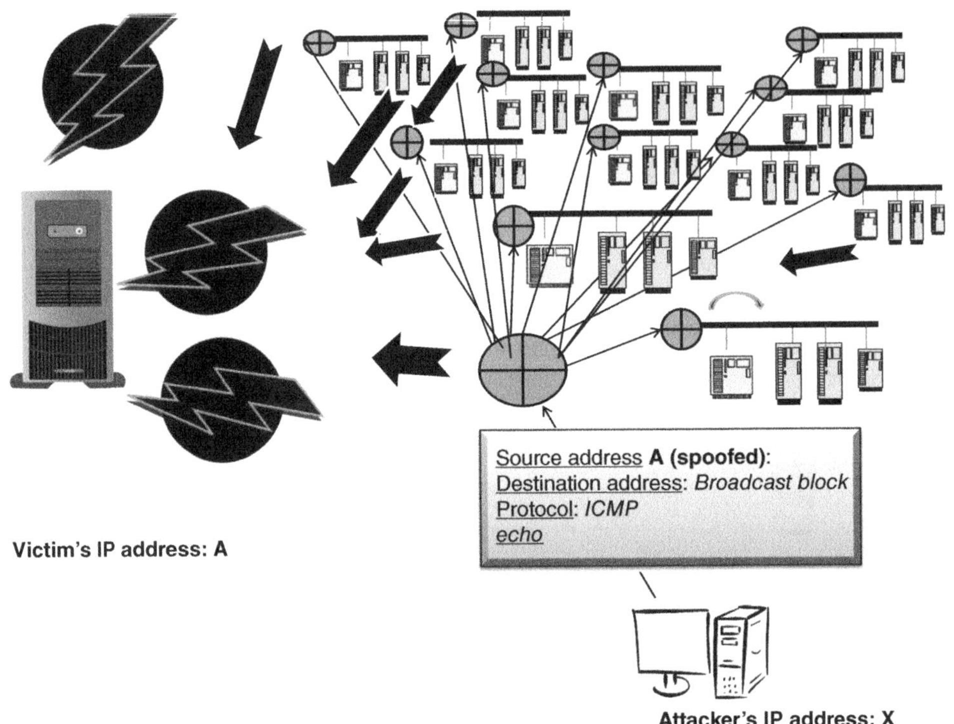

Figure 5.16 A *smurf* attack.

LANs, helpfully translate it to the link-layer broadcast requests (to which hosts are required to respond). The participating networks are said to act as *amplifiers*. When all these hosts in the amplifiers "reply" to the server, the latter quickly becomes overwhelmed with processing the traffic, to the point of being useless for anything else. The sheer amount of traffic may also overwhelm the network in which the server is based. To this end, the CERT advisory CA-1995.01[50] has noted: "Both the intermediary and victim of this attack may suffer degraded network performance both on their internal networks or on their connection to the Internet ... A significant enough stream of traffic can cause serious performance degradation for small and mid-level ISPs that supply service to the intermediaries or victims. Larger ISPs may see backbone degradation and peering saturation."

The reaction to the *smurf* attack resulted in changing the router configurations and also modifying the Internet standard not to require (as a default) that packets directed to broadcast addresses actually be forwarded to them. In the absence of these measures, the ingress filtering, by a carrier, of the IP packets whose source address does not match that of the network that issues it prevents a carrier from becoming an amplifier of the attack. This is mandated by RFC 2827,[51] which has the status of Best Current Practice. We also note that prevention of spoofing by an egress firewall of the originating carrier is the simplest solution of all (although it would

[50] www.cert.org/advisories/CA XE "CA" -1998-01.html

[51] www.ietf.org/rfc/rfc2827.txt

not prevent attacks on the host within that carrier's network, which would in turn require that all egress firewalls implement this feature). Another measure taken was the restriction of ICMP traffic by network administrators. That should explain why it may be desirable for firewalls to look at the *protocol* field.

So much for *smurfing*, except that the use of ICMP was non-essential; it was merely a device for carrying an attack. The ideas of *amplification* (through broadcast) of a malicious "request" and *reflection* by multiple servers "responding" to the request were abstract enough and powerful enough to have become a method for creating numerous denial-of-service attacks.

George Pólya famously said in [10]: "What is the difference between method and device? A method is a device which you used twice." Sure enough, the same person who wrote the *smurf.c* program followed up, using the same method, with the *fraggle.c* (a larger program than the former, but still only 136 lines long). That attack did not use ICMP at all. Instead, it used UDP traffic to ports 7 and 19, which are associated with testing. (Port 7 is connected to the *echo* service; port 19 to the *chargen* service, which responds with random strings.)

The effect of the *fraggle* is similar to that of the *smurf.* Clearly, disabling these services on *all* hosts as a default would prevent this specific attack, but that outcome would be, too much to expect from system administrators. Unless the attack had already clogged the network (or just the link) before reaching the firewall, not much could be done. Otherwise, the firewalls can help here by eliminating the traffic destined for these ports—the closer to the perimeter of the network the better—and also by logging the respective activities. (Log analyzers can issue alarms to the proper response teams.) Even more important, the firewalls are always effective at the source of the problem, where the packets with spoofed addresses can be eliminated before causing any harm. Unfortunately, the amplification attacks have not ended with these as described; they seem to have no end, period.

As we mentioned earlier, DNS has been targeted by attacks of this type. In the *DNS Amplification* attack, illustrated in Figure 5.17, an attacker spoofs requests to *open*[52] recursive resolvers, which in turn flood the target host (whose IP address was spoofed) with the DNS response traffic. The CERT Alert TA13-088A[53] provides a detailed description of the attack. Note that the requests can be constructed to demand all possible zone information (by using type "ANY"). Sadly, DNSSEC makes things even worse, for the resulting responses are much larger than those that do not use DNSSEC because of the signatures. Finally, *botnets*—possibly located in different networks—can be used to further magnify the effect, resulting in a large-scale *Distributed Denial-Of-Service* (*DDOS*) attack.

A variation of this type of attack can also involve authoritative name servers that do not provide recursive resolution, but in this case it is possible to mitigate the attack by limiting the response rate.

Again, source IP address verification according to IETF standards is the best protection against this attack, but this requires the cooperation of all providers—the IP packets with spoofed addresses must never be allowed to leave their networks. Here, the egress firewalls are indispensible. To mitigate the reflective DNS attacks, NIST recommends that firewalls

---

[52] *Open* means open to the public. Typically, one uses recursive resolvers inside the service provider's network, which is accessible only to the customers of that network, so any attempt at malicious activity can be stopped. The Open Resolver Project (http://openresolverproject.org/) keeps track of open recursive resolvers.

[53] www.us-cert.gov/ncas/alerts/TA13-088A

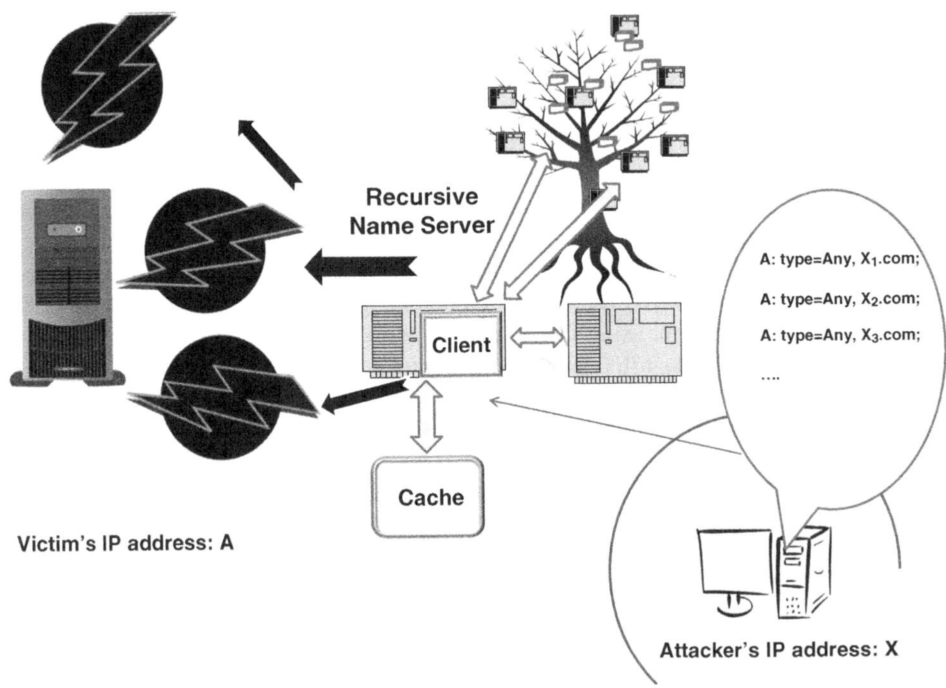

Figure 5.17 A reflective DNS attack.

keep track of DNS requests on the egress interfaces and never permit the "response" to a non-existing query to enter the network.

The firewalls that provide only packet filtering are called *stateless*, because they examine each packet without considering the overall traffic context, as opposed to *stateful* firewalls, which actually follow the state of transport-layer connections. (We have already come close to using stateful firewalls: one can argue that the implementation of the NIST recommendation of the previous paragraph in effect requires a stateful application-layer firewall for it involves keeping track of all outstanding DNS queries.)

5.2.3 Stateful Firewalls

The original motivation for developing these types of firewall was the mitigation of the *SYN* attack, described in great detail in [11], whose author also wrote (the informational) RFC 4987[54], which the IETF published in 2007. The attack exploits typical implementations of TCP (specifically, the TCP connection establishment phase).

It is as important to understand what exactly is happening here as *why* it is happening.[55] The relative complexity of the connection establishment mechanism is caused by the necessity to synchronize the initial sequence number values at both the sender and the receiver. The

[54] www.ietf.org/rfc/rfc4987.txt

[55] Lest the reader thinks that the problem can be remedied by changing the TCP.

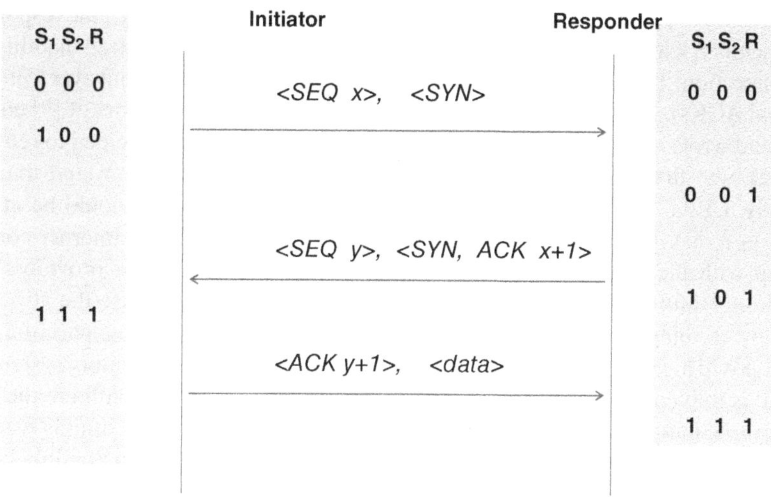

Figure 5.18 TCP connection establishment. Source: RFC 675.

original TCP specification[56] explains: "For an association to be established or initialized, the two TCP's must synchronize on each other's initial sequence numbers. Hence the solution requires a suitable mechanism for picking an initial sequence number [ISN], and a slightly involved handshake to exchange the ISN's. A 'three way handshake' is necessary because sequence numbers are not tied to a global clock in the network, and TCP's may have different mechanisms for picking the ISN's. The receiver of the first SYN has no way of knowing whether the packet was an old delayed one or not, unless it remembers the last sequence number used on the connection which is not always possible, and so it must ask the sender to verify this SYN."

Figure 5.18 depicts the exchange that ends up in successful connection establishment. The state of both the receiver and the responder is maintained in the three bits (S_1, S_2, R) respectively indicating whether

- the initial *SYN* with the sequence number was sent $(S_1 = 1)$;
- the sequence number was acknowledged by the other party by sending back as the *ACK* parameter, the original value incremented by 1 $(S_2 = 1)$; and
- the *SYN* was received $(R = 1)$.

The connection is established when both parties reach state (1, 1, 1).

In an unsuccessful exchange, the acknowledgment never arrives, in which case the party that was expecting it returns to state (0, 0, 0) upon expiration of the respective timer.

In what follows, we will concentrate on the responding host (which, for our purposes, is a server against which the attack is carried). Maintaining a connection requires memory. The corresponding memory (typically, an array cell) is allocated by a host upon receiving the first SYN, that is—on transition to state (0, 0, 1). The block is naturally supposed to be kept until the connection returns to state (0, 0, 0). Thus, as a minimum, the memory block is kept until the timeout.

[56] www.ietf.org/rfc/rfc0675.txt

If, too many SYN packets arrive in a sufficiently short period of time, then the responder will run out of memory, which in turn would result in either a crash or, at the least, an inability to open any new connection. To tie up the server, an attacker can do just that (without ever following up with the final ACKs). RFC 4987 cites an interesting account that the authors of [7] envisioned this attack and wrote a paragraph about it in the 1994 edition, but then decided to remove it.[57]

The attack was first described in 1996 in what CERT called "underground magazines." Subsequently, CERT issued advisory CA-1996-21.[58] Since the attacks could be effectively carried out in a distributed manner, with the spoofed IP addresses, the Internet community followed up with the requirements for filtering—stressing the need for providers' ingress firewall action. Unfortunately, this measure alone is not sufficient because the attack can be carried out by seemingly legitimate hosts once they are hijacked to become part of a botnet.

Other proposed measures could be carried out only by changing the operating system kernels (where TCP is implemented). One such feature provided the ability to configure the limits of the *backlogs* (the number of half-opened connections) so that once such a limit is reached, the half-opened connections are closed and their memory is freed, this action possibly combined with ignoring SYN requests. The backlogs could be increased for large servers. The timer values could also be tinkered with.

The problem though is caused by early memory allocation, and a potential solution has to do something about postponing it. One efficient technique (which also hinted at the subsequent firewall implementation) was *SYN-caching*, in which the actual memory was not allocated until the connection had been established. Of course, the problem here is that it requires a (non-trivial) change in the operating system of a host, but there is more than one operating system. Another technique, called *SYN Cookies* (described by its author at http://cr.yp.to/syncookies.html), uses cryptographic techniques to encode the state of half-opened connections using the bits reserved for sequence numbers. When the connection completes, the state can be reconstructed in the newly allocated memory slot. The disadvantage of this technique is that certain TCP options become unavailable when it is used (as the bits are taken). As [11] reports, the techniques can be combined in a powerful hybrid.

An example of a stateful firewall solution is depicted in Figure 5.19.

The firewall (presumably itself protected with techniques like SYN-caching or SYN Cookies) responds to the initiator of the TCP connection, attempting to establish its own connection before the responder knows anything about the request. If it succeeds, it establishes another connection with the responder, and from then on relays the data between the initiator and the responder, neither of which is aware of a *proxy* (or *midbox*) in the middle.

The proxy arrangement has been carried into applications protocols, as we will see, but a stateful firewall does not necessarily have to be a proxy. In a less extreme example, a firewall may merely keep track of all connections (by maintaining a table of all *<Source IP address, Destination IP address, Protocol, Source port, Destination port>* quintuples), rather than establishing two endpoints. This type of firewall can still do more than a stateless one.

---

[57] The original narrative by Bill Rosen (http://memex.org/meme2-12.html) states: "The technique, known as SYN Flooding, was documented by 1984 (sic!), if not earlier, when Bill Cheswick and Steve Bellovin published their book 'Firewalls and Internet Security: Repelling the Wily Hacker.' 'We had a paragraph in the book about it,' Cheswick told me from his office at Bell Labs, 'which we removed because we knew of no way to fix it. We're sorry about it now. We should have put it in.'"

[58] www.cert.org/advisories/CA XE "CA" -1996-21.html

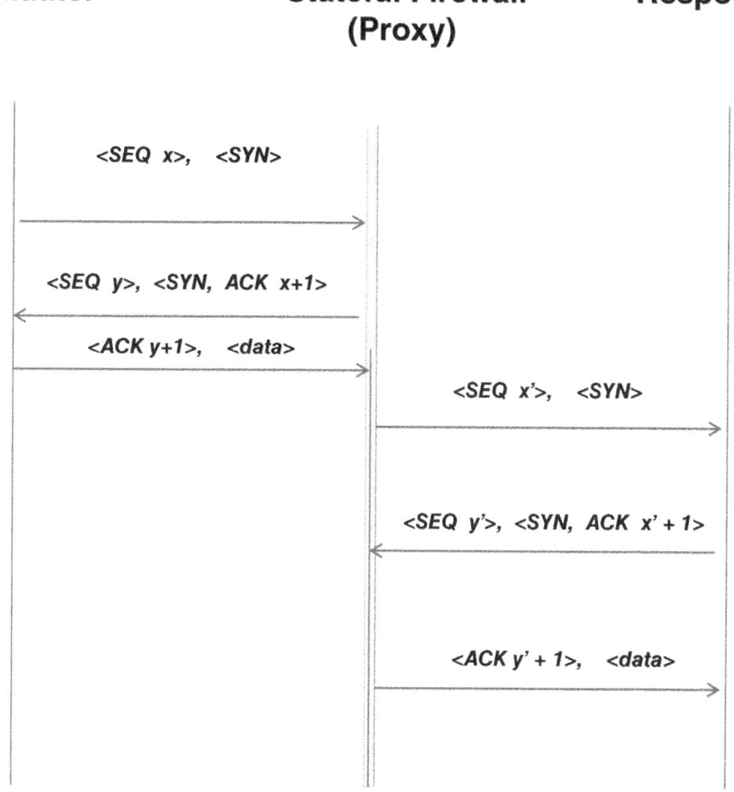

Figure 5.19 Stateful firewall (an example of a TCP connection establishment).

For instance, such a firewall can support a policy that no session may last longer than a specified period of time (an important policy if one considers charging for a connection based on its duration, especially when a pre-paid card is used). Keeping track of open connections coincides with the function of NATs, a point we will explore in the next section of this chapter.

5.2.4 Application-Layer Firewalls

It has been a tradition in the IETF to publish RFCs of an absurd and humorous nature on April 1.[59] To this end, RFC 3903,[60]written by Mark Gaynor and Scott Bradner in 2001,

[59] Perhaps the most famous of these has been RFC 1149 (http://tools.ietf.org/rfc/rfc1149.txt), "A Standard for the Transmission of IP Datagrams on Avian Carriers," published on April 1, 1990 by D. Waitzman. The adaptation procedure is described as follows: "The IP datagram is printed, on a small scroll of paper, in hexadecimal, with each octet separated by whitestuff and blackstuff. The scroll of paper is wrapped around one leg of the avian carrier. A band of duct tape is used to secure the datagram's edges. The bandwidth is limited to the leg length." According to an often-cited IETF anecdote, when a network provider included a question of compliance with RFC 1140 in a Request for Information document, some vendors claimed such compliance in their responses.

[60] www.ietf.org/rfc/rfc3093.txt

proposed the "Firewall Enhancement Protocol (FEP) to allow innovation, without violating the security model of a Firewall." More specifically, the "proposal" is "to layer any application layer *Transmission Control Protocol/User Datagram Protocol* (*TCP/UDP*) packets over the *HyperText Transfer Protocol* (*HTTP*) protocol, since HTTP packets are typically able to transit Firewalls." That was indeed a funny joke! At the time, nothing could look more grotesque than carrying IP datagrams over the transaction-oriented application protocol, which was designed for retrieving fairly small files—called pages—on which the World-Wide Web depended.

We will discuss HTTP later in the book; here we observe—not without amazement—that what appeared absurd in 2001 in fact became the norm three or four years later! Effectively, the HTTP started to be used as a transport protocol for remote procedure calls and even for video streaming! The reason was precisely that mentioned in RFC 3093—HTTP could traverse firewalls unhindered. Furthermore, certain peer-to-peer applications (including instant messaging) used port 80—typically reserved for HTTP. All of that, of course, meant that HTTP could no longer traverse firewalls the way it did: the content of the "HTTP messages" has to be analyzed.

A significant threat in terms of malware has been posed by *active content* (e.g., Java programs), which therefore needs to be examined. But even "normal" HTTP methods have been used for harmful purposes (such as causing buffer overflow attacks) and to deal with this, it was important at least to validate the input parameters' lengths.

Hence, application firewalls have been built for HTTP, e-mail, interactions with SQL servers, and voice-over-IP applications. Even a seemingly innocuous data structure specification language—the *Extensible Markup Language* (*XML*) presented a need for XML firewalls, chiefly to understand the service specifications that are written in it. For example, the XML-based *Web Services Description Language* (*WSDL*) has been developed to describe service programs (to be executed remotely) that are offered by a site.

Analysis of the application protocol payload is called *deep packet inspection*. But, application firewalls often need to go way beyond just checking the payload. In fact, in many cases, to understand the payload, one needs to know the particular state of the protocol. Hence, application firewalls are often *stateful*. In the extreme version, an application firewall acts as a proxy in that it terminates the protocol in question and restarts other instances with the entity behind the firewall that it protects. The situation is similar to that depicted in Figure 5.19. Things can become pretty complex, and this complexity can be (and has been) exploited by intruders. The very attacks that could result in taking control of a host may now result in taking control of the firewall, which is not surprising since the firewall is executing the protocol that a protected host was supposed to be executing and looking at the data that a protected host was supposed to look at. Just as Nietszche warned in [12]: "He who fights with monsters should be careful lest he thereby become a monster. And when thou gaze long into an abyss, the abyss will also gaze into thee."

It has become common for enterprises to deploy firewalls to separate *zones*—sometimes even within a single organization. The idea is to establish a fully protected internal network—often called the *trusted zone*—behind the firewall, while also maintaining another network—called the *demilitarized zone* (*DMZ*), which operates according to a different policy. A typical use case for DMZ is to host an enterprise's public web server.[61] DMZ operates under a different policy, and so it is separate from both the outside world and the protected zone.

[61] The next section will clarify further why this is necessary.

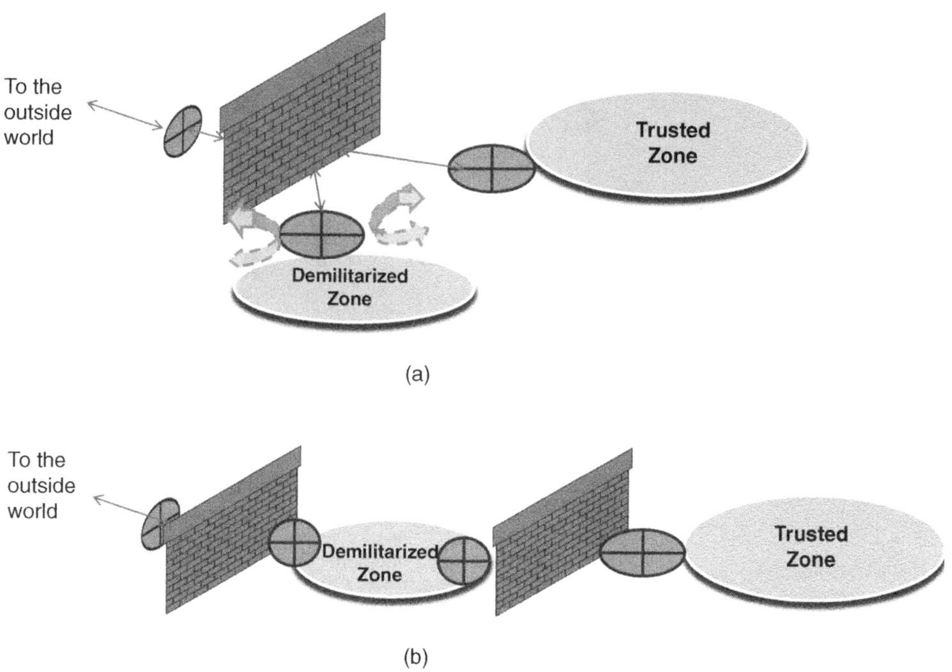

Figure 5.20 Network zoning: (a) with a single firewall; (b) with two firewalls.

Zoning can be accomplished with a single firewall that has at least three network interfaces, as depicted in Figure 5.20(a). One interface is connected to the outside world, the other to the DMZ (so that both the traffic from- and into the outside world, as well as traffic from- and into the protected zone, go through this interface); the third interface is connected to the trusted zone. This arrangement is the least expensive to effect, but it presents dangers (consider misconfiguration or a single-point failure).

The dual-firewall arrangement of Figure 5.20(b) is more expensive, but is considered to be much safer.

As we are going to describe the network address translation function, we note that—although it is distinct from that of the firewall—it is often implemented as part of a firewall.

5.3 NAT Boxes

With a 32-bit IP address field, there are about 4.3 billion IP addresses—clearly not enough to assign to every person's computer, phone, washing machine, tooth pick, and what not. This was understood as early as in the 1990s, although the idea of assigning IP addresses to things other than computers came later—phones, around 1997; washing machines, around 2003 as part of the Smart Grid plan; and tooth picks … well, we surmise that tooth picks are "things" as in the "Internet of Things."

IPv4 has stubbornly remained around though, as have the solutions to address the shortage of the IPv4 addressing space. The idea is to reuse the pool of existing IP addresses in a network following a clever scheme.

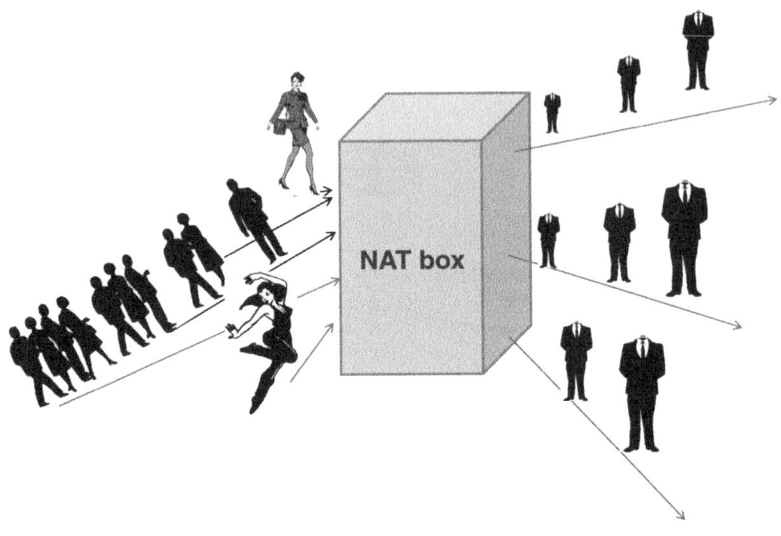

Figure 5.21 NAT in a nutshell.

In this scheme, first the IP address space is divided into two parts—private and public—with the private addresses to be used only *inside* the network, that is for intra-network communications. Second, for each IP packet that goes outside, its source IP address is changed to the public IP address. Such address substitution is precisely a function of a NAT box. With that, a NAT box can assign the *same* public address to all packets that go through it. Hence, if a network has n entities, inside only one IP address—shared by all of them—it is used for external communications. Not only does this scheme allow the reuse of IP addresses, but it also *anonymizes* the network addresses behind the NAT box,[62] as depicted in Figure 5.21.

Of course, such a trick could not be pulled off without introducing new (and serious) problems, the first of which is caused by the necessity to translate the incoming packet's destination IP address to the proper private IP address. This problem can be solved in a fairly straightforward way, but the solution itself is problematic for, as we will see, no entity external to a network can initiate communications with any entity within a network. This is a violation of a major Internet principle. In fact, we will see that the scheme has broken a number of Internet principles. But then, the people who considered NAT an abomination have learned (and taught others) how to live with it. As the deployment of NAT has progressed—along with further growth of the number of Internet hosts and further IP address space depletion—so has grown the number of new problems and their solutions. Still, the NAT boxes are evolving while still serving their two major purposes mentioned above: (1) effective management of scarce IP addresses and (2) obfuscation of the internal network structure.

[62] While this feature is by no means a substitute for security measures, it does help security. For this reason, the feature has often been referred to as "network privacy." It allows network operators—both in the enterprise and in the service provider space—to make the internal entities addressable only on a need-to-know basis. With that, some entities remain non-addressable from outside. In addition, essential competitive information— the internal network structure and device deployment numbers—is also protected.

Again, it is hard to overestimate the importance of the latter. We had mentioned this in a footnote earlier, but this subject warrants an expansion. First of all, in an enterprise network (say that of a bank or—for a more striking example—a military facility), there are hosts that for obvious reasons *should* never be visible to the outside world. Indeed, the firewalls can help here, but the major issue is that such hosts must not be addressable from the Internet, period. Second, given the way the Internet has been designed, not only hosts, but also routers can be reached by their IP addresses. When it comes to carrier networks, the ability to reach their routers through network management interfaces is a dangerous thing. (This issue should not be confused with that of connecting peer routers directly, which is accomplished at the link layer.) The PSTN has stayed fairly secure in large part, owing to the fact that its switches and other network elements were not addressable, and thus accessible, from outside. The ISPs have learned that they had better follow the same model, which NAT enables.

With the advances in home networking (in which there is a NAT function deployed within the home gateway), combined with the growth in enterprise networking, carriers needed to introduce NAT-on-top-of-NAT, which is often called *carrier-grade-* or *large-scale NAT*.

In the rest of this section we discuss:

1. The allocation of private IP addresses;
2. The architecture and operation of NAT boxes;
3. The protocols that enable operations (of many existing Internet protocols) in the presence of NATs—the *Interactive Connectivity Establishment* (*ICE*) protocol, *Session Traversal Utilities for NAT* (*STUN*) protocol, and the *Traversal Using Relay NAT* (*TURN*) protocol; and
4. Large-scale NAT.

5.3.1 Allocation of Private IP Addresses

Definitive guidance on the subject was first issued in 1994, in RFC 1597,[63] co-authored by the engineers who represented three essential segments of the Internet industry—software vendors, enterprise networking, and Internet registry.[64] Explaining the advantages of introducing the private address space—IP address conservation and operational flexibility—the RFC observes that the (uncoordinated) use of private IP addresses had already taken place and warned about the consequences:

> "For a variety of reasons the Internet has already encountered situations where an enterprise that has not been connected to the Internet had used IP address space for its hosts without getting this space assigned from the IANA. In some cases this address space had been already assigned to other enterprises. When such an enterprise later connects to the Internet, it could potentially create very serious problems, as IP routing

[63] www.ietf.org/rfc/rfc1597.txt

[64] Yakov Rechter—the inventor of BGP, among other things—worked at IBM at the time; Bob Moskowitz, an IETF security expert who later co-chaired the IPSec working group and otherwise was involved with all security protocols, was in charge of security at Chrysler Corporation; Daniel Karrenberg and Geert Jan de Groot were with the Réseaux IP Européens (RIPE) Network Coordination Centre. RIPE is the regional Internet registry for Europe, the Middle East, and Central Asia; Eliot Lear was with Silicon Graphics.

cannot provide correct operations in the presence of ambiguous addressing. Using private address space provides a safe choice for such enterprises, avoiding clashes once outside connectivity is needed."

Interestingly, we witnessed just such a clash six years later, when we were in charge of establishing the IETF network for the March 2001 IETF meeting (the first IETF meeting in the 21st century, sponsored by Lucent Technologies). Much expertise was supplied by Bell Labs and Lucent Technologies business units, and the network had passed all the tests within the Bell Labs premises. The network was designed and built to accommodate more than 3,000 hosts, with both wireline and wireless connections. Yet, on its deployment, a strange phenomenon manifested itself: many participants had no outside connection at all, even though the network multi-homed on two ISPs to ensure reliability.

Here is what had happened. For the internal IETF network, Lucent Technologies used the IP addresses from its private space, but the specific block of IP addresses in question was inherited from AT&T following its trivestiture in 1996. Something obviously fell through the cracks, for someone in AT&T forgot to delete these addresses from its space. Fortunately, the problem was diagnosed and fixed within a couple of hours, but we will always remember the anxiety it caused...

In 1996, the (informational) RFC 1597[65] was replaced by the best-current-practice RFC 1918,[66] which remains in force. As specified, IANA has reserved the following three blocks of IP address space for private networks:

1. 10.0.0.0–10.255.255.255 (10/8 prefix);
2. 172.16.0.0–172.31.255.255 (172.16/12 prefix);
3. 192.16A0.0–192.16A255.255 (192.168/16 prefix).

This is equivalent to the allocation of, respectively, a single Class-A network number, 16 contiguous Class-B network numbers, and 256 contiguous Class-C network numbers.

Any entity can use them in its own domain without asking IANA or anyone else: "An enterprise that decides to use IP addresses out of the address space defined in this document can

[65] www.ietf.org/rfc/rfc1597.txt

[66] www.ietf.org/rfc/rfc1918.txt. Note that 1918 was the year of the end of the First World War. Bob Moskowitz told us a fascinating story of the development. Everything started in 1983, at the Houston IETF meeting, when Bob, in a corridor conversation with Jon Postel, requested four Class-B network address spaces, which the Chrysler Corporation (then Bob's employer) needed for its engineering, manufacturing, and other organizations—all of which required separate networks. Jon replied that he could give only two Class-B addresses, period, as they were being depleted. Then Bob suggested that in this case it would be essential to develop the notion of a private address space to be reused within the enterprise networks. In disbelief, Jon replied with the suggestion that Bob write an RFC elaborating the concept. At this point, Yakov Rechter—who overheard the conversation and followed it for some time—joined in and expressed his interest in co-writing the RFC with Bob. This is how RFC 1597 was born. Its publication, however, created controversy, and soon two camps were formed—one in support of forming a private address space and the other against it. Jon Postel requested that both camps make peace and document their agreement in a best-practice RFC. After prolonged discussions there was an agreement, and the newly formed document differed from RFC 1597 merely in the text that described the pitfalls and dangers of the private address space. Jon Postel, well known for his deadpan humor, then assigned the new RFC the number 1918 claiming that all other numbers before that were taken. There were several RFCs issued at the same time as RFC 1918 (February 1996), however, and no one in the IETF doubted the meaning of the number.

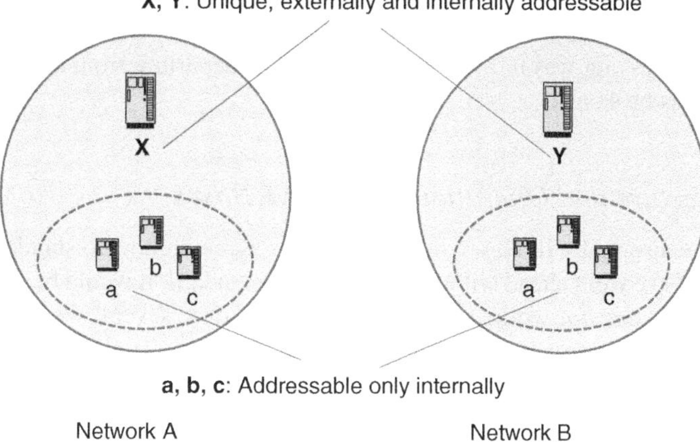

Figure 5.22 Private and public addressing networks *A* and *B*.

do so without any coordination with IANA or an Internet registry. The address space can thus be used by many enterprises. Addresses within this private address space will only be unique within the enterprise, or the set of enterprises which choose to cooperate over this space so they may communicate with each other in their own private internet." Of course, none of these addresses can be used externally, but this is what IANA and the Internet registry have to ensure.

In contrast, any entity that is made visible to—and accessible from—the outside world must have an address from the globally unique address space. These addresses can be assigned only by an Internet registry (which, in turn, gets allocated the address space by IANA).

The hosts that are assigned network addresses from the private space are called *private hosts*; similarly, the hosts that are assigned globally-unique addresses are called *public hosts*. Figure 5.22 illustrates the arrangement.

The private hosts (placed within a punctured oval) in both networks, *A* and *B*, have private IP addresses, $\{a, b, c\}$, which are meaningful only within the network they are in. (It is important to note that in addition to an ability to communicate among themselves, they can communicate with *any* host within their respective networks independent of that host's address.) The hosts with IP addresses *X* and *Y*, both of which are globally unique, are *public*. They are addressable by any host on the Internet. In the particular example of Figure 5.22, eight hosts use only five IP addresses.

With a change of its IP address, a host can move from being private to being public (and the other way around).

Naturally, routing information of private networks is not propagated outside. It is also a job of edge routers (or, to be more precise, the firewalls) to ensure that no packet with either a private source or a private destination address (1) leaves the network in which it originated or (2) enters any network. *A propos* (2), an edge router that rejects an incoming packet with a private IP address or routing information associated with such an address is not expected to treat this as a protocol error. It must simply toss the packet out.

In the same vein, the DNS resource records or any other information relevant to a network's internal private addresses must never leave the network. (This is yet another policy to be enforced by firewalls.)

Again, with all the benefits of private addressing for IPv4 space preservation, the major problem with this approach is that the IP addresses were *envisioned* to be global. The mere fact that private addressing was introduced has signaled a departure from the original Internet vision. A taboo was broken.

5.3.2 Architecture and Operation of the NAT Boxes

It was exactly because many IETF engineers could not agree on how to standardize a broken taboo that the industry went ahead without waiting for a standard. It would be incorrect though to say that the IETF has *not* worked on NAT; to the contrary, several working groups dealt with, and have been dealing with, NAT. It is just that there is no standard for NAT, although there are standards (described in the next section) on how to live with NAT boxes.

The subtle issue here is that the architecture per se is not necessarily subject to standardization—the protocol is. The adage is that the standard does not have to deal with how a box is built; it merely has to describe the box's behavior. That maxim is incorrect though, and the NAT box is a poster child for demonstrating how the internal structure and behavior may be indivisible.

An informational RFC 1631[67] published in 1999, while by no means a standard, sheds light on what needs to be implemented.

Let us start with the definition of the minimal function of a NAT box. It has to translate *S*—a set of private source IP addresses—into *only one* source IP address, *i*, but do it so that on receiving a packet with the destination address *i*, it would translate it back into the *unique* $i' \in S$. Obviously, this cannot be achieved without modifying some other field in the IP header. The only field available for modification is the source port number. But if the source port number changes, it must be saved, along with the source IP address. Let us take a look at Figure 5.23.

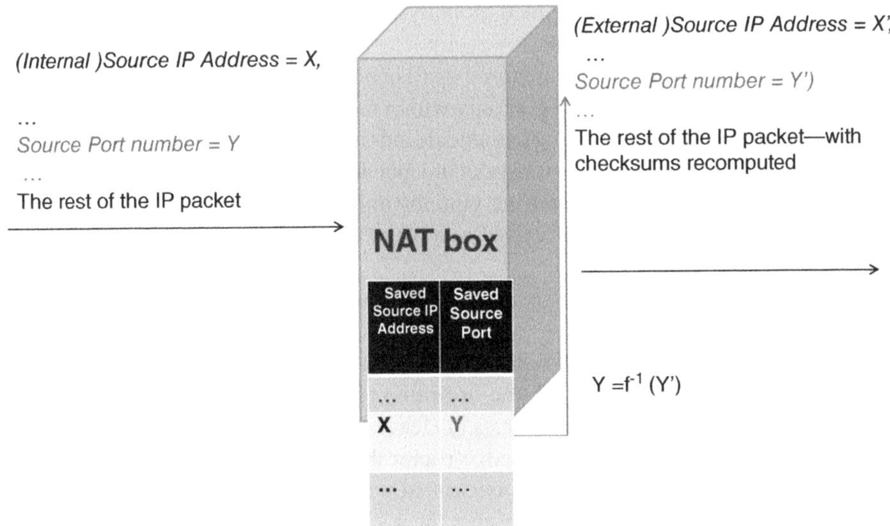

Figure 5.23 A NAT box—outgoing traffic.

[67] www.ietf.org/rfc/rfc1631.txt

Let X and Y be the private source IP address and source port number of an IP packet that arrives at a NAT box from inside. For the future backward translation to work, the NAT box must save the pair (X, Y) in the translation table and transform the pointer to that table entry into the value Y'.[68] The packet that leaves NAT now has the NAT box's public IP address X' along with the source port number Y'. But now that the IP header has changed, so must the checksums change for each IP header as well as the transport protocol headers. (We remind the reader that the source port number is part of the transport-layer header.) Right at this point, another taboo is broken—the layering principle has been violated, as the network-layer entity needs to look at and modify a transport PDU. (A NAT box is essentially performing a router function.)

Not only that, but several Internet application-layer protocols have already violated the layering principle in that they had carried—in the absence of a universal resource locator scheme that was invented and implemented much later than these protocols—the IP addresses *within* the application protocol payload. To this end, RFC 1631 suggests that "NAT must also look out for ICMP and FTP and modify the places where the IP address appears. There are undoubtedly other places where modifications must be done." This would be rather a complex task,[69] further complicated because of the tradition of specifying the application protocols (such as the protocols for e-mail, multimedia session initiation, and hypertext transfer) as ASCII text! This is how breaking one taboo immediately resulted in breaking quite a few others …

As far as the incoming traffic is concerned, the behavior of the NAT box is uniquely determined, as Figure 5.24 demonstrates.

Since X' is a constant associated with the NAT box, only Y' can be used to determine the original pair (X, Y).

At this point it should be clear why with this scheme no entity behind the NAT box can be contacted from outside before that entity initiates the contact. In fact, as may be expected, this

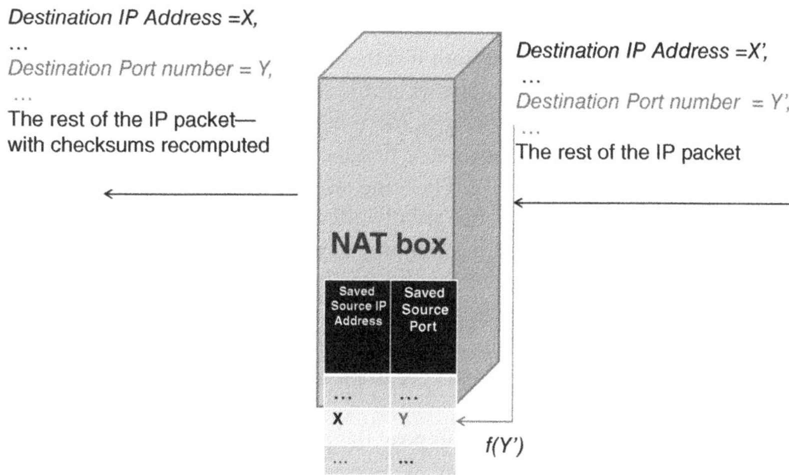

Figure 5.24 A NAT box—incoming traffic.

[68] In fact, Y' can be just that pointer (an index, i, to the array of entries), but the rules for the port number selection, further complicated by the requirement for port number randomization, suggest that in the general case an invertible function f be used such that $i = f(Y')$. As a result, the translation in the reverse direction is straightforward.

[69] And an impossible one when the application payload is encrypted.

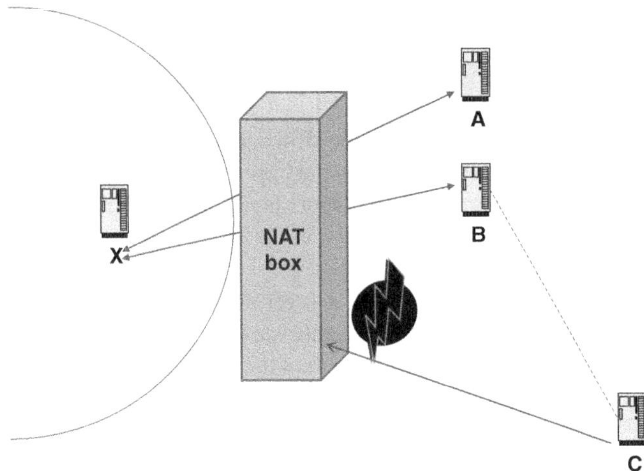

Figure 5.25 An unsolicited "response."

matter is complicated further. The translation scheme that we just presented requires that the size of the table for keeping the (X, Y) pairs be proportional to the number of hosts in the private network. For big carriers, this table is already, too big to be implemented practically, and so the number of entries in the table must be smaller than the logical maximum. To support this requirement, the entries must be removed from the table after they spend there some time—determined by the timing parameter. Implementations vary here, but no matter what is done, it is quite possible for an external interlocutor of an entity in the private network behind the NAT box never to be able to reach it until it restarts the conversation. That necessitates the "keep-alive" routines that increase the network traffic without carrying any payload.

This problem gets worse as NAT becomes more complex, because of the constant introduction of new features. It is important to note that the translation mechanism is invariant to feature introduction. What changes is *what* is being stored and for how long.

These features—never standardized, but greatly affecting the behavior of the NAT boxes—are, too many to consider here, and their taxonomy alone is overwhelming. For the purposes of this book, we only hint at what happens here.

Let us consider a requirement that a host in the private network may receive messages *only* from those external hosts with whom it had initiated a conversation. Not only is this requirement reasonable, it is essential to implement in order to protect against reflective denial-of-service attacks discussed in the previous section.

Consider the situation of Figure 5.25. Suppose the private host X starts conversations with the external hosts A and B. Both A and B can, of course, respond because they know the unique port number that allows them to identify X. But nothing prevents a (potentially malicious) host C from learning this port number (for instance, by sniffing the traffic to B or simply by making B disclose this number—it is by no means secret, and is not protected cryptographically). Once C knows this number, it can start sending messages to X. According to requirements, the NAT box must not allow this message to go through, but with the arrangement we just described the NAT box has absolutely no means of doing so!

The only solution is for the NAT box to store the parameters of each opened *session*—that is not only the source IP address and source port number, but also the destination IP address and the destination port number. This would immediately double the size of the table.

More stringent requirements result in saving the protocol number, the timer interval for each session, and other parameters. Unfortunately, all this is still only the tip of the iceberg ...

The reader has probably observed that much of this could have been eliminated, had the NAT boxes been considered separate from firewalls; however, the implementations invariably keep the NAT function as part of the firewalls, further blurring the distinction between essentially different functions.

To deal with the complexity, the IETF created the NAT working group, which, however, did not produce a much-needed standard. RFC 2663[70] further complicates things, introducing multiple "flavors," including one (two-NAT), in which DNS is involved. This is definitely an interesting read, but as other NAT-related RFCs had mentioned, RFC 2663 is informational—it specifies no standard.

An excellent analysis of NAT architecture and deployment, along with a review of application protocol interworking with NAT, is contained in an early 2001 monograph [13], but quite a few things—notably those we discuss in the next section—developed later (the development motivated first by IP telephony and later by more general real-time multimedia requirements).

Meanwhile, the IETF followed up with the *Behavior Engineering for Hindrance Avoidance* (*behave*) working group, with the objective of creating "documents to enable IPv4/IPv4 and IPv6/IPv4 NATs to function in as deterministic a fashion as possible." This group, which has concluded, produced about three dozen documents[71], enough to fill a small library, thus bringing the volume of literature dedicated to NAT behavior close to that dedicated to human psychiatry ...

For a concise history of NAT development, along with the nuanced pro and contra arguments, we highly recommend [14]—an article in the *IETF Journal*—written by the IETF insider (and inventor of the RSVP protocol), Lixia Zhang. Here is one of Dr. Zhang's observations: "The misjudgment on NAT costs us dearly. While the big debate went on, NAT deployment was rolled out, and the absence of a standard led to a number of different behaviors among various NAT products. A number of new Internet protocols were also developed ... during this time ... All of their designs were based on the original model of IP architecture, wherein IP addresses are assumed to be globally unique and reachable. When those protocols became ready for deployment, they faced a world that was mismatched with their design. Not only did they have to solve the NAT traversal problem, but also the solution had to deal with a variety of NAT box behaviors."

The word "behaviors" is key here, for just figuring out the mapping at the NAT box does not guarantee NAT traversal. We have already described informally the differences in behavior. An early (2003) attempt to characterize such behavior was taken in the (now obsolete) RFC 3489[72]:

- With the *full cone* NAT, an external host can send a packet to the internal host without prerequisites.

[70] http://tools.ietf.org/search/rfc2663, 1999.

[71] http://datatracker.ietf.org/wg/behave/charter/

[72] www.ietf.org/rfc/rfc3489.txt

- With the *restricted cone* NAT, an external host cannot initiate a conversation with an internal host; it can speak only if it has been spoken to. In other words, the NAT box keeps track of the destination IP addresses to which the internal host had previously sent messages, and allows traffic only from those addresses.
- With the *port-restricted* cone NAT, the previous restriction is narrowed to allow responses only through the port on which the conversation was initiated. Here the NAT box keeps track of the pairs (*Destination IP address, Destination port number*) to which the internal host had previously sent messages, and allows IP packets whose (*Source IP address, Source port number*) pairs match the above.
- With the *symmetric* NAT, the table entries are sessions (*Source IP address, Source port number, Destination IP address, Destination port number*), and each session is mapped to a different port number.

In 2007, the IETF issued a best-current-practice RFC 4787[73] on NAT behavior as related to unicast UDP packets. The RFC acknowledges though: "The classification of NATs is further complicated by the fact that, under some conditions, the same NAT will exhibit different behaviors. This has been seen on NATs that preserve ports or have specific algorithms for selecting a port other than a free one. If the external port that the NAT wishes to use is already in use by another session, the NAT must select a different port. This results in different code paths for this conflict case, which results in different behavior." One rather sad observation is that instead of setting the standard for NAT and leading the industry, the IETF ended up trying to keep up with the standardless situation. Larger and larger documents appeared, occasionally "obsoleting" (sic) earlier documents, each of them nearing the length of the TCP specification (by far the most complex one in the Internet). None of these documents makes easy reading either, partly because the state of our understanding of the Wild-West nature of NAT development is commensurate with the state of writing the very documents that describe it…

We will look now at ways to deal with the NAT traversal problem.

5.3.3 *Living with NAT*

An early mechanism, described back in 1999 (in RFC 2663), is fairly simple, and is still being used. It is called *Application Level Gateway* (*ALG*). RFC 2663 describes it as follows:

> "Application Level Gateways (ALGs) are application specific translation agents that allow an application on a host in one address realm to connect to its counterpart running on a host in different realm transparently. An ALG may interact with NAT to set up state, use NAT state information, modify application specific payload and perform whatever else is necessary to get the application running across disparate address realms."

Actually, the idea is very straightforward. The mechanism is exactly the same as that which allows a person who may play chess very badly—in fact, a person who might not even know how to play chess!—to play simultaneously with the best two chess players in the world (say *X* playing white and *Y* playing black), and end up either winning at least one game or drawing both. To achieve this, the incompetent player would start the game with *Y* by repeating the first

[73] https://www.rfc-editor.org/rfc/rfc4787.txt

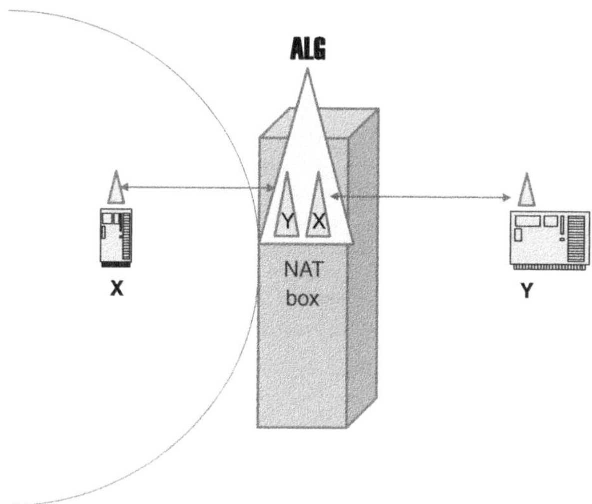

Figure 5.26 Application-Level Gateway (ALG).

move of *X*, then proceed by repeating the move that *Y* made in the game with *X*, and so on. In reality, all this means is that *X* plays with *Y*. If the game is drawn, that means the incompetent player has drawn both games; if the game is won, it means that the bad player won one game (and lost the other). The power of a middleman!

And this is precisely how an ALG works, as shown in Figure 5.26. A process running on host *X* always initiates the conversation (because it is inside the private network), thinking it is talking to its interlocutor on host *Y*. Instead, the ALG inserts itself into the middle of the conversation, by maintaining two processes—one impersonating *Y* to *X* and one impersonating *X* (now equipped with the NAT public address) to *Y*. At least the ALG can just copy the data, but it can also perform a firewall function, modifying or even censoring the packets. To this end, ALG is a kind of stateful firewall.

Before addressing other solutions for NAT traversal, we should emphasize that the fact that only a host within a NAT-shielded network can start a conversation with any host outside means that no two hosts located in different NAT-shielded networks can communicate, period. (Once again we see that breaking the end-to-end principle results in a chain of far-reaching consequences.)

As it happens, this was a major problem that the development of IP telephony faced originally (as in the PC-to-PC scenario described in [15]). Interestingly enough, the problem is still very real today—a significant amount of energy in the IETF *Real-Time Communications in Web Browsers s* (*RTCWeb*) working group[74], created in 2011 to eliminate plug-ins and enable multimedia streaming directly between browsers, has been spent on its charter item "Define the solution—protocols and API requirements—for firewall and NAT traversal."

From the time the development of IP telephony started, the objective of NAT traversal was two-fold: (1) to discover an entity hidden by a NAT box and (2) to establish a *pinhole*[75] for the

[74] http://tools.ietf.org/wg/rtcweb/charters

[75] *Pinhole* is, unfortunately, a commonly used but vaguely defined term, because of the convolution of the NAT and firewall concepts. For the purpose of this book, we define it as the port to an internal host in the NAT translation

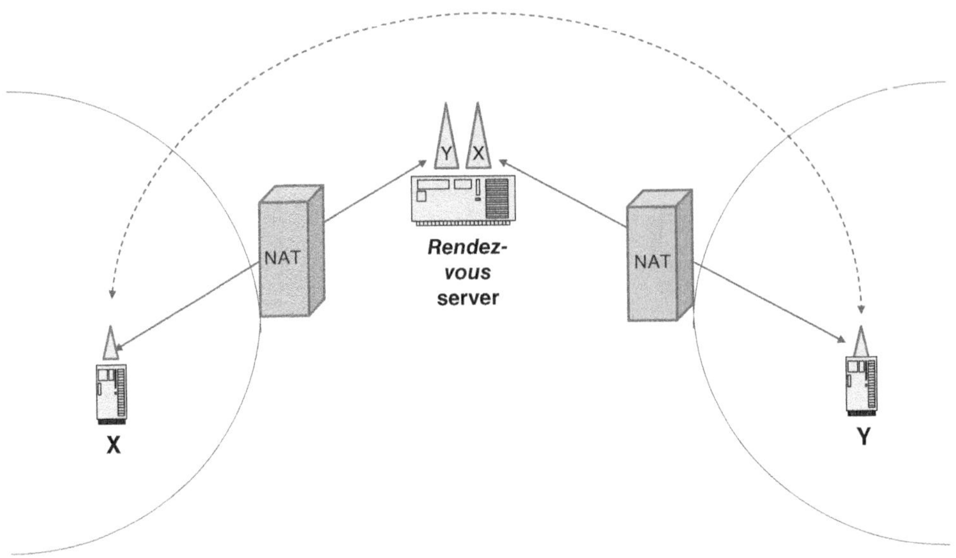

Figure 5.27 A *rendez-vous* relay.

necessary port in the firewall. The discovery is the hardest problem. It has multiple solutions, of which some may work in some circumstances but not in others.

Let us start with the most straightforward solution, which always works. The drawback is that it is the most expensive of all, and perhaps impractical at scale.

The solution is called *Traversal Using Relays around NAT* (*TURN*), and it is described in RFC 5776.[76] TURN was originally designed to work with the *Session Initiation Protocol* (*SIP*) and *Session Description Protocol* (*SDP*),[77] as part of IP telephony, but it can be applied more universally, which we will discuss later.

Figure 5.27 presents the idea: make a central (i.e., publically addressable) server a relay point to connect two NAT-hidden hosts (or *peers*) in separate networks. Each peer can establish its own connection to the relay server, which will then relay packets so that the peers communicate with each other.

Given that the nature of communications is multimedia, it follows that the relay server must have a very high-bandwidth connection to the network, and also high capacity. This requirement can be significantly relaxed though if it is possible for the peers to establish a

record. By starting a conversation, the host creates a pinhole (through which it can be reached back). The problem here is that the firewall function may forbid traffic to certain ports, and so the NAT function must instruct the firewall function to "open the pinhole." Sometimes this instruction can interfere with the firewall policy.

[76] www.ietf.org/rfc/rfc5766.txt

[77] SIP was designed for multimedia session control. It has been widely used in the enterprise (SIP phones), and has a significant application to telecommunications, culminating with the 3GPP *IP Multimedia Subsystem* (*IMS*), in which SIP is the centerpiece protocol. SDP is hardly a protocol—but rather a simple ASCII text file that lists the attributes of processes participating in a session. These attributes include the IP addresses and port numbers, which are later to be used in a media session by the Real-Time Transport Protocol (RTP) and Real-Time Control Protocol (RTCP). The introduction to these protocols and a description of their places in establishing and maintaining a multimedia session are given in [15]. There are also dedicated monographs to SIP and IMS.

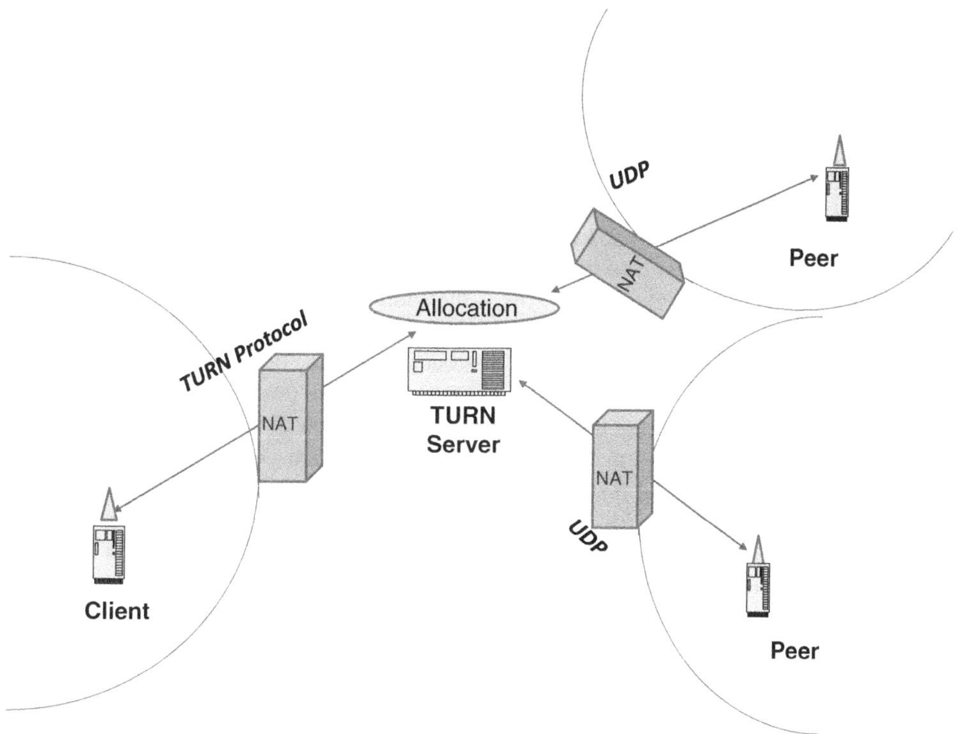

Figure 5.28 Traversal using relays around NAT (TURN).

multimedia transport connection among themselves so that relaying is used only for initial signaling (which needs significantly less of both the bandwidth and processing capacity). Unfortunately, this is not always possible. We will return to this point later.

What is used in real life though are variations of the above model. *Traversal Using Relays around NAT* (TURN) is the name of the protocol enabling the scheme of Figure 5.28.

It is important to note that the TURN server is *not* a *rendez-vous* point. Its operation is asymmetric—rather like that of a telephone switch—in that a TURN client must know the IP address and port number of a peer it wishes to communicate with. (This information can be found through peer discovery via a true *rendez-vous* server—such as a SIP server, to which a peer would register—or it can be distributed through e-mail or similar out-of-band means.) With that, the reason the TURN server is needed at all is because as long as it is public and known, it has a much better chance of penetrating firewalls than its client. To this end, the client turns to TURN only after it has failed to reach the peer.

The TURN protocol is used only between the client and the TURN server, and it must be initiated by the client. A client can learn the IP address and port number of the TURN service from a configuration or through DNS. (The value of the *SRV* parameter is *TURN*.) It is also possible to reach TURN via an anycast address.

The client uses TURN commands to create and manipulate a data structure (called *allocation*) on the TURN, which is the switching point for all the peers the client wishes to communicate with. As is the case for many Internet protocols, TURN defines a keep-alive mechanism: the *allocation* is kept for as long as the client repeats a *refresh* request within a specified period of time. The client also specifies permissions for peer connections. Now, the TURN server does not establish a connection with any peer—all communications with peers are done over UDP.

The client encapsulates the application data inside a TURN message. The TURN server extracts these data and sends them over UDP. When the peer sends the data in the other direction, the TURN server relays it to the client inside a TURN message.

The issue of addressing is solved by *allocation*, which contains the *transport address* (i.e., the [IP address, port] pair) of the client. This is the source address used in all messages to a peer, and thus becomes the destination address in messages from the peer. The TURN message always contains an indication of the peer that has been the source of the message.

Back to the original problem: what can an application protocol (such as SIP or SDP), which uses IP addresses and port numbers hard-coded in-line, do in view of NATs, which will change the protocol headers but not the in-line data? It cannot do much unless it finds out exactly what its external IP address and port number is. Incidentally, with the high volume of NAT publications, there seems to be a bit of inconsistency in terminology. Some specifications call the combination of an external transport address a *mapped address*; others call it a *reflective address*. For the rest of this section, we will use the latter term since this is the one used in the protocol designed to solve the problem at hand. The name of this protocol is *Session Traversal Utilities for NAT (STUN)*.

The first version of STUN was published in 2003, in RFC 3489.[78] Back then "S" actually stood for "Simple," and the name of the protocol was *Simple Traversal of User Datagram Protocol (UDP) Through Network Address Translators (NATs)*. STUN was described as "a lightweight protocol that allows applications to discover the presence and types of NATs and firewalls between them and the public Internet." It so happened that nothing at all was simple—or at least as simple and straightforward as it used to be in the original Internet design—and five years later the new RFC (RFC 5389[79]) was published. It had "obsoleted" (sic[80]) RFC 3489, which by then was called the "classic STUN." The reason for the radical change was that "experience since the publication of RFC 3489 has found that classic STUN simply does not work sufficiently well to be a deployable solution." To this end, "Classic STUN provided no way to discover whether it would, in fact, work or not, and it provided no remedy in cases where it did not. Furthermore, classic STUN's algorithm for classification of NAT types was found to be faulty, as many NATs did not fit cleanly into the types defined there." There was also a security vulnerability (the mapped addresses could be spoofed under certain circumstances).

We believe that it was after this experience that the IETF started to discourage the use of the words "simple" and "light" in the names of its protocols. For sure, nothing has ever been simple about NAT. Yet, the idea of STUN *is* simple, as illustrated by Figure 5.29: to get its reflective address, an application process running on a host should just send a request to a

[78] www.ietf.org/rfc/rfc3489.txt

[79] www.ietf.org/rfc/rfc5389.txt

[80] "Obsoleted" is a term of the RFC series, which, according to tradition, never continues with the same RFC number when an RFC is modified. If a modification is a mere update, the older RFC is marked as "updated," but when the older RFC is no longer in force, it is marked as "obsoleted by" the new RFC.

Figure 5.29 Learning the reflective address from a STUN server.

STUN server, which then responds with the reflective address in the payload. Indeed, it is as simple as looking into a mirror!

What has complicated and ultimately ruined the initial design of STUN is that NAT boxes refuse to behave according to the predicted logic. Some people considered the Internet broken then and there, but others applied *realpolitik.* RFC 3489 chose to abandon the idea of providing a complete solution, and instead packaged STUN as a tool with several defined "usages" (i.e., specific circumstances where STUN can be applied). In addition, the STUN protocol can now be used over both TCP and UDP as well as the *Transport Layer Security* (*TLS*) protocol, which runs on top of TCP.

The protocol supports *request/response transactions* and *indications* (which require no response). With both, the single method specified is *Binding.* In transactions, *Binding* is used by the client to find out the reflective address it is bound to; in indications it may be used, for example, to keep the binding alive.

An important feature of STUN is that its messages can be multiplexed with those of other protocols. To help with demultiplexing the value of the transaction correlation ID (called *magic cookie*) is a bit string specially constructed to avoid ambiguity. (There is an extension, which uses a *fingerprint* attribute to aid in the same task.)

An interesting feature of STUN deals with helpful NAT boxes that try to detect the in-line transport addresses and rewrite them themselves. Hence the obfuscation technique: a STUN server applies an *exclusive-or* (*XOR*) bit operation[81] on the value of the reflexive address and a part of the magic cookie, which is what ends up being transmitted as the reflexive address value.

[81] The XOR operation is defined as follows: $\text{XOR}(0,0) = \text{XOR}(1,1) = 0$ and $\text{XOR}(1,0) = \text{XOR}(0,1) = 1$. Therefore, for any two strings A and B, $\text{XOR}[\text{XOR}(A,B),B] = A$, which makes it trivial to recover the value A given $\text{XOR}(A, B)$ and B. This technique actually makes the *One-Time Pad* cryptographic algorithm.

STUN addresses security by providing the mechanisms for both authentication and integrity checking. The mechanisms are optional—subject to the "usage" selection—and they are based on two credential mechanisms: with the *long-term* credential mechanism the user name and password are pre-provisioned; with the *short-term* mechanism they are shared through an out-of-band exchange. With either mechanism, the authentication is achieved through a challenge/password response, and the key for integrity checking is derived from the password.

Just as with other request/response protocols surveyed above, STUN can be used in an amplified distributed denial-of-service attack, but the nature of the attack is different from what we have seen before. Rather than sending (fairly small) faked responses, an attacker needs to provide multiple clients not with *their* reflective addresses, but with that of the target of an attack. Once the clients (hopeful of receiving their own huge video streams on this address) hand the address to their peers, all the traffic will be directed to the victim. RFC 5389 notes that to effect the attack, an attacker would need to insert itself between the STUN server and multiple clients.

A simpler DoS attack can be carried out to "silence" a client, if the attacker—again acting as the man-in-the-middle between the STUN server and the client—provides the latter with a fake transport address. This attack is not specific to STUN though, since a potential attacker can just as well deny other services to the client. An attacker can easily modify the nature of the attack by providing the client with its own transport address, so that it can *eavesdrop* on the traffic destined for the client.

A more serious attack is that of an attacker assuming the identity of a client. This, however, is a more generic problem than just that of STUN, and its solution lies in the means of distributing and guarding shared secrets.

So far we have not addressed the STUN server discovery, which is the last item in our discussion of STUN. Noting that the server discovery is problematic when STUN is multiplexed, RFC 5489 defines an optional DNS procedure, as follows: "When a client wishes to locate a STUN server in the public Internet that accepts *Binding* request/response transactions, the SRV service name is 'stun'. When it wishes to locate a STUN server that accepts *Binding* request/response transactions over a TLS session, the SRV service name is 'stuns.' STUN usages MAY define additional DNS SRV service names."

The implementations of TURN and STUN servers exist in open source, which makes them particularly useful for deploying in the Cloud.

As a segue to the last topic of this section, let us observe one new complexity with the use of NAT boxes. As already observed, the size of a NAT box cannot exceed 61,440.[82] The physical memory limitation is yet another constraint, which can make the number of entries even smaller. One approach to deal with this problem is to deploy different NAT boxes at the perimeter of the network so that different prefixes of destination IP addresses use different NATs.[83] This situation is reflected in Figure 5.30.

Consequently, a process on a host within a given network may have *different* reflexive addresses depending on which TURN server it obtained them from.

---

[82] Since the port number—the key to an entry—is 16 bits long, and the first 4096 ports are reserved, the upper bound for the number of entries is equal to $2^{16} - 4096 = 61,440$.

[83] By using the term "NATs" rather than "NAT boxes," we underline that here actual translations are different. (Two different NAT boxes can perform the same translation.)

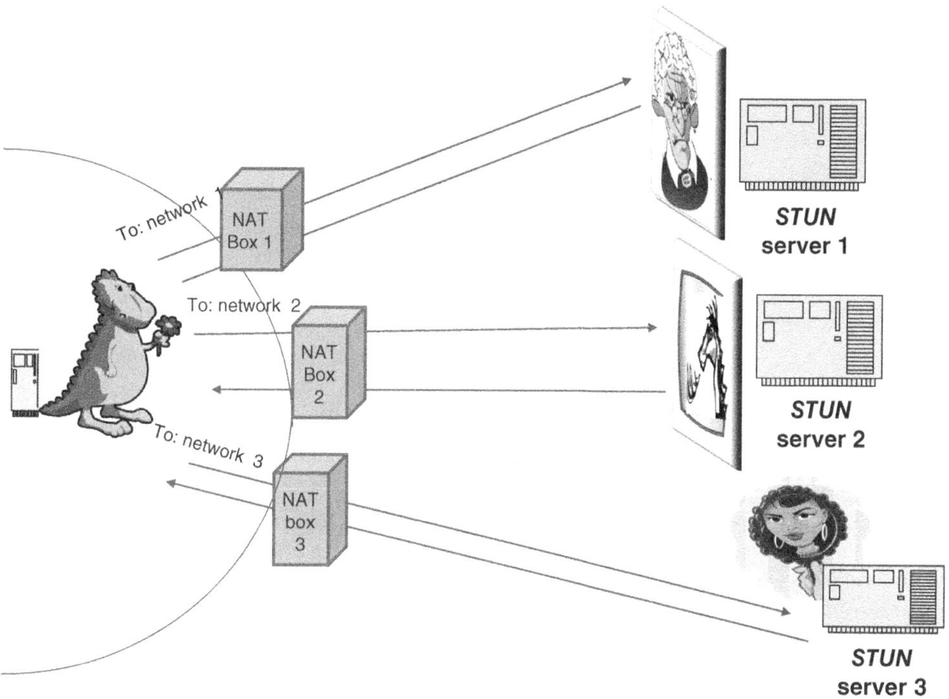

Figure 5.30 Different NATs for different paths.

Now we are ready to describe one definitive mechanism that uses STUN and TURN for NAT traversal. The name of this mechanism is *Interactive Connectivity Establishment* (*ICE*). It is by no means universal in that it applies only to a set of so-called *offer/answer* protocols, which allow two processes to arrive at a common view of a multimedia session using the SDP protocol. SIP is one such protocol, and it serves as the original inspiration for defining the common features of the offer/answer family. For the purposes of this book, we can assume that the protocol in question is indeed SIP.

ICE is defined in RFC 5245.[84] The ultimate objective of ICE is to find two transport addresses best suited for establishing an RTP/RTCP session between two peers. With that, the peers are assumed to communicate between themselves through SIP, which knows how to traverse NAT. (Of course, the transport addresses used for this signaling are likely to be different from those best suitable for carrying the media stream over UDP.) These transport addresses are exchanged through SDP. ICE achieves this objective by accumulating the transport addresses, testing them for connectivity, and selecting the best-performing ones.

[84] www.ietf.org/rfc/rfc5245.txt. This RFC was published in 2010, and—as is the case with other NAT-related RCS—it has *obsoleted* two earlier versions of ICE.

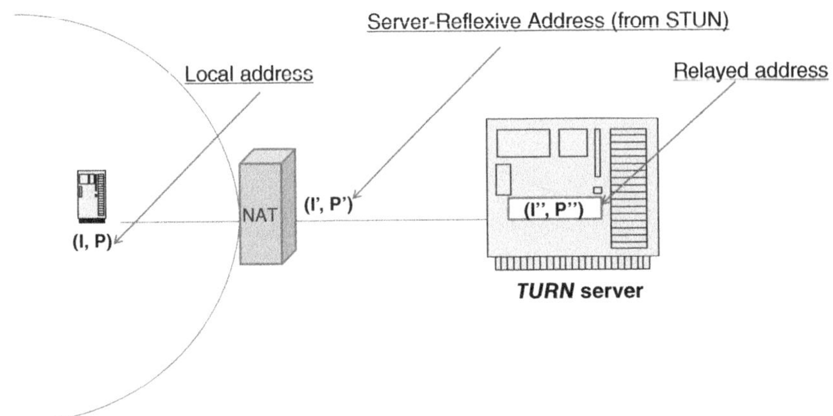

Figure 5.31 Candidate transport addresses (after Figure 2 of RFC 5245).

Altogether there are three types of addresses, as shown in Figure 5.31:

1. *Local address* (i.e., a transport address as related to a host's network interface card);
2. *Server-reflexive address* (i.e., an address obtained from a STUN server on another side of a NAT box); and
3. *Relayed address* (obtained from a TURN server in response to *Allocate*).

In each address type there may be multiple candidate addresses for every given peer process. Indeed, in the presence of multiple network interfaces (multi-homing) there are as many local addresses. As Figure 5.31 demonstrates, there may be several NAT boxes[85] on different paths, and so different STUN servers may supply different server-reflexive addresses. Finally, there may be more than one TURN server and as many relayed addresses.

ICE operates in three steps, as depicted in Figure 5.32.

First, the client that initiates the session collects the candidates and sorts them according to a calculated *priority* (see the RFC for the algorithm to compute this priority). Once finished, these are sent to the peer (via an SDP offer). The peer performs the same operations, so in the end the sorted candidate lists are exchanged.

At this point, each peer keeps checking connectivity for each pair of transport addresses (STUN running on each peer's host can be used for this purpose) and informs its interlocutor about the check results. In the end, both peers have one or more working pairs.

RFC 5245 carefully considers the optimization options and security considerations, especially for connectivity testing.

5.3.4 Carrier-Grade NAT

So far we have tacitly assumed that NAT boxes are deployed only at one layer. This is no longer the case though, because Internet service providers faced IPv4 address exhaustion, too, especially with the growth of home networking.

[85] As we will see in the next subsection, NAT boxes can be nested.

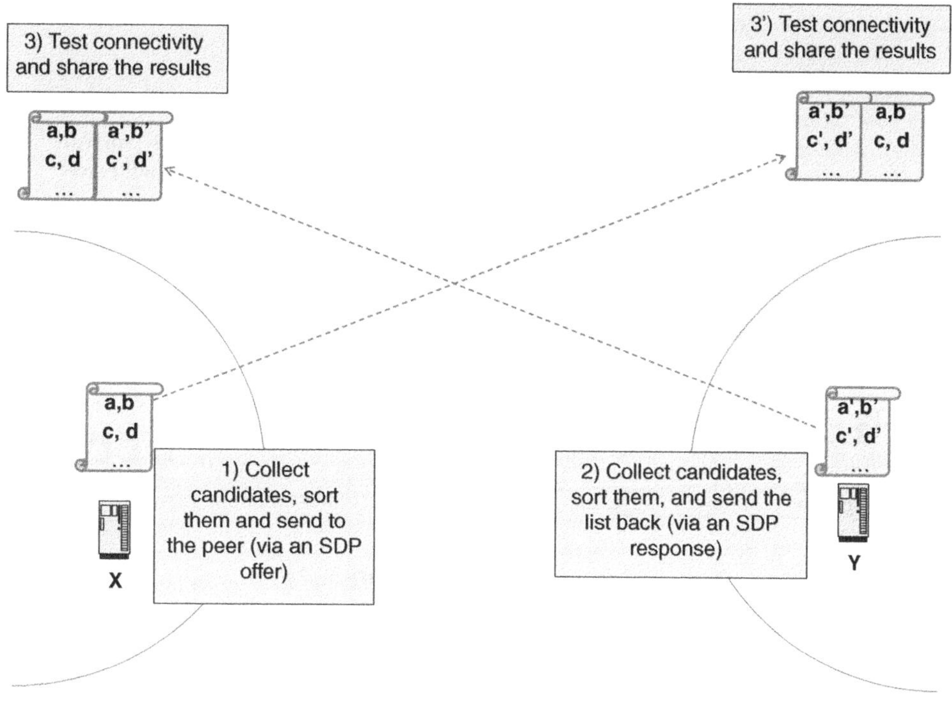

Figure 5.32 ICE operation.

Up into the late 1990s (the history described in [15]), it used to be that a single home computer simply dialed into the provider's network, at which point it was assigned a temporary IP address. This situation has changed drastically. A single home may have many devices now, and all of them are expected to be on all the time.

The addresses for these devices come from the private address space, and the residential gateway provides the NAT service. (Note that it is not only big enterprises or people's homes that are involved, as it is customary for libraries, hotels, bars, and cafés to provide access to the Internet, too.)

For some very large carrier networks it has become impossible to assign to each residential gateway—or enterprise CPE gateway—a public IP address. The solution, depicted in Figure 5.33, has been to assign each of them a private-space address still, and hence deploy another NAT box (this time with the public IP address) at the border with public Internet.

This type of NAT has been called *Carrier-Grade NAT* (*CG NAT* or *CGN*). As it happens, in an industry known for its love of jargon, one name was not enough. Another name denoting the same object is *Large-Scale NAT* (*LS NAT* or *LSN*). And if this were not enough, other terms have been added—playing on the nature of the translation. Common NAT provides IPv4-to-IPv4 translation, and so it has been given the name *NAT 44*. Since CG NAT deployment effects IPv4-to-IPv4-to-IPv4 translation, it is also called *NAT 444*. And so we have three names and four additional acronyms—all of which apply to the same thing. And this is not the end yet: because some NAT boxes also provide IPv4-to-IPv6 translation, we also get the name *NAT 46*. The authors have not seen *NAT 446* or *NAT 644* yet, but they expect these names to appear,

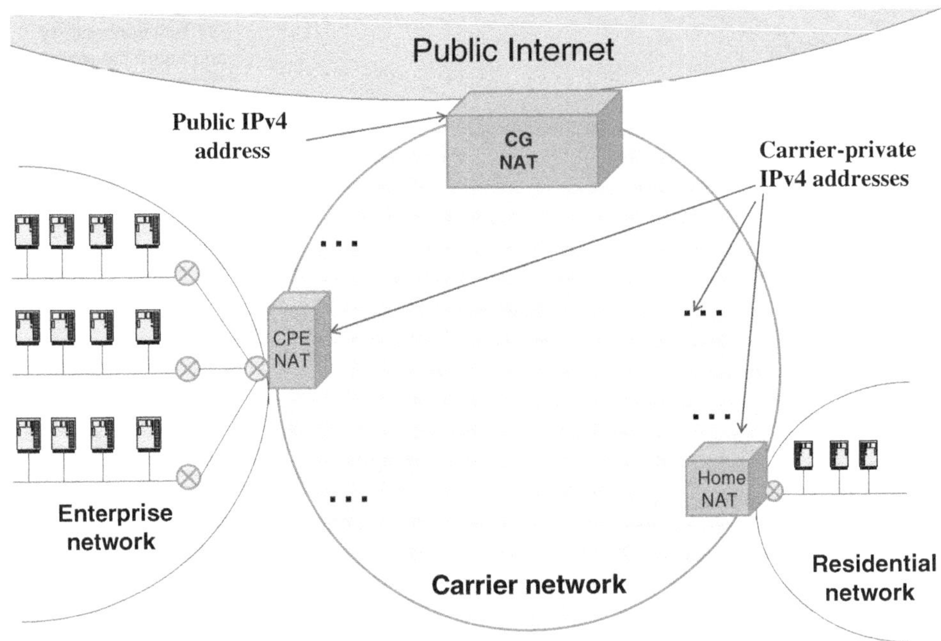

Figure 5.33 Carrier-grade (large-scale) NAT.

too, especially because CG NAT boxes may deal with IPv6 addresses. Nobody expects NATs to be deployed when the whole world turns to IPv6, and so the apocalyptic potential *NAT 666* may very well signify the end of the Internet.

In fact, RFC 6264,[86] while acknowledging that "global IPv6 deployment was slower than originally expected," proposes "an incremental CGN approach [through tunneling] for IPv6 transition. It can provide IPv6 access services for IPv6 hosts and IPv4 access services for IPv4 hosts while leaving much of a legacy ISP network unchanged during the initial stage of IPv4-to-IPv6 migration."

It is not only the terminology that gets complex here. One essentially new and urgent matter is the need for a new private address space. Just as the public IPv4 addresses may not be used inside NAT-protected networks, so the private addresses used by the hosts in home or enterprise networks may not be assigned to gateways and other entities at the next level of translation.

One alarming practice, which emerged in the first decade of this century, was "address squatting." This simply means using the yet-unregistered part of the fast-depleting IPv4 address space. As pointed out by ICANN 's Leo Vegoda in [16]: "Many organizations have chosen to use unregistered IPv4 addresses in their internal networks and, in some cases, network equipment or software providers have chosen to use unregistered IPv4 addresses in their products or services. In many cases the choice to use these addresses was made because the

[86] www.ietf.org/rfc/rfc6264.txt

network operators did not want the administrative burden of requesting a registered block of addresses from a *Regional Internet Registry* (*RIR*)."

Ultimately, in 2012, the Internet community has agreed on the best current practice here, as published in RFC 6598.[87] The practice is to extend the private address space further than specified in RFC 1918 to allocate the IPv4 prefix for the shared address space. Specifically responding to the squatting practice, RFC 6598 forbids numbering the CG-NAT second-level interfaces (e.g., those of gateways) from the pool of "usurped globally unique address space (i.e., squat space)," explaining that when "Service Provider leaks advertisements for squat space into the global Internet, the legitimate holders of that address space may be adversely impacted, as would those wishing to communicate with them." And even "if the Service Provider did not leak advertisements for squat space, the Service Provider and its subscribers might lose connectivity to the legitimate holders of that address space."

But what is left to the service provider then? One of two things:

- Reusing the private address space carefully so that the same address is never assigned to two entities, of which one is inside and the other outside the gateway; or
- Using some new address space (which, incidentally, is the only case when the first option is unenforcible) "in an unmanaged service, where subscribers provide their own CPE and number their own internal network."

The new address space has been specifically designated "with the purpose of facilitating CGN deployment." Subsequently, the *American Registry for Internet Numbers* (*ARIN*) has adopted the following policy: "A second contiguous/10 IPv4 block will be reserved to facilitate IPv4 address extension. This block will not be allocated or assigned to any single organization, but is to be shared by Service Providers for internal use for IPv4 address extension deployments until connected networks fully support IPv6. Examples of such needs include: IPv4 addresses between home gateways and NAT444 translators."

And so the depletion of the IPv4 address space has been postponed once again ... This has not happened without cost though. RFC 6598 lists several examples where certain services become impossible to provide with CG NAT.

Some of these services appear to be of the type one could live without—like console gaming (when two subscribers using the same IPv4 address try to connect with one another. Others include peer-to-peer-to-peer applications and video streaming. More important services in this category are geo-location services that need to identify the location of a CG NAT server and "6-to-4" (i.e., IPv6-to-IPv4) translation, which requires globally reachable addresses.

Now it is easy to follow up on our earlier promise to clarify the enigmatic use case for DMZ, in which an enterprise places its public web server there. Of the two firewalls in Figure 5.20(b), the NAT box is implemented in the one that separates the trusted zone from DMZ. No public server can possibly function behind the NAT, and so the DMZ is the only place (still protected by another firewall) in the enterprise where it can be located. (Similarly, in the case of Figure 5.20(a), the NAT box is located so that it does not interfere with the traffic between the DMZ interface and the public access interface.)

[87] www.ietf.org/rfc/rfc6598.txt

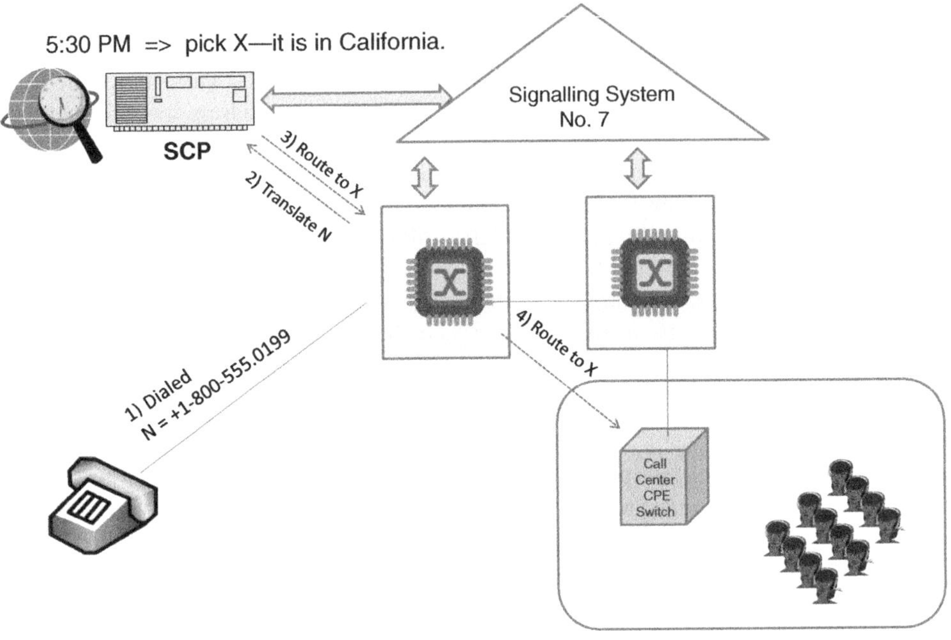

Figure 5.34 A load balancing example: choosing a call center with the 800 service.

We are now ready to move to the next function that is often implemented in firewalls—the load balancing.

5.4 Load Balancers

The concept of load balancing is very intuitive. This is how one chooses the most appropriate resource (out of several identical resources) to perform a given function. Imelda Marcos, for example, has been known for her huge collection of shoes (about 3000 pairs), part of which is displayed in the National Museum of the Philippines. We surmise that she would select a pair considering such factors as the time of day, the weather, and the outfit she planned to wear.[88]

A similar example is from telephony. We have chosen this because it is still widely in use and also because it is very illustrative of virtually all uses of load balancing in IP networks. The example is the so-called 800 (also known as Freephone) service, described in detail in [17] and illustrated in Figure 5.34.

When a person needs to call a company's customer service, the number to reach it indicates a special connection that should be free to a caller; instead the called party (in this case, the company) is billed for it. In the USA, this number is assigned special prefixes—the 800 prefix was the first one to appear when AT&T rolled out the service in the early 1980s—to signal that it should be treated differently from "normal" numbers.

[88] Note that in this example the word "balance" applies to Mrs. Marcos's act of load-balancing her shoes by choosing a particular pair—this should not be confused with her keeping her own balance while wearing them.

When such a number is dialed, the telephone switch immediately knows that it cannot route it and that it needs a special instruction to process it.[89] Hence, the switch turns for instruction to a computer called the *Service Control Point* (*SCP*). (All the signaling data among the switches and NCP flow through a separate data communications network operating on the *Signalling System No. 7* protocols standardized by ITU-T.)

The SCP, in turn, invokes a custom-written service logic program, which makes the translation. In our example, the program looks at the time of the call to decide which call center should be reached. Since the time of day happens to be 5:30 PM, the program figures that the center in New Jersey will be closed for the day, and therefore the most suitable center is that in California (where it is 2:30 PM). Hence the route to the on-premises call center switch in California is specified. For calls starting three hours later, the call center in Bangalore will be specified for the next eight hours, and after that the New Jersey call center. The sun never sets over the company! Note that the translation is handled dynamically, according to the service logic program. (Also note that this example is by no means that of an antiquated technology—Google has been providing a *follow-me* variant of this service as part of Google Voice.[90]

In this example, each call is assigned to a call center based on the center's availability. But with IN it is also possible to choose one out of several call centers based on the distribution of the load: calls will be routed to a center that has been handling fewer calls than the other ones. To this end, the calls can be evenly distributed among the call centers statistically, with assigned weights. In the extreme case, SCP can be used to protect the telephone network from overload by applying *call-gapping*, that is dropping a defined percentage of calls (in which case the caller would hear a fast "busy" signal).

The load-balancing features described above are pretty much uniform across multiple environments. The rest of this section describes load balancing in a modern server farm, provides a practical example of implementing and deploying load balancing, and discusses the use of DNS for the purposes of load balancing.

5.4.1 Load Balancing in a Server Farm

As it happens, the above set of features is pretty much the same as that used in the modern server farm depicted in Figure 5.35. The servers are processes (each process possibly running on a dedicated host) executing a task in response to a client. World Wide Web servers (returning Web pages) were perhaps the first widely used example, followed by SIP servers (for IP telephony), DNS servers, and so on. A load balancer gets the request, which it then forwards to the server it selects.

The back-end servers don't necessarily have to be in the same location; in fact, they can be geographically dispersed (in which case, of course, their collection won't be called a "farm"). In fact, it is not even necessary for the back-up servers to be "servers." Load balancers can be implemented in the routers at the edge of a network, in which case they distribute traffic over spare links.

---

[89] As we mentioned in the previous chapter, this is strikingly similar to the SDN concept. In fact, one of the IN-supported services was called *Software-Defined Network*. But the translation part of it is also very similar to what DNS does: at the minimum, a non-routable number is translated into a routable one, and it is translated *dynamically*.

[90] https://support.google.com/voice/answer/115061?hl=en

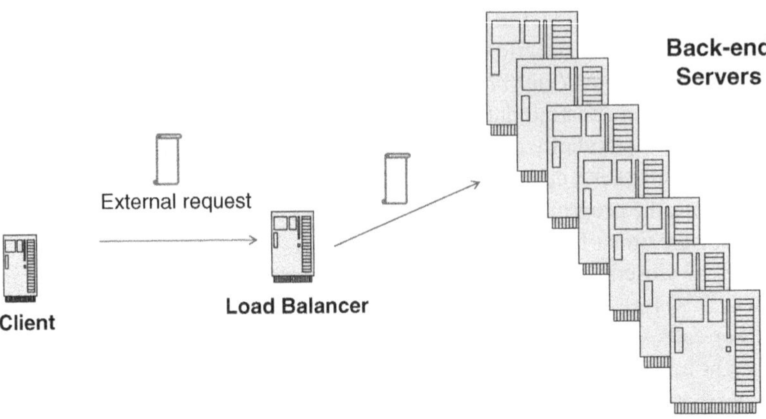

Figure 5.35 A server farm.

A few major benefits of this arrangement are as follows:

1. Speeding up processing (using parallelism—all servers are capable of performing every specified task);
2. Improving reliability (if one or more servers go down, the performance degrades gracefully, being restored when the servers are brought back); and
3. Supporting scalability (with highly parallel tasks, adding new servers increases performance linearly).

The last two items are essential Cloud Computing characteristics, which makes the usefulness of load balancers in Cloud Computing obvious.

There is a benefit for security, too—somewhat similar to that provided by NAT—in that the internal structure of the back-end operation is hidden from outside. When a load balancer is implemented (as is often the case) within the firewall, it can actually terminate a security session, thus saving the back-end servers from maintaining the security state. More important, load balancers are used to mitigate various denial-of-service attacks, notably the SYN attack—by implementing the SYN cookies and delayed binding.

As we can see already, the nature of a load balancer is dual: it is both a middle-man and a scheduler. The latter is the most essential function of a load balancer, and so we will concentrate on that in the rest of this section.

The first pertinent matter here is choosing a scheduling algorithm. There are services for which a back-end server can be selected randomly—with a statistical specification of the proportion of the tasks assigned to each back-end server. A geographic (or network-specific) location of a back-end server can be yet another factor, which may be critical for some applications. With that, a scheduling algorithm can also be based on the feedback mechanism: a load balancer can monitor the load and the health of each server and adjust the task assignments accordingly.

So far, we have tacitly assumed that the type of task suitable to load balancing applications is a one-time request/response transaction. Yet, load balancing has been made to work with session-oriented applications. The major issue here is where to keep the state of a session so that a newly assigned back-end server can know the exact context of a request that has arrived.

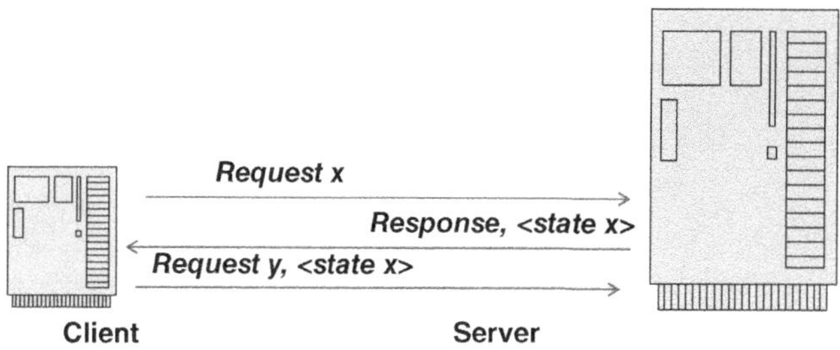

Figure 5.36 Saving session state at the client (a cookie).

Some application protocols—notably HTTP—store the entire state of the session at the client. (Interestingly, this mechanism was apparently developed not with load balancing in mind but to solve the scalability problem. When the number of clients is expected to be significantly large, it becomes impractical or even impossible to store the server-side state of each session on the server. Instead, the protocol forces the client to store that state and then present it to the server in the next message,[91] as depicted in Figure 5.36.

The body of the state information is called a *cookie*. This is a core mechanism enabling many Web applications. Consider shopping online—moving from page to page, putting things in your basket, and so on. The server does not keep the history of the browsing. Instead, it returns a cookie to the client, which the latter is expected to present with the next request. Once the server receives the cookie, it restores the state. Incidentally, this explains why a cookie should be cryptographically protected (lest a rogue client fools the server by modifying the cookie to indicate that the payment has already been made when in fact there was none) and encrypted (to protect both the privacy of the customer and the business interests of the online enterprise).

There are applications, however, which do not use the cookie mechanism. In this case, in order to enable load balancing, the session state is stored in a central database. This, of course, creates a significant reliability problem because of the single point of failure.

There is ongoing research on load balancers, particularly their use in assuring *self-healing* properties of the network. One interesting approach (demonstrated in [18]) is based on analogies with chemistry. For server load balancing, [19] is a comprehensive monograph.

There is no mystery to load balancing, as the next section will attest.

5.4.2 A Practical Example: A Load-Balanced Web Service

In practice, it is very simple to create and deploy load balancing in the Cloud using open-source software.[92] In our example that follows, we use the World-Wide Web service and more

[91] Note the striking similarity with the operation of the CPU. The state of each process is saved in that process's memory—not in CPU—whence the CPU obtains it every time it needs to execute the process.

[92] This example comes from a lab assignment in CS-524 (Introduction to Cloud Computing) that we have been teaching at Stevens Institute of Technology. The authors owe the design of the example to Bo Yu, a brilliant developer, who was our Teaching Assistant in the Spring Semester of 2014.

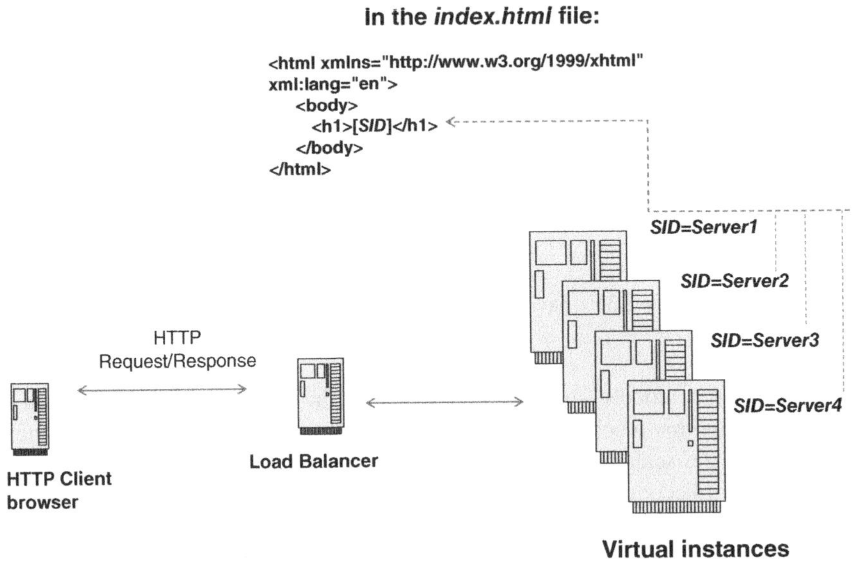

In the *index.html* file:

```
<html xmlns="http://www.w3.org/1999/xhtml"
xml:lang="en">
    <body>
      <h1>[SID]</h1>
    </body>
</html>
```

SID=Server1
SID=Server2
SID=Server3
SID=Server4

HTTP
Request/Response

HTTP Client browser

Load Balancer

Virtual instances

Figure 5.37 An example of an Nginx-based load-balanced web service.

specifically, *Nginx*[93] server software. We recommend that a reader try this as a practical task, using, for example, Amazon's EC2 service.

Our task is to create a website maintained on four identical servers, which are load-balanced by the fifth server, as shown in Figure 5.37. To achieve this, we can create five virtual machines running the Linux operating system as Amazon EC2 instances and deploy the Nginx server on each of them. One machine will use the Nginx server to act as a load balancer among the other four.

For each of the four servers, the *index.html* file (located in the directory/usr/share/nginx/html) should be updated with the text identifying the server id as demonstrated in Figure 5.37 (with the string *SID* being replaced by *Server1*, *Server2*, *Server3*, or *Server4*).

The only thing left to do (and this is the most interesting thing) is to configure the load balancer. This turns out to be as straightforward as configuring the server. The load balancer's configuration file is located at */etc/nginx/nginx.conf*. Figure 5.38 contains the sample code.

In our example, the *weight* of each server has the value 1, which means that at run time the traffic will be distributed equally among the four servers, but the weight values can be assigned arbitrarily, and we recommend that the reader experiment with assigning servers different proportions of the traffic, by setting weights correspondingly. To cause the new configuration to take effect, one needs to execute the shell command: */etc/init.d/nginx reload*.

5.4.3 Using DNS for Load Balancing

It is possible to achieve load balancing even without employing a dedicated front-end server. The load balancing in this case is performed by the DNS translation function, which returns the

---

93 http://nginx.org/

```
events {
        worker_connections 768;
    }
http {
    upstream myapp {
        #ip_hash;
        server [SERVER1_PUBLIC_DNS_NAME] weight=1;
        server [SERVER2_PUBLIC_DNS_NAME] weight=1;
        server [SERVER3_PUBLIC_DNS_NAME] weight=1;
        server [SERVER4_PUBLIC_DNS_NAME] weight=1;
    }
    server
    {
        listen 80;
        server_name myapp.com;
        location /
         {
            proxy_pass http://myapp;
         }
    }
}
```

Figure 5.38 Configuring the load balancer.

IP address of a specific server within the farm. There are two aspects to the DNS-supported load balancing: (1) specifying the addresses of the servers and (2) specifying the load-balancing algorithm.

We will deal with the former aspect first. There are (at least) two ways to specify the addresses, which are presented in Figure 5.39.

In both cases we deal with an abstract service, *<service>*, which could be any application service (*www*, *ftp*, *mail*, *sip*, etc.) supported in both the client and DNS server. Figure 5.39(a) shows the response record, which translates *serv.example.com* into a list of four IP addresses. The alternative, depicted in Figure 5.39(b), is to translate *serv.example.com* into a list of authoritative servers for the four zones so that each zone is administered by the very server to pick up the load.[94] The latter approach slows things down, but it has an advantage in dealing with overload: if the server is, too busy, it won't respond to the DNS query, and so will appear non-existent.

As far as the algorithm for selecting the return order of multiple records is concerned, it is defined—in the *bind* implementation[95]—by using the *rrset-order* specification. Specifically, the *ordering* attribute may take values of *fixed*, *random*, or cyclic (the default). When the ordering is fixed, records are returned exactly in the order they are defined; when it is random, the order is random; when it is cyclic, the order is permuted cyclically—resulting in the *round-robin* schedule.

One problem with the DNS-supported load balancing is caching—the cache returns the same answer for the duration period specified by the TTL parameter. An extreme way of dealing with this problem is to make the TTL value equal to 0, but that would increase the load

[94] To achieve that, the host in question must also run the DNS server software (perhaps a very basic and simplistic version).

[95] The relevant Bind9 Manual chapter is at www.bind9.net/manual/bind/9.3.2/Bv9ARM.ch06.html#rrset_ordering.

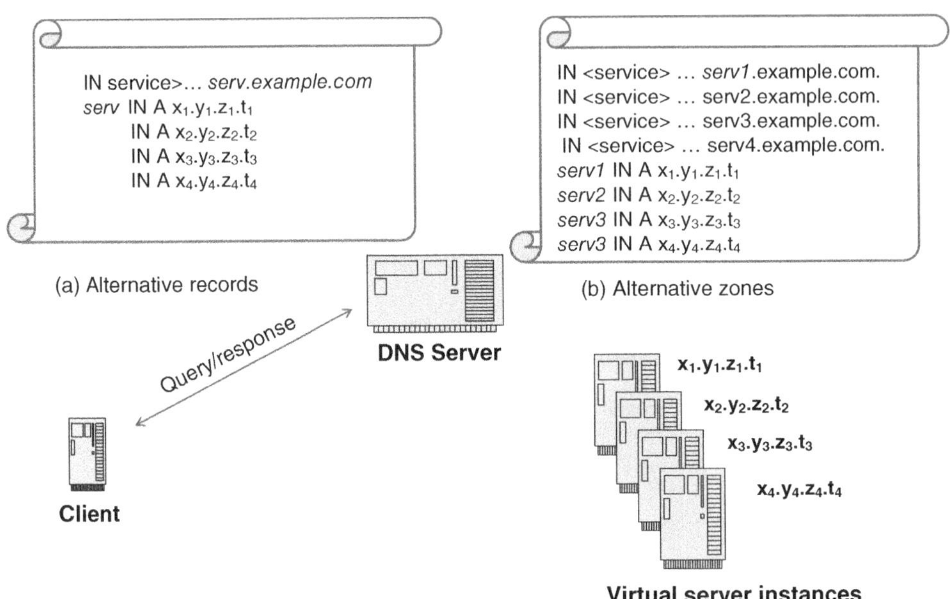

Figure 5.39 Load balancing with DNS.

on the DNS servers. The cache problem is perhaps the most serious to deal with. A number of problems are also caused by the server's availability (or rather lack thereof): if a server is unavailable, the DNS server may still return its address. (Associating the server with its own zone, described earlier, disposes of exactly this problem.) In a less extreme case, the DNS, while unaware of the servers' respective loads, may only provide service distribution rather than load distribution.

To overcome this difficulty, some DNS servers have been enhanced to interact[96] with each server to gather the information on its respective load and then make scheduling decisions based on that information. An earlier (ca. late 1990s) implementation of this type of server is the *Lbnamed* DNS server developed by Rob Riepel of Stanford University. The documentation, software distribution, and accompanying tutorial are available at www.stanford.edu/~riepel/lbnamed/.

With time, the DNS load balancing capabilities have evolved along the lines of intelligent network processing (cf. Figure 5.33)—guided by dedicated service logic. The latter is invoked at the DNS server when a query is received, and it is capable of processing many factors, including the geographic location of the client that issued the request (so as to find the server that is closest to the client).[97] (In a private conversation with an Acamai representative at a conference, we were told that "whatever IN considered we have in our DNS servers!") This confirms once more that solid concepts are invariant to technological fashions—what was good for PSTN is still good for the Internet.

[96] Such interactions are not standardized and depend on the implementation.

[97] We will return to this subject when discussing content delivery services.

There are relevant products on the market. For an example[98] confirming the above observation, we refer the reader to a White Paper [20].

References

[1] Nabokov, V.V. (1979) *The Gift.* Collins Collector's Choice: Five Novels. Collins, London, p. 445.

[2] Gabrilovich, E. and Gontmakher, A. (2002) The homograph attack. *Communications of the ACM*, **45**(2), 128.

[3] Son, S. and Shmatikov, V. (2010) The hitchhiker's guide to DNS cache poisoning. Proceedings of the 6th International ICST Conference on Security and Privacy in Communication Networks (SecureComm), Singapore, September, pp. 466–483.

[4] Goldsmith, J.L. and Wu, T. (2006) *Who Controls the Internet? Illusions of a Borderless World.* Oxford University Press, Oxford.

[5] Scarfone, K. and Hoffman, P. (2009) *Guidelines on Firewall and Firewall Policies.* Recommendations of the National Institute of Standards and Technology, NIST Special Publication 800-41, Revision one. US Department of Commerce, Gaithersburg, MD.

[6] Avolio, F. (1999) Firewalls and Internet security, the second hundred (Internet) years. *The Internet Protocol Journal*, **2**(2), 24–32.

[7] Bellovin, S.M., Cheswick, W.R., and Rubin, A.D. (2003) *Firewalls and Internet Security: Repelling the Wily Hacker*, 2nd edn. Addison-Wesley Professional, Boston, MA.

[8] Eichin, M.W. and Rochlis, J.A. (1989) With microscope and tweezers: An analysis of the Internet virus of November 1988. www.mit.edu/people/eichin/virus/main.html (presented at the 1989 IEEE Symposium on Research on Security and Privacy).

[9] United States General Accounting Office (1989) Virus highlights need for improved Internet management. Report to Chairman, Subcommittee on Telecommunications and Finance, Committee on Energy and Commerce, House of Representatives. IMTEC-89-57, June 12. www.gao.gov/assets/150/147892.pdf.

[10] Pólya, G. (1945) *How to Solve It.* Princeton University Press, Princeton, NJ.

[11] Eddie, W.M. (2006) Defenses against TCP SYN flooding attacks. *The Internet Protocol Journal*, **9**(4), 2–16.

[12] Nietzsche, F.W. (1886) *Beyond Good and Evil.* Cited from the 2006 Filiquarian Publishing edition, New York, p. 82.

[13] Dutcher, B. (2001) *The NAT Handbook.* John Wiley & Sons, Inc., New York.

[14] Zhang, L. (2007) A retrospective view of NAT. *IETF Journal*, **3**(2), 14–20.

[15] Faynberg, I., Lu, H.-L., and Gabuzda, L. (2000) *Converged Networks and Services: Internetworking IP and the PSTN.* John Wiley & Sons, Inc., New York.

[16] Vegoda, L. (2007) Used but unallocated: Potentially awkward/8 assignments. *The Internet Protocol Journal*, **10**(3), 29–33.

[17] Faynberg, I., Gabuzda, L.R., Kaplan, M.P., and Shah, N. (1996) *The Intelligent Network Standards: Their Applications to Services.* McGraw-Hill, New York.

[18] Meyer, T. and Tschudin, C. (2009) A Self-Healing Load Balancing Protocol and Implementation. Technical Report CS-2009-001, University of Basel.

[19] Bourke, T. (2001) *Server Load Balancing.* O'Reilly & Associates, Sebastopol, CA.

[20] Elfiq Networks (2012) Application and Service Delivery with the Elfiq iDNS Module. Technical White Paper, Elfiq Inc., Montreal. www.elfiq.com/sites/default/files/elfiq_white_paper_idns_module_v1.63.pdf.

[98] We are not even attempting to carry out a market or product survey in this book.

6

Cloud Storage and the Structure of a Modern Data Center

Data centers are the workhorses of Cloud Computing.

A data center is where servers, storage, and communication gear reside along with the necessary utilities (e.g., power, cooling, and ventilation equipment). Co-locating equipment this way is natural, since the environmental needs and physical security needs are often common. It also simplifies operations and maintenance. A case in point is that ten computers in a single room are easier to safeguard physically than when the same ten computers are distributed across five rooms.

Most data centers consume vast amounts of energy unnecessarily, wasting 90% or more of the electricity they draw from the grid [1].[1] One reason[2] for such inefficiency is under-utilization of servers: typical utilization figures range from 6% to 12%. Virtualization of data centers offers a way to increase server utilization and reduce energy consumption. It also sets loose the traditional delineation of data centers by hardware, physical casing and wiring, floor space, and other physical attributes.

The resulting *virtual data centers* no longer have well-defined physical boundaries. It goes without saying that a physical data center may host multiple virtual data centers. If the virtual data centers are intended for more than one organization, the physical data center is *multi-tenant*.

But it is also possible to have a virtual data center spanning multiple physical data centers. For instance, an organization may outsource part of its IT infrastructure while maintaining a private data center. In this case the two data centers, which are separate geographically and administratively, are stitched together through an appropriate virtual private network (or tunneling) mechanism to ensure isolation.

[1] Google's data centers are exceptions. They use 50% less energy than typical data centers. This is achieved by, to name just a few steps raising the server floor temperature to 80°F, using outside air for cooling, and building custom servers that are 93% efficient. See www.google.com/about/datacenters/.

[2] Another reason is the practice of keeping servers running all the time.

Cloud Computing: Business Trends and Technologies, First Edition. Igor Faynberg, Hui-Lan Lu and Dor Skuler.

Naturally, on-demand allocation of virtual resources and dynamic relocation of the allocated resources are two essential features that enable virtualization of a data center. Where to allocate and relocate resources may be based on criteria such as performance requirements, load balancing, improved resilience, disaster recovery, and regulatory compliance. The mapping of physical to virtual resources is a matter of implementation. Overall, in addition to virtualization technology, it is also necessary to have a Cloud management system that manages all the resources across the underlying infrastructure and provides a uniform interface to applications [2]. Our discussion of the Cloud management system takes place in Chapter 7.

This chapter discusses the enablers of data center virtualization. We start with a bird's-eye view of a traditional data center, introducing its high-level functional architecture. The core components of this architecture are the *compute*[3] (sic), storage, and networking. One characteristic of traditional data centers is the use of a dedicated, specialized network for storage traffic to bolster performance. This is costly. Fortunately, technological advances are making it possible to use a single network for all traffic without causing performance problems. Thus emerges the next-generation data center, which we are going to describe along the way.

Then we zoom in on storage-related matters, since computing and networking each have their own chapters. We draw upon the shared storage model [3] from the *Storage Networking Industry Association* (*SNIA*) to introduce the taxonomy of storage. We study three types of storage that are distinguished by how they connect to the host: direct-attached storage, network-attached storage, and the *Storage Area Network* (*SAN*). The technology to interconnect the processor and storage devices ranges from the *Small Computer System Interface* (*SCSI*), with a maximum cable length in the order of 10 meters, to *Fibre Channel* (*FC*) or Ethernet, with a maximum cable length in the order of 10 kilometers. For a long time, SCSI was the dominant technology used for direct-attached storage. Its parallel bus design, however, limits the speed and cable length. It is being replaced by the *Serial Attached SCSI* (*SAS*) technology, which makes the interconnection faster and over longer distances. The direct-attached storage is difficult, if not impossible, to share though.

The network-attached storage addresses this limitation. In particular, it allows file sharing over an IP network. But file sharing does not quite work for database applications, which require storage access at a lower level. In addition, storage throughput is limited by the underlying networking media.

This is where SAN enters. SAN is tailored to interconnect storage systems at high speed while supporting resource pooling and block-level access to the pooled resources. It is predominantly based on FC, a popular technology in data centers, which combines the qualities of a serial I/O bus and a switching network.

Obviously, deploying and managing a separate, bespoke network just for storage is expensive, as it entails specialized hardware as well as extra staff to operate it. Consequently, there has been constant interest in finding a way to use a single converged network to carry all types of traffic (while doing so effectively for storage-related traffic). We review the development in this area, focusing on the two primary approaches in data centers: *FC over Ethernet* (*FCoE*) and *Internet SCSI* (*iSCSI*). (It is interesting that at about the same time when iSCSI was being developed, a standard interface for object storage was in the works as well. This happened for a good reason. Object storage, which we discuss next, has been viewed as a missing link toward

[3] *Compute* (as a noun) is a new (and rather ugly and imprecise) term coined in the industry to refer to computing resources as opposed to storage resources.

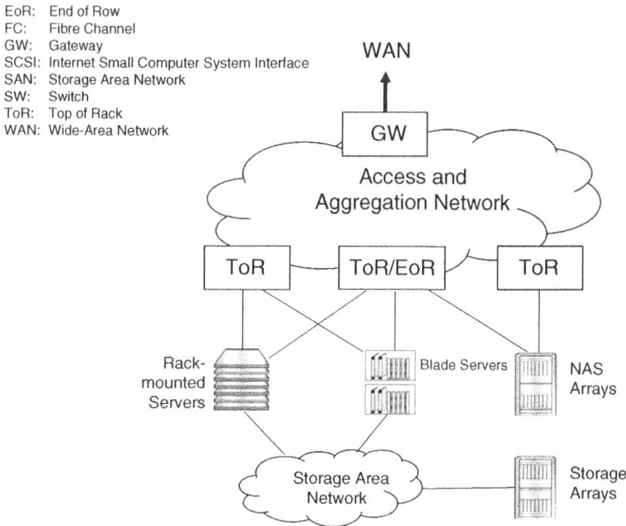

Figure 6.1 Traditional data center.

fulfilling the promise of the shareable storage enabled by iSCSI: unmediated host access with granular access control.)

The next topic discussed in this chapter is *storage virtualization*, which is a mechanism for shielding applications from the underlying detail of physical storage. Virtualization of network storage is important to Cloud Computing because it enables effective resource pooling and simplifies management tasks, such as *snapshots* and *migration*.

Finally, we discuss *solid-state storage*. In terms of storage media, technologies exist with varied performance and cost. At the one extreme is *Random Access Memory* (*RAM*); at the other extreme is magnetic tape. Somewhere in the middle is the relatively new flash memory base of solid-state technology. Like RAM, flash memory is semiconductor-based and so no moving parts are involved. It is also faster than hard disk and cheaper than RAM. These qualities make the flash memory technology a viable member of the storage hierarchy and a serious challenger to that of hard disk. Moreover, given its superior performance in random read operations, flash memory has become essential to Cloud Computing. The quest for high performance in Cloud Computing also prompts developments such as *RAMCloud* [4] and *Memcached* [5], which we examine as well. Both developments exploit RAM but focus on different aspects. RAMCloud in essence aims to build a remote cache practically of infinite capacity, while *Memcached* supports a simple key-value store for caching arbitrary data within the respective memory units for a pool of commodity computers.

The limits on the size of this book don't allow us to address some important aspects of data centers such as configuration, power, and thermal management. We refer to [6] for a complementary overview.

6.1 Data Center Basics

Figure 6.1 depicts the high-level functional architecture of a traditional data center. The hardware modules are organized into rows of racks of a standard dimension to ease deployment.

This section introduces the key components, which, once virtualized, become the building blocks of virtual data centers.

6.1.1 Compute

The *compute* components are high-performance computers called *servers*, which are accessible via a network. They are expected to be reliable and capable of handling large workloads. Servers span a wide range in cost and capabilities. In comparison with desktop computers, they are much more expandable in terms of computing[4] and input/output capacity. Servers also have different form factors than desktop computers. They come in the form of either rack-mounted or blade servers. These forms are optimized to reduce their physical footprint and interconnection complexity (cabling spaghetti). Such optimization is necessary in the face of an ever-increasing number of servers that need to be put in the constrained space of a data center.

A rack-mounted server is inserted horizontally into a rack (typically 19 inches wide). It is denoted by its height, which varies discretely in the rack unit, of 1.75 inches (known as *RU* or simply *U*), defined by [7]. Namely, a 1U server is 1U high, a 2U server is 2U high, and so on. Most single- and dual-socket servers are available as 1U servers.

A rack housing rack-mounted servers may be a simple metal enclosure or it can be a complex piece of equipment armed with power distribution, air or liquid cooling, and a keyboard/video/mouse switch that allows a single keyboard, video, and mouse to be shared among servers.

A blade server (or simply a blade) is even more compact than a rack-mounted server. The smaller form factor is achieved by eliminating pieces that are not specific to computing—such as cooling. As a result, a blade may amount to nothing more than a computer circuit board that has a processor, memory, I/O, and an auxiliary interface. Such a blade certainly cannot function on its own. It is operational only when inserted into a chassis that incorporates the missing modules. The chassis accommodates multiple blades. It also provides a switch through which the servers within connect to the external network. Worth noting here is that the chassis also fits into a rack much like a rack-mounted server.

A given rack space can house more blade servers than rack-mounted servers. The chassis–blade arrangement offers other benefits as well: reduced power consumption, simpler cabling, lower cost, and so on. This makes blade servers more attractive in the Cloud Computing environment.

6.1.2 Storage

In terms of how it is connected to servers, storage may be classified as *Direct-Attached Storage* (*DAS*), *Network-Attached Storage* (*NAS*), and *Storage Area Network* (*SAN*). For simplicity, Figure 6.2 depicts only NAS and SAN.

DAS, as the term implies, is directly attached to a processor through a point-to-point link. (The dominant technology in this case is the hard-disk drive.) In contrast, NAS and SAN reside across a network. This network is purpose-built for, and dedicated to, storage traffic in

[4] Servers tend to fashion chips with multiple processors (or cores), such as Intel® Xeon®, and AMD Opteron™ processors.

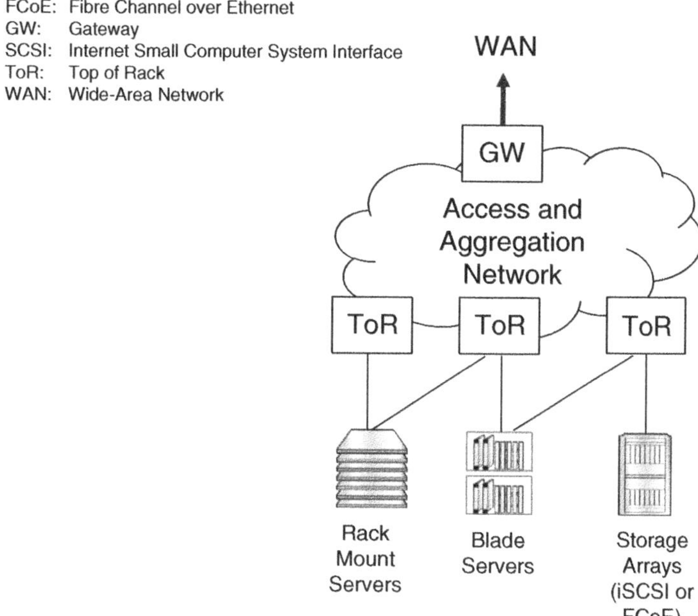

Figure 6.2 Next-generation data center.

the case of SAN. One major difference between NAS and SAN lies in the semantics of the interface. The NAS units are files or objects, while the SAN units are disk blocks. Another key difference lies in the underlying transport. SAN relies on specialized transport, FC, which is optimized for storage traffic. NAS does not require anything special apart from the IP network. We will discuss the integration of both types of access after taking a closer look at the forms of storage.

For now, we note that NAS and SAN are readily applicable to Cloud Computing but DAS has a limitation. An essential feature of Cloud Computing is flexible allocation of virtual machines based on, among other factors, resource availability and geographical location. In the DAS case, when a virtual machine moves to a new physical host, the associated storage needs to move to the same host, too, which is likely to result in consuming both much bandwidth and much time.

Storage is further classified as online storage and offline storage. Online storage is accessible to a server, while offline storage, which is intended for archiving, is not. Magnetic tape libraries and optical jukeboxes are common implementations of offline storage. They usually come with automatic control via a robotic arm that can locate, fetch, mount, dismount, and put back a tape or disc. Google data centers, for example, have employed robotic tape libraries for backup.

Besides magnetic tapes and optical discs, common storage media include magnetic disks and integrated circuits (i.e., solid-state electronics). Among these, magnetic hard disks are most prevalent.[5] Because of their mechanics, they are much more suited to sequential than

[5] Hard disks have also dominated secondary memory in the computer memory hierarchy since 1965. The disk access speed has always been much slower than the CPU speed. The order of magnitude of the gap is seven and it is still growing.

random access. Here, solid-state storage comes to the rescue. Originally used in mobile devices such as smart phones, digital cameras, and MP3 music players, solid-state storage is faster (from 100 to 1000 times) and sturdier than hard disks, but it is more expensive. As the price of solid-state storage continues to drop, however, it has become a viable option. It is particularly applicable to Cloud Computing, which makes I/O operations more random than ever because of hardware sharing across unrelated applications. We will discuss solid-state storage further in Section 6.2.5.

6.1.3 Networking

The servers of a data center need to be interconnected, and they need to connect to the outside world as well. As the number of servers increases, more cables have to fit into a given space. *Top-of-Rack* (*ToR*) and *End-of-Row* (*EoR*) are two approaches to connectivity resulting in different cabling options. In the ToR approach, each rack has a switch at the top to which all servers in the rack connect. As a result, the cable connecting a server to the ToR switch does not need to be longer than the height of the rack. A ToR switch typically provides external network access. Normally, it is sufficient for a ToR switch to have just enough ports to support the servers within the same rack.

In the EoR approach, each row (of racks) has a switch at its end to which all nearby servers and switches in other racks in the same row connect. This may require long cables of different lengths running between the servers and switches. Depending on its actual length and required bandwidth, a fiber-optic cable may be needed (where a copper connection would suffice in the ToR case). Here the cost of cabling could exceed the cost of a server supporting multiple links.

An EoR switch is placed in a rack (possibly all by itself due to its size). It may provide network access and aggregation.

Both ToR and EoR switches are typically implemented using Ethernet technology. We will return to this subject later. For now we just note that Ethernet technology is particularly important to data centers because of its potential to eliminate employing separate transport mechanisms (e.g., FC) for storage and interprocessor traffic. Figure 6.2 depicts a next-generation data center with common Ethernet transport.

Finally, note that the data-center aggregation network connects to the *Wide Area Network* (*WAN*) through a gateway. On the other side of the WAN may be a single user device or a full-blown data center.

6.2 Storage-Related Matters

As the number of users and devices connecting to the Internet keeps rising, the world is deluged with data. Every day brings with it more than an exabyte[6] (i.e., 10^{18} bytes) of traffic on the Internet. In 2011 alone, more than 1.8 exabytes of data were created globally (with about three-quarters of the data created by human users). The total amount of data is staggering, and it is still growing. The need to store and process the data puts an enormous strain on Cloud storage.

[6] The standard prefix *exa* was adopted at the 15th General Conference on Weights and Measures in 1975. To address "the very large scales of measurement that scientific advances required," additional prefixes for multiples (i.e., *zetta* (10^{21}) and *yotta* (10^{24})) were adopted in 1991. As the big data trend continues, there will soon be a need for new prefixes beyond yotta.

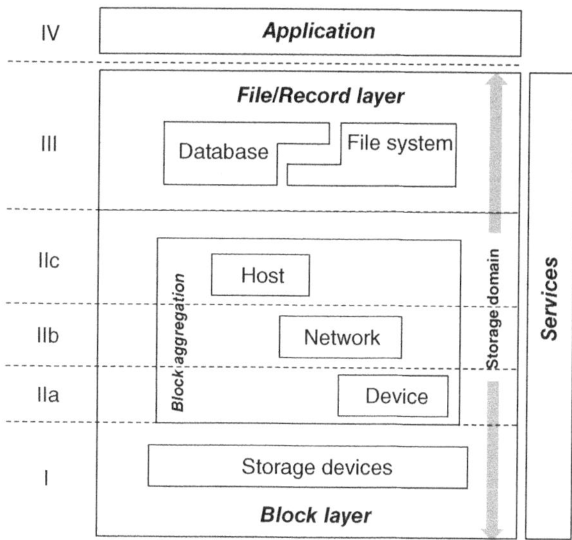

Figure 6.3 SNIA shared storage model.

There are three aspects to keeping up with this pressure. First, the storage capacity needs to increase constantly; second, the stored data need to be secured; and third, access to the data needs to be made more efficient.

To help examine matters related to Cloud storage, we draw upon the *shared-storage model* [3] from the SNIA. Initially developed in 2001, the model reflects the then trend that storage should be managed as an independent resource shared among multiple computing systems. More than ten years later, Cloud Computing not only continues this trend but also amplifies it in a major way.

As shown in Figure 6.3, the SNIA model consists of multiple layers, with each layer providing certain services in an implementation-neutral manner to the higher layers. As a result, the higher layers are shielded from the implementation details of the lower layers and the design complexity of the system is reduced. In this sense, the model is similar to the OSI model [8].

At the top is the application layer that uses the services provided by the underlying storage domain. Example applications are web servers, search engines, analytics engines, and online transactions engines. The application layer is included in the model only to show the relationship between the storage domain and its clients; storage-specific applications have a special place. The services subsystem (denoted by the services box in Figure 6.3) captures the basic functions such as discovery, management, security, and backup.

Beside the services subsystem, the storage domain is divided into the file/record layer, the block aggregation layer, and the block layer. The file/record layer serves the application layer and is normally implemented in software. It presents data in terms of files, file records, and similar items that are easily accessible to applications. This involves mapping the application-accessible parcels to the underlying logical building blocks (i.e., logical volumes[7]). Database management and file systems in wide use belong here. A file system

[7] A logical volume may combine non-contiguous physical partitions and span multiple physical storage devices.

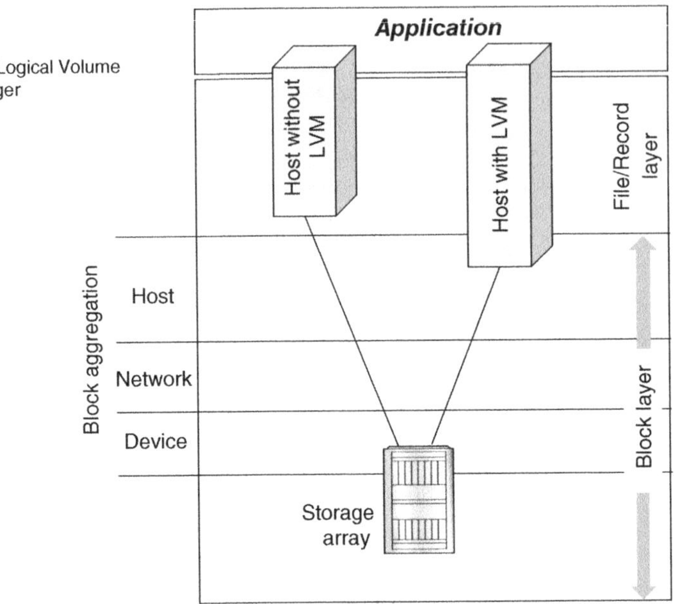

Figure 6.4 An example of direct-attached storage.

maps bytes to files to volumes.[8] Similarly, a database management system maps records to tables to volumes. The file/record layer may be implemented in a host alone or as a network file system. The latter is a special case of network-attached storage, to be discussed later.

The block aggregation layer provides services to the file/record layer. It provides block-based aggregation independent of the actual storage devices, how the devices are interconnected, and how storage is distributed among them. To this end, aggregation may be achieved through virtualization at the host, network, or device level, involving tasks such as space management, *striping*,[9] and mirroring.[10] In particular, the transport of data to and from storage devices is governed by a set of peripheral interface and storage network standards, which we will address later.

The block layer provides services to the block aggregation layer, providing low-level storage of fixed-size blocks and functions such as numbering of logical units, caching, and access control.

6.2.1 Direct-Attached Storage

DAS, the most common storage arrangement, is dedicated to a single host. At least initially, the defining characteristic of this type of storage is that (1) the host and storage devices are interconnected through point-to-point links and (2) the host controls the devices. Figure 6.4

[8] A volume refers to all the blocks of a file system. It may consist of blocks from a storage medium or several storage media. In the former case, it is also called a partition.

[9] Striping concerns partitioning logically sequential data and storing the partitions across multiple devices that are accessible in parallel. As a result, the overall data throughput is increased.

[10] Mirroring is duplicating data in a second set of devices for failure protection.

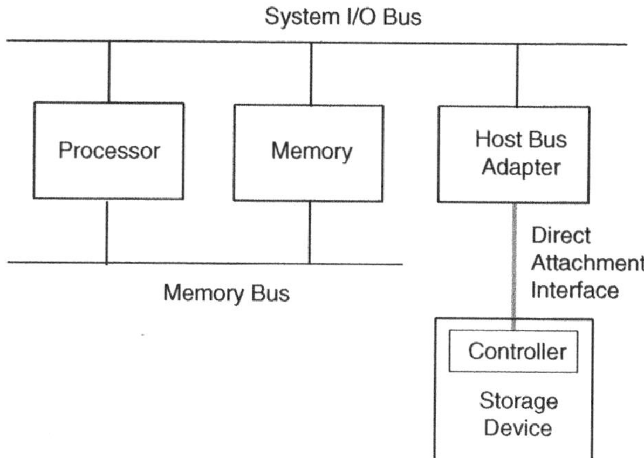

Figure 6.5 A schematic direct-attachment interface.

shows an example (in relation to the SNIA model) where a block-oriented protocol is used over direct links, and block aggregation is done by either the host (through a logical volume manager) or the storage array controller. A block-oriented protocol handles data in terms of fixed-size blocks. In contrast, a file-oriented protocol handles data in terms of variable-size files, which are then divided into blocks handled by the storage. Network-attached storage such as *Network File System* (*NFS*) employs a file-oriented protocol, which we will discuss in the next section.

Since DAS is not subject to network delay, it is suitable for keeping local data such as boot image and swap space. Depending on the location of the storage device with respect to the host, DAS may be internal or external. The internal hard-disk drive of a host is an example of internal DAS. Naturally, the total capacity of internal DAS is in part constrained by the amount of physical space within a computer enclosure. External DAS will be more flexible in this regard. Whether DAS is internal or external, there is the need for an interface for the host and storage device to communicate with each other to carry out I/O operations. Figure 6.5 shows exactly where the interface belongs. The bus adapter on the host and the controller on the storage device implement the interface. The host bus adapter serves as a bridge between the system I/O bus and the direct attachment interface, and shields the details of the storage device. As a result, a storage device with a standard interface can be attached to hosts of distinct processors and architectures. The *Small Computer System Interface* (*SCSI*) is an example of this type of standard interface. Applicable to both internal and external DAS, SCSI is in common use in data centers.

SCSI was first standardized by the *American National Standards Institute* (*ANSI*) in 1986 as X3.131-1986. The standard is based on the *Shugart Associates System Interface* (*SASI*), introduced around 1979 by Shugart Associates, then a premiere disk drive manufacturer.[11] In

[11] Its actual development was done in the X3T9.2 Task Group of the International Committee on Information Technology Standards (INCITS). The X3T9.2 Task Group was the predecessor of the X3T10 Technical Committee. X3T10 was later shortened to just T10. The technical committee is responsible for SCSI specifications, including those on serial attached SCSI.

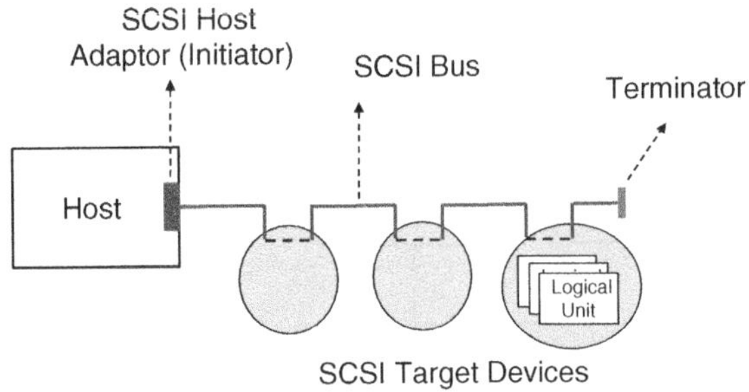

Figure 6.6 An example SCSI configuration.

light of the ensuing developments, the original standard is also known as SCSI-1. It defines a parallel bus for attachment of various types of peripheral devices, including hard-disk drive, tape drive, CD-ROM, scanner, printer, and host bus adapter. Multiple devices (or more precisely their controllers) can be attached to the same bus via daisy-chaining (as depicted in Figure 6.6), resulting in the multi-drop configuration. There is, however, a limit on the number of devices that can be chained. The limit depends on the data bus width. A k-bit-wide bus supports at most k devices, including the host bus adaptor. The limitation is due to the underlying design of mapping each single enabled bit to a particular address assignable to a device. Figure 6.7 shows the mapping for an eight-bit data bus. Note that the address (or identifier) of a SCSI device implies a certain priority level, which is an important factor in bus arbitration during contention. The same prioritization scheme is used in cases with wider buses. Namely, the more significant a bit is, the higher priority is assigned to its corresponding address. As it turns out, backward compatibility is important, and so a somewhat convoluted scheme is in place to preserve the priority rankings of the first byte of the bus.

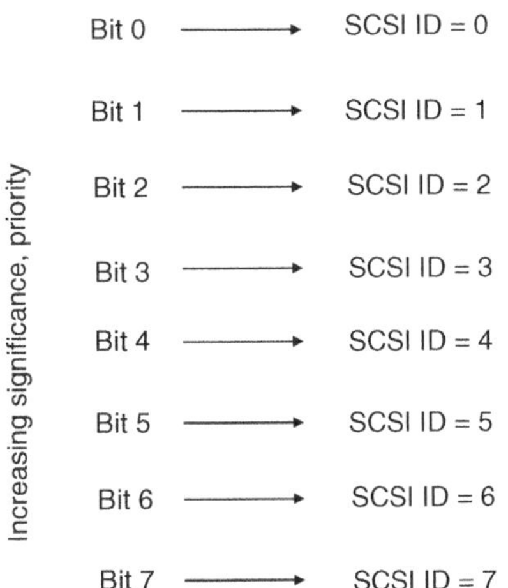

Figure 6.7 SCSI addressing for an 8-bit data bus.

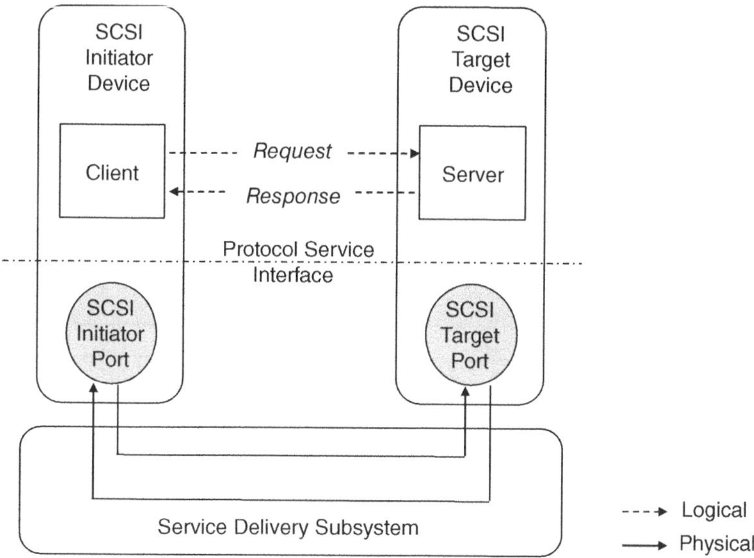

Figure 6.8 SCSI client–server model.

A device can be further associated with multiple logical units addressable by *Logical Unit Numbers* (*LUNs*). To the operating system, a LUN appears as an I/O device. An example of a multiple-LUN device is a CD jukebox, where each CD is a logical unit that can be addressed separately. Naturally, to serve any I/O purposes the devices on the same bus need to be able to communicate with one another as well as with the host. At a high level, SCSI communication is based on the master–slave model shown in Figure 6.8. In SCSI parlance, the entity issuing requests is called the *initiator* and the entity responding to requests, the *target*. A request may be for an I/O operation (a *command*) such as *read* or *write*, or for a task management function such as aborting an operation. In the case of an I/O operation, the data transfer takes

Version	Data Bus Width (bit)	Clock Rate (MHz)	Throughput (MBps)	No. of Devices
SCSI-1	8	5	5	8
Fast SCSI (SCSI-2)	8	10	10	8
Fast Wide SCSI (SCSI-2)	16	10	20	16
Ultra SCSI (SCSI-3)	8	20	20	8
Ultra Wide SCSI (SCSI-3)	16	20	40	16
Ultra2 SCSI	8	40	40	8
Ultra2 wide SCSI	16	40	80	16
Ultra3 SCSI	16	40	160	16
Ultra-320 SCSI	16	80	320	16
Ultra-640 SCSI	16	160	640	16

Figure 6.9 Comparison of different SCSI versions.

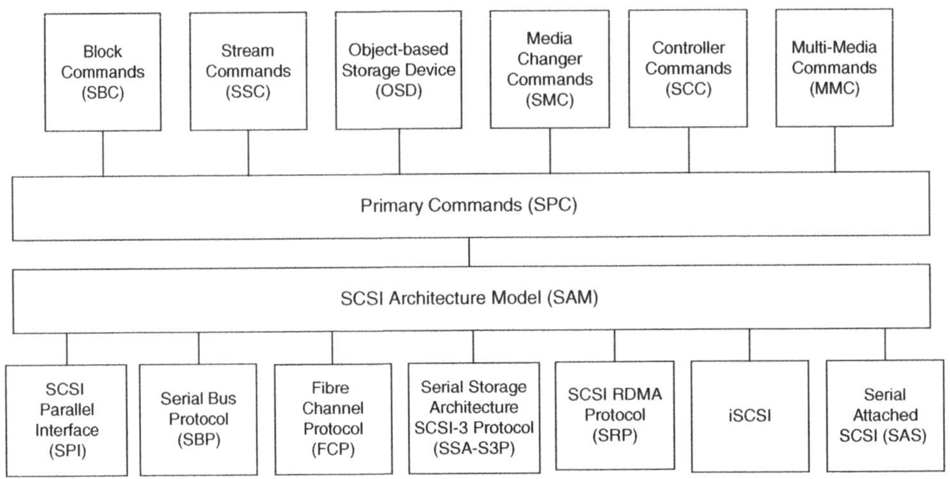

Figure 6.10 Organization of SCSI standards.

place between the request and the final response. The direction of the data transfer is from the initiator to the target in a *write* operation, and the other way around in a *read* operation.

The SCSI standard supports a set of commands, each command assigned its own operation code. The specifics of a command are communicated to the target via a *Command Descriptor Block* (*CDB*) over the bus (which is part of the service delivery subsystem). Because the bus is shared, SCSI specifies how exclusive control of the bus is arbitrated among multiple devices. Usually the device with the highest-priority address wins the arbitration. The winning device becomes the initiator, in a position to select and command a target device to carry out the desired I/O operations. It thus follows that the *Host Bus Adaptor* (*HBA*) is assigned the highest-priority identifier to secure the role of the initiator.

Over the years, SCSI has gone through several iterations of improvement in various aspects—including reliability and performance—making SCSI useful to data centers. Figure 6.9 compares different SCSI versions in terms of bus width, clock rate, throughput, and number of devices supported. On top of the various improvements, SCSI has evolved from a self-contained standard addressing a myriad of aspects (such as protocols and cabling) to a family of standards with a layered structure separating physical interconnections from transport protocols and I/O commands. Figure 6.10 is a snapshot[12] of the forever-evolving SCSI family, which covers varied types of I/O device and interconnections. At the center is the *SCSI Architecture Model* (*SAM*), the glue that holds the family together. It specifies a functional abstraction of the common behaviors of I/O devices and interconnections in terms of objects,[13] protocol layers, and service interfaces. Adjacent protocol layers, in particular, interact with each other through well-defined service requests, indications, responses, and confirmations (see Figure 6.11). The layered structure allows flexibility in choice of interface

[12] www.t10.org/scsi-3.htm

[13] For example, a relationship between an initiator and a target is represented by the object named *nexus*.

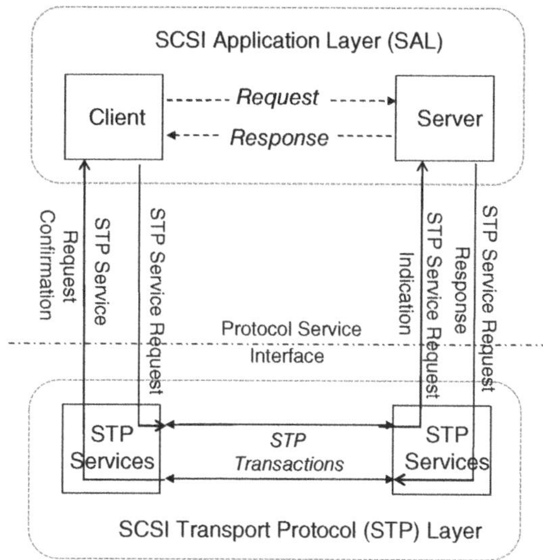

Figure 6.11 SCSI interlayer relationship.

hardware, software, and media in actual implementations. It also allows each layer to advance independently.

One important advance as a result is *Serial Attached SCSI* (*SAS*), first published as an ANSI standard in 2003. (The standard is called ANSI INCITS 376-2003). The shift to serial attachment aims to bypass the progressively intractable problems associated with parallel attachment as throughput increases. The key difference between the two lies in the physical layer. Traditional SCSI uses multiple lines to transfer data in parallel, which is subject to, among other things, cross-talk and inconsistent signal arrival times (i.e., timing skew). In contrast, SAS uses a single line to transfer data sequentially. Free from the problems associated with parallel attachment, SAS can support faster clocks and greater distances. At the time of this writing, 1.5 GBps is already available in the version known as SAS-3 and the throughput is expected to grow. In comparison, the fastest version of traditional SCSI (i.e., Ultra-640 SCSI) supports 640 MBps. SAS also offers other advantages, including better scalability (i.e., the capability to attach tens of thousands of devices) and simplified cabling. Because of its superiority, SAS is supplanting its parallel predecessors.[14]

The evolution of SCSI technology actually follows that of *Advanced Technology Attachment* (*ATA*), a low-cost, popular interface used in internal DAS in personal computers and electronic devices. Originally designed as a parallel interface for IBM PC AT, ATA has given rise to *Serial ATA* (*SATA*), which SAS has eventually leveraged. Among other things, SAS uses the point-to-point interconnection—just as SATA does, supports a superset of SATA signals (which are electric patterns sent on power-up for initialization, resetting, and speed-negotiation purposes), and adopts connectors that are compatible with SATA. As a result, it is possible to

[14] A "cousin" is SCSI-3. The corresponding command set is kept in the key protocol stack for the SAN, which was developed about the same time. We will discuss SAN later.

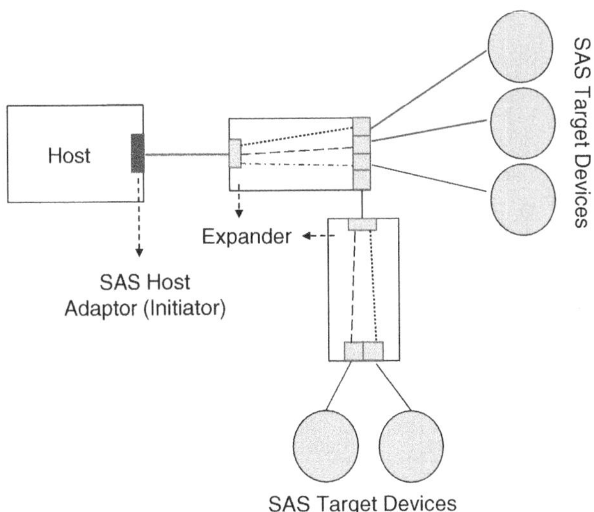

Figure 6.12 An example of SAS configuration.

interconnect a mixed set of SAS and SATA devices, which, in turn, increases the relevance of SATA technology along with its later extension for external storage (called *eSATA*) to the needs of data centers.

The point-to-point interconnection is a departure from daisy chaining. It requires a special device (called an *expander*) when there are more than two SAS devices to be interconnected. The device (distinct from a SAS device which serves as an initiator, a target, or both) is essentially a virtual-circuit switch allowing an initiator to connect to multiple targets. It does so using three routing methods: *direct*, *table*, and *subtractive*. In direct routing, the expander recognizes that the targets of connection requests are directly attached and route the requests accordingly. In table routing, the expander routes connection requests to an attached expander based on a routing table (which is provisioned or created through a discovery procedure). In subtractive routing, the expander routes unresolved connection requests using the other two methods to another expander that may be able to resolve the requests.

Expanders come in two flavors: edge expanders and fan-out expanders. One difference between them is the number of expanders that can be attached. An edge expander can be attached to multiple SCSI devices but just one other expander. In contrast, a fan-out expander can be attached both to multiple SCSI devices and multiple expanders. Figure 6.12 shows an example configuration involving an HBA, five SAS storage devices, and two expanders. The HBA connects to each storage device point-to-point through the dedicated virtual circuits provided within the expanders. It is straightforward to interconnect more SAS devices by adding extra expanders. The relative flexibility in the use of expanders explains why SAS can support many more devices than traditional SCSI can. The gains, however, come at the expense of simplicity. A set of new needs arises, including those for connection and configuration management, a robust addressing scheme (which is not tied to the physical layout of the parallel bus), and a communication mechanism between a SAS device and an expander.

ATA: Advanced Technology Attachment
SSP: Serial SCSI Protocol
STP: Serial ATA Tunneled Protocol
SMP: Serial Management Protocol

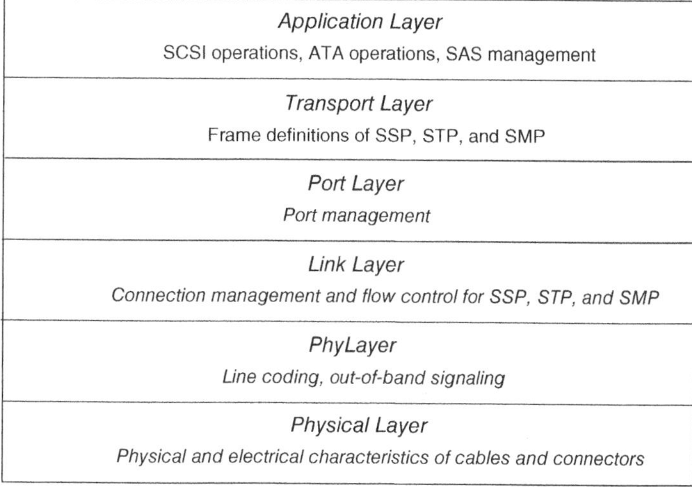

Application Layer
SCSI operations, ATA operations, SAS management
Transport Layer
Frame definitions of SSP, STP, and SMP
Port Layer
Port management
Link Layer
Connection management and flow control for SSP, STP, and SMP
PhyLayer
Line coding, out-of-band signaling
Physical Layer
Physical and electrical characteristics of cables and connectors

Figure 6.13 Serial attached SCSI architecture.

The SAS architecture supports three protocols:

1. *Serial SCSI Protocol* (*SSP*), which is for communication between two SAS devices and between a SAS device and an expander. It preserves the SCSI command set while adding support for multiple initiators and targets. SSP is the primary protocol in SAS;
2. *SATA Tunneled Protocol* (*STP*), which allows a SAS initiator device to communicate with a SATA target device through an expander. The expander, serving as a gateway, speaks STP on the initiator side and SATA on the target side. The protocol extends SATA to support multiple initiators; and
3. *Serial Management Protocol* (*SMP*), which is for communication with expanders. It covers discovery and configuration management.

Figure 6.13 shows the SAS architecture. Again, as in the OSI model, each layer provides services to the layer above and utilizes the services provided by the layer below:

- *Physical layer* deals with the physical and electrical characteristics of cables, connectors, and transceivers.
- *Phy layer* deals with line coding, out-of-band signals, and other preparations (e.g., speed negotiation) necessary for serial transmission. The name of the layer reflects the logical construct *phy* that represents a transceiver (consisting of a transmitter and a receiver) on a device. A phy has an 8-bit identifier that is unique within a device. The identifier is assigned by a management function. Its value is an integer equal to or greater than zero and less than the number of phys on the device. On line coding, SAS prescribes 8b/10b,

following the lead of FC (to be discussed later). 8b/10b was originally developed by IBM researchers [9] for high-speed data transmission. The moniker reflects a key characteristic of the coding scheme: the 8-to-10-bit transformation of data blocks before transmission. The transformation is optimized to have enough transitions (i.e., 0 to 1 or 1 to 0) in each encoded block to keep the sender and receiver in sync, and to have the number of 0s and 1s as equal as possible to minimize the direct-current component. The 8-to-10 expansion gives enough room for such optimization while incurring a 25% transmission overhead. In comparison, Manchester encoding, which is used in 10-MBps Ethernet, has a 100% transmission overhead. The large overhead becomes a problem as the speed increases.

- *Link layer* defines the primitives and their encodings on the wire and handles—among other things, connection management and flow control. Three link layers are defined—for SSP, STP, and SMP, respectively.
- *Port layer* is primarily responsible for managing the phys on a port. A port contains one or more phys and is assigned a unique identifier by the device manufacturer. The identifier is the address used in all communications. It is 64 bits long in the World Wide Name format, which is also supported in FC (to be discussed later).
- *Transport layer* addresses the transport services as defined in SAM and framing (including the frame formats) for SSP, STP, and SMP. In the case of SSP, the frame format incorporates the CDB data structure and other constructs to carry the information related to SCSI operations.
- *Application layer* supports SCSI operations, ATA operations, and SAS management. To send commands to a server, for instance, an application client invokes the appropriate transport services (typically implemented as procedural calls).

The monographs [10, 11] provide additional information on ATA, SCSI, and their serial counterpart technologies.

6.2.2 Network-Attached Storage

NAS provides file- or object-level access over a local area network. Placing storage on the network facilitates information sharing among many computers and simplifies the related storage management. In this respect, NAS is a good fit for Cloud Computing, the observation validated by the rapid development of high-capacity, high-availability NAS systems for data centers.

A network file system is the earliest and most well-known manifestation of NAS. It is accessible to an arbitrary number of remote clients through an application-layer protocol as though it were local. Figure 6.14 depicts the arrangement. To help explain NAS, we review the key concepts of file systems and then the widely implemented NFS, originally developed at Sun Microsystems [12].

A file system native to a host is maintained by the operating system. At the highest level, a file system appears as a collection of files and directories[15] (or folders). Files and directories can be created, deleted, opened, closed, read, and written. They can also be moved from directory to directory. Most file systems support a hierarchical structure: a directory may have

[15] A directory may be treated as a special file that contains information about the files and subdirectories therein.

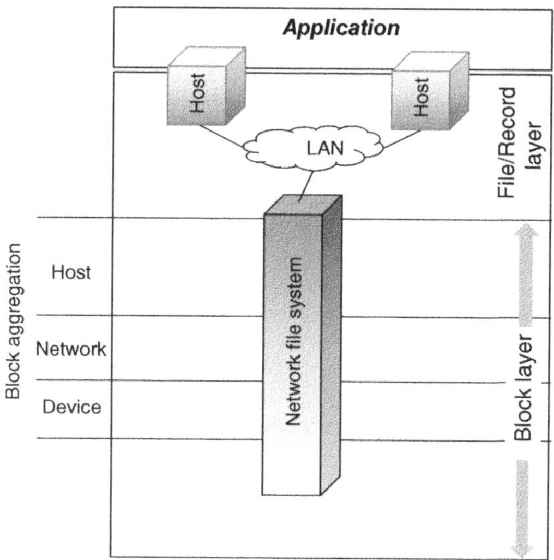

Figure 6.14 A network file system.

subdirectories; a subdirectory may have sub-subdirectories; and so on. Figure 6.15 shows such a directory.

A file system manages space in terms of blocks, in step with the back-end storage directly attached to the host. A block is a fixed-size sequence of bytes that is addressable as a whole. A file is implemented as a link list of blocks. How the file is represented to a user differs from one operating system to another. Earlier operating systems defined files as lists of records of specified format. In contrast, in the Unix operating system—as well as in Linux—the file is merely a sequence of bytes.

The block size is constrained by the logical organization of the underlying storage medium. It is traditionally set to a multiple of the smallest unit that can be handled on a magnetic disk—the dominant storage medium for the last 50 years or so.

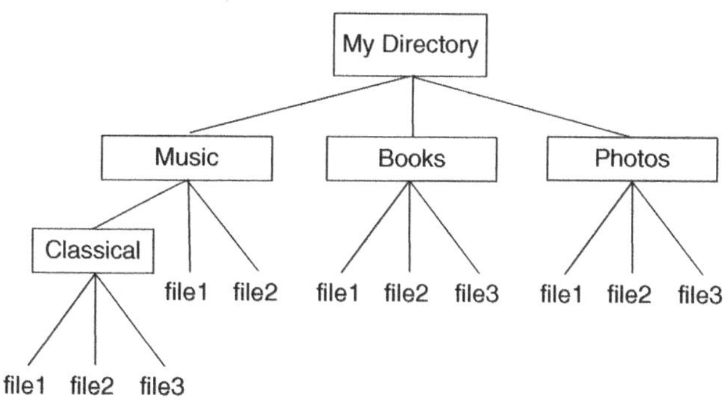

Figure 6.15 A hierarchical directory.

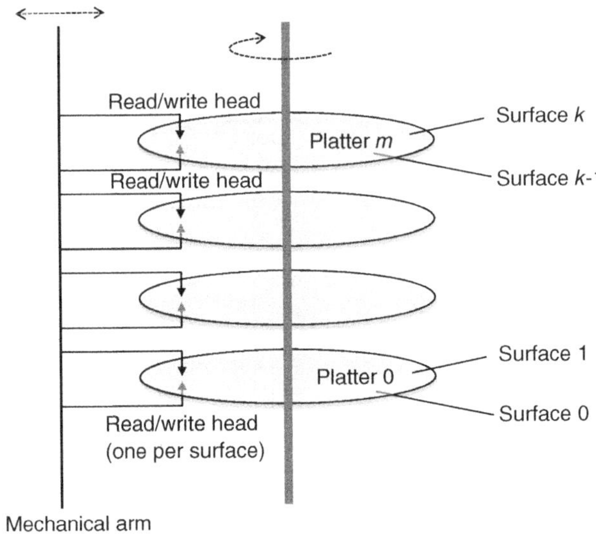

Figure 6.16 Structure of a magnetic disk drive.

A magnetic disk is a stack of platters, each platter coated with a magnetic material (such as ferric oxide) on both surfaces. It is also known as a hard disk, because the platter is made of a rigid material. Figure 6.16 shows the organization of a typical hard-disk drive. The stack of platters rotates on a common axis at a constant speed, and the disk arm with set of read/write heads—one head for each surface—moves along parallel radial lines. Reading and writing is achieved by means of electromagnetic interactions between the head and the coated material in a tiny surface area right across it on the associated platter. Obviously, the smaller the area, the higher the disk's overall capacity. Advances in physics and engineering have allowed the areal density to increase steadily. In particular, the Nobel Prize-winning discovery of giant magneto-resistance in 1988 by physicists Albert Fert and Peter Grünberg [13] made possible an areal density of over 100 gigabit/inch^2. A case in point is that a 160-gigabyte iPod classic fits into one hand, while the first gigabyte-capacity hard-disk drive (IBM 3380) was as big as a refrigerator.

As shown in Figure 6.17, each platter's surface is divided into concentric circles called *tracks*. (The set of tracks of the same radius on different surfaces collectively forms a *cylinder*.) Each track, in turn, is divided into hundreds of pie-shaped sectors. A sector is the smallest unit that is addressable on a disk. As a result, the file block size is a multiple of the sector size. The exact block size used, however, involves trade-offs. For example, if the block size is very large, most files will tie up larger-than-needed blocks and waste storage space. On the contrary, if the block size is very small, most files will span many blocks, which are likely non-contiguous. Access to the files, therefore, is subject to multiple seek and rotational delays.[16] In addition,

[16] The operation to position the disk head over a given cylinder is called *seek* and the time taken to perform this operation is called *seek time*. Once the head is over the desired track, more time is needed to rotate to the right sector under the head. This time is called *rotational delay*.

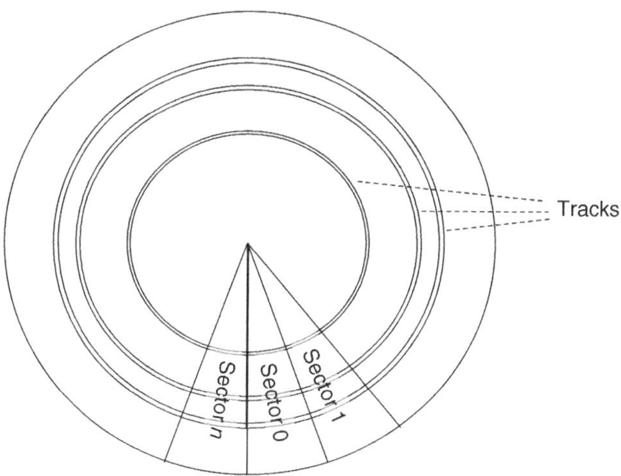

Figure 6.17 Organization of a platter's surface.

a very small block size may incur large data structures for tracking free blocks. A common scheme for keeping track of free blocks is to employ a characteristic function called a *bitmap*. The value of the *n*th bit indicates whether the *n*th block is free (value 1) or allocated (value 0).[17] Large bitmaps, multiple seeks, and rotational delays all degrade performance. It is worth noting that the Google File System[18] [14] uses 64-kilobyte blocks. The large block size is chosen in support of Google's need to process millions of files that are over 100 megabytes in size.

For management purposes, an operating system stores information about the file system (e.g., type, layout, and the bitmap for free blocks) and about each file (e.g., the pointer to the first block, the owner, last modification time, and access permissions).

If a system crashes during a file update operation, the file data may become corrupted. Modern file system management is able to repair—to some extent—corrupted data. There are algorithms for block and file consistency, but in a large system these take a substantial time to run. Fortunately, there are alternatives, such as *journaling*. Here the system keeps a log—appropriately called a *journal*—of all intended updates in a separate storage area.[19]

The updates that must be completed either in full, or not at all, are grouped together as an atomic transaction. As the actual updates are being made, the file system keeps track of the progress. In the event of a failure, the information contained in the journal can then be used during recovery to fix any inconsistency by redoing the required updates or undoing the incomplete updates. Fittingly, the former is called *redo* (or *new-value*) journaling and the latter *undo* (or *old-value*) journaling. Journaling is efficient because only the latest log needs to be examined instead of the entire file system. If it also logs the actual file content, file

[17] The bitmap itself is stored at a well-known location and consumes disk space.

[18] *Colossus* is the next-generation file system succeeding the Google File System, based on the lessons learned from the latter.

[19] The location for the storage of the journal is important because of the need for high-performance access. We will return to this topic later when discussing solid-state storage.

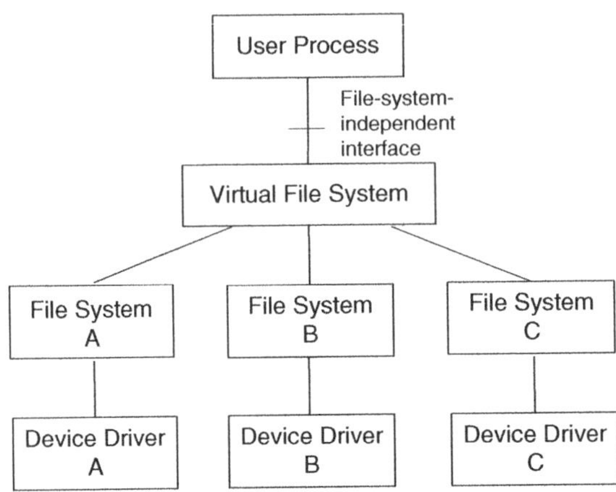

Figure 6.18 File system abstraction.

recovery is possible, too. It goes without saying that the extra operations due to journaling may affect performance. Nevertheless, the trade-off is such that most modern file systems support journaling. Doeppner's book [15] discusses journaling in more detail.

Listed below are examples of common file systems:

- Unix *File System* (*UFS*);
- *Linux extended file system* (*ext2* or *ext3* or *ext4*);
- *Windows New Technology File System* (*NTFS*);
- ISO 9660 (also known as *Compact Disc File System*).

Among these examples, ISO 9660 stands out, which is not tied to any particular operating system by design. It leads to a general need for an operating system to support multiple types of file system. Also worth noting is that the image of an ISO 9660 file system can be captured as a file (of the extension *.iso*) for electronic transfer. Known as an *ISO image*, this format has been used to distribute software modules and even virtual machine images.

An operating system may support different file systems directly, without making an attempt to integrate them. In this case the presence of different file systems is visible to user processes. Alternatively, the operating system may add an abstraction layer on top of the file systems to hide their differences—such as that shown in Figure 6.18. Many modern operating systems (notably those similar to Unix) implement such a layer as inspired by the *Virtual File System* (*VFS*) that Sun Microsystems first pioneered [16]. The VFS layer provides a file-system-independent interface to user processes, supporting standard system calls for file operations such as *open*, *read*, and *write*. It also provides an interface to the underlying file systems. As long as the underlying file systems support the interface, the VFS layer is not concerned about their specifics, including where the files are stored. Indeed, Sun's original VFS includes support for remote file systems such as NFS, which we are now ready to discuss.

NFS was designed in the 1980s by Sun Microsystems for file sharing between networked computers with possibly varied operating systems. Figure 6.19 shows Sun's implementation, which most Unix-like operating systems follow closely. As shown, NFS is integrated with

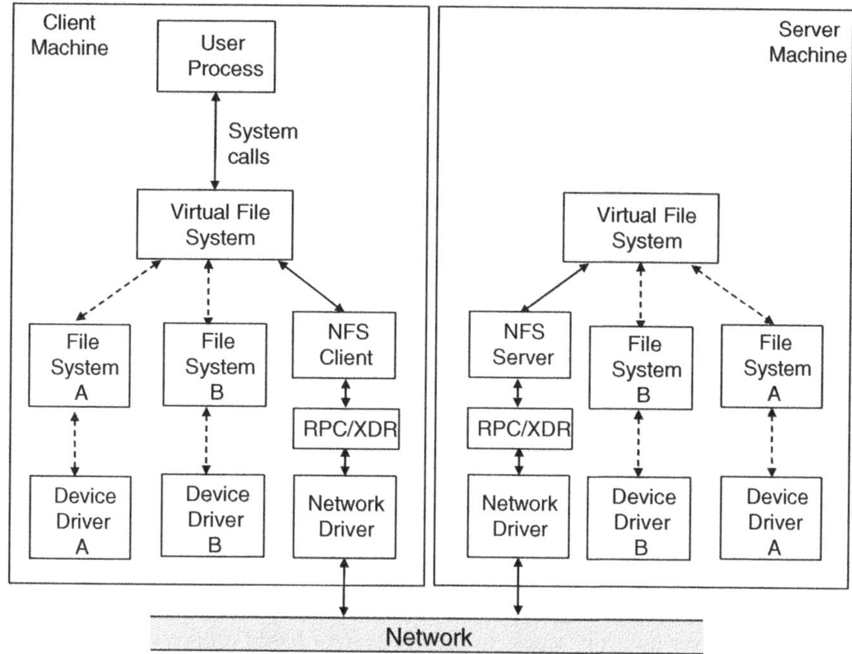

Figure 6.19 A functional view of NFS.

the operating system through a virtual file system, which is a natural fit here. When a user process attempts file access through a system call, the VFS determines whether the file is remote or local. If it is remote, the appropriate NFS procedure is invoked. The NFS proper is client/server-based. The NFS client initiates requests through the NFS protocol, which relies on the *Remote Procedure Call* (*RPC*) [17]. The NFS server only responds to requests, taking no actions on its own. The use of RPC hides the network-related details. To support machines of different architectures (big- or little-Endian), RPC, in turn, needs a presentation-layer protocol. The Sun's RPC message protocol [18], as standardized by the IETF, relies on the *External Data Representation* (*XDR*) standard. Similar to the *Abstract Syntax Notation 1* (*ASN.1*), XDR [19] is a generic over-the-wire representation of basic data types (e.g., string, integer, Boolean, and array). It defines the size, byte order, and data alignment.

Upon receiving an RPC call, the server invokes the appropriate operation in the VFS on the server machine, which eventually results in local file system operations. To return the result, the path across the network in Figure 6.19 is retraced. An advantage of this architecture is that the client and the server are symmetric. It is, therefore, straightforward to implement both a client and a server on the same machine.

Specifically, to make a file system accessible to remote clients, an NFS server exports it. To access a directory of the remote file system, an NFS client grafts (or *mounts* in Unix parlance)

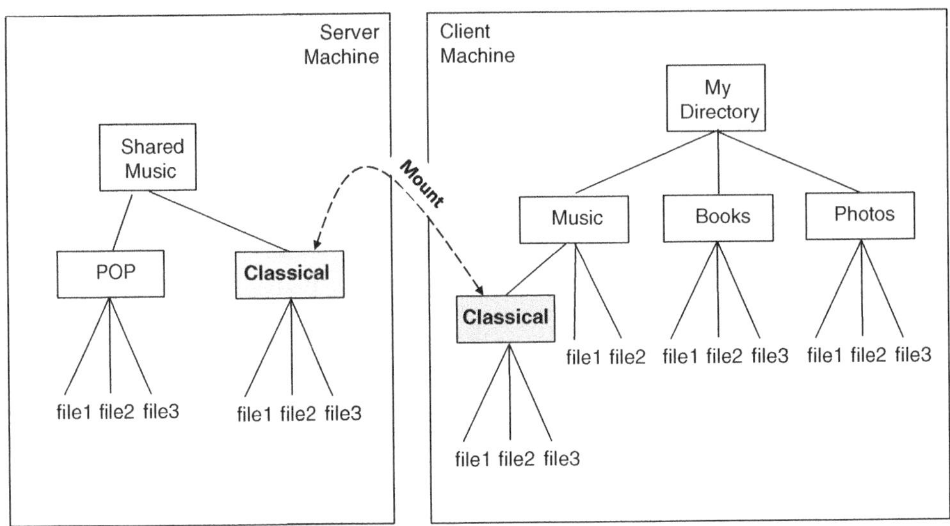

Figure 6.20 An example remote file system.

it to the local file system through the *mount* protocol. Upon receiving the mount request from the client, the server controls access to the file system based on pre-set policy and responds accordingly. Once the client receives a successful response, the remote directory becomes part of the local file system (such as shown in Figure 6.20) and is accessible to user processes through regular system calls. The actual interactions between the client and the server for file access are through the NFS file protocol. Most of the corresponding RPC routines map well to the regular Unix system calls for file operations. As an example, Figure 6.21 shows the *open*, *read*, and *close* operations of a remote file.

An interesting nuance: the *close* system call does not result in an RPC invocation. There are two reasons for this. First, the NFS protocol does not have the *close* routine because of the original stateless design of servers (which do not keep track of past requests) to facilitate crash discovery. Second, in this case there is no file modification.

A remote file operation, even if it has an RPC counterpart, does not necessarily result in an RPC invocation. No such invocation is needed when the information is stored in the client cache, which reduces the number of remote procedure calls and improves performance. Nevertheless, caching makes it difficult to maintain file consistency. For example, a *write* operation to a file at one site may not be visible at other sites that have this file open for reading.

NFS has gone through several iterations since its inception. In the process, the constraints of the stateless design have been relaxed, file consistency has been improved, and security strengthened. NFS and its evolution are explained in depth in [15].

Before leaving the topic of NAS, we observe that it is often implemented as *Redundant Arrays of Independent Disks* (*RAIDs*). Employing RAID technology allows recovery from a number of individual disk failures and overall improves the NAS performance and availability.

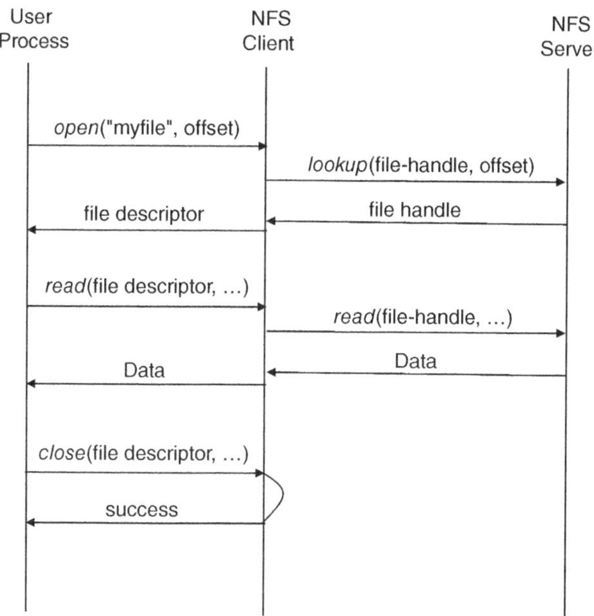

Figure 6.21 Examples of remote file operations through NFS.

6.2.3 Storage Area Network

Historically, DAS is a stove-piped technology, which makes it difficult to share storage resources and stored information. NAS alleviates the problem but still leaves room for improvement. In particular, storage throughput is limited by the particular networking technology in use and block-level I/O access is unavailable. This is where SAN comes in. In essence, SAN is a high-speed network that is tailored to interconnecting storage systems to allow resource pooling and block-level access to the pooled resources. SAN is predominantly based on FC, a standard technology combining the qualities of a serial I/O bus and a switching network. The bus qualities (reflected in the choice of the word "channel") allow hosts to see storage devices that are attached through FC as locally attached and to have reliable transmission as in SCSI. The network qualities allow flexibility in supporting multiple protocols and dynamic attachment of storage devices over a long distance.

The development of FC standards first started at ANSI in 1988, culminating in the specification ANSI X 3.230-1994. It is continuing in the T11 Technical Committee of INCITS, side by side with T10 that is responsible for the closely related SCSI project.

An open standard, FC has a layered structure as shown in Figure 6.22. FC-0 defines the physical and electrical characteristics of transceivers, connectors, and cables for serial lossless transmission (with a low bit error ratio) at different rates. To date, the fastest FC (known as 32GFC) supports 3.2 GBps per direction. Both fiber-optic and copper types of cabling are supported. It is even possible to have a mix of copper wire and optical fiber in an end-to-end path.[20]

[20] The choice of spelling ("fibre" rather than "fiber") in the technology name is intended to convey this broad cabling support.

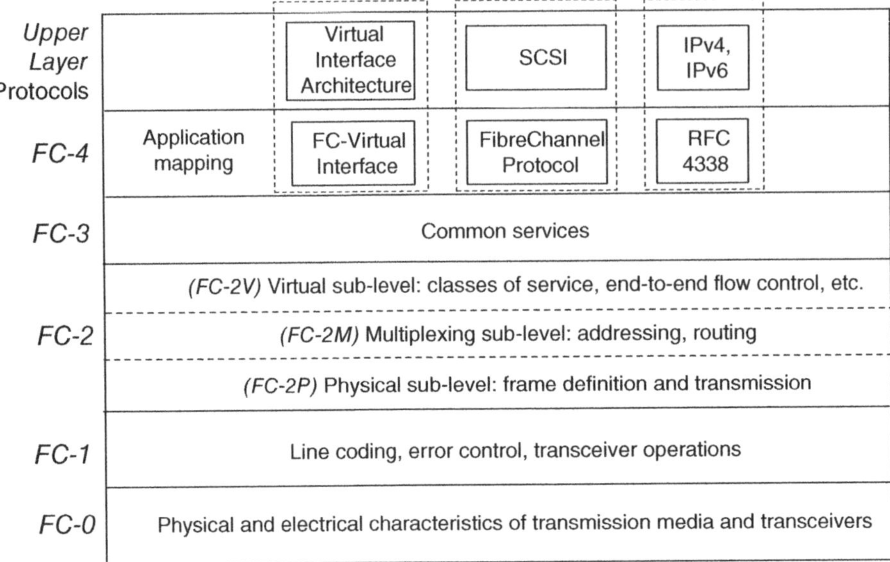

Figure 6.22 FC structure.

FC-1 is concerned with line coding and related transceiver operations. In particular, it defines a set of coding schemes suitable for high-speed data transmission, including 256b/257b, 64b/66b, and 8b/10b. In general, these coding schemes allow clock recovery at the receiver, enable detection of bit errors during transmission and reception, and help achieve transmission block alignment. You might recall that SAS utilizes 8b/10b coding. The coding scheme has a transmission overhead of 25% and is not efficient enough for the faster versions of FC. Figure 6.23 shows the coding scheme used by each of the FC versions available to date. In a nutshell, the 64b/66b coding scheme (also used in 10- and 100-gigabit Ethernet) transforms every 64-bit block to a 66-bit block before transmission. The 256b/257b scheme builds on 64b/66b by further transforming every four 64b/66b blocks to a 257-bit block before transmission. FC-1 also defines a number of *ordered sets* (i.e., certain encoded bit patterns). Among

FC Version	Coding Scheme	Line Rate (GBaud)	Throughput (MBps)
1GFC	8b/10b	1.0625	100
2GFC	8b/10b	2.125	200
4GFC	8b/10b	4.25	400
8GFC	8b/10b	8.5	800
10GFC	64b/66b	10.53	1,200
16GFC	64b/66b	14.025	1,600
32GFC	256b/257b	28.050	3,200

Figure 6.23 FC and line coding.

them are frame delimiters for marking frame boundaries, and primitive signals to signal a port's readiness to transmit and receive.

FC-2 consists of three sublevels named *physical* (FC-2P), *multiplexing* (FC-2M), and *virtual* (FC-2V), respectively. FC-2P addresses the format of frames (the basic units for carrying information on a physical link), and matters germane to transmitting and receiving frames, such as per-link flow control. The frame format includes a *Cyclic Redundancy Check (CRC)* field to detect and correct transmission errors.[21]

The flow control mechanism prevents a transmitter from sending to a receiver more frames than the latter can handle. It requires a feedback mechanism to allow the transmitter to regulate its transmission. If overwhelmed, the receiver will drop frames. The dropped frames need to be retransmitted, which worsens the congestion. Flow control is of particular importance in FC, given the requirement for lossless frame transmission. To this end, FC uses a flow control mechanism based on a notion of credits. A credit is the maximum number of buffers[22] available for receiving frames on the receiver. It is negotiated buffer-to-buffer (i.e., per link) or end-to-end between the involved ports (i.e., the transmitter and receiver) during a login procedure (to be discussed later). The transmitter does book-keeping to ensure that it sends a frame if and only if the receiver has a free buffer. In the case of per-link flow control (which is applicable to fabric ports), the transmitter does so through the help of a primitive signal (i.e., R_RDY) from the receiver. The signal indicates that the receiver is ready to receive with a free buffer. The transmitter tracks the number of available buffers, decrementing it by one upon sending out a frame and incrementing it by one upon receiving an R_RDY.

FC-2M is concerned with end-to-end connectivity, addressing, and path selection. Three types of connection are supported: *point-to-point*, *fabric*, and *arbitrated loop*. The point-to-point topology is the simplest, with a direct link between two ports (which are analogous to the SAS ports discussed earlier). It has the same effect as DAS, while supporting longer distances and working at a higher speed.

The fabric topology is most flexible. It involves a set of ports attached to a network of interconnecting FC switches through separate physical links, as shown in Figure 6.24. The switching network (or fabric) has a 24-bit address space structured hierarchically, according to domains and areas. An attached port is assigned a unique address during the fabric login procedure (which we will discuss later). The exact address typically depends on the physical port of attachment on the fabric (or switch, to be precise). The fabric routes frames individually based on the destination port address in each frame header.

Finally, the arbitrated loop topology allows three or more ports to interconnect without a fabric. Figure 6.25 shows an example together with an alternative using a hub (a simple device without any loop control capabilities) to simplify cabling. On the loop, only two ports can communicate with each other at any given time through arbitration.

In all three types of topology, communication may be simplex, full-duplex, or half-duplex; and a port may be on an HBA, a storage device controller, a hub, or a switch.

In the case of fabric topology, the *Fabric Shortest Path First (FSPF)* protocol as defined in ANSI INCITS 461-2010 is used to select a path on a fabric. FSPF is a link-state routing

[21] The CRC algorithm stipulated is the Frame Check Sequence (FCS) specified in Fiber Distributed Data Interface—Media Access Control.

[22] A buffer is a logical construct that holds a single frame.

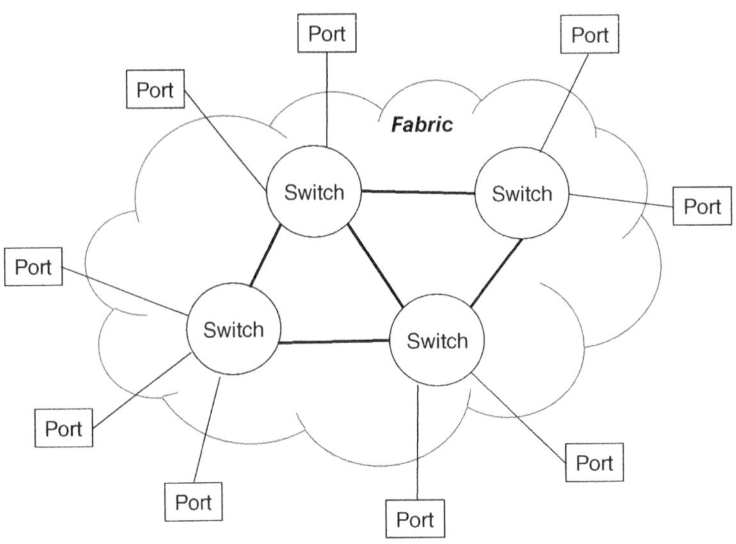

Figure 6.24 An example of fabric topology.

protocol similar to the standard *Open Shortest Path First* (*OSPF*) routing protocol[23] commonly used in IP networks.

Through FSPF, a switch in a fabric can keep track of the state of all the interswitch links throughout and maintain an up-to-date topology of the fabric consistently. The link state information includes the cost associated with each link, which is inversely proportional to its speed.[24] Based on the link state and topology information, each switch computes the respective total costs of all possible paths to other switches and selects those with the least costs. The total cost of a path is simply the sum of the costs of all links therein. Figure 6.26 shows an example, where the least-cost path between switch A and switch C is through switch B.

Obviously, a selected path is valid only for a given topology. A switch has to redo path computation whenever there is a topology change. Say link A–B in Figure 6.26 is down. Then path recomputation will yield two paths of the same cost. In this case, there is a need for a tie breaker, which could be based on load balancing considerations.

FC-2V is concerned with classes of service, end-to-end flow control, naming schemes, segmentation and reassembly in support of upper-layer protocols, among other things. At the time of this writing, three service classes are specified to support, respectively, the acknowledged frame delivery (Class 2), non-acknowledged frame delivery (Class 3), and interswitch frame delivery (Class F). Both Class 2 and Class 3 are datagram services. Frames are individually routed through the fabric without any guarantee of delivery order. Class 2 supports notification of frame delivery status, while Class 3 does not.

[23] http://tools.ietf.org/html/rfc2328

[24] According to ANSI INCITS 461-2010, link cost = S*(1.0625e12/link baud-rate), where S is an administratively defined factor. By default, S is set to 1.0.

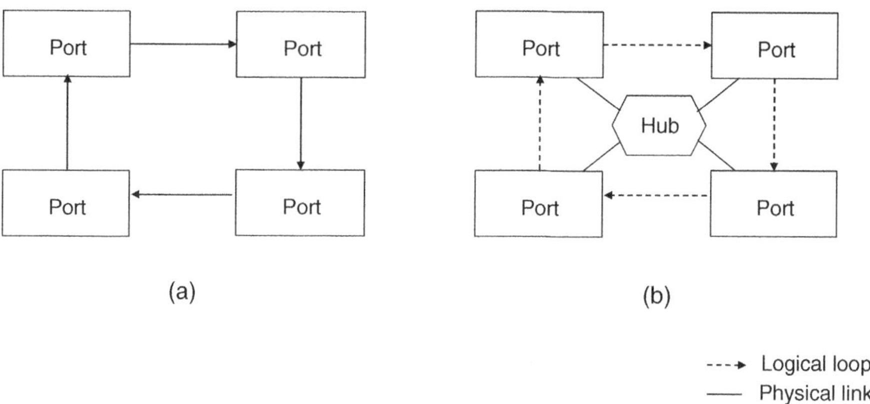

Figure 6.25 An example of the arbitrated loop.

Delivery acknowledgment enables end-to-end flow control and improves error handling. End-to-end flow control is also based on credits, which communicating ports negotiate at login time. A transmitter may not send additional frames when the number of outstanding delivery acknowledgments has reached the negotiated credit. Note that delivery acknowledgment is done at the frame level (through ACK_1 frames) and has more overheads than acknowledgment done at the primitive-signal level.

The naming mechanism is similar to that of addressing in FC. Several schemes for identifying ports, nodes (e.g., storage devices and HBAs), fabrics, and other FC entities have been specified. In practice, the 64-bit *World Wide Name (WWN)* is what is implemented. WWNs are similar to MAC addresses, and they are administered by the IEEE in the same way. WWNs are assigned to FC entities by manufacturers.

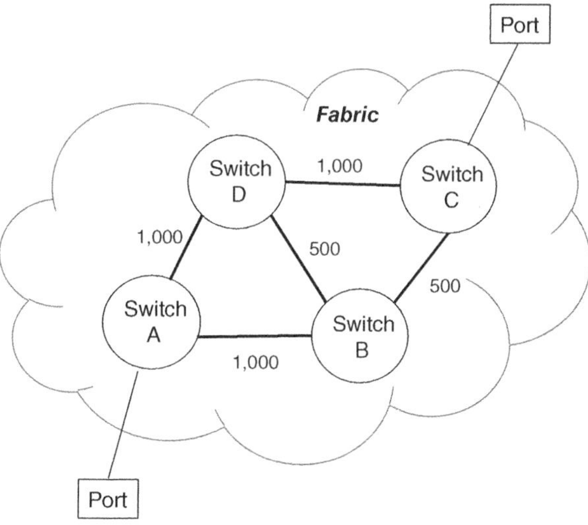

Figure 6.26 A weighted-path network.

All things considered, WWNs can potentially provide the basis for FC routing. But, as already noted, FC routing is based on a special 24-bit port address. This has happened because of concerns that the much longer WWN address might make routing, too slow to meet the overall performance objective.

Hence, a port ends up with two identifiers. In FC parlance, the *address identifier* is 24 bits long; the *name identifier* is 64 bits long. They serve different purposes. The name identifier is useful in services such as zoning. Based on their name identifiers, FC devices can be grouped into isolated zones so that they cannot see and communicate with each other across zones. Zoning may be based on address identifiers but it is harder to administer; address identifiers, unlike name identifiers, are subject to change when devices alter attachment ports on the fabric. The restrictiveness of address-identifier-based zoning, however, is a plus from the security point of view.

FC-3 is concerned with the link services to FC-4 for managing both the communication between FC devices and the interaction between the fabric and an attached device. FC-3 provides a link service further subdivided into basic and extended services.

The set of basic link services is small. It is intended to support aborting a sequence (which is a flow of frames resulting from fragmentation of a single upper-protocol data unit) and notifying a service requestor of the result (i.e., request completion or rejection).

In contrast, the set of extended link services is much larger. It supports, in particular, procedures for login and logout.

The login procedure is mandatory. It consists of two steps: fabric login and port login. A port on an FC device must perform the fabric login step first before attempting to do anything else. The step involves sending a frame carrying the fabric login command and other information to a well-known port address. If it completes successfully, the device port discovers the topology type (e.g., fabric or point-to-point), at which point it is assigned an address (if a fabric is present). The rest of the procedure settles some service parameters (such as supported classes of service and the credits for per-link flow control). Then the port login step is performed, which settles the values of other service parameters (such as port names and the credits for end-to-end flow control).

The login procedure results in a long-lived session. As long as the session is active, I/O operations can be performed between the two ports. Otherwise, a new login session must be established.

The logout procedure simply terminates a login session and frees up its resources. The login procedure does not have in-built authentication, despite the word "login." Traditionally, FC devices are trusted.

The top layer, FC-4, is concerned with bridging the transport below and applications above to make FC devices accessible to applications in a transparent way. For example, an SCSI-aware application can access an FC device without modification. To this end, FC-4 defines the mapping between application protocols and the underlying FC constructs. The mapping is specific to an application protocol. A set of application-specific mappings has been defined, including, in particular, the *Fibre Channel Protocol* (*FCP*) for SCSI. FCP provides transport protocol services, as defined in the SCSI architecture model (discussed earlier). To name a few, it addresses the encapsulation of the information related to SCSI operations (e.g., CDBs), address mapping, and capability discovery. Through FCP, an FC storage device can appear as an SCSI device to an application.

Among other mappings that have been defined are the *FC-Virtual Interface* (*FC-VI*) for the *Virtual Interface* (*VI*) *Architecture* [20], and RFC 4338[25] for IPv4/IPv6. The VI architecture aims to provide processes with high performance needs a protected, directly accessible interface to the network hardware without involving the specific operating system services. It supports *Remote Direct Memory Access* (*RDMA*) in addition to traditional send and receive messaging constructs. RDMA has been applied to distributed scientific applications and proven effective. The versions used in practice, however, are not identical to RDMA in the VI architecture. *InfiniBand™* is a notable example. In light of Cloud Computing, devising effective mechanisms for supporting RDMA in virtual machines is a topic for ongoing research.

6.2.4 Convergence of SAN and Ethernet

FC SAN has been popular in data centers because of its superior performance. But the need to deploy and manage a separate, bespoke network for storage is a drawback. Doing so entails the procurement of specialized hardware (i.e., tailored HBAs, connectors, cables, and switches) as well as the involvement of dedicated operational staff. Convergence of SAN and Ethernet is about using Ethernet networks for all types of traffic, including storage. A key motivation is the prospect of reduced capital and operational expenditure.

As the reader may remember from Chapter 2, the same motivation resulted in IT transformation and network function virtualization.

SAN's layered structure facilitates the approaches to convergence demonstrated in Figure 6.27. These approaches correspond to swapping out the lower-layer modules of the FC protocol. In the extreme approach (i.e., approach 3), no trace of FC[26] is left.

The other two approaches, developed by the INCITS T11 Technical Committee, are kinder to FC. The idea is to keep various modules to help the transition to new deployments. Common to the three approaches is the use of the IEEE 802.3 MAC and physical layers in place of FC-1 and FC-0. Approach 1 further calls for replacing FC-2M and FC-2P with an FCoE layer, approach 2 replacing FC-3 to FC-2P with FCIP over TCP/IP, and approach 3 replacing FCP to FC-2P with iSCSI) over TCP/IP. The rest of the section focuses on approach 1 (FCoE) and approach 3 (iSCSI), the primary convergence approaches.

The main characteristic of FC is that it incurs no frame loss due to buffer congestion. Approach 1 relies on lossless Ethernet links to preserve this characteristic. To this end, the Ethernet *PAUSE* mechanism[27] is essential. The mechanism allows a congested Ethernet switch to request an adjacent switch (through a PAUSE frame) not to send frames its way for a certain duration. If the congestion persists beyond the valid period of the request, the switch can send a new PAUSE request. On the contrary, if the congestion alleviates sooner than expected, the switch can cancel the outstanding request by sending a new PAUSE request with the duration set to zero. The PAUSE mechanism works on a per-link basis. Its invocation is handled

[25] http://tools.ietf.org/html/rfc4338

[26] This explains why the IETF (rather than the INCITS T11 Technical Committee) is responsible for the related standards.

[27] See IEEE 802.3-2008—Annex 31B.

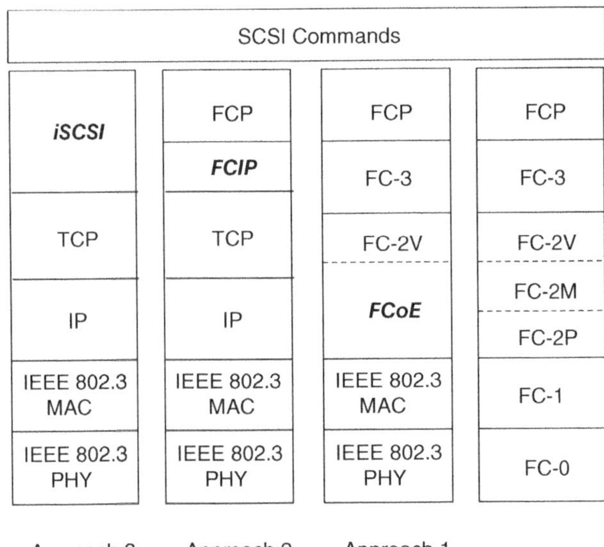

Figure 6.27 Examples of converged storage protocol options.

independently by each switch, based on the local load conditions. Furthermore, once invoked, PAUSE applies to all traffic on the same link.

The way that PAUSE works is not ideal when the converged network is to be shared by different types of traffic. Storage performance will suffer even if PAUSE is caused by the traffic that is unrelated to storage.

Fortunately, there is a remedy, which is the *Priority-based Flow Control* (*PFC*) mechanism specified in IEEE 802.1Qbb.[28] PFC allows PAUSE to be applied separately to traffic of different priority classes. Traffic priority classification is through a 3-bit tag, as defined in IEEE 802.1Q.[29] With finer control granularity, different classes of traffic (with eight classes the maximum, as limited by the tag length) will not interfere with each other. It is also possible to pause non-storage traffic to allow storage traffic to get through and help meet the storage performance requirement.

Besides lossless Ethernet, approach 1 requires a new layer, namely FCoE as defined in the *Fibre Channel-Backbone-5* (*FC-BB-5*) specification.[30] FCoE's job is to fill the gaps resulting from the use of Ethernet for transport, such as FC frame encapsulation, emulating point-to-point links, and access to common services. An FCoE frame is an Ethernet frame that encapsulates an FC frame in its entirety without any change. Keeping the FC frame intact simplifies integration of FCoE and existing FC SANs. As depicted in Figure 6.28, the encapsulated FC frame has a relatively low overhead, with just additional delimiters to mark the beginning and end of the frame and padding to meet the minimum Ethernet frame size requirement. FCoE frames

---

[28] www.ieee802.org/1/pages/802.1bb.html

[29] www.ieee802.org/1/pages/802.1Q.html

[30] See ANSI INCITS 462-2010. The specification also defines mechanisms to support FC over different types of backbone network, including TCP/IP SONET/ SONET/SDH/OTN/PDH, and MPLS.

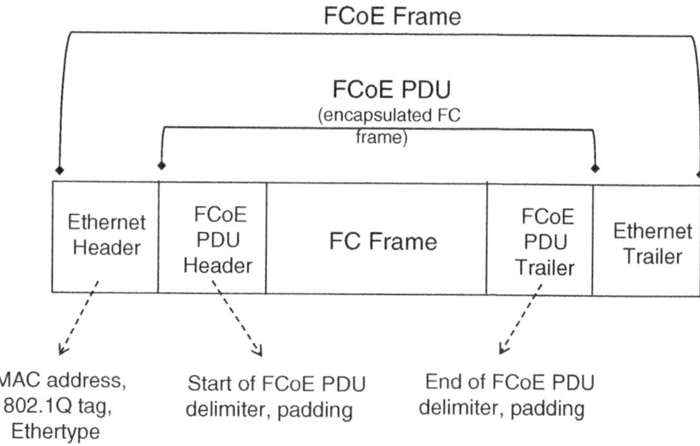

Figure 6.28 FCoE frame structure.

are distinguishable from other types of frame via a special *Ethertype* value. (Ethertype is a two-byte header field in the Ethernet frame to indicate the nature of the payload. The Ethertype value determines what the receiver does with a received frame. IPv4 and IPv6 are among the common Ethertype values. To avoid conflict, the Ethertype values are managed by the IEEE Registration Authority[31].)

FCoE-aware entities are classified into *FCoE Nodes* (*ENodes*) and *FCoE Forwarders* (*FCFs*). The former are relatively simple, in practice known as converged network adapters that consolidate FC HBAs, and Ethernet NICs. The latter are essentially FC switches in an Ethernet network, supporting the node and FC switching functions. Their central task is forwarding FCoE frames. For each frame received, an FCF decapsulates the FC frame and determines the forwarding MAC address based on the destination address in the FC frame. Then the FCF has to encapsulate the FC frame again in a way suitable for forwarding out of an Ethernet port, with the Ethernet source address set to the FCF MAC address and the Ethernet destination address the forwarding MAC address. If the FCF also supports native FC ports (thus the SAN gateway function), re-encapsulation may not be necessary. It is possible for the FCF to forward an FC frame bound for an FC SAN out of a native FC port.

To emulate point-to-point links over the Ethernet shared media, FCoE relies on the logical constructs of virtual ports and links.

Virtual ports emulate FC ports. They are created dynamically on ENodes and FCFs. Each virtual port is associated with an element (known as an *FCoE Link End Point* (*FCoE_LEP*)), which handles the encapsulation and decapsulation and also deals with the Ethernet transmission. Two virtual points can be interconnected through a virtual link identified by at least the MAC addresses of the associated FCoE_LEPs. The link serves as a tunnel to transport encapsulated FC frames between the two MAC addresses over an Ethernet network. Figure 6.29

---

[31] The Ethertype public listing is available at http://standards.ieee.org/develop/regauth/ethertype/eth.txt.

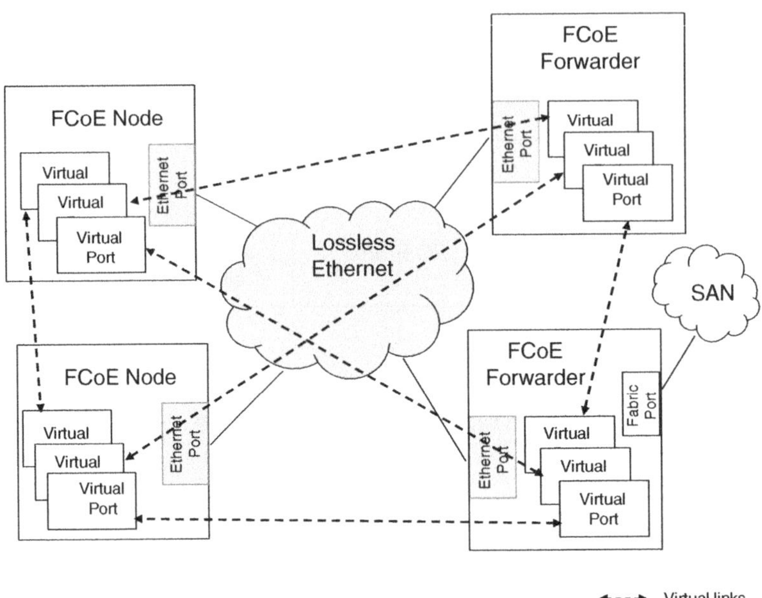

Figure 6.29 A conceptual FCoE architecture.

shows virtual ports and links in a conceptual FCoE network. (For simplicity, FCoE_LEPs are not shown.) From the figure, we observe that:

- An FCoE node may establish multiple virtual links with different FCFs through a single Ethernet port.
- An FCF may establish multiple virtual links with different ENodes through a single Ethernet port.
- An FCF may establish multiple virtual links with different FCFs through a single Ethernet port.
- An ENode may establish multiple virtual links with different ENodes through a single Ethernet port.

Now we can explain how the FCoE entities and virtual ports are discovered and how the virtual links are set up.

In FC, an end device is provisioned with a direct physical link to a switch. To perform fabric login, for example, the device simply sends a request to the corresponding well-known port address over the link. In FCoE, there is no direct physical link anymore between an ENode and an FCF. Instead, there are intermediate Ethernet links and switches. To perform fabric login, the end node has to have an appropriate virtual link set up first. If this is done manually, the procedure will be both ineffective and error-prone.

Hence the *FCoE Initialization Protocol* (*FIP*). The FIP messages are also carried in Ethernet frames. A special Ethertype value distinguishes these frames from the FCoE frames.

FIP addresses FCoE entity discovery, virtual link instantiation, and virtual link maintenance. Figure 6.30 shows the related interactions between an ENode and FCF. (The interactions between two ENodes or two FCFs are similar.) The entity discovery procedure is typically

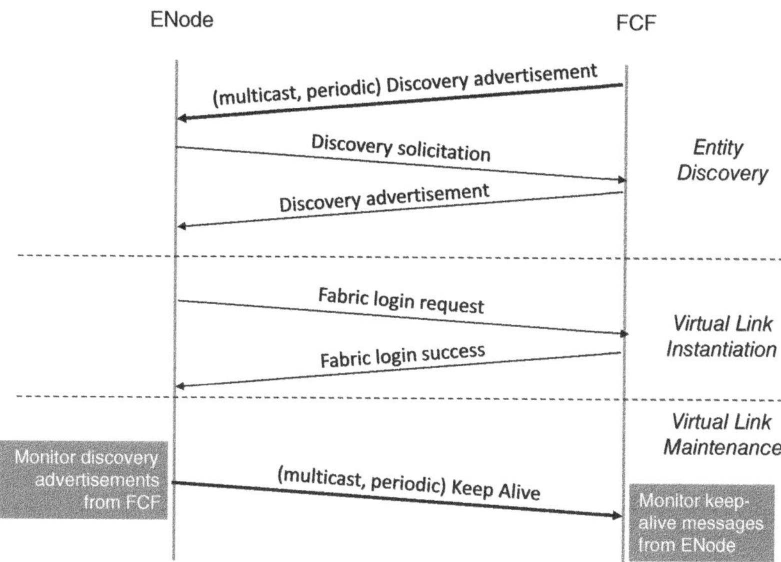

Figure 6.30 High-level FIP operations.

hinged on FCFs sending, periodically, multicast discovery advertisements to a known multicast address.

An ENode selects a compatible FCF based on the advertisement and sends a discovery solicitation at which the capability negotiation starts. Upon receiving the solicitation, the FCF responds to the ENode with a solicited discovery advertisement, confirming the negotiated capabilities.

Once receiving the solicited discovery advertisement, the ENode can proceed with setting up a virtual link to the FCF. The procedure here is similar to the fabric login procedure in FC.

Successful completion of the login procedure results in creation of a virtual port on the ENode, a virtual port on the FCF, and a virtual link between them.

The MAC address of the virtual port on the ENode is typically assigned by the FCF, although it may be assigned by the ENode. A MAC address in the former case is known as a *Fabric-Provided MAC Address* (*FPMA*). It is constructed by concatenating the 24-bit MAC prefix of the FCF and the 24-bit address identifier of the virtual port assigned by the FCF. This method ensures that the MAC address is unique within the fabric. Virtual ports and links can be deleted explicitly through a logout procedure. Successful completion of the procedure frees up all related resources, including MAC addresses and virtual port address identifiers.

A virtual link may span a series of Ethernet links and switches. Hence, a broken link due to a fault in an intermediate link or switch might not be immediately apparent to the associated FCoE entities. FIP deals with the problem by making the associated entities periodically check the state of a virtual link. An ENode does so by monitoring multicast discovery advertisements and sending keep-alive messages to the FCF. An FCF does so by monitoring the keep-alive messages from the ENode (in addition to its ongoing task of issuing multicast discovery advertisements).

A virtual port on the FCF is considered unreachable if the ENode logs two missing advertisements. In this case, the ENode deletes the associated virtual port and link. Similarly, a

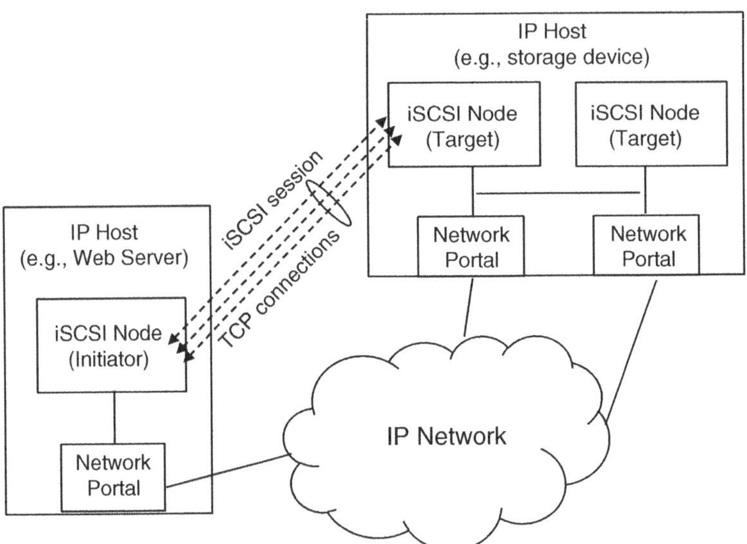

Figure 6.31 iSCSI conceptual model.

virtual port on an ENode is considered unreachable if the FCF logs two missing keep-alive messages. In this case, the FCF deletes the associated virtual port and link.

For good measure, FCoE services are typically provided over VLANs so that storage traffic is isolated appropriately. These VLANs may be pre-provisioned, but if this is not the case, there needs to be a mechanism to discover them. To this end, FIP includes an additional procedure that FCoE entities can perform before anything else. The VLAN discovery procedure is straightforward. An ENode (or FCF) sends a VLAN discovery message to a pre-set multicast address. The FCFs receiving the message respond to the ENode with a list of the identifiers of FCoE-capable VLANs.

iSCSI is a development enabled by the ubiquitous connectivity that came with the development of the Internet. As demonstrated in Figure 6.27, TCP is leveraged here[32] for the features that are essential to SCSI operations: reliable in-order delivery, automatic retransmission of unacknowledged packets, and congestion control.

Initially there was a concern about potential performance problems, but the choice of TCP was validated by the *Virtual Internet SCSI Adaptor* (*VISA*) project [21], carried at the University of Southern California's Information Sciences Institute in the 1990s. The project demonstrated that the TCP/IP overhead was not as great as feared, and could be compensated for by employing more powerful processors. Discussions of the related standardization effort in the IETF followed, and led to the formation of the IP Storage Working Group in the last quarter of 2000. The effort resulted in the publication of a series of RFCs, starting with the core RFC[33] specifying the iSCSI protocol in 2004. The paper [22] by K. Meth and J.

[32] The *Stream Control Transmission Protocol* (*SCTP*) is similar to TCP in its support for the features essential to SCSI operations. At the time of standardization of iSCSI, however, the SCTP was considered, too new to be relied on.
[33] http://tools.ietf.org/html/rfc7143

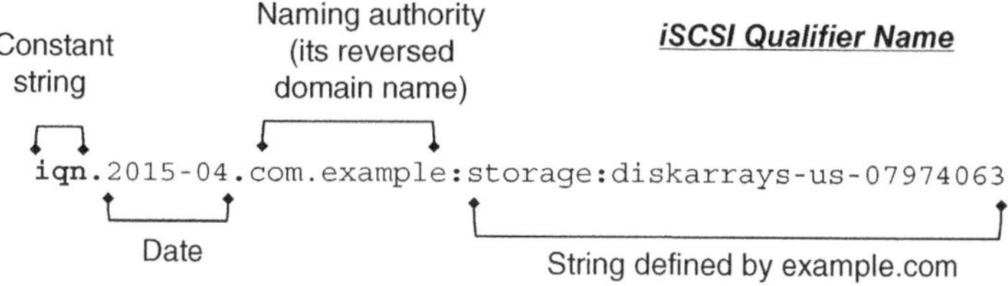

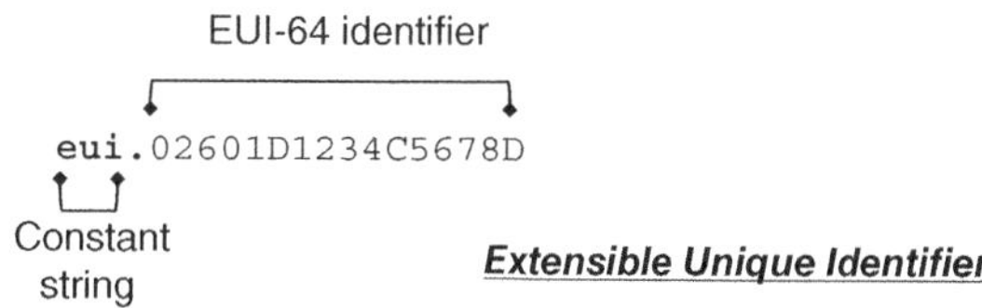

Figure 6.32 iSCSI names.

Satran at IBM Haifa Research Laboratory gives a good explanation of the design of the iSCSI protocol.

To explain how iSCSI works, let us first review the conceptual model in Figure 6.31. The central construct here is the iSCSI node representing an iSCSI communication endpoint (initiator or target). The node is accessible from an IP network through one or more network portals.

The node is identified by a globally unique iSCSI name, which depends on neither the node location nor its IP address. Multiple iSCSI nodes may be reachable at the same address, and the same iSCSI node can be reached at multiple addresses. As a result, it is possible to use multiple TCP connections for a communication session between a pair of iSCSI nodes to achieve a higher throughput. We will return to this important aspect later. Figure 6.32 shows the two formats defined for iSCSI names: *iSCSI Qualified Name* (*iqn*) and *Extensible Unique Identifier* (*eui*). With the iqn format, the names can be issued by any organization that owns a domain name. In contrast, the names in the eui format are assigned by the IEEE Registration Authority.

Figure 6.33 outlines the format of the iSCSI PDU. Only the basic header segment field is mandatory. This field carries critical information such as the iSCSI PDU type and SCSI CDB.

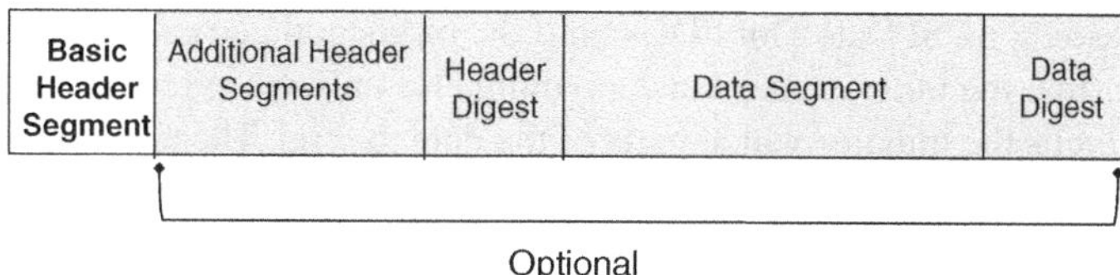

Figure 6.33 Format of the iSCSI protocol data unit.

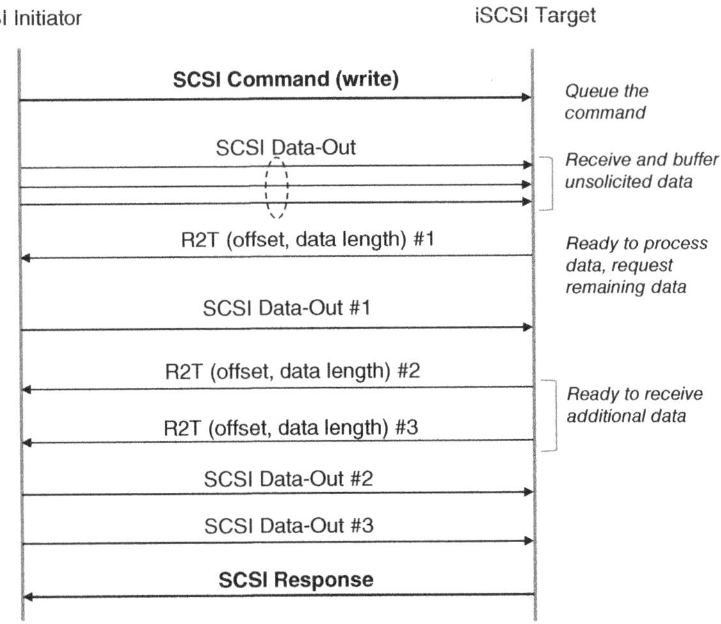

Figure 6.34 A work flow for the *write* operation.

The two optional fields with the label *digest* carry the checksums for detecting changes (e.g., the changes caused by noise) to the header and the data.[34] To reduce the processing cost, the basic header is of a fixed size, 48 bytes in length to accommodate a normal SCSI CDB. In the case of a larger CDB, the use of additional header segments will be necessary.

The iSCSI PDU type identifies the key function of the PDU. Several PDU types are defined. Naturally some have direct counterparts in SCSI, such as *SCSI Command*, *SCSI Response*, *SCSI Data-In*, and *SCSI Data-Out*. Those that do not are introduced to provide the necessary adaptation functions to the underlying TCP/IP. Among such PDU types are *Login Request*, *Login Response*, *Logout Request*, and *Logout Response* to support connection management and capability negotiation; and *Ready to Transfer* (*R2T*) to support target-driven flow control.

To illustrate the roles of different types of iSCSI PDUs, Figure 6.34 depicts an example information flow for the *write* operation.

Each SCSI *command* PDU must have a matched *response* PDU indicating if the command is carried out successfully. Before the SCSI response is issued, data transfer may be necessary between the initiator and the target. This transfer is carried out by the SCSI Data-In and SCSI Data-Out PDUs. In the example, the initiator, after the *write* command, sends the intended data to the target in several SCSI Data-Out PDUs until the pre-negotiated cap of unsolicited data[35] is reached. After that the initiator may send anything else only when requested by the target.

An R2T PDU tells the initiator which parts of the data to send. The target sends R2T PDUs without waiting for responses to the old ones. Upon receiving an R2T PDU, the initiator

[34] http://tools.ietf.org/html/rfc3385

[35] In the case of a read operation, the target, after receiving the read command, will send the requested data to the initiator in one or more SCSI Data-In PDUs.

sends the requested data in an SCSI Data-Out PDU. The target-driven scheme allows local optimization based on the load and configuration of the target. But the scheme comes at the cost of transmitting extra R2T PDUs, which might become unacceptable when the amount of data is small and the network delay is long. This is why iSCSI allows the initiator to transfer data to the target without solicitation, as seen earlier in the flow. (Also available is another even more efficient scheme known as *immediate data*, which allows data to be sent as part of the SCSI command PDU.) The maximum amount of unsolicited data is negotiated during a login procedure that takes place after a TCP connection is set up between the initiator and the target. We will discuss the login procedure later.

One problem with using TCP/IP as transport is under-utilization of the underlying physical media. As a remedy, the notion of an *iSCSI session* is introduced. An iSCSI session is a set of TCP connections linking an initiator and a target. This set may grow and shrink over time, allowing us to aggregate multiple TCP connections to achieve a higher throughput.

With the availability of multiple connections comes the problem of using them correctly in the context of carrying out I/O. It is certainly reasonable to use separate connections for control and data transfer to ensure that a connection is always available for task management. Yet such a scheme requires monitoring and coordination across multiple connections, which can even require different adaptors on the initiator or the target.

To avoid this complexity, iSCSI employs a scheme known as *connection allegiance*. With this scheme, the initiator can use any connection to issue a command but must stick to the same connection for all ensuing communications.

The iSCSI sessions need to be managed. A big part of session management is handled by the iSCSI login procedure. Successful completion of the login procedure results in a new session or adding a connection to an existing session.

A prerequisite for the procedure is that the initiator knows the name and address of the storage device (i.e., the target) to use. One approach is to have such information pre-configured in the initiator. Then any change will require reconfiguration.

An alternative approach is based on the *Service Location Protocol*.[36] It allows the initiator to dynamically discover available targets. To start the login procedure, the initiator first sets up a connection to a known TCP port[37] on the target. Once the connection is established, the initiator performs the login steps through *Login Request* and *Login Response* PDUs. Mutual authentication may take place through a negotiated authentication method, with the *Challenge Handshake Authentication Protocol* (*CHAP*)[38] as the default authentication method. As a minimum, the operational parameters are negotiated—among which are the maximum amount of unsolicited data, the maximum size of SCSI Data-In PDUs, and whether to include cyclic redundancy checksums in PDUs for error protection. When everything is in order, the target sends a Login Response PDU with an indication that the login procedure has completed successfully. Only then can the new connection associated with the session be used for SCSI communication.

Effective distribution of loads across multiple TCP connections and recovery from errors are also part of session management. iSCSI supports a three-level hierarchy for error recovery, with ascending increase in complexity.

[36] http://tools.ietf.org/html/rfc3721

[37] The well-known TCP port number for iSCSI assigned by IANA is 3260.

[38] http://tools.ietf.org/html/rfc1994

At the bottom is *session recovery*, which rebuilds a defunct session all over again. It involves cleaning up all the associated artifacts (such as closing all TCP connections and aborting all pending SCSI commands with error indications) and then re-establishing a new set of TCP connections.

Next is the *digest failure recovery*, which, in addition to session recovery, allows the receiver of a PDU with a mismatched data digest to request that the PDU be resent.

Finally, the *connection recovery* includes the digest failure recovery and also allows a pending command on a broken connection to be transferred to another connection (which may need to be created).

Each recovery procedure is suitable for a specific environment. For example, in a LAN where errors of any kind are rare, it would be sufficient to just have session recovery. Overall, an iSCSI session can remain active for as long as it is possible to have a connection between the initiator and the target. The session terminates when the last connection closes. To make multiple connections appear as a single SCSI *interconnect* between the initiator and the target, iSCSI employs sequence numbers and tags.

In iSCSI, the identifier of a session consists of an initiator part and a target part. The former (the initiator session ID) is explicitly assigned by the initiator at the session establishment; the latter is implied by the initiator's selection of the TCP endpoint at connection establishment. To ensure that the initiator session ID is unique for every session that an initiator has with a given target (especially when the initiator is distributed), a hierarchical namespace controlled by a registration authority is prescribed.

We must emphasize that the mutual authentication step that may be part of the login procedure is only a one-time affair. It has no bearing on whether the ensuing communication is still between the authenticated nodes. Moreover, iSCSI itself does not provide any mechanisms to protect a connection or a session. All native iSCSI communication is in the clear, subject to eavesdropping and active attacks. In an untrusted environment, iSCSI should be used along with IPsec.[39]

6.2.5 Object Storage

NAS provides controlled access to shared data at the file level in a manner independent of an operating system. Its design requires every file-related I/O request from a client to go through a file server, which acts as an adaptor to the device storing the file. Thus the file server is a potential bottleneck limiting the I/O throughput. One way to address this limitation is to allow the client to have direct access to the storage device by sharing metadata [23]. The achieved performance gain, however, comes at the expense of security. A traditional block-storage device is relatively simple. It can read and write blocks of data in terms of zeros and ones, but does not have the faculty to understand the meaning of the data or discern constructs such as files or directories. Access control is possible only for the whole device. The client is given access to either everything or nothing at all. This is clearly problematic. Here object storage comes to the rescue.

A comparatively new technology—called *object storage*—allows data sharing across multiple operating systems securely and at the speed of direct storage access. Its chief characteristics

[39] http://tools.ietf.org/html/rfc3723

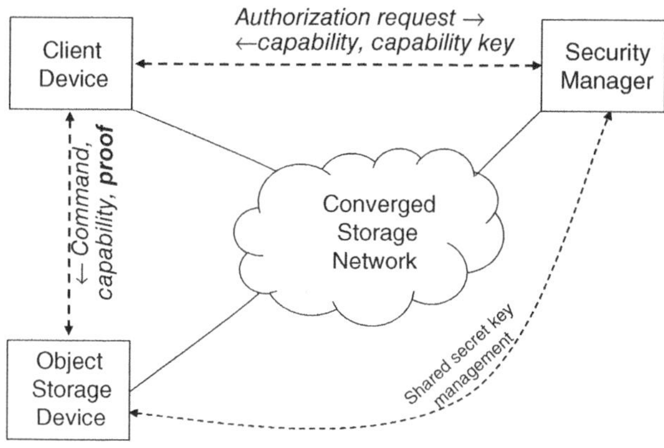

Figure 6.35 Object storage access control model.

are (a) a new device interface at a higher abstraction level than blocks and (b) additional intelligence in the device itself. Through the new interface (which has been standardized by the INCITS T10 technical committee), a storage device appears as a collection of objects. An object is an ordered set of bytes that is uniquely identifiable in a flat namespace. An object can hold any type of data, be it a file, database, or even an entire file system. What gets to be part of an object is up to the storage application. As objects are being created, deleted, modified, or cloned, the associated tasks of allocating and releasing blocks are handled by the storage device. To keep track of the used and free blocks, the device relies on per-object metadata.

The additional device intelligence refers to the capabilities to understand metadata, manage space, and support granular access control. Such on-device capabilities permit new performance optimization mechanisms (e.g., file pre-fetching and data reorganization), simplify application clustering, and enable automated storage management.

Granular access control is fundamental in Cloud Computing. The access control mechanism as standardized in ANSI INCITS 458-2011[40] is based on the notion of *capability* and *credential*. A capability describes the access rights of a client to an object, such as *read*, *write*, *create*, or *delete*. A *credential* is essentially a cryptographically protected tamper-proof capability, involving the *keyed-Hash Message Authentication Code* (*HMAC*)[41] of a capability with a shared key. More specifically, a credential is a structure:

<capability, object storage identifier, capability key>,

where

capability key = HMAC (secret key, capability||object storage identifier).

Figure 6.35 depicts the conceptual model. The security manager is responsible for granting credentials according to policy upon a client's request. The secret key for computing the capability key is shared between the security manager and the object storage device. The latter

[40] ANSI INCITS 458-2011, Object-based Storage Device Commands—2 (OSD-2).

[41] See FIPS 198 (2002), The Keyed-Hash Message Authentication Code (HMAC) and FIPS 180-1 (1995), Secure Hash Standard.

will carry out a command if and only if the client provides proof that it possesses a valid credential. Thus, the storage device serves as the access policy enforcer.

Now the question is what makes reasonable proof. Could a credential itself serve as proof, much like a driver's license that attests to the driver's qualification for driving a certain class of vehicles?

To answer this question, let us consider the basic requirements of a proof of interest. At a minimum, it should be verifiable, tamper-proof, hard to forge, and safe against unauthorized use. A credential meets all but the last requirement; there is no in-built mechanism to bind it to the acquiring client or to the communication channel between the client and the storage device. (In contrast, a driver's license has a photograph of the driver to bind the license to the driver, although such a strong binding is not necessary for the problem at hand.) This is clearly not good, especially if the credential is subject to eavesdropping over an improperly protected storage transport. Thus, another proof scheme is in order.

The standardized scheme derives a proof based on the capability key. The proof is a quantity computed with the capability key over selective request components according to the negotiated security method. The following security methods are possible:

- *NOSEC*. That is, no access control whatsoever. In this case, the storage device performs a command without requiring a proof. This method is useful only in a fully isolated environment where the links are secure and there is a trust relationship between the client and the storage device.
- *CAPKEY*. In this case, the proof is the integrity-check value of the identifier of the channel between the client and the storage device. As a result, the particular channel in use is pinned. (The channel identifier is assigned by the object storage device, from which the client can obtain the information.) The scheme assumes that the channel itself is secure. It prevents unauthorized use of the credential over a different channel, while allowing delegation, namely forwarding the credential to another client [24]. For a given channel, the scheme is fairly lightweight. The client does not need to request a credential or compute the integrity value for each command separately.
- *CMDRSP*. In this case, the proof is the integrity-check value of the command in the request. The scheme is tailored to environments where the channel between the client and the storage device is unsecure but it is impractical to provide integrity protection for the user data. In addition to command origin authentication and integrity protection, it also provides anti-replay protection through the use of a *nonce*[42] in each request. The paper by M. Factor *et al.* [25] explains the corresponding nonce management mechanics.
- *ALLDATA*. In this case, the proof contains multiple integrity check values, including that for CMDRSP. The additional integrity check values are computed over the data sent to and received from the storage device, respectively. So on top of what is afforded by CMDRSP, the scheme provides protection against replay and alteration of the data exchanged between the client and the storage device. As CMDRSP, it is tailored to environments where communication channels are insecure.

[42] The word *nonce* refers to a string that is supposed to be used (as part of a communications exchange) only once. This is a mechanism for ensuring the *freshness* property. As an example, consider the checkbook—each check in it is supposed to be unique (so that a copy can be distinguished from the original), and a number of mechanisms, including sequence numbers and watermarks, are used to ensure uniqueness.

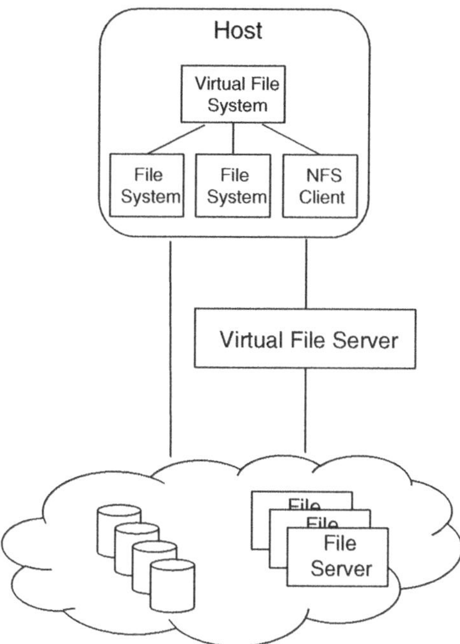

Figure 6.36 File-level storage virtualization.

Note that the access control mechanism does not involve actual client authentication. The resulting decoupling of the client and the storage device improves scalability, allowing the latter to scale independently of the client specifics. However, it gives rise to the need for a way to revoke credentials when they become accessible to a rogue client. Here, two options are available.

One option is that the security manager and object storage device change the relevant secret keys. Relatively easy to implement, this option, however, has a systemic effect beyond a single object. As soon as the secret keys are changed, all outstanding credentials become invalid.

With the other option, the security manager resets the policy access tag of the problematic object in the storage device. The tag is also part of the capability structure. A valid credential must have a policy access tag matching what is stored in the device.

6.2.6 *Storage Virtualization*

Storage virtualization [26] is concerned with abstraction of physical storage to shield applications from its underlying details, such as the actual media, access interface, and location.[43] As a result, physically dispersed, heterogeneous storage systems can appear as a single aggregated entity, and vice versa. For example, ten 800-gigabyte hard disks can emulate an 8-terabyte virtual disk to the operating system. Conversely, an 8-terabyte hard disk is partitioned into

[43] In this sense, the familiar file system construct is a form of storage virtualization.

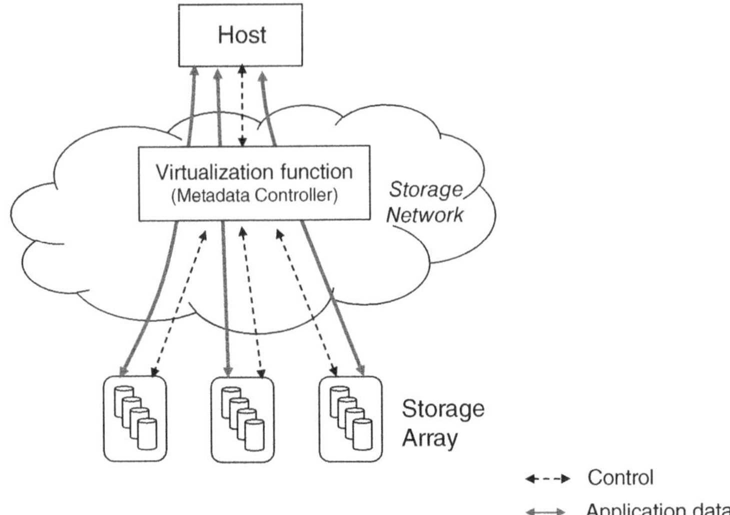

Figure 6.37 In-band storage virtualization.

eight 1-terabyte virtual disks that can be allocated to different hosts separately. The flexibility to allocate storage logically also allows dynamic resource management and improves overall resource utilization.

In general, storage virtualization entails (a) management of the metadata that map logical storage into physical devices and (b) translation and redirection of the I/O operations according to the mapping. The file-level virtualization builds on top of the block-level virtualization. The former calls for storage volumes being presented as files. As shown in Figure 6.36, with the use of a virtualization entity multiple file servers can appear as a single virtual file server.

With the block-level storage virtualization, storage appears to the operating system as a set of logical volumes or virtual disks. (A logical volume may combine non-contiguous physical partitions and span multiple physical storage devices.)

As shown in Figure 6.36, there are three approaches to block-level virtualization depending on where virtualization is done: the host, the network, or the storage device. In the host-based approach, virtualization is handled by a volume manager, which could be part of the operating system. The volume manager is responsible for mapping native blocks into logical volumes, while keeping track of the overall storage utilization. Ideally the mapping should provide a capability to be adjusted dynamically to allow the capacity of virtual storage to grow or shrink according to the latest need of a particular application. A major drawback of the approach is that per-host control is not favorable to optimal storage utilization in a multi-host environment, not to mention that the operational overhead of the volume manager is multiplied.

In the storage device-based approach, virtualization is handled by the controller of a storage system. Because of the close proximity of the controller to physical storage, this approach tends to result in good performance. Nevertheless, it has the drawback of being vendor-dependent and difficult (if not impossible) to work across heterogeneous storage systems.

In the network-based approach, virtualization is handled by a special function in a storage network, which may be part of a switch. The approach is transparent to hosts and storage

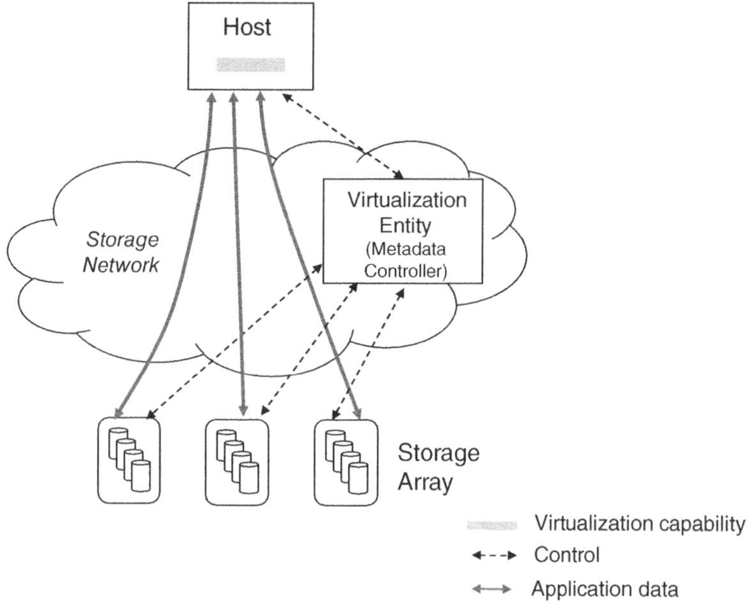

Figure 6.38 Out-of-band storage virtualization.

systems as long as they support the appropriate storage network protocols (such as FC, FCoE, or iSCSI). Depending on how control traffic and application traffic are handled, it can be further classified as *in-band* (symmetric) or *out-of-band* (asymmetric).

Figure 6.37 illustrates the in-band approach, where the virtualization function for mapping and I/O redirection is always in the path of both the control and application traffic. Naturally the virtualization function could become a bottleneck and a single point of failure. Caching and clustering are common techniques to mitigate these problems. On the positive side, the central point of control afforded by the in-band approach simplifies administration and support for advanced storage features such as snapshots, replication, and migration. The snapshot feature is of particular relevance to Cloud Computing. It can be applied to capture the state of a virtual machine at a certain point in time, reflecting the run-time conditions of its components (e.g., memory, disks, and network interface cards). The state information allows rolling back after applying a patch or a failure. Nevertheless, there is a trade-off as in this case the performance of other virtual machines on the same host may suffer when the snapshot of a virtual machine is being taken.

Figure 6.38 illustrates the out-of-band approach, where the virtualization function is in the path of the control traffic but not the application traffic. The virtualization function directs the application traffic. In comparison with the in-band approach, the approach results in better performance since the application traffic can go straight to the destination without incurring any processing delay in the virtualization function. But this approach does not lend itself to supporting advanced storage features. More important, it imposes an additional requirement on the host to distinguish the control and application traffic and route the traffic appropriately. As a result, the host needs to add a virtualization adaptor, which, incidentally, may also support

	Relative Access Time	Relative Cost	Retention Time
SRAM	$\sim10^{-7}$	$\sim10^{4}$	the duration when it is powered
DRAM	$\sim10^{-5}$	$\sim10^{2}$	<< 1 second
Flash	$\sim10^{-2}$	~10	years
Magnetic Disk	1	1	years
Magnetic Tape	$\sim10^{-4}$	0.5	years

SRAM: Static Random Access Memory
DRAM: Dynamic Random Access Memory

Figure 6.39 A comparison of storage technologies.

caching of both metadata and application data to improve performance. Per-host caching, however, faces the challenging problem of keeping the distributed cache consistent.

The network-based approach is most suitable for Cloud Computing, given its relative transparency and flexibility in storage pooling. With this approach, storage can be assigned to VM hosts, which, in turn, can allocate the assigned virtual storage to VMs through their own virtualization facilities as described in [27]. The choice between the in-band and out-of-band approach, however, is not as clear and depends on the application. It would be ideal to have a hybrid approach combining the best of two worlds. Apparently, this is possible with an intelligent switch that, in effect, handles the control traffic out-of-band and the application traffic in-band [28].

6.2.7 Solid-State Storage

Storage technologies vary widely in performance, cost, and other attributes. Figure 6.39 gives a glimpse of the differences. The access time and cost shown there are relative to those of a magnetic disk. The access time of a magnetic disk is in the order of milliseconds. The *Static Random Access Memory* (*SRAM*), *Dynamic Random Access Memory* (*DRAM*), and flash memory are much faster than the hard disk. With no moving parts and fully electronic processing, they are also superior in other aspects (e.g., shock resistance and energy efficiency). In the case of DRAM, data are stored as electric charge in the capacitors. Since the charge leaks over time, the capacitors need to be refreshed regularly. The need for constant refreshing explains why this type of RAM is named *dynamic*. With SRAM, data are held in transistors rather than in capacitors. There is no need for refreshing, which makes SRAM faster than DRAM. Nevertheless, both SRAM and DRAM are volatile in that they need power to retain the stored data. In contrast, flash memory is non-volatile.

Flash memory is a kind of *Electrically Erasable Programmable Read-Only Memory* (*EEP-ROM*).[44] It keeps data in floating-gate islands, which can retain electric charge for a long period of time (years). A relatively new flash memory technology was invented by Dr. Fujio Masuoka

44 "Electrically-erasable" is significant because an earlier Erasable Programmable Read-Only Memory (EPROM) technology requires exposure to ultraviolet light (for over 10 minutes) to erase content. Programming EPROM also calls for a separate special device.

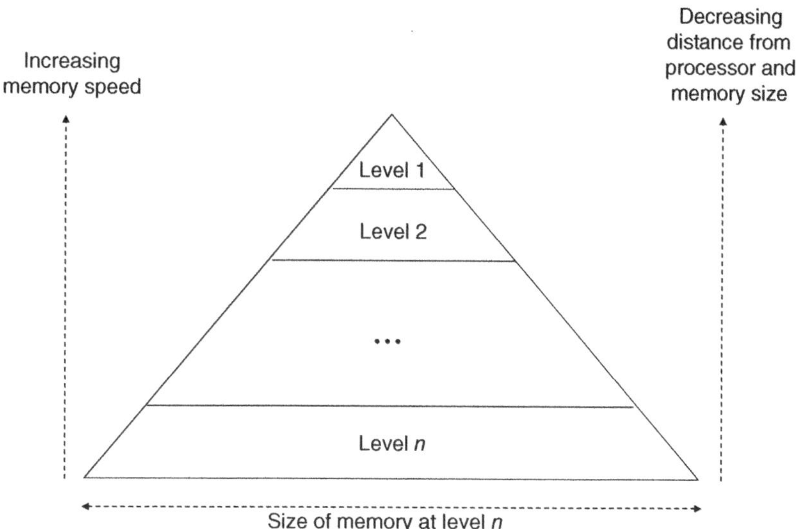

Figure 6.40 The memory hierarchy.

while he worked at Toshiba in the 1980s. It was named *flash* because of the capability to erase a big chunk of memory fast. Dr. Masuoka actually devised two types of flash memory in 1984[45] and 1987, respectively. The first type is known as *NOR flash* because its basic construct has properties resembling those of a *NOR gate*. NOR flash is fast (at least faster than hard disk), and it can be randomly addressed to a given byte. Its storage density is limited however.

The later type of flash memory removes this limitation (while also reducing the cost). It is called *NAND flash* because its basic construct has properties similar to those of a *NAND gate*. NAND flash, however, allows random access only in units that are larger than a byte. The NAND flash has made a splash in consumer electronics [29], and it is used much more widely than NOR flash—in digital cameras, portable music players, and smart phones.

The way to deal with the wide disparity in storage technologies is to implement storage hierarchically. Figure 6.40 depicts the memory hierarchy, where the lower the level of the memory, the closer is its distance to the processor, the faster its speed, the higher its cost, and the smaller its size. The constraint of the memory size at different levels implies that data can be stored in full only at a high level where the memory has a sufficient size. Furthermore, the data kept at a certain memory level can only be a subset of what is kept at a level above it.[46] Overall, the memory hierarchy aims to create an illusion of infinite fast memory. The general strategy for placing data in the memory hierarchy is to keep data items that are more recently accessed closer to the processor and to include their neighbors as well when copying the data items to a lower level. For an in-depth discussion of memory hierarchy, we recommend the textbook on computer architecture by John L. Hennessy and David A. Patterson [30].

[45] Dr. Masuoka noted in an interview [31] that he invented NOR flash in 1982 but presented the first paper about it in 1984. As a result, in most literatures, 1984 is attributed as the birth year of NOR flash.

[46] In a strict memory hierarchy, information can be copied from one layer to an adjacent layer only.

Until recently, a common memory hierarchy has been SRAM for caches, DRAM for main memory, and hard disk for paged memory. The continued advances in solid-state storage technology have introduced other practical options.

In particular, NAND flash has emerged as the first serious challenger to a hard disk. It is increasingly used between SRAM and hard disk in the memory hierarchy. When used this way, flash memory is fashioned into solid-state drives that emulate hard-disk drives to help integration with the existing systems.

While solid-state drives will remain more expensive (in cost per byte) than hard-disk drives in the near future, they can deliver better I/O performances. Solid-state drives outperform hard-disk drives in random read operations by about three orders of magnitude. They are especially useful for applications involving a high percentage of random I/O operations. Web and online transaction processing services are familiar examples of such applications. Cloud services make an even better example, because they multiplex unrelated workloads on the same hardware—the I/O blender effect.

To be deployed in the Cloud, the solid-state drives must overcome three limitations inherent to NAND flash:

1. A write operation over the existing content requires that this content be erased first. (This makes write operations much slower than read operations.)
2. Erase operations are done on a block basis, while write operations on a page basis[47];
3. Memory cells wear out after a limited number of write–erase cycles.

Given the limitations, directly updating the contents of a page in place will cause high latency because of the need to read, erase, and reprogram the entire block. Obviously, this is not desirable, which gives rise to the practice of *relocate-on-write* (or *out-of-place write*). Here, a free page is written with the latest data, while the old page is marked as invalid.

Write performance is improved at the expense of an ever-growing number of invalid pages. If not reclaimed, the invalid pages deplete the storage space quickly. To reclaim the storage, garbage collection is necessary.

For purely sequential write operations, garbage collection is straightforward. Blocks can be invalidated and reclaimed one by one as data are written page by page. No extra write–erase operations are incurred. For random write operations, in contrast, the situation is much more complex, and so more sophisticated algorithms are required. For instance, an algorithm could maximize the number of reclaimed pages or minimize the number of additional read and write operations. The effectiveness of a garbage collection algorithm depends on the degree of write amplification that it incurs.

With write amplification, the eventual number of write operations carried out on a NAND flash is greater than that requested by the host. Naturally, it is desirable to contain write amplification as much as possible for performance and endurance reasons. Such containment is of particular importance in Cloud Computing, since write amplification worsens as the amount of random write operations increases.

There are two techniques to reduce write amplification.

[47] Pages are grouped together in blocks. A typical block contains 32, 64, or 128 pages. (It tends to be larger than the block size in a file system.) Page sizes vary. A page may contain, for example, 512, 2048, or 4096 bytes.

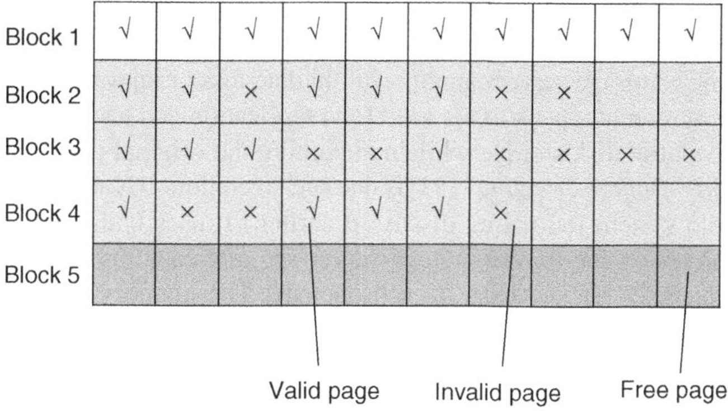

Figure 6.41 Hypothetical state of a NAND flash memory.

One technique is *over-provisioning*, namely limiting the user address space to a fraction of the raw memory capacity. Over-provisioning increases the number of invalid pages in the block selected for reclamation. It is effective and does not depend on special support from the operating system (or the file system).

The technique employs a special ATA command to inform the underlying storage what data are deleted. With hard disks, there is no need for such a command because the storage medium supports in-place writing. The command makes a great difference in the case of NAND flash as it saves time that is otherwise wasted during garbage collection.

To extend a NAND flash's lifetime in general, the practice of "*wear leveling*" is used to spread write–erase operations as evenly as possible. (Note that out-place-write intrinsically supports wear leveling.) The practice introduces write amplification. To see the effect, consider the extreme example shown in Figure 6.41.

In the figure, the cells correspond to pages, which may be valid, invalid, or free (unmarked); the rows correspond to blocks. The shade of each block denotes its age. The darker the shade of a block, the older it is. Block 5 is the oldest, reaching the end of life, while block 1 is the youngest, still having many write–erase cycles ahead of it. Given the state, the memory will become unusable soon unless another block is vacated to replace block 5, the free block.

Assuming the data stored in block 1 are static, it is the best block to vacate for two reasons: (1) block 5 won't need to be updated once programmed with the data of block 1; and (2) the memory's life is extended by the most cycles. Relocating the contents of block 1 to block 5 requires more *read* and *write* operations than any other option. Hence, wear leveling needs to address not only unused cycles but also the cycles wasted moving unchanged data. A good analysis of write amplification together with wear leveling is given in [32].

Despite its high cost, the unique performance need of Cloud services still leaves room for DRAM-based storage devices. To address the volatility problem, such devices come with built-in batteries or other backup power sources. Yet more interesting is the *RAMCloud* project at Stanford University [4]. The project aims to create a new class of storage for use in a data center that can keep all data in DRAM all the time. Commodity servers are the building blocks. Depending on the scale needed, hundreds or thousands of commodity servers can be clustered to form a single unified large-scale storage system. Expected to have exceptional performance, such storage systems face several challenges. Among other things (e.g., management of highly distributed storage and low-latency networking), the data stored on RAMCloud ought to be as durable as if they were on hard disk; a power failure must not cause permanent data loss; and failure of a single storage server cannot result in data loss or unavailability for over a few seconds. These requirements speak to the need for a replication and backup technique that can make use of non-volatile disk storage while maintaining the original performance advantage afforded by DRAM. "*Buffered logging*" [33] is one such technique. (Note that buffered logging is related to the file system journaling discussed earlier.) It uses both disk and memory for backup. Data changes on the master storage server are replicated as log entries on backup memories synchronously but on disks asynchronously. The memory copies are temporary. They are buffered and then transferred to disks in batches. Once replicated on disks, the log entries are removed from backup memories. Buffered logging keeps up performance but leaves behind a potential problem: the buffered data vanish if the master and all backups lose power simultaneously. An obvious solution to this problem is to fit each storage server with a small battery for it to flush buffered log entries to the disk after a power loss. Ironically, the special fitting deviates from the original assumption of using commodity servers.

In essence, RAMCloud provides a remote cache of practically infinite capacity to boost application performance. In this respect, it is influenced by *Memcached* [5], an open-source distributed caching system originally developed by Brad Fitzpatrick to improve the performance of *LiveJournal* [34]. *Memcached* supports a simple key-value store for small chunks of arbitrary data in DRAM on commodity computers. It is specific to caching to allow applications to bypass heavy operations such as database queries. Data durability is never part of the equation; each cached item is valid only for a certain period. *Memcached* is client-server-based, employing a request/response protocol (which may run over TCP or UDP).

A server stores data in a hash table. Keys are unique strings used to index into the table. For example, a result from a database query can be cached in a *memcached* server with the query string as the key. Although each data item has a limited lifetime, *memcached* does not implement garbage collection to actively reclaim memory. Instead, memory is reclaimed only when an expired item is being retrieved or when the space is needed for caching a new item. In the latter case, one of the least-recently-used[48] items is subject to eviction. If an expired item exists, it is selected for reclaiming first. Otherwise, a still-valid item is selected.

Depending on the size of DRAM available on a server, caching the workload data may need more than one server. In this case, the hash table is distributed across multiple servers, which form a cluster with aggregated DRAM. *Memcached* servers, by design, are neither aware of one another nor coordinated centrally. It is the job of a client to select what server to use, and the client (armed with the knowledge of the servers in use) does so based on the key of the data item to be cached.

How should the hash table be distributed so that the same server is selected for the same key? A naïve scheme might be as follows:

$$s = H(k) \bmod n,$$

where $H(k)$ is a hashing function, k the key, n the number of server, and s the server label, which is assigned the remainder of the division of $H(k)$ over n. The scheme works as long

[48] Strictly speaking, less-recently-used items are what are meant here; there is just one least-recently-used item.

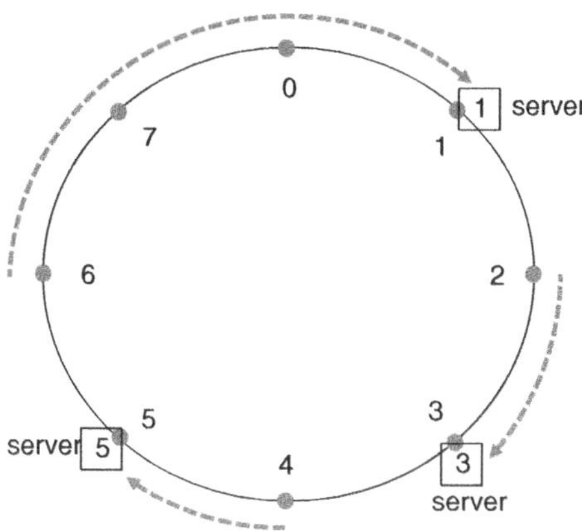

Figure 6.42 A circle in consistent hashing.

as n is constant, but it will most likely yield a different server when the number of servers grows or shrinks dynamically—as is typically the case in Cloud Computing. As a result, cache misses abound, application performance degrades, and all servers in the latest cluster have to be updated.

Obviously this is undesirable, and so another scheme is in order. To this end, *memcached* implementations usually employ variants of consistent hashing [35] to minimize the updates required as the server pool changes and maximize the chance of having the same server for a given key. The basic algorithm of consistent hashing [36] can be outlined as follows:

- Map the range of a hash function to a circle, with the largest value wrapping around to the smallest value in a clockwise fashion;
- Assign a value (i.e., a point on the circle) to each server in the pool as its identifier[49]; and
- To cache a data item of key k, select the server whose identifier is equal to or larger than $H(k)$.

In [36], the server selected for key k is called k's successor, which is responsible for the arc between k and the identifier of the previous server. As an example, Figure 6.42 shows a circle of three servers, where server 1 is responsible for caching the associated data items for keys hashed to 6, 7, 0, and 1; server 3 for keys hashed to 2 and 3; and server 5 for keys hashed to 4 and 5.

An immediate result of consistent hashing is that a departure or an arrival of a server only affects its immediate neighbors. In other words, when a new server p joins the pool, certain keys that were previously assigned to the original p's successor will now be reassigned to server p, while other servers are not affected. Similarly, when an old server p leaves the pool, the keys previously assigned to it will now be reassigned to p's successor while other servers are not affected. In the example in Figure 6.42, adding a new server 7 would result in reassigning keys 6 and 7 to the new server; removing server 3 would result in reassigning keys 2 and 3 to server 5.

[49] The assignment can be done through a hash function, which may be different from but has the same range as H

The basic algorithm allows the server pool to scale effectively and provides a sound foundation for further enhancements. An enhancement for achieving better load distribution among servers is described in [37].

Overall, *memcached* proves to be an effective, scalable mechanism to improve application performance. It is widely used by high-traffic websites such as *Facebook*, *Twitter*, and *YouTube*. In particular, Facebook has deployed thousands of *memcached* servers to support its social networking services, creating the largest key-value store in the world—where over a billion requests per second are processed and trillions of items are stored [38].

References

[1] Glanz, J. (2012) The Cloud factories: Power, pollution and the Internet. *The New York Times*, September 22. www.nytimes.com/2012/09/23/technology/data-centers-waste-vast-amounts-of-energy-belying-industry-image.html?pagewanted=all.

[2] Pianese, F., Bosch, P., Duminuco, A., *et al.* (2010) Toward a Cloud operating system. Network Operations and Management Symposium Workshops (NOMS Wksps). IEEE/IFIP, pp. 335–342.

[3] SNIA Technical Council (2003) The SNIA shared storage mode. www.snia.org/sites/default/files/SNIA-SSM-text-2003-04-13.pdf.

[4] Ousterhout, J. (n.d.) RAMCloud. Stanford University. https://ramCloud.stanford.edu/wiki/display/ramCloud/RAMCloud.

[5] Dormando (n.d.) What is *memcached*? http://memcached.org/.

[6] Kant, K. (2009) Data center evolution—a tutorial on state of the art, issues, and challenges. *Computer Networks*, **53**(17), 2939–2965.

[7] Electronic Industries Alliance (1992) EIA-310-D: Cabinets, Racks, Panels, and Associated Equipment. Electronic Industries Alliance, Arlington.

[8] ISO/IEC (1994) ISO/IEC 7498-1: Information Technology—Open Systems Interconnection—Basis Reference Model: The Basic Model. International Organization for Standardization, Geneva.

[9] Widmer, A.X. and Franaszek, P.A. (1983) A DC-balanced, partitioned-block, 8B/10B transmission code. *IBM Journal of Research and Development*, **27**(5), 440–451.

[10] Jacob, B., Ng, S.W., and Wang, D.T. (2008) *Memory Systems: Cache, DRAM, Disk*. Elsevier Science, Amsterdam.

[11] Paulsen, K. (2011) *Moving Media Storage Technologies: Applications & Workflows for Video and Media Server Platforms*. Elsevier Science, Amsterdam.

[12] Sandberg, R., Goldberg, D., Kleiman, S., *et al.* (1985) Design and implementation of the Sun network filesystem. Proceedings of the Summer USENIX Conference. USENIX, the Advanced Computing Systems Association, Berkeley.

[13] Nobel Prize organization (2007) Class for Physics of the Royal Swedish Academy of Sciences. The Nobel Prize in Physics 2007. www.nobelprize.org/nobel_prizes/physics/laureates/2007/advanced-physicsprize2007.pdf.

[14] Ghemawat, S., Gobioff, H., and Leung, S.-T. (2003) The Google File System. SOSP '03, Bolton Landing, NY, pp. 29–43.

[15] Doeppner, T.W. (2011) *Operating Systems In Depth: Design and Programming*. John Wiley & Sons, Inc, Hoboken.

[16] Kleiman, S.R. (1986) Vnodes: An architecture for multiple file system types in Sun Unix. Proceedings of the Summer USENIX Conference.

[17] Birrell, A.D. and Nelson, B.J. (1984) Implementing remote procedure calls. *ACM Transactions on Computer Systems*, **2**(1), 39–59.

[18] Thurlow, R. (2009) RFC 5531, RPC: Remote Procedure Call Protocol Specification Version 2. Vol. RFC 5531. http://tools.ietf.org/html/rfc5531.

[19] Eisler, E. (2006) RFC 4506, XDR: External Data Representation Standard. http://tools.ietf.org/html/rfc4506.

[20] Dunning, D., Regnier, G., McAlpine, G., *et al.* (1998) The virtual interface architecture. *IEEE Micro*, **2**(18), 66–76.

[21] Van Meter, R., Finn, G.G., and Hotz, S. (1998) VISA: Netstation's virtual Internet SCSI adapter. *ACM SIGOPS Operating Systems Review (ACM)*, **32**(5), 71–80.

[22] Meth, K.Z. and Satran, J. (2003) Design of the iSCSI Protocol. Proceedings of the 20th IEEE/11th NASA Goddard Conference on Mass Storage Systems and Technologies (MSS'03), IEEE, pp. 116–122.

[23] Azagury, A., Dreizin, V., Factor, M., *et al.* (2003) Towards an object store. Proceedings of the 20th IEEE/11th NASA Goddard Conference on Mass Storage Systems and Technologies (MSS'03), IEEE, San Francisco, CA, pp. 165–176.

[24] Azagury, A., Canetti, R., Factor, M., *et al.* (2002) A two layered approach for securing an object store network. Proceedings of the First International IEEE Security in Storage Workshop, IEEE, San Francisco, CA, pp. 10–23.

[25] Factor, M., Nagle, D., Naor, D., *et al.* (2005) The OSD security protocol. Proceedings of the Third International IEEE Security in Storage Workshop, IEEE, San Francisco, CA, pp. 11–23.

[26] Troppens, U., Erkens, R., Mueller-Friedt, W., *et al.* (2011) *Storage Networks Explained: Basics and Application of Fibre Channel SAN, NAS, iSCSI, Infiniband and FCoE.* John Wiley & Sons Ltd, Chichester.

[27] Vaghani, S.B. (2010) Virtual machine file system. *ACM SIGOPS Operating Systems Review*, **44**(4), 57–70.

[28] Smoot, S.R. and Tan, N.K. (2012) *Private Cloud Computing: Consolidation, Virtualization, and Service-Oriented Infrastructure.* Morgan Kaufmann, Waltham, MA.

[29] Harari, E. (2012) Flash memory—the great disruptor! In Winner, L. (ed.), *IEEE International Solid-State Circuits Conference Digest of Technical Papers (ISSCC).* IEEE, San Francisco, CA.

[30] Hennessy, J.L. and Patterson, D.L. (2012) *Computer Architecture: A Quantitative Approach.* Morgan Kaufmann, Waltham, MA.

[31] Computer History Museum (2012) Oral history of Fujio Masuoka, September 21. http://archive.computerhistory.org/resources/access/text/2013/01/102746492-05-01-acc.pdf.

[32] Hu, X.-Y., Eleftheriou, E., Haas, R., *et al.* (2009) Write amplification analysis in flash-based solid state drives. Proceedings of SYSTOR 2009: The Israeli Experimental Systems Conference, The Association for Computing Machinery, New York.

[33] Ousterhout, J., Agrawal, P., Erickson, D., *et al.* (2011) The case for RAMCloud. *Communications of the ACM*, **54**(7), pp. 121–130.

[34] Fitzpatrick, B. (2004) Distributed caching with *memcached. Linux Journal*, **124**, 5.

[35] Karger, D., Lehman, E., Leighton, T., *et al.* (1997) Consistent hashing and random trees: Distributed caching protocols for relieving hot spots on the World Wide Web. Proceedings of the 29th Annual ACM Symposium on Theory of Computing, ACM, New York.

[36] Stoica, I., Morris, R., Karger, D., *et al.* (2001) Chord: A scalable peer-to-peer lookup service for internet applications. Proceedings of the 2001 Conference on Applications, Technologies, Architectures, and Protocols for Computer Communications, ACM, New York, **31**(4), pp. 149–160.

[37] DeCandia, G., Hastorun, D., Jampani, M., *et al.* (2007) Dynamo: Amazon's highly available key-value store. Proceedings of the 21st ACM SIGOPS Symposium on Operating Systems Principles, ACM, New York, **41**(6), pp. 205–220.

[38] Nishtala, R., Fugal, H., Grimm, S., *et al.* (2013) Scaling memcache at Facebook. Proceedings of the 10th USENIX Conference on Networked Systems Design and Implementation, USENIX Association, Berkeley, CA.

7

Operations, Management, and Orchestration in the Cloud

The first words in the title of this chapter refer to the means of supporting the *Operations and Management* (*OA&M*) of the Cloud infrastructure. While the practice of operations and management has been fairly well understood and even partly standardized, the word "orchestration" remains somewhat ambiguous, one of the most misused words in the industry. Yet the concept of orchestration is critical to Cloud Computing. Our first task is to clarify this concept.

Things were simpler in the 19th and 20th centuries,[1] when *orchestration* simply referred to the task, performed by a composer, of writing a score for an ensemble of musical instruments (typically a symphonic orchestra). The same word has also referred to the musical discipline—taught in conservatories as part of a composition curriculum—of writing for orchestra. The discipline catalogs the musical characteristics (range, timbre, technical difficulties, and idioms) of the representatives of various groups of instruments (strings, woodwind, brass, and percussion)—the subject also referred to as *instrumentation*—and teaches how different individual instruments may be combined or juxtaposed to achieve the sound color and balance envisioned by a composer. It should be noted that the physical characteristics of the instruments employed in the modern symphonic orchestra have been largely standardized, and orchestra performers have been trained according to this standard. That makes the instrumentation part rather precise (in specifying, for example, which trill is easy to play on a trombone, and which one is impossible to play). On the other hand, the orchestration proper—that is, the part that deals with combining the sound qualities of various instruments to achieve new effects—can do nothing more beyond listing a few generic principles and then bringing in various examples from the work of masters to illustrate the effects created. If one follows these examples as rules, one cannot create new effects. Yet, great composers (notably Richard Wagner in the 19th century and Maurice Ravel and Igor Stravinsky in the 20th century) have revolutionized orchestration by discovering new and striking sound combinations that fit their respective artistic visions. Once their music became known and accepted, their scores became

[1] The Merriam-Webster online dictionary (www.merriam-webster.com/dictionary/orchestration) dates the first use of this word to 1859.

Cloud Computing: Business Trends and Technologies, First Edition. Igor Faynberg, Hui-Lan Lu and Dor Skuler.

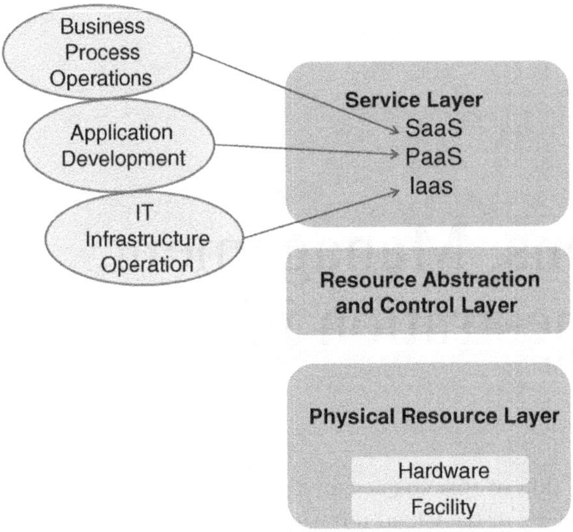

Figure 7.1 Service orchestration (after NIST SP 500-292).

a new source for teaching orchestration. We refer interested readers to an excellent book on orchestration [1], from which at least one author has learned much.

The meaning of *orchestration* in Cloud Computing is not that dissimilar from that of its original counterpart in music. In the Cloud, the "instruments" are the resources described in the previous chapters. The word "instruments" refers to both physical resources (i.e., hosts, storage, and networking devices) and software resources (hypervisors and various operating systems), all of which are "played" with the single purpose of introducing and supporting Cloud services.

Two NIST Cloud architecture publications [2, 3] address this subject with the following definition:

> "Service Orchestration refers to the composition of system components to support the Cloud providers' activities in arrangement, coordination and management of computing resources in order to provide Cloud services to Cloud Consumers."

The NIST Cloud Computing reference architecture [3] illustrates the task of orchestration (depicted here in Figure 7.1).

The NIST three-layered model represents the grouping of the components that a Cloud provider deals with. On the top is the service layer where the service-access interfaces are defined. The middle layer contains the system components that provide and manage access to the physical computing resources through software. The control aspect here relates to resource allocation, access control, and monitoring. NIST refers to these as "the software fabric that ties together the numerous underlying physical resources and their software abstractions to enable resource pooling, dynamic allocation, and measured service." At the bottom of the stack is the physical resource layer, which includes all hardware resources—computers, storage components, and networks, but also "facility resources, such as heating, ventilation and air conditioning (HVAC), power, communications, and other aspects of the physical plant."

How exactly these resources are coordinated is not specified in [3]; we will provide some "under-the-hood" views later in this chapter. (In particular, we will extend the above model in Section 7.3.) What is important is that the NIST description underlines the distinction between *service orchestration* and *service management* tasks performed by a Cloud provider. Service management includes "all of the service-related functions that are necessary for the management and operation of those services required by or proposed to Cloud consumers." The three service management categories are *business support*, *provisioning and configuration*, and *portability and interoperability*.

In the business support category are the tasks of customer-, contract-, and inventory management, as well as accounting and billing, reporting and auditing, and pricing and rating. The actual operation of the Cloud is the subject of the provisioning and configuration category, whose tasks include provisioning, resource change, monitoring and reporting, metering, and SLA management. Finally, data transfer, VM image migration, and the all-encompassing application and service migration are the tasks of portability and interoperability, accomplished through the unified management interface.

To understand what is actually involved, it is necessary to distinguish the components and observe the respective evolution of each of them separately.

In the first section of this chapter we discuss the evolution of the concept of orchestration in the enterprise (i.e., IT) industry—where the concept was actually born at the turn of the century.

In the second section, we review the discipline of network and operations management, with the emphasis on the evolution of the operations support systems. Note that, the word "network" aside, network management is a purely software matter. Network management is used both in the enterprise and telecommunications industries, but naturally it originated in the telecom world. In the context of this discussion we will also review several widely implemented standards.

The third section of this chapter synthesizes the above concepts in the context of Cloud, where hosted services (along with the appropriate orchestration tools) have been offered to an enterprise by the Cloud provider (who naturally needs its own tools to orchestrate the services). As might be expected, there is not much in the way of history here, let alone standards; but the history is being made right now, at the time of this writing, and it is happening very fast with multiple open-source initiatives!

The fourth and last section of this chapter deals with the subject of identity and access management. We have mentioned that before, and we repeat it now: the success of security in general and identity management in particular has been considered by many the single most important matter that the industry needs to deal with. Needless to say, the authors—who have been working on this very subject for more than a decade—subscribe to this view.

7.1 Orchestration in the Enterprise

The origin of the term dates back to the information technology movement developed in the early 2000s. The movement has been known as *Service-Oriented Architecture* (*SOA*). As we will see later in this section, SOA "died" in 2009—at least this is when its obituary was written—but the overarching idea and the objectives of the movement are still alive and well!

The major motivation was to break the old model of developing and maintaining monolithic applications[2] by harnessing modularity and enabling distributed processing.

Of course, modularity has been the holy grail of software since at least the 1960s, and much has been accomplished in the years that have passed. ALGOL-60—the progenitor of all structured high-level programming languages used to date—provided the mechanisms for modules to have independent variable naming so that they could interact with one another only through clearly defined parameter-based interfaces. Once the interfaces were defined, the modules could be developed independently (by the programmers who, presumably, never needed even to talk to one another). These modules could then be compiled and the resulting *object code* stored in *libraries*, which would eventually be linked with the main-line application code. One essential point here is that one—presumably better-performing—module could always substitute for another as long as both modules adhered to the same interface.

In the 1980s the evolution of this paradigm forked into three independent developments, which influenced the service orchestration concept.

The first development, fostered by the Unix operating system *shell* interface, provided programmers with powerful means to execute a set of self-contained programs, without any need for compilation or linking with the main-line code. These programs could even be arranged so that one fed its output into another (through the *pipe* interface). It is important to underline that, unlike with the previous *job-control language* environments provided by other operating systems, the *shell* environment was really a well-thought-through collaborative programming platform. Anyone can write a new "command," compile it, and make it available to others. Furthermore, the same "command" name can be shared by different modules as long as they are stored in different directories. The set of directories to fetch a module from is indicated by an environmental variable, which can be changed on the fly.[3] And, again, the *shell* programs don't need to be recompiled when changed, because they did not need to be compiled in the first place—they are being interpreted. Finally, a module invoked in a *shell* script can be written in any language (including *shell* itself).

The second development, called *object-oriented programming*, significantly simplified the interface to the modules (previously thought of as procedures). Whereas previously programmers needed to understand every detail of the data structures on which library procedures operated, with object-oriented programming the data structures have become encapsulated along with the *methods* (i.e., the procedures) that perform operations on them. Only methods are visible to a programmer, who therefore no longer needs to care about the data structures. The latter can be quite complex,[4] but a programmer who uses an object does not need to understand this complexity; only the programmer who implements the object *class* (an equivalent

[2] Everything discussed in this section has to do with application development, and ultimately programming.

[3] Unfortunately, the ease of collaborative mix-and-match is at cross purposes with security. The very ingenious mechanism that helped collaboration has introduced a significant security problem. One could (and many people actually did) write a deadly program, give it the same name as a frequently used one, and put it in a directory specified by the environmental variable *PATH*. Unless each module resets this variable (or carefully checks it before proceeding), there is no guarantee that the modules it calls are what they are supposed to be. The same problem has persisted in the frameworks that allow homonymous modules.

[4] Consider a procedure for multiplying complex numbers, which allows each parameter to be represented either as a (*Re*, *Im*) pair or—in trigonometric form—as a (*modulus*, *argument*) pair so that the programmer can mix and match representations as he or she wishes.

of a *type* that defines a data structure) does. With that, the objects instantiated to a given class started to be thought of as *services*.[5] The first object-oriented language, *SIMULA*, was actually developed in 1967—at about the same time as ALCOL-67, and it was a natural superset of ALGOL, created solely for the purpose of simulating systems. (It was, in fact, used in simulating complex hardware systems.) Since every system consists of "black boxes"—some of the same type (or *class*, in object-oriented parlance), the paradigm was born naturally. Of course, the objective of SIMULA was modeling rather than effective code reuse. It took about 20 years to standardize SIMULA, the task carried out by the SIMULA Standards Group (1) and completed in 1986. By the time that was done, in 1983, a new language—*C++*—was released by a Bell Labs researcher, Dr. Bjarne Stroustrup, who had quietly worked on it since 1979. C++ borrowed much from SIMULA, but it has been based on (and, in fact, compiled to) the C language, which was designed as a systems programming language (or, in other words, allowed a programmer to cut corners unceremoniously in order to work closely with the hardware at hand). It is this efficiency—combined with the full implementation of the object-oriented paradigm—that made C++ so popular. It has been ratified by ISO as the ISO/IEC 14882 standard. An earlier version was issued in 1998, but the present standard in force is ISO/IEC 14882:2011, which is known in the industry as *C++11*. There is a much recommended book [4] on the subject, issued by its inventor and first developer. C++ is also a progenitor of a plethora of other popular interpreted object-oriented languages, notably Java, designed for an increasingly lighter-weight application development (vs. system programming, in which C++ still rules).

From a programmer's point of view, the new object-oriented languages have implemented *parametric polymorphism* (a feature that allows programmers to define subroutines with both a flexible number of parameters and—to some extent—flexible typing of parameters). This has significantly improved the flexibility of the interface between the program that uses the service and the program that provides a service. The interface is called the *Application Programmer's Interface* (*API*).

The third development was *distributed computing*. For a comprehensive monograph, we highly recommend [5]. As part of this development, much has been researched and standardized in the way of remote execution. An essential objective here was to shield a programmer from the complex (and often tedious) detail of keeping track of the actual physical distribution of the computing resources. To this end, a programmer should even be unaware of the actual distribution. For all practical purposes, the API had to look exactly as the one already provided by operating systems or any application library—the interface being that of a procedure call (or, in the object-oriented model, the method invocation).

With this objective in view, the *Remote Procedure Call* (*RPC*) model has been developed. In this model, a programmer writes a *local* procedure call—what else other than local could it be, anyway?—but the underlying software "transfers" the call to another machine by means of an application protocol. The model was primarily intended for client/server interactions, where the client program invokes "remote" procedures on the server. The issues here are non-trivial (consider passing parameters *by reference* from a client to a server, or crash recovery—especially on the server side).

---

[5] In the spirit of the previous footnote, an operation (addition, multiplication, division, etc.) on complex numbers is an example of such a service.

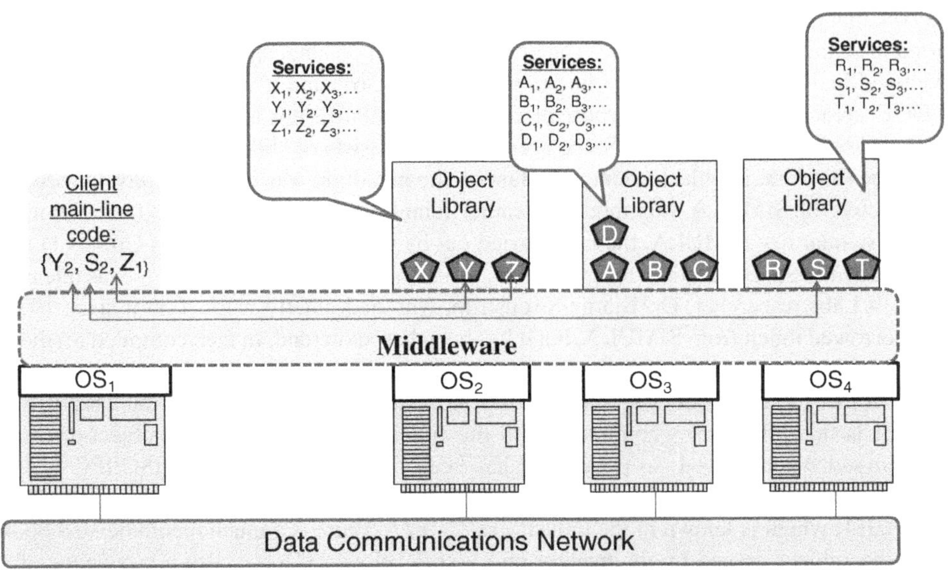

Figure 7.2 Distributed object-oriented computing model.

Aside from the algorithmic part covering concurrent execution, the industrial infrastructure has been developed for advertising the *services*[6] provided by the objects across the machines and for accessing such services. To this end, more than one infrastructure has been developed, as quite a few standards organizations and fora were involved. These included ISO/IEC, ITU-T, *Object Management Group* (*OMG*), and—later, with the success of the World-Wide Web—the *World-Wide Web Consortium* (*W3C*) and the *Organization for the Advancement of Structured Information Standards* (*OASIS*), to name just a few.[7]

The common model that shaped up around the mid-1990s is depicted in Figure 7.2.

Here, the client program can invoke remotely the methods of various objects residing across the infrastructure. The infrastructure may include different machines, which run different operating systems. The only requirement of a "physical" nature is that these computers be interconnected through a data network.

Each object library can, of course, be implemented in its own language. The mechanisms of remote invocation have been largely invariant to both the original language and the operating system on which the respective code is to be executed. This has been achieved through *middleware*, which provides its own primitives (local API) to insulate the programming environment from the operating systems and thus ensure universal portability. As the environment also allowed the object libraries to advertise their services, some models included the concept of

[6] Another overloaded term, which here strictly means the *methods* (i.e., operations on the objects) supported on a given server.

[7] In the telecommunications industry, standardization and some research and development have been performed in the *Telecommunications Information Networking Architecture Consortium* (*TINA-C*), which existed between 1993 and 2000, and to whose early work the authors contributed on behalf of Bell Labs. The results of TINA-C generated enough interest in the industry to be cited in [4]. There is a separate book on TINA-C [6].

a *service broker*, whose job was to match the client service requirements to various service providers' libraries.

One disturbing development that took place in the mid-1990s, when all eyes were focused on the Internet and the World-Wide Web, was the en-masse rejection of the standards that had been written before then (and most standards that enabled the infrastructure had been written before then). This was not necessarily bad for the standards people, who suddenly got new and exciting jobs; nor was it bad for the new standards fora that mushroomed and pushed aside the older organizations, which had been struggling with completing the standards based on technology that was labeled "old" almost overnight. It was also good for people who had fresh ideas on how to "simplify" programming, because the ebb of fashion propelled many an untested idea into standards. Technology was moving fast, and few companies—and fora that depended on them—risked being left behind. Eventually, when the bubble burst, they were left behind anyway, but the fast development of untested technology proved to be ruinous even for the technology itself!

At the root of the problem was a truly religious aspect of the new wave of distributed processing technology: it was believed that all application-layer protocols had to be ASCII-text-based. The truth is that the *Simple Mail Transfer Protocol* (*SMTP*) was indeed ASCII-text-based, which was advantageous at a time when most terminals were teletype-like and using ASCI text was helpful in testing and debugging (and also for breaking in by hackers, although that most certainly was not a design objective!). Similarly, the main protocol of the Web—the *Hyper-Text Transfer Protocol* (*HTTP*), initially had to deal only with the transfer of the ASCII-encoded (HTML) files. Since the amount of protocol-related data was small compared with the payload, text-based encoding was justified. But these decisions, which were necessary—or at least justifiable at a time when SMTP and then HTTP were being developed—later somehow became interpreted as the maxim that *all* Internet application protocols must be text-encoded. The maxim soon became a *belief*, joining other false beliefs (such as that IPv6 is "better for security" than IPv4). As the application protocols grew, the absurdity of applying the maxim became evident. Not only has the amount of data become huge, but parsing it became a problem for real-time protocols. In fact, the new version of HTTP [7] presently developed in the IETF HTTPbis working group uses binary encoding, providing the following explanation for the change: "... HTTP/1.1 header fields are often repetitive and verbose, which, in addition to generating more or larger network packets, can cause the small initial TCP congestion window to quickly fill.... Finally, this encapsulation also enables more scalable processing of messages through use of binary message framing."

The effect of text encoding on distributed object-oriented computing first manifested itself in abandoning the *Abstract Syntax Notation* (*ASN.1*) encoding standard—which required compilation into a binary format[8]—in favor of the *Extensible Markup Language* (*XML*).[9]

---

[8] ASN.1 has been defined in the X.680–X.695 series of ITU-T recommendations, available at www.itu.int/ITU-T/studygroups/com17/languages/. It was developed in the early 1990s, exactly to overcome the problem of specifying bit strings in the protocol definitions. With ASN.1, the encoding is specified in PASCAL-like data structures, which are then compiled according to binary encoding rules. The compilation is indeed an extra step, but the overall scheme produces efficient binary encoding.

[9] XML has been developed in W3C: www.w3.org/XML/. It is a universal text-based encoding scheme, which is known for producing "verbose" output when not used sensibly, but no one has defined what constitutes sensible use of XML.

Nothing is wrong with XML, but using it indiscriminately can be catastrophic.[10] Even though HTTP itself provided a mechanism for remote API access, W3C decided to develop an RPC mechanism that ran on top of HTTP. Hence a new protocol—*SOAP*, the acronym originally expended as *Simple Object Access Protocol.*[11] "The word *simple* proved to be a misnomer, and so the expansion of the acronym was dropped in SOAP version 1.2.[12] SOAP became quite fashionable, and the complex SOA infrastructure was developed on top of it.

While SOAP was (and still is) used as a remote procedure call mechanism, its serialization in the XML format made it perform much worse than the RPC in the *Common Object Request Broker Architecture* (*CORBA*) developed by OMG.[13] That alone required extra work (and extra standards) for embedding binary objects, but what has proven worse is that SOAP competed directly with the HTTP since it used HTTP as transport. Although, strictly speaking, running on top of the HTTP was not a requirement, the default SOAP/HTTP binding took off, in part because that ensured firewall traversal. (The reader may remember the April 1 RFC mentioned earlier—here is an example of the stuff of a rather cynical joke suddenly materializing as reality.) The result was not only a political confrontation (no one wants his or her application protocol to be a mere transport for someone else's application protocol!) but also a dilemma: either accept the strict client–server structure of the HTTP, in which *every* communication must be started by a client, and which therefore makes server notifications impossible to implement[14] or invent more and more mechanisms to make up for the limitation. But the most serious argument against the RPC approach in general, and SOAP in particular, was that the remote procedure call—as a concept—could not easily adapt to the structure of the Web, which involves *midboxes*—proxies and caches. As it happened, the industry went on inventing more mechanisms and adding more complexity.

Finally, there was a revolt against SOAP in the industry, with the "native" Web discipline called *REpresentation State Transfer* (*REST*). The REST API won, at least for Web access.[15] We will discuss the REST principles in the Appendix. For now, we only mention that turning toward the REST style has become necessary because of the "API" in "REST API"—it is something of a misnomer in that it does not involve procedure calls per se. Instead, the programmer writes the application-layer PDUs, the protocol being—for all practical purposes—HTTP. There is no REST standard; REST is merely a style, as we will see later.

Talking about standards, CORBA has been around, and so have SOAP and a few others which may have made fewer headlines. One should never forget Andrew Tanenbaum's aphorism: "The nice thing about standards is that you have so many to choose from!"

---

[10] Here is a personal story from an author who has been using a popular music-writing program since 2003. The tool that combines score editing with immediate playback has been invaluable, but from the moment its new version was developed with XML to encode the sounds, the tool became very slow—to the point of being unresponsive—and caused constant crashes. Ultimately, the author had to acquire a much larger and more expensive computer just to be able to use the same features that had worked perfectly in previous versions...

[11] www.w3.org/TR/soap/

[12] www.w3.org/TR/2007/REC-soap12-part0-20070427/

[13] www.omg.org/spec/

[14] Imagine using a polling mechanism instead of interrupts.

[15] An opinion, posted in 2010 in a blog—http://royal.pingdom.com/2010/10/15/rest-in-peace-soap/ (retrieved on May 3, 2014)—had a catchy heading: "REST in peace, SOAP," but the supporting data are compelling. Four years later, REST was affirmed as the practice of choice.

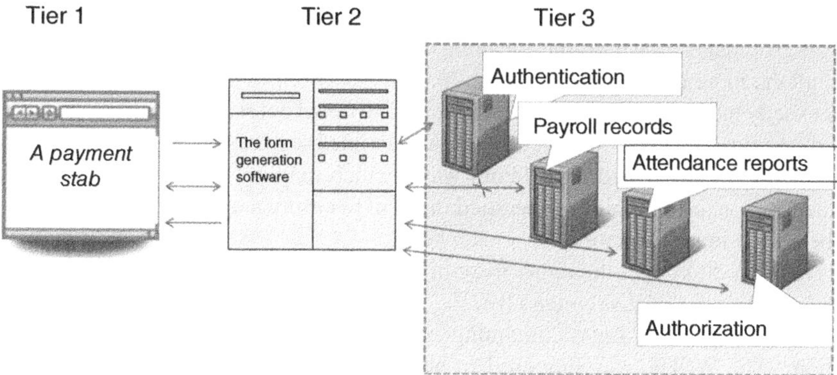

Figure 7.3 An example of the three-tier enterprise model.

In the case of REST vs. RPC though, the division of labor is rather straightforward, owing to the widely implemented three-tier model, which emerged in the enterprise and has become the model of choice for providing software-as-a-service. In this model, Tier 1(a client) issues HTTP-based queries, Tier 2 (a server) provides the *business processes logic* and data access, and Tier 3 (often a set of hosts running database software) provides the actual data. It is the REST paradigm that is used by clients to access the front end (the second tier) of the service delivery infrastructure; the back-end communications may use RPC and other distributed processing mechanisms.

In the example of Figure 7.3, the client requests a pay stub for a particular employee from the Tier-2 server. The server, in turn, generates the form after querying the corporate databases that contain the payroll records and attendance reports. Of course, this act is performed only after authenticating the user who had requested this information and ensuring that the user is authorized to receive it. (Another example is the now ubiquitous Web-based e-mail service. A Web client speaks REST with the Tier-2 server, which uses the actual mail–client protocols to send and receive e-mail messages from an SMTP mail server.)

Competing standards and non-interworking implementations aside, the advantages for modularity brought about by the architecture and mechanisms outlined so far are clear: nothing could be made *more* modular than the infrastructure that provided buckets of ready-to-execute service modules, which, on top of everything, could be invoked from anywhere. But its promise went even further—it was expected to reduce IT costs by making programming so easy as to allow the very people who define the business do it, thus eliminating their dependency on in-house specialized software development.

An industry effort to deliver on the promise came in the form of the SOA, which introduced the term *orchestration*.

7.1.1 The Service-Oriented Architecture

To begin with, we note that there has been much misunderstanding in the industry on what "SOA" means. At the beginning of his authoritative monograph [8], Thomas Erl writes: "I cannot recall any one term causing as much confusion as 'service-oriented.' Its apparent ambiguity has led vendors, IT professionals, and the media to claim their own interpretations. This, of course, makes grasping the meaning of a technical architecture labeled as 'service-oriented' all the more difficult."

This is exactly the problem: *interpretation.* It is a truism, of course, that a vision (in the case of the SOA the vision being remote execution of API-defined services on a distributed computing platform) can be implemented in different ways, which may not necessarily interwork with one another. But once something is specified in detail to ensure a unique interpretation, it risks being labeled "an implementation."

To this end, the SOA specifications were piling up. First, W3C produced the XML-based *Web Services Description Language* (*WSDL*[16]) for "describing network services as a set of endpoints operating on messages containing either document-oriented or procedure-oriented information." The WSDL was supposed to be abstract and extensible so as to bind to any protocol, but the specification centered on one binding—specifically binding with SOAP 1.1 over a subset of HTTP.

The standard for the next necessary SOA component—the registry to enable publication and subsequent discovery—was developed by OASIS in the form of the (also XML-based) *Universal Description, Discovery and Integration* (*UDDI*) standard.[17]

Yet another set of SOA components addressed *quality of service* (a concept which, in this context, has nothing to do with the QoS in data communications), which also included a set of parameters for security (built on the OASIS *Security Assertion Markup Language* (*SAML*) standard), reliability, policy assertion, and *orchestration per se*. The standard for the latter, the *Web Services Business Process Execution Language* (*WSBPEL*),[18] was produced by OASIS based on an earlier specification created by the joint efforts of IBM, Microsoft, and BEA, in turn inspired by the IBM *Web Services Flow Language* (*WSFL*) and Microsoft *XLANG*.

In a nutshell, WSBPEL uses XML-encoded facilities to specify business process requirements in a manner similar to that used in specialized programming languages to specify the execution of concurrent processes. Both provide facilities for describing parallel activities and dealing with exceptions. A number of other WS specifications were laid out to deal with management and coordination as part of the broad quality-of-service discipline.

Unfortunately, the SOA effort was not the success it had promised to be. By the end of 2005, the UDDI standard alone contained over 400 pages—something few developers had time to deal with, especially since the specifications were filled with the arguably unnecessary new terminology, as is the wont of many standards documents. In December 2005, the *SOA World Magazine* (http://soa.sys-con.com) published an article[19] commenting on the decisions made by IBM, Microsoft, and SAP to close their UDDI registries.

On January 9, 2009, Anne Thomas Manes, a Burton Group analyst, wrote in her blog an obituary for the SOA.[20] Citing the impact of the recession (and the resulting refusal of IT organizations to spend more money on the SOA), Ms Manes noted that "SOA fatigue has turned into SOA disillusionment. Business people no longer believe that SOA will deliver spectacular benefits." The blog though was by no means derisive—it characterized the situation as "tragic

[16] www.w3.org/TR/wsdl

[17] https://www.oasis-open.org/committees/uddi-spec/doc/tcspecs.htm

[18] https://www.oasis-open.org/committees/tc_home.php?wg_abbrev=wsbpel

[19] http://soa.sys-con.com/node/164624

[20] http://apsblog.burtongroup.com/2009/01/soa-is-dead-long-live-services.html

for the IT industry" because "service-orientation is a prerequisite for rapid integration of data and business processes" and expressed the need to develop it for the SOA "survivors"—web mash-ups and SaaS. To this end, the blog actually suggested that it is the term "SOA" that is dead, while "the requirement for service-oriented architecture is stronger than ever."

This was the common sentiment in the industry at that time. When one author googled "why SOA failed," over three million results came up. On the business side, the blame was almost uniformly laid on the lack of resolve in the IT industry to change. The business people in turn blamed the proponents of the SOA for failing to communicate the importance of the SOA to the business. "Shortage of talent" was yet another explanation, and there were many more.

In our opinion, the SOA history was similar to that of the OSI in the late 1980s. In fact, the fates of the OSI and the SOA are strikingly familiar in at least three aspects, one of which is that both have produced sound metaphors and foundation architectures, which survived the test of time. The second similarity is that both the OSI and SOA standards were challenged by the Internet community. Just as the SOAP-based SOA was declared dead, the REST paradigm was picking up. The third aspect is a fundamental change in the way things were done: The Internet connected private networks and enabled partial outsourcing of networking; the appearance of the Cloud enabled outsourcing of IT services.

Four years later, in an article[21] in *InfoWorld* magazine, David Linthicum noted that SOA practices are absolutely necessary in the Cloud. Perhaps the problem with SOA in the 2000s was the problem with a specific solution to SOA. Furthermore, the SOA referred to earlier was about the application development *within* the enterprise. In the context of the Cloud, we need a much broader definition. This is why we chose in this book not to describe SOA in any detail. The major surviving SOA concept is that of *workflows*.

7.1.2 Workflows

In describing a task—any task—one lists all the activities that are involved in carrying the task to completion. Some of these activities may run in parallel; others need to wait for the completion of prerequisite activities. A workflow is a specification that defines and orders all the activities within a task. Naturally, to automate a task involving a distributed system, its workflow must be defined in such a way that it is executable in a distributed environment.

In a way, the whole development of computing has been based on workflows. Hardware is built based on the discipline of *logic design*, dealing with building circuits by connecting the building blocks—the *logic gates*—that perform basic operations. Figure 7.4(a) depicts such a circuit.

In the 1980s there was a research movement to build workflow-based computers—then called *data-flow machines*—from elementary blocks. The blocks are chained as specified by a directed graph, and each block is activated when it receives a message (token). A 1986 MIT memorandum [9] describes the model and issues involved in developing such machines. Figure 7.4(b) (after [9]) gives an example of a data-flow machine that calculates a conditional expression.

In a way, the data-flow machines were workflows built in hardware. It might have developed this way, had it not been for the industry's realization that standardized, ubiquitous computing

[21] www.infoworld.com/d/Cloud-computing/soa-dead-not-if-youre-using-paas-app-dev-220491?source=footer

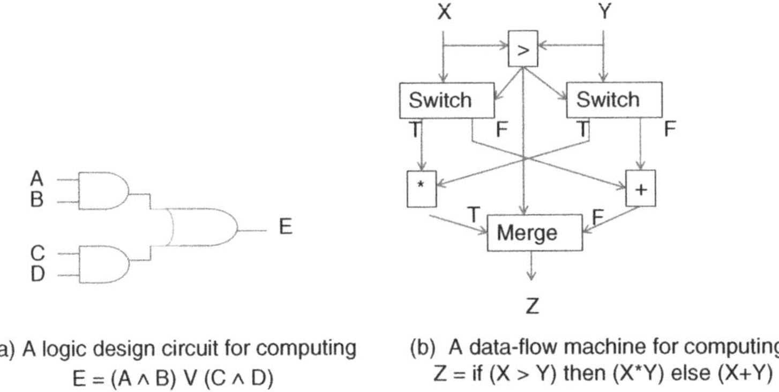

Figure 7.4 Flow-based computing examples.

platforms provided the means for a much more economical (and arguably more flexible) software implementation approach. The trick was to develop software building blocks that could be mixed and matched just as the pieces of silicone could.

Before the introduction of structured computer languages, the algorithms were specified using flowcharts. The flowcharts were suitable for a single-process specification, but proved to be quite unwieldy for describing parallel activities in distributed processing. This is where software-based implementation of data-flow machines—which is, again, what workflows are really all about—helped.

One example, which came from the authors' personal experience, was *service creation* in telephony. The *intelligent network* technology, already referred to in this book, was developed in the late 1980s through the 1990s. Its major objective was to enable rapid development of telephony services. "Rapid" meant that the service developers—while being blissfully unaware of the network structure and the distributed nature of the processing—could put services together with the help of a graphical interface by simply chaining icons. Each icon represented a *service-independent building block* (such as *queue_call* or *translate_number*). Thus, a complex 800-number service, which involved time- and location-based translation, playing announcements and gathering input, and so on, could be programmed in minutes. Of course, the execution of each service-independent building block was in itself a complex distributed activity. Yet, since it was contained in a ready module, the service programmer was not concerned with that complexity. In modern terms, each service was programmed as a *workflow*. An attempt was even made to coordinate the call establishment with billing and charging processes. (As no standard was developed, several service-creation environments existed, but it was not trivial to merge them. In the mid-1990s the authors researched the means of unifying several such environments in AT&T, reporting on the results in [10].)

Figure 7.5 elucidates the general concept of workflow specification and execution. On the left-hand side, a workflow program is represented as a directed graph of activities. (This *almost* looks like a flowchart, although, as we will see, there is a significant difference.) Specifically, *Activity 1* is the first such activity, which starts the workflow. Each activity—with the exception of the last, *terminal*, activity—has an output directed toward the next activity, said to *consume* the output, in the chain. In principle, activities can loop back, although the figure does not display such an example.

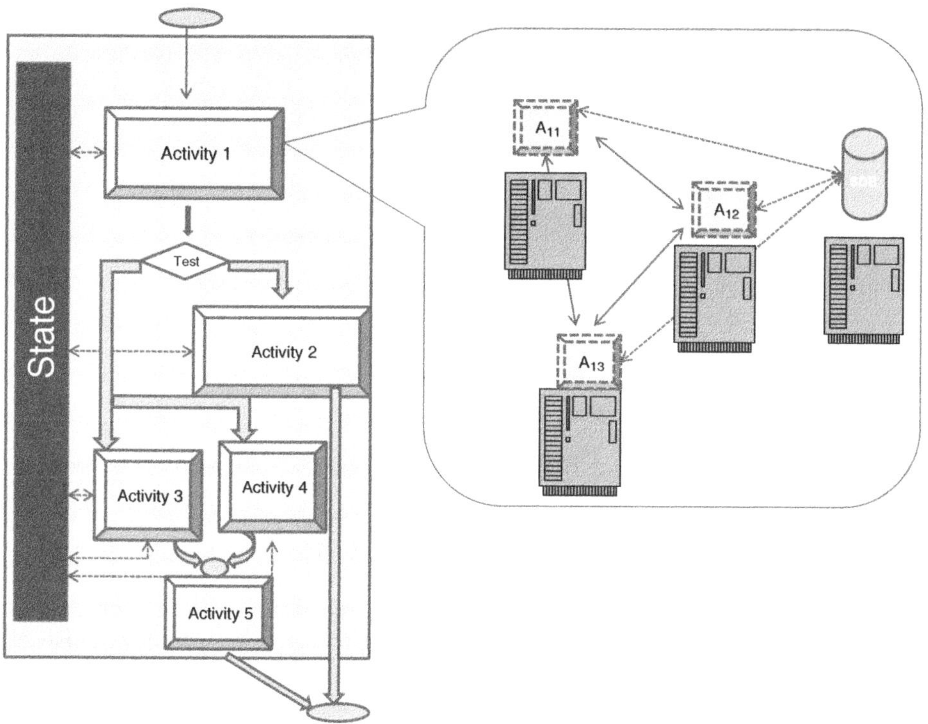

Figure 7.5 Workflow as a directed graph of activities.

Once an activity completes, the next activity can be selected via a conditional *test*. In our example, the test block determines whether *Activity 2* is to start after *Activity 1* and consume its output. If not, two activities—*Activity 3* and *Activity 4*—are to execute concurrently. The example demonstrates that it is possible to synchronize the execution of both activities, by making the *checkpoint* (*CP*) wait for the completion of both activities before filtering their respective outputs to *Activity 5*. Supporting concurrency makes a workflow specification different from that of a flowchart. Another difference is that a workflow specification maintains its explicit *state* (depicted in a block on the left), which is read and updated by all activities.

So far we have discussed only a *specification* of a workflow. The execution is a different matter altogether, and it is explained by the right-hand side of Figure 7.5, which expands *Activity 1*. As we can see, here it is executed by three processes—A_{11}, A_{12}, and A_{13}—which run on three different machines. The *state database* is maintained (in this example) on yet another machine. Of course, it is non-essential that A_{11}, A_{12}, and A_{13} run on separate hosts—they could be distributed between two hosts or even run on the same host; nor is it essential that they are processes rather than threads within a single process. The ingenious part of the arrangement is that the choice of the execution host and the form of the execution is absolutely flexible—it is left to the run-time environment. Similarly, the location of the state database (which, in fact, may also be distributed) is irrelevant as long as it meets the performance requirements. To increase reliability, and also to improve performance, the state database may be replicated. Soon, we will see this principle applied to the design of OpenStack.

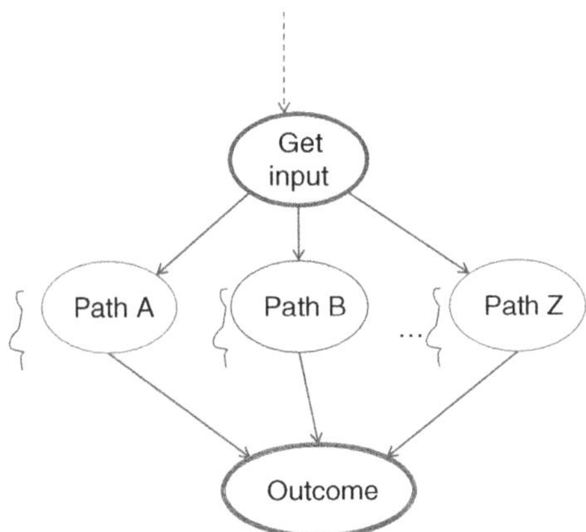

Figure 7.6 Path analysis.

One other aspect of improving performance is workflow optimization. If a workflow specification language is formally defined (so that it can be parsed), it is possible to apply the compiler theory to eliminate redundancies and—most important—optimize scheduling of parallel activities. But it is also possible to analyze the performance of a workflow statistically, as it repeats, to discover performance problems. This approach, illustrated in Figure 7.6, is called *path analysis*, and it is particularly useful in the workflows that implement diagnostic tools.

Starting from some place within a workflow where an input has been gathered there may be several ways—represented by paths through the workflow graph—to achieve an outcome. An inference that among the paths $A, B, \ldots, Z$ the path B is a shortcut in terms of the execution time may very well suggest to the workflow designer that other paths be eliminated to streamline the workflow.

There is a significant volume of literature and a number of products related to workflows. We refer only to a few examples.

An earlier grid-related research project, *GridAnt*, is described in [11] along with a survey of the then-existing commercial products. A research paper [12] provides an overview of several workflow optimization algorithms and proposes an extended one (the Boolean verification algorithm) that deals with the workflows that contain conditional branches and cycles.

As far as products are concerned, the Microsoft Windows Workflow Foundation is described on a dedicated site.[22] This site also contains an excellent tutorial.

Amazon provides the *Amazon Simple Workflow Service* (*AWS*) API along with the *AWS Flow Framework* to invoke these APIs[23] from user programs. A developer needs to specify coordination logic (sequencing, timing, and failure response) as well as the code for each step of the workflow. To this end, a library of commonly used programming patterns in support of coordination logic is also available.[24]

---

22 http://msdn.microsoft.com/en-us/library/dd851337.aspx

23 http://aws.amazon.com/swf

24 http://aws.amazon.com/code/2535278400103493

So far we have discussed the generic use of workflows in applications. Later in this chapter we will return to this subject, but we will narrow the focus of the discussion to the application of workflows to the specific task of Cloud orchestration. Yet, before doing so, we need to review the concepts and techniques of network and operations management.

7.2 Network and Operations Management

As we noted earlier, the discipline of network management predates that of data communications. It started with telephone networks, and it has been driven solely by automation. As the telecommunication network equipment evolved from human-operated switching boards to computer-controlled switches that processed call requests automatically, the need to control individual calls morphed into the need to control the equipment that controlled the calls. Furthermore, with the introduction of time-division multiplexing, the operation of the transmission equipment itself has become complex enough to warrant real-time monitoring and administration activities.

In the Bell Telephone System [13],[25] as in all other major telephone companies, these activities—commonly called *network-related operations*—were part of the overall company operations, which included provision of services to the customer, service administration, and maintenance operation. Incidentally, we are not mentioning these for purely historical (or even historic) reasons—these activities remain at the heart of the Cloud today! Interestingly enough, a good deal of software technology concepts, as we see them today, were developed to streamline network operations.

The administrative processes were initially performed manually, but during the magic 1970s they had been increasingly moving to computerized processing. Separate systems were developed—one for each piece of equipment to be administered. Initially, Bell System was purchasing various mainframes to host the operations support software, but when the DEC PDP-11 line became available (as did the Unix operating system, which was first developed for PDP-11), its minicomputers were used for the development of the *Operations Support Systems* (*OSS*s).[26] Ultimately, because the Unix operating system could run on any computer, the particular choice of hardware became less and less relevant. In the late 1980s, the largest part of the software research and development in Bell Laboratories[27] was dedicated entirely to the design of OSSs.

OSSs required more or less the same capabilities that any business administration would, but on a much larger scale because the telecom domain contained thousands of pieces of autonomous computer-based equipment (not to mention hundreds of millions of individual telephone lines!), further governed by various business processes and US government regulations.

---

[25] As the authors remember, in the 1980s, every Bell Laboratories employee was handed this impressive 900-pager on the first day of his or her job. It is interesting that after more than 30 years, the book is still technically relevant and useful to other than historians. It can still be acquired in book stores and on the Web.

[26] AT&T's own *3B* line of computers were mostly used in telephone switches, although its smallest offspring—the Unix *PC*—was a general personal computer.

[27] Area 59.

In the 1980s, the objective of the OSS development was to have a universal OSS which would govern all activities, but this was a tall order.[28]

To begin with, the business activities were disconnected across the company. When a telephone service was requested, it had to be processed by the business office. Sure enough, a customer record was created in one or another database—most likely in several—but it could not reach the local switch's database automatically. According to a Bell Labs anecdote of the time, an operator of the switching exchange management system, which was accessed through a dedicated terminal, needed to turn in a swivel chair to use another terminal to log into the order system to read the customer order record and then turn back to retype the information into the switching system. Apparently, this is when the term "swivel chair integration" was coined.

To be precise, the independent operations support systems were—and largely still remain in the telecom world—as follows:

- Trunks integrated record-keeping system.
- Plug-in inventory control system.
- Premises information system.[29]
- Total network data system.
- Switching control data system.
- Central office equipment engineering system.
- A number of facility network planning systems.

In addition, in the 1970s AT&T developed a central network management system, which was showcased at the Network Operations Center, Bedminster, NJ.[30] There, the updates from all over the network were displayed on a wall-sized map of the United States, indicating the state of the network. The network managers, working at individual terminals, were able to take corrective action when necessary. This was the first decisive step toward *network* (vs. *element*) management. In the second half of the 1980s, central network traffic management systems were developed by AT&T's Network Systems division for sale to regional operating companies and abroad.[31]

Back to the unified OSS vision. Again, the major obstacle in its way was that in Bell System alone multiple systems had evolved separately, without any common platform.[32] Rewriting all this software was out of the question, but even if a decision were made to rewrite it, there was still no standard which different vendors could implement. As the vision was built around the ISDN technology, in which telephony services were combined with data communications services, the first step was (naturally) to integrate the management of the data communications

[28] It still is today, but it should now be clear what orchestration aims at and how it can solve the problem.

[29] Related to enterprise clients.

[30] The history of AT&T network management, along with a photo of the Bedminster network operations center, can be found at www.corp.att.com/history/nethistory/management.html.

[31] A 1991 publication [14] describes the deployment of the *Netminder*™ traffic management system in France Telecom's new network operations center.

[32] In some OSSs, whose earlier versions relied on the swivel-chair, human-entered input, but which were then upgraded to receive this input directly from switches, the form of the input was kept the same and so—just to keep the interface the same to prevent any changes to the OSSs' code—the switches were programmed to pretend they were humans responding in ASCII text to the OSS prompts!

network. The latter had morphed into a discipline of its own, starting with the ISO OSI network management project with its five-item framework. This framework is still all-encompassing; we describe it in the next section.

7.2.1 The OSI Network Management Framework and Model

The first aspect of the framework is *configuration management*, and it is concerned with the multitude of parameters whose values need to be maintained within specified ranges on all the devices in the network. The values of some parameters may be changed directly by the network owner; others can be read-only.[33]

The second aspect of the framework deals with *fault management*. The word "fault" broadly refers to any abnormal condition in the network. One big design task here, of course, is to define clearly all events that correspond to changes from "abnormal" to normal. Another design task is to select those events that are worthy of being detected on the one hand, and on the other hand to ensure that the reporting of these events does not overwhelm the system's processing power. A typical event constitutes a change of a parameter value beyond a certain threshold. The change is (often) logged and reported in real time through an *alarm* mechanism. (Recalling an earlier discussion of the computer architecture and operating system, this situation is very similar to a CPU interrupt flag being raised by a device, and, indeed, just as an operating system needs to supply an interrupt handling routine, so does the network management system needs to supply a proper operating procedure.) Note that in order to detect a change (as well as to react to it), the configuration management mechanisms need to be invoked.

The third aspect of the framework is *performance management*. This, again, relies on the configuration management mechanism to measure the utilization of the network resources in real time. A longer-term part of this activity is *capacity planning*. It is pretty obvious that when a given resource becomes overwhelmed so as to affect the overall network performance, it may be high time to replace it with a larger one (but determining which resources contribute to a bottleneck is a complex problem). As replacing or beefing up the equipment is often expensive, effective capacity planning can save much money.

The fourth aspect is *identity and access management*, addressed in the last section of this chapter. In a nutshell, the task of access management is to ensure that every single attempt to learn any information about the network—or to change anything in it—is captured and allowed to proceed only after it is determined that the attempting entity is properly authorized to do so. Typically, the attempts to access critical data are logged and otherwise processed through the fault management mechanisms.

The fifth and final aspect is *accounting management*. This involves the whole range of activities that deal with charging for the use of resources. In an enterprise network comprising several organizations, this may mean determining a proportion of the overall communications bill that each organization should pay. In an operator's network, this is the activity that determines the revenue.

---

[33] Consider the case of a company that owns several LANs and leases the lines from a telecom operator to interconnect these LANs. The company's network management system can change the values of the parameters that control the enterprise's own devices, but it can only *read* the values of parameters that control the operator's devices.

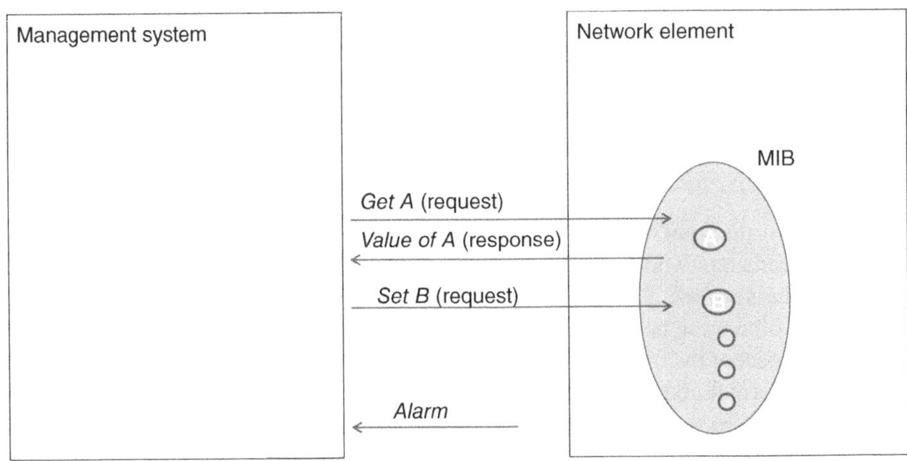

Figure 7.7 The basic network management model.

While the framework has been clear—and it remains unchanged for the Cloud—the development of network management standards has proven to be rather erratic, with competing parallel activities carried by several organizations and still inconclusive results.

Historically, the above five aspects, spelled out in a different order—*Fault*, *Configuration*, *Accounting*, *Performance*, and *Security*—and thus known by the acronym *FCAPS*, formed the basis for the ISO work, later carried out jointly with ITU-T. In parallel, and according to the same model, the IETF was developing its own protocol series. We will briefly address both, but we start with the common basic model, as depicted in Figure 7.7.

Each managed device is associated with the *Management Information Base* (*MIB*), which actually defines the configuration parameters. The management system may request (*Get*) the value of a parameter as well as change (*Set*) this value. Which values may be changed externally (and, if so, by whom) is part of a MIB specification. (There are also other capabilities with respect to the parameters—such as learning which parameters are defined within the MIB—and many nuances to defining the managed objects.) An *alarm* or *trap* message is a notification from the device, which can only be processed as an interrupt at the machine hosting the management system.

ITU has developed, jointly with ISO/IEC JTC 1, the *Common Management Information Protocol* (*CMIP*), defined in [15] and other ITU-T recommendations in the X.700 series. As CMIP was using the OSI application-layer services (such as the OSI *Remote Operations Service Element*) that were unavailable in the Internet, the IETF had decided to proceed with its own protocol, and here the development of the network management standards forked.

Based on CMIP and other modules, ITU-T has come up with a large set of specifications (the M.3000 series) called the *Telecommunications Management Network* (*TMN*), while the IETF has produced the so-called *Simple Network Management Protocol* (*SNMP*), now in its third version *SNMPv3*. The enterprise IT industry has deployed SNMP exclusively, while TMN is deployed in the telephone networks—notably in *WorldCom*, as reported in [16]. This divergence is rather unfortunate, as it has contributed to enlarging the difference between telephony and IT—the very difference that the network management standardization effort was supposed to eliminate!

The SNMP STD 62 standard was completed in 2002, reflecting more than 10 years of SNMP development. By 2003, when the IETF Internet Architecture Board had a workshop,[34] SNMP was widely deployed, with some MIBs implemented on most IP devices. Hence the industry had obtained enough operational experience to understand the technology limitations. The major one was that SNMP dealt primarily with the device monitoring aspect of network management (as opposed to the configuration aspect).

We should stress that device monitoring was—and remains—an important function because it has provided, among other things, notifications ("traps") of the state of physical equipment (such as a server board or a simple fan). Knowing that hardware works properly and detecting a malfunction as early as possible is the foundation of the operations discipline. In modern data centers, such SNMP traps are fed into specialized monitoring systems (such as *Nagios*)[35] used as part of the modern solutions based on the development operations (*devops*) methodology.

Although the use of SNMP for configuring devices was not unheard of (after all, the protocol explicitly supports changing device parameters via a SET method!), many standard MIB modules lacked writable objects. With SNMP, it is not easy to identify configuration objects, and, as RFC 3535 documented, the naming system itself seemed to be in the way of playing back a previous configuration of a reconfigured system. But even if all MIBs were perfect, SNMP is, too low level for network operators—who lamented that not much had been done in the way of developing a bird's-eye view of application building blocks.

Nor might the development of such building blocks help, as the SNMP software started to reach its performance limits. Retrieving routing tables, for example, proved to be very slow. Another set of problems was caused by the objective of keeping things simple (as the "S" in SNMP might indicate). Sure enough, the protocol was simple enough—compared with CMIP—but this has merely left the complexity to the developers to deal with. Now it was the network management application that was supposed to checkpoint the state of SNMP transactions,[36] and be prepared to roll a device back into a consistent state. Designing such an application required significant experience with distributed processing, and even for the experts it was by no means a simple task. This was at cross purposes with the plan to make network management applications "easy" to develop (i.e., cobbled by non-programmers from some elementary building blocks). More generally, as RFC 3535 states, there was "often a semantic mismatch between the task-oriented view of the world usually preferred by operators and the data-centric view of the world provided by SNMP. Mapping from a task-oriented view to the data-centric view often requires some non-trivial code."

And then the "simplicity" resulted in under-specification, which hindered interoperability:

> "Several standardized MIB modules lack a description of high-level procedures. It is often not obvious from reading the MIB modules how certain high-level tasks are accomplished, which leads to several different ways to achieve the same goal, which increases costs and hinders interoperability."

[34] The results of the workshop have been documented in RFC 3535: www.ietf.org/rfc/rfc3535.txt.

[35] Nagios (www.nagios.org/) is an open-source software project.

[36] The choice of UDP as transport protocol made this aspect even worse in this context, as G. Houston noted in his 2002 article at www.potaroo.net/ispcol/2002-05/2002-05-snmpng.html.

Part of the problem with the ineffectiveness of SMNP with respect to configuration management is the very model in which the network manager (presumed to be "intelligent") deals with a "dumb device." Initially, the devices (a modem is a good example of one) were indeed not programmable, but by the late 1990s the situation had changed drastically. To appreciate the difference, consider what happened to the concept of a home network, which evolved from a bulky modem, connecting a computer to a telephone line, to an Ethernet LAN hub (although relatively few people had this in their homes), and then to the present WiFi base-station router with built-in firewalls and a NAT box. Beside the obvious differences, here is a fairly subtle one: the complexity introduced with all this equipment required that configuration changes be made according to a specific *policy*.

For more detail on SNMP, we refer the reader to the next chapter.

7.2.2 Policy-Based Management

The IETF started to address the problem gradually, strictly on a specific need basis. The first such need was the policy configuration in support of QoS. Here, the device (typically, a router) is by no means dumb: its configuration needs to change continuously—in response to users' requirements– and so the management system needs to propagate the change into a device from a local copy. Here, the model introduced a new challenge—the need to maintain a synchronized state between the network manager and the device. Another challenge came from the potential interference among two or more network managers administering the same device.[37] That case introduced the potential to corrupt the device with contradictory changes.

And then there is a need for policy-based management. While a device may have to change in response to users' requests, it is hardly acceptable to allocate network resources based *only* on user requests—that is, always give whatever one asks. Network providers wanted to have a mechanism that would enable granting a resource based on a set of policy rules. The decision on whether to grant the resource takes into account information about the user, the requested service, and the network itself.

Employing SNMP for this purpose was not straightforward, and so the IETF developed a new protocol, for communications between the network element and the *Policy Decision Point (PDP)*—where the policy-based decisions were made. The protocol is called *Common Open Policy Service* (*COPS*); we review it in the Appendix.

As an important aside, COPS has greatly influenced the *Next-Generation telecommunications Network* (*NGN*) standards, which have been developed since 2004 in both ETSI and ITU-T. NGN is characterized, among other things, by (1) the prevalent use of IP for end-to-end packet transfer and (2) the drive to convergence between wireline and wireless technologies.[38]

In contrast to specialized networks optimized for specific applications, NGN has been envisioned as a general multi-service network that would meet a wide range of application

---

[37] These two challenges were elucidated in G. Houston's article, mentioned in the previous footnote.

[38] Even though only a relatively small part of a communication path in wireless networks—namely the path between a handset and a wireless base station—is actually wireless, with the rest of the path very much "wired," the telecommunications operators historically kept both the networks and the services offered separate. 2005 seems to be the critical year for driving convergence. See [17] for a comprehensive monograph on the subject.

performance needs and security requirements. To this end, service control was to be separate from transport as well as from the mechanisms required to allocate and provide—often in real or near-real time—network resources to applications.

One specific set of such applications emerged to support the so-called *triple-play services*, which encompass *Voice-over-IP* (*VoIP*), *IP television* (*IPTV*), and Internet access. These applications required—and still require—special QoS treatment.

As we saw in Chapter 4, the performance needs of applications are characterized by four key parameters: bandwidth, packet loss, delay, and jitter (i.e., variation in delay), which determine the quality of service. Overall, the needs of the triple-play services are different with respect to QoS. For example, some popular data applications (such as e-mail and web access) require low to medium bandwidth and are quite relaxed as far as delay and jitter are concerned. In contrast, VoD flows have relaxed requirements on delay, but they do need high bandwidth and cannot tolerate much packet loss or jitter. VoIP, while tolerating some packet loss, needs much lower bandwidth than VoD, but it can tolerate neither long delay nor jitter.

In addition to the QoS-related resources, networks often need to grant other resources (e.g., IP addresses or service-related port numbers) to the endpoints and the processes that execute on them. As we may recall from Chapter 5, this specific need arose from NAT LSNAT deployment, which has been employed to hide the internal network topology. These diversified and already complex tasks were further complicated by the very structure of the NGN, which combines several network types, including *Asynchronous Transfer Mode* (*ATM*), *Digital Subscriber Line* (*DSL*), Ethernet, and fixed and mobile wireless access networks.

The key to fulfilling this complex duty was a dynamic, policy-based resource management framework, known as the *Resource and Admission Control Functions* (*RACF*), described in [18] (the ITU-T standard published in [19]). An important point to emphasize is that RACF was put in place to interwork the real-time processing with OSSs; RACF have both functions, and their protocols combine both sets of building blocks.

Even though RACF was influenced directly by COPS, its framework also relied on a number of IETF protocols other than COPS.[39] Starting from their inception, the *Third-Generation Partnerships*—3GPP and 3GPP2—have been following and influencing the development of the IETF building blocks in support of the *IP Multimedia Subsystem* (*IMS*).[40]

[39] These protocols include the *Remote Authentication Dial-in User Service* (*RADIUS*), its follow-up, *Diameter*, and *Media Gateway Control* (*MEGACO*). RADIUS was an early authentication and authorization protocol used in remote dial-in applications, but is easily extendible to other access mechanisms. Diameter started as an improvement on RADIUS, but has evolved into a generic peer-to-peer protocol that can be used by a wide range of applications that require authentication, authorization, and accounting functions, which should explain why it had become an essential candidate for resource control. The MEGACO protocol has been developed by the IETF MEGACO group, jointly with the ITU-T Study Group 16, and it is also known by its ITU-T project name H.248. MEGACO/H.248 was initially developed to manage the media gateway between the circuit and packet networks, and later extended to support generic packet-to-packet border gateways. It is noteworthy that, unlike *Diameter* or *RADIUS*, MEGACO/H.248 is not a peer-to-peer protocol; it is a client–server or (to use its own terminology) a master–slave protocol. In some circumstances, this feature limits its usefulness at the PDP-to-PEP interface.

[40] IMS was developed by 3GPP, starting from 1998, in a decisive step toward IP–wireless convergence. The IMS architecture and standards are described in [20]. In the first decade of the 21st century, 3GPP has adopted these building blocks for *Service-Based Local Policy* (*SBLP*), which is evolving into the *Policy and Charging Control* (*PCC*) mechanism. The 3GPP2 model is called service-based bearer control. Although they differ in the protocols specified for the respective interfaces, they are very similar to the point of being identical at the conceptual level.

While the Third-Generation Partnerships were focusing on the needs of wireless carriers, the ETSI *Telecommunication and Internet Converged Services and Protocols for Advanced Networks* (*TISPAN*) group embarked in 2003 on a project that dealt with fixed access. Its approach to resource management was reflected in its *Resource and Admission Control Subsystem* (*RACS*), published in [21].

We should emphasize again that the need to control *Network Address and Port Translation* (*NAPT*) and NAT traversal was an important driver for the ETSI work. When service providers started deploying VoIP, they discovered the complications—which we now know very well—caused by the end users being located behind NAT devices (as is the case for most broadband access users). This problem could be circumvented with session border controllers supporting hosted NAT traversal. Standalone session border controllers, however, do not fit well in the overall IMS approach. In contrast, the RACS model supports NAPT and hosted NAT traversal as part of policy enforcement under the control of a policy decision function that interfaces with IMS session control.

In 2004, ITU-T embarked on the RACF effort with the objective of preserving the separation of services and transport while enabling dynamic, application-driven, policy-based end-to-end QoS and resource control capabilities (in particular, resource reservation, admission and gate control, NAPT, and hosted NAT traversal within the network domain and at network boundaries. From its onset, the scope of the RACF included various types of access and core networks. To this end, RACF was the first attempt to create a flexible end-to-end resource management solution by blending (rather than replacing) the existing standardization results within a common framework.

As we can see, COPS has solved the problem of policy-based management, but it has not solved the problem of managing configurations effectively. Going back to RFC 3535 (which, as the reader may remember, reports on the 2002 IAB workshop), the prevailing complaint from the operators was the lack of a consistent, all-encompassing configuration discipline. Neither COPS nor the ever-growing IETF set of MIBs was helpful here.

Hence, one objective of the workshop was to determine how to refocus the IETF resources.[41] The workshop made eight recommendations—both positive (which activities to focus on) and negative (which activities to stop). Of these, the only positive recommendation that enjoyed "strong consensus from both protocol developers and operators" was that "the IETF focus resources on the standardization of configuration management mechanisms." Two other recommendations, apparently supported more by the operators than the protocol developers, were that the resources be spent "on the development and standardization of XML-based device configuration and management technologies" and *not* be spent on the HTML-over-HTTP-based configuration management.[42]

To the IETF's credit, it turned out to be quite nimble, responding decisively. In 2003, the NETCONF WG was created, and three years later it had published the first version of the NETCONF protocol. That was augmented in the next two years to incorporate notifications

[41] RFC 3535 has put this in rather blunt terms: "During these meetings, several operators have expressed their opinion that the developments in the IETF do not really address their requirements, especially for configuration management. This naturally leads to the question of whether the IETF should refocus resources, and which strategic future activities in the operations and management area should be started."

[42] As it happened—and we will return to the subject later—the NETCONF battle was the one lost by the REST camp. The RPC camp won then, but it started to lose systematically around 2009, by which time the REST camp regrouped.

and several classical distributed processing and security mechanisms, and the protocol kept evolving for the next eight years. The present version of the base NETCONF protocol was published as RFC 6241[43] in June 2011. (Its extensions have been published in separate RFCs.) We review NETCONF in detail in the next chapter.

Meanwhile, the industry has created several configuration management tools, which have been used extensively in today's Cloud. In the rest of this section we review two well-known examples: *Chef* by Chef[44] (formerly Opscode) and *Puppet* by Puppet Labs.[45]

With Chef, an administrator describes the structure of the distributed system (which might include web servers, load balancers, and back-end databases) using what is called *recipes*. These recipes describe how the entities within the structure are deployed, configured, and managed; they are stored at the *Chef server*. The *Chef clients* are installed on the respective nodes (which could be virtual machines). The job of the Chef clients is to keep the software on its respective node up to date, which it achieves by checking the compliance with the latest recipe installed at the Chef server and automatically updating the software as necessary. At the moment of this writing, the company provides free experimentation as a learning tool (and even limited free software distribution) at its website, which we highly recommend to the interested reader.

Puppet automates the same configuration tasks similarly, as it is also based on the client–server model. The main difference from Chef is in the specification method. The Puppet specification (which uses its own DSL) is declarative—it specifies the dependencies and the client ensures that these are followed. The Chef specification, in contrast, is procedural—written in the Ruby language. Just as Chef, Puppet is available as open source. There is an incisive article [22] comparing the two.

7.3 Orchestration and Management in the Cloud

We are ready to start putting together the pieces of the puzzle developed in this chapter and elsewhere in the book. The elements of the management of the physical elements of the data centers and the network interconnection have already been introduced. The piece that we have not touched on is the management of the *life cycle* of a Cloud service.

In addition to many technical aspects (such as creation and bootstrapping of images), here the business aspects enter the picture. An excellent introduction to the subject matter has been produced by the *Distributed Management Task Force (DMTF)*[46] organization, and so we will use the definitions and concepts described in the DMTF white paper, *Architecture for Managing Clouds*.[47] We address the life cycle of a service in the next section. The sections that follow review the orchestration and management in OpenStack.

We need to emphasize here that orchestration can be implemented at various levels. As we started this section with a musical simile, we will complete it with the same. Ultimately, in an orchestra each musical instrument needs to have its own part. These parts may be shared among

---

43 www.ietf.org/rfc/rfc6241.txt

44 www.getchef.com

45 http://puppetlabs.com/

46 www.dmtf.org. DMTF was founded in 1992 with the purpose of "bringing the IT industry together to collaborate on systems management standards development, validation, promotion and adoption."

47 http://dmtf.org/sites/default/files/standards/documents/DSP-IS0102_1.0.0.pdf

the "clusters" of musicians (e.g., first or second violin sections), but ultimately the individual parts are combined into sections, and then into a single score—the overall composition that the conductor deals with.

In the extreme—and somewhat degenerate—case, each VM in the Cloud can be configured, monitored, relocated, and so on, manually by its own administrator. This task can be automated using tools (such as Chef or Puppet).[48] This is where the VM (an "instrument") is accompanied by its own score. At the next level, the whole infrastructure (the VMs along with the network components to interconnect them) can be orchestrated according to a uniform "score"—and this is what the OpenStack example will demonstrate. But things can go even further! At the top layer, a "score" can be written that combines business policies with the infrastructure specification. This can be achieved with the *Topology and Orchestration Specification for Cloud Applications* (*TOSCA*), an OASIS standard, which we will review in the Appendix.

7.3.1 The Life Cycle of a Service

The three entities involved here are the Cloud service provider, the Cloud service developer, and the Cloud service consumer.

Suppose the Cloud service developer needs to create a (typical) web services infrastructure—say three identical servers and a load balancer along with a back-end database. Writing a program that issues individual requests to the Cloud service provider for creating all the instances—and networks—is problematic in more than one way.

First, suppose the instances for a load balancer and two servers have been created successfully, but creating the virtual machine for the third server has failed. What should the user program do? Deleting all other instances and restarting again is hardly an efficient course of action for the following reasons. From the service developer's point of view, this would greatly complicate the program (which is supposed to be fairly simple). From the service provider's point of view, this would result in wasting the resources which were first allocated and then released but never used.

Second, assuming that all instances have been created, a service provider needs to support elasticity. The question is: How can this be (a) specified and (b) effected? Suppose each of the three servers has reached its threshold CPU utilization. Then a straightforward solution is to create yet another instance (which can be deleted once the burst of activity is over), but how can all this be done automatically? To this end, perhaps, maybe not three but only two instances should have been created in the first place.

The solution adopted by the industry is to define a service in more general terms (we will clarify this with examples), so that the creation of a service is an atomic operation performed by the service provider—this is where orchestration first comes into the picture. And once the service is deployed, the orchestrator itself will then add and delete instances (or other resources) as specified in the service definition.

Hence the workflow depicted in Figure 7.8. The service developer defines the service in a *template*, which also specifies the interfaces to a service. The template (sometimes also called a *recipe* in the industry) specifies various resources: VM images, connectivity definitions, storage configuration, and so on.

---

[48] This automation can even be extended to clusters of identical VMs.

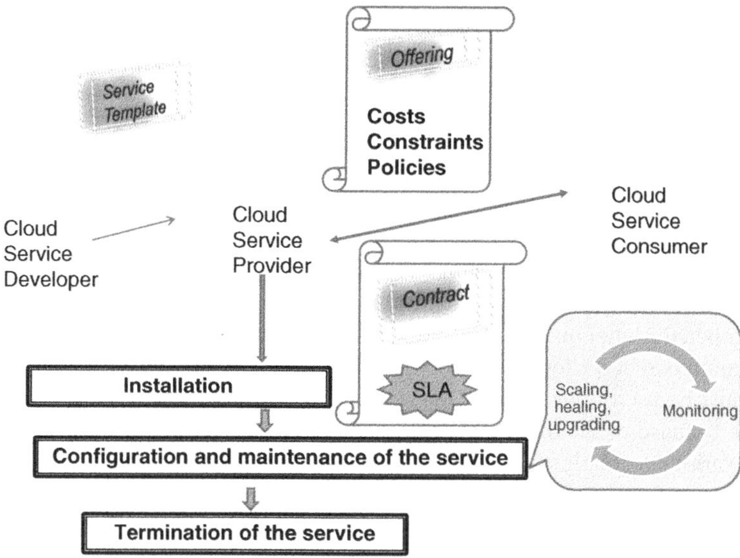

Figure 7.8 The service life cycle.

The service provider creates an *offering* for a service consumer by augmenting this template with the constraints, costs, policies, and SLA. On accepting the offering, the consumer and provider enter into a *contract*, which contains, among other items, the SLA and a set of specific, measurable aspects of the SLA called *Service-Level Objectives* (*SLOs*).[49]

At this point, the provider may modify the template to fit the contract requirements. Based on the template, the provider then deploys (or *provisions*) the service instance. Provisioning involves committing the resources necessary to fulfill the contract.

Once deployed, the service is maintained until the contract is terminated and so the service ends and the resources committed to its support are redeployed. From the orchestration point of view, an essential part of service maintenance is *monitoring*. Here the relevant events are collected and acted on automatically so as to *scale*—up or down—the capacity or *heal* the service in case of a breakdown. Similarly, upgrades are handled automatically in this phase, too. The auto-scaling and auto-healing capabilities are two major functions of orchestration.

As we can see, the model implies that the business objectives and interface definitions be expressed (i.e., encoded) in some form. The formal language constructs for doing so are developed in the *Telemanagement Forum* (*TMF*).[50] The synergies between the DMTF and the TMF have been explored in the joint DMTF/TMF White Paper, *Cloud Management for Communications Service Providers*.[51]

[49] SLOs are used to determine compliance in the audit. The measurements are expected to be logged.

[50] www.tmf.org. The TMF was created in 1988 under the name *OSI/Network Management Forum* to help its members interpret OSI standards so as to develop interoperable network management solutions. In 1998, the organization was renamed the *Telemanagement Forum* and has been growing since then.

[51] www.dmtf.org/sites/default/files/standards/documents/DSP2029%20_1.0.0a.pdf

Let us start with *onboarding*.[52] Here a service developer needs to specify which applications run on which virtual machines, what kinds of events an orchestrator needs to handle (and what exactly to do when such an event occurs), and what information to collect.

An *application recipe* (or *template*) describes the services that the application requires, each service further defined as a group of service instances (running on separate VMs). These are provided as file descriptors. Services are further specified in individual recipes that specify (a) the number of instances, (b) the hardware and software requirements, and (c) the life cycle events along with their "interrupt handlers," which are the pointers to the respective scripts. In support of network and operations management, a recipe can also specify *probes* for monitoring and configuration management. In addition to pre-defined probes available to a service developer, the latter may plug in independent scripts. One aspect of Cloud management and orchestration is that a Cloud provider's resources that are needed to fulfill obligations to customers must be used optimally (as far as the cost is concerned). Optimization here is a complex task because of the many constraints, which include compliance with a customer's policies and various regulations.

The other aspect is providing a customer with the orchestration tools so the customer may control its own infrastructure. Ultimately, what is good for the goose is good for the gander: a provider may share some of its own orchestration tools with customers. Inasmuch as the orchestration involves interworking with business activities, employing workflow-supporting tools is becoming an expected feature. For instance, the VMware® vCenter™ Orchestrator™ provides[53] a pre-built workflow library along with tools to design customized workflows. The new blocks for workflows can be created using a JavaScript-based scripting engine. The policy engine launches the appropriate workflows in response to external events (and according to defined policies).

Another important example—and in a way a benchmark for orchestrators—is the *Amazon AWS CloudFormation* service[54], which provides a mechanism for managing the AWS infrastructure deployments. As we will see, the OpenStack orchestrator, *Heat*, has adopted the terminology as well as the template format of AWS CloudFormation, and in its early orchestration offer did much to interwork with the same tools and interfaces that AWS CloudFormation had given its users.

With the AWS CloudFormation, all resources and dependencies are declared in a template file. Each template defines a collection of resources pertinent to a service, along with the dependencies among them. The collection, which actually represents an infrastructure, is called a *stack*.[55] The idea is that the multitude of resources within a given stack are treated as a single entity, which can be created (or deleted) with a single *create* or *delete* command.

Furthermore, when a template for a stack is updated, the stack gets updated (automatically), too. Furthermore, once a template is specified, the whole stack can be replicated or even moved into a different data center or even a different Cloud.

---

[52] This term—catching on in the industry—is defined in Jelle Frank van der Zwet's White Paper (www.interxion.com/Documents/Whitepapers%20and%20PDFs/Interxion_CloudOnboarding_Whitepaper_EN_online.pdf) thus: "In the context of migration to a Cloud environment, 'onboarding' refers to the deployment of applications, data or both to the chosen Cloud infrastructure (public, private or hybrid)."

[53] www.vmware.com/products/vcenter-orchestrator/features.html

[54] http://docs.aws.amazon.com/AWSCloudFormation/latest/UserGuide/Welcome.html

[55] This term has been adopted widely, notably by the OpenStack organization, where it seems to influence even its name.

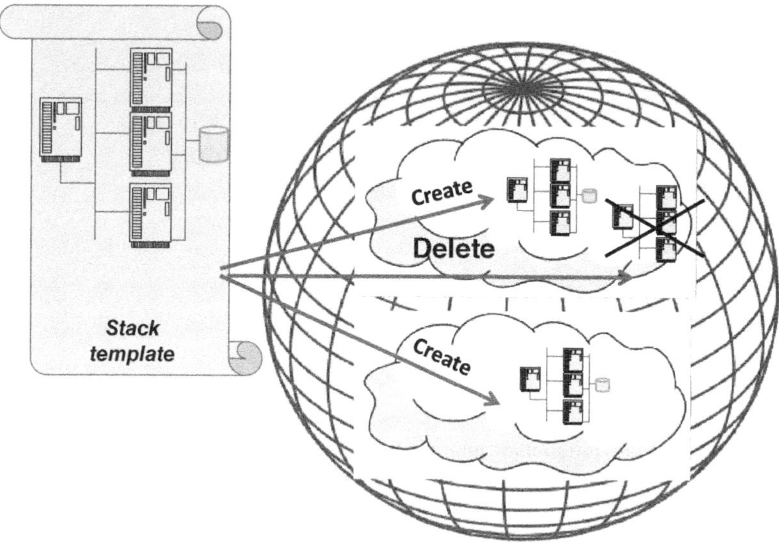

Figure 7.9 Operations on a stack (an example).

Figure 7.9 illustrates this concept. Here, the template defines the infrastructure that we discussed earlier: a load balancer distributing the traffic among three identical servers. To make the service look realistic, we also added the back-end database. Two networks are involved: one to be shared among the load balancer and the servers, and the other among the servers and the database. With a sequence of {*create, delete, create*} operations, the whole infrastructure is first created in one Cloud and later replicated in another. (Of course, this assumes that both Cloud providers support the same template. As we will see in the next section, the OpenStack project has achieved just that by creating a standard along with the software for implementing it!)

In line with the ideas outlined at the beginning of this section, we stress that when a stack is created (or deleted), all resources specified in a template are instantiated (or deleted) simultaneously. During the lifetime of a stack, the declared interdependencies among the resources are maintained automatically.

To begin with, Amazon deployed CloudFormation endpoints—with known URLs—across the world regions. Referring to the local geographic endpoint reduces latency. As we will see, some functional capabilities rely on the choice of endpoints.

The template is written in the *JavaScript Object Notation* (*JSON*) format.[56] In addition to the *version* and *description* fields, it has the following entries: *resources*, *parameters*, *mappings*, *conditions*, and *outputs*. We review them, in that order, with the help of Figure 7.10.

The term *resource* refers to a VM instance or any other AWS pre-defined object (such as a security group, or an auto-scaling group—we will see specific examples soon).[57] Each resource is assigned a resource name, which must be unique within a template. The *resource type* is

[56] The format has been standardized in the IETF—see https://tools.ietf.org/html/rfc7159.

[57] The list of resource type references is provided at http://docs.aws.amazon.com/AWSCloudFormation/latest/UserGuide/aws-template-resource-type-ref.html.

```
{
  "AWSTemplateFormatVersion" : <date>
  "Description" : <string>

  "Resources" :
    { <resource-name/type/properties list>          Mandatory
    },

  "Parameters" :
    { <parameter list>
    },

  "Mappings" :
    { <mapping/key/value list>
    },

  "Conditions":
    { <name/intrinsic function/arguments list>
    },

  "Outputs" :
    {
    }
}
```

Figure 7.10 The AWS CloudFormation template.

another part of the resource specification. In addition, a set of resource properties associated with a resource may be declared, too, each declaration taking the form of a *name/value pair*. A property's value may be known only at run time, and so the template syntax allows the use of an intrinsic function instead of a static value. The *resource* entry is the only mandatory one; the rest are optional.

A *parameter* is just a name string, whose specification may list the conditions that constrain the values that parameters can take.

Mappings automate the parameters' value assignments. One can define a subset of parameter's values and associate it with a key. A typical example of a key is the name of a region; all region-specific values (e.g., current time or local regulations) are assigned to the respective parameters automatically.

Conditions are but a programmatic tool. These are Boolean functions that compare parameter values, either with one another or with constants. If the result of a comparison is positive, resources are created. All conditions are evaluated when a stack is (a) created or (b) updated (and only then).

Outputs are parameters declared specifically in support of the feedback mechanism. The end user can query the value of any *output* via a *describe-stack* command. Again, conditions can be employed to guide the value assignment.

Going back to our earlier example of a web service, we can see how a template may be constructed in support of auto-scaling— an orchestrator-provided service that enables elasticity. In AWS in particular, auto-scaling enables launching or terminating an instance according to user-defined policies as well as run-time characteristics (such as an application's "health" gauged through monitoring). Scaling can be achieved *vertically*, by changing the compute capacity of an instance, or *horizontally*, by changing the number of load-balanced instances. It is particularly the horizontal scaling that demonstrates the unique economic advantages of the Cloud environment: in the physical deployment, there is a need to keep additional servers on standby in anticipation of increased load—or actually load balance all of them, while they are under-utilized—but in the Cloud environment an additional server instance may be deployed on the fly, the moment the demand reaches a specified threshold. Conversely, when the demand drops sufficiently, a superfluous instance can be shut down. As a result, the expenditure for the extra resource is incurred only when the resource is needed.

A template[58] for operating the environment that involves a group of web servers would specify under the *Resource* header a group of the type "`AWS::AutoScaling::AutoScalingGroup`," with the *properties* that list the availability zones, the *configuration name* (another resource, pointing to the image of the instance to launch), and both the minimum and a maximum size of the group.

If notification of the events to the operator (an interesting feature!) is desired, the notification topic can also be specified as a resource with the type "`AWS::SNS::Topic`," which would refer to the appropriate resource—the endpoint (the operator's e-mail)—and specify the protocol ("*email*"). In this case, the common group specification would also list specific notification message strings (e.g., "instance launched," "instance terminated," or "error," the latter also supplying an appropriate error code).

Next, the scale-up and scale-down policies can be specified, using the resource type "`AWS::AutoScaling::ScalingPolicy`". The actual alarm event that triggers scaling up (or down) can be specified as the resource, too: "`Type`": "`AWS::CloudWatch::Alarm`." For instance, if the requirement for scaling up is a burst of CPU utlilization exceeding 80% for 5 minutes, the properties of the scaling-up alarm will include, using the "WS/EC2" namespace, "`MetricName: CPUUtlilization`," "`Period: 300`," and "`Threshold: 90.`" The "`AlarmActions`" will refer to the name of the scale-up policy defined above. The intrinsic function used here is "`ComparisonOperator`," with the value "`GreaterThanThreshold.`"

Another resource that needs to be specified is the load balancer itself, of the type "`AWS::ElasticLoadBalancing::LoadBalancer`," with properties that include the port number to listen to and—given that we deal with web servers—the instance port number and the protocol (HTTP).

Last but not least, a resource describing the instance security group of the type "*InstanceSecurityGroup*" must be created. The typical use is enabling *Secure Shell* (*SSH*[59])-based access to the front end, the load balancer, only.

The *Parameters* section defines the structures referred to above: the types of instances allowed, specific port numbers, the operator's e-mail, the key pair for SSH access, and the (CIDR) IP address patterns.

The *Mappings* section supplies the parameters' values (pre-defined in AWS), and the *Outputs* will list the only output—the URL of the website provided by the server. This can be achieved using intrinsic functions. The scheme of the URL is, of course, always "http"; the rest of the string is obtained via an intrinsic function *GetAtt*, with two parameters—the name of the elastic

---

[58] Cf. the actual ready-to-use sample template with the superset of capabilities described here, which can be found at https://s3-us-west-2.amazonaws.com/Cloudformation-templates-us-west-2/AutoScalingMultiAZWithNotifications.template.

[59] We address this protocol later in the chapter, in the context of our public key cryptography review.

load balancer resource, specified in the *Resources* section, and the string "`DNSName.`" These two strings can be concatenated using the intrinsic function *Join*,[60] with an empty delimiter. Thus, if the name of the elastic load balancer is *MyLB*, the *Outputs* section will look as follows:

```
"Outputs":
    {
     "URL":
        {Value":
          {"Fn::Join": ["",[http://",
             {"Fn::GetAtt": ["MyLB",
               "DNSName"]
          }]]
        }
    }
```

We went into this level of detail in describing the AWS CloudFormation example for a good reason, as already mentioned—it is a benchmark. To this end, the same template is accepted by the orchestrator in OpenStack, which we review in the next section. Of course, the template merely defines *what* needs to be done; the *how* is a different matter. The fact that OpenStack is an open-source project allows us to understand the inner workings of Cloud orchestration—and even to participate in the development of its software.

As we said earlier, orchestration can be performed at different levels. We will address one implementation of the orchestration at the stack level in the next section and return to the orchestration that involves business logic in the TOSCA discussion in the Appendix.

7.3.2 Orchestration and Management in OpenStack

First, a few words about OpenStack itself. In the organization's own words,[61] its software "... is a Cloud operating system that controls large pools of computing, storage, and networking resources throughout a datacenter, all managed through a dashboard that gives administrators control while empowering their users to provision resources through a web interface."

The project is supported organizationally by the OpenStack Foundation. The latter's funding comes—at least in part—from corporate sponsorship, but otherwise the OpenStack Foundation has attracted thousands of members with its personal membership, which is free of charge. The strategic governance of the OpenStack Foundation is provided by its Board of Directors, which represents different categories of its members. The Technical Committee defines and directs the technical direction of the OpenStack software. The software users' advocacy and feedback is carried out by the User Committee. The structure and up-to-date information on the OpenStack Foundation can be found on its site: www.OpenStack.org/foundation/.

In fact, in describing the OpenStack components, this section is a culminating point of the book in that it finally brings together the material of other chapters. The software

[60] *Join* [*x*"*d*,"*y*] concatenates the string *x*, the delimiter "*d*," and the string *y*.

[61] www.OpenStack.org/software/

components of the OpenStack correspond exactly to the functions studied in the previous chapters—there is a component for *compute* (i.e., administration of the host that provides a CPU shared by the hosted VMs), which enables virtualization; there is a component in charge of *networking*; and there is a component in charge of storage. Interacting with all these there are management functions, which notably include those of orchestration and identity and access management (to be addressed in the last section of this chapter). Note that we were careful in calling these pieces "components," because neither of them represents a simple architectural entity—such as a machine or a process or a library. As we will see shortly, some components combine executable images, various libraries, and shell scripts.

In line with the API terminology that we discussed earlier, the part of a component that implements an HTTP server (and is thus accessed via a REST API) is referred to by the OpenStack documentation as a *service*. It is important to understand that deployment of the OpenStack software on physical hosts is a separate matter altogether. Overall, there is no single way to deploy these components. We will provide specific examples; for now we note that the deployment issues pretty much boil down to ensuring reliability commensurate with the operating budget.

First, let us take a closer look at the components. Each component is associated with a separate project in charge of its software development. The names of the components and their associated projects are used interchangeably by the OpenStack documentation.

The OpenStack *Compute* component (developed in a project called *Nova*) contains functions that govern the life cycles of all virtual machines inasmuch as their creation, scheduling, and shutting down are concerned. Within the *compute*, the *controller* processes—the *Cloud controller*, *volume controller*, and *network controller*—take care of the computing resources, block-level storage resources, and network resources, respectively.

The OpenStack *Networking* component (developed in the *Neutron* project) is concerned with enabling network connectivity for all other components. The *OpenStack Administrative Guide*[62] refers to this as "Network-Connectivity-as-a-Service for other *OpenStack* services." The services provided by this component support network connectivity and addressing, but—importantly—there is also a place for plugging in other software. The native Neutron software presently supports configuring the TLS support for all API, and it implements *Load-Balancer-as-a-Service* (*LBaaS*) and *Firewall-as-a-Service* (*FWaaS*).

Neutron also allows to create routers, which are gateways for virtual machines deployed on the nodes that run the *Neutron L3 agent* software. Among other things, the routers perform NAT translation for the *floating IP address*—the public IP address that belongs to the Cloud provider. It is a unique feature of the Neutron design that this address is not assigned through DHCP or set statically—for that matter the guest operating system is unaware of it as the packet delivery to the floating IP address is handled exclusively by the Neutron L3 agent. This arrangement provides much flexibility, as the floating (public) and private IP addresses can be used at the same time on any network interface.

To deal with detailed network management, Neutron supports plug-ins. As may be expected, there is an open-source SDN project—part of the Linux Foundation—called *Open*

[62] http://docs.OpenStack.org/admin-guide-Cloud/

Daylight.[63] We refer the reader to the project's website, which provides fine examples of the plug-ins that implement both SNMP and NETCONF. The latter, naturally, makes a lot of sense in the SDN context. There are, of course, other implementations, including several proprietary ones. The plug-ins run at the back end. The front-end REST API allows, among other things, creating and updating of tenants' networks as well as specific virtual routers.

As far as storage is concerned, there are two projects in OpenStack: *Swift* and *Cinder*. The former deals with unstructured data objects, while the latter provides access to the persistent block storage (here again there is room for plugging in other block-storage software).

Also related to storage—of a rather specialized type—is the *Service* component (developed in the *Glance* project). True to its name, the service deals with storing and retrieving the registry of the virtual machine images. The state of the image database is maintained in *Glance Registry*, while the services are invoked through *Glance API*.

The authentication and access authorization component is worked in the OpenStack *Keystone* project, which deals with the identity and access management. Given the singular importance of this issue, we have dedicated a separate section—the last section of this chapter—to these issues.

Finally, there are three management and orchestration components. The user interface is available both in the "old" CLI form and through the web-based portal, the OpenStack *Dashboard*, developed as part of the OpenStack *Horizon* project. Two other components are (1) *telemetry*, developed in the OpenStack *Ceilometer* project,[64] which is in charge of metering (achieved through monitoring) and (2) *service orchestration*, developed in the OpenStack *Heat*[65] project. To address these, we need to make a deeper excursion into the OpenStack architecture and illustrate it with some deployment examples.

In approaching this subject, one must keep in mind that formally software modules can run anywhere—and the OpenStack design has gone a long way in defining high-level software interfaces (including REST API and RPC) to ensure that the way in which the management activities interact with one another is independent of hardware deployment. It is important to clarify what the word "interact" means here. Depending on the context, it can mean one of two things: (1) a subroutine call—which is a programming construct employed within an activity or (2) passing a message—which is the means of interaction among the activities.[66] Another important thing to keep in mind is that in order to ensure reliability, both data and code are expected to be replicated across several machines, and so an *activity* here may in fact be supported by several identical processes. When a unit of code runs though, it does run on a particular machine, and so to illustrate the essential sequence of events it is helpful to see a minimum deployment with no replication. Once it is understood though, the next thing

[63] www.opendaylight.org/project

[64] In the earlier releases of OpenStack software, metric collection and alarm configuration were developed in the OpenStack *Cloud Watch* project (the namesake of the AWS Cloud Watch service, which enables setting of alarms, collection of metrics, and monitoring of log files). Now this project has been replaced by *Ceilometer*.

[65] We have tried not to get into the etymology of the OpenStack project names, although this would be an interesting study in itself. When it comes to orchestration projects, their names are quite appropriate and by no means random. The word "ceilometer" is not recognized by our word processor, so we looked it up on the Web. According to the US National Science Digital Library, a ceilometer is "a device using a laser or other light source to determine the height of a Cloud base." Makes sense! As for *Heat*, the OpenStack website volunteers an explanation of the name: "Why 'Heat'? It makes the Clouds rise!"

[66] Or even higher-level activities that are a result of distributed execution of SIBs discussed earlier.

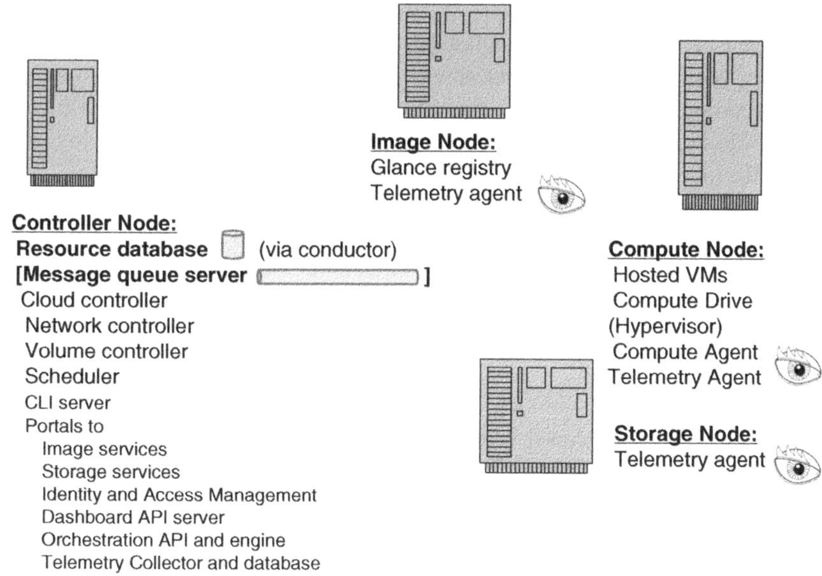

Figure 7.11 Mapping the OpenStack components into a physical architecture: an example.

to understand is that the software components can and may need to be deployed differently depending on requirements related to performance, reliability, and regulations.

Figure 7.11 provides the first deployment example. The hosts in the data center on which the virtual machines are hosted are called *compute nodes*. Hence, each data center must have at least one compute note. In addition to running a hypervisor and hosting guest VMs, a compute node runs various applications that belong to the management infrastructure. Some of these applications—we call them *agents*—initiate interactions with other components (and so act as *clients*); others respond to communications initiated elsewhere (and so act as *servers*). As often happens, some may act either as clients or as servers, depending on the circumstances.

As far as hypervisors are concerned, OpenStack interworks with several major ones through specific *compute drivers*, but the degree of interworking varies.[67]

The *compute agent* is actually creating and deploying virtual machines. It acts as a server to the *scheduler* (which we will discuss in the context of the *controller node*), but it acts as a client when dealing with the central resource database, image node, and storage node, which respectively maintain the *Glance* image registry and either type (block or object) of storage.

The *telemetry agents* present in all three nodes collect the performance data used in orchestration, which we will address soon.

Finally, the controller node is at the heart of Cloud management. To begin with, it contains the global resource database,[68] which we have already mentioned when introducing the compute

[67] The list of hypervisors supported, along with the description of the drivers indicating the degree of support, is published at https://wiki.OpenStack.org/wiki/HypervisorSupportMatrix.

[68] In OpenStack, the database software of choice is *MySQL*—available from the namesake open-source project (www.mysql.com/).

agent. Since in practical large-scale deployments this database is replicated, there is a front end (called *Nova Conductor*), which handles the compute agent interface.

The *scheduler* is in charge of the placement function.[69] It makes the decision on where (i.e., on which compute node) a new virtual machine is to be created and on which storage node a new block storage volume is to be created. The former purpose employs the *Nova Scheduler* and the latter the *Cinder Scheduler.*

This takes care of the entities in Figure 7.11, except for the *Message Queue Server* (which we labeled in brackets). We momentarily defer the discussion of this because—in the rather simplistic deployment example where all controller components are running on the same host—it appears superfluous. Before reviewing the actual means of interaction among the components, we will walk through a simple flow of events resulting in the creation of a virtual machine:

1. The flow starts with a remote user invoking the API (more precisely, the *Nova API server*) in the controller with the request to provision a VM. The controller then requests that the scheduler query the resource database to determine a proper compute node (which is easy in our case since we have only one) and order its compute agent to provision a virtual machine;[70]
2. The compute agent complies with the request, queries the resource database to get the precise information about the image, fetches the image identifier from the image node registry, and, finally, loads the image itself from the storage node, and orders the hypervisor to create a new tenant VM;
3. The compute agent passes the information about the new VM back to the controller node and requests that the network controller provide the connectivity information;
4. The network controller updates the resource database and completes the network provisioning; and
5. Similarly, the compute agent interacts with the volume controller to create the storage volume and attach it to the VM.

Needless to say, to simplify the discussion and to get the basic flow through, we have omitted several essential capabilities. This simple sequence, of course, did not involve orchestration, which would have been unnecessary in this case because (1) the "stack" here contains only one virtual machine rather than an infrastructure of several machines and (2) we assumed that the service offered by the stack does not require auto-scaling or any other service that required monitoring and automatic intervention. Orchestration will get into the picture soon, when we discuss a more complex example.

But the most patent omission is that of all matters of identity and management, including the authentication of the original request and its authorization. We discuss this subject separately in the next section, and we will see that the activities related to identity management permeate all steps.

---

[69] In the Appendix, we have a special section dedicated to this complex and interesting subject, which requires knowledge of optimization techniques and is thus treated as an advanced topic.

[70] The attentive reader may ask what protocol is used here. We intentionally defer naming this and all other application protocols until we finish the description of the flow.

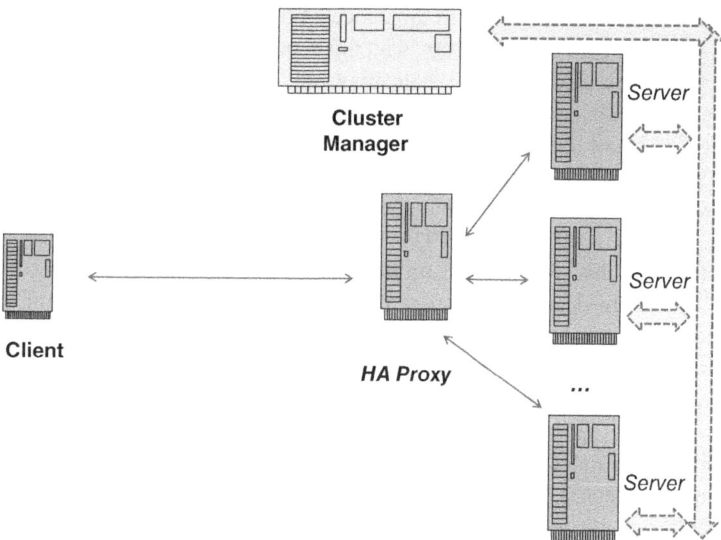

Figure 7.12 A high-availability cluster.

Now we are ready to clarify further the nature of communications at the application level among various pieces within each OpenStack component. The underlying idea is to have *no* shared data between any two peers (i.e., a client and a server).[71]

The OpenStack software has been written with the objective of creating highly-available systems. *High availability*, an aspect of a broader concept of reliability, is defined in [5] as the "ability of the system to restore correct operation, permitting it to resume providing services during periods when some components have failed." High availability is achieved through redundancy, by replicating the pieces of a system—in our case, the network, storage, and *compute* components—that can become single points of failure.

Replicated servers run on a group of machines called a *cluster*. All these servers together must appear as *one* server to the client, as illustrated in Figure 7.12. Hence, one of the machines is designated a proxy, which distributes client requests among the rest of the servers and also balances their load. The proxy itself is not a single point of failure, because every other machine in the cluster is ready to take on both the front-end and load-balancing functions.

Incidentally, the mechanism we have just described is pertinent to the so-called *active–active* mode (in which all servers are running at the same time), but it is not the *only* mechanism to achieve high availability in a cluster. Another mode is *active–passive*, in which an extra server is kept ready (as a hot standby) but not online, and is brought online in case of failure or overload of the active server. OpenStack supports both modes.

But how does the cluster "know" when to assign the proxy function to another server, or when to bring the hot standby online? For that there is yet another function—the *cluster manager*. Its job is to observe the health of the cluster, according to its configuration, and

[71] Note that this is different from replication. For example, database servers in a cluster may share replicated data among them.

reconfigure it in accordance with the circumstances. For this monitoring purpose, OpenStack presently uses software called *Pacemaker*, which is a product of Cluster Labs.[72]

By now, it should be clear why no state may be shared between a client and a server. (Suppose the client sends two requests. The first request is directed by the proxy to the top server in Figure 7.12 and the second to the server at the bottom. If the client and the server shared the state, and this state was modified by the first server, the second server would have no way of knowing that the state had changed!)

As we have noted several times, HTTP, the protocol of the World-Wide Web, has been designed exactly with this objective in mind—no state is shared between the HTTP client and the HTTP server. In decades of experience with the World-Wide Web, the industry has learned how to develop and deploy highly efficient servers and proxies. Consequently, it has made a lot of sense to take what was tried and true and apply it—while reusing all the software available—to a new purpose, which is much more general than providing web services.

The computational model here is rather straightforward. An HTTP server is a *daemon* process (or a thread) that is listening to a specific port. When it gets a message (an HTTP PDU), it parses it and performs a one-time action, which at the beginning was limited to fetching a file and passing it back to the client, but subsequently—as we will see when we address this in detail—has grown much more involved.[73] Two different servers may run on the same host or on different hosts—the interface to the services remains the same. It makes sense to combine global management services on a dedicated host, as is the case in our deployment examples.

To this end, all OpenStack modules that have "API" in their names (i.e., *nova-api*) are daemons providing REST services (discussed in the Appendix). Communications among daemons are carried out via the *Advanced Message Queuing Protocol* (*AMQP*).[74] The message queue of Figure 7.11 is the structure that enables this.

AMQP can be initiated from either end of the pipe. On the contrary, an HTTP transaction can be initiated only by the client because HTTP is a pure client/server protocol.

There are three aspects to the orchestration in OpenStack. The first aspect deals with the life cycle management specification of a Cloud application (i.e., the stack) and its actual instantiation; the second aspect deals with monitoring the state of the stack on the subject of compliance with specifications for running virtual machines; and the third aspect deals with taking a remediating action. As we mentioned earlier, the Heat component is in charge of the first and third aspects, while Ceilometer takes care of the second.

An early stated objective of Heat was compatibility with the AWS CloudFormation, so as to enable a service already working with the AWS CloudFormation to be ported to OpenStack. (Conversely, a service developed and running in a Cloud employing OpenStack could be moved to AWS; in fact, such a Cloud could *burst* into AWS.) To this end, OpenStack both recognizes the AWS CloudFormation template and provides the AWS CloudFormation-compatible API.

---

[72] http://clusterlabs.org/doc/

[73] The action—not the protocol!

[74] For example, the request to the scheduler mentioned earlier (step 1 of the flow) is carried over AMQP. The nova-compute daemon, which, among other things, creates and terminates virtual machine instances through the hypervisor's APIs, takes its requests from the message queue, one at a time.

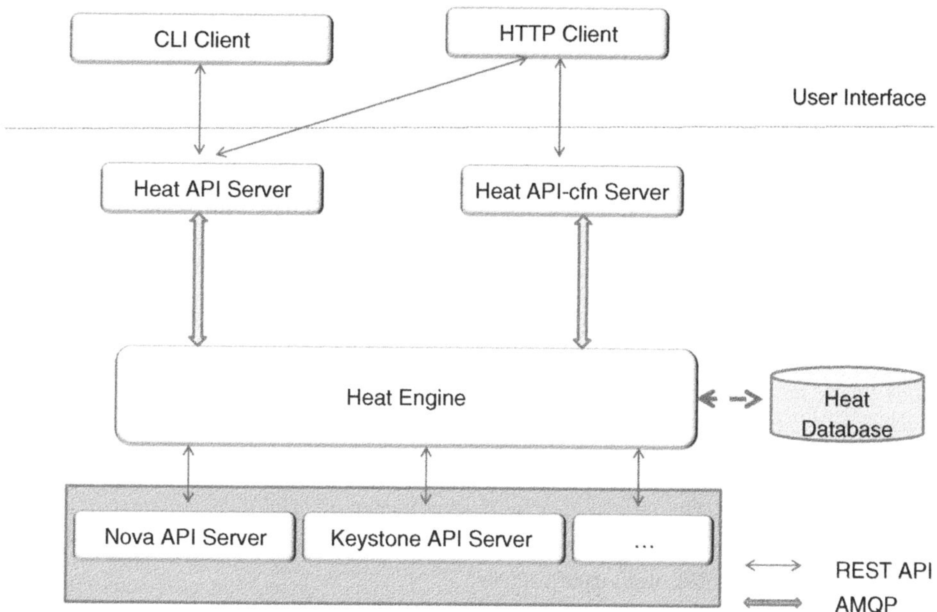

Figure 7.13 The Heat computing architecture.

Over time, the Heat project has developed its own template—appropriately called *HOT*[75]—which is actually an acronym for *Heat Orchestration Template*. The template itself has the same format—and semantics—as the *AWS CloudFormation Template*, but it is specified in a language called *YAML*[76] rather than JSON. One way or the other, the template is a text file that specifies the infrastructure resources and the relationship among them. The latter feature is programmatic in nature in that it can enforce the order in which virtual machines are created and assigned storage volumes and network connections.

Another programmatic feature is that a template is dynamic: when the template is changed, Heat modifies the service accordingly.

We will start with the description of a computational (i.e., described in terms of computing processes) architecture of the Heat part of the orchestration service architecture depicted in Figure 7.13.

The *Heat engine* is the process in charge of launching stacks according to their template specification.

The user interface function is performed by two servers—*Heat API* and *Heat API-cfn*—which respectively provide the REST API for the HOT- and AWS CloudFormation-compatible services. Either of these two merely serves as the front end to the Heat engine, with which it communicates over AMQP.

[75] The template is described at http://docs.OpenStack.org/developer/heat/template_guide/hot_spec.html#hot-spec.

[76] YAML is a left-recursive acronym: it stands for "YAML Ain't a Mark-up Language." For the description of the language, reference parser, and release information, see www.yaml.org/.

Needless to say, this architecture supports the distribution of processes across available machines in a far more flexible way than our earlier controller architecture picture suggested. All servers of the same type may be replicated and accessed through a high-availability proxy.

In addition to the REST API, the Heat component provides the command-line interface, but the CLI agent converts the commands to the REST API orchestration, so the Heat engine does not deal with CLI directly. The commands are semantically identical to the API in that they refer to the same capabilities. We briefly introduce the commands, in the order they relate to templates, stacks, resources, and the events associated with the resources:

- *template-show* requests a template for a given stack;
- *template-validate* requests that a template be validated with specific parameters;
- *stack-create* requests that a stack be created;
- *stack-delete* requests that a stack be deleted;
- *stack-update* requests that the stack be updated (according to the data described in a file, or URL, or with the new values of specific parameters);
- *action-suspend* and *action-resume*, respectively, request the name-sake action on the execution of the active stack;
- *stack-list* requests the list of all user's stacks;
- *stack-show* requests a description of a given stack;
- *resource-list* requests the set of resources that belong to a stack;
- *resource-metadata* requests a resource's metadata attributes;[77]
- *resource-show* requests the description of a given resource;
- *event-list* requests the list of events for the selected resources of the current stack; and
- *event-show* requests the description of a specific event.

Heat also provides hooks for programmable extensions—the resource plug-in, which extends the base resource class and implements the appropriate handler methods for the above commands.

So far we have addressed the so-called *Northern API*—the user interface to orchestration. Both API servers act as the front end to the Heat engine. To effect the execution of the commands, the Heat engine, in turn, invokes *Southern API—Nova API*, *Keystone API*, and so on. In a nutshell, the sequence of invocations is suggested by an earlier workflow for creating an image.

The remaining piece of the workings of OpenStack orchestration is the mechanisms in support of alarms. An earlier example of a service template in fact refers to the *AWS CloudWatch* service, which was partly imitated in the earlier releases of Heat. The mechanisms were put in place for users to create and update alarms, along with the mechanisms for reacting to the alarms. For details, and a description of testing with simple but incisive use cases, we recommend Davide Michelino's Summer Student Report[78] from CERN.

---

[77] This notion and feature comes from the AWS CloudFormation Template, which allows us to add to a resource's description *metadata attributes*, which associate the resource with the structured data. For syntax and examples, see http://docs.aws.amazon.com/AWSCloudFormation/latest/UserGuide/aws-attribute-metadata.html.

[78] http://zenodo.org/record/7571/files/CERN_openlab_report_Michelino.pdf

Later, however, OpenStack decided to deprecate the use of the AWS CloudWatch API and instead rely on Ceilometer. Consequently, this is where the action in OpenStack is at the time of this writing.

To Ceilometer then! As we have mentioned already, its objective is *metering*—that is, measuring the rate of use of the resources. In the telecommunications business, metering is the first step in the overall charging process, the other steps being *rating* and *billing*. To this end, Ceilometer provides the API that a rating engine can use to develop a billing system, but we are not going to be concerned with this matter here. Our main interest—strictly for the purposes of this book—is in using metering to determine when an auto-scaling action is needed.

The task of Ceilometer is much complicated by an obstacle every OSS project had in the past: different parts of a large system invariably use different means for providing management data—and some parts don't provide any data at all. To deal with that, OpenStack had to create several mechanisms where one would have sufficed had the same methodology been used.

The Ceilometer model employs three types of actor: various *telemetry agents*, the *telemetry collector*, and the *publisher*. The collector aggregates data from the agents in charge of each of the five OpenStack components: *Compute*, *Networking*, *Block Storage*, *Object Storage*, and *Image*—and then transmits these data to the publisher, which stores it in the database or passes it on to external systems. Having introduced the terminology, we note that, for the purposes of this book, the collector and the publisher are really one entity, which we will call collector. (In the fairly simplistic arrangement of Figure 7.11, the agents are depicted as eyes and are assumed to send their data to the collector by means of notification.)

In an ideal system, each component has an agent that issues event notifications over a unified messaging system (called the *Oslo bus*). For detail, please consult the respective OpenStack documentation,[79] but note that the AMQP is compatible with the Oslo bus, which encompasses other messaging mechanisms. For simplicity, we will assume that all messages are sent over AMQP.

The first—and preferred–mechanism is effected by the *Bus listener agent*, which processes all notification events and produces the Ceilometer samples. Again, in a system where all components are capable of issuing event notifications, this is the only required mechanism. Absent the uniform notification implementation, the second—less preferred—additional mechanism is in order. Here, a *Push agent*, which actually creates notifications, needs to be added to every monitored node. And if, for whatever reason, this cannot be done, one reverts to the third mechanism—the *Polling agent*. The Polling agent does just what its name suggests: it checks remote nodes (via REST API or RPC) in a loop, which includes waiting for a specified interval.[80] This is the least preferred method, because its implementation gets in the way of resiliency.

The agents differ in what they do and where they run. (A *compute agent* runs on a compute host, for example.) A *central agent* is part of the central management system (the controller node, according to our earlier nomenclature); its responsibilities include accounting for the

[79] http://docs.OpenStack.org/developer/oslo.messaging/

[80] And, closer to hardware, there are *inspectors*, which use various protocols (such as SNMP) for collecting the data, which are then passed to the agents. For more on this, see the post from O. Serhiienko at http://superuser.OpenStack.org/articles/ceilometer-full-stack-monitoring-for-OpenStack.

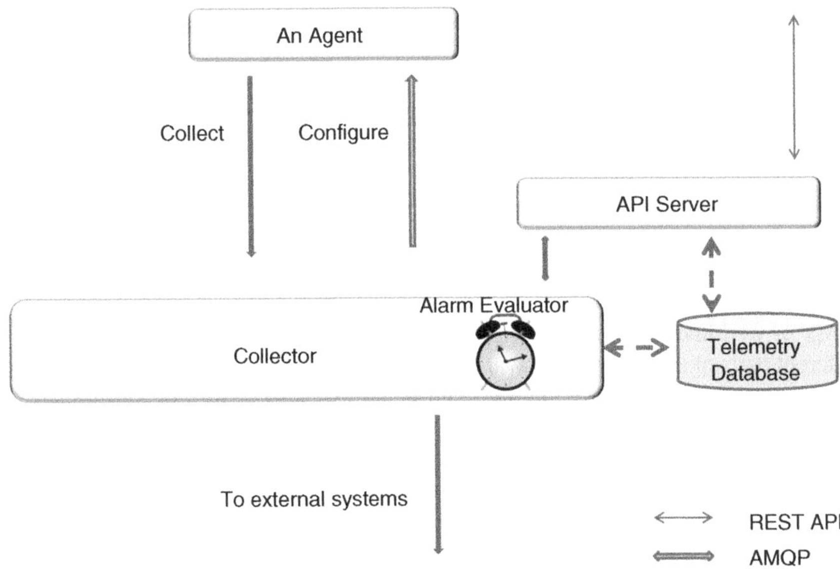

Figure 7.14 The Ceilometer computing architecture.

resources other than compute nodes or instances. The collector, of course, runs on the central management system, too. It should be clear though that there may be several different hosts that run different pieces of the central management system (or, in a high-availability cluster, each of the hosts may run all these pieces). Ceilometer also supports configuration of the agents.

The collected data are stored in the Ceilometer database. Ceilometer provides two sets of API: (1) for writing to the collector and (2) for accessing the database. As with all other components, the API server is a separate process.

The above architecture is summarized in Figure 7.14, which shows a logical message flow. In reality, all the components are "interconnected" by a real messaging bus—that is, they read and write into the same logical "wire."[81]

One other feature of Ceilometer—the one most essential for our purpose—is the ability to create alarms based on pre-defined thresholds (as in "tell me when CPU utilization reaches 70%"). OpenStack defines a separate module for that purpose,[82] but for simplicity we consider the *alarm evaluator* to be part of the collector.

To illustrate the interworking between the telemetry and orchestration proper (i.e., between Ceilometer and Heat), we will use Figure 7.15. We return to the auto-scaling example that we first introduced in the discussion of *AWS CloudFormation*.

In order to know when to scale up (or down) a stack, the Heat engine needs feedback on the CPU utilization of the stack instances. To enable this, one can define the alarms based on the compute agent's metrics. With the support of Ceilometer, the metrics get evaluated according

[81] According to http://docs.OpenStack.org/havana/install-guide/install/apt/content/metering-service.html.

[82] *Ceilometer-alarm-notifier.*

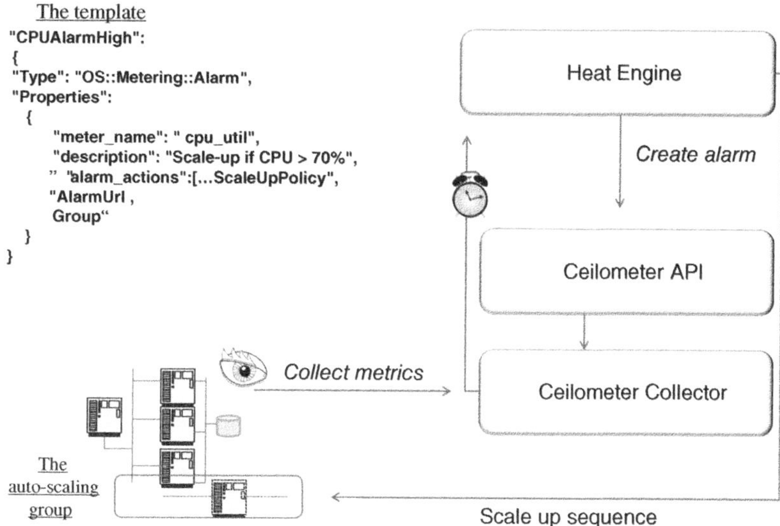
The template
"CPUAlarmHigh":
{
"Type": "OS::Metering::Alarm",
"Properties":
{
"meter_name": " cpu_util",
"description": "Scale-up if CPU > 70%",
" "alarm_actions":[...ScaleUpPolicy",
"AlarmUrl ,
Group"
}
}
Heat Engine
Create alarm
Ceilometer API
Collect metrics
Ceilometer Collector
The auto-scaling group
Scale up sequence

Figure 7.15 Interworking Heat and Ceilometer: an auto-scaling example.

to the template-specified rules, and exceptions are reported as alarm notifications. (Of course, it is not that Ceilometer itself reads the template—only the Heat engine does. Ceilometer only needs to provide an API flexible enough for the Heat engine to express the template rules for the auto-scaling group.)

In the upper-left-hand corner, part of a HOT template[83] is defined to set an alarm based on the CPU utilization of an auto-scaling group. Namely, when the CPU utilization exceeds 70%, the group of servers "scales up," that is a new server instance is added. A particular property, *alarm_actions*, is defined in the OpenStack manual as a "list of URLs (webhooks) to invoke when state transitions to alarm. (sic!)" The template also specifies the period to collect the metrics and the statistics used (e.g., *average*).

The alarm is set on the request of the Heat engine when the stack is created. When the alarm "sounds," the Heat engine follows up by creating a new instance, connecting it to the networks, and so on. Similarly, an alarm can be set to scale down (say when the average CPU utilization falls below 40%), so when extra instances become redundant, they are eliminated. Note that this feature is not simply an exercise in efficiency by a Cloud provider—it also saves money for the customer, who typically pays the Cloud provider for each instance. A true example of elasticity!

It is important to note that OpenStack supports integration of software configuration and management tools—specifically Chef and Puppet, which we mentioned in the previous section.

We discussed the workflow tools earlier. At the time of this writing, OpenStack is actively working on developing one as part of the *Convection* project.[84] In the project parlance, a

---

[83] This is a simplified version of an example presented by J. Danjou, N. Barcet, and E. Glynn at https://www.OpenStack.org/assets/presentation-media/CeiloPlusHeatEqualsAlarmingIcehouseSummit.pdf.

[84] https://wiki.OpenStack.org/wiki/Convection

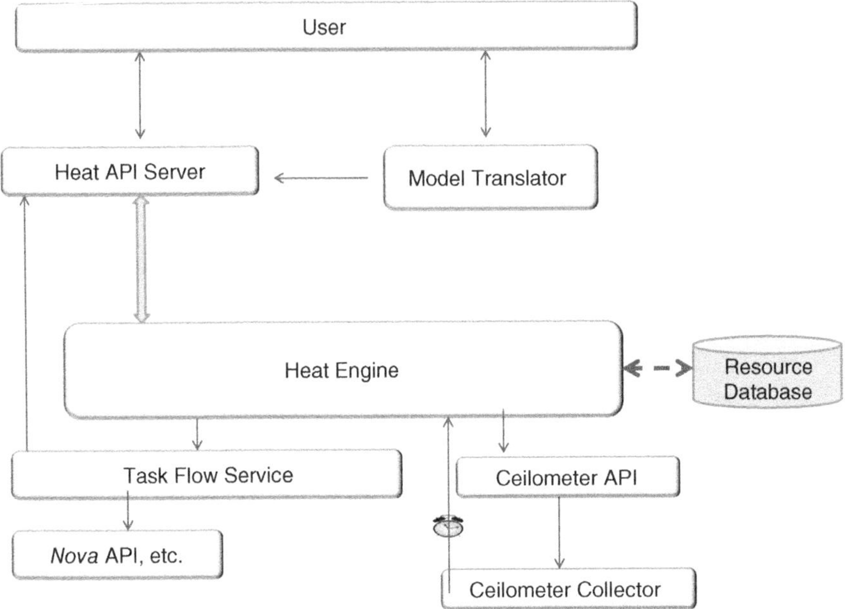

Figure 7.16 Integrated orchestration architecture.

workflow is called a *Task Flow*, and the plan is to offer *Task-Flow-as-a-Service* (*TFaS*), similarly to what Amazon AWS has done.

The vision of the service is such that a user would write and register a workflow. An application could then invoke this workflow (and, later, also check its status or terminate it). The orchestrator's job is to react to every change of state in a workflow and invoke the respective tasks.

The service is recursive in that the TFaS can be used by Heat itself to manage its own tasks. For example, a task flow could call Heat API to start a given task. According to this vision, "orchestration is concerned with intelligently creating, organizing, connecting, and coordinating Cloud based resources, which may involve creating a task flow and/or executing tasks."

Figure 7.16 summarizes the authors' understanding of the OpenStack orchestration vision by combining—and showing the interactions among—the pieces that we have described so far. Again, at the time of this writing this is merely a blueprint for future development.

A piece depicted in the upper-right-hand corner is a catch-all for other template specifications (cfn or TOSCA), each of which is interpreted here by an entity called a *model translator*. We will review some specification examples in the Appendix.

We conclude this section by considering another deployment example—from the networking angle—which is presented in Figure 7.17. This figure modifies Figure 7.11 to demonstrate the structure of a modern node in the Cloud data center. Just as in human anatomy books different layers of a body (e.g., muscles or a skeleton) are shown, here we take a look at a practical way to interconnect the components. To reduce the clutter, we have omitted the image nodes, but all other nodes are present—now replicated and assumed to work in clusters.

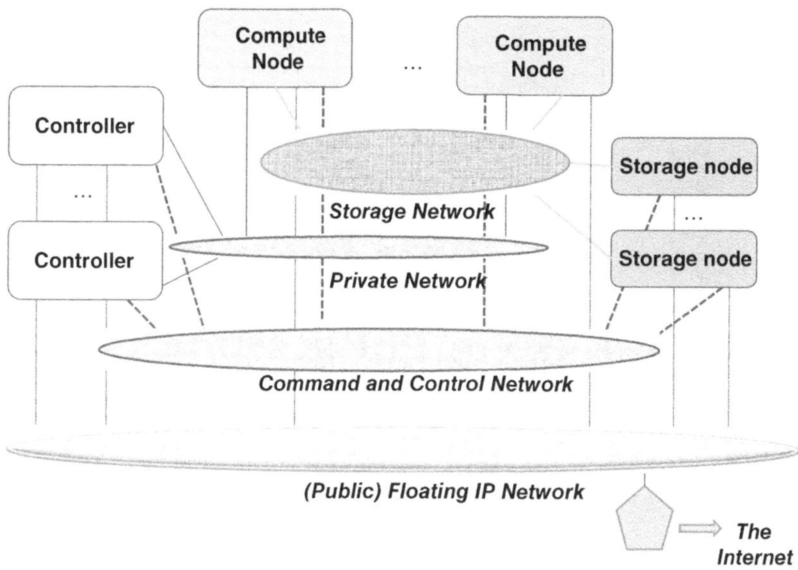

Figure 7.17 Networking with OpenStack nodes.

The following four (Layer-2) networks are completely separate from one another:

- The *storage network*, which is intended only for accessing storage and thus interconnects only the compute nodes and storage nodes.
- The *private network*, which exists only for communications among the hosted virtual machines.
- The *command and control network*, which exists only for the purpose of orchestration and management.
- The *public network*, which allows connection to the Internet and which, for this reason, employs floating IP addresses as discussed before.

Having these networks separate is more or less typical[85]—both for security purposes and for differentiating the capacity, as different purposes have different bandwidth demands. As a minimum, the private, public, and command and control networks are advisable.

7.4 Identity and Access Management

The discipline of *Identity and Access Management* (*IAM*) deals with matters of authentication and authorization. Both are indispensible to Cloud Computing: before applying any operation to a virtual machine (or a stack) throughout its life cycle, the management and orchestration

[85] Cf. Mirantis OpenStack® Reference Architecture (http://docs.mirantis.com/fuel/fuel-4.1/pdf/Mirantis-OpenStack-4.1-ReferenceArchitecture.pdf), p. 17, which demonstrates an architecture with *five* networks—the administrative and management networks are separate in that example.

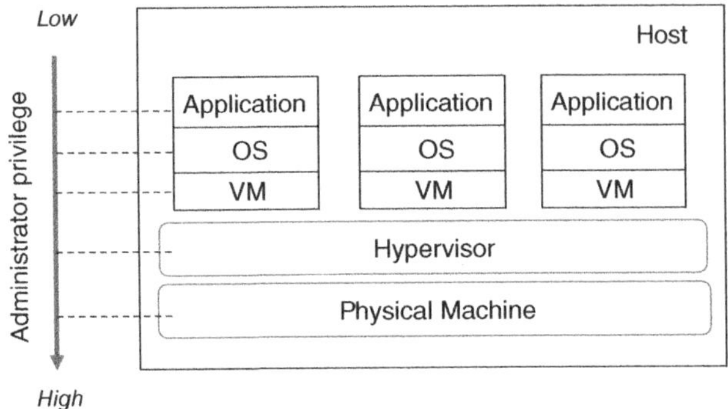

Figure 7.18 Relative administrative privilege.

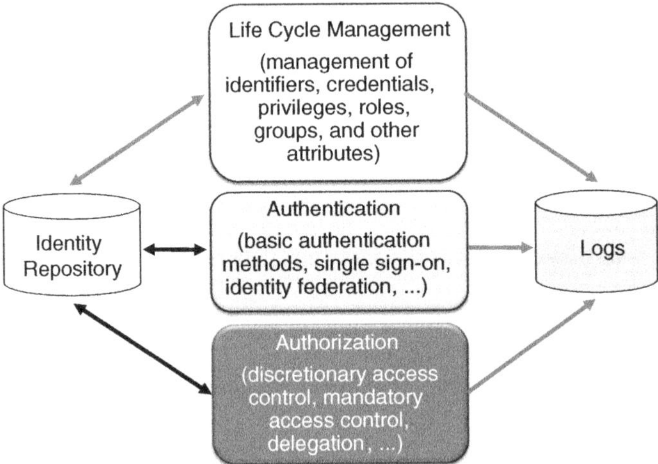

Figure 7.19 Scope of identity and access management.

system must know who is requesting the operation and whether the requesting entity has the right to the operation.

The need for the IAM is pervasive, and it is manifest in other contexts. Each machine—whether physical or virtual—needs to have its own IAM mechanisms (part of the operating system) to control access to programs and data. An application may further have its own IAM to control access to its services. The IAM functions at different contexts are hierarchical in terms of privilege; the one associated with the Cloud management system is most privileged. This resembles the administrative privilege hierarchy of a virtualized host, as shown in Figure 7.18. We will explain further the reason for the privilege hierarchy later; for the moment, let us recall Chapter 3, which introduced the concept of privilege levels and protection rings.

Figure 7.19 summarizes what falls in the realm of IAM generally. In short, it deals with the life cycle and correlation of the identity information representing different personas that correspond to an entity, and the authentication and authorization of the entity. The construct through which an entity can be consistently and comprehensively identified as unique is known as an *identity*. An identity may be associated with a person, project, process, device, or data object.

We define the identity as a structure that combines the entity name (*identifier*)[86] and the *credentials* for authenticating the entity. Creating an identity for a given entity requires proof of credentials, role setting, and provisioning of the associated data (including privileges) in the repository. Naturally, adequate security and privacy controls must be in place to protect all the identity-related information created. To this end, it is necessary to have a clear policy on how such information is used, stored, and propagated among systems. Such a policy may be provider specific or it may be dictated by governmental regulations (e.g., the Sarbanes–Oxley Act in the United States). To enable auditing and reporting of policy compliance, critical IAM activities (both online and offline) must be logged. Auditing trails of who used the system and which authorization decisions were made is also essential for incident management and forensics.

In this section, we will first discuss the implications of Cloud Computing as related to identity and access management. Then we will discuss the most pertinent state-of-the-art IAM technology by reviewing its building blocks. Here we just provide an outline, and leave the details to the Appendix. Finally, as a case study, we will examine *Keystone*, the OpenStack component that implements identity and access management.

7.4.1 Implications of Cloud Computing

To help us understand the implications of Cloud Computing, let us consider a flow for creating a virtual machine through a web-based portal. Let Alice be a user of the portal.[87] The flow is as follows.

First, Alice attempts to access the portal, which sets off an authentication and authorization step. Alice provides her credentials.

At this point the portal authenticates Alice and determines her entitlements. But being a user interface, it relies on another Cloud component (i.e., the identity controller) to do so. The portal invokes the identity controller through an identity API. Upon successful authentication and authorization, Alice is presented with the services and resources to which she is entitled. Next, using the portal, Alice asks to provision a virtual machine with certain properties. This triggers a chain of actions on behalf of Alice across various components:

1. The portal constructs and sends a request to the compute controller through a compute API. The request includes her credentials.
2. The compute controller validates the credentials.[88] If everything goes well, it allocates a compute node and orders the compute agent therein to provision a virtual machine.
3. Upon receiving the order, the compute agent proceeds in requesting the image from the image store through an image API. The request includes Alice's authorization. If the

[86] An entity may have more than one name (consider aliases), in which case multiple identifiers can be linked.
[87] Not only will this resolve the problem with selecting gender nouns, but it is also a well-known convention in security texts to call principles Bob and Alice. Bob will appear in the next chapter.
[88] Authentication and authorization may be done by a component (e.g., the identity controller) outside the compute controller.

authorization is valid, the image is downloaded. Then the hypervisor creates a new virtual machine.

4. After the virtual machine is created, the compute agent requests (via the networking API) that the network controller provision the specified connectivity. The request includes confirmation of Alice's authorization in a form that the network controller can check.
5. Upon successful validation of the authorization, the network controller allocates the networking resources and returns the related information to the compute agent.
6. The compute agent asks the volume controller to create the required volume and attach it to the virtual machine through a block storage API.
7. The volume controller allocates the volume and returns the related information to the compute agent. (Of course, this step also required authorization checking.)

Now Alice is notified that her virtual machine has been provisioned, together with the related information (e.g., an IP address and a root password) for accessing it.

From the above flow,[89] we can make the following five observations:

1. The portal is accessible to authenticated users only. So the first time Alice tries to have access, she has to log on, providing her credentials as dictated by the user interface. The specific credentials required depend on the authentication method supported by the Cloud service.
2. After Alice has logged on, the authentication and authorization steps repeat several times. Specifically, verification of Alice's privilege is in order whenever an API request is involved. The need for repeated authentication and authorization is understandable. Normally, the effect of authentication and authorization is limited to an API transaction and to the involved components in a distributed system. The need is further compounded by the objective of sharing no state in support of "massive scalability."
3. Alice is not required to provide her credentials every time they are needed. This is an important design matter, which is addressed by implementing *single sign-on*. As a result, additional interactions requiring her credentials after Alice has logged on can be handled without her intervention.
4. There is a need for a *delegation* mechanism to allow Cloud service components to act on behalf of Alice. Obviously, replicating Alice's original credentials across the distributed components is unacceptable (imagine giving your password to everyone whom you delegate any task to). A viable mechanism should use a temporary construct in lieu of Alice's original credentials. Needless to say, it is imperative that the construct have at least as good security properties as Alice's original credentials. However strange this requirement may look now, we will demonstrate (see the Appendix) that it can be fulfilled.
5. Beside Alice, there are other privileged users, such as Cloud administrators or process owners. They are subject to authentication and authorization as well.

The complexity of the matter increases as soon as automation, a hallmark of Cloud Computing, comes into the picture. Consider, for example, auto-scaling. As we have seen, an

[89] As far as identity and access management is concerned, essentially the same flow applies to other operations, such as start, suspend, stop, and de-provisioning.

orchestrator is responsible for creating a new virtual machine in response to a certain alarm. Such an alarm is typically triggered when the load of an existing virtual machine reaches a pre-set threshold. The flow for creating a virtual machine is pretty much the same as that involving Alice directly. The major difference here is that it is the orchestrator rather than the portal that constructs and sends a request to the compute controller through a compute API. The orchestrator acts on behalf of Alice. It gets the specification of the virtual machine from a template that she has provided beforehand. As before, to do what is necessary, the orchestrator will need to include Alice's authorization in the request to the compute controller. As before, the orchestrator should use a construct in lieu of Alice's original credentials and the construct should be valid for a short period of time.

But here lies a problem. The timing of scale-out alarms is unpredictable. It is quite likely that when an alarm does go off, an existing temporary construct has already expired. Therefore, it is necessary that the orchestrator obtain a fresh temporary construct dynamically—on demand.

Moreover, auto-scaling is not just about provisioning and starting a new virtual machine. The reason for having a virtual machine to begin with is to run applications. Once the virtual machine is up and running, the orchestrator also needs to install applications remotely, provision the application-specific data (e.g., credentials of application users and the administrator), configure the system and applications, and finally launch the applications. To carry out these tasks, the orchestrator needs to have access to application-specific data (i.e., *metadata*) pre-provisioned in the Cloud. And then there is a need to run scripts on the virtual machine, which may require special privileges. Fortunately, the orchestrator could do all of this, given proper permissions from Alice.

But that creates another problem. For one thing, the orchestrator must have special privileges on Alice's virtual machine. Therefore, it is essential that Alice be able to delegate roles with enough granularity to mitigate potential security risks. In addition, since the orchestrator assumes whatever power the special user has on the virtual machine, the privilege assigned to the special user shall be the bare minimum required for performing the tasks at hand.

Overall, Cloud administrators have privileges that may be abused. Thus, in a Cloud environment it is essential to have in place the controls that can limit the potential damage.

7.4.2 Authentication

When it comes to authenticating a person to a computer system, there are three common types of credential, as shown in Figure 7.20. Alice may be authenticated based on what she knows (e.g., a password), what she has (e.g., a hardware security token), or what she is (e.g., her fingerprint). Obviously, authentication based on what Alice knows is the simplest method as it requires no additional gadgets. This explains why passwords are used most widely.

The choice of an authentication method depends on the risk that can be tolerated. Obviously, the more privileged a user is, the stronger the authentication method should be. Just imagine the havoc that an adversary masquerading as a Cloud administrator could cause! Authentication based on more than one type of credentials (called *multi-factor authentication*) can significantly increase the level of assurance. Given the various privileged users involved, it makes sense for a Cloud infrastructure service to support at least two-factor authentication. The most common form of two-factor authentication combines a password (i.e., what Alice knows) and a dynamically generated code retrievable from a device (i.e., what Alice has).

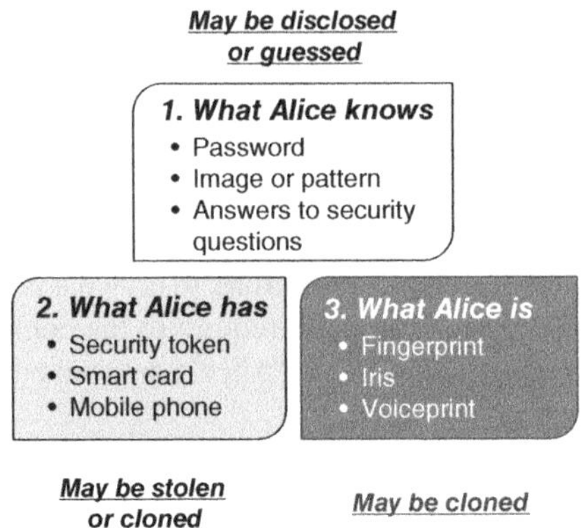

Figure 7.20 Credentials for user authentication.

In the presence of networking, it is necessary to use a cryptographic system. Any such system either uses shared secrets (*symmetric cryptography*) or relies on *public-key cryptography*.

The latter requires a pair of keys: one is known as the public key, which can be shared, and the other is known as the private key, which must be kept secret. Given a properly generated public key, it is computationally infeasible to derive the respective private key. A well-known and widely used public-key cryptographic system is *RSA*, which was developed at MIT in 1977 by Rivest, Shamir, and Adleman (hence the acronym) [23]. The property that it is computationally infeasible to derive the private key from the public key is based on the intractability of factoring a large number. One important feature of RSA is that the public- and private-key operations are commutative: a quantity encrypted with the private key can be decrypted with the public key. This feature allows us to use the scheme not only for secrecy, but also for signatures and authentication.

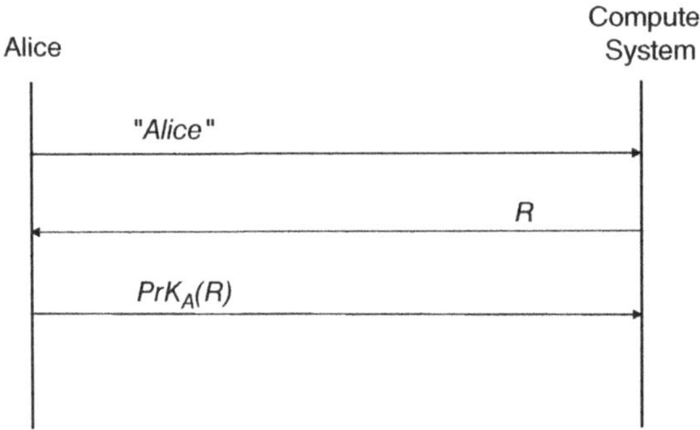

Figure 7.21 Public-key-based authentication (a simplified view).

Figure 7.21 illustrates the application of public-key cryptography to authentication. As shown, Alice announces herself. Upon receiving Alice's message, the authenticating system sends her a challenge R, which is typically a combination of a random number and a time stamp. Alice responds with $PrK_A(R)$, which is the challenge encrypted in her private key PrK_A. The system then decrypts $PrK_A(R)$ using Alice's public key. If the decrypted quantity is the same as the original challenge, the authentication has been successful. It goes without saying that availability of Alice's public key to the computer system is assumed. (How this is achieved is another matter, which we will discuss later.)

An important nuance here is that the key pair for authentication must be limited to that specific purpose only and not be used for signing as well. Signing involves the same operations as authentication, namely encrypting a document or its digest with Alice's private key, which can then be decrypted and verified by anyone else with her public key. If the same key is used for authentication and signing, it is possible to trick Alice into signing, for instance, an IOU by presenting it as a challenge—as shown in Figure 7.21.

Not only must the key pairs be different for the authentication and signing tasks, but the procedures for key generation and management need to be different, too. While private keys used for authentication and decryption may be escrowed (i.e., placed in a trusted third party's care), certain jurisdictions forbid key escrow of private keys used for digital signatures.[90] In Cloud Computing, keys are effectively escrowed, since privileged Cloud administrators can access stored private keys. Key escrow is problematic for regulatory compliance. To meet such requirements, a *hardware security module*—a piece of storage equipment that has a separate administrative interface from that of the hypervisor—is often used.

With public-key cryptography, there is a need for storing the private key on the one hand and for distributing the public key securely (i.e., proving the association of Alice and her public key) on the other hand. The former problem is somewhat simpler as it can be solved by the use of specialized devices, such as a *smart card*. The latter problem, however, has been a challenge since the time of the first known publication on public-key cryptography by Whitfield Diffie and Martin E. Hellman [24]. Ultimately, the industry *Public Key Infrastructure* (*PKI*) solution called for a management infrastructure in support of:

1. Issuing a *PKI certificate* that binds a public key to an identity along with a set of attributes.
2. Maintaining a database of the certificates.
3. Specifying mechanisms for verifying certificates.
4. Specifying mechanisms for revoking certificates (which includes storing them, too).

In this solution certificates serve as credentials. Loren Kohnfelder introduced some of its central elements in his Bachelor thesis [25] in 1978 at MIT, including the construct of a certificate, the idea of using the digital signature of a trusted authority (or *Certification Authority* (*CA*)) to seal binding, and the notion of certificate revocation. Naturally, a certificate should have a limited lifetime. This, however, is not good enough. While a certificate remains valid, things could go wrong to invalidate the binding. For example, an adversary could get hold of the private key. Certificate revocation allows a CA to void a certificate.

The use of a CA's signature to bind a public key to an identity gives rise to the question of how the signature is verified. If the signing algorithm is based on public-key cryptography, the question is the same as that of public-key distribution. So it can be solved by the same method: a CA is issued a certificate by another CA of a higher rank. The step can be repeated as many times as needed, resulting in a chain of certificates (or a chain of trust). Figure 7.22

---

[90] For instance, the State of New Jersey used to forbid private key escrow for signatures; the recent *STATE OF NEW JERSEY IT CIRCULAR Title: 181 Encryption and Digital Signatures Policy* (http://www.nj.gov/it/ps/14-26-NJOIT_181_Encryption_Digital_Signatures_Policy.pdf) goes even further, stating that "Keys used for digital signatures, digital certificates, and user authentication shall not be included in a key escrow arrangement with a third party."

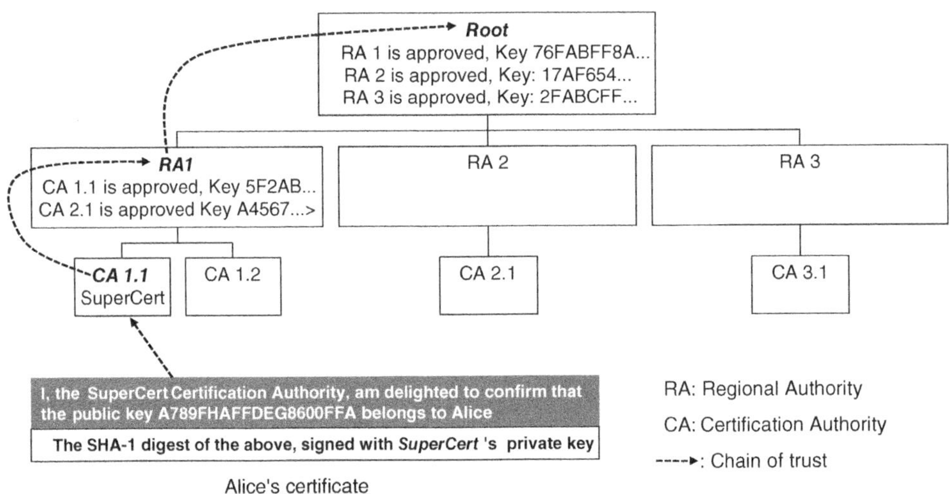

Figure 7.22 Conceptual illustration of the chain of trust.

shows a chain of trust conceptually. At the top of the chain necessarily is a *trust anchor* with a root certificate that is self-signed. Given that anyone can generate a key pair and a self-signed certificate, such trust anchors must be well-known and few. The hierarchical certification model has been standardized by ISO and ITU-T, which published Recommendation ITU-T X.509 [26]. An X.509 certificate captures, among other things, the holder's name and public key, the issuing CA's name and signature, the signature algorithm, the expiration time, and the issuing CA's certificate. Although there are other standards for certificate formats, X.509 is the most widely used. Part of its success is due to its built-in extensibility. Other organizations, notably the IETF, have specified extensions.

We would like to emphasize that web security depends on this standard: the TLS protocol uses X.509 certificates for server authentication.[91] Naturally, the X.509 dependency is carried over to Cloud Computing. The dependency is, in fact, stronger, because certificates are used not only for server but also client authentication.[92]

Public-key cryptography may be used without a PKI. A case in point is the SSH protocol, which is indispensible in Cloud Computing. (For one thing, SSH is the primary secure means for automated access to a virtual machine.) As specified in RFC 4252[93] and RFC 4253,[94] SSH supports the use of certificates for client and server authentication.

One problem with the SSH standard is that it has introduced multiple options. While the use of certificates is supported, it is not mandatory, and that results in rather problematic deployment scenarios. In particular, the server may send just the public key and a hash (also

[91] As does its predecessor, the *Secure Socket Layer (SSL) protocol*.

[92] The reader may wonder why certificate-based authentication has not taken off for human-user authentication. One main reason is that it is harder to make people safeguard their private keys. Yet, uncompromised private keys are fundamental to PKI security. Another main reason is that certificates cost money.

[93] https://tools.ietf.org/html/rfc4252

[94] https://tools.ietf.org/html/rfc4253

	Object 1	Object 2	Object 3	Object 4
Subject 1	read, write, execute	read, write, execute	read	read
Subject 2	read, execute	read, execute	null	null
Subject 3	read, execute	read	read, write	write

Figure 7.23 Access control matrix.

known as a *fingerprint*) of the key upon a connection request. The client may accept the public key blindly when first receiving it. Such a trust-on-first-use approach is subject to nasty attacks, but it is still practiced.

Our opinion is that in Cloud Computing, this practice has to change. A logical solution would be to mandate the use of certificates for both the client and server authentication. Unfortunately, this is impractical to date. Open-source software underpins Cloud Computing, but the certificate formats implemented in open-source SSH software (including *OpenSSH*,[95] which is bundled with all Linux distributions) are proprietary. Best practice is to keep a copy of the hash in a secure data store (such as the DNS, defined in RFC 4255[96]) that can be queried by the client during its very first contact with the server. The client verifies the fingerprint received from the server against that in the secure store and proceeds with the connection only if the fingerprints match.

7.4.3 Access Control

One way to keep track of who is authorized to access what is by maintaining a table (called an *access control matrix*) where the rows correspond to subjects and the columns correspond to data objects. The matrix reflects the protection state of a system. A subject is an active entity (e.g., a user or process), while an object is a passive one (e.g., a file). Each entry in the matrix (denoted A_{ij}) specifies the rights (such as read or write access) to a given object (denoted O_j) that a subject (denoted S_i) has. Figure 7.23 shows such a matrix, where subject 2 is least privileged, with access rights to only object 1 and object 2. In comparison subject 1 is more privileged, with access rights to all objects. In fact, subject 1 could be a system administrator. He only has read access to object 3 (say payroll data) and object 4 (say auditing trail) because of the least-privilege principle. These objects are readable and writable by subject 3 (which could very well be a process). The matrix provides a powerful model for designing access control systems and determining whether a system is secure [27].

The access control matrix is naturally sparse and so it requires special implementation considerations. In a nutshell, only non-empty matrix elements need to be stored, but their positions need to be recorded. Two common approaches are storing relevant cells by columns

[95] www.openssh.org

[96] https://tools.ietf.org/html/rfc4255

and rows, respectively. The column approach yields the *Access Control List* (*ACL*), and the row approach yields the *capability list.* We discuss these in more detail in the Appendix.

Access control can be either *discretionary* or *non-discretionary*, depending on who has the authority to set rights to an object. With *Discretionary Access Control* (*DAC*), the owner of an object may change the permissions for that object at will. DAC is implemented in most operating systems using access control lists. Under the scheme, an owner can revoke the rights, partially or fully, to an object given to any subject with particular ease. The owner just deletes the subject's rights in question from the object's access control list. Nevertheless, access control lists have limitations. Notably, they are unsuitable for handling cases where a user needs to delegate certain authority to another user for a period of time. Needless to say, dynamic delegation (which is essential in the Cloud Computing environment) has to rely on a separate mechanism.

The multitude of access control lists in a normal system also makes it difficult to ascertain privileges on a per-user basis. This is problematic when user privileges need to be updated quickly to reflect a sudden change of personnel or an incident. The use of the group construct adds another wrinkle. An access control list could contain both a user and a group to which the user belongs. If the user's right is revoked, but the group's right is not, the user can still access the object. Clearly, there is room for improvement!

In non-discretionary access control, a subject may not change the permissions for an object, even if the subject creates the object. The authority that can do so exists at a system level. *Mandatory Access Control* (*MAC*) is an example of restricting the flow of information between personnel of different ranks in military and civilian government agencies. MAC typically requires that every subject—as well as every object in a computer system—be assigned a security level within a hierarchy by a system-wide authority, according to a policy. Access eligibility is based on the dominance relation between the assigned security levels of the subject and the object. A subject can access an object if and only if the object is at the same or a lower level in the hierarchy. In the US military, for example, information is classified into *Top Secret*, *Secret*, *Confidential*, or *Unclassified.* In order to access information classified as Secret, a staff member must have an equivalent or higher security clearance level. Such a scheme assumes the use of a *Trusted Computing Base* (*TCB*) to enforce the policy over all subjects and objects under its control.

The first publication [28] on trusted computer system evaluation criteria (called the Orange Book, because of the color of its cover) from the US Department of Defense in the 1980s expressly defines MAC as "a means of restricting access to objects based on the sensitivity (as represented by a label) of the information contained in the objects and the formal authorization (i.e., clearance) of subjects to access information of such sensitivity." The definition is based on the *Bell–LaPadula model* [29], which has influenced the development of much computer security technology. The resulting systems are called multi-level security systems, because of the multiple security levels used in the model.

The Bell–LaPadula model essentially addresses control of information flow through the policy of no "read up" or "write down." Enforcement of the policy guarantees that information never flows downward. A useful outcome is protection against Trojan horse malware. Consider a scenario where Alice, a privileged user, ends up running an infected program. Without MAC, the associated process could access the file keeping personnel salary information in her organization (which is inaccessible to her adversary Andy), and write its content to another file (named "salary2," for example) accessible to Andy. With MAC, the process cannot write to salary2 at a security level lower than that of Alice; and if salary2 is at a high security level, Andy cannot read it.

The Bell–LaPadula model inspired the *Biba model* [30], which addresses the integrity of classified information. Specifically, the Biba model prescribes the policy of "read up" and "write down", which is actually forbidden by the Bell_LaPadula model. The rationale is that the integrity of an object can only be as good as the integrity of the least-trustworthy object among those contributing to its content. The Bell–LaPadula model also spurred many other developments to address its limitations. Of particular relevance to Cloud Computing are two important developments: *type enforcement* and *Role-Based Access Control* (*RBAC*), described below.

Type enforcement [31] is due to E. Boebert and D. Kain. According to [32], the idea was triggered by the problem of verifying that a multi-level security system meets the requirement that sensitivity levels be accurately included in printed output. Apparently a solution component involves the use of pipelines. The TE approach essentially addresses the inability to enforce pipelines in the Biba model. Consider an application for sending data over a network confidentially. A pipeline in this case would consist of a process preparing the original data (P_1), an intermediate process to encrypt the data (P_2), and a process for handling network transmission (P_3). The read-high policy can ensure the integrity of the data flow but cannot enforce the pipeline structure. In other words, any data readable by P_2 is also readable by P_3 as well. Yet P_2 could be bypassed and clear-text data could be transmitted to the network.

With type enforcement, each object is assigned a *type* attribute, and each subject a *domain* attribute. Whether a subject may access an object is governed by a centralized table called the *Domain Definition Table* (*DDT*) that has been pre-provisioned. The table includes, conceptually, a row for each type and a column for each domain. The entry at the intersection of a row and column specifies the maximum access permissions that a subject in that domain may have to an object of that type. The table, in effect, is another access matrix. It is checked whenever a subject seeks access to an object. Access is denied if the attempted access mode is not in the table. Type enforcement was later extended by L. Badger *et al.* [33] to become *Domain and Type Enforcement* (*DTE*), which introduces a high-level language for access control configuration and implicit typing of files based on their positions in the file hierarchy. TE and DTE are more general than traditional multi-level security schemes. They can enforce not only information flow confidentiality and integrity, but also assured pipelines and security kernels.

A prominent implementation of mandatory access control is the *SELinux* kernel extension to Linux based on the *Flask* effort[97] at the US National Security Agency (NSA). In addition to multi-level security and type enforcement, SELinux also supports multi-category security. So-called *categories* add another dimension to control. A category is a set of subjects that have equal rights according to a given policy. For instance, the category assignments and a policy could be such that two subjects, a and b, which belong to category X, may be allowed to communicate with each other and with subjects in the category X', but no subject in category X may communicate with a subject in category Y.

As far as implementation is concerned, categories are represented by their respective identifiers or labels. A central authority assigns a subject to a category, by associating the subject

[97] www.cs.utah.edu/flux/fluke/html/flask.html

with a respective label. The same procedure is carried out for the objects. With all other policies in place, the category-based policies provide an additional and independent set of controls.

SELinux underpins the *sVirt* service, aimed at enforcing virtual machine isolation. With sVirt, each VM is assigned, among other things, a unique label.[98] In addition, the same label is assigned to the resources (e.g., files and devices) associated with the virtual machine. Isolation of virtual machines is assured by forbidding a process to access a resource of a different label. If the hypervisor is implemented correctly, a virtual machine may not access the resources (such as the disk image file) of another machine. But no practical hypervisors can be proved secure and bug free. In light of the situation, sVirt adds extra protection.

The US NIST spearheaded the development of the role-based access control technology. (A comprehensive monograph [34] on RBAC, among other useful information, provides a detailed history, dating back to the invention of the cash register in 1879.) RBAC has its roots in the enterprise, where each individual has a well-defined function (or *role*), which, in turn, defines the resources the individual is authorized to access. As [34] reports, NIST first began studying access control in both commercial and government organizations in 1992, and concluded that there were critical gaps in technology. They specifically found that there was no implementation support for subject-based security policies and access based on the principle of least privilege.

To address these problems, [35] proposed the initial RBAC model, which was subsequently named—after its authors—the *Ferraiolo–Kuhn model*. This model formally defines the role hierarchies, subject–role activation, and subject–object mediation as well as their constraints, using set-theoretic constructs. At its center are three rules concerning (1) role assignment, (2) role authorization, and (3) transaction authorization. The first rule postulates that a *subject* can execute a transaction only if it has been assigned a role, which then, according to the second rule, must be authorized for the subject. In addition, according to the third rule, the transaction itself must be authorized. In other words, access to any resource can take place only through a *role*, which is defined by a set of permissions. (In contrast to the case of ACLs, removing a subject's role immediately disables the subject's access to a resource.) Another important feature of the model is that roles are hierarchical rather than flat (as is the case with ACL groups), and they can be inherited. The feature eases aggregation of permissions among roles. For instance, permissions assigned to a junior manager can be aggregated and assigned to a senior manager. Another important feature is that constraints (in the form of policy rules rooted in separation of duty[99] and least privilege) can be used to enforce high-level security goals, such as preventing conflicts of interest. For instance, policy rules can be defined to prevent a user from being assigned or activating simultaneously two conflicting roles (say system administrator and auditor).

Following the original proposal, RBAC research mushroomed both in the USA and internationally, and its applications began to emerge in areas such as banking, workflow management,

---

[98] *Label* is actually part of the security context of a subject or object in SELinux. In addition to "label" (confusingly called "level" in SELinux), the security context contains three more fields: user, role, and type.

[99] Separation of duty is the principle that more than one role is required for performing a critical task and no single individual is assigned all the roles. RBAC supports static and dynamic separation of duty. The key difference between the two is that in dynamic separation of duty the constraints are set at run time.

and health care. By the end of 2003, the industry had formed a consensus on the ANSI RBAC standard [36]. The standard has been widely accepted as the basis for national regulations. For instance, the US Health Insurance Portability and Accountability Act (HIPAA) prescribes the use of RBAC specifically. It is also worth noting that before the advent of RBAC, an access control model was considered either mandatory or discretionary. RBAC changes that view. Providing a flexible policy framework but no specific policies, it can support both discretionary and mandatory access control [37].

7.4.4 Dynamic Delegation

Dynamic delegation is a relatively new development. Traditional identity and access management systems can handle delegation that is set up beforehand (but never on the fly). Consider the following proverbial use case originated on the Web. Alice stores her photos at the website TonVisage.com, run by the company TonVisage. Access to these photos is password-protected. Only Alice knows her password, and she wants to keep it that way. But now Alice wants to print her photos—taken during a-once-in-a-lifetime trip to the Himalayas, and make a real, physical album. To achieve this, she plans to use a printing service offered by PrintYerFace.com, which promises, for a relatively small price, to edit Alice's photos professionally and print them on beautiful thick paper bound in an album. How can PrintYerFace get Alice's photos? Alice certainly does not want to divulge her TonVisage login and password to anyone. Perhaps she could be asked to mail her photos in. This, however, would be an inconvenience to her. It would also be a burden to TonVisage given the storage space needed for the photos and the company's business plan for adding a million users each year. In addition, the competition is there: Alice, for instance, can put her photos on a stick and walk to a local print shop. Commonsense dictates that things should be made as simple as possible for Alice: a temporary permission for reading her photos of the Himalayas at TonVisage.com is all that she should pass to PrintYerFace.

To support the use case, the *OAuth* community effort[100] developed the initial open solution in 2007. It's not that a solution didn't exist; there were actually, too many proprietary solutions employed by the so-called Web 2.0 companies such as Google, AOL, Yahoo!, and Flickr. The solution (known as OAuth 1.0) was later brought to the IETF and became the basis of OAuth 2.0, the formal standard developed eventually under a specifically chartered working group there.[101] The OAuth effort in the IETF attracted much interest. The Web 2.0 companies participating in the community work were soon joined by network equipment vendors and major telecommunications providers. Over time, new applications far more serious than printing of photographs have emerged, in particular automated management of virtual machine life cycles in Cloud Computing.

The first OAuth output of the IETF is an informational RFC on OAuth 1.0.[102] Although not an official standard, it was intended as an implementation specification and it has been used as such. The RFC differs from the original community specification chiefly in that it has

[100] The history is documented at http://OAuth.net/.

[101] http://datatracker.ietf.org/wg/OAuth/charter

[102] http://tools.ietf.org/html/rfc5849

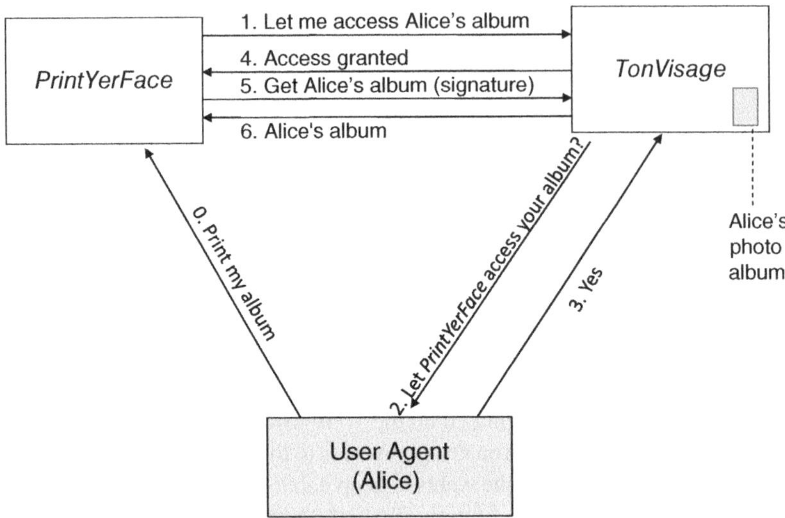

Figure 7.24 Conceptual OAuth 1.0 workflow.

addressed some security problems by making TLS mandatory in cases where it is necessary, clarifying the use of time stamps and other nonces, and improving cryptographic signatures.

Getting back to Alice's use case, Figure 7.24 shows conceptually how TonVisage can obtain her permission to gain access to her photos based on OAuth 1.0. The initial request from Alice to PrintYerFace to print her album was not part of the standard exchange (because the request itself did not need any new standardization), which is why we assign it a sequence number of zero. On receiving her request, PrintYerFace, in turn, requests access to Alice's photo album at TonVisage in message 1. Now TonVisage needs to obtain Alice's permission to actually pass the album to PrintYerFace, which is achieved by exchanging messages 2 and 3.

There are two major issues here, as far as the authentication of the subjects involved is concerned: first, TonVisage needs to understand that messages 2 and 3 are part of the conversation with Alice (and not someone impersonating her); second, TonVisage must know that it is actually receiving a request from and releasing information to PrintYerFace. The first issue is dealt with simply by authenticating Alice by her password with TonVisage. The second issue is addressed by having TonVisage and PrintYerFace share a set of long- and short-term cryptographic secrets. A long-term shared secret allows PrintYerFace to authenticate to TonVisage; a short-term shared secret allows PrintYerFace to prove that it has proper authorization. Dynamically generated by TonVisage, the short-term secret is returned to PrintYerFace in message 4. Using a combination of the long- and short-term secrets to sign its request for Alice's album, PrintYerFace can finally get the album as shown in messages 5 and 6.

The OAuth 1.0 scheme, however, has drawbacks. For one thing, PrintYerFace (i.e., the client in the OAuth 1.0 jargon) needs to acquire different kinds of long-term and temporary credentials and use a combination of them to generate signatures. This proves, too complex to be implemented correctly by web application developers. In addition, OAuth 1.0 leaves much to implementations; the specification still warns of a legion of potential catastrophes that sloppy implementations may engender. For one thing, the confidentiality of the requests is not provided by the protocol, and so the requests can be seen by eavesdroppers. In addition, if TonVisage (i.e., the *server* in the OAuth 1.0 terminology) is not properly authenticated, transactions can be hijacked. Furthermore, to compute signatures, the shared secrets used for signing must be available to OAuth code in plain text. This requirement is, unfortunately, too easy to implement by storing the secrets in plain text on servers. If this is done, an attacker who breaks into the server will be able to perform any action by masquerading as the clients whose shared secrets are obtained in the attack.

If this were not enough, more potential problems arise because the actual OAuth code on the client host typically belongs to a third party. This can be mitigated if the server uses several factors in authentication, but again it is not part of the protocol specification, it's just something a "smart" server should do. The proverbial phishing attack is yet another evil that can be overcome only by users who now need to be "smart" to understand what sites they are dealing with. Other security problems have to do with the length of secrets and their time-to-live. Again, without confidentiality, eavesdroppers can collect authenticated requests and signatures and then mount an offline attack to recover the secrets.

These are by no means all known security problems, but it should be clear by now why OAuth 1.0 needed a serious follow-up. A new framework and protocol can not only address security problems but also support new use cases, such as automated life cycle management of virtual machines. New use cases entail new requirements, in particular the flexibility to use a separate, dedicated server to handle authentication and authority delegation. Because of the requirement, the OAuth 2.0 framework as specified in IETF RFC 6749[103] includes four actors. In addition to the resource owner (e.g., Alice), client, and server employed in OAuth 1.0, another server specific to authorization is introduced. The new server naturally is called the authorization server, while the original server is qualified as the resource server. The introduction of the authorization server has actually been motivated by Cloud Computing, which may involve multiple resource servers that rely on the same authorization server. The authorization server provides services through service endpoints in terms of the *Uniform Resource Identifiers* (*URIs*).

Figure 7.25 shows conceptually the OAuth 2.0 workflow for the same use case. It is similar to the OAuth 1.0 workflow, especially if TonVisage also serves as the authorization server. The major difference lies in how PrintYerFace proves that it has Alice's authorization. Instead of providing a signature as in the case of OAuth 1.0, PrintYerFace shows an *access token* issued by the authorization server. The token represents a set of temporary rights. Moreover, it may not be bound to a particular client. Such an access token is known as a *bearer token*. The holder of a valid bearer token may access the associated resources by providing the token alone. An analogy here is a concert ticket. It is thus essential that the bearer tokens be properly protected, both in motion and at rest. Making the tokens as short-lived as possible, of course, helps contain any damage caused by disclosure.

Obviously, upon receiving a resource request, the resource server must validate the access token included and ensure that (a) it has not expired and (b) its scope covers the requested resource. How the resource server validates the access token is outside the scope of OAuth 2.0.

[103] http://tools.ietf.org/html/rfc6749

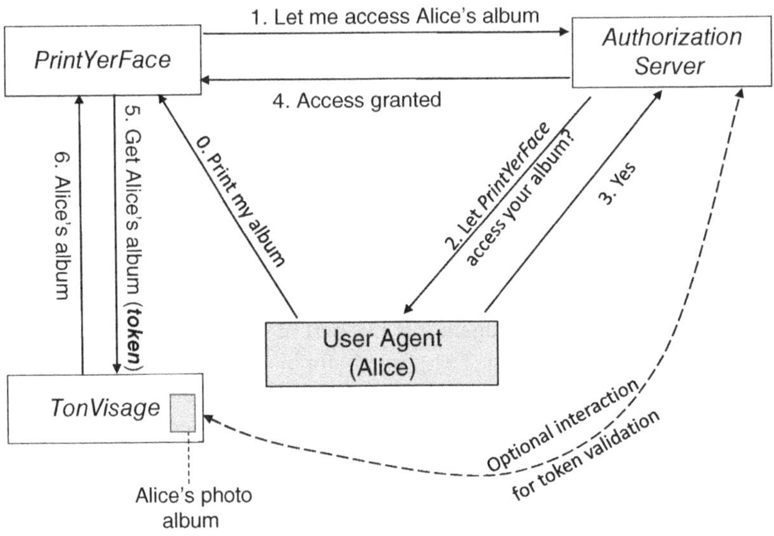

Figure 7.25 OAuth 2.0 conceptual workflow.

We can, however, observe that there are two options for where token validation is actually done:

- *Resource server*. In this case, the token needs to be in a standard format and capture verifiable information. A standard is the *JSON Web Token* (*JWT*)[104] specification from the IETF. The JWT representation is particularly compact, which allows so-represented access tokens to be carried within HTTP authorization headers or URI query parameters. (The latter option is not recommended though; the URI parameters are likely to be logged.) The representation also allows critical information to be signed and encrypted.
- *Authorization server*. In this case, the token format is dictated by the authorization server since it is responsible for both issuance and validation of access tokens. The authorization server may provide the token validation service through a specific endpoint.

Both options are relevant to Cloud Computing, and we will return to them later in the case study of OpenStack Keystone.

7.4.5 Identity Federation

Identity federation, first introduced in the enterprise and web industries, allows a user to gain access to applications in different administrative domains without using domain-specific credentials or explicit re-authentication. This is achieved primarily by separating the identity management component from each application and outsourcing it to a general *Identity Provider* (*IdP*). The resulting distributed architecture entails the establishment of trust between the

[104] https://tools.ietf.org/html/rfc7519

application provider and the IdP, and trust between the user and the IdP. An application can then rely on the IdP to verify the credentials of a user, who, in turn, can enjoy the convenience of fewer credentials and single sign-on. In the nomenclature of identity federation, the user is known as the *principal* (or *claimant* or *subject*) and application the *relying party*.

An essential requirement here is that multiple service providers use a common set of mechanisms to discover the identities of users, relying parties, and identity providers. It is also essential that sensitive information exchanged among these entities, and possibly across multiple domains, be secure (e.g., that confidentiality and integrity are protected). Several mechanisms in support of identity federation exist. In the Appendix, we will review three mechanisms of particular importance: the *Security Assertion Markup Language (SAML)*, *OpenID*,[105] and *OpenID Connect*[106] (which is actually an application of OAuth 2.0).

7.4.6 OpenStack Keystone (A Case Study)

Keystone is the gatekeeper of OpenStack services, providing centralized authentication and authorization. Not only virtual machine users but also OpenStack services are subject to its control. It provides core services called the *identity service* and the *token service*.

The identity service handles basic authentication of users and management of the related data. A user may be a person or a process. User authentication based on passwords is supported natively, but it is possible to use other authentication methods through external plug-ins. In addition to the user, Keystone supports the constructs of domain, project, group, and role. The first three constructs have to do with the organization of personnel and resources, with domain at the highest level. Accordingly, a project, which encapsulates a set of OpenStack resources, must belong to exactly one domain. Similarly, a group, which is made up of users, must belong to exactly one domain. The role construct is a different story. Representing a set of rights, it provides the basis for access control. A user must have a role assigned in order to access a resource, and the role is always assigned on a project or domain. Keystone uses a single namespace for roles. A well-known role is *admin*. When it comes to users, the identity service also supports identity federation to allow an organization to reuse its existing identity management system, saving the need for provisioning in Keystone the existing users of the organization. Keystone has the flexibility to support multiple identity federation protocols, such as SAML 2.0 and OpenID Connect. Support for SAML 2.0 is already available.

Central to the *token service* is the notion of a token. Figure 7.26 shows a simplified workflow to illustrate its function. Again, we consider the case of provisioning a virtual machine. The user is authenticated by Keystone first before gaining access to Nova or another service. Upon successful authentication, the user is given a temporary token that denotes a set of rights. From this point on, to get a service, the user (or rather the user agent Horizon) encloses the token in the service request. The user can receive the service only if the token is validated and the rights represented by the token comply with the access policy of the service. If the token has expired, the user can obtain a new token and try to get the service again.

As shown in Figure 7.26, Nova asks Keystone to validate the token as Keystone is responsible for both token generation and token validation. This is not the only way to do things though. We

[105] http://openid.net

[106] http://openid.net/connect/

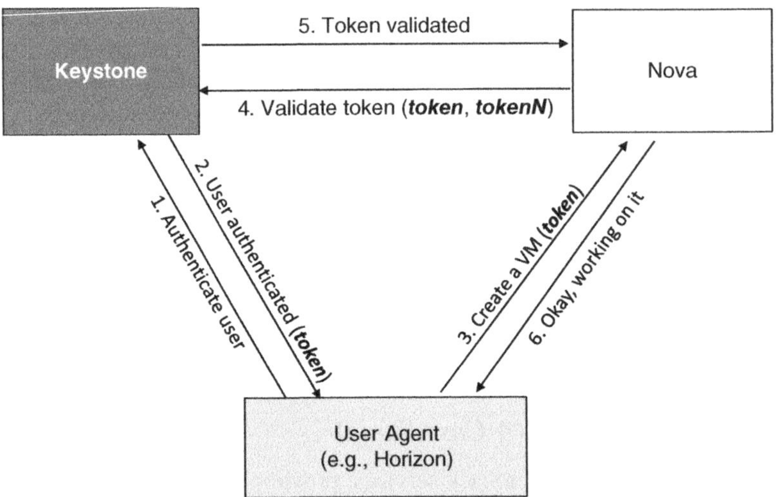

Figure 7.26 A simplified workflow for VM provisioning.

will discuss another approach and the trade-offs later. For now, it is important to note that when asking Keystone to validate the user token, Nova (or any other service) also needs to provide its own token (denoted *tokenN* in the figure) to authenticate itself. Nova acquires a token the same way as an end user does. It needs to pass authentication. But there is a difference. Nova cannot enter the password or other types of credential interactively as a human being. It can only retrieve its credentials stored at a pre-set location. The simplest solution is to keep the credentials in a file. Indeed, this is what is done throughout OpenStack as a default. In the case of Nova, there is a specific configuration file and the password for authentication to Keystone is there in plain text! We will discuss the basic mechanism for storing passwords in the Appendix. The mechanism shields passwords from even the most privileged administrator (i.e., root). But it works only when the authentication process is interactive.

To provision a virtual machine, Nova actually needs services from other OpenStack components. The additional steps are shown in Figure 7.27. *Glance* keeps a registry of images (including the URI of a particular image in block storage), while *Swift* is the object storage where images are stored as objects. When requesting a service from another component, Nova encloses the user token as well. This is necessary simply because each OpenStack component runs independently in favor of scalability. The token allows Glance and Swift to know the intended user and its privileges. Such a token-based approach has an important quality: improved usability without sacrificing security. The user can sign on once and access multiple services with neither explicit re-authentication nor disclosure of the password. Finally, as done by Nova earlier, Glance and Swift, respectively, have to ask Keystone to validate the token, and they have to provide their own tokens (denoted *tokenG* and *tokenS*, respectively) when doing so.

A token typically captures the issuance time, expiration time, and user information. It may also define the *scope*—the information about roles concerning a domain. A token is called "unscoped" if it does not contain such information. Such a token is useless for resource access,

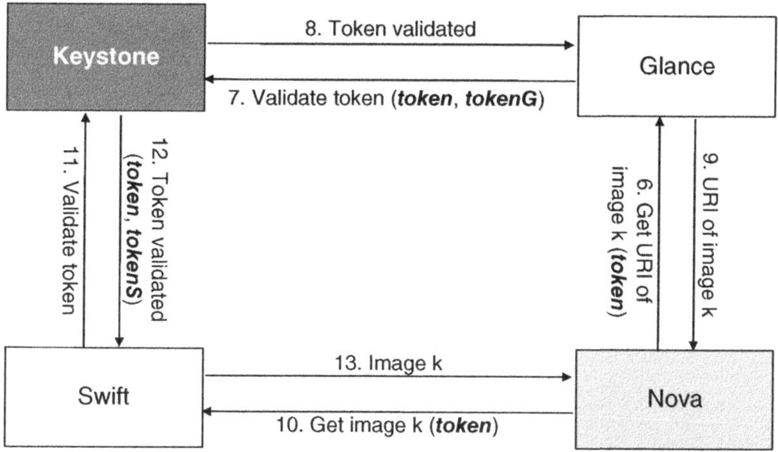

Figure 7.27 Additional steps for VM provisioning.

but it can be used as a stepping stone to discover accessible projects and then have it exchanged for a *scoped* token. A token may even capture a catalog of services to which the user is entitled.

By now, it should be clear that Keystone tokens are *bearer* tokens. As the basis for service access, they must be protected from disclosure, forgery, and alteration. Disclosure protection is a huge subject itself, hinging on comprehensive communication and information security. Forgery prevention and integrity protection are a different matter, affected by the structure and format of tokens. While custom tokens can be used through external modules, Keystone natively supports three types of tokens as of the Juno release respectively named *Universally Unique IDentifier* (*UUID*), *Public Key Infrastructure* (*PKI*), and *compressed PKI*.

A UUID token is a randomly generated string that serves as a reference to a piece of information stored in a persistent token database. By itself, it is meaningless. A service has to invoke Keystone to verify any received UUID tokens. (This is, in fact, what we saw in the workflows earlier.) A UUID token is valid if there is a not-yet-expired matching token in the database. The constraint that only Keystone can verify tokens makes it a potential bottleneck. There is, however, an upside. The size of a UUID token is small and fixed (i.e., 128 bits) so that it will never cause an API call to fail in practice.[107] In addition, it is relatively hard to forge a valid UUID token. Keystone uses UUID version 4 as specified in IETF RFC 4122.[108] Such a UUID has 122 bits pseudo-randomly generated. This means that the probability for creating a UUID that is already in the database is 2^{-122}. Finally, altering an existing token gives rise to a brand new one. Again, the probability for the new token to be in the database is 2^{-122}.

Unlike a UUID token, a PKI token is not merely a pointer to a data structure, but a data structure itself. This structure stores the user identity and entitlement information. To prevent modification of the contents, the data structure contains a digital signature. An immediate

[107] OpenStack API server implementations build on existing open-source HTTP server software. Although the HTTP standard imposes no limits on the size of a header field, such software does so for operational and security reasons. For example, the Apache 2.4 server by default limits the size of a header field to 8190 bytes.

[108] http://tools.ietf.org/html/rfc4122.html#section-4.4

```
{
    "token": {
        "expires_at": "2017-05-27T22:52:58.852167Z",
        "issued_at": "2017-05-27T21:52:58.852167Z",
        "methods": ["password"],
        "domain": {
                "id": "3a5140aecd974bf08041328b53a62458",
                "name": "Wonderland"
        },
        "roles": [{
                "id": "9fe2ff9ee4384b1894a90878d3e92bab",
                "name": "admin"}
        ],
        "user": {
            "domain": {
                "id": "3a5140aecd974bf08041328b53a62458",
                "name": "Wonderland"
            },
            "id": "3ec3164f750146be97f21559ee4d9c51",
            "name": "Alice"
        }
    }
}
```


Figure 7.28 An example token (unsigned).

benefit of such a token is that it is verifiable by a service endpoint. So the concern about bottlenecks and weak scalability in the case of UUID tokens is gone. Specifically, a PKI token is a *Cryptographic Message Syntax* (*CMS*)[109] string (encoded in base-64[110] notation). This token contains a digitally-signed block of data. The specifics of the data are context-dependent. As a result, the token size varies. Figure 7.28 shows, as an example, a token in JSON before signing. Note that it includes the obligatory information on the list of methods used for user authentication. In addition, to allow an authenticated user with a token to get another token of a different scope, *token* is recognized as an authentication method as well. When an authenticated user does so, the list of authentication methods will include both "password" and "token."

By default, RSA-SHA256 is the algorithm used to produce a signature in Keystone. This means that the digest of the data block to be signed is computed using the SHA256 algorithm[111] and the signature is computed by encrypting the digest using an RSA private key. A PKI token is valid if the signature is valid, among other things.[112] To facilitate signature validation by another service endpoint, Keystone supports retrieval of the signing and other relevant certificates through its API.

One characteristic of a PKI token is its large size. A token could easily be several thousand bytes in size. Especially if the token includes a catalog of the services accessible to the user,

[109] See the corresponding IETF specification at https://tools.ietf.org/html/rfc5652.

[110] See the corresponding IETF specification at https://tools.ietf.org/html/rfc4648.

[111] See the corresponding IETF specification https://tools.ietf.org/html/rfc6234.

[112] Other token validation criteria are that the expiration time has not passed, and the token has not been revoked.

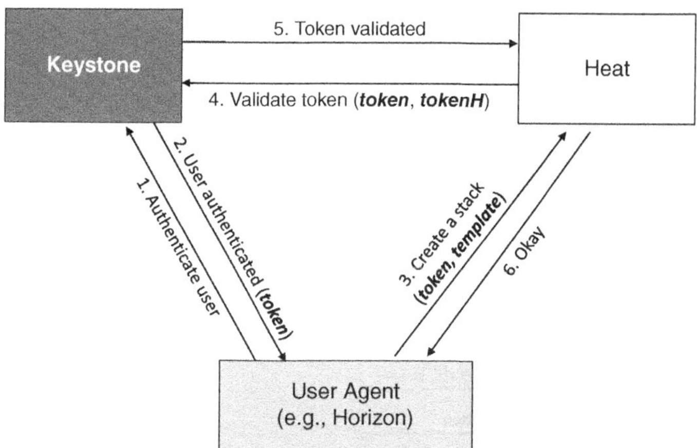

Figure 7.29 A simplified workflow for auto-scaling.

its size could reach the practical limit of an HTTP header and break the operation. To reduce the token size, Keystone supports compression though.

Unfortunately, there is no guarantee that the size of a compressed PKI token always stays within the limits of an HTTP header. Because of the tradeoffs between UUID and PKI tokens, the default token type in Keystone is not a settled matter. It was UUID from the beginning, became PKI in the Grizzly release, and swung back to UUID since the Juno release.[113]

So far, we have seen how Keystone tokens enable single sign-on and basic delegation. As useful as they are, these tokens are short-lived (by design). They might expire (and in real life actually tend to expire!) when the deadline for an action at hand is unknown. (Imagine the task of launching a new server when the CPU utilization of the existing server reaches 60%. Depending on the clients' activity, this may happen in a few minutes, a few years, or never!)

Thus we need some other mechanism to obtain tokens dynamically. For this purpose, Keystone introduces the construct of *trust* to capture who delegates authority, who is the delegate, the scope and duration of the delegation, and other pertinent information.

Trust is not unlike a power-of-attorney document. The delegating entity creates it and hands it to the delegate. Now the delegate presents the trust to get a token. The idea underlying this arrangement is that a token is short-lived but the trust is long-lived.

In Keystone parlance, the delegating entity is called the *trustor* and the delegate, the *trustee*. Only the trustor can create a trust. Based on the trust, the trustee (but no one else) can obtain a fresh token in order to carry out a delegated task. The token will have the same scope as the trust. Such a token is known as a trust token. Its structure is the same as that of a normal token, if not for an additional data block to carry trust-related information. Naturally, the trust may not be expired when used for getting a token.

To explore how trusts work, let us go through the related part of the workflow for spinning up a new stack (e.g., a virtual machine as a degenerate case) automatically. Figure 7.29 shows a

[113] OpenStack releases are named alphabetically. The releases to data are available at https://wiki.OpenStack.org/wiki/Releases/.

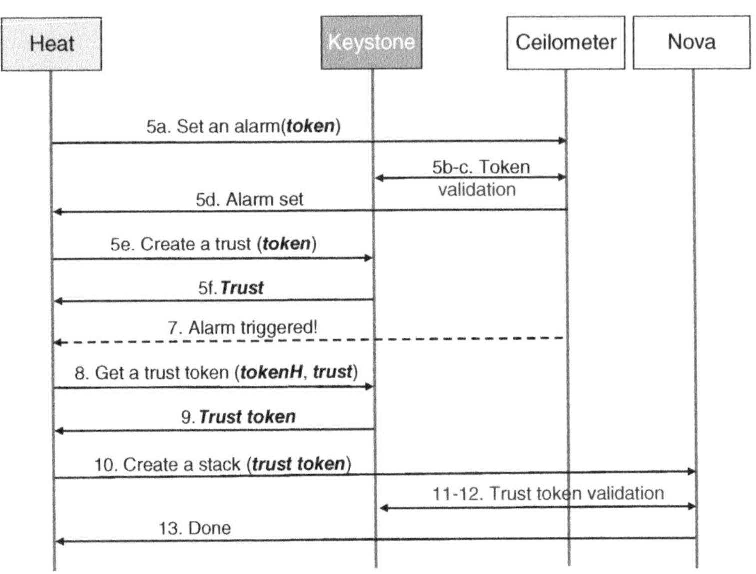

Figure 7.30 Additional steps for auto-scaling.

greatly simplified workflow for instantiating a template to provision a stack and for scaling-out automatically when the running stack is overloaded. Steps 1 to 5 are essentially the same as before when Heat is not involved. After step 5, some heavy lifting will take place to launch the first stack. Here we will focus on the extra steps required to set up the stage for automation. These steps are shown in Figure 7.30. First we set an alarm (steps 5a to 5d), then we create a trust to allow Heat (as the service user) to have Alice's delegation (steps 5e and 5f). After these steps, Heat is in the monitoring mode, waiting for the alarm to go off at Ceilometer. Finally, an alarm notification arrives as shown in step 7.[114] Upon receiving the notification, Heat proceeds to get a trust token as shown in step 8. Here Heat needs to present its own token to prove that it is the trustee identified in the trust. Upon successful authentication, Heat receives a trust token, which allows it to launch a new virtual machine on behalf of Alice.

Figure 7.31 shows an example of a trust. The structure is pretty much self-explanatory except for the "impersonation" field. If it is set to false, the user field of the trust token based on the trust will represent the trustee. Otherwise, the user field will represent the trustor. In other words, the trustee impersonates the trustor when presenting the trust token for validation. This is the case in our example where the trust token has Alice as the user. Impersonation is enabled by default in Keystone, given the goal of providing automated life cycle management of a user's stacks. Two other fields also have default values set toward the same goal: "*expires_at*" and "*remaining_uses*". The "expires_at" field, if unspecified, will have the effect that the trust is valid until explicitly revoked. Similarly, the "remaining_uses" field, if unspecified, will have the effect that the trust can be used to get a token an unlimited number of times. Finally, trusts

[114] A dotted line is used to reflect the fact that a separate notification mechanism, which does not involve Keystone for authentication, is used.

```
{
    "trust": {
        "expires_at": "2016-05-27T21:52:58.852167Z",
        "id": "c703057be878458588961ce9a0ce686b",
        "impersonation": true,
        "project_id": "fb49a0ecd60c4d2092643b4cfe272106",
        "remaining_uses": null,
        "roles": [{
        "id": "9fe2f79ee4384b1894a9083bd3e92bab",
        "name": "admin"}
        ],
        "trustee_user_id": "29beb2f1567642eb810b042b6719ea88",
        "trustor_user_id": "3ec3164f750146be97f21559ee4d9c51"
    }
}
```


Figure 7.31 An example trust.

are immutable once created. To update a trust relationship, the trustor deletes the old trust and creates a new one. Upon deletion of the old token, any tokens derived from it are revoked. If the trustor loses any delegated privileges, the trust becomes invalid.

Support for identity federation results in a new authentication workflow. When receiving an authentication request, Keystone, instead of handling the request itself, redirects it to the external identity provider. Upon receiving the redirected request, the identity provider performs the steps to authenticate the user, and then redirects the result as an attestation to Keystone. If the user is attested authentic, Keystone generates an unscoped token, based on which the user can find out the accessible projects and obtain another token with a proper scope. Tokens generated for a federated user are distinct—they carry information related to federation, such as the name of the identity provider, the identity federation protocol, and the associated groups.

Overall, the token service supports generation, revocation, and validation not only of tokens but also of trusts. As a centralized service, it has been influenced by OAuth 2.0 and can be mapped directly to the latter's authorization server. Also similar are the money-like quality of tokens—that any bearer of a token may use it—and the use of JSON for token description. Nevertheless, the Keystone token service has its own protocol (in the form of a REST API) because very different use cases are targeted. The use cases involve essentially two actors (i.e., the user and Cloud infrastructure service provider), and they are high in automation but low in interactivity. As a result, a different user consent model for delegation suffices—a user's consent to delegate is implied as soon as the user is authenticated to get a service.

References

[1] Blatter, A. (1997). *Instrumentation and Orchestration*, 2nd edn. Shirmer, Boston, MA.

[2] Hogan, M., Liu, F., Sokol, A., and Tong, J. (2011) NIST Cloud Computing Standards Roadmap—Version 1.0. Special Publication 500-291. National Institute of Standards and Technology, US Department of Commerce, Gaithersburg, Maryland.

[3] Liu, F., Tong, J., Mao, J., *et al.* (2011) NIST Cloud Computing Reference Architecture. Special Publication 500-292. National Institute of Standards and Technology, US Department of Commerce, Gaithersburg, Maryland.

[4] Stroustrup, B. (2013) *The C++ Programming Language*, 4th edn. Addison-Wesley, New York.

[5] Birman, K.P. (2012) *Guide to Reliable Distributed Systems: Building High-Assurance Applications and Cloud-Hosted Services*. Springer-Verlag, London.

[6] Lapierre, M. (1999) *The TINA Book: A Co-operative Solution for a Competitive World*. Prentice-Hall, Englewood Cliffs, NJ.

[7] Thompson, M., Belshe, M., and Peon, R. (2014) Hypertext Transfer Protocol version 2. Work in progress. https://tools.ietf.org/html/draft-ietf-httpbis-http2-12 IETF.

[8] Erl, T. (2005) *Service-Oriented Architecture: Concepts, Technology, and Design*. Prentice-Hall, Englewood Cliffs, NJ.

[9] Culler, D.E. (1986) Data Flow Architectures. MIT Technical Memorandum MIT/LCS/TM-294, February 12. http://csg.csail.mit.edu/pubs/memos/Memo-261-1/Memo-261-2.pdf.

[10] Slutsman, L., Lu, H., Kaplan, M.P., and Faynberg, I. (1994) Achieving platform-independence of service creation through the application-oriented parsing language. Proceedings of the IEEE IN'94 Workshop, Heidelberg, Germany, pp. 549–561.

[11] Amin, K., Hategan, M., von Laszewski, G., *et al.* (2004) GridAnt: A client-controllable grid workflow system. 37th Hawaii International Conference on System Science, pp. 210–220. (Also available in an Argonne National Laboratory preprint: ANL/MCS-P1098-1003 at www.mcs.anl.gov/papers/P109Apdf.)

[12] Kalenkova, A. (2012) An algorithm of automatic workflow optimization. *Programming and Computer Software*, **38**(1), 43–56. Springer, New York.

[13] Rey, R.F. and Members of the Technical Staff of AT&T Bell Laboratories (1983) *Engineering and Operations in the Bell System*, 2nd edn. AT&T Bell Laboratories, Murray Hill, NJ.

[14] Ebner, G.C., Lybarger, T.K., and Coville, P. (1991) AT&T and TÉLÉSYSTÉMES partnering in France. *AT&T Technical Journal*, **71**(5), 45–56.

[15] International Telecommunication Union (1998) International Standard 9596-1, ITU-T Recommendation X.711: Information Technology—Open Systems Interconnection—Common Management Information Protocol: Specification.

[16] Dick, K. and Shin, B. (2001) Implementation of the Telecom Management Network (TMN) at WorldCom—Strategic Information Systems Methodology Focus. *Journal of Systems Integration*, **10**(4), 329–354.

[17] Schneiderman, A. and Casati, A. (2008) *Fixed Mobile Convergence*. McGraw-Hill, New York.

[18] Anderson, T.W., Busschbach, P., Faynberg, I., *et al.* (2007) The emerging resource and admission control function standards and their application to the new triple-play services. *Bell Labs Technical Journal*, **12**, 5–21.

[19] International Telecommunication Union (2011) ITU-T Recommendation Labs.: Resource and Admission Control Functions in Next Generation Networks, Geneva.

[20] Camarillo, G. and Garcia-Martin, M.A. (2008) *The 3G IP Multimedia Subsystem: Merging the Internet and the Cellular Worlds*, 3rd edn. John Wiley & Sons, Inc., Hoboken.

[21] European Telecommunications Standards Institute (2005) Resource and Admission Control Subsystem (RACS), Functional Architecture. ETSI ES 282 003, v.1.6.8, December. www.etsi.org/services_products/freestandard/home.htm.

[22] Wayner, P. (2013) Puppet or Chef: The configuration management dilemma. Network World. www.infoworld.com/article/2614204/data-center/puppet-or-chef–the-configuration-management-dilemma.html.

[23] Rivest, R.L., Shamir, A., and Adleman, L. (1978) A method for obtaining digital signatures and public-key cryptosystems. *Communications of the ACM*, **21**(2), 120–126.

[24] Diffie, W. and Hellman, M.E. (1976) New directions in cryptography. *IEEE Transactions on Information Theory*, **22**(6), 644–654.

[25] Kohnfelder, L.M. (1978) Towards a practical public-key cryptosystem. B.S. thesis, Massachusetts Institute of Technology.

[26] International Telecommunication Union (2012) Information Technology—Open Systems Interconnection—The Directory: Public-Key and Attribute Certificate Frameworks. ITU-T Recommendation X.509, December. www.itu.int.

[27] Bishop, M. (2014) Mathematical models of computer security. In Bosworth, S., Kabay, M.E., and Whyne, E. (eds), *Computer Security Handbook*, 6th edn. John Wiley & Sons Inc., Hoboken, Chapter 9.

[28] Brand, S.L. (1985) DoD 5200.28-STD Department of Defense Trusted Computer System Evaluation Criteria (Orange Book), National Computer Security Center, pp. 1–94.
[29] La Padula, L.J. and Bell, D.E. (1973) Secure Computer Systems: Mathematical Foundations. MTR-2547-VOL-1, Mitre Corporation, Bedford, MA.
[30] Biba, K.J. (1977) Integrity Considerations for Secure Computer Systems. MTR-3153-REV-1, Mitre Corporation, Bedford, MA.
[31] Boebert, W.E. and Kain, R.Y. (1985) A practical alternative to hierarchical integrity policies. Proceedings of the 8th National Computer Security Conference, Gaithersburg, MD.
[32] Boebert, W.E. and Kain, R.Y. (1996) A further note on the confinement problem. IEEE Security Technology '96, 30th Annual 1996 International Carnahan Conference, Lexington, Kentucky.
[33] Badger, L., Sterne, D.F., Sherman, D.L., *et al.* (1995) Practical domain and type enforcement for UNIX. Proceedings of IEEE Symposium on Security and Privacy, Okland, CA.
[34] Ferraiolo, D.D., Kuhn, R., and Chandramouli, R. (2003) *Role-based Access Control.* Artech House, Boston, MA.
[35] David, F. and Kuhn, R. (1992) Role-based access controls. Proceedings of 15th NIST/NCSC National Computer Security Conference, Baltimore, MD.
[36] American National Standards Institute (2004) Role Based Access Control. ANSI INCITS 359-2004, February, New York, NY.
[37] Bonneau Osborn, S., Sandhu, R., and Munawer, Q. (2000) Configuring role-based access control to enforce mandatory and discretionary access control policies. *ACM Transactions on Information and System Security (TISSEC)*, **3**(2), 85–106.

Appendix

Selected Topics

The purpose of this Appendix is to provide more information on selected topics that have been referenced earlier in the book:

- The first topic concerns the relevant operations and management standards developed in the IETF;
- The second topic is the development of modeling languages in general and the TOSCA standard in particular;
- The third topic is dedicated to the notion of the REST API in the context of the World-Wide Web architecture;
- The fourth topic covers the basic mechanisms that enable identity and access management.

A.1 The IETF Operations and Management Standards

The standards introduced here are the Simple Network Management Protocol (SNMP), the Common Open Policy Service (COPS), and the Network Configuration (NETCONF) protocol, respectively.

A.1.1 SNMP

The OSI approach to network management in the Internet was neither ignored nor completely abandoned. It was, indeed, simplified and constrained to focus on smaller, specific problems. Until fairly recently, the main objective of network management was *monitoring*—not configuration management. As we will soon see, the SNMP protocol ended up being much less than universal; a new set of protocols was needed for configuration management. In addition, access management (and overall security of network management) was not systematically approached until SNMPv3.

Cloud Computing: Business Trends and Technologies, First Edition. Igor Faynberg, Hui-Lan Lu and Dor Skuler.

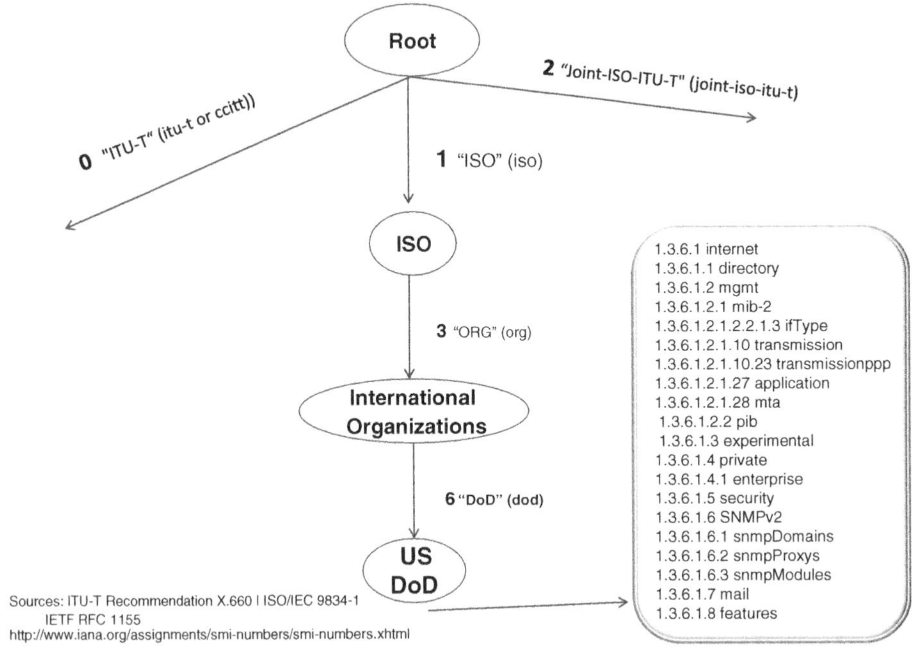

Figure A.1 The tree of SMI ASN.1 object identifiers.

The 1990 IETF RFC 1155[1] defines the *Structure of Management Information* (*SMI*). As in the OSI, the MIBs were defined using ASN.1, but the use of ASN.1 is restricted, as we will explain shortly. Each type of object has been assigned—via an *object identifier*—a name specified down to its encoding. An object identifier is assigned according to the administrative policies.

An object identifier is a path through a global naming tree structure.[2] The edges are labeled by Unicode strings, which in turn are encoded as integers. Each edge indicates the respective administrative domain (which may change as the tree is being traversed). Figure A.1 depicts the root of the tree with three edges, which are respectively administered by ITU-T (0), ISO (1), and ISO and ITU-T (2), jointly.

Under the ISO administration there is space for international organizations (3), which provided space (6) for the US Department of Defense. The rest of the SMI paths are listed on the right-hand side of the figure. The "internet (1.3.6.1)" subtree is reserved for objects managed by the *Internet Assigned Number Authority* (*IANA*).

To allow independent object definition, the "private space (1.3.6.1.4)" is defined, with the 1.3.6.1.4.1 space allocated to enterprise objects.

---

[1] www.ietf.org/rfc/rfc1155.txt

[2] RFC 1155 is somewhat imprecise (and, in any event, outdated) in describing the tree structure, for which reason we use the description of the ITU-T Recommendation X.660, as presented at www.itu.int/en/ITU-T/studygroups/2013-2016/17/Documents/Special-Topics/Jointly_administered_registers_as_defined_in_X660.pdf. The latter document contains all the present top namespace definitions.

Formally, all identifiers are defined through the *OBJECT IDENTIFIER* construct recursively—by referring to previously defined constructs. Thus, one writes:

```
internet OBJECT IDENTIFIER ::= {iso org (3) dod (6) 1};
private  OBJECT IDENTIFIER ::= {internet 4}; and
enterprise OBJECT IDENTIFIER ::= {private 1}.
```

RFC 1155 permits only the primitive (non-aggregate) ASN.1 types.[3] It restricts the use of constructor types to lists and tables, and defines a number of application-wide types (such as *NetworkAddress*, *IpAddress*, *Counter*—a 32-bit one, *TimeTicks*—in 0.01 sec intervals, etc.). RFC 1155 further defines the format of a MIB. The latter is a quintuple comprising:

1. Object name (a textual *OBJECT DESCRIPTOR* along with the OBJECT IDENTIFIER);
2. The object structure proper, called *syntax*, which must resolve to an allowed structure type;
3. A definition of the "semantics" of the object-type—written for people rather than machines to ensure "consistent meaning across all machines;"
4. Access (*read-only*, *read-write*, *write-only*, *or not-accessible*[4]);
5. Status (*mandatory*, *optional*, or *obsolete*).

The SNMP framework architecture is laid out in the RFC 3411,[5] which is part of the Internet Standard 62. The SNMP system is realized by exchanging the SNMP protocol messages among the SNMP entities. At least one of these entities is a manager; the others are present in the devices or network elements. In its more general form, the architecture of an entity is presented in Figure A.2.

An entity has the SNMP engine and applications. The engine executes the protocol and also takes care of the security services—in particular, confidentiality and authentication. Within an administrative domain, each engine (and hence each entity) is unique, and it is assigned a name—*snmpEngineID*.

The engine consists of the *Dispatcher, Message processing subsystem*, and *Access control subsystem*.

The dispatcher supports (concurrently) multiple protocol versions but provides a single abstract interface to SNMP applications.

The message processing subsystem[6] relies on the modules specific to the SNMP version.

Finally, the security subsystem provides the namesake services according to a given model. The model is characterized by the threats it protects and the protocols it employs. Only the *user-based model*[7] is mentioned explicitly, but the plan is to allow any model as a plug-in).

---

[3] Which are *NULL, INTEGER, OCTET STRING*, and *OBJECT IDENTIFIER*.

[4] Inaccessible really means "inaccessible to SNMP." One important example is a cryptographic key, which must be kept secret. Several such objects are defined in the SNMPv3 model (RFC 3414), but they are not accessible to the SNMPv3 protocol.

[5] www.ietf.org/rfc/rfc3411.txt

[6] The term *subsystem* refers to an all-encompassing abstract mechanism. When designed to deliver a specific set of services, it is called a *model*. A model is realized in an implementation.

[7] Described in the companion STD 62 RFC 3414 (www.rfc-editor.org/rfc/rfc3415.txt). This document is self-contained, comprehensive, and straightforward to read.

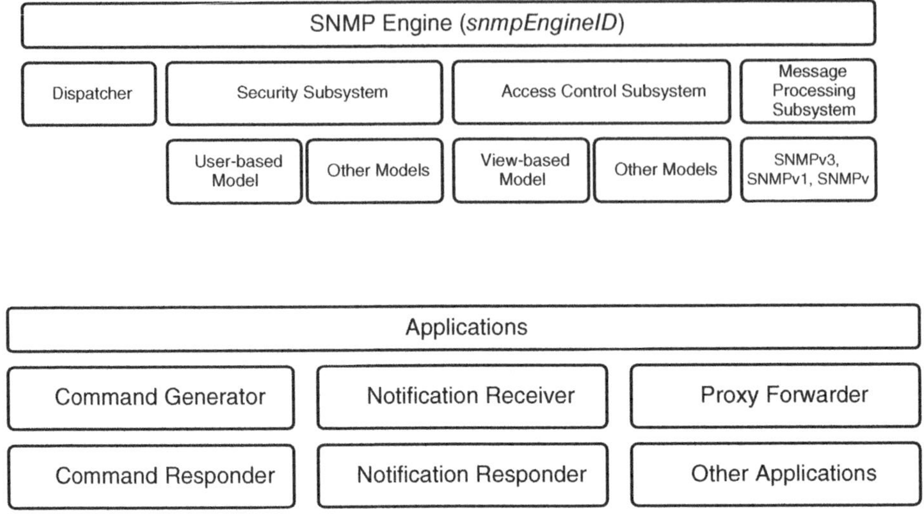

Figure A.2 SNMP entity (after RFC 3411).

Access control subsystem, which provides the authorization service (and thus may have been arguably considered a part of the security subsystem). Similarly to the security subsystem, the access control subsystem relies on one or more specific access control models. RFC 3415,[8] yet another part of STD 62, specifies the *view-based access control model*, which determines the access rights of a group, representing zero or more objects that have the same access rights. As the standard explains, "For a particular context, identified by *contextName*, to which a group, identified by *groupName*, has access using a particular *securityModel* and *securityLevel*, that group's access rights are specified with respect to *read-view*, *write-view*, and *notify-view*." Each view represents a set of object instances authorized for its respective action (i.e., reading or writing objects, or sending objects in a notification).

As far as applications within an SNMP entity go, they include *command generators*, which monitor and manipulate management data; *command responders*, which provide access to management data; *notification originators*, which initiate notification messages; *notification receivers*, which process asynchronous messages; and *proxy forwarders*, which merely forward messages toward the recipients. These applications are well-defined, but other applications are not excluded, so the architecture leaves a place to plug in an application.

A.1.2 COPS

COPS is specified in RFC 2748,[9] but the context for this work has been set in RFC 2753,[10] which provides the motivation, describes the terminology, and otherwise specifies the framework. We will introduce this context briefly.

[8] www.rfc-editor.org/rfc/rfc3415.txt

[9] www.ietf.org/rfc/rfc274Atxt

[10] www.rfc-editor.org/rfc/rfc2753.txt

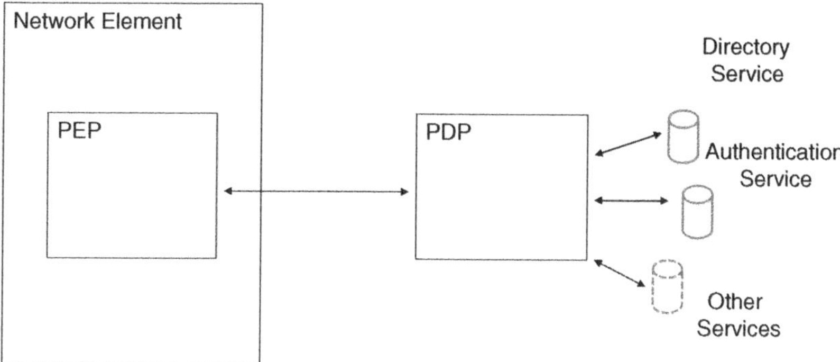

Figure A.3 Policy control architecture (after RFC 2753).

First of all, the objective of the framework is to describe the execution of policy-based control over the QoS admission control decisions, with the primary focus on the RSVP protocol as an example.[11]

Among the goals of the framework are support for pre-emption, various policy styles, monitoring, and accounting. Pre-emption here means the ability to remove a previously granted resource so as to accommodate a new request.[12] As far as the policy styles go, those to be supported include bi-lateral and multi-lateral service agreements and policies based on the notion of relative priority, as defined by the provider. Support for monitoring and accounting is effected by gathering the resource use and access data. The framework also states the requirement for fault tolerance and recovery in cases when a PDP fails or cannot be reached.

Figure A.3 presents the policy control architecture. Its main components are the PDP, where the policy-based decisions are made and the *Policy Enforcement Point* (*PEP*), which queries the PDP and ensures that the latter's directives are executed. The PEP is part of the network element in which admission control takes place. Figure A.3 depicts the general case where PDP is outside the network element; however, the PEP and PDP may be co-located within the same physical "box." To this end, the framework allows both a co-located PDP module—called a *local PDP* (*LPDP*)—and a remote PDP module to be used.

Interactions between the PEP and the PDP are typically triggered when the PEP acts on an event (such as making a decision on whether to admit a given packet). The PEP itself may also trigger the interactions by sending a notification. In the former case, the PEP queries the PDP, supplying the admission control information. The latter could be a *flowspec*, the amount of bandwidth requested, or a description of the event that triggered the policy decision request (or a combination of these). The PDP responds with the decision, and the PEP acts on it by accepting or denying the original request. PDP may also send additional information—unrelated to admission control—or respond with an error message.

[11] Later in this section, we will see how ETSI, ITU-T, and 3GPP further extended the framework to include not only other QoS resources (e.g., the *diffserv* code points) but also the whole range of other resources under an operator's control: private IP addresses, port numbers, NAT pinholes, etc.

[12] It is a bit more subtle than just robbing Peter to pay Paul. The objective here—as the authors surmise—is to optimize the network (and the service delivery) under extreme load conditions. Pre-emption also allows us to deal with deadlocks—the perennial problem of resource management.

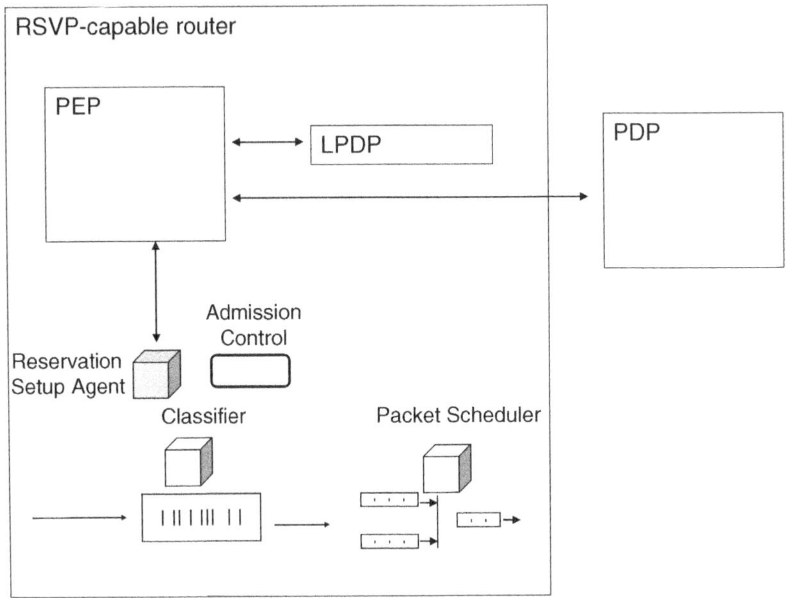

Figure A.4 Policy control in an RSVP router (after RFC 2753).

In order to formulate the decision, the PDP may, in turn, request additional information from the directory services or other services—most notably the *Authentication, Authorization, and Accounting* (*AAA*) services. Yet another function of the PDP is to export information relevant for monitoring and accounting purposes.

Meanwhile, RFC 2750[13] updated RSVP to include policy data as a payload in its protocol, to be processed by routers and PDPs, but otherwise opaque to every other entity. We use Figure A.4 to explain the interaction with RSVP.

When any RSVP-related event requires a policy decision, the reservation setup agent consults the PEP module. The latter first checks the LPDP—to obtain a partial policy decision (if available)—and then queries the PDP, attaching the partial decision fetched from the LPDP. The final policy decision is returned to the reservation setup agent.

A typical case is an admission control request (with which the associated policy elements are passed). The PDP may request, however, that at the same time the PEP raise a policy-related exception to the reservation setup agent. For example, the PDP may approve the request to proceed with the soft-state installation and forward the reservation upstream, but the session time may be limited, and so a respective notification regarding the path expiration would also need to travel upstream. This example illustrates the necessity of non-trivial interactions between COPS and RSVP.

Hence, whenever the PDP returns an error, it has to specify whether the event that generated the admission control request be processed as usual (but with the addition of error notification) or the processing be halted.

[13] www.rfc-editor.org/rfc/rfc2750.txt

Conversely, the PDP can itself initiate a communication (by issuing a notification) to the PEP when a decision made earlier needs to be changed or an error was detected. If the notification needs to propagate along the reservation path, the PEP has to convey this information to the reservation agent.

The actual COPS protocol, created for the general administration, configuration, and enforcement of policies, is consistent with the above framework.

Something intrinsically new about COPS—as compared with SNMP or CMIP—is that COPS employs a *stateful* client–server model, which is different from that of the remote procedure call. As in any client–server model, the PEP (client) sends *requests* to the remote PDP (server), and the PDP responds with the *decisions*. But all the requests from the client PEP are *installed* and remembered by the remote PDP until they are explicitly deleted by the PEP. The decisions can come in the form of a series of notifications to a single request. This, in fact, introduces a new behavior: two identical requests may result in different responses because the states of the system when the first and second of these requests arrive may be different—depending on which states had been installed. Another stateful feature of COPS is that PDP may "push" the configuration information to the client and later remove it.

The COPS stateful model supports two mechanisms of policy control, called respectively the *outsourcing model* and the *configuration model*. With the outsourcing mechanism, PEP queries PDP every time it needs a decision; when the configuration mechanism is employed, PDP provisions the policy decision within the PEP.

Unlike SNMP, COPS was designed to leverage self-identifying objects and therefore it is extensible. COPS also runs on TCP, which ensures reliable transport. Although COPS may rely on TLS, it also has its own mechanisms for authentication, protection against replays, and message integrity.

The COPS model was found very useful in telecommunications, where it was both applied and further extended for QoS support. As far as Cloud Computing is concerned, the primary application of COPS is SDN.

A.1.3 Network Configuration (NETCONF) Model and Protocol

Figure A.5 presents the NETCONF architecture.

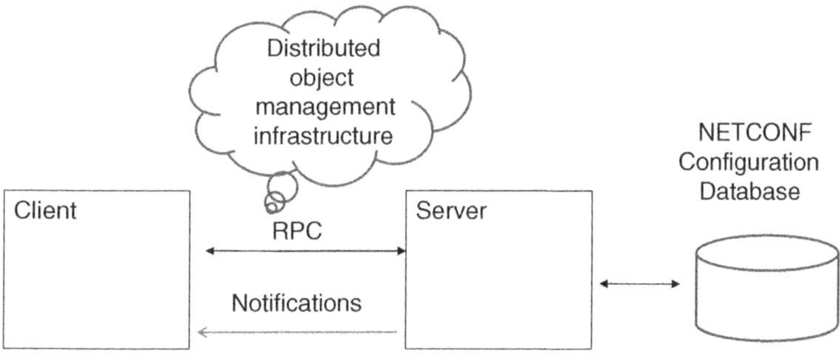

Figure A.5 NETCONF architecture.

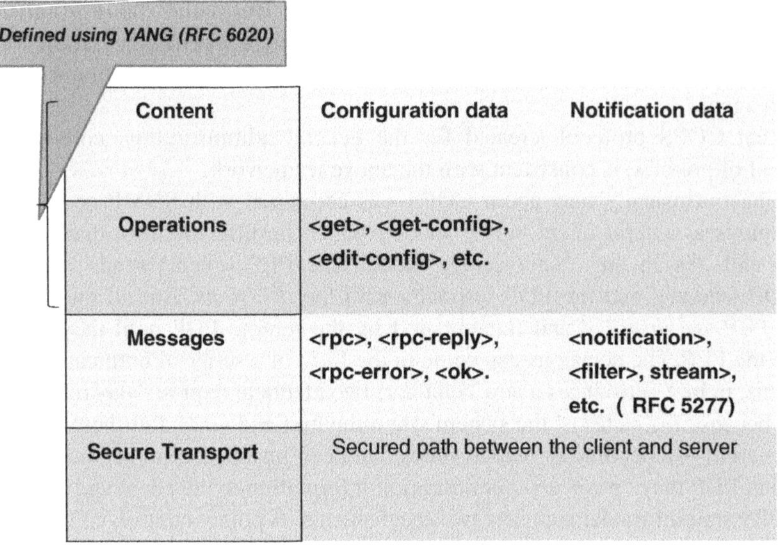

Figure A.6 NETCONF layers.

The architecture has been developed—at least initially—with the command-line interface in mind, which explains some of its peculiar features. The protocol follows a client–server model in that a client issues commands carried in a remote procedure call and obtains the result on the return. The server executes commands over the *configuration datastore*. RFC 6241 defines this term as follows: "The datastore holding the complete set of configuration data that is required to get a device from its initial default state into a desired operational state." The *datastore*, in turn, is defined as "... a conceptual place to store and access information." As far as the implementation is concerned, "A datastore might be implemented, for example, using files, a database, flash memory locations, or combinations thereof."[14]

In this design, there are two major points of departure from both the client–server protocol and CLI. In the departure from the strict client–server model, the NETCONF architecture supports asynchronous communications—it gets notifications from the server. These are effectively interrupts as far as the client is concerned, and so the client has to be developed to supply proper interrupt handlers. In the departure from the CLI model, NETCONF uses structured XML-encoded data. In summary, NETCONF specifies[15] a distributed object-oriented infrastructure.

This infrastructure, along with all other pieces of NETCONF, is conveniently presented in four layers as in Figure A.6. Following RFC 6241, the layers are explained by the respective examples—depicted on the right-hand side.

[14] Why this definition needed to mix the operating systems objects (files), specific file systems (databases), and physical devices (flash memory) is unclear, but one gets the point of what is meant.

[15] The Cloud in the picture symbolizes this infrastructure, and so the symbol has nothing to do with Cloud Computing in this context.

(a)
```
<rpc message-id="123"
     xmlns="urn:ietf:params:xml:ns:netconf:base:1.0">

     <deck-the-halls
      xmlns="http://example.net/Cloud/deck-the-halls/1.0">
         <fixture boughs_of_holly>
         </fixture>
     </deck-the-halls>
   </rpc>
```

(b)
```
<rpc-reply message-id="123"
     xmlns="urn:ietf:params:xml:ns:netconf:base:1.0">
   <ok/>
 </rpc-reply>
```

Figure A.7 (a) Invocation of the *deck-the-halls* RPC method; (b) reply with the positive result.

We start with the lowest one, called *secure transport.* (Note that all four layers are modules *within* the OSI application layer. The choice of the word "transport"[16] in the name of the layer is somewhat unfortunate, as the name conflicts with the OSI terminology; however, the confusion is avoided if one keeps in mind that NETCONF is strictly an application-layer protocol and that the key word in the term "secure transport" is "secure.") What the term really tries to reflect is that all NETCONF messages must be passed over a secure interface. Initially, the example in mind was that supported by the *Secure SHell* (*SSH*) protocol, as opposed to *telnet*—in which CLI commands were transmitted in the clear. (Again, SSH was developed for CLI—with SSH, one gets access to the *shell* interpreter, which otherwise could be reached with the unsecure telnet.) Over time, however, other protocols—notably TLS—have been accepted here. It is mandatory that this layer provides authentication, data integrity, confidentiality, and replay protection.

The next layer, *messages*, is merely a transport-independent framing mechanism for encoding both RPC-related and notifications-related structures. The four elements of the RPC structure are listed in the example entry of Figure A.6; the notification elements are listed in RFC 5277.[17] In what follows, we will provide an example of the specification of an RPC call.

Figure A.7 presents both the XML encoding of the client's invocation of the *deck-the-halls* method, whose single parameter is the string *boughs_of_holly*, and the server's reply. First, the *<rpc>* element has a mandatory attribute *message-id*, a string, whose purpose is to uniquely identify the message (so as to be returned with the respective *<rpc-reply>*). This string is chosen by the sender of the RPC. We chose it to be "123," following the tradition of encoding an integer.

The *<rpc>* element is defined by NETCONF, and the appropriate namespace is referred to by the *xmlns* string. The name of the method, *deck-the-halls*, follows. Since this method has been introduced by us, we have to provide the URI of the namespace in the *xmlns*

[16] What is particularly interesting is that "transport" here really means "session," and in fact the word "session" is used throughout this RFC as well as its companion RFCs! It is implied that a session is established, and many things—for instance, subscription to notifications—happen in the context of this session.

[17] www.ietf.org/rfc/rfc5277.txt

string that follows. The only parameter, which we appropriately call *<fixture>*, is the string *boughs_of_holly*, a constant value.

In case of a successful execution, the *<rpc-reply>* is returned with the *<ok>* element. (Otherwise, it can be returned with *<rpc-error>*, in which case the error cause would be specified.)

Back to the layers of Figure A.6. At the third layer, *Operations*, the NETCONF-defined base protocol operations, are processed. These operations are *<get-config>*, *<edit-config>*, *<copy-config>*, *<delete-config>*, *<lock>*, *<unlock>*, *<close-session>*, and *<kill-session>*. The first four are self-explanatory; the verb in each name specifies an operation that is performed on the configuration (or part of it). There are many nuances with the choice of parameters in the reply options, which are well explained in the RFC.

The *<lock>* operation is to request that the server deny (presumably for a short time) the entire datastore modification requests from other clients (including the SNMP clients, clients executing CLI scripts, or human users). The lock is active until the *<unlock>* operation is issued or—to preclude a permanently locked system—for the duration of the session. If the datastore is locked, then *<edit-config>*, *<copy config>*, or *<delete-config>* requests from other clients will be denied. (No semaphore or monitor infrastructure is maintained at the server; it is a client's job to retry.)

There is, however, a much more nuanced approach to the execution of the *<lock>* operation on the server side, and we will address this shortly. Let us first finish with the two remaining operations. Of these, *<close-session>* results in releasing all locks—and other resources—and terminating the underlying *secure transport* session. (This seems a bit awkward, since there is no *<open-session>* operation;[18] the whole idea here is to force the release of the locks and other resources.) The *<kill-session>* achieves the same result, but with some other client's session, which naturally means that this operation may succeed only if the client that issued it has proper authorization.

A nuance mentioned in the previous paragraph is that, with respect to configuration updates, NETCONF supports and partly implements the transactional model known as *ACID—Atomic, Consistent, Isolated, and Durable.* (For a detailed discussion of this subject, see Chapter 20 of [1].) In a nutshell, these properties refer to a group of operations that constitute a transaction in the distributed environment. Incidentally, this is a classical orchestration construct.

The first major problem here is ensuring that either the whole group of operations succeeds—consider what may happen in the distributed environment when one or more hosts suddenly crash in the middle of the transaction—or, in case of a failure, the effect of all operations that had already executed is undone.

A typical example of a vulnerable transaction here is getting money from a cash machine. This involves debiting an account and dispensing the cash. If the machine cannot dispense the cash, the account must never be debited, but the machine must not give the cash out before the account is debited.

Atomicity is the property whose presence solves this problem. It is implemented by logging and tracking the effect of all successful transaction operations as *candidates* before actually performing the changes. In case of a failure of an operation, the logs are flashed, and so the transaction *rolls back* to the initial state. Otherwise, when all operations have completed

[18] The opening of the session is achieved by (1) establishing a secure transport connection and (2) discovering the NETCONF *capabilities* (a set of specified protocol extensions) supported by the server.

successfully and the involved entities *commit* to the transaction, it is carried out. (Even if the server crashes in this last phase, it will still execute the committed transaction, according to the log, after it reboots.)

Here the *consistency* property means that if the associated data had been consistent before the transaction started, then these data will remain consistent after the transaction has completed. The *isolation* property deals with the visibility of the steps in an unfinished transaction; it is implementation-dependent. The *durability* property is concerned with the preservation of the system state (for example, in logs) to deal with crashes.

To this end, NETCONF defines the effect of its *<commit>* operation as follows: "The *<commit>* operation instructs the device to implement the configuration data contained in the candidate configuration. If the device is unable to commit all of the changes in the candidate configuration datastore, then the running configuration MUST remain unchanged. If the device does succeed in committing, the running configuration MUST be updated with the contents of the candidate configuration."

NETCONF defines the *<rollback-on-error>* capability, in which case the *<error-option>* parameter of the *<edit-config>* operation may be set to *rollback-on-error*. To avoid inconsistency in the case of shared configurations, the RFC recommends that a client lock the configuration. That is why the standard explicitly forbids granting a lock "if any of the following conditions is true:

- A lock is already held by any NETCONF session or another entity;
- The target configuration is <candidate>, it has already been modified, and these changes have not been committed or rolled back; or
- The target configuration is <running>, and another NETCONF session has an ongoing confirmed commit."[19]

As we can see, the *Operations* layer is quite involved. (Reading all of the 112 pages of RFC 6241 will definitely confirm this observation, even more so the respective programming effort.) For a developer to deal with the implementation, a programmatic representation is needed, which is what is supposed to make up the fourth, *Content*, layer of the model. But RFC 6241 stops short of defining this layer—delegating the job to another standardization effort to specify "the NETCONF data models and protocol operations, covering the Operations and the Content layers." Fortunately, the IETF NETMOD working group has completed such a specification, called *YANG*,[20] and published in RFC 6020.[21]

In this book we won't be able to review YANG in any detail, but the interested reader will find the RFC very well written. We only note that YANG is the de-facto NETCONF modeling language. It is well structured, so following a module one can find both its high-level view

[19] *<confirmed-commit>* is another NETCONF-defined capability.

[20] YANG is not an acronym but as in "Yin and Yang (陰-陽)"—the two opposite but dialectically inter-related concepts in Chinese philosophy, which pre-dated any written text. These were first introduced in writing around 700 BC in I. Chin's *Book of Changes*. One distinctive characteristic is that Yin is "female, passive, negative" while Yang is "positive, active, male." For instance, the Sun is Yang, but the Moon is Yin. Yin and Yang are inseparable. Similarly, RFC 6020 specifies YIN as the XML-based representation of YANG (a data-modeling language): "YANG modules can be translated into an equivalent XML syntax called YANG Independent Notation (YIN) (Section 11), allowing applications using XML parsers and Extensible Stylesheet Language Transformations (XSLT) scripts to operate on the models. The conversion from YANG to YIN is lossless, so content in YIN can be round-tripped back into YANG."

[21] www.ietf.org/rfc/rfc6020.txt

and the ultimate encoding in NETCONF operations. By design, YANG has also been made extensible, thus allowing other SDOs to develop its extensions and individual programmers to produce plug-and-play modules.

YANG also maintains (limited) compatibility with SNMP: the SMIv2 MIB modules can be automatically translated into YANG modules for read-only access. There are several products and open-source projects—listed at http://trac.tools.ietf.org/wg/netconf/trac/wiki.

Naturally, NETCONF is used extensively in the SDN for configuring virtual switches. As noted in Chapter 7, there are NETCONF plug-ins used for this purpose as part of the open-source SDN project *Open Daylight*.

A.2 Orchestration with TOSCA

Already introduced earlier, the *Topology and Orchestration Specification for Cloud Applications* (*TOSCA*) is an OASIS standard [2]. At the time of writing, it is being adopted by the industry. TOSCA is a DSL for life cycle software management. It is also a modeling language in that it describes the structure (a *model*) of a service so as to express *what* needs to get done in order to run it as opposed to the programmatic *how*. The *how* part is generated automatically by the interpreter.

These types of language have not appeared overnight. A more general idea of *domain-specific modeling* as the means to improving software productivity through automatic code generation, derived from a high-level specification, has been supported by the *Domain-Specific Modeling* (*DSM*) *Forum*,[22] whose site provides much interesting information (including authoritative bibliography) on the subject.

As an historical (and historic!) aside, as with several key technologies reviewed in this book, the major breakthrough with the domain-specific language development was achieved toward the end of the magic 1970s. Professor Noah Prywes, whom we first met at the very beginning of this book, published a seminal paper [3] that introduced the "*Module Description Language* (*MODEL*) designed for use by management, business, or accounting specialists who are not required to have computer training." The MODEL language described the "input, output, and various formulae associated with system specification" but provided no sequencing information. The latter was the job of the *MODEL Processor*, which generated code (possibly after resolving inconsistencies or ambiguities in the process of interaction with the programmer). In the 1980s and 1990s, Professor Prywes and his graduate students at the University of Pennsylvania designed a full system for the distributed software life cycle specification, which could also be used for reverse engineering [4]. This was one successful example of technology transfer. The actual MODEL product, based on the research results, was developed and marketed by the *Computer Command and Control* company.

Let us go back to TOSCA. We start by expanding the explanation of its role in application orchestration with the help of Figure A.8, which is based on incisive material provided by our colleague Sivan Barzilay. An *application* here is expected to employ multiple virtual machines—including virtual networking appliances—interconnected in a particular way and ruled by a set of policies. A typical example here is deployment of a virtual network function (such as IMS) in an operator network.

[22] www.dsmforum.org/

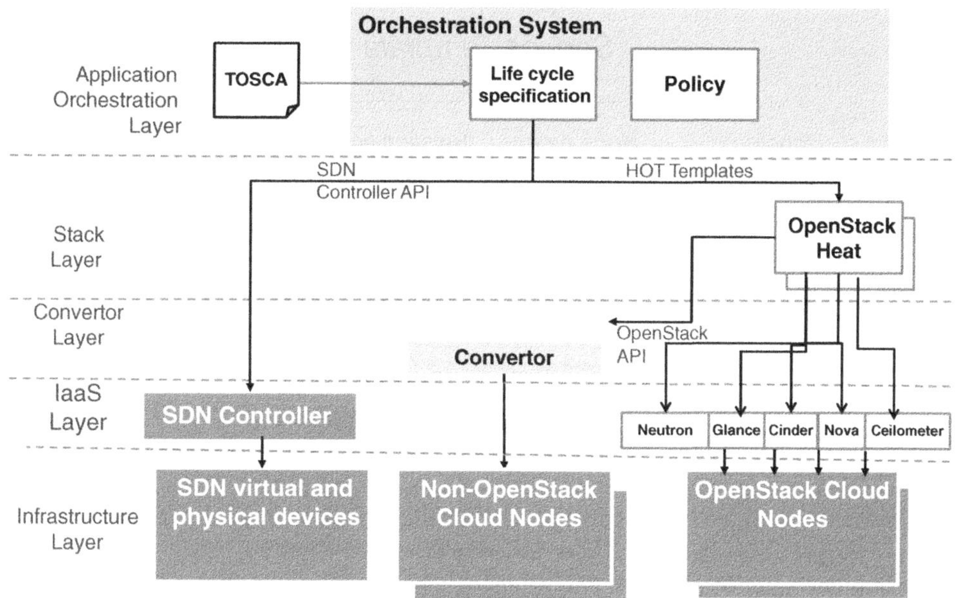

Figure A.8 Orchestration layering framework (courtesy of Sivan Barzilay).

Managing network function virtualization at the lowest—*infrastructure*—layer is far too complex, as we have already demonstrated in Chapter 7 when discussing the evolution of telephony network management.

At the IaaS layer, we know how to orchestrate stacks. Specifically, we are familiar with the OpenStack mechanisms for orchestration, which are of course applicable to the Cloud nodes (data centers) that are based on the OpenStack software. But what if there are nodes that deploy alternative implementations? To maintain the uniform service specification in this case, we need to terminate the Heat API at the *convertor* layer, where the back-end functions will then take over the conversion task.

At the stack layer, we combine virtualization with data communications (and SDN); hence the need to integrate orchestration of stacks with network topology entities. Once again, this aspect is particularly critical to network function virtualization where an application in fact is networking as a service.

Naturally, to integrate wide-area networking with stack orchestration, another layer of abstraction—and specification—is needed so as to port the services across different platform implementations. This is precisely what TOSCA aims to accomplish.

The core TOSCA specification [2] describes the components of a service as well as the relationship among these components. In addition—and this is the key point—the specification language allows one to specify the operational behavior through *management procedures* for both creating and modifying the services in orchestration. Thus, the TOSCA *Service Template* describes the invariants of topology and orchestration procedures that hold across different environments throughout the life cycle.

To shed more light on the specifics, let us start with the namespace. TOSCA uses XML and defines two namespace prefixes: the namespace with prefix *tosca* (http://docs.oasis-open

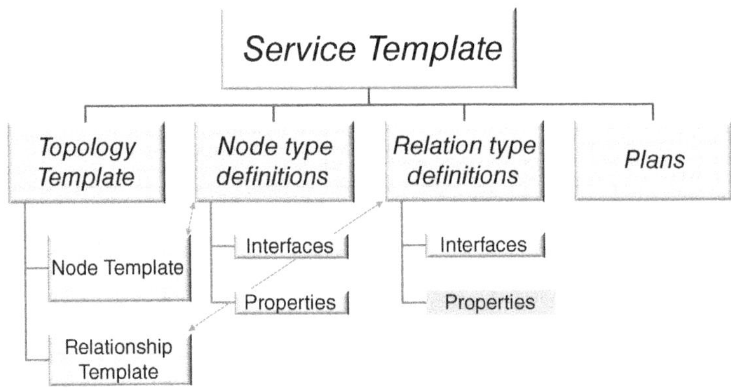

Figure A.9 The structure of a TOSCA template.

.org/tosca/ns/2011/12) is the default; the other prefix is *xs*. For the XML schema, refer to www.w3.org/2001/XMLSchema. TOSCA extensibility mechanisms support the export of entities (attributes and elements) from other namespaces as they don't contradict any entity in the TOSCA namespace.

The description of the abstract syntactic structure of the service template is accompanied by Figure A.9. (We will soon take a look at a specific example, to illustrate the abstraction.)

The elementary components of the service are called *nodes*, the *node types* being declared at the highest level of the specification (along with the *relationship types*, *Topology Template*, and *Plans*). For example, the node types in a web service deployed in the Cloud might be a web server application, called *My_App*; a web server, *X_Web_Server*; the underlying operating system (a Linux distribution), *Y_Linux*; the virtual machine that hosts the application, *Virtual_Machine*; and, finally, the Cloud service providing the virtual machine, *Z_Cloud*.

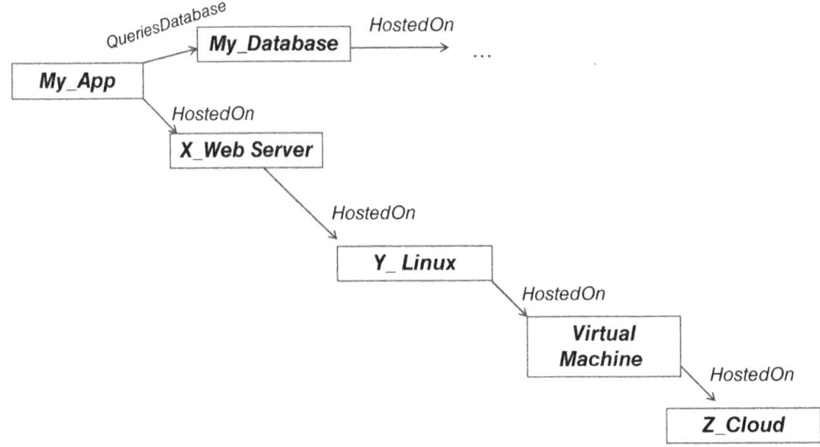

Figure A.10 A topology template example.

(a)

```
tosca_definitions_version: tosca_simple_yaml_1_0_0_build_1

description: My most simple server template

inputs:
 image_name:
   type: string
   default: tinyCentos
   keypair_name:
   type: string
   default: TEST-KEYPAIR-FOR-BDD

node_templates:
   server1:
   type: Ournodes.Compute
   properties:
   num_cpus: 1
   mem_size: 1024
   image_name: { get_input: image_name}
   keypair_name: { get_input: keypair_name}
```

(b)

```
heat_template_version: '2013-05-23'
resources:
 server1_119677379087827598:
  metadata: {deploymentId: '119677379087827597',
      deploymentNodeId: '119677379087827598'}
  properties:
   availability_zone: zone0
   flavor: default
   image: 41d1769d-a6fc-4849-8c70-8f5b0d64fcb5
   key_name: TEST-KEYPAIR-FOR-BDD
   metadata: {deploymentId: '119677379087827597',
      deploymentNodeId: '119677379087827598'}
   name: cPaaS_server1_119677379087827598
   networks:
   - port: {get_resource:
      server1_119677379087827598_mgnt_port}
  type: OS::Nova::Server
 server1_119677379087827598_mgnt_port:
  properties:
   fixed_ips:
   - {ip_address: 10.38.237.63, subnet_id: 66bc11c4-2312-4c55-
      a169-20ca0d21f5f1}
   network_id: 8796324e-7a75-43f7-8be8-32581d846f5c
   security_groups: [d8be0483-77da-41b5-bc17-a55c2eaa0384]
  type: OS::Neutron::Port
```

Figure A.11 An example of translation of (a) the TOSCA template into (b) the corresponding HOT template (courtesy of Sivan Barzilay).

Each node type defines the *properties* of the service component and the respective *interfaces* to the operations to be performed on the component. In the case of a server-type node, the properties might include the number of CPUs, memory size, the name of the image to instantiate and—as an essential security property—the SSH key pairs' location (cf. Figure A.11 later). (The values of the above parameters can be obtained through a specified input procedure.) The interfaces specify the operations on the node during the life cycle of a service. Each operation (e.g., *create*, *start*, or *stop*) comes along with the pointer to a script actually implementing the operation, as in:

```
create: scripts/server_library/install_server.sh.
```

This is one place in TOSCA that provides the interface for procedural plug-ins. The *relationship types* specify the relations (or connections) among the nodes of given types, the idea being that the service is a *directed graph* whose *vertices* are the nodes and whose *edges* are the relationships.

Relationship types specify which nodes they can connect. The direction is denoted by explicitly declaring the source and target elements. (The direction, as we will see shortly, is essential for establishing the processing order.) The *interface* part allows us to plug in the code—just as in the node type case.

This graph-based representation (and the subsequent derivation of the actions obtained by traversing the graph) is the reason for the use of the word "topology" in TOSCA. With the earlier examples of nodes, we could use a relationship type *HostedOn*, as in "*My_App* [is] *HostedOn X_Web_Server*." But *My_App* may also consume the services of a database represented by the node *My_Database*, and to specify this relationship we would introduce a new relationship type, *QueriesDatabase*.[23]

Overall, the TOSCA topology template consists of a set of node templates and relationship templates. Figure A.10 illustrates a fragment of a topology template for our schematic web service.

The final element of the TOSCA service template is *Plans*. Here the management aspects of service instances are defined via a workflow. In the choice of a specification language, TOSCA defers to other standards, such as the OASIS own *Web Services Business Process Execution Language* (*BPEL*) or the *Business Process Modeling and Notation* (*BMPN*)[24] produced by the Object Management Group, although it allows use of other languages. Either way, a workflow refers to the operations defined as part of the node and relationship templates (e.g., as in the *interface* specifications).

Figure A.11 (provided to us by Sivan Barzilay) is a simple example of translating a TOSCA template into a HOT template which can be understood by the AWS CloudFormation and OpenStack. But how is a specification interpreted so as to support the sequence of life cycle operations? A node template provides a rather straightforward answer to the question of how to deploy and manage the node. The relationship specifies the order of processing the node templates (and, as we noted earlier, it may inject additional processing logic). For example, for the relationship type *HostedOn,* the host should naturally be created and configured before the node it hosts. Similarly, for the client-server relationships, the server must be processed before any of its clients.

For additional reading, we recommend an incisive paper [5], which also describes the life cycle of a service in view of a TOSCA template created by the Cloud service provider during the service offering phase.

There has been significant effort in the industry to adopt TOSCA. As with many other initiatives, there is an open-source project, which is appropriately called *OpenTOSCA*.[25] Pleasing to the authors' tastes, the naming conventions for the OpenTOSCA ecosystem output seem to be rooted in oenology: in addition to the TOSCA run-time environment, the *OpenTOSCA Container*, it provides a graphical modeling tool called *Winery* and a self-service portal for the applications available in the container, called *Vinothek.*

As we mentioned earlier, there is considerable effort in OpenStack to interwork with TOSCA. TOSCA is also the subject of ongoing research. One pressing item here is the definition of a policy framework, which, as an important example, can be used to specify security policies. Among the major drivers is certification of Cloud services (as, for example, addressed in [6]). Once certified, a service should remain unchanged; hence the need to capture certification requirements in a formal service description.

Noting that "TOSCA lacks a detailed description of how to apply, design, and implement policies,"[26] [7] demonstrates how security policies can be defined. The paper considers two approaches. The first approach is plan-based, and so the workflows in the build, management,

---

[23] This relationship type is usually named *ConnectsToDatabase.*

[24] www.omg.org/spec/BPMN/20100524/MODEL

[25] www.iaas.uni-stuttgart.de/OpenTOSCA/

[26] Surely the present version of the TOSCA standard does allow us to specify policies, but, as [7] notes, such specifications are merely annotations, with various aspects of policy definition and processing left open to interpretation.

and termination *plans* are modified to support the annotated policies. The second approach does not involve any modification of plans; instead, the relevant *operations* are modified.

But while the research is ongoing, the OpenTOSCA code is already being used successfully in production. As reported in [8], the design, specification, and Cloud deployment of an *Enterprise Content Management (ECM)* system using OpenTOSCA and OpenStack can be achieved by a single graduate student in the course of an MS project.

A.3 The REST Architectural Style

The concept of the REST architectural style has been described in [9] and elaborated on in Chapter 5 of Roy Fielding's PhD dissertation [10]. "A stubborn misconception in the industry is that REST is "HTTP-based." Although Dr. Fielding has worked on the design, specification, and implementation of HTTP—whose specification he co-authored—he has stressed that REST is a style, which is completely protocol-independent. Nor is an HTTP-based API REST by default.

As [9] states, "REST is a coordinated set of architectural constraints that attempts to minimize latency and network communication while at the same time maximizing the independence and scalability of component implementations. REST enables the caching and reuse of interactions, dynamic substitutability of components, and processing of actions by intermediaries, thereby meeting the needs of an Internet scale distributed hypermedia system."

"Caching" and the presence of the "intermediaries" here are quintessential architectural entities in the World-Wide Web, and in order to discuss REST, we need to review the architecture of the World-Wide Web. As we will see, the key to understanding the style lies in the last three words of the quote: "distributed hypermedia system." In the next section, we review the latter concept; the two sections that follow briefly highlight aspects of the World-Wide Web architecture and outline the REST style.

A.3.1 The Origins and Development of Hypermedia

The word *hypermedia* refers here to the system of sound and video references. Syntactically, hypermedia are *hypertext*, as the actual links are ASCII-encoded. An early vision of hypermedia was expressed by Professor Vannevar Bush in 1945, in his famous article [11]:

> "Consider a future device for individual use, which is a sort of mechanized private file and library. It needs a name, and, to coin one at random, 'memex' will do. A memex is a device in which an individual stores all his books, records, and communications, and which is mechanized so that it may be consulted with exceeding speed and flexibility. It is an enlarged intimate supplement to his memory."

The implementation idea (unrealized in that form) was to use microfilm as the storage medium for "Books of all sorts, pictures, current periodicals, [and] newspapers." These would be indexed and searched, mechanically, based on the codes entered on a typewriter keyboard and projected to a screen. The conception of associative linking—the key concept of hypertext—was part of the vision: "It affords an immediate step, however, to associative indexing, the basic idea of which is a provision whereby any item may be caused at will to select immediately and automatically another."

According to his seminal 1965 paper [12], Theodor Holm Nelson started to work on the computer-based[27] implementation of Bush's concept in 1960. The term "hypertext" was introduced in [12] "to mean a body of written or pictorial material interconnected in such a complex way that it could not conveniently be presented or represented on paper." Same goes for "films, sound recordings, and video recordings," which "can now be arranged as non-linear systems—for instance, lattices—for editing purposes, or for display with different emphasis." Along with "hypertext" came the word "hyperfilm," denoting a "browsable or vari-sequenced movie," which is "only one of the possible hypermedia that require our attention."

Of course, the paper went much further than merely defining the terms—it presented the information structure, file structure, and even a language for expressing the file format.[28]

In parallel with this development, two University of Pennsylvania professors, Noah Prywes—whom we now meet for the third time—and Harry J. Gray had been building the *Multi-List* system, outlined in a 1959 paper [15] and further described in [16], which was envisioned for library function automation through the software-based associative memory implementation in which the memory was organized in the linked-list structure. As reported in [17], Andries van Dam, a computer graphics pioneer, used *Multi-List* in his doctoral research at the University of Pennsylvania. In1966 he defended his doctoral thesis "A Study of Digital Processing of Pictorial Data," and was awarded the second PhD in Computer Science in history.

Subsequently, Nelson and van Dam joined forces to develop—together with a team of Brown University students—the *Hypertext Editing System* (*HES*) on IBM 360 [18]. That project later morphed into a more advanced one, but here the major elements of hypertext processing as we know it have been present. The project involved multi-user access (not only for reading, but also for modifying files). The text displayed on a computer terminal could be selected with a *light pen* (a pre-cursor of what has become a mouse), tagged, and annotated. On top of validating the hypertext idea, HES demonstrated that line editing (which, incidentally, was still around even two decades later) can be replaced with full-screen editing and formatting.

We will fast-forward to 1980, when Sir Timothy Berners-Lee developed his hypertext-based system *ENQUIRE* at CERN; to 1989, when he followed up with a different design—now uniting the hypertext technology with that of the Internet—and built the first website; and finally to 1990, when he released the first web browser, called *WorldWideWeb*.

The hypermedia component of the architecture referred to a resource (which initially was a document represented by a file, but later evolved to what could be produced on the fly by a program). The universal resource naming scheme, which we reviewed earlier, allows us to locate resources at servers by means of DNS look-up. A browser, located at the client device, interprets the web pages written in the *Hypert-Text Mark-up Language* (*HTML*), and fetches the resources.[29]

[27] One fascinating thing about this paper is that it correctly predicted that computers would be both user-friendly and sufficiently inexpensive to become writing and research tools.

[28] It is interesting that at about the same time Vladimir Nabokov (who was not a computer scientist and actually wrote in long hand) published a novel, *Pale Fire* [13], which is effectively written in hypertext, as observed in [14].

[29] Of course, the client does *not* have to be a browser, which is a gateway to the human user. A user may be an automaton—a process or a thread—which is where the relevant API comes to place. Yet modern browsers, such as Chrome, support the programmatic API-based interface.

- ftp://ftp.ietf.org/rfc/rfc3986
- http://www.ietf.org/rfc/rfc3986.txt
- ldap://[2001:db8::7]/c=GB?objectClass?one
- mailto:Cloud.Administrator@example.com
- news:comp.infosystems.www.servers.unix
- tel:+1-816-555-1212
- telnet://192.0.2.16:80/
- urn:oasis:names:specification:docbook:dtd:xml:4.1.2

Figure A.12 URI examples.

A resource is assigned a *Universal Resource Identifier* (*URI*), defined in RFC 3986.[30] A URI can be a *Universal Resource Name* (*URN*), which uniquely identifies a resource but does not specify its location, or it can be a *Universal Resource Locator* (*URL*), which actually specifies the resource location. The "or" is not exclusive: a URI can be both a URN and a URL.

A URI is a mere identifier; it does not have to refer to an accessible resource. An operation associated with a URI reference is defined by the protocol and the relevant metadata. RFC 3986 stresses that the typical operations that a system may attempt to perform on a resource—*access*, *update*, *replace*, or *find attributes*—are defined by the protocols that make use of URIs.

The syntax of URI is defined formally thus:

```
URI = <scheme> ":" <hier-part> ["?" <query>] ["#" <fragment>].
```

The *scheme* is typically the relevant protocol (such as *http*, *mailto*, or *SIP*), but it can be just a string *urn*, implying that the URI is a URN. The *<hier-part>* contains the DNS name of the host where the resource is located, the port to be used (this is optional, and the default is 80), and the path to the resource (modeled after the Unix file system). The rest is the optional *search* part. Figure A.12 lists several URI examples. (Note that, as is evident from the first two examples, a single resource may have different URIs.)

Here is another example illustrating the search part of the URI string. When we googled "an example of URL," the browser displayed the following URI with the result: https://www.google.com/webhp?sourceid=chrome-instant&ion=1&espv=2&ie=UTF-8#q=an%20example%20of%20url.

This example not only underlines the flexibility of the web hypermedia realization, but also demonstrates how the URIs store and "drive" the state of an application. The latter is a major tenet of the REST architectural style; we will return to this subject later. The reader will appreciate the quote from [9]: "Hypermedia was chosen as the user interface because of its simplicity and generality: the same interface can be used regardless of the information source, the flexibility of hypermedia relationships (links) allows for unlimited structuring, and the direct manipulation of links allows the complex relationships within the information to guide the reader through an application. Since information within large databases is often

[30] http://tools.ietf.org/html/rfc3986

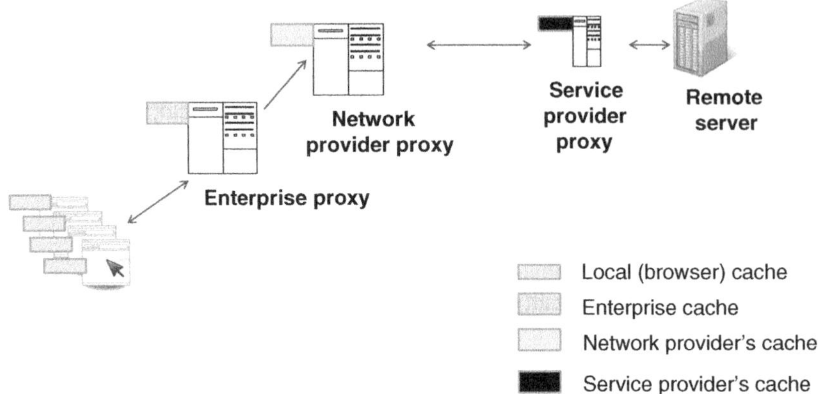

Figure A.13 Caching with proxies (an example).

much easier to access via a search interface rather than browsing, the Web also incorporated the ability to perform simple queries by providing user-entered data to a service and rendering the result as hypermedia."

The structure of a web page, which also provides a *representation* of the relevant resources, is specified using the *HyperText Markup Language* (*HTML*). HTML is standardized by W3C—an organization founded and headed by Sir Berners-Lee. The latest version, HTML 5.0,[31] supports, among many other things, native (rather than plug-in-based) audio and video, browser storage, and in-line vector graphics.

Part of the resource representation is *metadata* (such as media type or last-modified time). Another data component is *control data*, whose purpose will become clear soon when we review data caching in the next section.

A.3.2 Highlights of the World-Wide Web Architecture

From the onset, the web design has been concerned with reducing bandwidth use (which also meant faster access to resources and, in many cases, also meant reducing networking fees). In the distributed environment, this can be achieved by a tried-and-true method—replicating data in one or more *caches*. Caching of the data starts at the client, where a page, once fetched, can be stored by the browser; further replication is performed by the *proxies*.

Figure A.13 illustrates this with an example where the proxies are deployed at the enterprise, the network provider, and the service provider. (We should note that deploying proxies not only provides physical storage for caching, but also enables content filtering, protocol translation, gathering of analytics, and end-user anonymity—all important features in the use of the World-Wide Web today. Needless to say, these very features come with well-known disadvantages where they are misused.)

[31] http://dev.w3.org/html5/spec/introduction.html#history-1

In the extreme case, when a server is down, a cache may still provide its services—from an end-user point of view a situation akin to observing the light of a star that has gone dark.

The known presence of caches naturally constrains any protocol deployed in this architecture, since an endpoint (a client or a proxy) that uses a cache has to know whether the cache is valid (i.e., contains the same information that the server does).

Another constraint is due to the *dynamic* nature of web pages. An ultimate HTML document does not have to be stored at the server—it can be created dynamically at the server as well as at the client, or at both, with a client and a server playing their respective parts.

In order to illustrate the working of the World-Wide Web, it is necessary to highlight the features of its original protocol, HTTP, defined in RFC 2616.[32] HTTP runs over TCP (now using persistent connections) and so it has a "reliable pipe."[33] HTTP is a request/response protocol, whose requests are issued by a client, with responses returned by a server.

All HTTP messages are ASCII-encoded. The message *headers* are actually pure ASCII text, while the body of a message may contain the ASCII-encoded binary data.

HTTP has been geared toward implementing an object-oriented paradigm; consequently it is defined with a list of methods,[34] which act on the resources identified in the request URI:

- *GET* obtains the resource representation;
- *HEAD* obtains only the HTTP header (typically to check the metadata associated with the resource);
- *POST* "requests that the origin server accept the entity enclosed in the request as a new subordinate of the resource;" (We will review an example of interpretation later.)
- *PATCH*[35] partially modifies the resource's representation;
- *DELETE* requests that the resource be deleted;
- *OPTIONS* requests information about the communication options available on the request/response chain associated with the resource;
- *TRACE* initiates a loop-back of the original message;
- *CONNECT* requests connection to a proxy that can be a tunnel.

The responses are grouped to reserved buckets of code as follows:

- *100–199*: Information;
- *200–299*: Success with data (if present);
- *300–399*: Redirection;
- *400–499*: Client error (also request for authentication, as in *401*, accompanied by a challenge);
- *500–599*: Server error.

[32] www.ietf.org/rfc/rfc2616.txt

[33] Such a pipe does not provide confidentiality, non-replay, or integrity services. Such services—and also server authentication—can be effected by running HTTP on top of the *Transport Layer Security* (*TLS*) protocol, standardized in RFC 5246 (http://tools.ietf.org/html/rfc5246). TLS runs on top of TCP and provides a secure tunnel between a client and a server. By itself HTTP supports mechanisms for client authentication.

[34] Allowing extensions for the new methods.

[35] This method—an extension standardized in 2010—is published in RFC 5789 (http://tools.ietf.org/html/rfc5789).

These are mostly self-explanatory, but two brief observations are in order. First, *redirection* is a powerful (and potentially dangerous) feature, which—true to its name—instructs the client to go to another server for information. Processing here may be complex—for example, loops must be avoided and, in some cases, the decision on whether to allow redirection cannot be made by the browser itself. Yet redirection can be a tool for constructing services. As we will see in the last section of this chapter, HTTP-based API systematically uses redirection in the implementation of token-based identity management schemes, such as those used in the *Open Authorization* (*OAuth*) protocol.

Second, *client error* may be used not to indicate an error, but rather to request additional processing. For example, the *401* response requests authentication of the client, for which it provides a *challenge* to be answered by the client so as to prove its identity. Similarly, in view of the proxies, the *407* response invokes the same procedure, except that the client has to authenticate to a proxy.

The last observation already hints that HTTP is well aware of the proxies, but there is much more to this. The nuances of dealing with caches are in the headers. A critical information element, which (typically) contains a hash of a given page, is called an *Entity Tag* (*ETag*), because it serves as a tag to the content of the page. *ETags* are used to check the freshness of the cache. When the resource representation is fetched (via the GET method) the first time, its ETag is stored along with the cached representation. The subsequent GET requests carry the ETag with an *if-none-match* request header field, making the request conditional: if the page is fresh (i.e., it hashes to the same quantity as the value of the ETag), there is no need to transfer the page. The same mechanism can be used with PUT to prevent it from modifying a page which the client does not know about.

Keeping time values also helps with validating freshness. The *last-modified* entity header field, returned in the response, records the date and time when the page was modified. The client can use the conditional GET with the same value in the *if-modified-since* header. The data elements that enable conditional processing are those that [9] refers to as *control data.*

A.3.3 The Principles of REST

These principles apply to the practice of programming a service in the presence of the web architecture. To begin with, it is impossible to dictate browser implementations, and so the client concerns and the server concerns must be separated—there ought to be no client-to-server interface binding. This is fundamentally different from the RPC approach, in which such binding is prescribed.

Considering the scale of a web service, the server cannot keep the state of the application separate for each client, and so the server must be stateless. (Yet another reason for this is that a server is likely to be replicated, with several instances of it being load-balanced.) It follows that each request from a client to a server ought to contain all the information necessary for the server to understand the request.

Not every mechanism for supplying state-related information is acceptable to REST. There is a well-known mechanism in HTTP, called *cookies*, as specified in RFC 6265.[36] A server places a "cookie"—a data structure describing the client state—in response to the initial

[36] http://tools.ietf.org/html/rfc6265

request from a client, and this cookie is then exchanged (and possibly updated by the server) in all future interactions so that the cookie keeps the state of the client. This approach is not considered in line with the REST style, which prescribes driving the application state transitions through hypermedia (URI). In fact, [10] takes a strong exception to this in Section 6.3.4.2, noting a clash with the user's backing up (as in clicking on the *Back* button in the browser) "to back-up to a view prior to that reflected by the cookie, the browser's application state no longer matches the stored state represented within the cookie. Therefore, the next request sent to the same server will contain a cookie that misrepresents the current application context, leading to confusion on both sides."

In the presence of intermediaries and caches, extra interactions ought to be eliminated, so that the correct cache that is closest to the client responds and eliminates further request propagation. To achieve this, all data within a response from a server are labeled as cacheable or non-cacheable.

The interface between a client and a server is constrained through (a) identification of resources, (b) manipulation of resources via their respective representations, (c) self-descriptive messages,[37] and (d) using hypermedia as the means of state transition.[38]

The REST style also prescribes layering (to encapsulate legacy services and to protect new services from legacy clients[39]) and the use of code-on-demand, where the code can be brought—by means of hypermedia—to be executed at the client.

The REST style prescribes defining fixed resource names or hierarchies (in fact, any "typed" resources where the types need to be understood by clients); the instruction on constructing appropriate URIs must come from a server—as is done with HTML forms or URI templates. Reliance on any specific protocol is actually *proscribed.*

The last point is often misunderstood. In his blog,[40] Fielding stresses that REST API must be defined in a protocol-independent manner. In fact, HTTP is not the only web application protocol. As we mentioned earlier, the IETF, recognizing the deficiency of single-transaction request/response protocols (which cannot support asynchronous "responses" such as notifications and thus necessitate expensive and awkward polling mechanisms), has developed and standardized a new full-duplex protocol called *WebSocket.*[41]

We finish this section with an example that demonstrates how hypermedia can drive the state of a service. To make this example concrete, we explicitly use HTTP, at the same time demonstrating the power of the *REDIRECT* method.

Consider a simple but rather typical service where a user orders something where a receipt is desirable. The user requests an item, represented by URI *X*, gets a form in response, fills in the form, and submits it.

If the service is implemented as in Figure A.14(a), where a form is obtained via *GET X* and returned to the server via *POST X*, the application ends up in a *transient* state. The browser may move elsewhere, and the user would never be able to return to the receipt by backing up. Unsure of the success of form submission—or desperate to get a receipt—the user might go

---

[37] In other words, the messages that can be understood by all intermediaries (proxies).

[38] [10] (Section 5.1.5) phrases this constraint: "hypermedia as the engine of application state."

[39] For instance, true to this scheme, with the web-based e-mail service, the SMTP mail service protocols are encapsulated within a layer invisible to the web user.

[40] http://roy.gbiv.com/untangled/2008/rest-apis-must-be-hypertext-driven

[41] http://tools.ietf.org/html/rfc6455

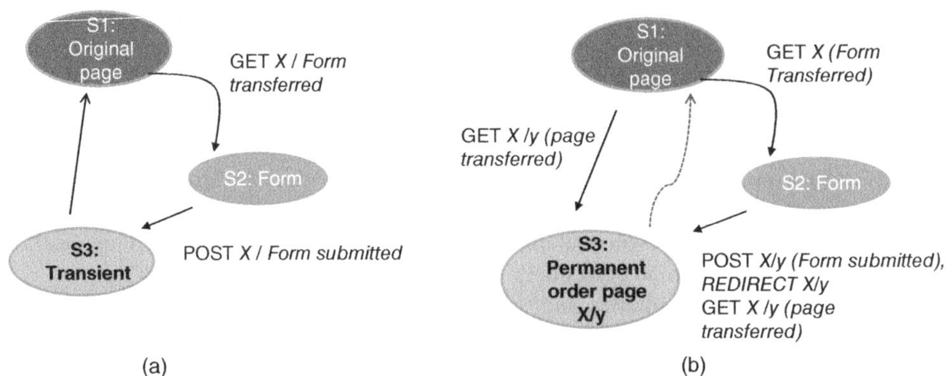

Figure A.14 Eliminating the transient state: (a) a service with a transient state; (b) the same service with a permanent state.

through the same steps again, thus submitting a second form. (And so the user might end up paying for and owning two items, where only one was needed in the first place.)

Figure A.14(b) depicts an alternative implementation, which fixes this problem. Here, POST appends suffix *y* to *X*, thus creating a subordinate resource *X/y*. The response redirects the user to *X/y*, which represents a new permanent state, and so any subsequent *GET X/y* will result in returning the receipt.

A.4 Identity and Access Management Mechanisms

This section introduces further detail on the identity and access management mechanisms referenced in Chapter 7. Most of these mechanisms are standardized. We first examine password management. Then we introduce *Kerberos*, which is widely used for authentication in enterprises. Kerberos is, in fact, a complete system with a well-defined architecture and communication protocol. It supports mutual authentication and single sign-on by design. After Kerberos, we move to the topic of access control. We start with a review of two common approaches to implementing access control matrix: storing the information in its non-empty cells by columns and by rows. The column approach yields access control lists, while the row approach yields capability lists. Next, the Bell–LaPadula model, a foundation of advanced access control technology, is reviewed. Afterward, we address the *Security Assertion Markup Language* (*SAML*), OAuth 2.0, and OpenID Connect, which have to do with identity federation. Finally, we discuss the *Extensible Access Control Markup Language* (*XACML*), which supports policy-based access control. Building on SAML, XACML aims at specification of access control policies and queries.

A.4.1 Password Management

Authentication using passwords is problematic in part because of the limitations of our memory. Best practice prescribes that passwords be sufficiently long (e.g., over 10 characters in length), contain non-alphanumeric characters, appear to be meaningless, be changed regularly, and so on. Yet we cannot remember passwords that are considered strong. The situation only becomes progressively worse as Cloud services grow. Instead of one password, we each have many and cannot remember them. In the past, when forgetting a password, a user called a customer support center. These days, the user can reset the password by following a web link received at a pre-registered e-mail address.[42] Given the vulnerabilities of e-mail end to end, the resetting steps may include a form of auxiliary authentication, which inevitably introduces additional side-effects. Usually, auxiliary authentication is based on the user's answers provided previously to a selective list of pre-set *security questions*. "What is your mother's maiden name?" is a standard question. In general, the questions are about common facts of the user. Here a dilemma arises. On the one hand, to maximize the chance that the user remembers the answers without writing them down, only truthful (or straightforward) answers should be provisioned in the system. On the other hand, such answers tend to be known or knowable by others in the age of Google. The dilemma can be eased somewhat by having the user customize the security questions so that the answers are obscure. For example, if a user had a history teacher with the nickname Turtle at high school, the user can choose to have the question "What does Turtle teach?" Increasing the number of security questions also helps. Overall, the set of answers to security questions is essentially another secret. The secret is relatively long-term and, in fact, needs to be protected accordingly.

Another major problem with passwords has to do with how they are stored in an authentication system. Keeping them in plain text with normal access control is obviously insufficient. An attacker breaking into the authentication system can easily steal the stored passwords and impersonate the users. Moreover, system administrators who have legitimate access to the stored passwords could misbehave. A standard practice is to cryptographically hash the passwords and store only the hash values. Cryptographic hashing is achieved with so-called *one-way* functions. This is not a formally defined concept. Roughly speaking, for a function $H(p)$ to be one-way, it must have the property that it is "easy" to compute $H(p)$ from p but "very hard" to solve an equation $H(p) = Q$ for p. And even when one such solution is known, it is still "very hard" to find another one. "Easy" and "hard" are, of course, imprecise terms. What they refer to is computational complexity. If something can be computed fast (say, within seconds) it is "easy," but if there is no known algorithm that would compute this in less than say 1000 years on a modern computer, then it might be considered "hard."

With the password hashing scheme, to verify a password entered by the user, the authentication process computes its hash and checks the result against the stored hash value.[43] Thus no one, not even the root, can look up a user's password. This is quite a feat! Encryption of passwords, for example, cannot achieve the same effect, since it is reversible. Whoever has access to the encryption key, legitimately or illegitimately, can know the password.

---

[42] Some websites support password recovery. To this end, the website keeps user passwords as they are and administrators can know them. You should stay away from such sites.

[43] It should be improbable that two different passwords yield the same hash value. Otherwise, there are potential exploits. Here is a classic example. Alice finds that the hash value of her password is the same as that of Bob's (say by reading the password file of the operating system) and logs in as Bob using her own password. In this case, a remedy is to limit access to hashed passwords to only privileged users. This scheme has been implemented as *shadow passwords* in Unix.

Roger Needham and Mike Guy are credited with inventing password hashing in 1963 [19], but standard cryptographic hash algorithms (e.g., MD5[44] and SHA-256) emerged much later. For a while, only "home-brewed" algorithms were used. One such algorithm was implemented in *Multics* and found to be flawed during a review, true to the common wisdom that cryptography is a hard subject. The Multics incidence prompted Robert Morris and Ken Thompson to develop a new hash function [20] for Unix, and this was ultimately proved cryptographically secure in 2000 [21].

Despite its virtue, the password-hashing scheme is vulnerable to dictionary attacks. Such an attack uses a pre-constructed dictionary of possible passwords (such as common names and words from the Oxford English dictionary) and their hash values using a known algorithm. The dictionary will take time to build, but this needs to be done only once. An attacker who manages to get hold of hashed passwords can then look up the hashes in the dictionary. If there are matches, the passwords are now identified. Dictionary attacks can be serious, since there are always people choosing bad passwords and dictionary look-ups are easy. Fortunately, when developing Unix at Bell Labs in the 1970s, Robert Morris and Ken Thompson anticipated the attacks and devised a technique to counter them [20]. The technique is hinged on including an n-bit random number (called the *salt*) when the hash of a password is computed. In other words, what is hashed is not just the password but the concatenation of the password and the salt. The salt is specific to each password and is changed whenever the password is changed. It is stored in the clear together with the hash value. Now when verifying a password entered by the user, the authentication process looks up the salt, computes the hash value of the concatenated salt and password, and compares the result with the stored value. As a result, the dictionary for pure password hashes no longer works and has to be reconstructed for every salt value. With an n-bit salt, this means 2^n new dictionaries. When first introduced in Unix, salts were 12 bits long. These days, with ever-more-powerful processors and cheaper storage, salts should be much longer (at least 64 bits in length) to increase the cost of pre-computation. Another way to mitigate dictionary attacks is to iterate the hashing operation multiple times. This, however, has an impact on run-time authentication performance.

A.4.2 Kerberos

Kerberos was initially designed to authenticate a human user on any workstation (versus the user's own machine) in a distributed environment based on what the user knows. Its major goal has been to provide mutual authentication between a user of *any* computer and any designated resource (server) that belong to the network. Kerberos has been a solution of choice in the enterprise world, given its built-in support for single sign-on. Developed at MIT,[45] Kerberos has been standardized by the IETF. RFC 4120[46] contains the core specification of Kerberos v5. Most operating systems support Kerberos[47] today, including Microsoft Windows™.

[44] MD5 has been shown to be insufficiently collision-proof and its use is no longer recommended. Please see www.win.tue.nl/hashclash/rogue-ca/.

[45] MIT has also developed Kerberos open-source software, which is currently managed by its Kerberos and Internet Trust Consortium (http://kit.mit.edu/).

[46] http://tools.ietf.org/html/rfc4120

[47] Some of the implementations are based on the open-source software developed at MIT, which is also hosting the Kerberos and Internet Trust Consortium (http://kit.mit.edu/) to manage the Kerberos software project.

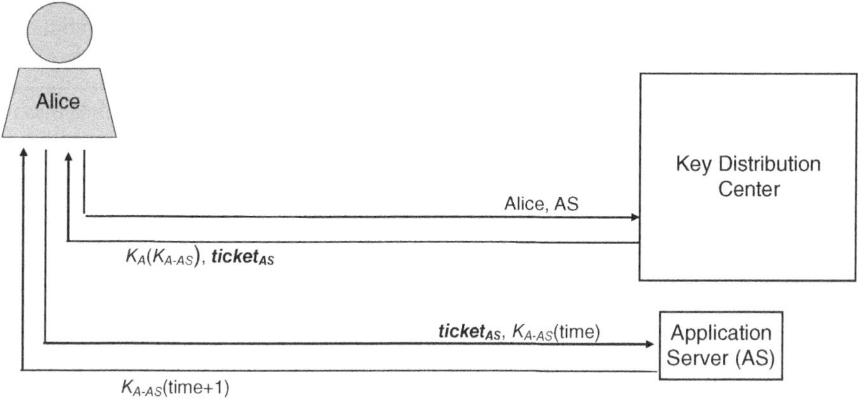

Figure A.15 Kerberos at work (simplified).

Fundamentally, user authentication is password-based in Kerberos. Yet passwords are never exchanged directly. This is done through a scheme based on the Needham–Schroeder protocol [22], which uses cryptographic operations to achieve mutual authentication and confidentiality protection. Central to the scheme is a *Key Distribution Center* (*KDC*), which shares a secret key with every user (as well as every server) in an administrative domain (known as a realm). Figure A.15 shows how the scheme works in principle.

Alice wants to access an application server providing, say, an e-mail service. She logs into the KDC, giving her name and the application server's name. Upon receiving Alice's information, the KDC generates a session key ($K_{A\text{-}AS}$) for Alice and the application server to share, encrypts the key with Alice's secret key (resulting in $K_A(K_{A\text{-}AS})$), encrypts the key (together with Alice's name) with the application server's key (resulting in $Ticket_{AS}$, known as a ticket to the application server), and sends the two encrypted blobs to Alice. She decrypts the session key, encrypts the time stamp with the session key, and sends it together with the ticket (which is unreadable to her) to the application server. By decrypting the ticket, the application server learns the session key and Alice's name. Now both Alice and the application server are armed with the session key. They can authenticate each other by demonstrating knowledge of the key. This is achieved by Alice sending the encrypted time stamp and application server response in kind, except that the time stamp is incremented to avoid reply attacks. Alice gets serviced upon successful mutual authentication. Alice can use the same ticket to get the service later, as long as the ticket remains valid. She needs to get a new ticket if this is not the case.

As far as the user interface is concerned, the secret key is transparent. Alice still supplies her name and the password when logging into the KDC. It is the Kerberos client's job to convert the password into the secret key and immediately erase it. (Naturally, whenever Alice changes the password, her secret key is re-derived and the KDC is updated accordingly. Changing password can actually be implemented as a service accessible through a Kerberos ticket.) But there are two problems with the authentication flow shown in Figure A.15. The first problem

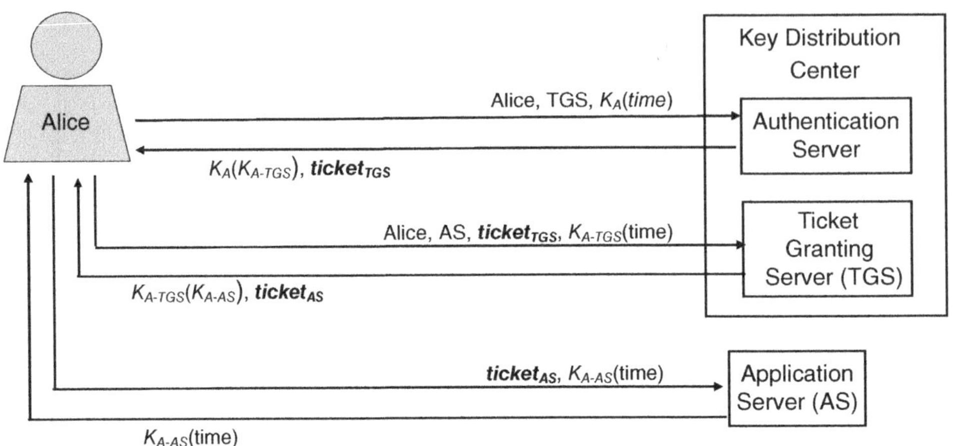

Figure A.16 Kerberos at work (improved).

is that there is no way for the KDC to know whether Alice is indeed the one sending the request. It sends a reply regardless. This is harmless since nobody but Alice will be able to understand the reply. Nevertheless, an adversary can just keep sending requests to attack Alice's key, especially if it is derived from a password. To address this problem, when Alice sends a request, she may include an encrypted time stamp with her secret key. Now the KDC can know whether the sender is really Alice and send a reply only if this is the case.

The other problem is that the client necessarily remembers Alice's secret key during her entire login session to prove her identity when needed. This makes the long-term secret key vulnerable to attack. To address the shortcoming, a special application server is introduced to the KDC to act as a buffer. Called the *Ticket-Granting Server* (*TGS*), it is responsible for issuing tickets to any other application servers and shares a secret key with the authentication server in the KDC—as shown in Figure A.16. Now Alice gets a short-lived session key (i.e., $K_{A\text{-}TGS}$) and a special ticket (called a ticket-granting ticket) when first logging in. The client uses $K_{A\text{-}TGS}$ and $Ticket_{TGS}$ to interact with the TGS on her behalf, whenever she seeks permission to access a server. As long as $K_{A\text{-}TGS}$ and $Ticket_{TGS}$ are valid, they can be used to get a ticket without Alice re-entering her password.

Kerberos also supports the provision of tickets to other *realms* (e.g., organizations outside a given enterprise, with which the enterprise has an established relationship). The resulting cross-realm authentication is transparent to the user, who never needs to re-authenticate after entering the login and password for the hosting realm. The way it works is by having the TGS in one realm (say realm B) be registered in the other realm (say realm A). Alice (who belongs to realm A) can then access an application server in realm B by first obtaining a ticket from the TGS in realm A for the TGS in realm B, and then using that ticket to obtain from the TGS in realm B a ticket for an application server.

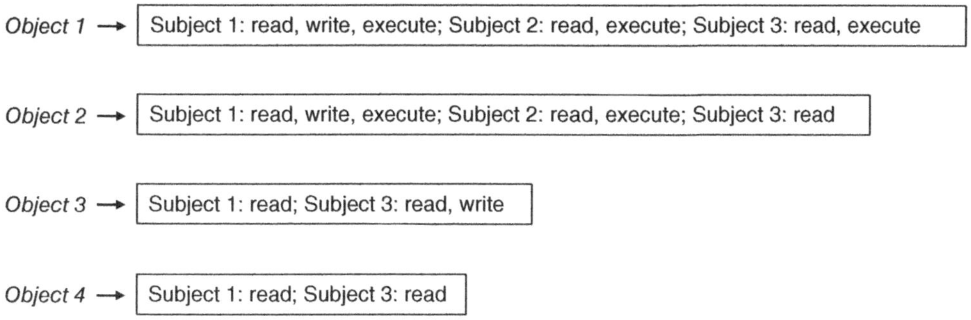

Object 1 → Subject 1: read, write, execute; Subject 2: read, execute; Subject 3: read, execute

Object 2 → Subject 1: read, write, execute; Subject 2: read, execute; Subject 3: read

Object 3 → Subject 1: read; Subject 3: read, write

Object 4 → Subject 1: read; Subject 3: read

Figure A.17 Access control lists.

To summarize, the key features of Kerberos are that it:

1. Authenticates the human user based on *what he or she knows* (i.e., a password), which the user can change at will;
2. Supports single sign-on to all network resources from a host outside the network;
3. Shields the user from all protocol complexities (including those associated with the generation and management of cryptographic keys, which actually provide much stronger authentication than a simple password scheme would);
4. Protects the end user by ensuring that the permanent key is never stored anywhere outside the network key distribution center.

A.4.3 Access Control Lists

Access control lists are object-specific. An access control list specifies the subjects who can access a given object and the rights of each subject. The list is kept and managed centrally, often as part of an operating system. When a subject tries to access an object, the central system searches the ACL associated with the object. If the subject together with the necessary rights are on the list, access is granted. Otherwise, access is denied. Figure A.17 shows the ACLs corresponding to the example access control matrix in Chapter 7. We can see that ACLs could still be tedious; for one thing, the size of an ACL grows with the number of eligible users and the ACL is subject to churns if the user population changes frequently. Hence, it would be useful if redundant information on the list can be reduced. One approach to this end is to use the *group*[48] concept. A group consists of multiple subjects sharing the same rights. As a result, an ACL can refer to just a group rather than every subject in the group. In this sense, a group is a special subject. A regular subject can be assigned to one or more groups and can access an object based on an individual subject's or group's rights.

[48] Groups as defined here resemble roles. A more nuanced definition of a group allows its membership to be based on arbitrary rules. As such, a group is broader than a role, which is tied to a specific set of privileges (e.g., job functions).

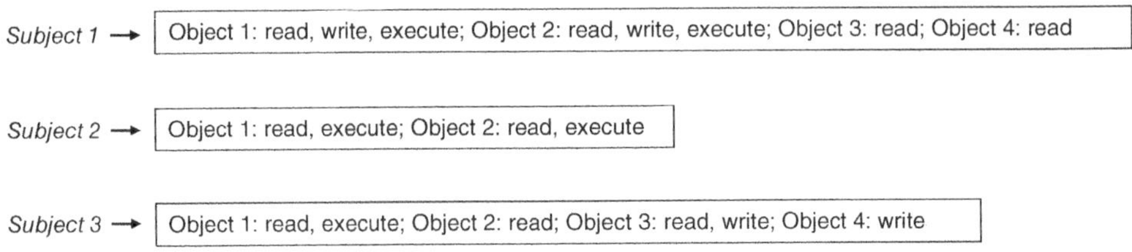

Figure A.18 Capability lists.

ACLs were used by Multics and became widespread in Unix systems.[49] An ACL associated with a file is typically represented as three triplets identifying the respective rights of the owner, the group, and the rest of the world (i.e., *other*). Each triplet consists of flags controlling whether the file can be read, written, and executed, respectively. A file with all the flags set will have the ACL that reads rwxrwxrwx; it is readable, writable, and executable by all. A file with more strict access would have the ACL that reads rwxr-----; it is readable, writable, and executable by the owner only. The Unix implementation of ACLs is a form of abbreviation to contain their sizes; it limits the permissions that the owner can assign. For instance, it is impossible for Alice (as the owner) to allow Bob to read her file, Chris to write to it, Debbie to read and write to it, and Eve to execute it. Various Unix-based operating systems have augmented the abbreviated ACLs with varied levels of sophistication.

Overall, with ACLs, it is easy to verify, at the time of access, whether a given user is indeed authorized for access. It is also easy for an owner of an object to revoke the rights given to a subject; the owner just deletes the subject's rights from the object's ACL. To downgrade the rights given to a subject is easy too. The specific rights are removed from the subject's entry in the ACL. Nevertheless, ACLs have limitations. As a start, ACLs are unsuitable for handling cases where a user needs to delegate the authority to another user for a period of time, say a manager asking a subordinate to approve purchasing requests while he is on vacation. There is also the inherent difficulty of ascertaining privileges on a per-user basis from the multitude of ACLs. Yet such a determination is necessary when certain user's access rights need to be revoked. The use of groups also adds another wrinkle. An ACL could contain both a user and a group to which the user belongs. If just the user's right to an object is revoked, the user can still access the object through the group membership.

A.4.4 Capability Lists

Capability lists are subject-specific. A capability list contains the *capabilities* granted to a given subject. A *capability* specifies a particular object along with the permitted operations on the object. Dennis and Van Horn [23] introduced this term in describing a mechanism for controlling access to objects in memory. Conceptually, a capability is similar to a Kerberos ticket or OAuth token, as described earlier. Figure A.18 shows the capability lists corresponding to the example access control matrix in Chapter 7. The subject's set of capabilities

[49] It is natural that ACLs are part of an operating system. For ACLs to work, naming and authenticating subjects (users, processes, and the like) are essential, and both are already handled by the operating system.

determines exactly which objects the subject may access. There is no need to authenticate the subject.

When accessing an intended object, a subject must present the corresponding capability. Normally, the subject obtains the capability beforehand and stores it for later use.[50] As a result, it is essential that a subject cannot forge or modify a capability and then use it. In other words, a capability shall be tamper-proof and authenticable. An effective approach to this end is through cryptography. An example is the PKI tokens in OpenStack Keystone, which are signed and verifiable.

As another example, Andrew Tanenbaum *et al.* [24] developed a scheme for the Amoeba distributed operating system. The scheme works as follows. A capability consists of an authenticable checksum in addition to the usual object identifier and rights. The checksum is computed with a cryptographically secure one-way function (e.g., HMAC) over the object identifier, rights, and a secret key (actually a random number as implemented) known only to the access control system. When attempting to access the object, the subject sends the capability to the system as part of the request. The system computes the checksum using the object identifier and rights in the capability, and the secret key that it holds. If the checksum matches the one in the capability, the request is granted. Otherwise, it is rejected. If a subject changes the object identifier or rights, the checksum in the capability will become invalid; the subject also cannot produce the right checksum without the secret key. This scheme should remind you of the object storage access control mechanism discussed in Chapter 6, which works essentially in the same way.

Another implication of a capability-based system is that a subject can pass copies of capabilities to other subjects without interacting with an authority, giving them access to objects. This is a double-edged sword. On the one hand, sharing and delegation become simpler. On the other hand, it is harder to track who gives which capabilities to whom, and whether the new holders of the given capabilities are authorized. It is, therefore, difficult to revoke the access rights of a selective set of subjects to an object. A work-around is to invalidate all outstanding capabilities associated with the object and to issue new capabilities to the eligible subjects. This can be achieved by changing the secret key in Amoeba and keeping track of revocation events in OpenStack Keystone.

A.4.5 The Bell–LaPadula Model

The Bell–LaPadula model [25] addresses control of information flow through two policy rules (called *properties*). One is *the simple-security property* that a subject can read only an object at the same or lower security level. Hence, a general can read a soldier's documents but a soldier cannot read a general's documents. But the *no-read-up* rule is insufficient to stop leakage of information downward. A general could read a confidential document and write what he read to an unclassified document accessible to a soldier. To prevent this, a subject must not be allowed to write down the security hierarchy. Thus comes the *confinement property* or **-property*,[51] which postulates that a subject can modify an object only at the same or higher security level.

[50] This is quite different from an ACL-based system, which itself needs to manage the lists.

[51] According to legend, the authors used "$*$" as a temporary place holder for a forthcoming satisfactory name.

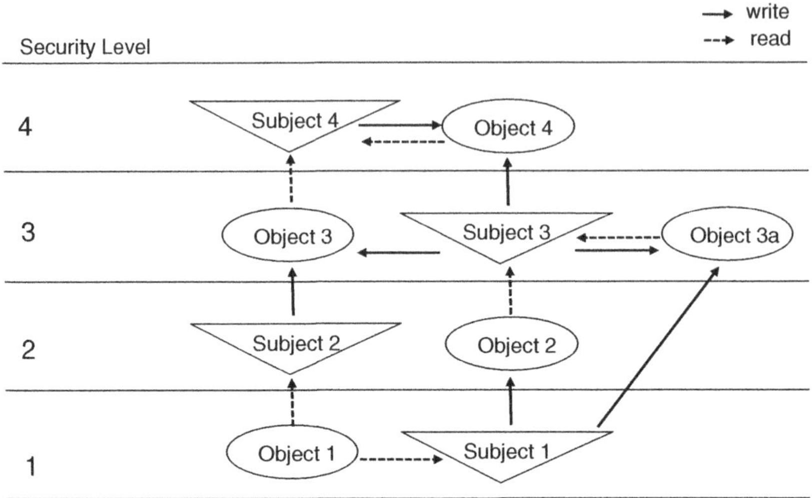

Figure A.19 Flow of information in a Bell–LaPadula system.

(This rule prevents a situation in which a general copies the content of a *Top-Security* file and pastes it to an *Unclassified* file.)

When both rules are enforced, as shown in Figure A.19, information can flow only upward. But this is problematic in practice. At some point, troops have to learn from their commanders where to go. Bell and LaPadula solved this problem by exempting a special group of trusted subjects from the rules. Another assumption of the Bell–LaPadula model is that the security levels of the involved actors stay the same (which is called the tranquility property). If security levels are allowed to change, information could flow in an undesired direction.

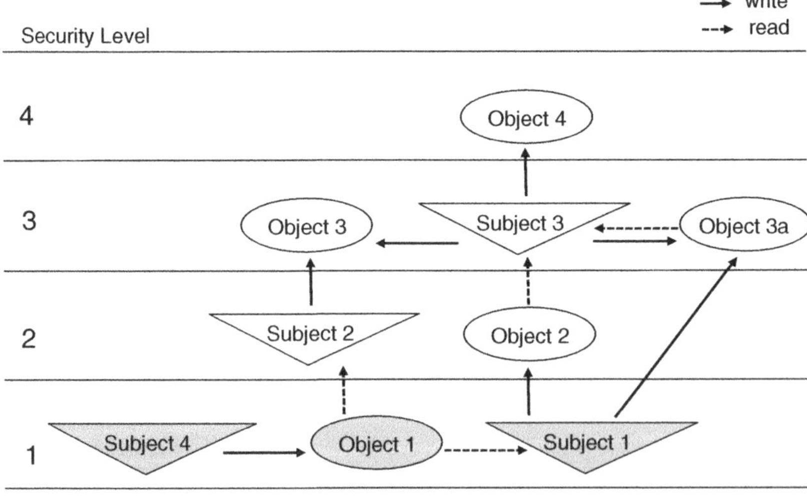

Figure A.20 Altered information flow in a Bell–LaPadula system.

Figure A.20 shows such a case, where Subject 4 lowers its own security level after reading from Object 3 in the previous example and writes to Object 1, leaking sensitive information as a result. The tranquility property actually has two versions: strong and weak. The strong version forbids changing security levels during system operation, while the weak version allows changes as long as the established security policy (e.g., no "read up" or "write down") is not violated.

Aimed at keeping secrets, the Bell–LaPadula model does not concern itself with either the trustworthiness or the integrity of the secrets. There is a danger here. With a naïve application of the model, a soldier may overwrite his superior's intelligence report. So it is possible for a general to get wrong information even though only the general can read the report. The gist of the problem is that the trustworthiness of an object created by a subject can be downgraded but not upgraded by the trustworthiness of the objects that the subject reads. Ken Biba addressed this problem by turning the Bell–LaPadula model upside down. His model [26] introduces two reverse properties: *read up* and *write down*. Analogous to the Bell–LaPadula properties, they are named as follows:

1. The *simple integrity* property that a subject can read only objects at the same or a higher security (or integrity) level.
2. The $*$*-integrity* property that a subject can write only objects at the same or a lower security (or integrity) level.

These properties reflect the so-called *low-watermark* principle: the integrity of an object composed of other objects is as good as that of the least trustworthy one among the composing group. Essentially, properties reflect the policy rules. When enforced, they ensure that the integrity of information is maintained; information can flow in the direction of high to low integrity. The Biba model is the first formal, verifiable model based on information flow integrity. As in Bell–LaPadula, the strict uni-directional flow of information makes it difficult to directly apply the Biba model to practical applications. More often than not, exceptions to break the flow constraint are required, and they have to be done on a case-by-case basis.[52] Furthermore, protection of information disclosure and integrity usually need to be addressed together, and yet the Biba and Bell–LaPadula models are contradictory, preventing communication between security levels.

A.4.6 Security Assertion Markup Language

SAML is a widely implemented standard based on XML.[53] It was originally developed by OASIS and then adopted by other efforts. The adoption by the *Identity Federation Framework (ID-FF)* project at Liberty Alliance[54] and the Shibboleth open-source project,[55] in particular,

[52] Microsoft's ill-fated Windows Vista actually implements a default policy of "*no write up*." Internet Explorer is assigned a low integrity level. But objects, by default, have medium integrity level. This is to limit damage by browser-based attacks; IE cannot open any directories, files, or registry keys for write access, unless they are explicitly assigned low integrity.

[53] www.w3.org/TR/REC-xml/

[54] Liberty Alliance (www.projectliberty.org/) has been merged into the Kantara Initiative (http://kantarainitiative.org/), a forum for "fostering identity community harmonization, interoperability, innovation, and broad adoption."

[55] https://shibboleth.net/

led to concurrent adaption of SAML 1.0, while it was undergoing various revisions in OASIS. The ID-FF project, driven by provider need, introduces the notion of the circle of trust and builds on SAML to effect identity federation therein. In contrast, the Shibboleth project addresses single sign-on and privacy-preserving access control, given its root in research and education-oriented Internet2.[56] Multiple SAML-based efforts, however, yielded incompatible variants. Fortunately, the stakeholders got together in time to correct the course and develop a harmonized version. The result is SAML 2.0, which was approved by OASIS in 2005. This is the version that has been supported by most SAML implementations.

SAML 2.0 is composed of a family of specifications.[57] At the core is the specification [27] that defines the notion for security assertions and the protocols for exchanging assertions between an identity provider and a relying party. (The core specification was also published as ITU-T Recommendation X.1141 [28] in 2006.) A security assertion is typically issued by an identity provider and used by a *relying party* to authenticate and authorize a subject (e.g., an end user). The assertion consists of a set of statements about the subject and contextual information such as the issuer, recipient, issuance time, and expiration time. A statement may concern authentication, or attribute, or authorization decision. An authentication statement describes an authentication transaction, including pertinent information such as the authentication method and time of the transaction. (SAML 2.0 does not dictate a particular authentication method and can support a range of authentication methods with varied strengths, such as password, Kerberos ticket, and X.509 certificate.) An attribute statement describes the attributes associated with the subject. Finally, an authorization decision statement asserts whether to allow a subject to access the requested resource. To ensure its integrity, a SAML assertion is digitally signed by the issuer.

SAML 2.0 defines a set of request–response protocols, each of which is for a specific purpose. For example, Assertion Query and Request Protocol allows a relying party to inquire about or request a SAML assertion (pertaining to attributes or authentication or authorization decision) about a subject; Authentication Request Protocol allows a subject to obtain an authentication assertion from the identity provider; and Name Identifier Mapping Protocol allows a relying party to obtain the new identifiers of a subject from the identity provider. The protocols, however, are not defined at a level that can be used directly for communication between the involved parties. They have to rely on an existing communication protocol (e.g., HTTP) for transporting messages (i.e., requests and responses) through protocol mappings. In the SAML nomenclature, mappings of SAML messages onto standard communication protocols are called bindings [29]. For example, the HTTP Redirect binding defines how SAML messages can be carried as part of URL parameters. Since the URL length is limited in practice, specialized encodings are needed. Furthermore, exceedingly large messages will need to be transported through other bindings. One such binding is HTTP POST, which allows SAML messages to be transported as part of the base-64-encoded content. It goes without saying that the transport has to be protected (typically through TLS), regardless of the bindings.

Figure A.21 shows as an example a message flow for identity federation through the SAML HTTP Redirect binding. The assumption here is that the relying party and identity provider have a pre-established relationship. The flow is high-level and goes as follows. Upon detecting

[56] www.internet2.edu/

[57] http://docs.oasis-open.org/security/saml/v2.0/

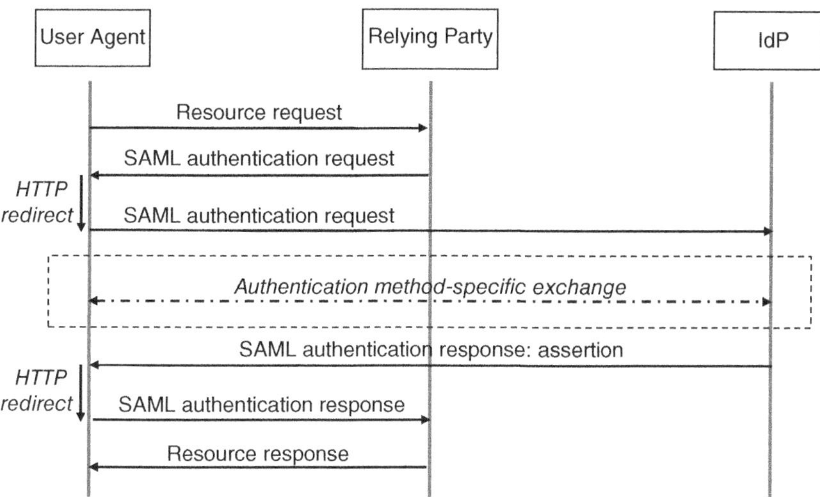

Figure A.21 SAML message flow for identity federation.

that the user (through the user agent) requesting resource access has not been authenticated, the relying party issues a SAML authentication request, which is redirected to the identity provider. Then the identity provider performs the steps to authenticate the user. Again, the steps are specific to the authentication method of choice and beyond the scope of SAML. Upon completion of the authentication steps, the identity provider sends the SAML authentication response carrying the assertion, which is redirected to the relying party. According to the authentication response, the relying party then responds.

A.4.7 OAuth 2.0

This section provides the additional detail on OAuth 2.0[58] that we promised in Chapter 7. We begin with the types of *authorization grants* defined in OAuth 2.0, which are as follows:

1. *Authorization code.* This type of authorization grant is generated and verified by the authorization server for one-time use by the client and is suitable for cases where the client is interacting with a user via a user agent. The code can only be used once, and is bound to the client. The binding with the client necessitates authentication by the authorization server when the client obtains an access token. It is worth noting that the authorization server alone dictates the structure of the authorization codes; it is responsible for both issuing and verifying authorization codes.
2. *Implicit.* This type of authorization grant aims to optimize the performance of an in-browser client (implemented in JavaScript). With such a client, there is no assured way to authenticate it. So the client is given an access token directly, saving it the need to take an extra step and exchange the authorization grant for the access token.

[58] https://tools.ietf.org/html/rfc6749

3. *Resource owner password credentials*. Of course, this grant type seems to defy the very goal of OAuth—never to divulge a user's password. Hence, it should be used only when there is a high degree of trust between the resource owner and the client, such as when the client is part of the user device.
4. *Client credentials*. This type of authorization grant allows the client to access the protected resources under its control or under the control of the authorization server by prior arrangement.

OAuth 2.0 also allows new grant types to be defined. One emerging new grant type is the SAML 2.0 Bearer Assertion.[59] Issued by an identity provider (as we discussed earlier), an assertion contains security-related information (e.g., identity and privileges) about a subject, which is usable by the authorization server. A bearer assertion is a particular type of assertion that the holder does not need to provide any other proof (e.g., a cryptographic key) to use it. Hence, it is paramount that such assertions be properly protected both at rest and in motion. Given that different actors are involved in issuing and processing assertions, there is a need for a standard way to specify them, namely SAML 2.0 here.

The authorization server typically requires that the client authenticate itself before issuing an access token. Bound to HTTP, OAuth 2.0 supports authentication based on passwords (e.g., using the HTTP basic or digest authentication scheme[60]) and assertions.[61] Obviously token requests and responses need to be protected appropriately; they include sensitive information (such as passwords, authorization codes, and access tokens). Mechanisms to this end include TLS 1.2, the HTTP "cache-control" header field (to effect no caching of sensitive information in HTTP caches), and sending OAuth-related information in the message body rather than the request URI (to prevent sensitive information from being logged at the user agent or possible intermediaries).

To optimize user experience, the OAuth 2.0 protocol simply utilizes the HTTP redirection constructs. Figure A.22 further shows the related message flow. The use of HTTP redirection, however, comes at a cost. For example, it is difficult, if not impossible, for a user to verify the redirect URI, given all the tricks that can be used for the graphical user interface. A user, thus, could authorize a rogue site without knowing it. To mitigate the problem, a countermeasure is for the authorization server to keep a white list of redirect URIs. In other words, all legitimate clients need to register their redirect URIs with the authorization server beforehand. Nevertheless, this is not common practice. Another problem is cross-site request forgery. The redirection back to the client from the user provides a venue for an adversary to inject its own authorization code or access token. A countermeasure is to allow the client to keep track of the authorization state. To this end, OAuth 2.0 supports a parameter in the protocol to carry state information. When redirecting the user agent to the authorization server, the client may include this parameter. It is then repeated in all related follow-up messages, up to the message that carries the authorization result back to the client. Since the value of the parameter is set and processed by the client alone, the client has total control of its structure. For state management, it can capture an authorization session identifier or some specific

[59] https://tools.ietf.org/html/rfc7522
[60] http://tools.ietf.org/html/rfc2617
[61] https://tools.ietf.org/html/rfc7521

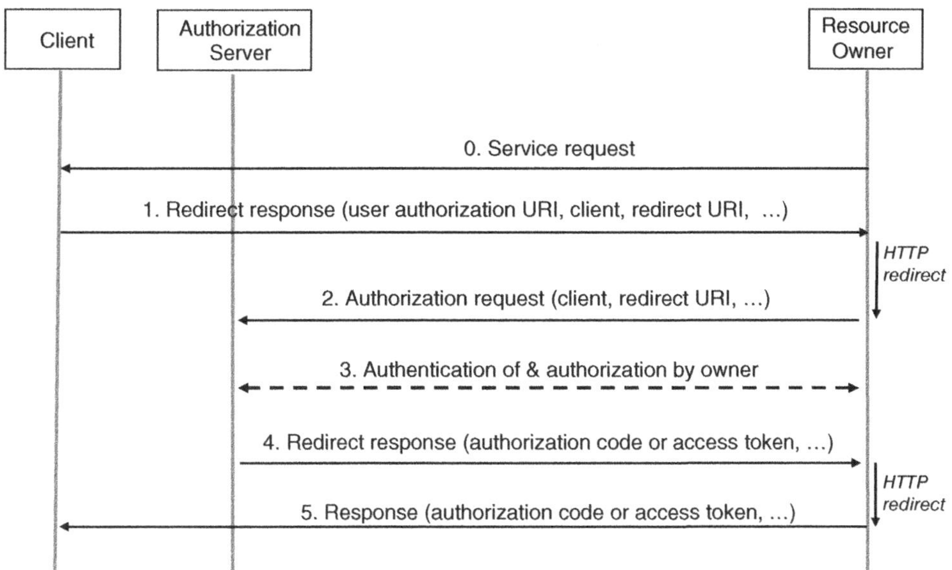

Figure A.22 OAuth 2.0 user authorization message flow.

local state information. For additional security protection, it can include a signature. Again, because sensitive information (e.g., the authorization code and token) is transmitted across the network, the authorization exchange should be carried out over a secure transport protocol such as TLS.

A.4.8 OpenID Connect

OpenID Connect (*OIDC*) is the latest reincarnation of OpenID, although the name is the only link to its predecessor. Developed by the OpenID Foundation,[62] OpenID is the first user-centric identity federation mechanism. With it, a user can select and maintain his identifier (typically a URI) as well as have a choice in selecting his identity provider. OpenID also comes with its own bespoke *federated authentication protocol* that is tightly coupled to HTTP [30]. Compared with SAML, OpenID has a more focused scope and a lighter approach. Still the use of XML and a custom message signature scheme makes correct implementations and their interoperation challenging. Then social networking services emerged and took off. The associated identity federation technology gradually overtook once-promising OpenID and eventually forced it to move on.

Building on OAuth 2.0, OIDC automatically acquires the former's virtues, including support for REST, JSON, standard signing and encryption mechanisms, and varied deployment scenarios. As a result, interoperability is improved. But user-centric features (e.g., user-defined

[62] Please see http://openid.net/

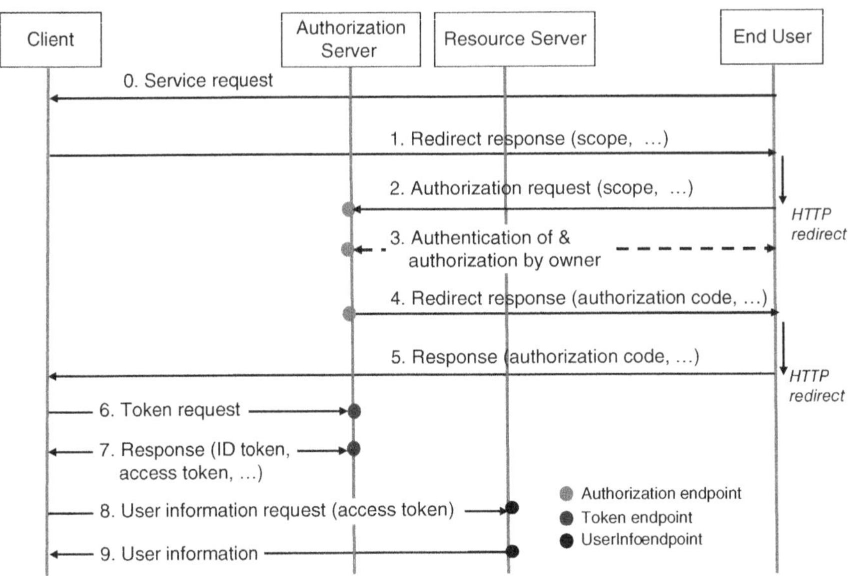

Figure A.23 OpenID connect message flow.

identifiers) are gone. According to the OpenID Foundation (the organization continuing to oversee OpenID's evolution), OIDC:

> "allows Clients to verify the identity of the End-User based on the authentication performed by an Authorization Server, as well as to obtain basic profile information about the End-User in an interoperable and REST-like manner. OpenID Connect allows clients of all types, including Web-based, mobile, and JavaScript clients, to request and receive information about authenticated sessions and end-users. The specification suite is extensible, allowing participants to use optional features such as encryption of identity data, discovery of OpenID Providers, and session management, when it makes sense for them."

Figure A.23 shows an example of the OIDC message flow, which essentially follows the authorization code flow in OAuth 2.0. The key differences according to the OIDC 1.0 core specification[63] include the following:

- A set of special values (e.g., opened, profile, and e-mail) is defined for the scope parameter. The presence of *openid* in the authorization request (e.g., step 1 and step 2) is mandatory. Multiple additional values may be included as well. The information about the end user that the client can obtain depends on the presence of these scope values;
- In addition to an access token, an ID token is also returned as part of the token response (i.e., step 7). The ID token is represented as a JSON *web token* with a JSON *web signature* based on an IETF standard.[64] It contains a set of claims made by the authorization server.

[63] http://openid.net/specs/openid-connect-core-1_0.html
[64] https://tools.ietf.org/html/rfc7515

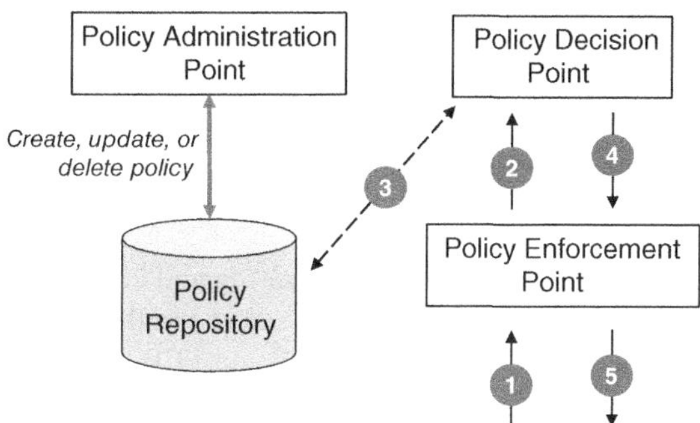

Figure A.24 Policy control workflow.

The claim set must include the information that identifies the issuer of the response, the intended audience (i.e., the client), the expiration time of the token, and the issuing time of the token. The information is used to further validate the token after its signature is verified as valid;

- Claims about the authenticated end user are treated as a protected resource accessible through the UserInfo endpoint of the resource server. To obtain claims about the end user, the client sends a request to the UserInfo endpoint, including an access token (as shown in step 8). The returned claims depend on the scope values in the access token. For example, if the value of the scope parameter is *profile*, the end user's default claims are returned. These claims reveal information such as full name, gender, birth date, and home page. Claims are normally represented as a JSON object, which may be signed, or encrypted, or both.

A.4.9 Access Control Markup Language

The *Attribute-Based Access Control* (*ABAC*) is evolved from the RBAC model discussed in Chapter 7. It allows varied attributes (in terms of values and relations) to be considered at the time of object access. The attributes may be provided by the subject as part of an access request or inferred from the environment (such as in the case of time and location). A development of ABAC is the *Extensible Access Control Markup Language* (*XACML*) [31, 32], standardized jointly by OASIS and the ITU-T. The language is designed for specifying access control policies and queries.

XACML follows a general policy control model, which employs the PDP and PEP described earlier for QoS support and, in addition, the constructs below:

- *Policy Administration Point* (*PAP*), which administers policies invoking typical operations such as create, update, and delete;
- *Policy repository*, which is a database or a collection of databases storing policies (typically in the form of rules, such as IF <condition> THEN <action>).

Figure A.24 shows how these different constructs are related to each other through an example workflow involving the following steps:

1. The PEP receives an access request for a protected resource (or an object);
2. The PEP passes the request to the PDP;

3. The PDP fetches the applicable policy from the policy repository;
4. The PDP, upon making the access decision, returns the result to the PEP;
5. The PEP returns the requested resource or rejects the access request, enforcing the decision.

XACML builds on and is consistent with SAML. It has two key components:

1. An XML-based language for expressing authorization and entitlement policies (e.g., who can do what, where, and when). Such policies are stored in the policy repository.
2. Request and response messages between the PDP and PEP, where the request message is for triggering and feeding into the policy evaluation process at the PDP, and the response message from the PDP is for capturing the actions or obligations that the PEP needs to fulfill.

True to an XML-based language, XACML is verbose and typically generated by machines. To support RBAC, two eponymous profiles [33, 34] have been developed for XACML 2.0 and 3.0, respectively. In both profiles, *roles* are expressed as *Subject Attributes*[65] in general. Depending on the application environment, there may be either one role attribute whose values correspond to different roles (e.g., "employee," "manager," or "officer"), or different attribute identifiers, each indicating a different role. Furthermore, the following policy types are defined in both profiles as well:

- *Role*, which associates a given role attribute and value with a *permission*;
- *Permission*, which contains the actual permissions (i.e., policy elements and rules);
- *HasPrivilegesOfRole*, which supports querying about whether a subject has privileges associated with a given role. It is also possible to express policies in which a user holds several roles simultaneously.

It is worth noting that in the RBAC profile of XACML 2.0, there is an extra policy type (i.e., *Role Assignment*) defined to handle the actual assignment of roles to subjects. But the question of what roles a subject can have generally is considered beyond the scope of XACML. The question is addressed by a Role Enablement Authority. According to the following text, common to the scope descriptions of [33, 34]:

> "Such an entity may make use of XACML policies, but will need additional information … The policies specified in this profile assume all the roles for a given subject have already been enabled at the time an authorization decision is requested. They do not deal with an environment in which roles must be enabled dynamically based on the resource or actions a subject is attempting to perform. For this reason, the policies specified in this profile also do not deal with static or dynamic "Separation of Duty" … A future profile may address the requirements of this type of environment."

[65] More specifically, a Subject Attribute is an <Attribute> element in an XACML Request associated with a subject. An <Attribute> element in an XACML Request may also be associated with a protected resource (Resource Attribute), an action on a resource (Action Attribute), or the environment of the Request (Environment Attribute).

References

[1] Birman, K.P. (2012) *Guide to Reliable Distributed Systems: Building High-Assurance Applications and Cloud-Hosted Services*. Springer-Verlag, London.

[2] OASIS (2013) Committee Specification 01: Topology and Orchestration Specification for Cloud Applications, version 1.0. http://docs.oasis-open.org/tosca/TOSCA/v1.0/cs01/TOSCA-v1.0-cs01.pdf.

[3] Prywes, N.S. (1977) Automatic program generation. Proceedings of National Computer Conference AFIPS '77, ACM, New York, pp. 679–689.

[4] Ahrens, J. and Prywes, N. (1995) Transition to a legacy- and reuse-based software life cycle. *IEEE Computer*, **28**(10), 27–36.

[5] Binz, T., Breiter, G., Leymann, F., and Spatzier, T. (2012) Portable Cloud services using TOSCA. *IEEE Internet Computing*, **16**(03), 80–85.

[6] Sunyaev, A. and Schneider, S. (2013) Cloud services certification. *Communications of the ACM*, **56**(2), 33–36.

[7] Waixenegger, T., Wieland, M., Binz, T., et al. (2013) Policy4TOSCA: A policy-aware Cloud service provisioning approach to enable secure Cloud computing. *Lecture Notes in Computer Science*, **8185**, 360–376.

[8] Liu, K. (2013) Development of TOSCA Service Templates for provisioning portable IT Services. Diploma Thesis No. 3428, University of Stuttgart, Faculty of Computer Science, Electrical Engineering and Information Technology.

[9] Fielding, R.T. and Taylor, R.N. (2000) Principled design of the modern Web architecture. Proceedings of the 22nd International Conference on Software Engineering, ACM, New York, pp. 407–416.

[10] Fielding, R.T. (2000) Architectural styles and the design of network-based software architectures. PhD dissertation, University of California, Irvine, CA. www.ics.uci.edu/~fielding/pubs/dissertation.

[11] Bush, V. (1945) As we may think. *The Atlantic Monthly*, **176**(1), 101–108. www.theatlantic.com/magazine/archive/1945/07/as-we-may-think/303881/.

[12] Nelson, T.H. (1965) Complex information processing: A file structure for the complex, the changing and the indeterminate. Proceedings of the ACM 20th National Conference, ACM, New York, pp. 84–100.

[13] Nabokov, V. (1963) *Pale Fire*. Lancer Books, New York.

[14] Rowberry, S. (2011) Pale Fire as a hypertextual network. Proceedings of the 22nd ACM Hypertext Conference, HT'11, ACM, New York, pp. 319–324.

[15] Gray, H.J. and Prywes, N.S. (1959) Outline for a multi-list organized system. Proceedings of ACM '59; Preprints of Papers Presented at the 14th National Meeting of the Association for Computing Machinery, ACM, New York, pp. 1–7.

[16] Prywes, N.S. and Gray, H.J. (1963) The organization of a multilist-type associative memory. *Transactions of the American Institute of Electrical Engineers, Part I: Communication and Electronics*, **82**(4), 488–492.

[17] Barnet, B. (2013) *Memory Machines: The evolution of hypertext*. Anthem Press, London.

[18] Carmody, S., Gross, W., Nelson, T.H., et al. (1969) A hypertext editing system for the /360. Center for Computer & Information Sciences, Brown University, Providence, RI. File Number HES360-0, Form AVD-6903-0, pp. 26–27 (cited from [17]).

[19] Bonneau, J. (2012) Guessing human-chosen secrets. PhD dissertation, University of Cambridge.

[20] Morris, R. and Thompson, K. (1979) Password security: A case history. *Communications of the ACM*, **22**(11), 594–597.

[21] Wagner, D. and Goldberg, I. (2000) Proofs of security for the Unix password hashing algorithm. In Okamoto, T. (ed.), *Advances in Cryptology—ASIACRYPT 2000*. Springer, Berlin, pp. 560–572.

[22] Needham, R.M. and Schroeder, M.D. (1978) Using encryption for authentication in large networks of computers. *Communications of the ACM*, **21**(12), 993–999.

[23] Dennis, J.B. and Van Horn, E.C. (1966) Programming semantics for multiprogrammed computations. *Communications of the ACM*, **9**(3), 143–155.

[24] Tanenbaum, A.S., Van Renesse, R., Van Staveren, H., et al. (1990) Experiences with the Amoeba distributed operating system. *Communications of the ACM*, **33**(12), 46–63.

[25] La Padula, L.J. and Elliott Bell, D. (1973) Secure Computer Systems: Mathematical Foundations. MTR-2547-VOL-1, Mitre Corporation, Bedford, MA.

[26] Biba, K.J. (1977) Integrity Considerations for Secure Computer Systems. MTR-3153-REV-1, Mitre Corporation, Bedford, MA.

[27] OASIS (2005) Assertions and protocols for the OASIS Security Assertion Markup Language (SAML) V2.0. http://docs.oasis-open.org/security/saml/v2.0/saml-core-2.0-os.pdf.

[28] International Telecommunication Union (2006) ITU-T Recommendation X.1141: Security Assertion Markup Language (SAML 2.0). www.itu.int.
[29] OASIS (2005) Bindings for the OASIS Security Assertion Markup Language (SAML) V2.0. http://docs.oasis-open.org/security/saml/v2.0/saml-bindings-2.0-os.pdf.
[30] OpenID Foundation (2007) OpenID Authentication 2.0. http://openid.net/specs/openid-authentication-2_0.html.
[31] International Telecommunication Union (2006) ITU-T Recommendation X.1142: eXtensible Access Control Markup Language (XACML 2.0). www.itu.int.
[32] International Telecommunication Union (2013) ITU-T Recommendation X.1144: eXtensible Access Control Markup Language (XACML 3.0). www.itu.int.
[33] OASIS (2005) Core and hierarchical Role Based Access Control (RBAC) profile of XACML v2.0. http://docs.oasis-open.org/xacml/2.0/access_control-xacml-2.0-rbac-profile1-spec-os.pdf.
[34] OASIS (2014) Core and hierarchical Role Based Access Control (RBAC) profile of XACML v3.0. http://docs.oasis-open.org/xacml/3.0/rbac/v1.0/csprd04/xacml-3.0-rbac-v1.0-csprd04.pdf.

Index

Cloud Computing: Business Trends and Technologies, First Edition. Igor Faynberg, Hui-Lan Lu and Dor Skuler.

Printed and bound by CPI Group (UK) Ltd, Croydon, CR0 4YY

12/01/2025

14624501-0005